Windows Sources Microsoft Office 97 for Windows SuperGuide

Windows Sources Microsoft Office 97 for Windows SuperGuide

Bruce Hallberg

ZIFF-DAVIS **ZD** PRESS

Ziff-Davis Press
an imprint of Macmillan Computer Publishing USA
Emeryville, California

Publisher	Stacy Hiquet
Acquisitions Editor	Lysa Lewallen
Copy Editor	Mitzi Waltz
Technical Reviewer	Dick Hol
Proofreader	Jeff Barash
Cover Illustration and Design	Megan Gandt
Book Design	Bruce Lundquist
Page Layout	M. D. Barrera and Bruce Lundquist
Indexer	Valerie Robbins

Ziff-Davis Press, ZD Press, the Ziff-Davis Press logo are trademarks or registered trademarks of, and are licensed to Macmillan Computer Publishing USA by Ziff-Davis Publishing Company, New York, New York.

"Windows" and "Windows Sources" are trademarks of Microsoft Corporation and "Windows Sources" is used by Ziff-Davis Press under license from Ziff-Davis Publishing and by Ziff-Davis Publishing under license from the owner. Windows Sources™ Microsoft Office 97 for Windows SuperGuide is an independent publication not affiliated with Microsoft Corporation. Microsoft Corporation is not responsible in any way for the editorial policy or other contents of the publication.

Ziff-Davis Press imprint books are produced on a Macintosh computer system with the following applications: FrameMaker®, Microsoft® Word, QuarkXPress®, Adobe Illustrator®, Adobe Photoshop®, Adobe Streamline™, MacLink®Plus, Aldus® FreeHand™, Collage Plus™.

Ziff-Davis Press, an imprint of
Macmillan Computer Publishing USA
5903 Christie Avenue
Emeryville, CA 94608

ISBN 1-56276-503-5

Manufactured in the United States of America
10 9 8 7 6 5 4 3 2

■ About the Authors

Bruce Hallberg

Bruce Hallberg, with more than 15 years experience in the computer industry, heads the Information Systems group for a biotechnology company located in California. His background includes consulting nationally with Fortune 1000 companies on accounting and management information systems. He is the author and co-author of over 15 books, including *Inside Windows NT Workstation 4*, *Inside Microsoft Exchange*, and the forthcoming *Windows Sources Excel 97 SuperGuide*.

Pam Borys

Once terrified of computers, P.A.M. Borys, President of Step by Step Training of Woburn, MA (pamborys@aol.com) provides consulting and training services for both Macintosh and Windows computer users. P.A.M. has co-authored or contributed to a number of books on popular business applications. Once active in the Boston Computer Society which ceased activity in September 1996, she is now helping to shape Computer Organizations of New England, to help fill the void left by the BCS.

Pam would like to thank Barrie Sosinsky and the Ziff-Davis Press team for all their thoughtful comments and help. Her thanks also go to her wonderful family, Jim, Beth, and Martin.

Trudi Reisner

Trudi Reisner is a computer technical writer specializing in software technical writing and course development. Trudi has written numerous books including Que's *10 Minute Guide to Excel 5*, *10 Minute Guide to Windows 95*, *Easy Excel 5 for Windows*, *Easy Microsoft Office 97*, and *Easy Word for Windows 95*. Trudi has also written user guides and software documentation manuals on manufacturing, clinical and financial, and font creation software, as well as courseware on Lotus 1-2-3 and Lotus Notes Web Navigator.

Barrie Sosinsky

Barrie Sosinsky is the author or co-author of more than 30 computer books and 75 magazine articles. His recent work includes *The BackOffice Bible* and *Building Visual FoxPro Applications* from IDG Books; *The Web Recipe Book* from Prentice Hall Technical; *Microsoft Publisher for Dummies* from Dummies Press, *The Warp Book* from Prima Publishing, and others.

Barrie's company, Killer Apps (Newton, MA), specializes in desktop database, Internet/intranet, electronic print, hypertext and workgroup solutions for clients, as well as technical writing and documentation.

Winston Steward

Winston Steward is a Respiratory Therapist and a musician, living in Los Angeles with his wife Barbara and his two children, Trevor and Larisa. He is the author of *Every Family's Guide to Computers* published by Ziff-Davis Press.

Winston wishes to thank MegaImage, Inc., of Pomona, California, for their marvelous laptop computer.

■ Contents at a Glance

■ Table of Contents

■ Acknowledgements

All books are team efforts; every part of the team contributes to a book's ultimate success. Just as a chain is only as strong as its weakest link, so too are the teams that bring books such as this to you dependent on all parts of the team functioning smoothly and competently together to achieve the goal.

With that said, there are a number of people who put many long and hard hours into the book you're holding:

Lysa Lewallen, the book's Acquisitions Editor, handled all of the contract issues, scheduling, and much of the coordination of the authors who worked on the book. She is a delight to work with, and was unfailingly pleasant even when deadlines were looming. Also, in the 15 or so projects on which I've worked, I've never seen a book's production turned around as quickly as with this book, and Lysa is responsible for making those arrangements.

Dick Hol, the Technical Editor, meticulously read every chapter, examined every screen shot, and followed every example to ensure the book is as accurate as possible. Dick is charming to work with and was usefully communicative about his thoughts on the various chapters. I've worked with many technical editors over the years, and have done the job myself on several occasions; Dick performed this function better than anyone I've ever seen.

The book's readability was improved dramatically by Mitzi Waltz's thoughtful copy edits (a copy editor makes sure the book is grammatically correct, pleasant to read, and that all the t's are crossed and i's dotted). Some copy editors follow rigorous rules of English when editing books, and in the process typically make the book much drier than otherwise. Mitzi, on the other hand, strikes just the right balance between "proper" English use and readability. Book authors often grumble about the edits made to their words. Not so with Mitzi's; out of hundreds of edits, they all improved the product, without exception.

Madhu Prasher, the Production Editor, did a yeoman's job of competently juggling all of the chapters as we approached the date the book went to the printer. With FedEx packages flying all over the country, back and forth, she never lost track of what was where, what was needed, and what I was late with. Madhu was integral to our ability to finish production very quickly.

Carol Burbo accepted all of the author submissions (made via e-mail, ftp transfers, and to a special BBS) and made sure they got to the right place expediently.

Valerie Robbins performed the difficult (and tedious) job of indexing all of the book's contents so that you can find information in the book quickly and easily.

Finally, I'd like to thank M. D. Barrera and Bruce Lundquist, the layout artists, for laying out the book in record time. Their work is very clean and pleasant to look at, and I think you'll find that the page design used in the book makes it easy to digest the information as easily as possible.

■ Introduction

Welcome to *Windows Sources Microsoft Office 97 for Windows SuperGuide*! This book is designed specifically to meet the needs of users who have invested in the Microsoft Office suite of applications, including Microsoft Word for Windows, Microsoft Excel for Windows, Microsoft PowerPoint, and Microsoft Outlook.

■ How *Windows Sources Microsoft Office 97 for Windows SuperGuide* Is Designed

Most of the parts in this book are dedicated to the separate applications in the suite. The other parts show you how to get more out of your Office suite of products by using more advanced features such as integration and networking. This approach enables you to use Office as most users use it—as separate applications—as well as understanding how to use these applications in harmony.

The *Office 97 SuperGuide* is written for those users who might be comfortable or even expert with one or two of the Office suite applications, but who must or want to learn the other applications in the Office line. Many users find that they spend so much time in one application, such as Word, that when they have to use another application, such as PowerPoint, they really are not that comfortable with it.

How many times have you had to complete a presentation, but you didn't know how to use PowerPoint, so you just created it in Word? Or, perhaps, you've been in a situation where your boss wants that report with charts, graphs, and pretty pictures done in "FIVE MINUTES," or else. But when you get back to your workstation, you can't get that sales history out of Excel so that it imports into Word just right. Eventually, you get frustrated with this approach, so you close Excel in a huff and rekey the data into a Word table and hand in a report blander than ice cubes boiled in water. The information is there, but it is not as presentable as you would like.

■ What's Different about This Book

The power of a suite of programs like Microsoft Office is the integration, or as Microsoft labels it, *component reuse,* you get when all your major applications work together seamlessly. This integration enables you to create sparkling presentations, "smart" spreadsheets, highly automated word processing documents, and powerful databases.

■ What Is Integration?

Although Windows has made it easier to integrate your applications, not many users are comfortable designing elaborate OLE and DDE links to make their various applications work together. Office is designed around the theory that users want to use two or three applications at once without having to reengineer or reformat data once time has been spent creating it. Users don't want to create worksheets in Excel that are filled with thousands of numbers, only to have that data available only to Excel. Why not use that data in another applications, such as Word or PowerPoint? This is the magic of Microsoft Office, and *Windows Sources Microsoft Office 97 for Windows SuperGuide* shows you how to do this.

Integration enables you to create a Word document, such as a sales letter, using an Excel worksheet to plug sales figures into the letter. Or, you might have an Excel database that keeps your inventory. For accounting purposes, you can have Excel send specific inventory data to Word to create a monthly report that you can turn in to your accountant or manager. Microsoft Office enables you to do all this and more.

■ Part 1: Office 97

Part 1 covers Microsoft Office 97 itself. There are many features of Office that aren't part of one of the core applications, such as Office Fast Find, the Office Assistant, the Office Shortcut Bar, and so forth. You learn about these topics in this section, as well as common user-interface styles shared between the Office applications.

For readers upgrading from Office 95 to Office 97, you'll find a discussion of all of the new features in Office in Part 1.

■ Part 2: Word

Part 2 is devoted to Microsoft Word 97 for Windows. Many users devote most of their working time using a word processor for correspondence, business proposals, memos, or other reports. For these users, the word processor is the key application on their desktop, with all other applications supporting its documents.

Using Word 97 for Windows to complete your work is easy. The goal of Part 2 is to introduce you to the basics of Word, including creating a document, changing text formats, and printing documents. Part 2 also gets you up and running on the more advanced uses and features of Word. You learn, for example, how to create tables and customize dictionaries, macros, and graphics.

Word is a powerhouse application and is simple enough that you can work with it as soon as it is installed. Word's more advanced features enable you to build complex documents such as an office newsletter. Whether you want to type a quick to-do list or create a one-page trifold brochure containing pictures and drop caps, you can do it in Word with equal ease. Word's advanced capabilities are as easy to use as its simple features.

■ Part 3: Excel

The third part of *Windows Sources Microsoft Office 97 for Windows SuperGuide* is devoted to Microsoft Excel 97 for Windows. Excel is one of the most popular spreadsheets available for Windows and is probably the second most popular application in the Office suite. With Excel 97, you can quickly and easily create powerful worksheets, colorful charts, and focused reports and presentations.

In Part 3 you are introduced to Excel's features; how to create and format worksheets; and how to build charts from the data you have in your worksheets. In later chapters, more advanced features are covered to help you get the most out of your Office investment. If you are interested in setting up loan calculations, mortgage analysis, or other powerful spreadsheet applications, this book shows you how to use functions, macros, and Visual Basic for Applications to get what you want.

■ Part 4: PowerPoint

When you need to put together a presentation replete with slides, handouts, and reports, use Microsoft PowerPoint. Part 4 gives you an introduction into this easy-to-use Office application. Although you might not do all of your work in PowerPoint, you might need to use it from time to time to put together that perfect presentation for the board of directors. For that reason, Part 4 shows you the best information and instructions to get the job done.

After you have put together your presentations on the computer, you can transfer them onto plain paper; color or black-and-white overheads; or 35mm slides; or you can show them on a video screen or computer monitor. To complete your presentation package, PowerPoint's printing options include formats ranging from audience handouts to speaker's notes.

Part 4 discusses using the PowerPoint AutoContent Wizard, entering presentation text in the outline, and viewing slides. You also learn ways to apply PowerPoint templates to a presentation, add to presentation shapes with text inside, and insert a new slide and clip art into a presentation.

What you will learn with PowerPoint and other Office applications is that many design and formatting tools are identical to those in Word and Excel. If you know how to use these applications, you already know how to use many functions in PowerPoint. This feature helps transfer your skill in one application to another, making the learning curve for that application much smaller.

■ Part 5: Access

Microsoft Access 97 for Windows is a powerful relational database application that lets you build data tables and then manage the data in sophisticated ways. You can relate information from one table to another, query data in your table, create custom reports for your data, design input forms, and much, much more.

In Part 5 you learn how to set up tables in Access, how to write queries and reports (using the Wizards available as well as getting started doing these things manually), how to relate tables, how to design forms, and everything else you need to productively use Access 97.

■ Part 6: Outlook

Everyone working in a typical business environment needs to manage their contacts, schedule, e-mails, and tasks. In Part 6, you learn how to use Microsoft Outlook to help you manage, manipulate, and use all your productivity-based information. Do you have a stack of business cards you've received from business contacts, hairdressers, and friends sitting in your desk drawer with a rubber band around them? Would you like a better way to manage them? Do you manage a number of people, and need to keep track of who's working on what projects, and when they're due? Would you like a better way to coordinate your schedule with others in your company? Do you need to stay in contact with a large number of people via e-mail?

If you answer yes to these or any other questions that deal with productivity data, you should consider using Outlook to manage your information.

In Part 6, you learn how to add contacts, set appointments (both single and recurring), create projects and delegate tasks within the project, send and handle your e-mail, and print your data in easy-to-use formats for quick reference.

The nicest thing about Microsoft Outlook is that it has been designed for normal people like you. Part 6 is designed to give you more than just a basic understanding of what you can do with Outlook; it shows you how to manage your busy life with it.

■ Part 7: Office Data Sharing and Integration

Have you ever created a Word document and decided to include a summary of data that you have stored in an Excel spreadsheet? Do you wish you could just place the data in there and not worry about updating that same data in the Word document every time you change or manipulate it in the Excel worksheet? With the integration features of Word and Excel (and the other Office applications), you can do just that. Link the data you want from Excel into the Word document using dynamic data exchange (DDE) and rest assured that your data will always be updated. No need to enter the same updates in two different documents.

DDE is an internal communications protocol Windows uses to enable one application to "talk to" or exchange data with another application. Normally used to transfer information between applications, DDE also can be used within an application. Part 7 shows you ways to create and use DDE links and share information between applications.

■ Part 8: Microsoft Office and the Internet

New to Office 97 are a number of capabilities that let you connect Office files and applications to the Internet, or to a company-wide intranet. You can create Web pages with many of the Office applications and use the resulting HTML files on the Internet or an intranet. You learn how to do this in Part 8. Other Internet features in Office are discussed in each application's individual section.

■ Online Content

This book includes a special bonus for readers: two extra books, the *Word Digital Solutions Guide* and the *Excel Digital Solutions Guide*. In these two books are hundreds of pages of questions and answers to the most commonly asked questions about getting the most out of Word 97 and Excel 97.

You can access these books by accessing the Internet and going to **http:// blah.blah.com/file.htm**. You will need a user name and security code to access the pages. The username is **superguide** and the password is **solutions**.

■ Special Conventions and Sidebars

This book includes special conventions that help you follow along with various discussions and procedures.

Before you look ahead, you should spend a moment examining these conventions.

Typeface Conventions

When you see normal typeface, you know that the same information literally appears onscreen:

This appears onscreen.

When you see this same typeface with bold lettering, you know that you are supposed to type the information, as in the following example:

Type this information.

Anytime you see a word, letter, or number highlighted with boldface, you know to type it in. You might, for example, be instructed to type **WIN** at the DOS prompt. When you see this, you should type WIN as instructed.

New terms, when defined, appear in *italic*. Sometimes italic is also used to provide *emphasis* in a sentence.

Key Combinations

This book uses a special convention to help you know which keys to press and in what order:

- Key1+Key2: When you see a plus sign (+) between key names, hold down the first key while pressing the second key. Then release both keys.

- Key1,Key2: When a comma (,) appears between key names, press and release the first key, then press and release the second key.

Notes, Tips, and Warnings

One way to fully understand and exploit the power of the Office applications is to find shortcuts, enhancements, tips, and other insider information. *Windows Sources Microsoft Office 97 for Windows SuperGuide* is packed with Notes and Tips to give you those shortcuts and enhancements just when you need them!

Another way to take advantage of the power of Office and to increase your efficiency with its applications is to know when you might get in trouble with a feature or procedure. *Windows Sources Microsoft Office 97 for Windows Super-Guide* provides warnings to help you get around these problem spots.

1

Office 97

- *Office*
- *Word*
- *Excel*
- *Access*
- *PowerPoint*
- *Outlook*

1

What's New in Office 97

OFFICE 97 ADDS A HOST OF NEW FEATURES TO THE MICROSOFT

Office suite of applications. Office 97 is, in fact, one of the largest

upgrades of Office seen in recent years.

In this chapter you will learn about the new features of Office 97, including:

- New Internet and Intranet capabilities.

- Ease-of-use improvements in all Office 97 Applications.

- Microsoft Outlook, a new personal information manager debuting in Office 97 that replaces both Schedule+ and Exchange Client.

- The Office Assistant, an on-line guide to help you work with Office 97 applications.

- Other major and minor improvements in all of the Office 97 applications.

If you're upgrading from Office 95 to Office 97, pay particularly close attention to this chapter so that you have a handle on all of the new features available to you. Many tasks are significantly easier in Office 97, once you understand how to take advantage of its improvements over Office 95.

■ Office

In this section you'll learn about changes to parts of Office that aren't tied to a specific application, or that are global to all applications.

Office Assistant

All Office 97 applications now share the Office Assistant, a helpful, animated on-screen guide that helps you accomplish your work. The Office Assistant, shown in Figure 1.1, can be called up and sent away at will.

The Office Assistant accepts natural-language queries when you want help. Simply type your query, which could be something like, "Tell me about Page Borders," and click on the Search button or press Enter. The Office Assistant will show you relevant Help topics. The Office Assistant can also be programmed in a number of ways, including:

- To appear only when you use certain features, like Wizards.

- To display any alerts from the application.

- To guess the help you need based on what you've done recently.

- To show tips on keyboard shortcuts, on using features more effectively, and on using the mouse more effectively.

You click on the Options button in the Office Assistant window to access these options, and to choose which Office Assistant you want (there are a

Figure 1.1

The Office Assistant displaying help for Word

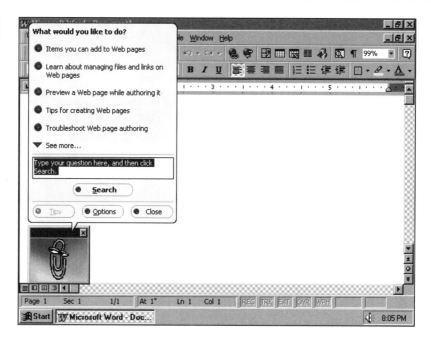

variety of charming characters from which to choose, each with their own animations and "personality").

IntelliMouse

Also new to Office 97 is the IntelliMouse, an updated version of the Microsoft Mouse that you're probably already used to. The IntelliMouse includes a roller button in between the two main buttons. The roller button can be used for special clicks, and can be used in Office 97 applications to browse information more easily.

OfficeArt

Office 97 includes Office Art, a powerful set of tools that you can use to add drawings to your documents. These tools include AutoShapes, which let you easily create complex shapes that can be formatted in a number of ways. AutoShapes can have gradient color fills and 3D perspectives, and can be easily rotated. Figure 1.2 shows an AutoShape created in Word to which some of these effects have been applied.

Figure 1.2

A couple of examples of
AutoShapes in Word

Visual Basic Development Environment

If you program in any or all of the Office applications, you'll appreciate the
new Visual Basic Development Environment (VBDE). Now that all Office
applications share Visual Basic for Applications, they also share the new
VBDE, shown in Figure 1.3. The VBDE lets you use a common development
environment for all of your Visual Basic for Applications (VBA) programs
written for Office applications.

Internet and Intranet Integration

Office applications now interface seamlessly with the World Wide Web. They
do so in a number of ways. First, most applications (Word, Excel, Power-
Point, and Access) can output their files into HyperText Markup Language
(HTML) format, which is used on the World Wide Web. Second, the Office
application documents can contain hyperlinks, which link to other Office documents or to Web pages on the Internet—clicking on a hyperlink takes you
immediately to the destination to which it points. Third, each Office application
has special Web tools that are used specifically with that application. For instance, Excel and Access can output tables to the Web. Excel has tools that import tabular data from Web pages or that can query information from the Web.

Figure 1.3

Visual Basic
Development Environment

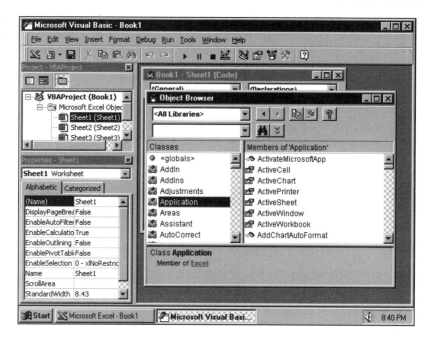

And you don't need to be on the Internet to use the Web tools in Office; you can use them to build your own Intranet in which people in your company can use a shared collection of Office documents that behave just like Web pages, but that also contain the power of the Office suite of applications.

Office Binder Improvements

The Office Binder has been improved in Office 97. Now, binders can be printed as a single print job, and can use a common header and footer, even when the binder is made up of documents from all of the different Office applications.

■ Word

Word 97 is perhaps the most improved application in Office 97. Aside from gaining the features common to all Office applications, such as the Office Assistant, Word has been updated to use Visual Basic for Applications instead of WordBasic. After making that fundamental change, Microsoft took the opportunity to add and improve many other areas of Word.

Letter Wizard

One particularly nice new productivity tool in Word is the Letter Wizard, an easy-to-use dialog box that helps you quickly prepare a letter template. The Letter Wizard, accessed through Word's Tools menu and shown in Figure 1.4, has four tabs that each offer you choices about your letter. Complete the information on the tabs, and Word will set up your letter, all ready for the body of the letter to be typed in.

Figure 1.4

Word 97's Letter Wizard

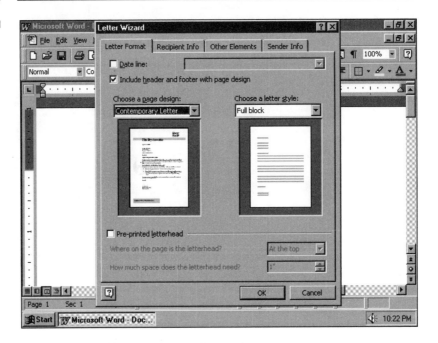

Automatic Grammar Checking

Word 95 introduced a handy feature called Spell-It, which automatically spell-checks documents as you type and marks words it doesn't recognize with a wavy red underline. Word 97 extends that functionality to its Grammar Checker, which marks out sentences that it thinks are ungrammatical with a wavy light-blue underline—right-click on a sentence with the wavy blue underline, and you'll see suggestions for fixing the sentence. The grammar checker built into Word 97 also uses natural-language algorithms that are more sophisticated about marking mistakes, and it offers better suggestions that those found in earlier versions of Word.

AutoSummarize

If you frequently prepare reports that include a summary of the report, you may find Word 97's new AutoSummarize feature helpful. Word uses advanced linguistic techniques to pull out the main ideas from a document and automatically writes a summary of the document. You can choose the length of the summary, and can preview the results before you accept them. Of course, you will generally need to edit the summary, but you'll find that Auto-Summarize gives you a good head start.

Automatic Hyperlinks

Word recognizes Uniform Resource Locators (URLs) from the Internet, UNCs (Universal Name Convention) that indicate filenames and e-mail addresses when they are typed into documents, and automatically creates hyperlinks for those entries. If you type one of these entries into a document, its text turns blue and it becomes a hyperlink. Click on the entry, and you are taken to the place indicated by the hyperlink automatically. When the hyperlink indicates an e-mail address, clicking on it opens a new message to that address.

Automatic Styles

Styles in Word 97 can now be created automatically. Type some text, format it as you like, and then apply a new style code using the Style drop-down list in Word's Formatting toolbar, and the style is created. Styles are also automatically updated when you change the formatting of a section that has an existing style applied to it.

AutoComplete

Word now automatically completes certain entries that you type. When you begin to type an AutoText entry, your name, or the current date, you will see a small yellow box appear above your typing that suggests the complete phrase. If you press the Enter key when the yellow box is visible, Word completes the rest of the words for you automatically. Figure 1.5 shows Word suggesting "Dear Mom and Dad," once "Dear M" is typed. Of course, if you're actually typing something else, just keep going and Word continues to work normally. The AutoComplete tip on the screen vanishes as soon as you type enough text to show Word that you're typing something different from what it's suggesting.

New Views

Word 97 includes a new view, Online Layout View, that lets you more easily preview and work with documents that you'll be publishing online. Online

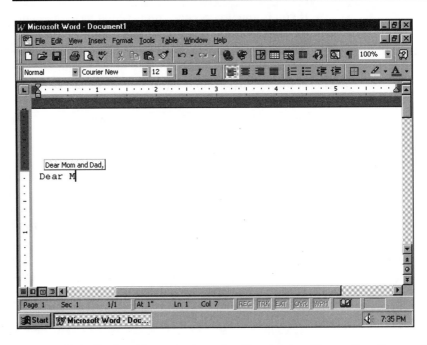

Layout View displays documents as they'll appear online, rather than as they might appear when printed.

By default, Online Layout View also activates another new feature called the Document Map, which shows an outline of your document in a window to the left of the main document window. You can navigate the document using the Document Map—simply click on a heading in the Document Map window, and the document window immediately shows that section of your document. Figure 1.6 shows Online Layout View with Document Map turned on. You can also activate Document Map for other views. You can access both features via their respective commands from the View menu of Word 97.

Versioning

Word 97 can now store multiple versions of a document in a single file. This feature, called Versioning, is found in the Versions command in the File menu. Figure 1.7 shows the Versions dialog box. In the Versions dialog box, you can choose the Save Now button to save a new version of the file. You can also use the Versions dialog box to open previous versions, or to delete previous versions of the file.

Figure 1.6

Online Layout View with
Document Map

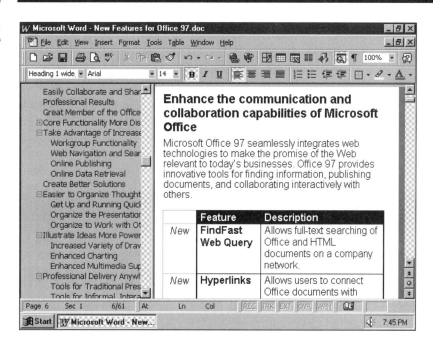

Figure 1.7

The Versions dialog box
is new to Word 97.

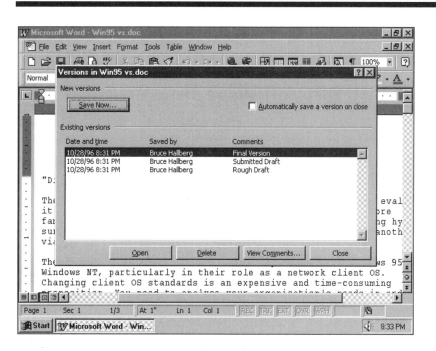

In-Place Comments

Earlier versions of Word let you store comments in your files, but now you can more easily review stored comments. Inserted comments are now marked with pale yellow background around the text that the comment is attached to. Simply place your mouse over a comment, and it appears on your screen, just like a ScreenTip on one of the toolbars. The comment even includes the name of its author, which is handy when multiple people have added comments to a document. Figure 1.8 shows an example comment appearing in this fashion.

Figure 1.8

An example of inserted comments

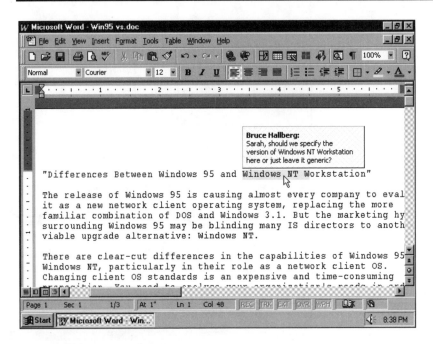

Portable Documents

One nice but subtle improvement in Word 97 is the concept of *portable documents*. Word 97 now compensates automatically for different installed printers, and retains a document's formatting even when another person opens the document and uses a printer with different capabilities than the one for which the document was generated.

Previously, the default printer that was selected when the document was generated had a lot to do with how the document's formatting appeared on the screen. Someone with a different printer selected would see the document slightly differently, and this often caused problems in companies that had many different printer types for different users. Now Word 97 uses new rules to lay out documents so that users should see documents similarly, even when they're using a different printer.

Animated Text

Word 97 now supports animated text. While animated text does not appear in a printed document, it does appear when others view the document in Word. You can access this feature from the Font dialog box: it is found when you use the Font command in the Format menu. In the Font dialog box, choose the Animation tab and then choose the effect you wish. Figure 1.9 shows the Animation tab of the Font dialog box.

Figure 1.9

The Animation tab of the Font dialog box

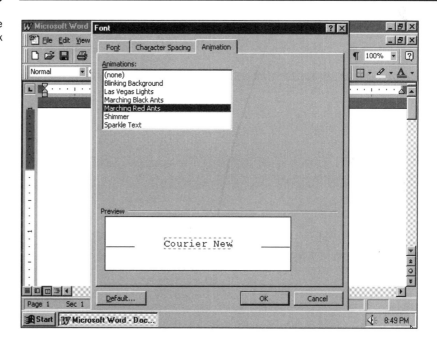

Table Drawing Tool

Earlier versions of Word let you set up complex tables that were not completely symmetrical. However, it was a fairly involved process that often took considerable time. Word 97 now lets you simply draw tables the way that you want them using the Draw Table command in the Table menu. Activating this command puts you in Page Layout view, and activates the Tables and Borders toolbar. You simply drag a box to start the table, and then drag inside the box where you want the table borders to appear. When you're finished, you have a normal table that appears exactly as you've drawn it. This feature is a real time-saver if you use tables often. Figure 1.10 shows an example of the Draw Table feature in action.

Figure 1.10

Drawing tables in Word 97

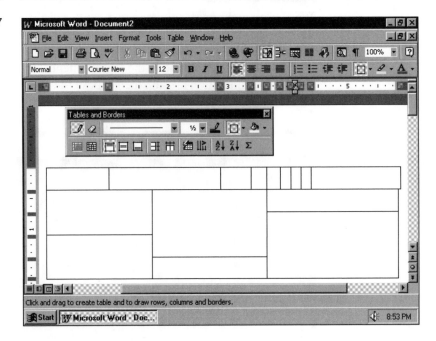

Page and Text Borders

Word 95 made you draw page borders manually with the square drawing tool. The problem with this approach is that your drawn page borders were hard to control, and you often couldn't get the proportions exactly correct. Word 97 enhances the Borders function with a new Borders and Shading dialog box, accessed with the Borders and Shading command in the Format menu. You can now use the Page Border tab in the dialog box to create page borders that are exactly as you want them. You can even use the Art drop-down list box to select from a variety of built-in border art, which you can use to spruce up your documents. In fact, Figure 1.11 shows this dialog box being used to add a Spruce border to a page.

Borders are also more sophisticated in that you can border selected text within a paragraph. Select the text that you want a border around, and access the Borders and Shading command in the Format menu. Then, use the Borders tab to choose the border that you want around the selected text.

Figure 1.11

The Page Border tab of the Borders and Shading dialog box

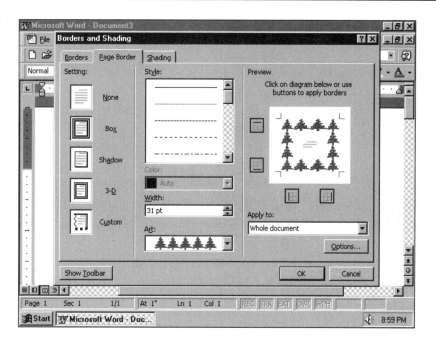

Miscellaneous Word Improvements

Bullets and Numbering has been improved with some new features. You can now create multilevel lists, which are often used in legal documents.

AutoCorrect has been made more intelligent, and can now catch some multiple-word errors so that, for instance, "int he" will be automatically changed to "in the." AutoCorrect can also catch some common multiple-word grammar errors, so that "go their" will change automatically to "go there."

Graphic images inserted into files are now compressed more efficiently, keeping file sizes to a minimum.

Text wraps around irregularly shaped embedded objects more intelligently, and you have more options for controlling how text wraps around such objects.

Word 97 integrates with Outlook much better than Word 95 integrated with Schedule+ and Exchange Client. You can now use the Outlook Journal feature to record work on a particular file, you can use your Outlook contact list as a source for mail merges and, with Word's Reviewing toolbar active, you can add tasks for a document to your Outlook task list.

■ Excel

Excel 97 includes a host of important improvements over its previous version. In this section you'll learn about Excel's increased capacities, new workgroup tools, easier and more powerful data queries, and improvements to how formulas are entered into Excel, as well as many other enhancements of particular note.

Shared Workbooks

Excel 95 let you create workbooks called "Shared Lists." In these, multiple people could access a file at the same time, but some important limitations existed. Excel 97 includes some extensive upgrades to this feature, now called Shared Workbooks:

- Changes from multiple users can now be consolidated automatically at intervals that you specify

- You can track changes made by different users for many days

- Each user can format the document and make other choices (such as printing choices) that are used for their own version of the open workbook

Figure 1.12 shows the Share Workbook dialog box's Advanced tab, which lets you control these features.

Improved Capacity

Excel 97's capacity has been increased dramatically over Excel 95's. You can now have cell entries that are up to 32,767 characters long (instead of 255) and each worksheet can have up to 65,535 rows (instead of 16,384). Also, the number of allowed data points in a chart data series has been increased from 4,000 to 32,000.

Improved Comments

Comments attached to cells can now be viewed just by placing your mouse over the comment. The comment, with the author's name, will pop up near the cell within a second or so.

Multiple Level Undo

Excel has now received a feature that Word has had for a while: multiple-level Undo. You can now Undo multiple actions, and you can use the Undo drop-down list box to select a number of actions to Undo at once.

Figure 1.12

The Advanced tab of the
Share Workbook
dialog box

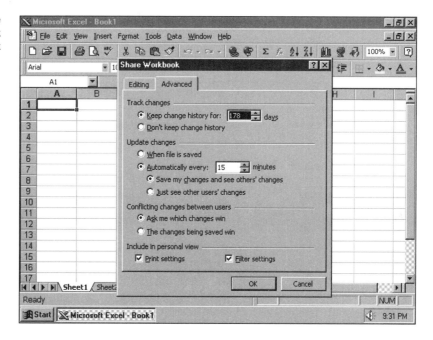

Formula AutoCorrect

Similar to Word's AutoCorrect, Excel's AutoCorrect feature now corrects 15
of the most common typing errors in formulas, such as double operators,
extra parentheses, and transposed cell references.

Natural Language Formulas

In Excel 95 you could enter formulas like =SquareFootage*RentalRate only
when you had properly defined the names of the cell ranges. Excel 97 is
much more intelligent in this regard: you can now use such formulas automatically. So long as the column and row headings are in the proper place in
relationship to the data, you can enter formulas based on those row and column headings, and Excel will understand them automatically.

Data Validation

It was possible to perform data validation on entries in earlier versions of Excel, but Excel 97 adds a Data Validation dialog box that makes setting up
data validation rules easy. You can define the data that is acceptable for any
given cell or range of cells, an input message that displays whenever a validated cell is selected, and an error alert that appears if the user tries to enter

a value that's not allowed. Figure 1.13 shows the Data Validation dialog box. You can access the Data Validation feature using the command of the same name in the Data menu.

Figure 1.13

The Error Alert tab of the Data Validation dialog box

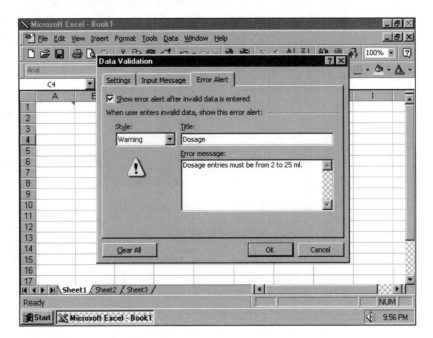

Track Changes

Another welcome change that Excel has inherited from Word is the Track Changes command found in the Tools menu. Using this command, you can automatically track changes made to a workbook or to a section of a work-sheet. These changes will be highlighted on screen, and you can choose to accept or reject specific changes. Figure 1.14 shows the Highlight Changes dialog box.

Collapse/Expand Dialog Boxes

There are many dialog boxes in Excel that let you use your mouse to select the range of cells that should be input into a particular field. In Excel 95, it was often difficult to move the dialog box out of your way so that you could select the range of cells you were interested in. In Excel 97, such dialog box fields have a Collapse/Expand Dialog Box button to the immediate right of the field that moves the dialog box completely out of your way while you select a range. Click the button again, and the dialog box reappears.

Figure 1.14

The Highlight Changes
dialog box

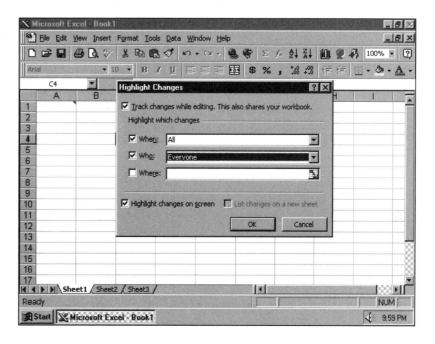

Range Finder

When you select a cell that contains a formula, the cells referenced by the formula are automatically highlighted in Excel 97, making it much faster to see the data on which the cell's results are based.

Custom Cells

You now have access to additional cell formatting enhancements that didn't exist in previous versions of Excel. You can rotate text within a cell to any angle, indent text within cells, and merge cells together so that one large cell exists where many cells previously existed. Also, the size of text in a cell can be automatically fitted to the cell's dimensions when you care more about the size of the cell than the exact size of font used within the cell.

Visual Printing

Placing page breaks has long been a hassle in Excel. Excel 97 addresses this by adding two new features. First, the View menu now includes a Page Break Preview view, in which you can easily see where page breaks will occur when the sheet is printed. Second, you can drag the page breaks and print-area borders to position them where you want them, easily and quickly.

Conditional Formatting

Excel 95 let you perform rudimentary conditional cell-formatting using cumbersome custom formatting codes. Excel 97 adds a new Conditional Formatting dialog box that lets you easily set special formatting that takes effect when the contents of the cell meet conditions that you specify. Figure 1.15 shows the Conditional Formatting dialog box with two simple formatting conditions applied.

Figure 1.15

Conditional Formatting
dialog box

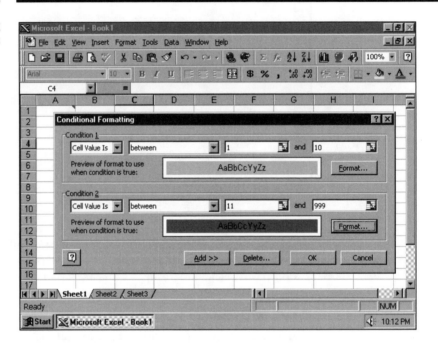

Formula Palette

Many users have trouble mastering formulas when they first start using Excel, and even experienced users can have difficulty with tricky formulas from time to time. Excel 97 adds the Formula Palette, a tool that combines the Function Wizard and the Formula Bar into a single tool that helps create formulas more easily than before. Figure 1.16 shows the Formula Palette active. Notice the dialog box's Collapse/Expand buttons at the right end of each of the formula parameters, Number and Form.

Figure 1.16

The Formula Palette in
Excel 97

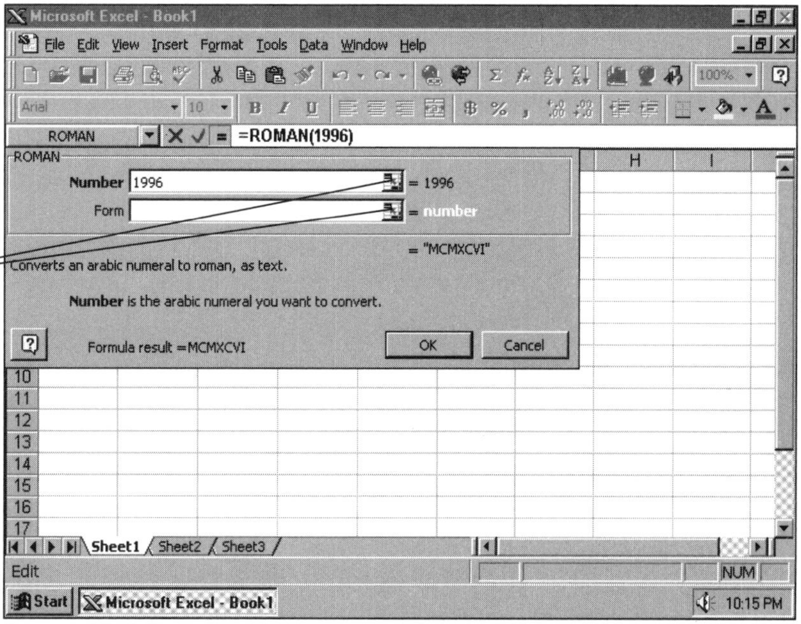

**Expand/
Collapse buttons**

Improved Queries

Many improvements have been made to Excel's querying abilities:

- You can query Web pages and import their data into your Excel workbooks.

- Queries can be written and then distributed to others to use.

- You can create parameterized queries, in which the query prompts the user for information that is used as part of the query. For instance, a query could prompt users for a customer ID number before retrieving a list of invoices linked to that customer ID number.

- Simple queries are easier to generate using the new Query Wizard in Excel 97.

Charting Improvements

Excel 97 includes a host of improvements in charting functionality. Key changes include:

- The Chart Wizard has been redesigned to be both more powerful and easier to use.

- Chart Tips now quickly display information about data points when you position your mouse over the data point momentarily.

- When charts are embedded in a worksheet, you can now select chart elements with a single click. In Excel 95, you first had to double-click on the chart to gain access to it, and then had to click on the element that you wanted to edit.

- There are a variety of new chart types. These include Pyramid, Cone, Cylinder, Bubble, Pie of Pie, and Bar of Pie charts.

- Chart axes that use dates or times now take into account that the axis is date- or time-scaled, and display the chart accordingly.

- You can easily include in your charts data tables that show the data being charted. Previously, you had to embed a chart in a worksheet, and create the data table above or below the chart. Now, the data table can be automatically created within the chart.

■ Access

Access received its big facelift as part of Office 95. However, some nice improvements have been included in Access 97 that make it a very worthwhile upgrade. In this section, you'll learn about these enhancements.

Improved Database Wizard

The Access Database Wizard has been improved to make creating databases easier than before. Over 20 different database wizards are included with Access 97. Each one will walk you through the process of creating a database. Figure 1.17 shows the Database Wizard setting up an asset-tracking database.

Internet Enhancements

Access 97 includes a number of Internet-related enhancements, including:

- Access can store Office 97 hyperlinks in its data fields, making data-organization easier than before.

- You can publish data from Access databases as HTML tables for inclusion in Web pages.

- Publish to the Web, a new feature in Access 97, lets you set up dynamic publications from Access databases to HTML-based Web pages. Publish to the Web requires the Microsoft Internet Information Server.

Figure 1.17

Creating a database with
the Database Wizard

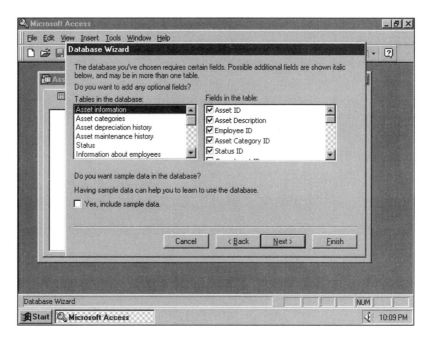

- HTML pages can be used within database records.

- Internet Replication lets you replicate Access databases over the Internet using the Internet's File Transfer Protocol (FTP).

Improved Performance

A key goal for Access 97 was improved performance. These changes all contribute to increased performance in Access 97:

- Delay loading, whereby Access doesn't load the entire application and all components. Rather, Access components are loaded only when they are needed. This improves the startup time for Access, and reduces the working memory footprint of the application for most uses.

- Forms and reports that do not use event procedures load much faster because the support code that handles event procedures isn't loaded when it's not needed by a form or report.

- ActiveX controls operate much faster in Access 97.

- Combo boxes operate faster than in Access 95.

A new Performance Analyzer scrutinizes your Access applications and suggests changes that can improve performance. Figure 1.18 shows the results of using the Tools, Analyze, Performance command on a database application.

Figure 1.18

Performance Analyzer suggests areas where you could improve database performance.

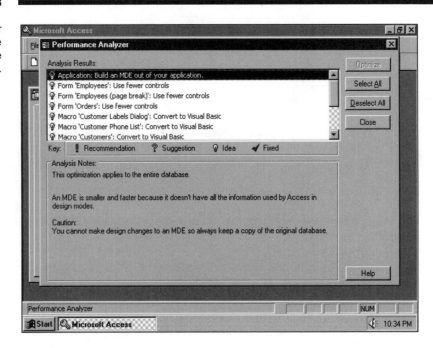

■ PowerPoint

PowerPoint has been extended in Office 97 to make generating presentations easier, to update PowerPoint with Office's new Internet capabilities, to improve performance, and to extend the overall functionality of the product.

Custom Shows

You can now create multiple "mini-presentations," called Custom Shows, within a single PowerPoint file, each one targeted to a different audience. You use the Custom Shows command in the Slide Show menu to prepare these custom shows. For each of the Custom Shows, you select which of your slides will be used, and in what order. You then present the appropriate Custom Show to each audience.

Expand Slide

The Expand Slide command, found on the Tools menu, takes all of the points on a single slide and creates new slides. The slide title on these new slides is made up of one of the original points. This feature lets you start with a summary slide, automatically creating slides that discuss each point in more detail.

Summary Slide

A new Summary Slide button on the Outlining and Slide Sorter toolbar lets you select multiple slides, and creates a summary slide on which each point is one of the slide titles. You can use this feature to create agenda slides once you've completed your detailed slides.

Microsoft Graph 97

Office 97 includes a new graphing module that eases the task of including charts in your slides. Graph 97 now includes many of the charting improvements also found in Excel 97. Graph 97 includes many of Excel's new chart types; handles time-scales more intelligently than before; allows picture, text, or gradient fills of chart elements; and even allows you to use animated charts.

Voice Narration

You can record the voice of a person delivering a self-running PowerPoint slide show, and attach this voice recording to the PowerPoint file. After you've done this, you can play the entire presentation back, complete with narration, and can also send the presentation file to others so that they can view and hear the complete presentation. To use this feature, access the Record Narration command in the Slide Show menu.

View on Two Screens

In cases when you have two presentation computers available, one for the presenter and one for the audience, the computers can be linked with a serial cable such that the presenter can view the PowerPoint Stage Manager and his or her notes, while the audience sees only the slides. Use the View on Two Screens command on the Slide Show menu to enable this feature.

Enhanced Export

To make your presentation viewable by those without PowerPoint, or to integrate a presentation onto a Web site, PowerPoint 97 can now export presentations into a number of different graphic file formats. These include JPEG

(JPG), Windows MetaFile (WMF), Encapsulated PostScript (EPS), PICT, and Graphics Interchange Format (GIF). Viewers for many of these formats are readily available.

Home Page Template

You can now use PowerPoint to quickly build your own home page for use on the Internet. With the AutoContent Wizard, you can create a template for your company home page in a snap.

New Presentation Modes

Three new features make it easier for you to set up PowerPoint shows for others. The first, called Save as PowerPoint Show, causes the presentation to be automatically displayed as soon as the file is opened by another person using PowerPoint 97. You can access this feature by using the PowerPoint Show format in the Save As dialog box.

You can also use the Set Up Show command in the Slide Show menu to control how the show will be viewed. You can set up the show to run in browse mode, in which a simplified set of commands is available for controlling the show. Another choice is Kiosk mode, with or without manual advance of slides, that sets up your show to be displayed in a trade show booth or in some other setting. PowerPoint 97 gives you many choices on how you want your shows to be displayed.

File Enhancements

A number of improvements in how PowerPoint saves its files enhance the performance of the application and conserve disk space. First, PowerPoint 97 automatically compresses embedded graphics in your presentation files in order to keep the size of the files as small as possible. Consequently, files load and save faster than before—with big presentations, this can be a significant benefit. Second, PowerPoint 97 now includes AutoRecover, in which your work is saved at regular intervals that you specify. If your computer loses power, your work up until the last save interval will be recovered when you restart PowerPoint. Third, JPEG files are stored in their native compressed format, further reducing file sizes.

Visual Basic for Applications

PowerPoint is now programmable with Visual Basic for Applications, the common programming language in the Office suite of applications. Using VBA, you can develop custom solutions that take advantage of the inherent power of PowerPoint. You can also record a series of actions into a macro program that can be played back at will, or further modified to suit your needs.

Miscellaneous Enhancements

PowerPoint now automatically checks your spelling as you prepare your presentations. The spelling checker functions in the background, underlining unrecognized words with a wavy red line. Right-click on such a word, and a suggested replacement will appear in a pop-up menu.

PowerPoint now uses the same color palette as the other Office applications, which makes it much easier to "mix and match" pieces generated in different Office applications into a coherent, properly colored whole.

Finally, PowerPoint 97 benefits from multiple-level undo and redo. You can even undo multiple actions with just a couple of clicks by using the dropdown list of actions next to the undo button on the toolbar.

■ Outlook

Possibly the most exciting addition to Office 97 is a new program called Outlook. Microsoft Outlook 97 combines the functions of both Exchange Client and Schedule+, with a number of new features in addition to those that Exchange Client and Schedule+ possessed previously. In this section, you'll learn about these new features . Figure 1.19 shows the main Outlook screen.

Figure 1.19

The main Outlook screen with the Inbox selected

The Inbox shows all the messages you've received.

Use the Outlook window to choose what information you view.

Other windows are available (such as Mail, which lists all your e-mail folders).

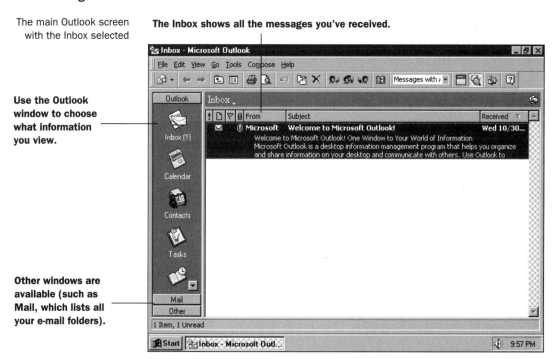

Interface Consistency

Outlook preserves the user interface of both Schedule+ and Exchange Client, with as few differences as possible. Because of this, learning Outlook is easier.

Mail Merge

You can use your Outlook contact list as a source for Microsoft Word mail-merge files. You can also choose a contact in your contact list and automatically start a letter to him or her by choosing the desired name and accessing the New Letter to Contact command from the Contacts menu. Using this command invokes Word's Letter Wizard, which fills out the recipient information for you.

Drag and Drop

You can drag and drop information from Outlook to other applications, or from other applications to Outlook. For instance, if you have a list of tasks in Word, you can select each line and drag it to a date in Outlook's calendar to create new action items on that date.

Attachments

Not only can you send attachments as part of e-mail messages, but Outlook lets you include attached files in other Outlook records, such as Contact records, appointments, and tasks. For instance, if you have a document that you need to discuss with someone, you can attach that document to the appointment record you create, making the document easy to access when the appointment actually begins. Alternatively, you can attach detailed information in a document to a task that pertains to the information in that document.

Task Links

You can create tasks for the document you are working with from within Office applications. If you are writing a proposal in Word and need to remind yourself to do some additional research, for example, you can create that reminder as a task from within your Word document.

AutoJournal

Outlook includes a journaling function that keeps track of time you spend on different activities. You can create your own journal entries, and you can also set Outlook to automatically track work with any Office document, with e-mail messages, and so on.

Document Explorer

Using the Other folder in the left-hand Outlook window, you can browse files on your computer from within Outlook, selecting the ones you want to work with or that you want to include in an Outlook record.

Messaging Enhancements

Outlook contains a number of improvements over Exchange Client in the area of messaging, including:

- **AutoName Check**. Earlier versions of Exchange Client didn't check the e-mail recipient's name you were typing until you actually sent the message or clicked on the Check Names button. Outlook now automatically looks up recipients as you type, letting you see if the right recipient is selected and saving you an extra step.

- **AutoPreview**. A nice addition to the Inbox, AutoPreview shows you the first few lines of unread messages in the Inbox. This feature lets you more easily determine which messages you want to read immediately, and which ones you want to deal with later.

- **Comma Separator**. If you choose, you can separate recipient names with commas rather than semicolons.

- **Contact Address Book**. You can store more than one e-mail address for each contact in your contact list.

- **Deferred Delivery**. You can choose to set a message to be delivered at a given time.

- **Easy Open Attachments**. You can open attachments without having to open the message that contains the attachment. Right-click on a message in your Inbox that has an attachment, and choose the View Attachments command from the pop-up menu.

- **Hyperlinks**. Hyperlinks to Web pages or to Office documents can be included within messages, and within other Outlook records.

- **Message Expiration**. If you choose, you can set expiration dates on messages, which will automatically delete a message at a selected time.

- **Message Recall**. You can retract a message from a recipient's Inbox, so long as the message is still unread. You can also choose to replace the message with a new version.

- **Reply Annotation**. If you change text in a reply, this feature automatically flags those changes with your initials.

- **Voting.** Outlook lets you create e-mail messages that contain voting fields, and automatically tracks vote responses for you.

Scheduling Improvements

Outlook contains quite a few enhancements to the scheduling and calendaring functions that were present in Schedule+, including:

- **All-Day and Multiple-Day Events**. You can create events that mark you as being busy without using 24-hour appointments.

- **AutoArchive**. Outlook will automatically archive entries that are a certain number of days old, keeping your Outlook mailbox's file size as small as possible.

- **Discontiguous Days**. You can view days that are not contiguous simultaneously to more effectively manage a complex schedule.

- **Time-Zone Swapping**. You can swap your time zone, such that all entries that are time-based will automatically be updated to reflect your new time zone.

- **World Holidays.** A number of different holiday lists are included with Outlook, and can be imported into your calendar. You can choose among different religions and different countries, adding the new list of holidays to your calendar automatically.

■ Summary

There are more improvements in Office 97 than can be easily discussed in this chapter. Many major advances have been incorporated into Office 97, but you will also find many small enhancements, each one making your work a little easier.

It takes time to learn any new piece of software, even when it's an upgrade of a collection of programs you've worked with for a while. You'll be discovering new features of Office 97 for quite some time. However, Microsoft has done a very nice job of making the improvements work as easily as possible, so you'll also find that using the new features of Office 97 isn't really all that difficult. The first part of the battle is in learning what the new features are. After that, you'll find that learning to actually use them is quite painless, and very rewarding.

- *Using the Office Shortcut Bar*

2

Using the Microsoft Office Shortcut Toolbar

THE OFFICE SHORTCUT BAR, A TOOL THAT LETS YOU MORE EASILY start Office programs and other programs on your computer, is included in Office.

In this chapter you will learn about the Office Shortcur Bar, including how to:

- Use the default toolbar provided with Office
- Move the toolbar and change its display properties
- Display and use other toolbars
- Customize the Office Shortcut Bar
- Use the toolbar to access the Office installation program

The Office Shortcut Bar is a very straightforward tool to use. Mastering it and taking advantage of its more advanced capabilities will enhance your productivity with Office 97 applications.

■ Using the Office Shortcut Bar

By default, the Office Shortcut Bar appears in the upper-right corner of your screen, as shown in Figure 2.1. The buttons on the Shortcut Bar let you perform basic Office tasks, such as starting Word, or adding a contact to Outlook.

Figure 2.1

The default Office
Shortcut Bar

| 1 | 2 | 3 | 4 | 5 | 6 | 7 | 8 | 9 | 10 | 11 |

1. Control menu
2. New Office document
3. Open Office document
4. New message
5. New appointment
6. New task

7. New contact
8. New journal entry
9. New note
10. Microsoft Bookshelf basics
11. Getting results book

You can create new office documents with the New Office Document button, which displays the dialog box shown in Figure 2.2. The New Office Document dialog box in Figure 2.2 differs from the one you see when you choose the New command in an Office application's File menu, because it includes the new document templates for all Office applications, as well as the supplementary tabs for all of the Office applications.

Moving the Shortcut Bar

You can move the Shortcut Bar to five different positions on your screen:

- The default position where it appears in an open application's title bar

Figure 2.2

The New Office
Document dialog box

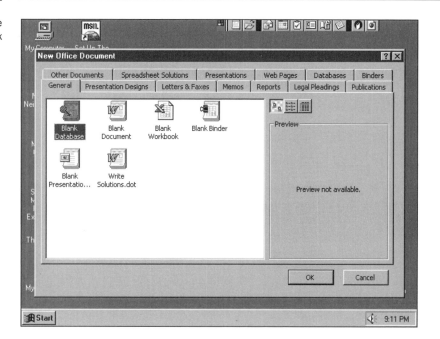

- Floating, where you can position it anywhere you like on your screen (see Figure 2.3).

- Against the right or left side of the screen, or the bottom of the screen (see Figure 2.4).

When the Office Shortcut Bar is at the top of the screen, but you want to display it at its full size instead of the small size shown in Figure 2.1, follow these steps:

1. Click the Control Menu for the Shortcut Bar.

2. Choose Customize from the menu that appears.

3. On the View tab of the Customize dialog box, deselect Auto Fit into Title Bar area.

Displaying Other Toolbars

The Office Shortcut Bar comes with a variety of Toolbars built in, but only the Office Toolbar will be active at first. To access the other Toolbars, follow these steps:

1. Right-click on a blank portion of the Shortcut Bar to display the Toolbar pop-up menu (see Figure 2.5).

Figure 2.3

The Office Shortcut Bar
floating on the desktop

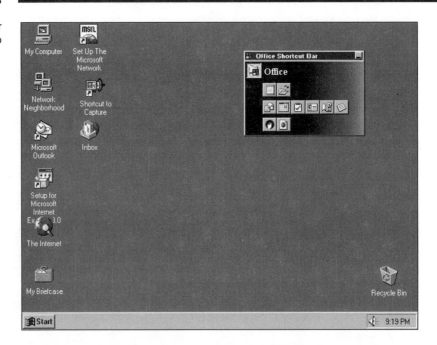

Figure 2.4

The Office Shortcut Bar
anchored to the bottom
of the desktop

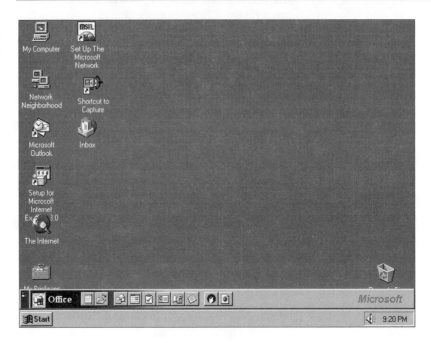

Figure 2.5

Choosing other toolbars

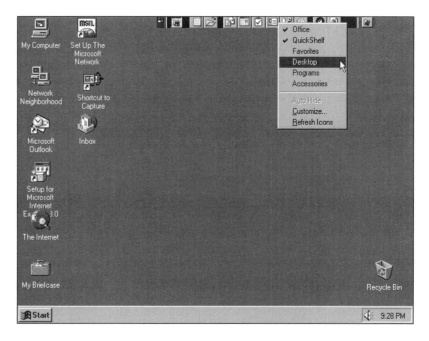

2. Select the Toolbar you want to access from the pop-up menu. Accessible Toolbars will have a check mark next to their commands on the pop-up menu.

   You can choose from these available Toolbars:

- Office, which displays the icons used with the Office suite of applications.

- QuickShelf, which displays icons related to using Bookshelf Basics.

- Favorites, which displays the icons for your favorite places on the Internet.

- Desktop, which displays icons that mirror those found on your Windows desktop.

- Programs, which lets you directly launch Office programs such as Word and Excel; and also other key Windows programs, such as the MS-DOS prompt, Microsoft Explorer, and so forth.

- Accessories, which displays the icons for the Accessory programs that come with Windows.

Adding and Removing Buttons

You can customize the buttons that appear on any of the Office Shortcut Toolbars by adding and removing buttons, or by rearranging buttons. To do so, access the Customize dialog box by right-clicking on a blank area in the Shortcut bar, and choose Customize from the pop-up menu that appears. You will then see the Customize dialog box. Click on the Buttons tab to move to that page of the dialog box (see Figure 2.6).

Figure 2.6

Customizing the buttons on the Office Shortcut Bar

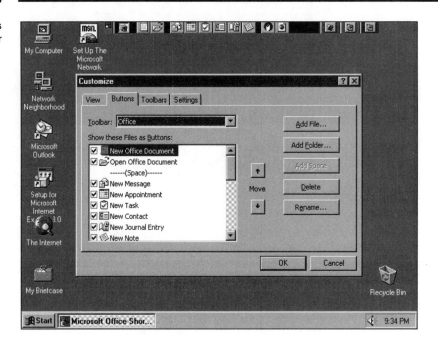

First, select the Toolbar you want to customize by using the Toolbar drop-down list box. You can then hide or show existing buttons by clicking in their checkbox. The checkmark will then indicate whether the button will be visible or not.

To add either a program or file to a toolbar, click the Add File button. You will then see the Add File dialog box, as shown in Figure 2.7. Use the dialog box to locate the program or file you want to add, select it, and click on the Add button.

Often, when you add a program or file to a Toolbar, its assigned name may not be what you want it to be. For instance, adding Microsoft Outlook to the Office toolbar results in a button called Outlook.exe, instead of simply Outlook. You can change this by selecting the button you just added

Figure 2.7

The Add File dialog box

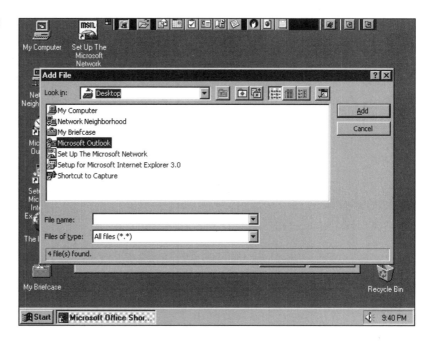

and then clicking on the Rename button. A Rename dialog box will appear in which you can type the name that the Shortcut Bar should use for your new button.

To change the position of a button in the Toolbar, select the item you want to move and then click on the Move up and Move down buttons to reposition the item.

To add a spacer to a Toolbar, select the button that is after the spot where you want the space to appear, then click on the Add Space button.

Finally, you can also add folders to Toolbars. Doing so can be helpful when you must frequently access a project folder that contains files that you work with often. Use the Add Folder button just as you used the Add File button, only this time select a folder name before clicking on the Add button in the Add Folder dialog box.

Adding Toolbars

If you want to create a new Toolbar, you can do so by using the Customize dialog box for the Office Shortcut Bar. Move to the Toolbars tab (see Figure 2.8) and click on the Add Toolbar button. You'll see the Add Toolbar dialog box shown in Figure 2.9.

Figure 2.8

The Toolbars tab of the
Customize dialog box

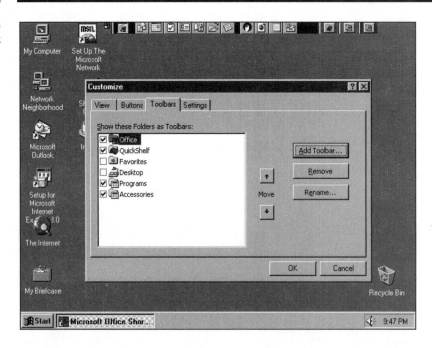

Figure 2.9

The Add Toolbar
dialog box

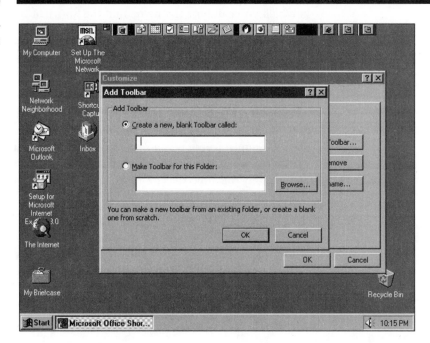

In the Add Toolbar dialog box you can either choose to create a blank toolbar, or to create a toolbar based on the contents of a folder. If you choose the latter, the toolbar will be populated with all the icons from the files and programs in the folder you have selected.

Changing the Toolbar's Appearance

There are many choices available to you if you wish to change the appearance of the Office Shortcut Bar. You can access these choices with the View tab of the Customize dialog box, shown in Figure 2.10.

Figure 2.10

The View tab of the Customize dialog box

In the View tab, you first choose the Toolbar you want to use when working with the Toolbar drop-down list box. You can then set these options:

- Use the Change Color button to control the background color of the toolbar.

- Create a gradient effect with the Use Gradient Fill checkbox. This causes the color of the toolbar background to fade out from one end of the toolbar to the other. A gradient fill can often make it easier to distinguish the toolbar on the screen.

- If you have chosen a gradient fill, you can choose the Smooth checkbox to change how it will appear on-screen. This option has no effect if you are using a video-display mode that supports 256 colors or less.

- Choosing Use Standard Toolbar Color forces the toolbar to use the selected Windows color scheme.

- Enlarge the buttons of the toolbar (and make them easier to see) with the Large Buttons checkbox.

- Control the availability of pop-up Tooltips with the Show Tooltips checkbox.

- If you select Always on Top, the toolbar is always visible and on top of any programs that are running on your desktop.

- If you have Always on Top deselected, you can choose the Auto Hide between uses checkbox. This makes the toolbar disappear until you move your mouse pointer to the side of the screen in which the toolbar is anchored. When you do, the toolbar pops up again and can be used. The toolbar hides itself again once you've moved your mouse pointer away from the edge of the screen.

- When you select Auto Fit into Title Bar area, the toolbar will always fit into the title bar of maximized Windows programs.

- Select Animate Toolbars to make the toolbars animate as you use them. This improves their visibility. You can also cause sounds to be played as the toolbars are moved with the Sound checkbox.

- Show Title Screen at Startup displays an Office 97 "splash screen" when the Office Shortcut Bar is opened.

Locating Office Templates

The Settings tab of the Customize dialog box shown in Figure 2.11 lets you tell Office where its templates are located. There are two types of templates, each found in a different location: your own private templates, which are usually found in the \Office97\Templates folder; and Workgroup templates, which are typically found in a network folder.

When you set a location for Workgroup templates, you indicate a folder that contains Office template files. This folder will generally also include other folders. Each folder in the Workgroup Templates folder will automatically display in any Office File New dialog box as a template tab. For example, if you set the Workgroup Templates location as F:\Company Templates, any templates stored in that folder will appear in the General tab of the File New dialog box. Any folders under F:\Company Templates will be shown as other tabs, with the templates stored in those folders appearing when you select

Figure 2.11

The Settings tab of the
Customize dialog box

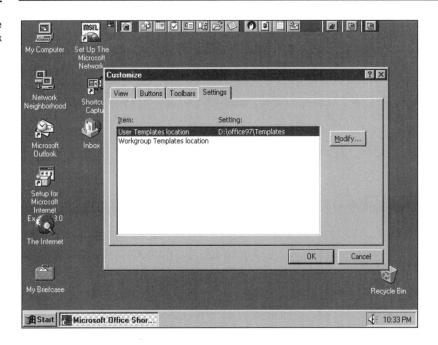

those tabs. You can, for instance, create the folders F:\Company Templates\ Legal or C:\Company Templates\Accounting and place relevant forms that your company uses in the appropriate folders so that everyone can access them easily.

TIP. *When you set the Workgroup Templates folder location in the Office Shortcut Bar, all Office applications automatically inherit that setting, and will also scan the Workgroup Templates location for valid Office templates. You do not have to set a Workgroup Templates location for each application if you set it for the Office Shortcut Bar.*

Customizing the Office Installation

You can add or remove Office components from the Office Shortcut bar by opening the Shortcut Bar's Control Menu and then choosing Add/Remove Office Programs. This action is the same one you use to start the Office Setup program from the CD-ROM that contains Office.

- *Introducing the Office Assistant*
- *Using Office Binders*
- *Managing Find Fast*
- *Managing Office Startup*

3

Using Office Tools

OFFICE 97 INCLUDES A NUMBER OF TOOLS THAT ARE COMMON TO all of the Office applications. These tools make using Office easier and faster. In this chapter you will learn about these tools, including:

- Office Assistant
- Office Binders
- Fast Find
- Office Startup
- Bookshelf Basics

■ Introducing the Office Assistant

Office 97 includes a powerful new tool called the Office Assistant. The Office Assistant uses artificial intelligence to assist you more efficiently. By default, the Assistant is available whenever you start an Office application, although you can close it with its Close button. To open the Assistant when it's not visible, click on the Office Assistant button of any Office application's toolbar. You can see the default Assistant in Figure 3.1.

Figure 3.1

The default Office
Assistant

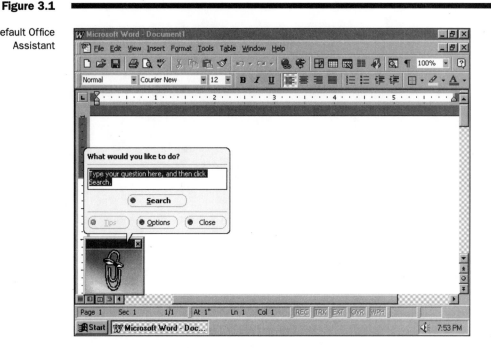

You can enter Help queries into the Office Assistant if you need assistance. To do so, simply click on the Office Assistant character, and the search window in Figure 3.1 will appear. Type your question and click the Search button to see relevant topics. You can phrase your question any way you'd like. Some examples of valid questions for the Office Assistant are:

- "Tell me about Page Borders"

- "How do I add a Page Border?"

- "Page Borders"

All you really need to construct your query is a keyword or phrase that describes what you need help with. If you don't receive information on the desired topic, try choosing a different word or phrase to describe what you want to do.

When you're using an Office application with the Office Assistant open and you perform some action that it has a tip for you about, you'll see a light bulb appear near the Office Assistant character, as shown in Figure 3.2. Click on the Office Assistant to see the tip itself.

Figure 3.2

A tip from Office Assistant

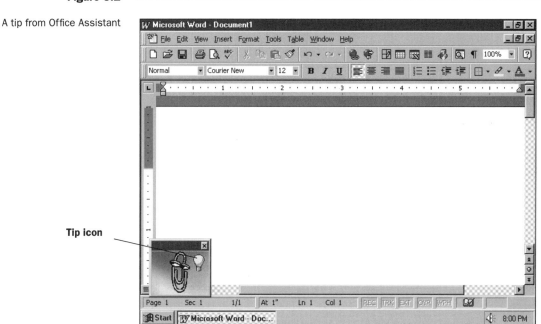

Tip icon

Tip. The Office Assistant remembers the tips you've seen, and doesn't display them again. You can reset your tips by accessing the Office Assistant and choosing Options, and then choosing Reset my tips from the Options page of the Office Assistant dialog box.

Choosing Your Assistant

A number of different Assistants are available for use with Office 97. You can choose one that suits your personality and needs. To choose a new Office Assistant, access the Assistant by clicking on it, and then choose the Options button from the dialog bubble that appears. You will see the Office Assistant dialog box appear. The Gallery page of the Office Assistant dialog box is shown in Figure 3.3.

Scroll through the various Office Assistant choices with the Back and Next buttons. When you see one that you want to use, click the OK button to activate that Assistant. You may need your Office 97 CD-ROM to install the Assistant you selected—you will automatically be prompted for it if it's needed.

Figure 3.3

The Gallery tab of the
Office Assistant dialog
box

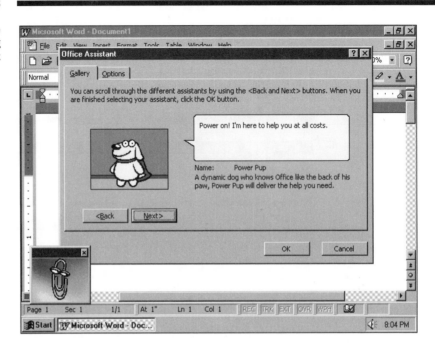

Changing Assistant Help Behavior

Tip. Different Office
Assistants are more
"active" than others: you
may find the animation
distracting, but still want
to use the Assistant. The
Office Logo Assistant is
the least active, while
the Dot and PowerPup
Assistants are the most
active.

There are a variety of settings available to change the way the Office Assistant functions. You can access these settings by clicking on the Assistant, choosing the Options button, and then selecting the Options tab of the Office Assistant dialog box (see Figure 3.4).

The following options are available to you:

- **Respond to F1 key**. Selecting this causes the Office Assistant to appear whenever you press the F1 key for help in any Office application.

- **Help with Wizards**. When selected, the Assistant will appear when you start using most of the Wizards in Office 97, and will offer additional help in using the Wizard.

- **Display Alerts**. Causes the Assistant to display any alerts from Office applications.

- **Move when in the way**. This option lets you leave the Assistant on the screen, but keeps it out of your way when you're working. If selected, the Assistant will shrink to a smaller size if not used in five minutes, and will automatically move out of the way of any dialog boxes that you use.

Figure 3.4

The Options tab of the
Office Assistant
dialog box

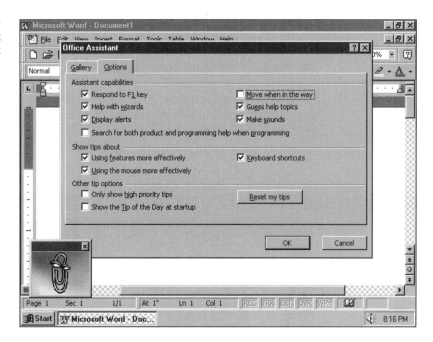

- **Guess help topics**. If you choose this option, when you access the Assistant it will automatically show you help for your most recently completed actions.

- **Make sounds**. This option gives you additional feedback from the Assistant in the form of sounds. It only works when you have a sound card installed in your PC.

- **Search for both product and programming help when programming**. If selected, the Assistant will provide both programming help and help with the Visual Basic Development Environment, when you are programming in Visual Basic.

- **Show tips about**. This section of the dialog box lets you select the types of tips that the Office Assistant will display. You can choose tips on using application features more effectively, on using the mouse more effectively, and on keyboard shortcuts that make using Office faster.

- **Only show high priority tips**. Choosing this option causes the Assistant to only show you the most important tips, such as those that might make a major impact on your productivity.

- **Show the Tip of the Day at startup**. This option causes a tip to display whenever you open an Office application.

- **Reset my tips.** The Office Assistant remembers the tips you've seen, and won't display them again. Clicking this button clears its memory of the tips you've seen.

■ Using Office Binders

Office Binders let you group multiple files that relate to a single project in one file that can be easily distributed and accessed by people working on that project. You can access the Microsoft Binders program from the Programs menu of your Start menu. Figure 3.5 shows a blank Binder started in this way.

Figure 3.5

A blank Binder

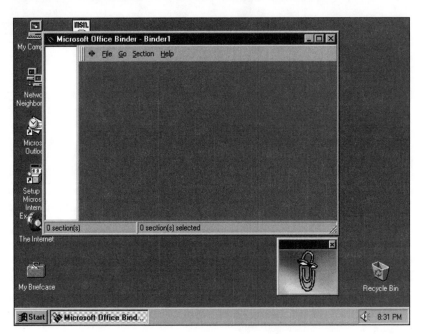

Use the File menu of the Binder's menu to save the Binder, open existing Binders, or create new Binders. You can also exit the Binder application from the File menu.

To add files to a Binder, open the Section menu and choose either Add or Add from File. Using the Add command creates a blank file in the binder—you'll see the Add Section dialog box shown in Figure 3.6. Choose the type of file you want to add, then click the OK button to add the file to the Binder.

Figure 3.6

The Add Section dialog
box

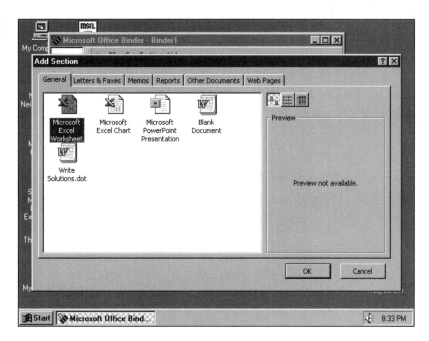

Choosing the Add from File command opens a standard File Open dialog box, from which you may select files to add to the Binder.

Binders not only let you group files together, but they let you actually work on the Binder files while in the Office Binder program. Figure 3.7 shows a more complex sample binder in which one of the documents is selected. In the main pane of the Office Binder application, you can see that Word (the application for the file in question) is active and usable.

TIP. *If you frequently prepare customer proposals, consider creating a Binder that has templates for all of the documents that you typically include. It will help you make sure that you've completed all of the forms for each proposal, and it will also make it easier to keep all of the related documents together for easy reference.*

Common Binder Actions

You can perform several actions on all of the files within a Binder. You can apply headers and footers to selected Binder files, including using a common page-numbering scheme; print all the files in a Binder; check the spelling on all of the Binder contents; and preview printouts for the entire Binder.

Figure 3.7

Editing documents within
a Binder

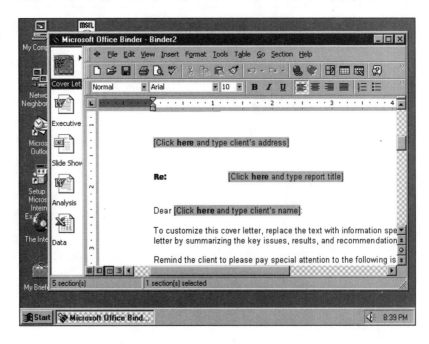

To check the spelling on an entire Binder, you must have the left pane visible on your screen. If it's not visible, click the Show/Hide Left Pane button. Next, select the sections (files) that you want to work with by holding down the Ctrl key and clicking each section in the section pane. Then choose the Spelling command from the Tools menu. All selected binder files will be checked.

To work with print settings for an entire Binder, access the Binder Page Setup command in the File menu. The Header/Footer tab in the Binder Page Setup dialog box will let you set the header and footer for the binder, and will also allow you to select which sections in the binder will use the header and footer that you create. Figure 3.8 shows this dialog box.

Use the Print Settings tab of the Binder Page Setup dialog box to choose which sections of a binder are printed, and how page numbers will behave for the sections that you print. You can choose to restart numbering at each section, or to consecutively number each section so that they all share common page numbering.

Tip. You can set page numbering for the Binder in either the Binder Page Setup dialog box or the Print Binder dialog box.

To preview a Binder's printout, choose the Binder Print Preview command from the File menu. You can print all of the Binder's contents with the Print Binder command, also found in the File menu.

Figure 3.8

The Header/Footer tab of
the Binder Page Setup
dialog box

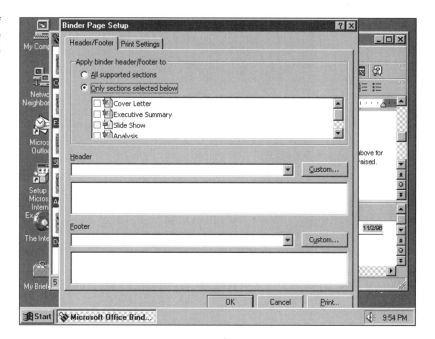

■ Managing Find Fast

Microsoft Find Fast indexes your Office 97 documents in the background, and provides this index automatically to Office programs when you use the Find File feature in their Open dialog boxes. Find Fast indexes can dramatically speed your search for a particular file, even in a complex hierarchy of many Office documents. Find Fast operates automatically: you don't need to do anything special to use its indexes when you perform searches for Office documents.

Find Fast runs automatically when you start your computer. Thereafter, it updates its indexes in the background while you work. It does this every couple of hours for each of the local hard drives connected to your computer. Indexes consume from 5 percent to 30 percent of the size of the files being indexed.

You can control Find Fast's indexes using the Find Fast icon in the Control Panel. When you access this icon, you'll see the Find Fast window shown in Figure 3.9.

Figure 3.9

The Find Fast window

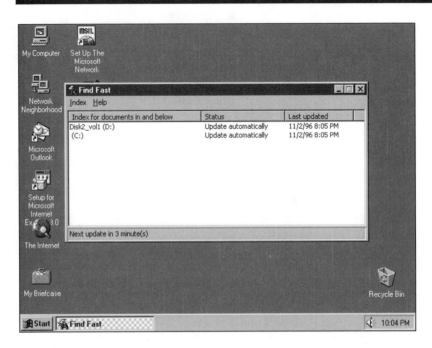

The Find Fast window shows you the status for each of the indexes it maintains. You can use the Index menu to control the different indexes. In the Index menu, you can perform these actions:

- **Create Index**. Creates a new index. You choose the folder that will be indexed (subfolders are indexed automatically as part of a selected folder), the types of documents that will be indexed, and three settings concerning the index. The three settings are Continue to update automatically, Speed up property display, and Speed up phrase searching. The latter two settings cause the indexes that are created to be larger than they otherwise would be. In the case of Speed up phrase searching, indexes increase to be 30 percent of the size of the indexed documents.

- **Update Index**. Changes the folder that an index references. You can also set or clear a checkbox that controls whether the selected index continues to be updated automatically. Finally, you can see statistics about the index by clicking on the Information button. You'll see the Index Information dialog box shown in Figure 3.10.

- **Delete Index**. If you want to recover the space an index consumes on your system, you can delete the index with this command.

Figure 3.10

The Index Information
dialog box

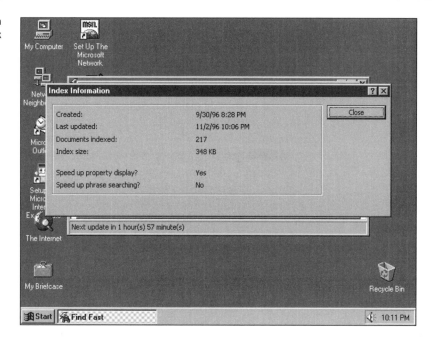

- **Update Interval.** Lets you change how often the index is updated. The
  default setting is for the index to update every two hours.

  Some index settings cannot be changed. You cannot change whether or
  not an index speeds up phrase searching or speeds up the property display,
  nor can you change the files that are included in the index. In order to
  change these settings, you must delete the index and then create a new one
  with the settings you want.

  NOTE. *On some machines and with some other software installed, Office Find
  Fast can cause problems. If you have trouble with applications crashing
  frequently, you may want to try disabling Find Fast before exploring other
  measures. You can disable Find Fast by removing its icon from the Startup
  folder—you should move it to another folder instead of deleting it—and then
  restarting Windows. If the problem doesn't go away and you don't think Find
  Fast was its cause, re-enable Find Fast by moving its icon back into the Startup
  folder, and restart Windows.*

■ Managing Office Startup

Office Startup is a program that automatically installs itself into your Startup folder. Its purpose it to pre-load some common Office 97 files, so that your Office applications will start more quickly.

You might want to disable Office Startup if you don't commonly use Office applications. Doing so reduces the amount of memory needed on your computer when you aren't running any Office applications, the trade-off being that Office applications will take a little bit longer to load when you do invoke them.

To disable Office Startup, move its icon out of the Startup folder, then restart Windows. You can re-enable it by moving its icon back into the Startup folder and then restarting Windows again.

There are no options to set for Office Startup.

- *Menus*

- *Dimmed Text, Ellipses, and Keyboard Shortcut
  Listings*

- *Customizing Menus*

- *Toolbars*

Learning the Office Common User Interface

ALL OF THE OFFICE APPLICATIONS SHARE CERTAIN COMMON FEAtures between their user interfaces. In other words, they all function similarly in certain respects. One of the big advantages of using a suite of programs, like Office 97, is that learning each individual application is easier than it would be otherwise. Once you learn a single application, the others are easier to master because they interact with you in similar ways.

In this chapter you'll learn about the common features of the Office 97 interface, and how to perform some actions that are similar among all of the Office 97 applications.

■ Menus

Early Windows programs standardized on two menus that almost all applications shared: the File menu and the Edit menu. The File menu, of course, contains commands for opening, saving, and closing files, as well as for printing files. The Edit menu contains commands that pertain to the clipboard, and to search and replace functions.

Office applications now include another menu found in most of the individual applications: an Insert menu. The Insert menu is for inserting objects into the file with which you're working. For instance, you can insert graphic images, text boxes, comments, and so forth from most Office applications.

In a new development, Office 97 menus now contain icons. The icons displayed next to the menu commands mirror the icons you see for those commands on the toolbars. Figure 4.1 shows the File menu from Excel. Notice that the New, Open, Save, Print Preview, and Print commands all have a toolbar icon to the left of the command.

Figure 4.1

The File menu from Excel

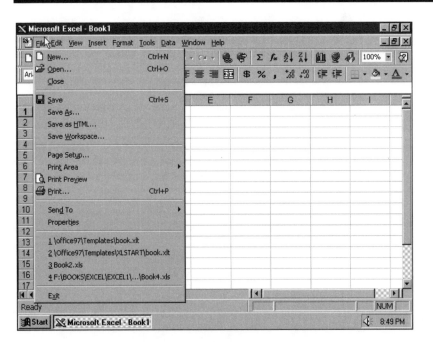

Another new feature in Office 97 is the ability to animate menus as they open. Right-click on a toolbar and choose Customize from the pop-up menu. Then, move to the Options tab. The Menu Animations drop-down list lets you choose from three animations: normal drop-down (None), Unfold, and Slide. You can also choose Random, which causes menus to use any of those methods. Try choosing each one to see if you like using them. Figure 4.2 shows the Options tab of the Customize dialog box.

Figure 4.2

The Options tab of the
Customize dialog box

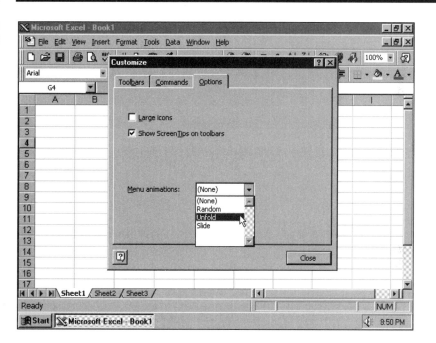

■ Dimmed Text, Ellipses, and Keyboard Shortcut Listings

Menus indicate options that cannot be executed by dimming commands. Usually this means that the command can't be executed *at this time* for some reason. For instance, Figure 4.3 shows Excel's Edit menu. The Undo command is dimmed because Excel was just launched, and no actions have been performed yet that can be undone. Similarly, the Paste commands are dimmed because there is no information in the clipboard to be pasted.

Ellipses in a menu indicate that the command, when chosen, will display a dialog box. In Figure 4.3 you can see that the Find command has ellipses after the command. Executing the Find command displays the Find dialog box.

Figure 4.3

Excel's Edit menu
showing dimmed
commands

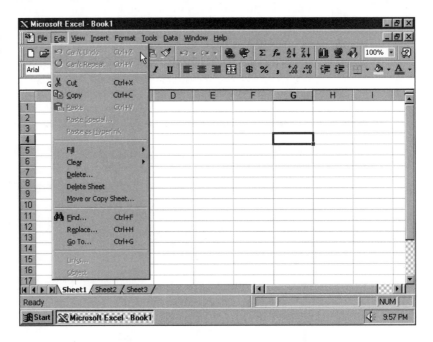

Menus also display shortcut keys that can be used to perform the same action. In Figure 4.3, you can see that the Cut command uses Ctrl+X, Copy uses Ctrl+C, and so forth. If a command has no shortcut key, none is shown in the menu.

■ Customizing Menus

You can customize the commands that appear on Office 97 menus, or even rearrange the menu's contents. You generally want to be careful in doing so, as a radically changed menu can make getting help difficult. Still, you may need to add commands to menus to make frequently used macros more readily accessible, or you may want to make changes for other reasons.

To customize the Office 97 menus on an application-by-application basis, right-click on the toolbar and choose Customize from the pop-up menu. Then, move to the Commands tab of the Customize dialog box (see Figure 4.4.)

With the Commands tab active, you can perform the following actions:

- Drag a menu to another position in the menu bar.

- Drag a menu off of the menu bar to get rid of it.

Figure 4.4

The Commands tab of
the Customize dialog box

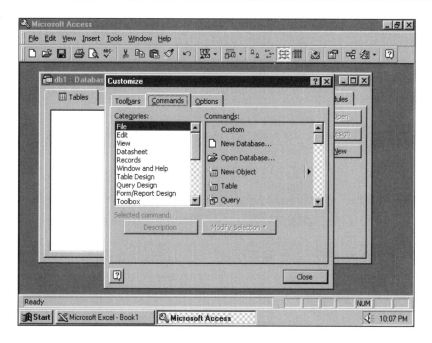

- Right-click on a menu, or on a menu command, to access its pop-up menu. The pop-up menu lets you reset a menu, delete it, change its name, and edit the menu.

- Drag a menu command from one position in a menu to another position. You can also drag a command to another menu entirely, or off of all menus to remove it from the menu structure.

- Add a command to a menu by first locating the command in the Customize dialog box's Commands tab. Then, open the menu that you want to contain the command, and drag the command from the Commands window to the position on the menu where you want the command to appear.

Using the Office 97 common Customize dialog box, which functions similarly in all Office applications, you can modify your menus to suit your needs easily.

■ Toolbars

Toolbars are handy: they let you quickly select commands with a minimum number of mouse-clicks. Different people have different working styles, though, and the default toolbars may not be perfect for you. Fortunately, Office applications let you modify how their toolbars appear and what commands are present on the toolbars.

Moving a Toolbar to a New Location

You can easily move a toolbar to another location on your screen simply by dragging it, using a blank area of the toolbar to drag. When you drag a toolbar, its outline appears while you drag it. If you drag it out of one of the four toolbar anchor areas (the top, right, left, and bottom of the application's window), the toolbar will "float" on top of your work area. Drag it back to an anchor area, and you can leave it attached to one side of the application's window.

Displaying and Hiding Toolbars

Most toolbar functions are carried out by right-clicking on one of the toolbars. Doing so displays the Toolbar menu shown in Figure 4.5. Simply click on a toolbar to show or hide it. The toolbar's current status is indicated by the checkmarks to the left of the toolbar's name.

Figure 4.5

The Toolbar menu

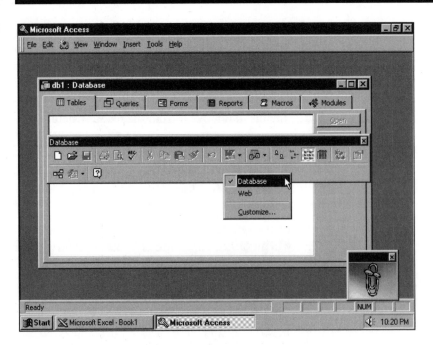

Modifying Toolbars

You can easily modify toolbars to suit your needs. Right-click on a toolbar and choose Customize from the pop-up menu to access the Customize dialog box. Use the Toolbars tab (see Figure 4.6) to work with toolbars.

Figure 4.6

The Toolbars tab of the
Customize dialog box

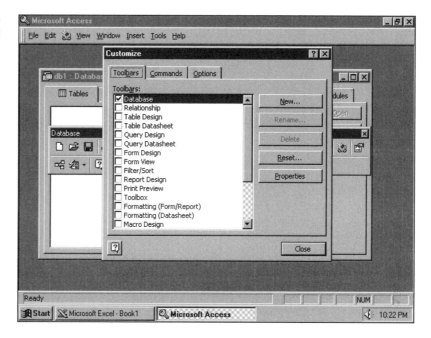

To modify the properties of a toolbar, select the toolbar in the Toolbars list and click on the Properties button. You will see the Toolbar Properties dialog box shown in Figure 4.7.

In the Toolbar Properties Dialog Box You Can:

- Change the toolbar that you're working with by selecting a toolbar from the Selected Toolbar drop-down list box.

- Change the docking properties of a toolbar with the Docking drop-down list box. You can choose Allow Any, Can't Change, No Vertical, and No Horizontal settings.

- Set or clear the Allow Customizing checkbox.

- Set or clear the Allow Moving checkbox.

- Set or clear the Allow Showing/Hiding checkbox.

- Set or clear the Allow Resizing checkbox.

Figure 4.7

The Toolbar Properties
dialog box

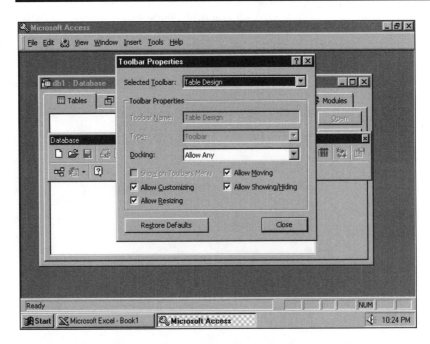

You can also click on the Restore Defaults button to return the selected toolbar to its default settings. This is handy if you make a mistake modifying a toolbar and can't figure out how to correct your mistake. Sometimes it's better to simply start over.

To modify the commands that appear on a toolbar, first make the toolbar visible and then access the Customize dialog box. Choose a command from the Commands tab and drag it to the toolbar on which you want the command to appear. You can also remove commands from toolbars by dragging the icons off of the toolbar when both the Customize dialog box and the toolbar are visible on your screen.

Create your own toolbars with the New command in the Toolbars tab of the Customize dialog box. Then drag commands from the Commands tab to the toolbar to populate it with the commands you want to access.

2

Word

- *Defining Document*

- *The Document Window*

- *The Document's Contents*

- *Master Documents*

- *Defining Template*

- *Understanding Styles*

- *Understanding Toolbars*

- *Defining Headers and Footers*

5

Understanding Word Concepts

EVERY PIECE OF SOFTWARE HAS A SET OF CONCEPTS—A MINDSET—
behind it. To exploit Word to your best advantage, you have to get
used to a few of the metaphors and concepts that drive the software's design. In this chapter, we'll cover the following items:

- What a document is

- What a template is

- How styles work

This chapter also will acquaint you with toolbars, headers and footers, and multiple document handling. After you are familiar with all these concepts, your work with Word will become more intuitive.

■ Defining Document

Word uses the metaphor of a *document* to describe the data you can enter and maintain with the word processor. A Word document has a lot in common with a document produced with a typewriter: For instance, both documents consist of printed pages containing text. However, a Word document can include much more.

Word documents can exist in your computer's memory, and can be stored on a disk. Word documents can be viewed on your computer's screen, or can be printed on your printer. Because they are electronic in form, Word documents can be sent by electronic mail as well as by postal mail. In addition, Word documents can contain several different kinds of data. They are not just text documents, as typewritten documents are.

■ The Document Window

To understand how Word for Windows extends the document metaphor, begin by looking at the way a document appears on the screen.

Each document appears in a *document window*, a "child" window that Word creates in its workspace when you create a document (see Figure 5.1.) Essentially, a document window is an on-screen container for your document. This window not only controls the appearance of your document, but also provides you with means of interacting with your document.

A Word document window is like the standard document window that you see in any other Windows application. It has the familiar title bar, control menu box, minimize button, maximize button, and scroll bars. These items are standard for any document window. They enable you to view the contents of a document, and to scroll that view.

Word adds two elements to this familiar scheme that give you much greater control over your document. At the top of the document and underneath the title bar is a horizontal ruler. At the left edge of the horizontal scroll bar are three view buttons.

Using the Ruler

The ruler allows you to control the margins, the paragraph indentation, and the tab settings for your document. (Figure 5.2 shows the ruler and its parts in detail.) The margin settings are controlled by the upward-facing pointers

Figure 5.1

A document window in
Word for Windows

Ruler

View window

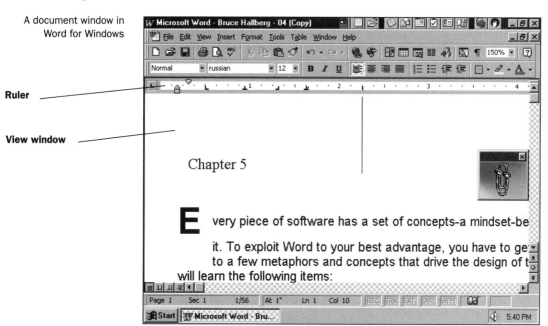

at the bottom edge of the ruler. Dragging these pointers adjusts the position of the right or left margin. When you drag these pointers, Word displays a vertical dashed line down your screen showing the position of the margin in the document. You can align margins easily in different portions of your document by matching this line to the position of the relevant characters on the screen.

The paragraph indentation setting is controlled by the downward-facing pointer at the top edge of the ruler. Dragging this pointer adjusts the indentation of the first line of a paragraph. When you drag the pointer, Word displays a vertical dashed line down your screen that shows you the exact position of the new indentation setting.

You can align indentations easily in different portions of your document by matching this line to the position of the relevant characters. You can use the ruler to create both hanging and standard indentations.

After setting the indentation for a paragraph, you will often want to move both the left margin setting and the indentation setting at one time. In this way, you preserve your indentation pattern while adjusting the margin. You can accomplish this type of adjustment by dragging the box under the left margin pointer.

Figure 5.2

The details of Word's horizontal ruler

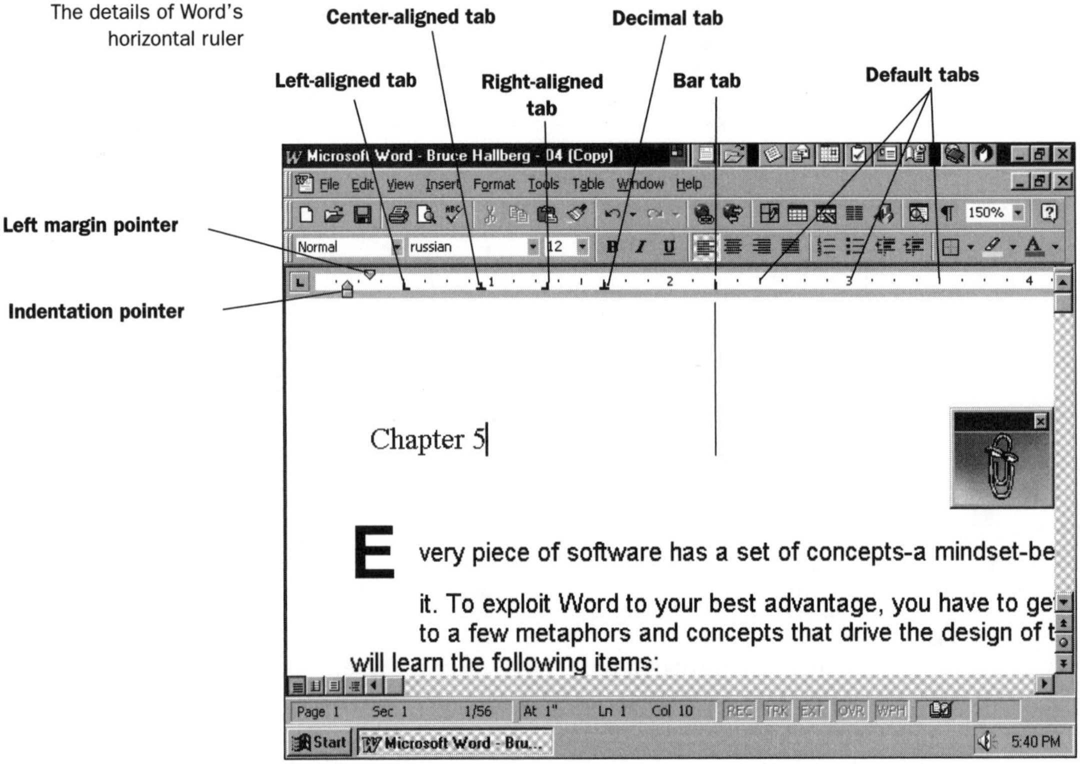
Center-aligned tab
Decimal tab
Left-aligned tab
Right-aligned tab
Bar tab
Default tabs
Left margin pointer
Indentation pointer
Microsoft Word - Bruce Hallberg - 04 (Copy)
File Edit View Insert Format Tools Table Window Help
Normal
russian
12
150%
Chapter 5
Every piece of software has a set of concepts-a mindset-be
it. To exploit Word to your best advantage, you have to ge
to a few metaphors and concepts that drive the design of t
will learn the following items:
Page 1 Sec 1 1/56 At 1" Ln 1 Col 10
REC TRK EXT OVR WPH
Start
Microsoft Word - Bru...
5:40 PM

As in the other margin and indentation adjustments, Word displays a vertical dashed line down your screen to indicate the position of the left margin. In this mode, Word does not display a line to indicate the position of the indentation pointer.

You can adjust tab settings by clicking or double-clicking on the ruler. Clicking on the box at the left edge of the ruler enables you to select which type of tab you will place on the ruler. Clicking on the box cycles you through the following four kinds of tab types:

- **Left-aligned** Characters extend to the right of the tab as you type; indicated by an L-shaped angle in the box.
- **Center-aligned** Characters are centered about the tab position; indicated by an angle with the vertical member centered over the base line.

- **Right-aligned**   Characters extend to the left of the tab as you type; indicated by a reverse L-shaped angle.

- **Decimal**   The decimal point aligns with the tab position; indicated by the symbol for a center-aligned tab with a decimal point to the right of the vertical member.

After you have selected the type of tab you want, follow these procedures to set the tabs:

- Click once on a marked position on the ruler to place a tab at that position.

As you are clicking to set a tab, Word runs a vertical dashed line down your screen to show you the position of the tab relative to the text on the screen.

You can see all of your tabs by accessing the Tabs command in the Format menu. This opens the Tabs dialog box, shown in Figure 5.3. The Tabs dialog box lets you specify the exact position of the tab on the ruler, as well as the tab's type and the positions of default tabs on the ruler.

Figure 5.3

The Tabs dialog box

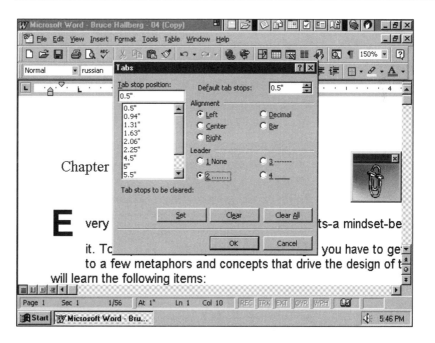

The exact position of the tab you are setting appears in the Tab Stop Position combination box in the Tabs dialog box; the positions of other tabs you have set appear in the list box portion of the combination box. To adjust the position and character of the tab, perform the following steps:

1. To specify a more exact position for the tab, enter a number representing the exact position you want in the text-box portion of the Tab Stop Position combination box.

2. Select the type of tab using the option buttons in the Alignment group. You can select from the four options already discussed, plus the Bar tab option. A *bar tab* places a vertical line through a paragraph at the tab position.

3. Use the option buttons in the Leader group to select characters that fill in the space between the last text on the line (or the margin, if there is no text) and the tab position.

4. Click on the Set button, then click on OK to complete the action of setting a tab at an unmarked position on the ruler.

The Tabs dialog box also allows the three following actions:

- You can clear the tab indicated in the Tab Stop Position combination box by clicking on the Clear button and then clicking on OK.

- You can clear all the tabs you have set by clicking on the Clear All button and then clicking on OK.

- You can adjust the width between the default tab stops using the Default Tab Stops spin box.

As you can see, a Word document adds all the settings provided on the ruler to the design of a document. Embedded in each document is the equivalent of the tabulator bar and margin setting controls on a typewriter. Word merges these document-control concepts into the design specifications of a Word for Windows document.

Changing the View

Word merges concepts used to create three different types of documents into its formula for a Word document. Writers often talk of outlines, drafts, and final copy. Word enables you to view any document in any of these three ways; you do not need to create separate documents for your outlines, drafts, and final copies. New to Word 97 is also a fourth view, called Online Layout view, in which you can see a document as it will appear on the Internet. In Word for Windows, you can shift among these points of view on a document by clicking on the view buttons at the left edge of a document's horizontal scroll bar (see Figure 5.4.)

Tip. A tabs leader enables you to place all the periods, or leader dots, between a chapter title and a page number in a table of contents or similar document. You do not have to type all those periods by hand!

Tip. You can clear a tab by dragging the tab mark off of the ruler. When you drop it away from the ruler, the tab stop is removed.

Tip. Default tabs are present in the document even when you have set no other tabs. They are indicated on the ruler by faint dots along the bottom edge.

Figure 5.4

The view buttons on the
horizontal scroll bar

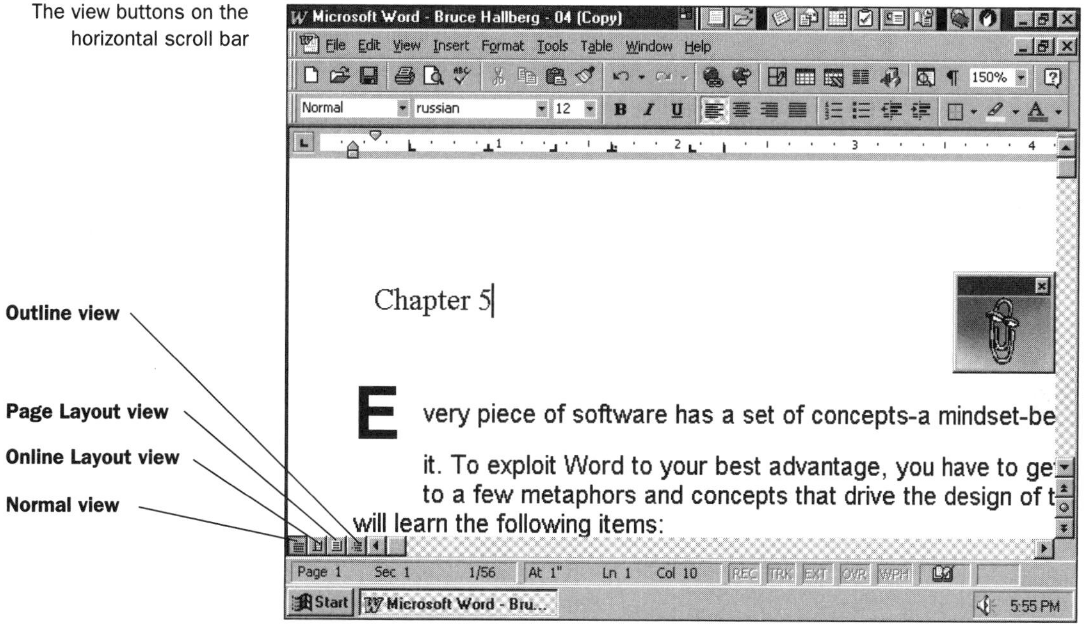

Outline view

Page Layout view

Online Layout view

Normal view

To see a document as an outline, click on the outline button. The Outlining toolbar appears, as shown in Figure 5.5. Now when you type, each block of text is either a heading for the outline or body text. The single-arrow buttons on the Outlining toolbar reformat a block of text as a heading. The left and right arrows also promote and demote headings to different levels within the outline's structure, whereas the up and down arrows move a heading up and down the list within its level in the outline.

You do not have to display every level of the outline at once. The number buttons indicate how many levels are displayed. Headings that contain undisplayed, or collapsed, levels appear underlined. The plus and minus buttons expand and collapse the topic containing the insertion point. You also can limit the display to the first line of any heading with the Show First Line button.

Using the Show Formatting button, you can switch between using special font and paragraph formats for each heading level, and not using these formats.

Tip. You also can adjust the view of your document by selecting the appropriate options from the View menu.

To see a document as a draft, click on the Normal button. You'll see a simplified version of your document, without special formatting applied, as shown in Figure 5.6. In this view, you can enter text, scroll, and apply proofreading tools more quickly than in other views. It is the best view for rapidly developing your document.

Figure 5.5

A document in
outline view

Promotion/demotion
buttons

Movement buttons

Levels displayed buttons

Show first line of
heading only

Show formatting of
heading

Outline toolbar

Expand/collapse
heading

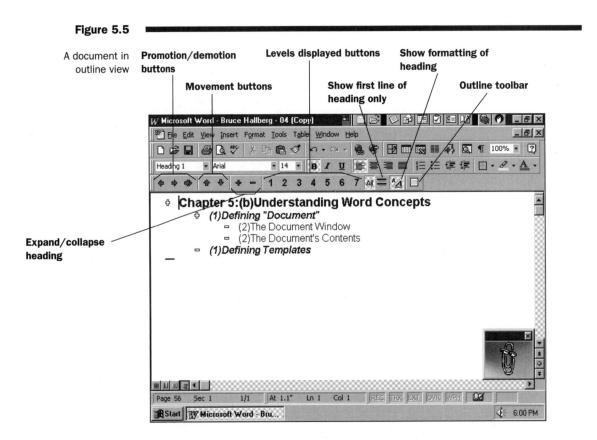

To see a document as final copy, click on the Page Layout button (see Figure 5.7). The view you have now shows you exactly how the document will look when printed. All formatting is applied, and all the document's contents are shown in their correct position on the page. You can edit the document to adjust its final appearance in preparation for printing, and Word provides some additional tools to help you.

Down the left side you can see a vertical ruler that displays the vertical margin settings. If you need to adjust these settings, double-click on the vertical ruler to display the Margins tab of the Page Setup dialog box. On the vertical scroll bar are two additional buttons displaying double arrows. These buttons advance you through the document, up or down, one page at a time.

Using Word's tools, you can rapidly shift between outline, draft, online layout, and final views of your document. A single document can represent what you ordinarily might see as three different documents.

Figure 5.6

A document in normal view

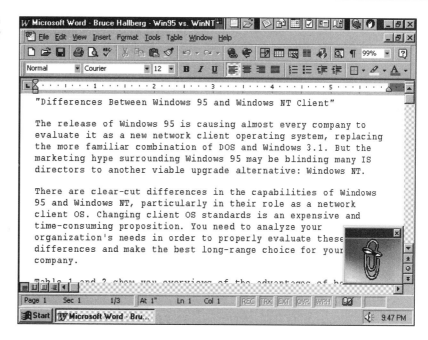

Figure 5.7

A document in page layout view

Vertical ruler

Page scrolling buttons

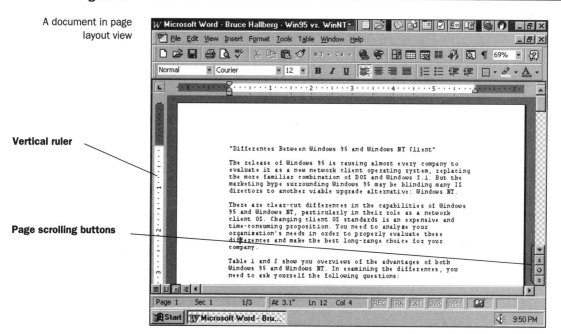

Zooming and Splitting

Word also has the ability to let you view more and less of a document. You can zoom in or zoom out on portions of a document, exploding and reducing the size of your view, and you can split a document into two "window panes" that show you different portions of the document simultaneously.

To zoom in on or out from your document, follow this procedure:

1. Open the Zoom drop-down list box on the Standard toolbar, the next-to-last control on the right (see Figure 5.8.)

2. Select the reduction or enlargement factor you want to use.

   Your document immediately shifts to that size on the screen.

Figure 5.8

Using the Zoom drop-down list box on the Standard toolbar

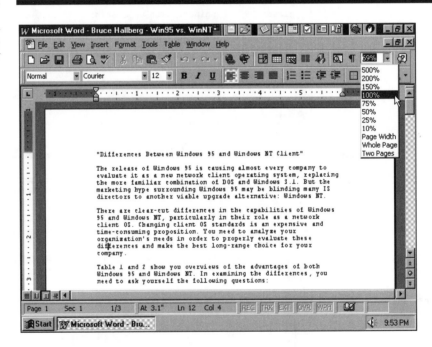

Tip. Zooming out beyond 50 percent makes a document difficult to read and edit, but does give you a sense of its overall look and structure. Zooming above 100 percent can ease eyestrain and help you to examine details like fine print at the bottom of a contract. To gain the maximum amount of screen space for viewing your document (at the expense of not having easy access to the menus or toolbars), open the View menu and select the Full Screen option.

To split your document into two panes, double-click on the split bar, the small rectangular button at the top of the vertical scroll bar, as shown in Figure 5.9. You can drag the split bar to adjust the relative dimensions of the two panes. Click on either pane to make it active for editing, just as you would on any other window. To return to a single-pane view of your document, double-click on the split bar again.

Figure 5.9

Using the split bar

Split bar

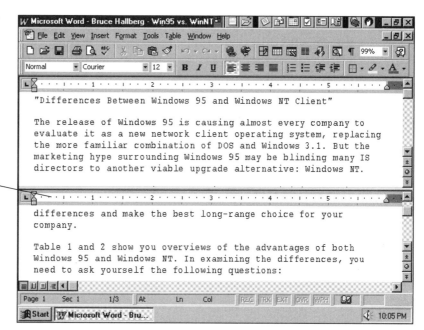

By merging the concepts of enlargement, reduction, and multiple views with its concept of the document, Word provides you with greater flexibility and control over your documents. Documents become objects that you manipulate electronically within your computer's memory the same way you might by spreading them out on a table and using a magnifying reader to study details. Documents provide you with all the tools you need to create and use them as a part of their functionality. You do not need lots of external tools to be able to use your documents.

■ The Document's Contents

Another way that Word revises your concept of a document can be seen when you look at the contents of a document. Normally a document contains words and, at higher levels of publishing, pictures, graphs, and tables. In Word 97 for Windows, documents can contain any type of data. You can create documents whose contents cannot be presented on paper.

To illustrate this concept, you need to examine only one of the accessory programs that comes with Windows, the Sound Recorder. If you have a microphone attached to the sound system in your computer, try the following exercise:

1. Open any Word document.

2. Position the cursor at a location where you would like to add a voice annotation to the document.

3. Open the Insert menu and select the Object option.

4. If the Create New tab is not on top, click on it.

5. In the Object Type list box, select Wave Sound, and then click on OK.

6. Click on the record button.

7. Record your message by speaking into the microphone.

8. Click on the Sound Recorder's stop button.

9. Open the Sound Recorder's File menu and choose "Exit and return to document." A sound icon appears in your Word document, as shown in Figure 5.10.

10. Close the Sound Recorder by selecting Exit from the File menu.

11. To play back your voice annotation, double-click on the sound icon.

Figure 5.10

A Word document that contains a voice annotation

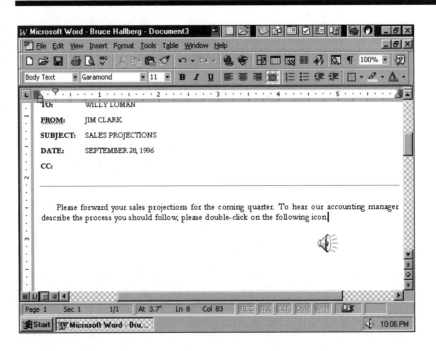

As you can imagine, you can add all sorts of non-text data to a Word for Windows document. If you own Video for Windows, for example, you can embed full-motion video clips to illustrate your text. You can include sound files of all types to illustrate your points. Using the options in the Insert menu, you can include data of any type prepared by any other application that can run under Windows.

Of course, you also can include pictures, tables, spreadsheets, and other illustration elements that can be printed on paper. If you are using electronic mail to route documents for review and revision, you can easily include voice comments as well as written comments in the documents. If you are creating the text of a slide-show presentation, you can embed the kind of data you need to make your points and present the slides electronically.

The application of Word's document metaphor radically redefines the nature of a document. Think of a Word document as a stack of paper plus a home theater system that's hooked up to one of the futuristic interactive cable systems, enhanced by the connectivity potential of the Internet. These are the communication possibilities that Word can provide for you, if your computer has the hardware to use them.

■ Master Documents

In Word 97 for Windows, documents can contain other documents in a hierarchical fashion. A document that serves this function is called a *master document*: a collection of separate documents, each contained in its own file, yet managed by another document file. As a result, the master document features of Word facilitate working with long documents like the text of a 1,000-page book.

Scrolling from the beginning to the end of such a work would take forever. Using the master document features, you can work with smaller chunks of the full document, so that scrolling and spell-checking no longer become horrendous problems. You also can work with the whole document.

Master documents are really special types of outlines. If you look back at Figure 5.5, you will note that there is an extra button on the Outlining toolbar. It is the last one on the right—the Master Document View button. When you click on that button you enter master document mode, in which you can convert an existing set of documents into a master document.

To create a master document from scratch, follow these steps:

1. Click on the New button on the Standard toolbar to create a new file.

2. Open the View menu and select the Master Document item.

Tip. You can view a master document in master document view, in which case you see the list of subdocuments. You also can view it in normal view, in which case you see the entire document as a single document. In normal view, sub-documents are indicated by section boundaries in the continuous text that you see. (Click the Paragraph button on the Standard toolbar to make the section boundaries visible.)

The new document you created is now a master document. You can outline your overall document using Word's outlining features, and you can group headings on your outline and define them as subdocuments.

After writing your outline, perform the following procedure to create subdocuments:

1. Select the headings on the outline that should represent the subdocument.

2. Click on the Create Subdocument button on the Master Document toolbar (see Figure 5.11.) The subdocument will be inserted at the location of your insertion point.

Figure 5.11

The Master Document toolbar, an extension of the Outlining toolbar

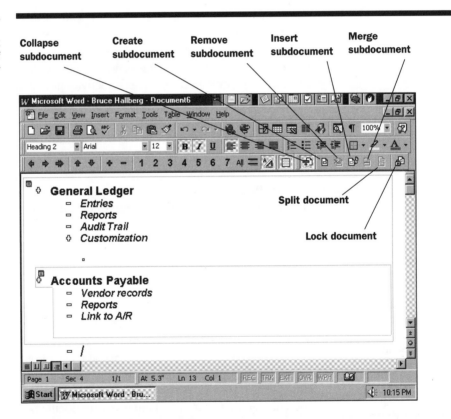

Word encloses each subdocument that you create on the outline in a box, and identifies that box's contents as a subdocument by displaying the subdocument icon in the upper left corner of the box.

To open a subdocument for editing, double-click on its subdocument icon. Word creates a new file, displays it in a document window, and displays the contents of the subdocument's segment of your outline for your additions and editing. To save the changes you have made to a subdocument, open the File menu and select the Save option, and accept the file name that Word has assigned. Close a subdocument just as you would close any other document.

To save your work on the entire project, return to the master document and select one of the save options from the File menu. Word automatically provides file names for the subdocuments based on the first header in the outline for the subdocument. As long as you keep the file name Word assigns to a subdocument file, you can edit it either outside of the master document as a separate file or from within the master document.

If you need to rename a subdocument, first open it from within the master document. You then can use the File, Save As menu option to rename the file. After renaming the subdocument, you should save the master document as well so that the new file name is recorded as a part of the master document.

You can remove subdocuments just as easily as you can create them by following these steps:

1. In master document view, place the insertion point inside the subdocument you want to remove.

2. Click on the Remove Subdocument button.

When you remove a subdocument, you do not lose any of its contents. Word makes the contents of the subdocument into a new segment of the master document. Instead of appearing as a subdocument that you open from the master document, the information appears as a part of the master document. If you want to delete the information, you should delete it from the master document.

If you need to add information stored in a separate file as a part of a master document, perform the following steps:

1. Open the master document.

2. Click on the Insert Subdocument button to display the Insert Subdocument dialog box (see Figure 5.12.)

3. Select the name of the file to insert in the File Name list box.

4. Click on OK.

The file becomes a part of the master document, and its original file name is reserved.

Note. *Master documents and subdocuments can be based on different templates. When you open subdocuments from the master document, however, Word applies the formatting used by the master document's template first and then picks up the features of the subdocument's template that don't conflict. When you open the subdocument outside the master document, Word applies*

Warning. Never change the name of a subdocument file when you edit it outside the master document. Doing so destroys the link between the subdocument and the master document.

Figure 5.12

The Insert Subdocument
dialog box

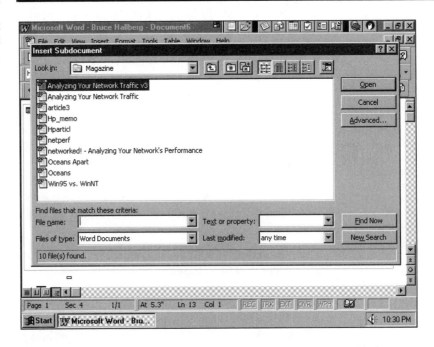

*the formatting used by the subdocument's template. You should eliminate as
many conflicts as possible between the master document's template and
subdocument templates to avoid surprise changes in a document's format.*

When managing a long project using a master document, you eventually
will find the need to merge two subdocuments into a single subdocument.
This situation might occur when you discover that two chunks of text covering the same issue in separate places need to be combined into one. To
merge two subdocuments, you need to make sure they are next to each other
in your master document's outline. If they are not, follow these steps:

1. Click on the subdocument icon for the subdocument you want to move
   up or down in the outline.

2. Drag the subdocument into its new position and drop it into place.

After the two subdocuments are next to each other, perform the following actions to merge them:

1. Select the subdocuments to merge. Holding the mouse button down but
   not pointing to the subdocument icon, drag the mouse over the text of
   the documents.

2. Click on the Merge Subdocument button.

Word merges the selected subdocuments into a single subdocument.

You might want to split a long subdocument into several shorter ones to improve the speed of working with the text. To split a subdocument, open the master document and perform the following steps:

1. Select the text that should be in the first new subdocument.

2. Click on the Split Subdocument button.

3. Select the text that should be in the second new subdocument.

4. Click on the split subdocument button.

Word breaks the old single subdocument into the chunks you have defined.

When you are working as a part of a group, you will want to lock subdocuments to prevent confusion about who is working on what section of the master document. Word keeps track of who created which subdocuments. When workgroup members open the master document, they each have read-write editing privileges on the subdocuments they created, but those created by others are locked, providing only read-only access.

You can open a document created by another user to make changes, but you must first unlock it. After you are done, you should lock it again.

To unlock a document, follow these steps:

1. In master document view, place the insertion point in the subdocument to be unlocked.

2. Click on the Lock Document button.

To lock a document, follow the same procedure. The Lock Document button switches the state of the document lock. When a document is locked, Word puts a padlock icon underneath the subdocument icon.

By bundling the document window, the ruler, the capability to split and zoom, and master documents into the concept of a document, Word 97 for Windows extends the document metaphor considerably. Working with a Word document can now mean editing a graphic, changing the volume of a sound, or adjusting the playback characteristics of a movie. These extensions can make your Word document a multimedia experience, without requiring you to be a multimedia expert.

Tip. If you want to avoid making accidental changes to a subdocument, always lock your subdocuments. You can read and review them, but you will not be able to make changes unless you first unlock the document.

■ Defining Template

Word uses a *template* to describe a set of directions for creating a document. Whenever Word creates a new document, it follows the directions stored in one of its templates. Templates all carry the file extension .DOT. If you open a file with this extension, it looks just like an ordinary Word document (in fact, it is). When Word constructs a new document, it copies all the characteristics of the template to the new document. When you save the new document, you save it as a .DOC file with its own name.

The characteristics of the document template are not modified when you save the document based on the template unless you have taken an action that explicitly modifies the template, such as recording a macro or creating a new style.

Tip. Chapter 7 explains styles in Word.

Templates in Word are files from which characteristics are inherited. As a result, to build a template, you simply create a Word document that has the characteristics you want, and save it as a template. When you create a new document based on the template, the new document inherits all the features you gave to the template. It appears on your screen with all those features in place, ready for you to make additions.

The best way to see how to create a template is to make and save one. Suppose that you want a memo format that clearly shows that a document is confidential. You would like to have your company name and information on the document, and a clear indication that the information in the document is to be treated with confidentiality. You could create a template for such documents by following these steps:

1. Open the File menu and select the New option.

2. In the New dialog box, select the Template option button and click on OK.

3. Enter the information you want for your company into the workspace. Figure 5.13 shows an example.

4. Place the insertion point where you would like a confidential label to appear.

5. Open the Insert menu and choose the Picture option and then choose WordArt.

6. In the WordArt Gallery dialog box, select a WordArt style and click on OK.

7. In the Edit WordArt Text dialog box, type the word **Confidential** and click on the OK button. Your WordArt image is inserted into your document. You can then position it within your document.

You have now created the image of the documents you want based on this template. To save the template, follow these steps:

1. Open the File menu and select the Save option, or click on the Save button on the Standard toolbar.

2. Word selects a portion of the first line you entered and offers it as a name. You can accept the name, edit it, or enter a new name for the document template, then click on OK. Word has limited the Save As dialog box to saving a template, because you already defined the file as a template.

Figure 5.13

Creating a confidential
memo template

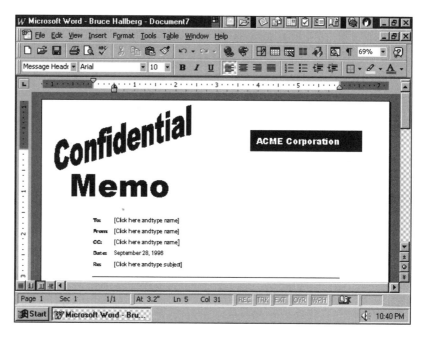

Word automatically saves the template file to your template directory, where it is ready for use the next time you create a new document.

Tip. You actually can
save any file as a
template. After you have
entered a file name in
the Save As dialog box,
open the Save File as
Type drop-down list box
and select Document
Template, then click
on OK.

Templates can contain anything a document can contain. They can be simple, like this confidential letterhead, or they can be complex. Imagine setting up a standard contract as a document template. All the text that never changes could become a part of the template. You could use bookmarks to indicate where you need to add the text related to each client who signs the contract. Writing a contract is then as simple as creating the document, moving to each bookmark, and entering the text necessary at each point.

You also can change a document's template, should you find it necessary to do so. You might have formatted a document using the Normal template, and discovered afterward that the person sitting two desks over has created a better template for just that kind of memo. To substitute the new template for the old one, you attach the new template to the document, following this procedure:

1. Select the Templates and Add-Ins option from the Tools menu to display the Templates and Add-ins dialog box (see Figure 5.14.)

2. Click on the Attach button to display the Attach Template dialog box. Select the template to attach from the File Name list box.

3. Click on OK in the Attach Template dialog box and then click on OK in the Templates and Add-ins dialog box.

Figure 5.14

Using the Templates and
Add-ins dialog box to
attach a template to a
document

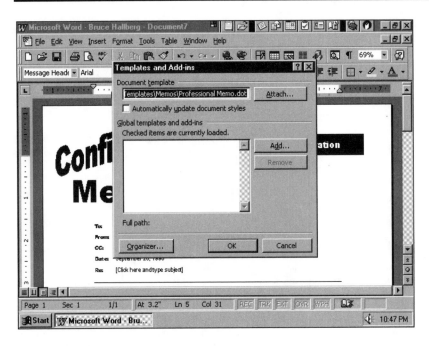

Templates are also the repository for things like styles and macros. The template can contain toolbars, custom menus, and default settings for dialog boxes. Using templates, you can set up each type of document you work with so that your work is focused on exactly the Word options necessary to the task at hand.

Templates define a plan of action for creating a document. When you create the template, you decide how the document will be created and how you will interact with the document after it is created. As a result, you should plan templates with your work flow in mind. Let the template perform repetitive tasks for you, allowing you to save time and focus on the items in the document that demand your attention.

Tip. If you want styles, toolbars, or other such items stored in a special template available to any document you open, load the template globally. Open the Tools menu, select the Templates and Add-Ins option, click on Add, select the name of the template in the File Name list box, and click on OK.

■ Understanding Styles

Word 97 for Windows uses *style* to mean a way of doing things with a format. Word extends this meaning into a concept that helps you accelerate much of the typical work you do in formatting a document.

In this context, a style is a collection of formatting commands or settings that you save as a unit. After you have saved this collection of formats, you can apply them to any block of text by placing the insertion point within the paragraph to be formatted, and selecting the style from the Style drop-down list box on the Formatting toolbar (which is just above the Ruler). The Style drop-down list box is always the one farthest left on this toolbar. It contains the styles currently available in the document.

Word provides a number of built-in styles that you can use to format your own documents. The Style drop-down list box on the Formatting toolbar shows you only the styles currently in use. If you want to see all the styles available to you, perform the following steps:

1. Open the Format menu and select the Style command.

2. In the Style dialog box, use the List drop-down list box to select All Styles. The Styles list box then displays all the styles available in the current template and in templates available globally (see Figure 5.15.)

3. To apply any style built into Word, select its name in the Styles list box and click on Apply. The paragraph containing the insertion point takes on the formats saved as that style.

Tip. Word provides two kinds of styles: paragraph and character styles. Paragraph styles contain formatting information that applies to paragraphs, including font settings. Character styles contain formatting information that applies only to characters. Paragraph style names appear in bold characters, while character style names do not.

Figure 5.15

Displaying available styles in the Style dialog box

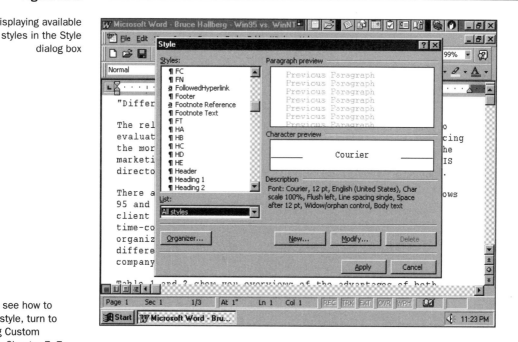

Note. To see how to create a style, turn to "Creating Custom Styles" in Chapter 7. To learn how to make a template available globally, see the preceding section.

Styles are saved as a part of a document or a document template. Accordingly, document templates can serve as collections of styles that you can apply to format the document based on the template. If you are wondering whether Word includes a template with appropriate styles for the document you need to create, investigate the Style Gallery. Open the Format menu and select the Style Gallery option. The Style Gallery dialog box appears, as shown in Figure 5.16.

Figure 5.16

The Style Gallery
dialog box

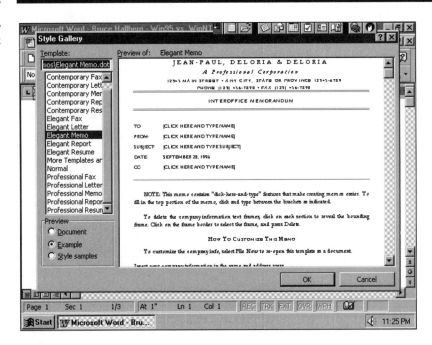

The Template list box displays the list of document templates in the \TEMPLATE directory (located in the directory into which you installed Office 97). By selecting a template from the list, the document shown in the "Preview of" box takes on the style of that template.

By default, Word shows you a preview of the document you are currently working on. Unfortunately, the current document is probably the worst example of the template and its styles, because none of the contents of the template are added to the document, and only the default paragraph text style is applied. As a result, you see very little of the automatic formatting available to you in the template. Better examples are provided by the alternate option buttons in the Preview group. You can choose to see an example document or a list of the styles available in the template, with each item in the list formatted in the style it names.

If you find styles available in a template that you would like to use in your current document, you have four choices:

- Copy the styles from their home template into your current document. The styles are available in that document only, unless you copy them again to another document. To exercise this choice, click on OK in the Style Gallery dialog box.

   Use this option if you are interested only in formatting your current document but not in creating similar documents on a regular basis.

- Attach the template to the document. Do this by canceling the Style Gallery dialog box and selecting the Templates and Add-Ins option from the Format menu. Click on the Attach button and select the template to attach from the File Name list box in the Attach Template dialog box. Click on OK in the Attach Template dialog box and then click on OK in the Templates dialog box. Keep in mind that the template you attach replaces the template that previously was attached.

   Use this option when you want to take advantage of other items that might also be stored in the template, such as macros and toolbars, and when you are certain that the template is not missing features you might need.

- Copy the styles into the NORMAL.DOT template. See Chapter 7 for more information about how to perform this operation.

   Use this option when you expect to use the styles stored in the template in the documents you create by choosing New from the File menu. Keep in mind that the styles will not be available in templates from which you have deleted some of the items stored in NORMAL.DOT.

- Make the template available globally. In this case, the styles in the template become available to every document in the Style dialog box. For the procedure, see the preceding section of this chapter.

   Use this option when you want the styles to be available to every document.

Tip. You can remove a character style from a selection by pressing Ctrl+spacebar.

■ Understanding Toolbars

Word provides toolbars to assist you with various editing tasks. Each toolbar consists of a bar-shaped window that appears beneath Word's menu and contains buttons and other controls that enable you to perform with a single mouse click tasks that otherwise might take several keystrokes or mouse clicks.

Toolbars display visual images that Word uses to represent to you how to perform these tasks. A toolbar therefore serves as a visual reminder of the nature and organization of the task represented by the toolbar. To facilitate your work, Word presents sixteen different toolbars, described in Table 5.1.

Table 5.1

Word 97 for Windows
Toolbars

TOOLBAR	FUNCTION
AutoText	Lets you quickly insert automatic text into your documents
Control Toolbox	Helps you insert Visual Basic controls into your documents
Database	Assists in inserting, building, and maintaining databases in Word documents
Drawing	Enables the drawing of pictures in Word documents
Formatting	Helps you to format a document
Forms	Enables you to insert custom fields on templates so that you can create online forms
Picture	Helps in placing and formatting inserted graphics
Reviewing	Helps in reviewing documents
Standard	Contains typical tools that you want to access frequently
Tables and Borders	Helps in placing borders around paragraphs and selecting shading options; helps in formatting tables
Visual Basic	Assists in editing, testing, and debugging macros
Web	Helps in navigating the Web from within Word
WordArt	Helps in constructing artful text

To use a toolbar, you use the controls on the bar just as you would if they appeared in a dialog box. You can adjust your view of the toolbars in two ways. First, you can determine which of several toolbars are displayed. The easiest way to adjust which toolbars appear on your screen is to click on any toolbar with the right mouse button. A floating menu that gives you access to all toolbar functions appears, as shown in Figure 5.17.

On the toolbar floating menu you can choose to have toolbars appear on-screen just by clicking on the menu item that bears the toolbar's name. A check appears next to the names of toolbars already chosen for on-screen display. To hide a toolbar from this menu, click on its checked menu item, and the toolbar will disappear from the screen.

In addition to being able to control your view of toolbars, you can select the Toolbar and Customize dialog boxes from this menu. For more about customizing toolbars, see Chapter 8.

Figure 5.17

The toolbar floating menu

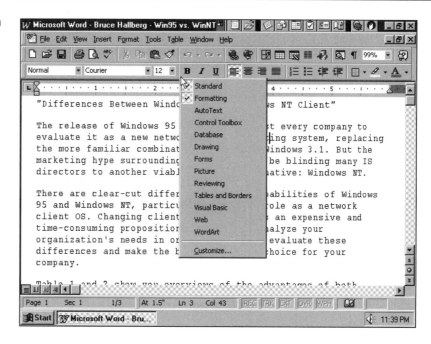

You'll also need to know how to float toolbars to avoid limiting a document's workspace. The toolbars shown in Figure 5.17 are *anchored;* that is, they are stationary and fixed underneath the Word menu. To make them *float* over your work as separate, movable, and sizable windows, double-click on the toolbar somewhere outside the controls. The toolbar now floats away from its anchored position and into the body of the document (see Figure 5.18).

You can adjust the size of the toolbar just as you would any window. To anchor the toolbar again, double-click on it.

To manage toolbars effectively, you must know how to access the Toolbar dialog box from the View menu. If you have hidden all your toolbars, you have no other means of getting access to them again. To change your view of the toolbars, follow this procedure:

1. Open the View menu.

2. Select the Toolbars option.

3. Check the toolbars you want to appear in the Toolbars list box. Uncheck those you do not want to appear.

4. Click on OK.

Figure 5.18

A number of floating
toolbars

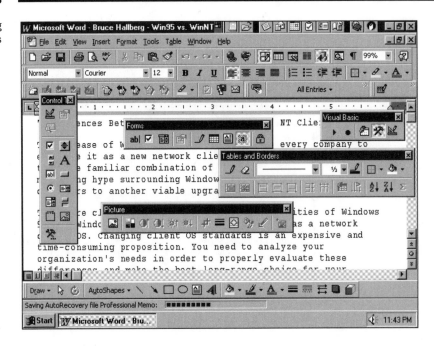

Using the Toolbars dialog box, you can also create new toolbars, customize existing toolbars, and reset toolbars to default tools. For more information about these processes, see Chapter 8.

■ Defining Headers and Footers

Word lets you place headers and footers in your documents. These are special regions of the page into which you can insert information that you want repeated on each page. The header appears at the top of the page and the footer appears at the bottom. Common uses for these regions are displaying running titles, printing page numbers, and printing information about the document itself, such as file name, print date, last edit date, or version number. Headers and footers remind us of the process printers use to place running titles, tool lines, and other graphics on each page.

Word reserves space for a header and footer in each document. If you insert nothing into these regions, then your text takes them over. On the other hand, if you do insert information, the header or footer is displayed.

Tip. The footer of a document is a good place to store any version-tracking information you want to keep as you revise a collaborative document.

Headers and footer are both commonly used to display page numbers. To add page numbers, perform the following procedure:

1. Open the Insert menu and select the Page Numbers option to display the Page Numbers dialog box (see Figure 5.19.)

2. Open the Position drop-down list box and select whether you want the page number in the header or the footer.

3. Open the Alignment drop-down list box and select whether you want right, left, center, inside, or outside alignment for the page number. Right, left, and center place the page number at the corresponding position within the header or footer. Inside and outside place the page number at the inside of the binding edge, or the outside of the binding edge if you are using mirror margins. The Preview box displays the exact position you have selected.

4. Check the Show Number on First Page check box if you want to display a page number on the first page of your document.

5. Click on the Format button to open the Page Number Format dialog box, shown in Figure 5.20.

Figure 5.19

The Page Numbers dialog box

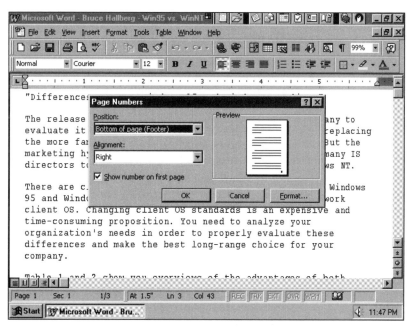

Figure 5.20

The Page Number Format
dialog box

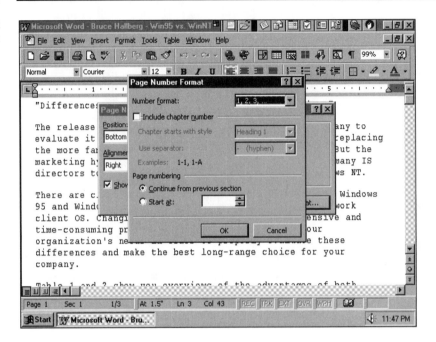

6. Use the Number Format drop-down list box to select the number format you want to use.

7. Use the option buttons in the Page Numbering group to determine whether the number sequence should Continue from Previous Section or Start At a particular number. If you choose Start At, enter the starting number in the spin box.

8. Check the Include Chapter Number check box to include the chapter number as a part of the page number. If you select this option, you must select a style using the Chapter Starts with Style drop-down list box. This tells Word how to recognize chapter beginnings. You also must open the Use Separator drop-down list box to indicate what character separates the chapter number from the page number in the page number string.

9. Click on OK in the Page Numbers Format dialog box and in the Page Numbers dialog box.

You also can directly edit the header and footer for each page. To prepare to do so, open the View menu and select the Header and Footer command. Your screen will switch to page layout view and the Header and Footer toolbar appears, as seen in Figure 5.21.

Figure 5.21

Editing the header and footer using the Header and Footer toolbar

1 **Insert AutoText**
2 **Insert Page Number**
3 **Insert Number of Pages**
4 **Format Page Number**
5 **Insert Date**
6 **Insert Time**
7 **Page Setup**
8 **Show/Hide Document text**
9 **Save as Previous**
10 **Switch between Header and Footer**
11 **Show Previous**
12 **Show Next**
13 **Close Header and Footer toolbar**

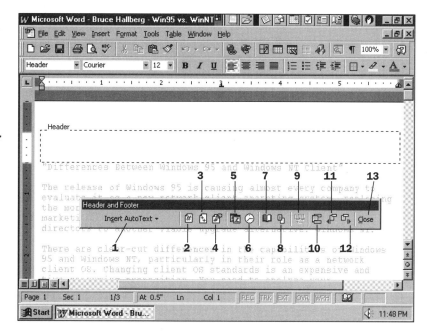

While the Header and Footer toolbar is visible, you can take the following actions to define your headers and footers:

- You can enter and edit text in the header or footer section of the document. You can use any text, field, or control that you can use anywhere else in a Word document.

- You can switch between editing the header and footer by clicking on the Switch Between Header and Footer button.

- You can move between headers and footers for each section of your document by clicking on the Show Previous or Show Next button.

- If you want to continue a header or footer from the previous section of the document, click on the Same as Previous button. The button stays depressed to indicate that all sections have the same header and footer. If you want to use different headers and footers in a section, place the insertion button in that section and click on the Same as Previous button again. It pops up to indicate that each section has different headers and footers.

- You can insert page number, date, and time fields by clicking on the buttons with those names.

Tip. Word enables you to define sections in your document, each of which can have different formatting characteristics and page numbering settings.

- You can hide the document text if it distracts you, or re-display it, by clicking on the Show/Hide Document Text button.

- You can access the Page Setup dialog box by clicking on the Page Setup button. The most important controls for headers and footers appear in the Headers and Footers group on the Layout tab and the From Edge group on the Margins tab. These controls enable you to select Different Odd and Even and Different First Page for headers and footers, as well as to set the distance from the edge of the page to the header and footer.

- You can exit the header and footer editing mode by clicking on the Close button or by selecting the Header and Footer option from the View menu.

■ Summary

Before you can master any software, you first have to understand how it works. Word processors are no different than any other piece of software in this regard. While all word processors let you enter text and format it to suit your needs, how they go about these tasks differs considerably between different programs. WordPerfect, for instance, works much differently than Word. Word Pro is another example of a word processor that's distinct from Word in how it operates.

The important thing is to remember that you can often make faster progress learning a program by making sure you have a firm grasp of the basics before moving on to more-advanced topics. In this chapter you learned the fundamentals of Microsoft Word 97, laying the groundwork for the topics covered in the remaining chapters.

- *Spelling and Grammar Checker*
- *Thesaurus*
- *Hyphenation*
- *AutoCorrect*
- *Document Statistics*
- *Multiple Language Support*
- *AutoText*

- *Find and Replace*
- *Bookmarks*
- *Highlighting*
- *Fields*
- *Symbols*
- *Macros*
- *Working with Multiple Documents*

Using Document Tools

WORD USES THE METAPHOR OF A TOOL TO REPRESENT THE AUTO-mation of a proofing process that you would ordinarily perform by hand when preparing a document. Word provides several tools that can help you improve your documents. These tackle tasks ranging from proofreading to maintaining lists of common phrases to automatically changing a date to match the current day. Using these tools simplifies and speeds up your work.

■ Spelling and Grammar Checker

Probably the most familiar document tool is the *spelling checker,* which compares each word in your document to the correct spellings stored in its dictionary, and asks you to verify the spelling of any words not in the dictionary. You can add words not in the standard dictionary to a custom dictionary, and you can maintain several custom dictionaries specific to specialized types of documents. The spelling checker, therefore, is a flexible tool that automates the process of proofreading for spelling errors.

Word has two processes for checking the spelling of documents: automatic and manual.

The *automatic* spelling checker works in the background while you are creating or editing documents. When the automatic spelling checker encounters a word that might be spelled incorrectly, it places a wavy red line under the word. Your work on the document is not interrupted, and you can choose whether or not you want to correct the word. If you do want to change the spelling, click the wavy red line with the right mouse button to display a list of suggested spelling corrections.

The *manual* spelling checker lets you stop your work on the document to launch Word's spelling check program. To access Word's spelling checker, perform the following steps:

1. Click on the Spelling and Grammar button on the Standard toolbar, open the Tools menu and select the Spelling and Grammar option, or press F7. The Spelling and Grammar dialog box will appear, as shown in Figure 6.1.

2. Verify the spelling of the word in the Not in Dictionary: text box. If it is correct, take one of the following steps:

    • Click on the Ignore button.

    • If you expect that the word will occur again later in your document, click on the Ignore All button. Word then will ignore the word for all spelling checks during the current Word session.

    • If you use the word frequently, click on the Add button to add the word to Word's Standard dictionary. Word will then accept the word as correctly spelled during all future Word sessions.

3. If the word in the Not in Dictionary: text box is incorrect, select one of the suggestions from the Suggestions list box. Or type the correct word in the Not in Dictionary: text box, and then perform one of the following steps:

    • Click on the Change button to correct the word.

Warning. Spelling checkers are wonderful, but they do not eliminate typographical errors. In fact, they can hide certain kinds of typos. After the spelling check is over, you can be certain that all the words in the document are correctly spelled; however, you cannot be certain that you have used the correct form of the word in the right place. The spelling checker, for instance, will not point out that "to" should have been spelled "too" when you meant "also." Such incorrect forms can be difficult to find once they all are correctly spelled.

Figure 6.1

The Spelling and
Grammar dialog box

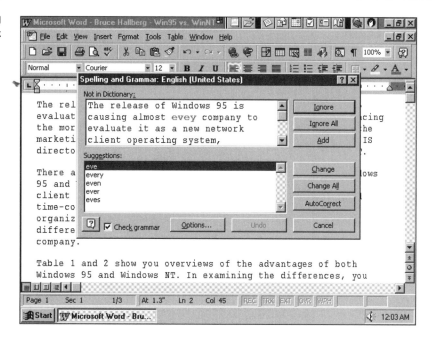

- Click on the Change All button if you expect to encounter the same misspelling throughout the document. Word then will change all encountered forms of the word to the form you specified as correct.

4. If you recognize the misspelling in the Not in Dictionary: text box as a common typing error that you make, click on the AutoCorrect button. Word adds this wrongly typed word and its correction to the AutoCorrect list, and will perform the correction on the fly as you type. (For more information about AutoCorrect, see the AutoCorrect section later in this chapter.)

5. If the error is caused by a repeated word, the Change and Change All buttons take on the labels Delete and Delete All. Use Delete and Delete All just as you would Change and Change All in dealing with these circumstances.

6. Click on the Undo button to undo the last spelling correction. Using this button, you can reverse the course of the spelling checker to correct any errors you might have made when clicking on buttons. Undo remains active as long as you can back up to an earlier correction and undo the action.

7. Click on the Options button to set the options for the spelling checker. The Spelling and Grammar Options dialog box will appear, as shown in Figure 6.2.

Warning. Be careful when selecting the Change All button, especially if the incorrect form is close to the correct spelling of two different words. You might encounter the word "all" incorrectly spelled as "al" in a document containing the male first name "Al." You could accidentally misspell Al's name throughout the document by clicking on the Change All button.

Figure 6.2

The Spelling and Grammar options dialog box

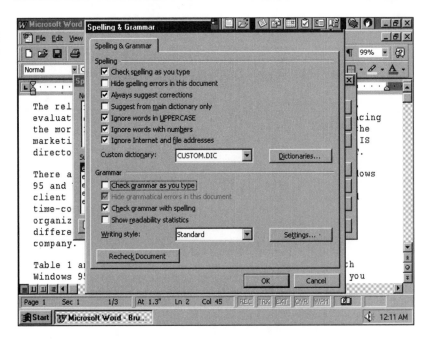

In the Options dialog box, perform the following steps:

- Use the check boxes in the Automatic Spell Checking section to turn automatic spell-checking on and off. Click on the "Hide spelling errors in this document" box to hide the wavy red line that appears under words that could be spelled incorrectly.

- Select "Always suggest corrections" if you want Word always to suggest alternate forms. (If you uncheck this box, you can always get suggestions by clicking on the Suggest button in the Spelling and Grammar dialog box.) Check "Suggest from main dictionary only" if you want suggestions only from the main dictionary. Uncheck this box if you want suggestions from custom dictionaries as well.

- Check the "Ignore words in UPPERCASE" box to ignore words in all capitals. Check the "Ignore words with numbers" box to ignore such words. Check the "Ignore Internet and file addresses" to cause Word to skip such addresses during its spelling check.

- Use the Custom dictionary list box to select which dictionary is active. You can also use the Dictionaries button to create new custom dictionaries, and to select multiple custom dictionaries to use by checking or un-

Tip. The fewer suggestions the spelling checker has to make, the faster it runs. Therefore, try to restrict the number or size of the custom spelling dictionaries that you use.

checking the box next to the dictionary's name in the Custom Dictionaries dialog box.

- Click on Recheck Document to check the spelling of a document again after you have changed options or opened another dictionary.

Word's spelling checker lets you define words that should not be included in the spelling check. The list of words to exclude from the spelling check is called the *exclude dictionary*. It must have the same name as the main dictionary it will be used with, end in an .EXC file extension, and be stored along with its main dictionary in the \WINWORD directory. For example, the American English dictionary shipped with Word is named MSWDS_EN.LEX. The corresponding exclude dictionary must be named MSWDS_EN.EXC.

The ability to exclude words permits you to use variant spellings not accepted by the main dictionary. For example, if you prefer *judgement* to *judgment*, a commonly accepted spelling variant in American English, you should add *judgment* to the exclude dictionary. This action causes Word's spelling checker to question the spelling *judgment*, so that you can change it to your preferred spelling of *judgement*.

To create an exclude dictionary, perform the following procedure:

1. Create a new file by clicking the New button on the Standard toolbar or by opening the File menu and selecting the New option.

2. Type the list of words to exclude. Press Enter after each word.

3. Open the **File** menu and select the **Save As** option.

4. Open the **Save As File Type** drop-down list box and select Text Only.

5. Enter the appropriate name for the exclude dictionary in the **File Name** text box.

6. Click on OK.

7. Start the spelling checker to complete the installation of the exclude dictionary.

Grammar Checker

Word provides a grammar-checking tool that can help you catch common errors in writing. The grammar checker examines your document sentence by sentence, searching for patterns that might indicate errors. This tool can also suggest improvements to each sentence that it flags as containing a possible error. You can accept the suggested change, seek an explanation of the possible error, edit the sentence, or ignore the possible error.

Warning. Although grammar checkers get better and better all the time, they do not catch all errors—and they flag some sentences as containing errors that are in fact correctly formed. For example, Word's grammar checker responds to the sentence, "This here be a boo boo" by suggesting only that you consider deleting the repeated word. You should proofread your document manually to catch any errors the automatic grammar checker missed.

The grammar checker operates in two modes, just like the spell checker: automatic and manual. Automatic mode runs in the background all the time, and marks possible grammar errors in your document with a wavy blue-green line under the sentence in question. Right-click on such sentences to see the grammar checker's recommendation.

To use the grammar checker in manual mode, open the Tools menu and select the Spelling and Grammar command to display the Spelling and Grammar dialog box, as shown in Figure 6.3.

Figure 6.3

The Spelling and Grammar dialog box

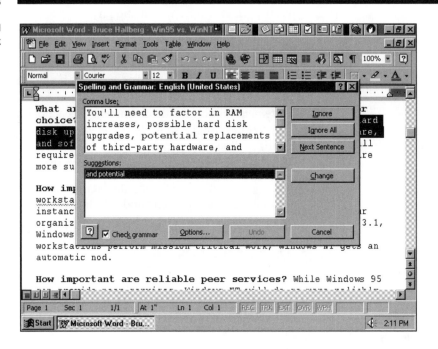

In the top field of the Spelling and Grammar dialog box you can see the problem area. In Figure 6.3, the grammar checker is warning about a possible comma-use problem. The Suggestions field contains possible solutions to the problem. At this point, you have the following choices:

- Click on the Ignore button to ignore the suggested change.

- Click on the Next Sentence button to move to the next sentence without either correcting the error or ignoring the error. You can bypass an error this way, allowing you to return later with the grammar checker after considering how you want to rewrite the sentence.

- Edit the sentence in the top field (this is called different names depending on the error type in question), making the changes you desire.

- Click on the Change button to make the suggested change, or to substitute your edited version of the sentence for the original. Your edited version takes precedence over the suggested change.

- Click on the Ignore All button to prevent the grammar checker from applying the rule indicated during the remainder of the grammar check.

- Click on the help button (the question-mark button in the lower-left corner of the dialog box) to get an explanation of the error from the Office Assistant, as shown in Figure 6.4.

Figure 6.4

The Office Assistant can explain proper grammar usage to you.

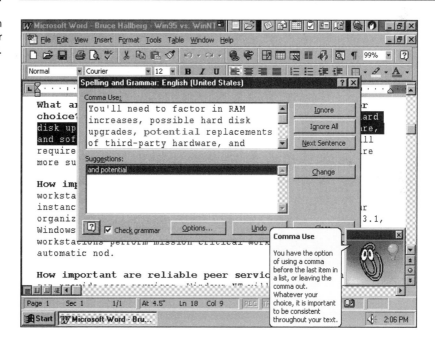

- Click on the Close button to end the grammar-checking session.

- Click on the Undo button to reverse the last action you took with the grammar checker. You can repeat this undo action to move backwards through the actions you have taken with the grammar checker.

You can adjust the rules the grammar checker applies to your text by clicking on the Options button, or by opening the Tools menu and selecting the Options item. When the Options dialog box appears, click on the Spelling and Grammar tab if it is not active (see Figure 6.5).

Figure 6.5

The Spelling and Grammar tab in the Options dialog box

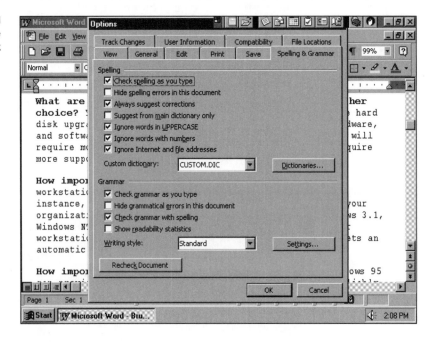

Now, perform the following steps:

1. Use the "Check grammar with spelling" check box to control whether the grammar checker runs along with the spelling checker.

2. Check or uncheck the "Show readability statistics" check box to control whether the grammar checker shows readability statistics after the grammar check is completed.

3. Select the type of writing you are grammar-checking in the Writing Style list box.

4. If you want to create a custom set of grammar and style rules, or if you want to change the rules applied to a predefined type of writing, click on the Settings button to display the Grammar Settings dialog box (see Figure 6.6) and take one or more of the following actions:

   • First, choose the Writing Style with which you want to work. This controls which rules in the Grammar and Style Options window are initially checked.

   • Use the Grammar and Style Options buttons to select which set of rules to check or to skip.

Figure 6.6

The Grammar Settings
dialog box

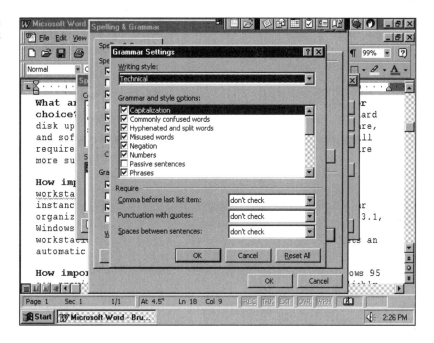

- Modify the three options in the Require area to meet your requirements.
- Click on OK to accept the changes you have made in the rule settings.

At the end of each grammar-checking session, Word displays a set of readability statistics, if you have selected that option (see preceding settings). These statistics can help you determine whether you have matched your writing appropriately to your intended readers.

Each of the means of calculating readability applies a slightly different method of calculating reading ease. In general, the lower the value, the easier the reading. You can use these statistics as guidelines for determining how well you meet the reading ability of your intended audience.

■ Thesaurus

Word includes a thesaurus to help you vary your vocabulary, and to find more-useful words by association with the less-useful word you might be able to think of. To use the thesaurus, place the insertion point on the word you want to look up. Then, open the Tools menu and either select the Thesaurus command from the Language menu or press Shift+F7 to display the Thesaurus dialog box (see Figure 6.7).

Figure 6.7

The Thesaurus dialog box

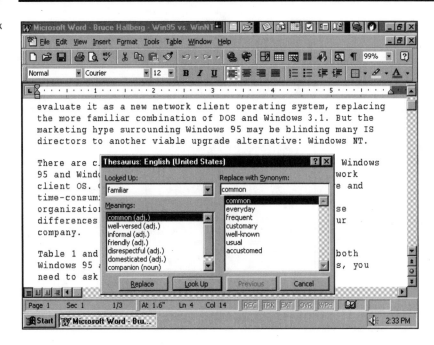

In the Thesaurus dialog box, perform one of the following actions:

- Verify that the word you want to look up appears in the Looked Up drop-down list box. (If the word was not found, Looked Up becomes the Not Found drop-down list box.) If it does not, enter the word in the text box portion of the Replace with Synonym combination box and click on the Look Up button.

  If the insertion point is not on a word when you invoke the thesaurus, the dialog box will be empty, and the Replace with Synonym combination box will be labeled Insert. Type the word to look up in the Insert control, and click on Look Up.

- Select the meaning you want to work with in the Meanings list box. (If the word was not found, Meanings becomes the Alphabetical List list box.) You can select antonyms and related words if you want to explore opposites or related word families.

- Select a synonym you want to work with from the list box portion of the Replace with Synonym combination box.

- Click on the Look Up button to look up synonyms for the word that currently appears in the text box portion of the Replace with Synonym combination box.

- Click on the Previous button or open the Looked Up drop-down list box to select words previously looked up during the thesaurus session.

- Click on the Replace button to replace the word containing the insertion point with the word that appears in the text box portion of the Replace with Synonym combination box.

■ Hyphenation

Word provides a hyphenation facility that lets you give your documents a professional look. It will automatically reduce excessive raggedness along a margin and squeeze down unusually long spaces between words in a fully justified document.

You can insert two types of hyphens into words using Word. *Optional hyphens* break a word only when the word appears at the end of a line and using the hyphen would improve the appearance of the ragged margin. *Nonbreaking hyphens* always appear in the word, but never break at the edge of a line. They are useful in compound words such as *Somerset-Upon-Thyme* or in hyphenated personal names that you don't want to wrap around a line. To insert an optional hyphen, press Ctrl+- (hyphen). For a nonbreaking hyphen, press Ctrl+Shift+-.

You can choose to read your text on-screen and guess where hyphens ought to appear. However, Word provides two alternative methods of inserting hyphens in a text: automatic and manual. Ordinarily, it is best to apply hyphenation toward the end of the writing process. Changes in the text alter the locations at which you need to apply hyphenation.

To apply hyphenation automatically, perform the following procedure:

1. Open the **Tools** menu and select the **Hyphenation** command from the **Language** sub-menu. The Hyphenation dialog box will appear, as shown in Figure 6.8.

2. Check the "Automatically hyphenate document" check box.

3. Check the "Hyphenate Words in CAPS" check box if you want to hyphenate words that use all capital (uppercase) letters; otherwise, Word will not hyphenate these words.

4. Use the "Hyphenation zone" spin box to adjust the width of the zone between the word and the margin where the hyphen break can occur. A wider zone produces a more ragged margin.

5. Use the "Limit consecutive hyphens to" spin box to set the maximum number of consecutive lines that can be hyphenated. (A text in which many consecutive lines are hyphenated can be difficult to read.)

Tip. Word treats a hyphen typed using the hyphen key as an ordinary punctuation mark.

Figure 6.8

The Hyphenation
dialog box

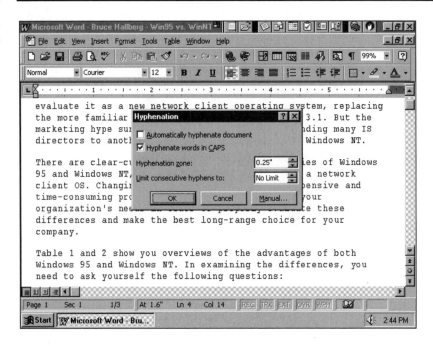

6. Click on OK, and Word will hyphenate the text.

   To insert hyphens manually, follow this procedure:

1. Open the Tools menu and select the Hyphenation command from the Language submenu to display the Hyphenation dialog box (refer to Figure 6.8).

2. Click on the Manual button to display the Manual Hyphenation dialog box (see Figure 6.9).

   Word searches through your document, displaying each word to be hyphenated in the Hyphenate At text box. For each word, perform one of the following actions:

- Click on the Yes button to accept the suggested hyphenation.

- If you disagree with the location of the suggested hyphen, click on the word in the Hyphenate At text box to indicate where the hyphen should go, then click on the Yes button.

- Click on the No button to prevent Word from hyphenating the word shown.

Figure 6.9

The Manual Hyphenation
dialog box

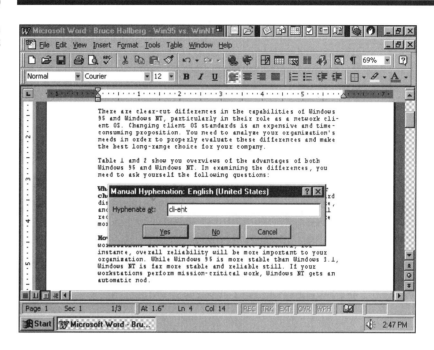

Tip. You can turn off
hyphenation for
individual paragraphs by
opening the Format
menu, selecting the
Paragraph option,
selecting the Line and
Page Breaks tab, and
checking the "Don't
hyphenate" check box.

Automatic hyphenation is faster and more convenient, but you should proof your document to make certain you agree with the hyphens inserted. Manual hyphenation is slower, but gives you control over the process at the screen. If hyphenation is the last step in producing your document, you can switch from manual hyphenation to print preview to verify the final look of the document. You are then ready for printing.

■ AutoCorrect

AutoCorrect is a Wizard that runs in the background as you type, watching for preprogrammed patterns in the stream of characters that you type. When AutoCorrect encounters one of these patterns, it substitutes a corresponding preprogrammed pattern.

AutoCorrect can therefore watch for the most frequent errors made when typing common words and automatically correct them for you. As a result, *teh* automatically becomes *the* as soon as you press the space bar after typing the word. You can extend this capability, however, to cover more than spelling errors. Common phrases can be AutoCorrect entries. You can set up the string *slogan* to expand into your company's slogan. You can set up key combinations that expand into frequently used addresses, chemical formulas, specialized vocabulary, and so on.

WARNING. *Keep in mind that AutoCorrect entries can take effect at unwanted times. If you store lots of specialized AutoCorrect entries, you will want their invoking strings to be unique and infrequently used words. One way to do this is to use abbreviations that are not otherwise correct. For instance, if you want to use AutoCorrect to insert your company slogan, you might enter the AutoCorrect text entry as "slgn" or "coslo" (short for "company slogan"). You know what these entries are and can use them, but you are certain not to need them in normal text.*

To build an AutoCorrect entry, perform the following steps:

1. Open the Tools menu and select the AutoCorrect command to display the AutoCorrect dialog box (see Figure 6.10).

Figure 6.10

The AutoCorrect dialog box

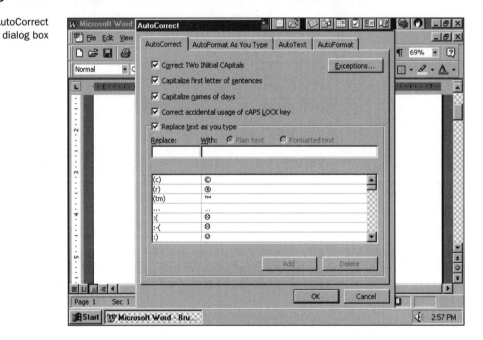

2. In the AutoCorrect dialog box, type the text to replace in the Replace text box.

3. Type the text to substitute in the With text box.

4. Click on the Add button.

5. Make sure the Replace Text as You Type check box is checked; otherwise, AutoCorrect is turned off and will not substitute text as you type.

6. Click on OK.

You can also designate exceptions to the AutoCorrect function by selecting the Exceptions button. Enter any abbreviations or terms that must appear with mixed capitalization and therefore should not be changed by AutoCorrect.

The next time you type the sequence of characters you designated to be replaced, AutoCorrect will substitute the characters you typed in the With text box.

AutoCorrect can substitute graphics and formatted text for a string of characters. Suppose you need your company logo and slogan to appear in the first heading for each section of your document. You have the logo and slogan already entered in your letterhead template. The logo has been scanned as a clip-art graphic, and the slogan is a block of 14-point text sitting to its right. To make the logo and slogan an AutoCorrect entry, perform the following procedure:

1. Select the graphic and the text as a unit.

2. Open the Tools menu and select AutoCorrect.

3. Type a name for the entry in the Replace text box.

4. Select either the Plain Text or Formatted Text option button. Formatted Text preserves the formatting of the text and the graphic image. Plain Text converts both formatted text and graphics to characters in the system font. The With box previews your entry for you.

5. Click on the Add button.

6. Make sure the Replace Text as You Type check box is checked.

7. Click on OK.

The following check boxes in the AutoCorrect dialog box allow you to correct additional text problems:

*   "Replace text as you type" switches the AutoCorrect Wizard on and off.

*   "Correct TWo INitial CApitals" switches the correction of this common Shift key error on and off.

*   "Capitalize first letter of sentences" switches this self-explanatory correction feature on and off.

*   "Capitalize names of days" switches the capitalization of these names on and off.

Tip. If AutoCorrect corrects something you did not want corrected, just click on the Undo button on the Standard toolbar.

AutoCorrect lets you change your entries anytime by simply editing the Replace and With text boxes. You can insert any entry into these boxes by clicking on it in the list box. (If your entry is formatted text or graphics, make the change in your document, select the changed material, and then open the AutoCorrect dialog box.) To complete the change, click on the Add or Replace button, whichever appears.

If you are editing the Replace box, the Add button appears. When you click on it, the entry you changed is not deleted in its original form. Instead, a new entry is added as a new Replace segment paired with the same With segment. If you edit the With text box, the Replace button appears, and the new entry is substituted for the old.

Occasionally you will need to delete an AutoCorrect entry. To do so, select the entry in the list box and click on the Delete button.

■ Document Statistics

Warning. Every time you use the word-count feature, Word repaginates your document and counts the relevant items. In a long document, this can take quite some time.

Often you need to make a document fit a length guideline. Word has a document-statistics facility that provides you with various length statistics. To use this facility, open the Tools menu and select the Word Count option. The Word Count dialog box appears, as shown in Figure 6.11, and Word updates the counts for you. If you wish to include footnotes and endnotes, check the Include Footnotes and Endnotes check box.

The counts reported are based on the counting rules shown in Table 6.1.

Figure 6.11

The Word Count
dialog box

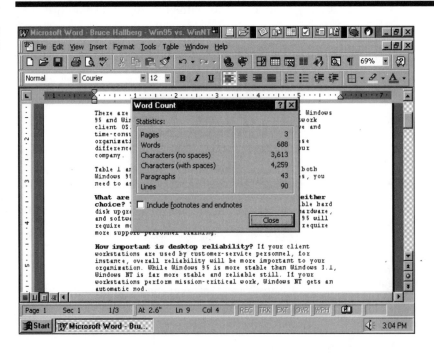

Table 6.1

Counting Rules for
Document Statistics

COUNT	RULE
Word	Words in the document, exclusive of footnotes and endnotes unless the check box is checked, and exclusive of headers and footers
Pages	Number of pages, as defined by page breaks in document and section breaks where relevant
Characters	Alphabetic characters, numeric characters, and punctuation marks
Paragraphs	Number of paragraphs, as defined by paragraph marks
Lines	Number of lines, including blank lines following paragraphs even if they are defined by paragraph marks

■ Multiple Language Support

Word allows you to work in multiple languages, even within the same document. You will not even know that Word is changing from one language format to another as you are working. You need only designate which sections of your text are written in which language, and Word handles the rest automatically.

If you have to work with people in Quebec with whom you must use French-Canadian words, for instance, you can designate such words as French Canadian using the Set Language command in the Language submenu of the the Tools menu. When Word encounters such a word in a spelling check, it will then automatically switch to the French-Canadian dictionary to look up the words so designated. If such a dictionary is not installed, Word will switch to the nearest equivalent, if possible: in this case, a French dictionary.

To change the language support for a portion of your document, perform the following procedure:

1. Select the text to be treated as a different language.

2. Open the Tools menu and select the Language submenu and then the Set Language command to display the Language dialog box (see Figure 6.12).

3. Select the language you want to use from the Mark Selected Text As list box.

4. If your text is primarily in a language other than the one you normally work with, you might want to set this language as the default language for Word. To do so, click on the Default button, then click on the Yes button in the dialog box that appears.

Tip. If you work with multiple languages frequently, make sure you have the appropriate dictionaries installed. If Word does not ship with the dictionary you need, you might be able to purchase one from a third-party vendor or find one available as shareware. You install such dictionaries as custom dictionaries. See the "Spelling Checker" section earlier in this chapter for the procedure.

Figure 6.12

The Language dialog box

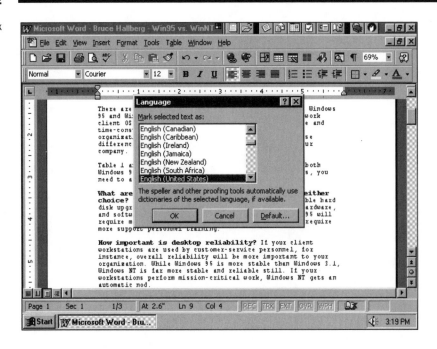

5. Click on OK.

After you have adjusted the language format, use the proofing tools just as you normally would. Word will treat the blocks of text you marked as being in the appropriate languages.

Tip. If you often work in multiple languages, consider creating a style for each language. Such styles can contain all the appropriate language formatting, and you can set them from the Formatting toolbar quite easily.

■ AutoText

Word provides the AutoText facility to help you create *boilerplate text,* common chunks of text that you use frequently. AutoText is the perfect place to store addresses, standard contract paragraphs, openings and closings for letters, distribution lists you use frequently, fax headers for clients, and other such items. Using AutoText, you can create boilerplate items, save them, and insert them into documents easily.

AutoText items are stored in a document template. Each item has a name that by default is the first few characters in the entry. You can, however, supply a name for each AutoText item when you create it. Because these items appear as entries in the AutoText dialog box, they frequently are called AutoText entries.

To create an AutoText entry, perform the following steps:

1. Enter the text, including graphics if you want, exactly as you want it to appear in any document.

2. Select the text (and graphics, if they are included). If you want the text to retain its formatting, be sure to select the paragraph mark as well. (Click on the Show/Hide Paragraph button on the Standard toolbar to reveal the paragraph mark, if necessary.)

3. Open the Insert menu and select the AutoText submenu and then the AutoText command. This displays the AutoText tab of the AutoCorrect dialog box, as shown in Figure 6.13.

Figure 6.13

The AutoText tab of the AutoCorrect dialog box

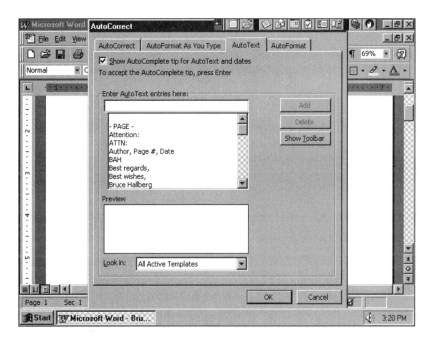

4. In the AutoText tab, enter a name in the Enter AutoText text box. Names can contain up to 32 characters, including spaces.

5. Open the Look In drop-down list box and select the document template in which you want the entry stored.

6. Click on the Add button.

To insert an AutoText entry into your text, follow these steps:

1. Place the insertion point at the beginning of a line or in an area surrounded by spaces.

2. Open the Insert menu and select the AutoText submenu. You will see the categories of AutoText, as shown in Figure 6.14.

Figure 6.14

The AutoText submenu

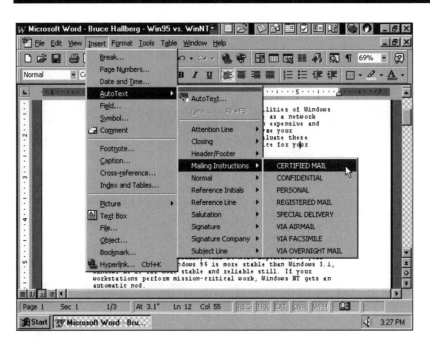

3. Select the category of the entry from the submenu.

4. Select the entry you want to insert into your document.

Alternately, you can type the name of the entry in your document and press F3 or Alt+Ctrl+V to invoke AutoText, then replace the typed name with the AutoText entry. AutoText inserts the entry you have named, or the closest match to the characters you have typed, at the insertion point.

If you ever need to change the content of an AutoText entry, insert it into a document, make the changes you want, and then repeat the entry-creation process described previously using the same name for the entry as it had before editing. To delete an AutoText entry, open the AutoText dialog box, highlight the name of the item to delete, and click on the Delete button.

■ Find and Replace

Word provides a powerful search-and-replace routine to help you locate information in your documents. Using this utility, you can locate just about anything and substitute something else for it, if desired. To access the Find utility, perform the following steps:

1. Open the Edit menu and select the Find option, or press Ctrl+F, to display the Find and Replace dialog box (see Figure 6.15).

Figure 6.15

The Find and Replace
dialog box

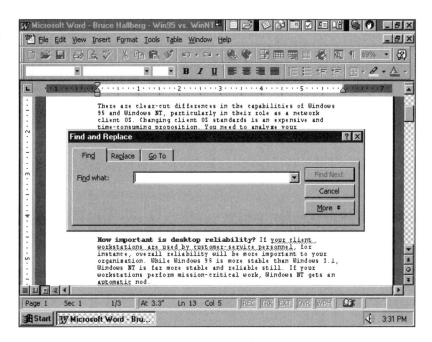

2. Enter the text to find in the Find What drop-down list box. The find strings from previous searches are stored in the list box portion of the control to facilitate repeated searches.

3. Use the More button to display an expanded-search dialog box that contains additional options. You can choose from the following options in the expanded-search dialog box:

   • Checking Match Case requires the matching item to be an exact upper- and lowercase match for the Find What string. *Intern* would not match *intern*, for example. Leaving the box unchecked allows a match with a string containing the same letters, but not necessarily the exact cases. *Intern* would match *intern*, *Intern*, and *INTERN*, for example.

Warning. Be careful of using Replace without checking Find Whole Words Only. You might replace the string in fragments of words, an action you probably do not intend.

- Checking the Find Whole Words Only box allows matches only with whole words. *Intern* would not match *internment*, for example. Leaving the box unchecked allows the Find What string to be matched with parts of words; therefore, *Intern* would match *internment*.

- Checking the Use Pattern Matching check box enables the use of the advanced wild cards, shown in Table 6.2, in your Find What string.

Table 6.2

Advanced Search Wild Cards

WILD CARD	USE	EXAMPLE
?	Single character	**w?t** finds *wit* and *wet*
*	Multiple characters	**w*t** finds *wit*, *wet*, *wheat*, and so on
[]	One of the characters	**w[ie]t** finds *wit* and *wet*. The [ie] section specifies that only those two letters can exist in that position in the word
[-]	Any character in range	**[p-t]at** finds *pat*, *rat*, *sat*, and *tat*. Any letters between "p" to "t" are found in the position indicated
[!]	Not the single character	**p[!a]t** finds *pit*, *pet*, *pot*, and *put*, but not *pat*
[!m-n]	Not the range of characters	**p[!a-e]t** finds *pit*, *pot*, and *put*, but not *pat* and *pet*
{n}	n occurrences of the character preceding the opening brace	**ble{2}d** finds *bleed* but not *bled*
{n,}	n or more occurrences of the character preceding the opening brace	**ble{1,}d** finds *bleed bled*
{n,m}	From m to n occurrences	**20{1,4}** finds *20*, *200*, *2000*, and *20000*
@	One or more occurrences of the character before the symbol	**ble@d** finds *bled* and *bleed*
<	Character or characters that begin the word	**<(intern)** finds *internment* and *internally*
>	Character or characters that end the word	**(intern)>** finds *comintern*

Checking the Sounds Like check box lets Word find words that sound like the one in your Find What string, but are spelled differently. Common variants like *Katherine* and *Catherine* or *sum* and *some* can be found this way.

- Checking the Find All Word Forms box allows Word to find a variety of forms of a word. For example, if you search for *looking*, Word will also find *looked* and *looks*.

- Click on the Format button to select Font, Paragraph, Language, and Style formats to search for. The items that appear on this button's menu open the same dialog boxes that you can open from Word's Format menu, in which you specify the format you want to look for. Using these options, you could look for italic text in paragraphs with hanging indents, for example. You do not need to enter text in the Find What drop-down list box to search for a format—you can search for the format alone. Click on the No Formatting button to clear formatting information from a search.

- Click on the Special button to search for one of the special characters that Word uses, like paragraph characters or section breaks.

- Click on the Find Next button to execute the search.

- Click on the Replace button to switch to the Replace dialog box in the midst of a find operation

To replace one piece of text with other text, perform the following steps:

1. Open the Replace tab in the Find and Replace dialog box, or open the Edit menu and select the Replace command, or press Ctrl+H. The Find and Replace dialog box appears, as shown in Figure 6.16.

2. Set the controls in the dialog box exactly as you would for a find operation.

3. Enter the text or format to replace the item with in the Replace With drop-down list box. You can use the Format and Special buttons to enter formats or special characters.

4. Perform one of the following actions:

   - Click on the Find Next button to find the next occurrence of the Find What string without replacing the currently found selection.

   - Click on the Replace button to replace the currently found selection and find the next selection.

   - Click on the Replace All button to replace all matching strings without having to confirm each replacement.

Tip. You can change the order of the words in the Find What drop-down list box and insert them into the Replace With drop-down list box by entering the number of each word in the Replace With drop-down list box preceded by a backslash. If the Find What string is "Darrow Clarence," you can enter \2\1 in the Replace With control to make the Replace With string "Clarence Darrow."

Figure 6.16

The Replace tab of the
Find and Replace
dialog box

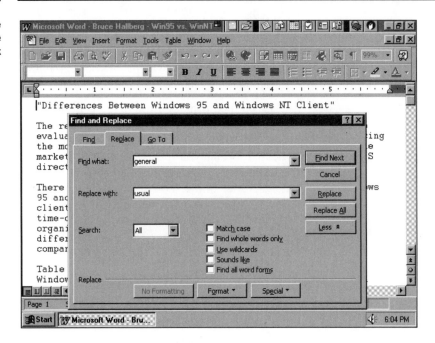

■ Bookmarks

Word provides a bookmark facility to help you easily find specific locations in a document. A *bookmark* is a named location in a document. It functions like a Post-it note inserted as a reminder tab in a book, except that each electronic reminder tab has its own name so that you can find it easily. After you have named a location in your document, however, you not only can move to that location quickly, but you also can insert information at that location.

To create a bookmark, perform the following steps:

1. Select the item you want to mark with a bookmark. This item can be text, graphics, or an insertion point location.

2. Open the Insert menu and select the Bookmark command, or press Ctrl+Shift+F5, to display the Bookmark dialog box (see Figure 6.17).

3. Enter a name for the bookmark in the text-box portion of the Bookmark Name combination box. The name must begin with a letter, and can contain only letters, numbers, and underscore characters. The name must be 40 or fewer characters in length.

4. Click on the Add button.

Figure 6.17

The Bookmark dialog box

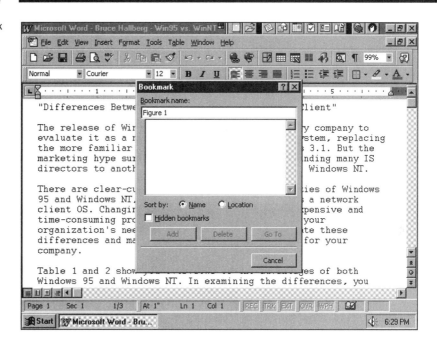

Tip. You can choose to view or hide your bookmarks. You make this selection using the View tab in the Options dialog box. Open the Tools menu and select the Options item to gain access to these settings.

The most common use for a bookmark is as a speedy means of locating a particular spot in a document. To move to a location marked by a bookmark, follow these steps:

1. Open the Insert menu and select the Bookmark option, or press Ctrl+Shift+F5.

2. Select the name of the bookmark in the Bookmark Name combination box.

3. Click on the Go To button.

When you edit items with bookmarks, you can use the following procedures to get the corresponding actions:

Tip. You also can move to a bookmark using the Go To dialog box. Double-click on the Status Bar or open the Edit menu and select the Go To option. Select Bookmark in the Go To What list box and select the bookmark name using the Enter Bookmark Name drop-down list box. Then click on the Go To button.

- Copy a marked item, or part of it, to another place in the same document. The bookmark stays in place. It is not moved or copied. The copy is not marked by a bookmark.

- Cut a marked item and paste it somewhere else in the same document. The bookmark moves with the item, and marks the item at its new location.

- Copy or cut a marked item and paste it to a location in another document. The bookmark both stays in place and moves to the other document. Both documents will now contain an identical bookmark. However, if the other document already has a bookmark of the same name, the bookmark does not move, and the pasted text is not marked with a bookmark.

Bookmarks let you perform calculations on marked numbers. Suppose you mention three sales figures in a memo, and want to add them to present a grand total at the end of the memo. If each figure is marked with the bookmarks figure1, figure2, and figure3, you can use this procedure to perform the calculation:

1. Open the Insert menu and select the Field option.

2. In the Field dialog box, select = (Formula) in the Field Names list box. It is the first item in the list when (All) is selected in the Categories list.

3. Enter **= figure1+figure2+figure3** in the Field Codes text box (see Figure 6.18).

4. Click on OK.

Figure 6.18

Entering a formula based on bookmarks in the Field dialog box

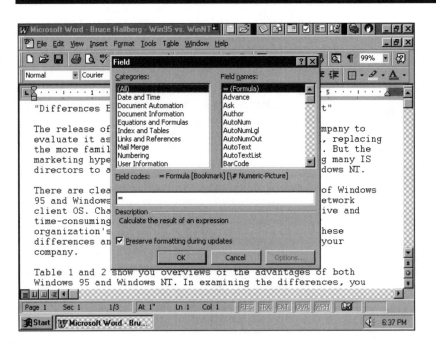

You will, of course, want to delete a bookmark occasionally. Word offers the following three methods for doing so:

- Open the Edit menu, select Bookmark, select the name of the bookmark in the dialog box, and click on the Delete button. The bookmark is deleted, and none of the text or other items marked are affected.

- Select the item marked by the bookmark, then press Del or Backspace. Both the item marked and the bookmark are deleted.

- Create a bookmark in a new location with the same name. The bookmark is moved to the new location, and the item previously marked is no longer marked by a bookmark. The item previously marked is not otherwise affected.

■ Highlighting

Word provides a feature called highlighting that lets you mark parts of your document for special attention, similar to the way you might use highlighting marker on printed documents. You can use this feature to draw your own eyes to a particular section of the document, or to note places that need attention when you share the file with another Word user.

There are two ways to apply highlighting to text: selecting the text and then applying the highlight, or painting the highlight color directly over text.

To highlight selected text, click the Highlight icon on the Formatting tool bar. By default, the highlight color is yellow. If you want to change the color, press the arrow to the right of the Highlight icon and choose a color.

To maneuver through your document as if you were holding a highlighting marker, follow this procedure:

- Press the Highlight icon with no text selected. The icon appears to have been pressed into the Formatting toolbar and your pointer changes its shape to resemble a marker.

- Drag the marker across any text you want to highlight. Continue to lift and then drag the marker until you have applied a highlight to every part of the document you want to draw attention to.

- To stop highlighting text, click the Highlight icon.

If you change the color of the highlight as you work with the marker, the text you have already highlighted will not change its highlight color. The new color will take effect with the next text you highlight. As a result, you can highlight different types of items with different colors. The Highlight icon contains a color indicator showing the current highlight color.

■ Fields

Word uses fields for automatic entry and updating of information. A *field* is a set of codes that instructs Word to perform a defined action. Although you can enter a field by hand, you have to know the appropriate codes for doing so. Word does not require you to learn these codes. The Field dialog box assists you in creating any type of field you want to use, and Word provides many types of pre-set fields to choose from.

As an example of how to use fields, consider how often you need to create a letter to a client, typing the date each time you do. You could place a date field in the template for the document that would automatically insert today's date when the document is created. To insert such a field, perform the following procedure:

1. Open the document template and place the insertion point where you want the date to go.

2. Open the Insert menu and select the Field option to display the Field dialog box (refer to Figure 6.18).

3. Select the category of field you want to insert from the Categories list box. In this case, select Date and Time. Select the type of date and time field you want in the Field Names list box—in this case, Date.

4. Click on the Options button to display the Field Options dialog box. Select the General Switches tab and select the date format you want, as shown in Figure 6.19.

5. Click on the Add to Field button and click on OK. Click on OK in the Field dialog box to insert the field.

6. Close and save the template.

Now each time you create a letter based on the template, the date is automatically inserted in the format you have chosen. When you reopen the document you have created, the date is not updated unless you specifically request it by selecting the field and pressing F9.

If you want to see the codes Word uses in a field, select the field and press Shift+F9; this keystroke switches the display of the actual codes. To switch all fields in this way at the same time, press Alt+F9. You can lock a field, preventing any updates, by pressing Ctrl+F11 or Ctrl+3. You can unlock the field by pressing Ctrl+Shift+F11 or Ctrl+4. If you need to *unlink* a field—that is, convert it to text that displays the last result of the field—select it and press Ctrl+Shift+F9.

Figure 6.19

The Field Options
dialog box

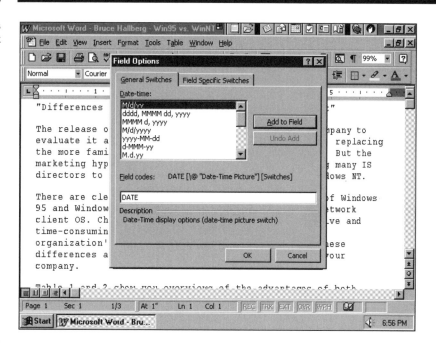

If your service bureau uses desktop publishing software that does not recognize Word fields, you can unlink your fields to convert them to plain text that can be imported into the program.

■ Symbols

Word has a special utility that lets you insert symbols into a document from any font, as well as from a list of commonly used special symbols like em dashes and trademark symbols. Using this utility, you can give your documents a professional look without having to look up and remember all the special ASCII-character codes for such symbols.

To insert a symbol, perform the following procedure:

1. Open the Insert menu and select the Symbol option to display the Symbol dialog box.

2. In the Symbol dialog box, select either the Symbols or Special Characters tab (see Figures 6.20 and 6.21), depending on whether you want to select the symbol from a font or from the list of special characters.

Figure 6.20

The Symbol dialog box
showing the Symbols tab

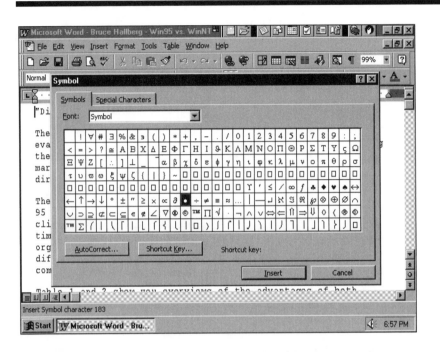

Figure 6.21

The Symbol dialog box
showing the Special
Characters tab

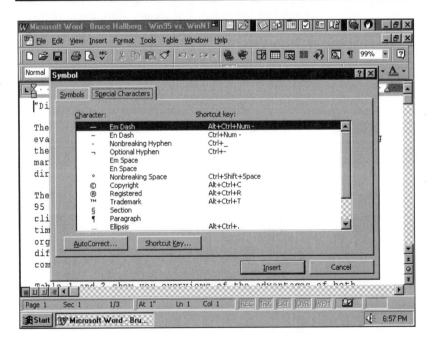

3. Using the Symbols tab shown in Figure 6.21, perform one of the following actions:

   • Select a font using the Font drop-down list box.

   • Select a character from the grid displayed and click on the Insert button. The character will be inserted at the insertion point.

   • Select a character from the grid displayed, and click on the Shortcut Key button. When the Customize dialog box appears, press the keystroke you want to use to insert the character in the future, click on the Assign button, and click on the Close button. You can insert the character now using the keystroke you just assigned.

4. Using the Special Characters tab shown in Figure 6.21, perform one of the following actions:

   • Select a character from the list displayed and click on the Insert button. The character will be inserted at the insertion point.

   • Select a character from the list displayed and click on the Shortcut Key button. When the Customize dialog box appears, press the keystroke you want to use to insert the character in the future, click on the Assign button, and click on the Close button. You can insert the character now using the keystroke you just assigned.

■ Macros

You might think that macros are mysterious things that you will never use. *Macros,* after all, are user-created commands, and you must use some sort of programming language to create them. Word, however, has you using them all the time. Macros are a part of the document metaphor, so much so that you could not have a document without macros. Each Word command that you invoke from the menu is, in fact, a macro created by the Word programmers for your use.

To demonstrate this point, follow these directions:

1. Open the Tools menu and select the Macro submenu and then the Macros command to display the Macro dialog box.

2. In the Macro dialog box, use the Macros In drop-down list box to select Word Commands (see Figure 6.22).

3. Scroll through the Macro Name combination box and select the Insert-Symbol macro.

4. Click on the Run button.

Figure 6.22

The Macro dialog box
with Word Commands
selected in the Macros
In list box

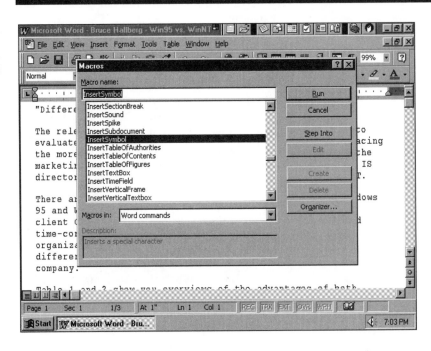

The Symbol dialog box should now be on your screen, and you can work with it just as if you had invoked it from the menu. The macro and the menu command are equivalent. (The menu, however, makes the Symbol dialog box much easier to find and use.)

All the Word commands are stored in the document template NOR-MAL.DOT. Any macro is stored as a part of a document template. As a result, you can keep macros that relate to special document types in the templates for those documents. In this way, Word integrates commands and documents entirely. Commands are parts of documents.

You might wonder why Word is structured this way. Building a word processor as a set of macros that you run as you work on your document has the following advantages:

- You can choose to use any command in any way at any time, whether it is on the menu, attached to a button, hidden away, or dimmed on the menu. You can always access a command through the macro dialog box.

- You can decide which commands are attached to the menu and to the toolbars.

- You can build your own Word commands that perform custom functions by combining the already familiar commands you use from the menu. You can use your own commands or Word's commands interchangeably.

- User-created commands are composed of existing, tested Word commands.

- With this structure, most users never need to learn the command names in order to create new commands. They can use the macro facility to record the command sequences generated by using the menu and to play these back to Word at will.

In Word, macros are not mysterious—you use them all the time. They are the core of the word processor, a part of every document, and a key concept behind the software. Chapter 9 shows the way to create your own Word macros and how to assign them to the menu or to toolbar buttons. For now, just be aware of how important these macros are to you.

■ Working with Multiple Documents

The reason that Word couples a document and a window together as a part of the document metaphor is that Word enables you to open multiple documents without having to open a separate copy of the word processor. Each open document runs in its own window and has all the capabilities associated with that window.

You can open as many documents as will fit in your computer's memory. You will, however, need to know how to manage multiple documents.

Each document window has the familiar maximize and minimize buttons. When a document is maximized, it occupies the entire Word workspace. Its ruler tucks up under the toolbars, its maximize button appears at the right end of the menu bar, and its control menu button appears at the left end of the menu bar. These features define the default appearance of any new document you open when you start Word.

When a document is not maximized, its window has a title bar and looks like any other document window used by any other Windows program, with the addition of the ruler and the view buttons already noted earlier in this chapter. When a document is minimized, it appears as an icon at the bottom of Word's workspace.

You can manage multiple document windows using Word's Window menu, shown in Figure 6.23.

The commands on the menu control the following actions:

- The New Window command opens a copy of the active document window. When you close the document, all copies of its window close as well.

- The Arrange All command arranges all the open document windows so that they are visible on-screen. If you have only a few documents open, their windows appear as horizontal bands in your workspace. If you

Figure 6.23

Word's Window menu

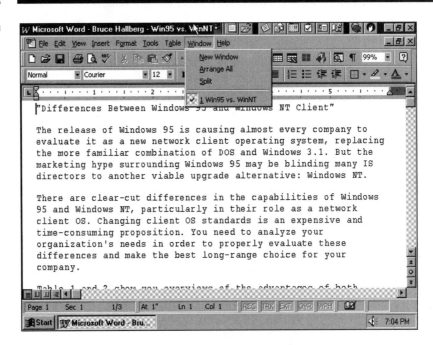

have more windows open, Word automatically arranges them in a tiled fashion on the screen. To change the active window, simply click on the window you want to be active.

- The Split command activates the split bar. Click in the active window where you want the split to occur.

- The list of document names allows you to switch to any document at any time. Simply select the name from the list. If your More Windows option is available (it appears when more than nine documents are open at once), selecting it opens the Activate dialog box (see Figure 6.24), which gives you access to the list of windows by means of a list box. Scroll through the list, select the document you need, and click on OK.

Through the facilities provided by the Window menu, you can keep track of all the documents on your screen. Word makes it easy to have multiple documents open and to avoid getting lost in a maze of multiple documents.

Figure 6.24

The Activate dialog box

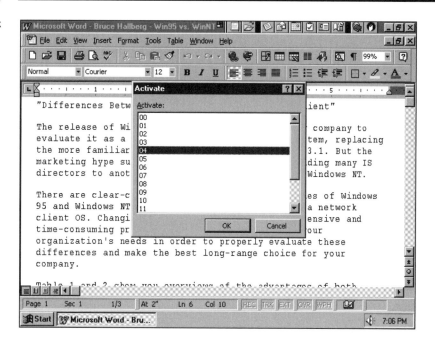

- *Creating a Custom Template*
- *Creating Custom Styles*
- *Modifying and Deleting Styles*
- *Merging Existing Styles*
- *Changing Case*
- *Using Drop Caps*
- *Creating Document Sections*

- *Using Columns*
- *Using Bullets and Numbering*
- *Using AutoFormat*

Using Advanced Formatting Tools

Now that you know the basic concepts upon which Word is built, it is time to teach Word how to support the way you work.

In this chapter, you will learn the following advanced features and techniques for using Word:

- Creating a custom template
- Modifying and deleting styles
- Merging existing styles
- Changing case
- Using drop caps
- Creating document sections
- Using columns
- Using bullets and numbering
- Using numbered headings
- Using AutoFormat

With these features, you can create professional-looking documents with a minimum of effort.

Having mastered the basics, you can apply your knowledge of Word to create sophisticated documents. Most users accommodate themselves to their software—that is, they learn how to perform tasks the way the software was designed to perform them. Word, however, accommodates itself to your working style. You don't need to build your documents a certain way just because Word does it that way; you can teach Word to build documents your way.

You need only two tools to set up Word to work the way you do: document templates and styles. The templates you create provide your documents with the formatting you want, and the styles you create and store in your templates define how you work with your documents. This combination provides you with a tool that facilitates your work by automating it as much as possible.

To illustrate how to use templates and styles to teach Word the way you work, this chapter presents a scenario to help you imagine building your own solutions to working problems. This scenario involves a consulting firm, Write Solutions, Inc., that specializes in helping companies find ways to simplify and automate writing tasks by taking advantage of the features built into their word processing software. The firm has clients in the United States, the United Kingdom, Belgium, and France. Members of the firm have French language skills, and often both correspondence and contracts must contain some passages in French. Of course, Write Solutions practices what it preaches—all its documents are based on Word templates, including its letterhead.

As an employee of this firm, your job is to set up Word to handle the letters its representatives must write. You do not write in French, but you need to incorporate passages written in French by others in your correspondence. You also want to match your writing as closely as possible to the conventions used in the United Kingdom when you write to clients in that country.

■ Creating a Custom Template

The first step in setting up Word to meet your goals is creating a new document template. Follow these steps to perform this task:

1. Open the File menu and select the New option.

2. In the New dialog box, select the Template option button on the lower right (see Figure 7.1).

Figure 7.1

Creating the new template using the New dialog box

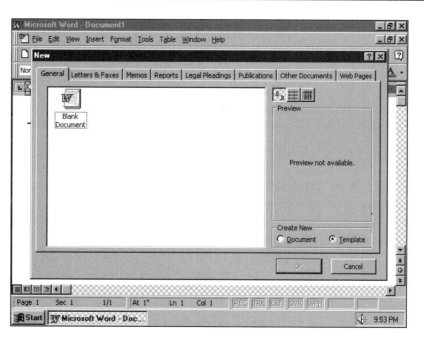

3. If the General page is not displayed, click on the General tab.

4. Click the icon for the existing template—in this case, the Blank Document template—on which you want to base this new template.

5. Click on OK to create the file.

After you create the new template, click on the Save button in the standard toolbar to save it under its own name. When the Save As dialog box appears, give the template the name Write Solutions and click on Save. After you name and save the template, you can add to it the information you need each document to have whenever you create correspondence.

Because documents based on this template will bear the Write Solutions letterhead, you can use the document header to contain the letterhead information. Open the View menu and select the Header and Footer option.

NOTE. *The Write Solutions letterhead information is in the Arial font that comes with Windows. The upper line is in 14-point Arial, and the lower line is in 9-point Arial. The phone number is placed at the first default tab after the address text. The rule between the two lines of text is the upper border for the second paragraph of the letterhead information. To create the rule, place the insertion point on the second line, open the Format menu, and select the Borders and Shading option. In the Borders tab of the Paragraph Borders and Shading dialog box, click on the upper border line in the Border box and click on OK.*

Follow these steps:

1. Click on the Page Setup button in the Header and Footer toolbar and select the Layout tab in the Page Setup dialog box. In the Headers and Footers group of the dialog box tab, check the Different first page box to prevent the letterhead information from appearing on each page of a multipage letter. Then click on the OK button.

2. Enter the letterhead information. Click on the Close button in the Header and Footer toolbar.

3. Enter a page break to create a second page. Open the View menu and select Header and Footer again. Click on the Switch Between Header and Footer button on the Header and Footer toolbar to move to the footer for the second page.

4. Click on the Align Right button in the standard toolbar.

5. Click on the Insert Page Number button in the Header and Footer toolbar. Press Enter.

6. Click on the Insert Date button in the Header and Footer toolbar. Press Enter.

7. Type **Write Solutions**. Select the text you have just entered and use the Font drop-down list box in the formatting toolbar to set the font to Arial.

8. Click on the Close button on the Header and Footer toolbar, and delete the page break that you entered into your template file. (You no longer need it there.)

Your completed header, as shown in Figure 7.2, can now serve as your letterhead.

Figure 7.2

The letterhead information for Write Solutions entered in the template

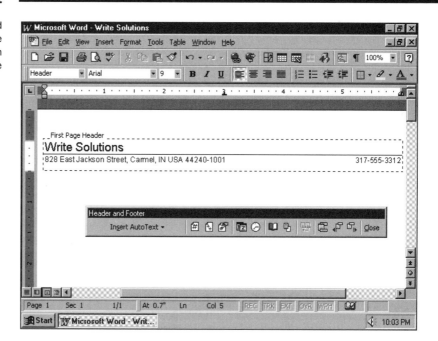

The people to whom you send correspondence now know the name of your firm from the letterhead you have created. They also can tell from the second and following pages which company the correspondence is from and on what date it was sent. This information helps if the pages of a long letter ever become separated. The final step in preparing this template is to add your name on the first line of the first page. Your clients can then tell who to contact in response to the correspondence.

After performing all these steps, save the template again to protect your work against loss. At this point, you are ready to consider what styles you might want to add to the document template you have just created.

■ Creating Custom Styles

To simplify working with documents based on your new template, you can create a selection of styles that automate the formatting of the document. The easiest way to create a style is by example. Format a paragraph of text the way you want it, then perform the following steps:

1. Open the Style drop-down list box on the formatting toolbar.

2. Clear the current style name by pressing Del.

3. Type a new name for the style.

4. Press Enter.

You can perform those steps on the Write Solutions template as follows:

Format your name the way you would like it to appear beneath the letterhead on the document. To keep the font consistent, select your name and set the font to Arial using the Font drop-down list on the formatting toolbar. Set the size to 8 points using the Font Size drop-down list. Next, open the Format menu and select the Paragraph option. In the Paragraph dialog box, select the Indents and Spacing tab. Use the After spin box to set the space after your name to 12 points. Choose OK. Then open the Style drop-down list box, clear the current style, type Name, and press Enter. You've just created a style for the name block on your letter.

Press Enter and type a date. Select the date text and change the font size to 9 points. Name this style Date. You will use it to format the date block on all documents.

Next type a sample inside address and apply formats from the appropriate dialog boxes until it looks the way you want it to. For example, set the font to Arial and the size to 9 points. Set the space after the paragraph to 0 points. Name this style Address. You now have a style for the inside address of letters you might write.

Figure 7.5 later in this section shows an example of each of these formats, if you need a visual target for creating these styles.

Create a similar style for the greeting. Set the space before the paragraph and after the paragraph to 12 points so that the greeting automatically spaces itself between the inside address and the body of the letter. Name this style Greeting.

Creating Language Styles

The body of your planned document places considerable demands on Word. You might be working with text in US English, UK English, or French. As a result, you need to create three body-paragraph styles, one for each language. In this way, you signal Word's document tools to apply the appropriate language information as they operate on the document. As a result, during a spelling check the French dictionary applies to the French paragraphs, the UK English dictionary to the UK English paragraphs, and the US English dictionary to the US English paragraphs automatically. Word also automatically applies the appropriate exception dictionaries that you may have created.

To create styles for the body of your document, type some sample text. Keep the 9-point Arial font and set the paragraph spacing to 0 points before and 12 points after. Select the text, open the Tools menu, and select the Language option. Select English (US) from the Mark Selected Text As list box and click on the OK button. Then open the Style drop-down list box and create a style named BodyUS. Repeat the process of selecting the language, this time choosing English (UK). Create a style called BodyUK. Repeat the process one last time, selecting French and creating a style called BodyFR. You now can create paragraphs in all three languages, and Word will automatically handle them appropriately.

Create a style in US English that has no lines before or after the paragraph. It should remain in the 9-point Arial font. Name this style Close. You will use it to format the closing of letters.

Creating Character Styles

The styles you have created so far are *paragraph styles*, so named because they involve paragraph formats. When you apply these styles to text, the paragraph containing the text is modified to fit the style. You also can create *character styles*—styles that apply only a font format to text. To create character styles, you must use the Style command on the Format menu.

You also can create paragraph styles using the Style command. The process is the same as for creating character styles, except that you set Style Type to Paragraph. The one advantage of creating paragraph styles in this way is that you can set the style of the text following the paragraph using the Style for Following Paragraph drop-down list box. The Format button in the New Style dialog box provides access to all the Format dialog boxes applicable to paragraphs.

To create a character style, perform the following steps:

1. Open the Format menu and select the Style command to bring up the Style dialog box (see Figure 7.3).

2. In the Style dialog box, click on the New button to bring up the New Style dialog box (see Figure 7.4).

3. In the New Style dialog box, open the Style type drop-down list box and select Character.

Figure 7.3

The Style dialog box

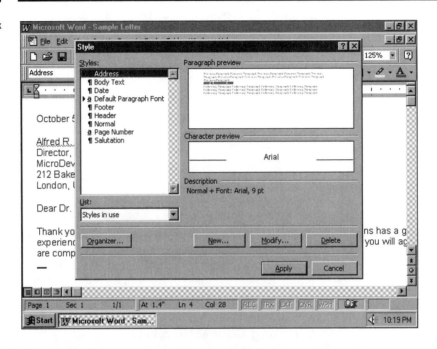

Figure 7.4

The New Style dialog box

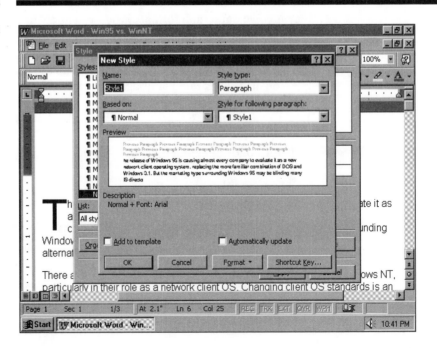

4. Enter a name for the style in the Name text box.

5. Select the style to base the new style on from the Based on drop-down list box. Word must always use information from an existing style as the basis for creating the new one.

6. Click on the Format button and select either Font or Language from the list that appears. Use the Font and Language dialog boxes to set the characteristics for your style.

7. Check on the Add to Template check box if you want to store the style to the current document template; otherwise, it is stored in the document only.

8. Click on OK. Word creates your new style.

9. Click on the Close button in the Style dialog box.

For the Write Solutions template, you might need a number of character styles: bold italics for foreign words and phrases embedded in your document, for example, and superscript and subscript styles for use in describing some elements of the programs your firm writes. Create these styles according to the procedure outlined. Name them ForeignPhrase, Subscript, and Superscript.

Style names can contain up to 253 characters, but cannot contain backslashes, braces, or semicolons.

Putting the Styles Together

To get a sense of the usefulness of your custom styles, create a brief document based on your Write Solutions template. Follow these steps:

1. Create a new document based on the Write Solutions template (use the New command in the File menu and then select Write Solutions in the General tab).

2. Press the End key to move to the end of the name block, press Enter, select the Date style, and type the date.

3. Press Enter, select the Address style, and type the address.

4. Press Enter, select the Greeting style, and type the greeting.

5. Press Enter, select the Body style appropriate to the country of your client, and type a body paragraph. Repeat this process until the body of the letter is complete.

6. Press Enter, select the Close style, and type the closing.

A portion of the completed letter is shown in Figure 7.5 with the styles applied to each paragraph showing in the style area. As you can see, the appropriate formatting is automatically applied to each section of the letter. You do not need to make repeated adjustments using the menu to change the format for each section of the letter. Each section is also set up for the appropriate spell-checking procedures.

Figure 7.5

A sample letter based on the Write Solutions template showing the use of custom styles

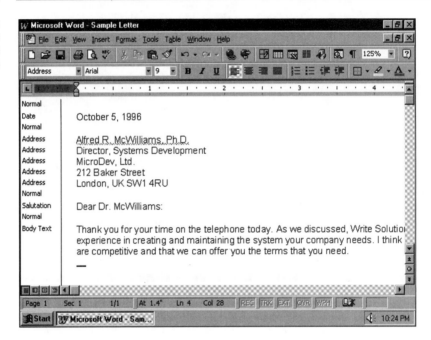

TIP. *You can open the style area on your screen by choosing Options from the Tools menu. Then use the Style Area Width spin box in the Window section of the View tab to adjust the size.*

Figure 7.6 shows the same letter in page layout view, showing the advantage of using the document template to contain the boilerplate text of the letterhead. Entering the text and the styles in the template once saves you a considerable amount of work as you create subsequent documents.

Figure 7.6

The sample letter based
on the Write Solutions
template in page
layout view

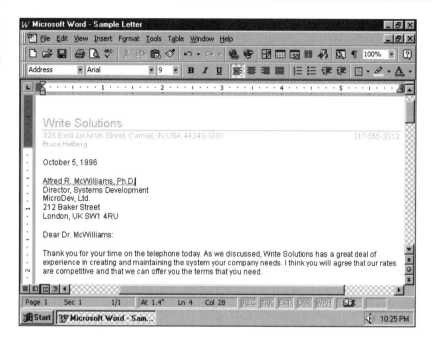

■ Modifying and Deleting Styles

Occasionally you might need to modify a style that you use for creating documents with the Write Solutions template. You might decide that because you write most of your documents in US English, for example, you would like to limit your use of UK English and French to single paragraphs only. You might like to automatically reset the following paragraph to the US English style. Making this change requires you to modify the style.

To modify a style, perform the following steps:

1. Open the Format menu and select the Style option to bring up the Style dialog box (refer to Figure 7.3).

2. Open the List drop-down list box and select the view that causes the style you want to modify to appear in the Styles list box (All styles or User-defined styles should display your styles).

3. Select the style in the Styles list box and click on the Modify button. The Modify Style dialog box appears (see Figure 7.7).

4. To change the name, enter a new name in the Name text box.

Figure 7.7

The Modify Style
dialog box

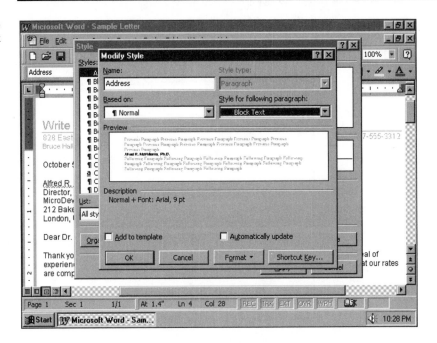

5. Open the Based On and Style for Following Paragraph drop-down list boxes to change these aspects of the style. (If you are working on a character style, the Style for Following Paragraph control will not be active.)

6. Click on the Format button and select the appropriate formatting dialog boxes. Make the changes you want to the style.

7. When you are finished, click on the OK button, then click on the Close button in the Style dialog box.

To change the BodyUK and BodyFR styles, select each in the Style dialog box, click on the Modify button, and set the Style for Following Paragraph for each to BodyUS. When you press Enter after you write a paragraph in either of these formats, the style for the new paragraph reverts to BodyUS.

When styles logically follow one another in a document, you might want to modify them so that each style selects the style for the next paragraph as the next style in the sequence. Address, for example, could format the next paragraph as Greeting. After you complete the inside address for the letter, press Enter to type the greeting using the appropriate style.

Occasionally you will need to delete a style from a document template. To delete a style, open the Style dialog box and select the style in the Styles list box. If you can delete the style, the Delete button becomes active. Click on the Delete button to delete the style.

■ Merging Existing Styles

As noted in Chapter 5, "Understanding Word for Windows Concepts," Word provides a large number of built-in styles you can use in documents. You might want to use some of these styles in your own custom templates, or you might want to move some of your custom styles from a custom template into the Normal document template to make them available globally. Word provides a facility for doing this type of copying and moving—the Organizer dialog box.

To access the Organizer dialog box, follow these steps:

1. Open the Format menu and select the Style option.

2. In the Style dialog box, click on the Organizer button to display the Organizer dialog box. Then select the Styles tab (see Figure 7.8).

Figure 7.8

The Organizer dialog box displaying the Styles tab

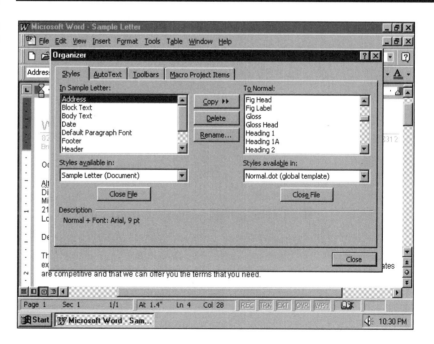

3. In the left half of the style organizer, set up one of the documents or templates that you want to work with. By default, Word places your current document in the left portion of the Organizer and Normal.DOT (the Normal document template) in the right portion. If this arrangement suits you, proceed to step 8. If not, follow steps 4 through 7.

4. Click on the Close File button on the left.

5. Click on the Open File button that replaces the Close File button.

6. In the Open dialog box that appears, select the file you want to work with and click on OK.

7. Repeat steps 4 through 6 with the Close File button under the list box and drop-down list box in the right portion of the style organizer.

8. Select a style in either list box, then choose from the following options:

   - Click on the Copy button to copy the style to the other document or template. (The arrow on the Copy button reverses direction depending on which list box contains the selected style.)

   - Click on the Delete button to delete a style. Confirm the deletion by clicking on the Yes button in the confirmation dialog box. The list boxes in the style organizer allow multiple selections. You can select contiguous style names using Shift+left mouse button. You can select discontiguous style names using Ctrl+left mouse button.

   - Click on the Rename button to rename a style. Type the new name in the Rename dialog box and click on the OK button.

9. When you have finished with the style organizer, click on the Close button.

Using the style organizer, you can copy styles among documents and templates, rename styles within documents and templates, and delete styles from documents and templates. After you have defined a set of styles, those styles need not stay isolated in your template or on your machine. You can easily make them available to colleagues, just as colleagues can share styles with you. You can mix and match styles to your advantage.

■ Changing Case

Word provides the capability to alter the capitalization of your text on the fly. This capability goes beyond changing the case of selected letters from upper to lower. Word provides several options.

The easiest way to become familiar with Word's case-changing capabilities is to type a sentence, select it, and then press Shift+F3. When you first press this key combination, the sentence changes to all uppercase letters. On the next press, the sentence changes to all lowercase. On the third press, the sentence changes to normal sentence capitalization: an uppercase first letter for the first word and the remainder in lowercase. For any group of selected characters, press Shift+F3 repeatedly to cycle the text through these three options. Just press this key combination until you have the results you want.

TIP. *Shift+F3 works on blocks of text longer than a single sentence. This key combination can be useful if you are not a skilled typist. Keep in mind, however, that Word will not preserve the capitalization of proper names in the sentences for which you adjust capitalization using this technique.*

In addition to the Shift+F3 key combination, Word provides the Change Case command on the Format menu. This command offers you even more flexibility. When you choose this command, if no text is selected, Word automatically selects the nearest word for you. If text is selected, Word operates on the selection you have made.

When you select the Change Case menu option, Change Case dialog box appears, as shown in Figure 7.9. Choose from the following options:

- Select **Sentence case** to place an initial capital letter on the selection and make the rest of the characters lowercase.

- Select **lowercase** to make the selection all lowercase characters.

- Select **UPPERCASE** to make the selection all uppercase characters.

- Select **Title Case** to make the selection have initial uppercase characters on each word.

- Select **tOGGLE cASE** to reverse the capitalization of the characters in the selection.

Figure 7.9

The Change Case
dialog box

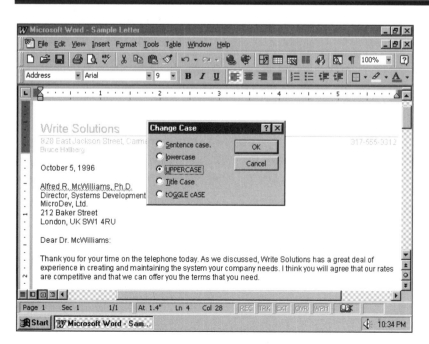

After you have made your selection in the dialog box, click on OK. Word applies the formatting you have chosen to the selection on the screen.

■ Using Drop Caps

Word also provides you with a simple way to create *drop caps,* large capital letters that mark the beginning of the first word in a section. Drop caps can make your documents visually attractive. They also serve a practical purpose—you can use them like bullets on a list to draw attention to a series of items. Drop caps help the person reading the document find the relevant sections. While you might not use them in formatting a letter that you prepare using the Write Solutions template, you might use them in preparing an article using that template. Figure 7.10 shows an example of a drop cap in use in an article prepared with the Write Solutions template.

To create a drop cap, follow this procedure:

1. Place the insertion point in the paragraph that will receive the drop cap.

2. Open the Format menu and select the Drop Cap option. The Drop Cap dialog box appears, as shown in Figure 7.11.

Figure 7.10

A drop cap in an article

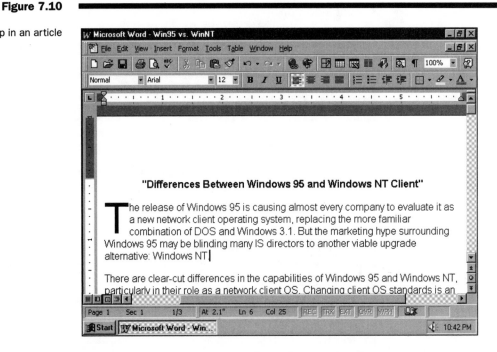

Figure 7.11

The Drop Cap dialog box

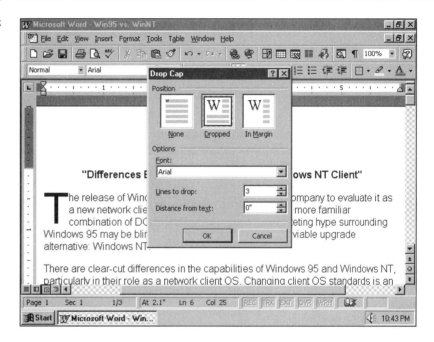

3. In the Drop Cap dialog box, select the position of the drop cap, either Dropped or In Margin.

4. Using the Font drop-down list box, select the font for the drop cap. The default is the font of the text in the paragraph.

5. Using the Lines to drop spin box, adjust the size of the drop cap in lines.

6. Using the Distance from text spin box, adjust the distance of the drop cap letter from the rest of the text on the right.

7. Click on OK. If you are not in page layout view, Word will ask if you want to switch to that view before you insert the drop cap. You need to be in page layout view to adjust the position and size of the drop cap by dragging with the mouse.

TIP. *You may want to use a different font for a drop cap than you use for the rest of your text. To create visual unity, however, it helps to use no more than two fonts in any given document. If you use Universal for titles and subheads and Palatino for body text, for example, use Universal for the drop cap at the head of a section to tie the elements together visually.*

After creating your drop cap, if you do not like it, you have the following options:

- Open the Edit menu and select Undo Drop Cap. You can select this option from the Undo button on the standard toolbar if the option no longer shows on the menu.

- Select the drop cap letter and press Del. You will need to retype the character you deleted from your text.

- Select the drop cap, open the Format menu, and select the Drop Cap option. You can adjust the controls in the Drop Cap dialog box to change the font, distance, and position of the drop cap until you are satisfied with it.

- Select the drop cap, select Drop Cap from the Format menu, and then select None in the Position group.

■ Creating Document Sections

In Word, you have complete control over the formatting you apply to any part of a document. A *section* is a part of a Word document that can be formatted separately from other sections. You define a section by inserting a section break into a document. Whatever comes before the section break can be formatted differently from whatever comes after the section break. You can create as many sections as you want in a document, and sections can be as short or long as you want them to be.

When you create a new Word document, it has a single section by default. To break a document into more than one section, you must perform the following steps:

1. Position the insertion point where you want to insert the section break.

2. Open the Insert menu and select the Break command.

3. In the Break dialog box, shown in Figure 7.12, use the option buttons in the Section Breaks group to select one of the following kinds of section breaks:

   - **Next Page**: The new section begins on a new page.

   - **Continuous**: The new section begins on the same page, unless the two sections have different settings for page size or page orientation, in which case the section starts on a new page.

   - **Even Page**: The new section begins on the next even-numbered page.

   - **Odd Page**: The new section begins on the next odd-numbered page.

Figure 7.12

The Break dialog box

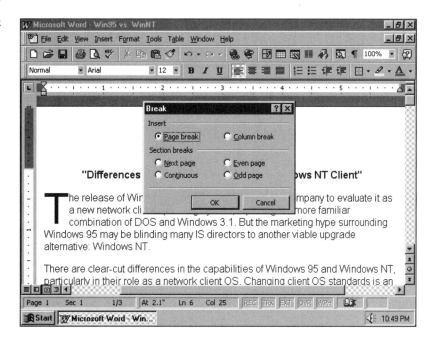

Word inserts a visible break line labeled End of Section into your document, which you can see in Normal view. If you ever need to delete a section break, select it and press the Backspace or Del key. If you delete a section, the formatting of the section above the break in the document becomes the same as the following section.

Defining sections lets you mix all sorts of formatting styles in the same document. Suppose you are creating a report on recent research and development efforts undertaken by Write Solutions. You want the abstract to occupy the width of the full page, the research report to have a two-column format, and the bibliography to have a full-page format. You can accomplish this formatting using sections.

Note. You can see and delete section breaks only in Normal view.

To set this document up, enter the text, applying the styles you have created. To format this document, create a TitleWS style that formats a centered title, a HeadingWS style that formats a left-aligned bold title, and a BiblioWS style that formats each bibliography entry. After you format your text, break it into three sections so that you can separately format the column section.

To create the sections, position the insertion point at the title of the research report, open the Insert menu, select the Break command, select a Continuous section break, and click on OK. Repeat these steps with the insertion point at the title for the bibliography. Figure 7.13 shows this report with the section break inserted after the abstract.

Figure 7.13

A report for Write
Solutions that
uses sections

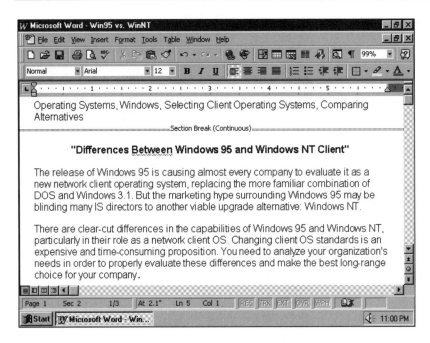

TIP. *To give each section a different header and footer, make sure that the Same As Previous button is not active on the Header and Footer toolbar. If the button is active, your new section has the same headers and footers as the previous section. To break this link, click on the button.*

■ Using Columns

To create columns in a section of a document, you have two courses of action: you can use the Columns button on the standard toolbar, or you can use the Columns command on the Format menu. Each action achieves the same result. But as usual in Word, the menu command gives you more control over the column-creation process.

To use the Columns button, place the insertion point in the section that is to have columns. Point to the Columns button, depress the left mouse button, and drag over the grid until the correct number of columns is highlighted (see Figure 7.14). Release the mouse button, and Word formats your section with the number of columns you indicated.

To use the menu command to create columns, perform the following steps:

1. Open the Format menu and select the Columns command.

Figure 7.14

Creating columns using the Columns button on the Standard toolbar.

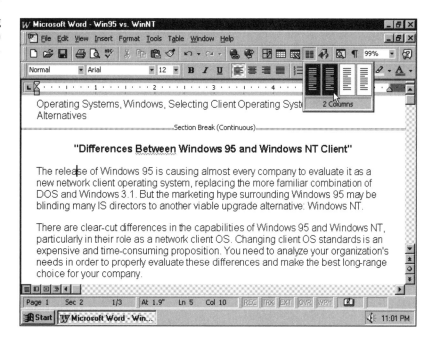

2. In the Columns dialog box, shown in Figure 7.15, you can set the following options:

  - To set up columns quickly in one of five preset formats, click on one of the controls in the Presets group to select **One**, **Two**, **Three**, **Left** (two columns, the narrower on the left), or **Right** (two columns, the narrower on the right).

  - To set a custom number of columns, enter the number using the **Number of Columns** spin box.

  - To place a vertical line between the columns, check the **Line Between** check box.

  - To set up custom column widths and spaces between columns, use the **Width** and **Spacing** spin boxes in the Width and Spacing group. Select which column you are working on using the **Col. #** control. To set equal column widths easily and quickly, check the **Equal Column Width** check box.

  - To start a new column at the insertion point, check the **Start New Column** check box, located beneath the Preview box.

Figure 7.15

The Columns dialog box

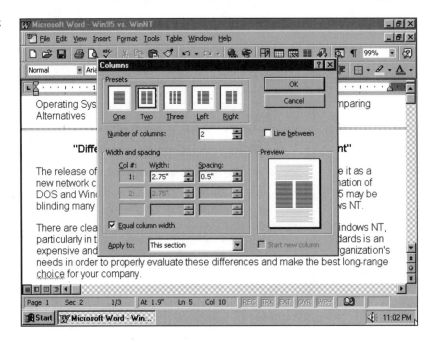

- Use the **Apply To** drop-down list box to control whether the column formatting applies to the entire document or simply from the insertion point forward. Word inserts a section break to protect the previous formatting if you elect to apply the column format from the insertion point forward.

3. When you have the column format set up properly, click on the OK button.

   To create the columns in the second section of your Write Solutions report, place the insertion point in the second section. Use the Columns button on the standard toolbar to select two columns. Word adjusts the format of the section, as shown in Figure 7.16.

   To fine-tune your columns, you need to master a few tricks:

- If you have unbalanced columns on the final page of your document, insert a continuous section break at the end of your document. Word automatically balances the columns for you when a continuous section break follows them.

- If a heading or text is orphaned at the bottom of a column, insert a column break ahead of the problem text to force it into the next column. Open the **Insert** menu, select the **Break** command, select **Column Break** in the dialog box, and click on the OK button.

Figure 7.16

The Write Solutions report with a two-column format in the second section

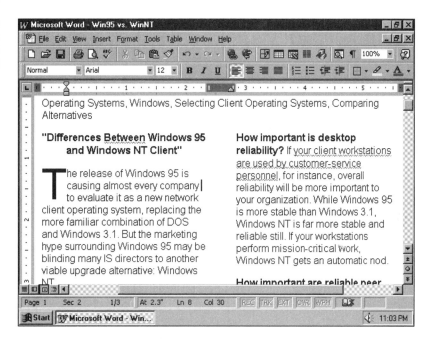

- If you need two paragraphs or some text and a graphic to stay within the same column, select the items that need to stay together, open the **Format** menu, select the **Paragraph** command, select the **Text Flow** tab, check the **Keep With Next** check box, and click on the OK button.

- If you have a document with a different header on the first page and you want to start your section on a new page, the first-page header will appear on the first page of the new section. If you want to maintain the same header and footer for the remaining pages throughout your document, do not want the first page header to appear in the new section, and need the new section to start on a new page, insert a continuous section break followed by a page break.

■ Using Bullets and Numbering

Word automates the process of creating bulleted and numbered lists for you. Word offers two buttons on the right side of the formatting toolbar: the Numbering and Bullets buttons. These buttons switch numbered and bulleted lists on and off for the paragraph that contains the insertion point, or for all paragraphs that you've selected. When you are numbering or adding bulleted items, these buttons appear pressed. When you are not using these features, these buttons appear normally.

NOTE. *The Bullets and Numbering dialog box contains a tab called Outline Numbered. In versions of Word prior to Word 97, this feature was called Numbered Headings and used to be accessed through the Heading Numbering command. Word 97 simplifies this design so that numbered headings are now contained in the Bullets and Numbering command of the Format menu.*

To enter a bulleted or numbered list, follow these steps:

1. Set up the paragraph's left indent the way you want it to be. If you want your list indented further than the rest of your text, you need to set that up in advance.

2. Click on the Bullets or Numbering button. The first bullet or number will automatically appear.

3. Type the items in your list. Each time you press Enter, a new bullet or the next number appears. Figure 7.17 shows this process in action.

4. When you finish your list, click on the button to exit bullet or numbering mode.

Figure 7.17

Entering a numbered list

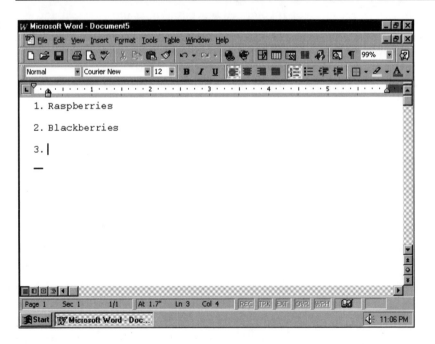

If you've already entered a list of items and decide later that it should be bulleted or numbered, select the list and click on the appropriate button. Word converts your list by adding the appropriate bulleting or numbering.

TIP. *Word supplies styles for formatting lists, bulleted lists, and numbered lists, which you can apply using the Style command on the Format menu. There are five forms of each list style. Each form is increasingly indented. The number ending the style name indicates the level of indentation. List5, for instance, is the furthest indented of the standard list styles.*

The buttons on the standard toolbar offer default bullets and numbering. Your list items are formatted with hanging indentation. The numbers are Arabic numbers followed by periods. The bullets are a standard round dot in a default size based on the font size associated with the paragraph marker.

If you want to modify these defaults or to use a different style of bullets and numbering, you need to apply the format using the Bullets and Numbering command from the Format menu. Using this command, you can create lists that are bulleted, numbered, or outline-numbered with the levels indicated by alternating numbers and bullets. To use this command, perform the following procedure:

1. Place the insertion point where you want to begin your list, or select the text that will be formatted as a list.

2. Open the Format menu and select the Bullets and Numbering option. The Bullets and Numbering dialog box, shown in Figure 7.18, appears.

3. The three tabs in the dialog box, Bulleted, Numbered, and Outline Numbered, offer different default styles. Select the style you want by clicking on its preview box, then click on the OK button.

Word applies the bullet, numbering, or outline-numbered style that you select. If you apply the style to a selection, the list is formatted. If you enter the list after applying the style, Word applies the style as you type.

You can create custom bullet and numbering styles using the Bullets and Numbering dialog box. On any of the tabs, click on the Customize button. A Modify dialog box for the tab appears, offering controls for adjusting the settings for the type of list you want to have. The Modify dialog box for the Bulleted tab is shown in Figure 7.19.

To modify the bulleted list options, you can choose from the following options:

- Select the bullet character from the Bullet character control by clicking on the preview that suits your needs. If you want a different bullet character, click on the Bullet button and select one from the Symbol dialog box that appears. Click on OK after you make your selection.

Figure 7.18

The Bullets and
Numbering dialog box

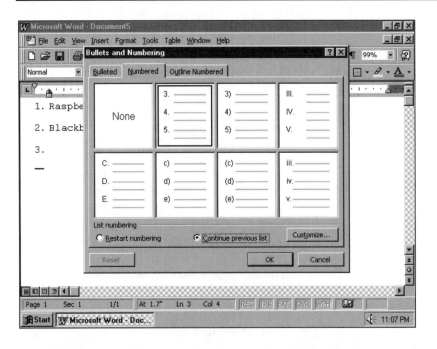

Figure 7.19

The Customize Bulleted
List dialog box

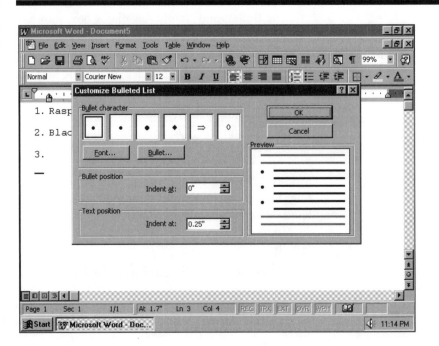

- Set the characteristics (point size and color, for example) of the bullet character using the Font button, which displays the Font dialog box.

- Use the Indent at spin box in the Bullet Position group and the Indent at spin box in the Text position group to determine the horizontal position of both the bullet and the text that follows it.

- Click on the OK button to apply your custom format.

When you create a new style, you replace one of the existing styles displayed by the tab.

The remaining two Customize dialog boxes have basically identical controls in the Position group; however, they offer different controls in the top portion of the dialog box specific to the format being modified. The Modify Numbered List dialog box is shown in Figure 7.20.

Figure 7.20

The Customize Numbered List dialog box

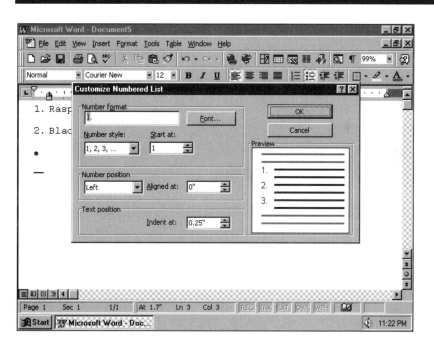

To adjust the numbered list format, you can choose from the following options:

- Modify the Number format field to contain any special text that you want before or after the number. The automatic number that Word generates appears as a grayed numeral 1 in the field; you can add text (such as parenthesis) before or after the number. You can also add or remove a period after the automatic number, or change anything else about the overall format for the automatic number.

- Use the Number style drop-down list box to select a number format.

- Click on the Font button to select the font and character styles from the Font tab in the Font dialog box. Click on OK after you have made your selection.

- Set the starting number in the Start at spin box.

- Use the drop-down list box in the Number Position group to set the alignment of the number.

- Use the Indent at to set the amount of space between the number and the text that follows it.

- Click on the OK button to apply your custom format.

The Customize Outline Numbered List dialog box is very similar to the Customize Numbered List dialog box, except that it adds a control for specifying the level of the list you are modifying (see Figure 7.21).

Figure 7.21

The Customize Outline Numbered List dialog box

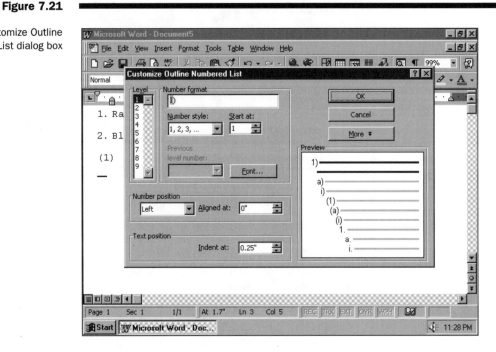

Choose from the following options to modify a multilevel list:

- Select the list level to modify using the Level list box. Your list can have up to nine levels.

- Modify the Number format field to contain any special text you want to appear before or after the number.

- Use the Number style drop-box to choose the style of numbering that is used.

- Click on the Font button to select the font and character styles from the Font tab in the Font dialog box. Click on OK after you have made your selection.

- Set the starting number in the Start At spin box.

- If you want to include a number from the previous level as part of the level you're modifying, select the level you want to include with the Previous level number drop-box. The Preview box shows the results of your selection.

- Use the Number position drop-down list box and the Aligned at spin-box to set the position of the number.

- Use the Indent at spin-box to set the distance between the number and the text that follows it.

- Click on the OK button to apply your custom format.

Using Word, you can create lists of any type you want—bulleted, numbered, multilevel, or plain. You can convert list types easily. After you have formatted a list as one style, select it and open the Bullets and Numbering dialog box. The tab representing the format of the list is automatically selected, and the Remove button is active. To remove the list format, click on the Remove button. You then can apply a new list format (or not) as you like.

TIP. *You can sort a list using Word. Select the list, open the Table menu, and select the Sort Text option. Word sorts numbered lists alphabetically, and automatically renumbers numbered lists after sorting.*

Bibliographies often appear in different formats for different audiences. Some publishers prefer the items numbered, for example, whereas some do not. Write Solutions is a company that has to work for both kinds of clients. Converting the bibliography from a numbered to an unnumbered format is a simple proposition, once the basic list has been typed into a document. Select the list, apply the appropriate list format, and the job is done. Figure 7.22 shows an example, a bibliography formatted as a numbered list.

Figure 7.22

A bibliography formatted
as a numbered list

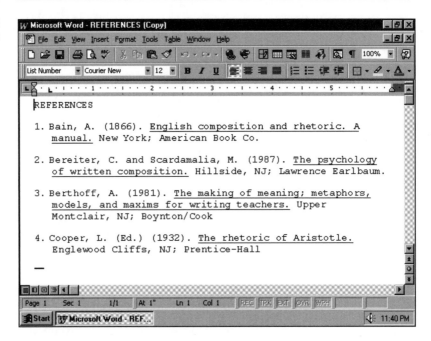

■ Using AutoFormat

Word can automatically format a document for you after you have typed it.
Word applies the built-in styles associated with the template on which the
document is based, according to rules Word contains that allow the analysis
of a document's parts. Word can recognize titles, headings, lists, and so on.
When it recognizes such a structure in your document, Word applies the
appropriate style to it.

Word comes with several document templates that it can use with the
AutoFormat feature, each representing different types of documents. To take
advantage of these templates, you can either base your document on the template when you create it, or copy the styles associated with the template
using the Style Gallery. To see a list of the document types available to you,
open the Format menu and select the Style Gallery option. The Style Gallery
dialog box offers previews of Word's companion document templates.

You can use AutoFormat to review the changes Word makes, accepting
some and rejecting others. Open the Format menu and select the AutoFormat option. Word then displays the AutoFormat dialog box, as shown in
Figure 7.23. Use the controls in the AutoFormat dialog box to control the
formatting process.

Figure 7.23

The AutoFormat
dialog box

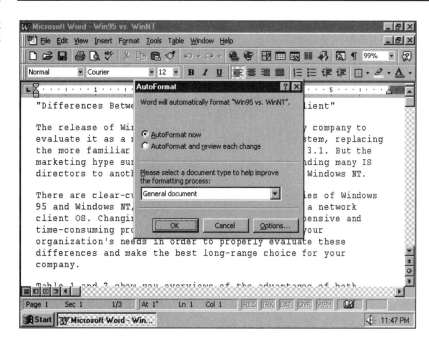

At this point, you can click on OK to proceed with the AutoFormat process or Cancel to cancel it, or you can choose Options to set options for the
process. If you click on Options, Word displays the AutoFormat tab in the
Options dialog box, as shown in Figure 7.24.

The AutoFormat tab controls what Word does as a part of the Auto-
Format process. Word can perform the following types of actions:

- Word can preserve existing formats. Check the Styles check box in the
  Preserve group to enable this.

- Word can apply styles to various document structures. Check any or all
  of the Headings, Lists, Automatic bulleted lists, and Other paragraphs
  check boxes in the Apply group to enable these actions.

- Word can replace certain characters with other characters. In the Replace group, check Straight quotes with "smart quotes" to replace regular quotation marks with the curly kind; check Ordinals to replace 1st
  with 1st; check Fractions to change numbers separated by a slash to
  true fraction symbols such as $^{1}/_{2}$; check Symbol characters with symbols
  to replace, for example, (C) with a true copyright symbol ©; check
  Bold and _underline_ with real formatting to automatically make
  text surrounded with asterisks bold and text surrounded with underline
  characters underlined (this can be very useful when formatting text

Figure 7.24

The AutoFormat tab in the Options dialog box

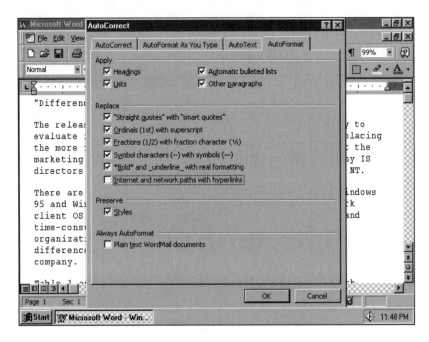

from text-only Internet messages); check Internet and network paths with hyperlinks to automatically create a Word hyperlink in place of any Internet addresses or network pathnames you type.

If you select the AutoFormat As You Type tab, you can see the formatting changes Word is making automatically as you enter text. You can adjust those AutoFormat changes to suit your own needs.

If you work with a typist who formats text the way you would on a typewriter, AutoFormat can convert such formatting to standard Word styles.

If you click on OK in the AutoFormat dialog box after choosing Auto-Format and review each change, the AutoFormat dialog box changes to show different options (see Figure 7.25). Use the buttons in this dialog box to control which changes you accept for the document.

Review the new formats Word has applied to the document. You can choose from among the following options:

- Click on the Accept All button to accept all changes. (You can always undo the changes using Word's Undo feature.)

- Click on the Reject All button to reject all changes.

- Click on the Style Gallery button to open the Style Gallery dialog box. Here you can review the types of document formats available by selecting

Figure 7.25

The AutoFormat dialog box after you start reviewing suggested formatting changes

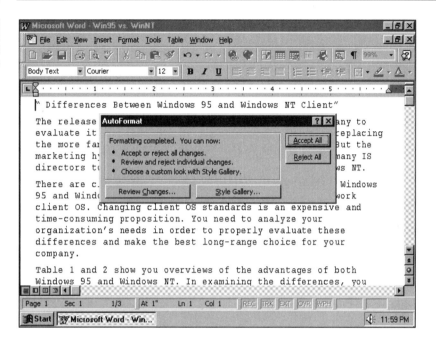

each in the list box, preview them in the Preview box, and choose the one you like by clicking on OK after having selected it in the list box. Word then repeats the AutoFormat process.

- Click on the Review Changes button to review each change, accepting or rejecting each change individually.

If you click on the Review Changes button, the Review AutoFormat Changes dialog box appears (see Figure 7.26). Use the controls in this dialog box to determine which changes to accept and which to reject.

You can perform the following actions:

- Click on the Find button (back arrow) or the Find button (forward arrow) to scroll to the previous change or the next change, respectively.

- Click on the Reject button to reject a change.

- Click on the Hide Marks/Show Marks button to turn the display of paragraph marks off and on.

- Click on the Undo button to undo previous actions. Each click undoes one action.

- Click on the Cancel button to accept all remaining changes.

Figure 7.26

The Review AutoFormat
Changes dialog box

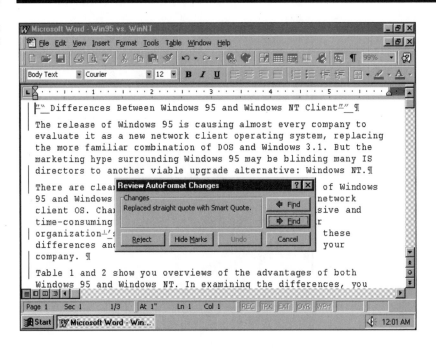

You can also scroll through your document using the scroll bars as you review AutoFormat changes.

While you are reviewing changes, Word displays its AutoFormat changes to you visually, using the cues shown in Table 7.1.

Table 7.1

Visual Cues to
AutoFormat Changes

CUE	CHANGE MADE
Blue Paragraph Mark	New style applied to paragraph
Red Paragraph Mark	Deleted this existing paragraph mark
Strikethrough Character Style	Deleted these characters or spaces
Underline Character Style	Added these characters
Bar in Left Margin	Changed the formatting of this text

AutoFormat thus helps you to quickly and efficiently identify the changes that have been made to each part or element of the document.

AutoFormat is a useful Word 97 feature. It lets you type in any way that feels comfortable to you, and then effortlessly convert your work into a correctly formatted document using styles. It also allows documents to be quickly converted from one style to another. If AutoFormat makes a mistake, you can easily correct it. AutoFormat can be a very useful first step, if nothing else, in the formatting of a complex document.

- *Making Word Work for You*
- *Customizing Toolbars*
- *Customizing Menus*
- *Customizing the Keyboard*
- *Setting Word Options*

Customizing Word

WHEN YOU CUSTOMIZE WORD, YOU MAKE THE WORD PROCESSOR do more work for you. Word will have to tell you what you need to know about a document, and do so in ways you can use and understand.

In this chapter, you will learn how to perform the following customization techniques:

- Customizing toolbars
- Customizing menus
- Customizing the keyboard
- Adjusting Word's options

By the time you complete this chapter, you will be able to perform tasks that make Word for Windows do your bidding.

Microsoft advertises Word as "the world's most popular word processor." One of the reasons for that popularity is that you can customize Word to suit your needs. Migrating from an earlier version of Word? You can get your familiar toolbar back if you want it. Don't like the way the menu is organized? You can rearrange it if you like. You can make Word work your way, instead of the other way around.

■ Making Word Work for You

Customizing Word is a matter of working with two items found on the Tools menu, Customize and Options. Each of these commands opens a tabbed dialog box. From the Customize dialog box, you can change the items that appear on toolbars, change key assignments, and add, rearrange, and subtract items from the menu. From the Options dialog box you can adjust many other features of Word, changing the behavior of the word processor by doing so. One other menu option, the Toolbars item on the View menu, also is involved in customization. Using the Toolbars dialog box that this item activates, you can create new toolbars, reset default toolbars, and select which toolbars are displayed. The following sections explain each of the customizations that you can perform to tune Word to your preferences.

■ Customizing Toolbars

You can use as many toolbars at the same time as you want with Word. You can also create your own custom toolbars, or change existing toolbars, through the Toolbars sub-menu (see Figure 8.1). Access this sub-menu box by opening the View menu and selecting the Toolbars item. You can also click your right mouse button when the pointer is on any toolbar to display a list of toolbars with the currently visible toolbars checked.

Using Multiple Toolbars

As noted before, Word lets you use multiple toolbars. To show a toolbar on the screen, simply select it from the Toolbars sub-menu. To hide a toolbar

Figure 8.1

The Toolbars sub-menu

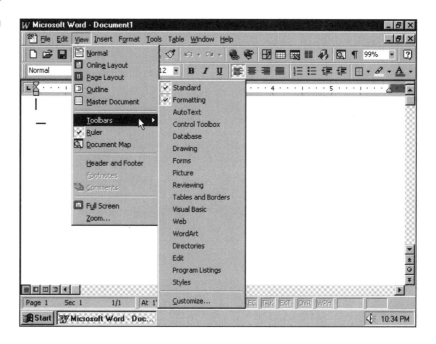

from view, select it again on the Toolbars sub-menu. The check next to the name of the toolbar appears and disappears to show you whether or not it's active (Figure 8.1 shows the Standard and Formatting toolbars checked in the sub-menu). Using multiple toolbars gives you immediate access to most of Word's features, but displaying multiple toolbars does reduce the size of the workspace, as shown in Figure 8.2.

TIP. *The number of toolbars displayed in the **Toolbars** list box changes depending on what you are using Word to do. If you are in outline view, for example, the Outlining toolbar appears on the list, although it does not do so otherwise.*

Changing the Appearance of Toolbars

You can modify the appearance of toolbars with the Options tab of the Customize command in the Tools menu (see Figure 8.3). You can use the check boxes of the Options tab to control the overall appearance of toolbars. These check boxes control the following characteristics of a toolbar:

- **Large icons** switches the size of the buttons between large and small. The large buttons are easier to see, especially if you work with one of the higher screen resolutions, like 1024 x 768.

Figure 8.2

Plenty of toolbars, but much less space to work in

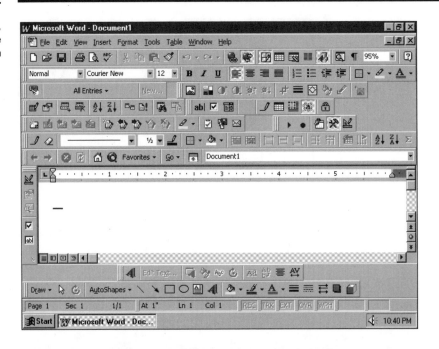

Figure 8.3

The Customize dialog box with the Toolbars tab shown

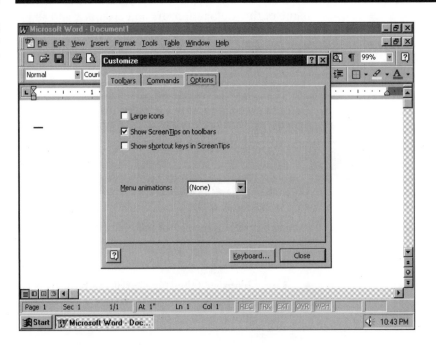

- **Show ScreenTips on toolbars** governs whether ScreenTips (formerly called "ToolTips") are displayed when you point the mouse pointer at a button. ScreenTips can be useful, but they might become distracting or annoying once you are familiar with the toolbars you display. You can turn ScreenTips off by unchecking this box.

- **Show shortcut keys in ScreenTips** controls whether ScreenTips also include information on what keyboard combination performs the same command as the toolbar button to which your mouse points.

  TIP. *Experienced users of word processing programs know that using the keyboard is almost always faster than using the mouse, because you don't have to move your hand away from the keyboard to reach for and use the mouse. However, the mouse is much easier to learn. The shortcut keys displayed in ScreenTips can help you learn all of the speedy keyboard shortcuts that increase your productivity.*

- **Menu animations** lets you improve the appearance of menus when you open them in Word. You can choose Unfold, Slide, or Random, which mixes the other two methods up randomly. You will not want to use this feature on slower computers, because menus may appear more slowly than otherwise when the animation is enabled.

Creating New Toolbars

To create a new toolbar, access the Customize command in the Tools menu, then select the Toolbars tab and click on the New button. Word will display the New Toolbar dialog box shown in Figure 8.4.

Enter a name for the toolbar (which is displayed in its title bar when it floats) in the Toolbar name text box. Open the "Make toolbar available to" drop-down list box to select the template that will contain the toolbar. Then click on the OK button.

Word creates your new toolbar as a floating toolbar (see Figure 8.5). You use the Commands tab to add buttons to your new toolbar.

To add a button to your toolbar, follow this procedure:

1. Move to the Commands tab of the Customize dialog box.

2. Select a category of Word commands in the Categories list box. Word shows the buttons and names of the commands for that category in the Commands box.

3. Click on a button to select it. To see what the command does, choose the Description button, which will display a help file for the command.

4. Drag the appropriate button, and drop it in the desired floating-toolbar location.

Figure 8.4

The New Toolbar
dialog box

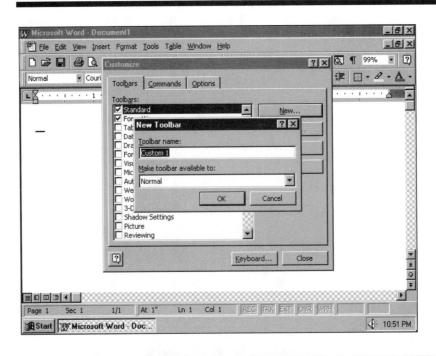

Figure 8.5

The floating toolbar and
the Commands tab of the
Customize dialog box

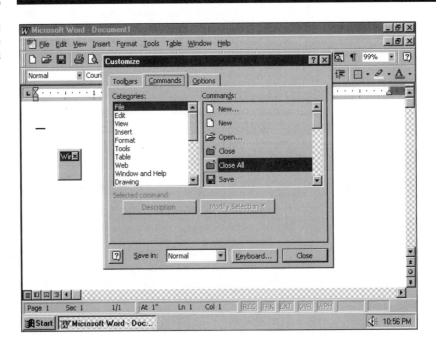

Once you have dragged a command entry to the floating toolbar, you can modify its properties by clicking on the Modify Selection button on the Commands tab of the Customize dialog box. You see the menu that appears when you click Modify Selection in Figure 8.6.

Figure 8.6

The Modify Selection menu

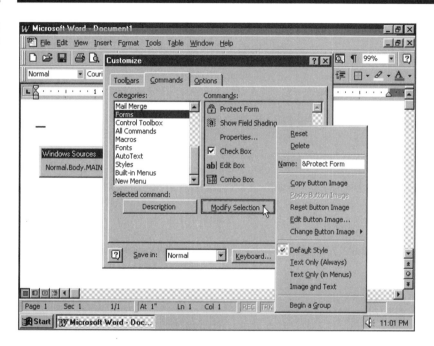

You can perform the following actions in this menu:

- Choose Reset to return the toolbar button to its default settings

- Choose Delete to remove the toolbar button from your toolbar

- Modify the name of the toolbar button with the Name field contained in the menu

- Use Copy Button Image to place the button's image onto the clipboard. You can then use Paste Button Image to use that button image on another toolbar button.

- Select Edit Button Image to activate an icon editor that lets you modify the button image to suit your tastes

- Choosing Change Button Image displays a sub-menu that contains a number of standard button icons. You can select one of these icons from the sub-menu to use it for the toolbar command.

- Use Text Only (Always) or Text Only (in Menus) to force the toolbar button to simply display its name, and no graphical image, always or only when displayed in a menu.

- Select Image and Text to display the toolbar button's command name and its image. Remember that this option, while informative, consumes more of your available screen space.

- Choose Begin a Group to build a grouping within your toolbar. Selecting this command divides your toolbar into a new group, with a small line separating the current command from the previous commands you added to the toolbar.

If you would like to create a custom graphical button, click on the Edit Button Image command in the Modify Selection menu. Word opens the Button Editor, shown in Figure 8.7. Select a color from the Colors palette and click on any square in the grid to change the pixels represented by that box to the color you have selected. You can see your work in the Preview box. And you can move your entire painting one square on the grid in any direction by clicking on the appropriate arrow button. Use the arrows to align your picture on the button.

Figure 8.7

The Button Editor

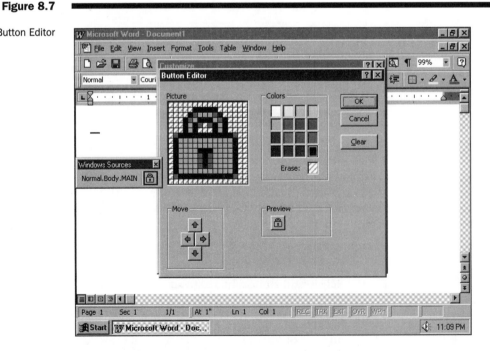

TIP. *Even if you click on the Cancel button in the Custom Button dialog box, Word places a button on your floating toolbar. To remove an unwanted button, open the Customize dialog box by selecting the Customize option on the Tools menu. Select the Toolbars tab, then drag the unwanted button from the toolbar and drop it on the Toolbars tab.*

Changing Existing Toolbars

You can change toolbars in several ways. To change the buttons on the toolbar, follow these steps:

1. Open the Toolbars dialog box by selecting the Toolbars sub-menu from the View menu and then choosing Customize.

2. Make sure the toolbar you want to change is visible by selecting the checkbox for the toolbar in the Toolbars list box.

   TIP. *You can also open the Customize dialog box to work on a toolbar by opening the Tools menu and selecting the Customize option, or by clicking the right mouse button when the pointer is on any toolbar and selecting Customize.*

3. Drag buttons from the **Commands** tab to the toolbar to add buttons, or drag buttons from the toolbar to the dialog box to delete buttons. To create custom buttons, follow the procedure described in the preceding section.

4. Click on the Close button when you are finished.

If you have changed one of Word's default toolbars, you can change it back to its original state easily. Follow these steps:

1. Open the Customize dialog box by selecting Toolbars from the View menu and then choose Customize.

2. Select the toolbar to reset in the Toolbars list box.

3. Click on the Reset button.

4. Select the template to which the change applies using the drop-down list box titled "Reset changes made to "*toolbar name*" for:" where "toolbar name" is the name of the toolbar you are modifying. Then click on the OK button.

If you have created a custom toolbar and no longer want it, you can delete it by following these steps:

1. Open the Customize dialog box by selecting Toolbars from the View menu.

2. Select the toolbar to delete in the Toolbars list box.

3. Click on the Delete button. (This button replaces the Reset button after you select the toolbar.)

4. Click on the Yes button in the confirmation dialog box that appears.

Obviously you can create toolbars that fit your working style and manage them easily in Word. You can also do the same sorts of things with menus.

■ Customizing Menus

You can customize Word's menus in much the same way as you can customize toolbars. You can add an entire menu to the menu bar or remove a menu from the menu bar. You can also add items to or delete items from any of the menus. You perform these actions using the Commands tab in the Customize dialog box, which you access by opening the Tools menu and selecting Customize. Figure 8.8 shows the Menus tab.

TIP. *Before you do any work on the menu, make sure you have selected the correct template in the Save In drop-down list box.*

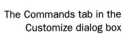
Figure 8.8

The Commands tab in the
Customize dialog box

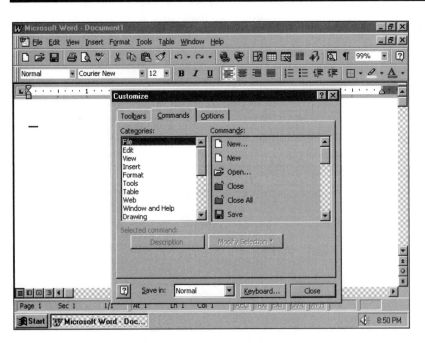

Adding and Deleting Menu Items

To add an item to a menu, follow this procedure:

1. Open the Tools menu, select the Customize option, and select the Commands tab.

2. Select the category of the item you want to add in the Categories list box.

3. Select the command you want to add in the Commands list box.

4. Drag the icon for the command onto the menu in which you want it added. When you drag onto the menu, the menu opens automatically.

5. Select the position on the menu where you want the item added and release the mouse button to drop it into place. The menu remains open after you have dropped the command into it.

6. If necessary, you can re-drag the command to a different menu, or a different position in the current menu. You can also right-click on the command to change its properties (such as its name, its button image, and so forth).

7. When you have finished making changes, click on the Close button.

   To delete a menu item, follow these steps:

1. Open the Tools menu, select the Customize command, and select the Commands tab.

2. Click on the menu you want to modify, which opens it. (The Customize dialog box remains on the screen.)

3. Drag the command you want to remove away from the menu and release the mouse button. You will see it vanish from the menu.

4. When you have finished making changes, click on the Close button.

Adding and Deleting Menu Bar Items

To add a menu to the menu bar, follow these steps:

1. Open the Tools menu, select the Customize command, and then select the Commands tab.

2. In the Categories box, scroll to the bottom and select the New Menu selection. The Commands box displays "New Menu" with an arrow to the right of it (see Figure 8.9.)

3. Drag the New Menu command to the position you desire in the menu bar and drop it into the menu bar.

4. Right-click on the New Menu item to change its name.

Figure 8.9

The New Menu command

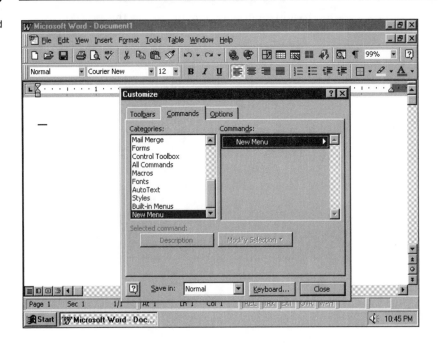

5. Drag new commands into the New Menu menu to create your menu.

6. When you have finished making changes, click on the Close button.

   To rename any existing menu, follow these steps:

1. Open the Tools menu, select the Customize command, and select the Commands tab.

2. Right-click on the menu you want to modify.

3. Choose the Name field and type a new name for the menu. Place an ampersand (&) before the hot key, and make sure the hot key does not conflict with any other item on the menu bar.

4. When you have finished making changes, click on the Close button.

CAUTION! *Once you rename a menu, you can change it back to its original name only by retyping the original name or resetting the menu. If you have to reset the menu, you might lose other changes you have made. Keep a record of the exact name as it was before you changed it to save wasted effort fixing a mistake.*

■ Customizing the Keyboard

The Word keyboard also is completely customizable. You can assign any command, macro, style, AutoText entry, or font to a key so that when you press that key the assigned action is performed. Word is shipped with many keys preassigned, and you can reassign these if you want. If you want to return to the default Word key layout, you can reset the keyboard to its original state.

TIP. *If you are wondering which keys are assigned which functions, you can always print a list of the key assignments. Open the File menu, select the Print option, select Key Assignments in the Print What drop-down list box, and click on the OK button.*

To make a keystroke assignment, follow these steps:

1. Open the Tools menu and select the Customize option.

2. In the Customize dialog box, click the Keyboard button.

3. Select the template you want to alter in the Save changes in drop-down list box.

4. Select a category of commands from the Categories list box, and select the exact command from the Commands list box.

5. Make sure that the Press New Shortcut Key text box has the focus. Press the key combination that you want to use to invoke the selected command. The current key assignment for the selected command appears in the Current keys list box and the Description box shows what the selected command does. If the keystroke you have chosen to assign is already assigned to another command, a Currently Assigned To message appears above the Description box to let you know which command your intended new keystroke already invokes.

6. Click on the Assign button.

7. When you have finished making changes, click on the Close button.

To remove a keystroke assignment from a command, follow these steps:

1. Open the Tools menu, select the Customize option, and click the Keyboard button in the Customize dialog box.

2. Select the template you want to alter in the Save changes in drop-down list box.

3. Select a category of commands from the Categories list box, and select the exact command from the Commands list box.

4. Select the key assignment to remove in the Current Keys list box.

5. Click on the Remove button.

6. When you have finished making changes, click on the Close button.

As noted, you can remove key assignments and make new assignments as often as you like. If, however, you want to return to the original key assignments, perform the following steps:

1. Open the Tools menu, select the Customize option, and click the Keyboard button.

2. Select the template you want to alter in the Save changes in drop-down list box.

3. Click on the Reset All button.

4. Click on the Yes button in the confirmation dialog box that appears.

You might find that you want to reassign keys so that the commands and macros you most desire to use from the keyboard are assigned to mnemonic keys. Word now is shipped with so many preassigned keys that you might find it impossible to find free keys that you can remember as representing a command. For example, you might find it convenient to assign the FigureCaption macro to the Ctrl+F keystroke, and the figure reference to the Ctrl+Shift+F keystroke, *F* being a good mnemonic key for *Figure*. However, Word already has assigned these keys, along with Alt+Shift+F and Ctrl+Alt+F, to other commands. Do not feel locked in by these assignments. Design your keyboard to meet your needs. You can always reset or change the key assignments later.

■ Setting Word Options

You can customize Word in many other ways. The Customize dialog box offers ways to change the features most commonly involved in customization. However, the Options dialog box (see Figure 8.10) gives you the ability to alter Word's behavior in many other ways. The 10 tabs in this dialog box control the way Word appears on the screen, the way Word interacts with files, and numerous other features. You should be sure to review each of the tabs to make sure that Word is taking the actions you want as it runs.

General

The General tab (see Figure 8.11) covers some miscellaneous features of Word, including screen appearance, help features, and measurement units.

Figure 8.10

The Options dialog box

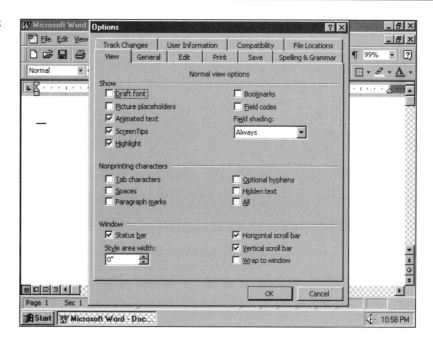

Figure 8.11

The General tab in the
Options dialog box

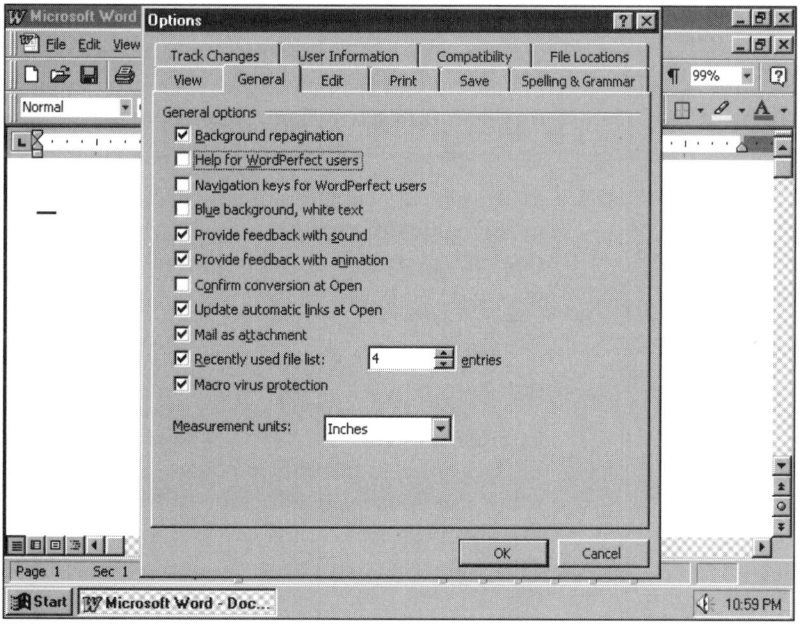

The controls within the General tab are described in the following list:

- The Background repagination check box governs whether Word repaginates documents as you are working. You probably want background repagination most of the time. But if you are working on a long document, the long pauses for repagination at certain working junctures might become annoying.

- The Help for WordPerfect users check box switches on and off special help for those migrating from WordPerfect for DOS. When you press a WordPerfect for DOS keystroke, Word displays help explaining the Word command that performs the same function.

- The Navigation keys for WordPerfect users enables and disables the Word emulation of WordPerfect keystrokes involving the PgUp, PgDn, Home, End, and Esc keys. If you prefer the WordPerfect key assignments for these keys, check this box.

- The Blue background, white text check box, when checked, converts Word's workspace to the named color scheme. Some people find it more pleasant on the eyes to work with this color scheme. Also, WordPerfect for DOS users may find the color scheme more familiar, since it mirrors WordPerfect for DOS's default colors.

- Provide feedback with sound governs whether Word beeps when you make a mistake, and whether it makes additional small sounds as you perform other actions, such as deleting a block of text. Check it if you need the audible reminder, uncheck it if you prefer silence from your word processor. (If you support many people who use computers, keep in mind as you help them that different people process visual and auditory cues differently, and while some will be annoyed rather than helped by additional auditory feedback, others may find it extremely useful.)

- Provide feedback with animation causes Word to animate certain actions, making them appear more graceful on the screen. Turning this option on will make some actions appear to take longer to process, and may even be bothersome when using Word on a slower computer. Many people that are new to Word, however, will find the animations helpful in understanding what is happening on the screen as they perform certain actions.

- Confirm Conversion at Open specifies whether or not a Conversion dialog box appears to confirm conversion from another word processor when you open such a document. If you do not select this option, Word takes its best guess at the original format of the document and automatically converts it to Word.

- Update automatic links at open causes Word to check any links within a document being opened, and to automatically update any that have changed since the document was last updated.

- Mail as attachment changes how Word sends files when you use the Send to Mail Recipient command on the File menu. Checking this option causes the current file to be sent as an attachment; when this option is not checked, the contents of the current file are instead sent as part of the message itself.

  TIP. *Word has special e-mail features that you can use directly from the menus. You can attach routing slips to a document that automatically send a document, either sequentially or at the same time, to the individuals who need to see it. Reviewers also can annotate a document or add revisions to a document using the Comment option on the Insert menu and the Revisions option on the Tools menu.*

- Change the Recently used file list entries to reflect how many recently opened files will appear at the bottom of Word's File menu. You can display up to nine entries.

- Macro virus protection enables a warning message that appears whenever a user opens a file that contains an automatically executing macro, which could potentially be a computer virus. The user can then choose whether to open such documents with or without the embedded macros enabled.

- The Recently Used File List check box governs whether the list of most recently opened files appears on the File menu. If you check it, set the number of files to include in the list using the spin box.

- The Measurement Units drop-down list box enables you to choose the unit of measurement that Word displays on its rulers and uses to calculate dimensions in most of its dialog boxes.

TIP. *Even though the Options dialog box does not offer hot keys for the tabs, you can move from one tab to another using the Ctrl+Tab key combination and the Ctrl+Shift+Tab key combination. The former cycles through the tabs to the right, the latter to the left. If a control on the tab has the focus, however, these keystrokes will cycle through all the controls on the tab before cycling through the tabs.*

View

The View tab (see Figure 8.12) governs which elements of a document you see on the screen. It offers three groups of controls that control what to show in the workspace, which elements of a document window to display, and which special characters to display on-screen. The View options vary slightly, depending on the view option selected from the View menu.

Figure 8.12

The View tab in the
Options dialog box

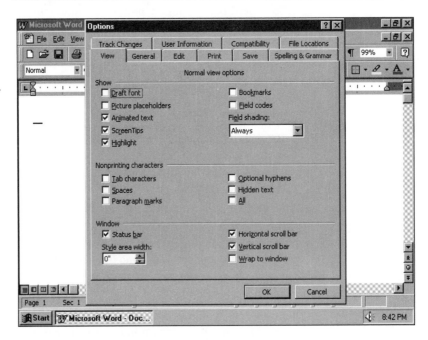

The Show group offers the following controls in Normal, Outline, and Master Document views.

TIP. *You can select among Normal, Online Layout, Page Layout, Outline, and Master Document views using the View menu.*

- The Draft font check box controls whether formats and graphics are displayed as a part of a document. When the box is checked, character formatting appears only as bold and underlined, and graphics appear as empty boxes. Using Draft font can speed your work with a draft, including printing, but does not give you an accurate view of your document's layout.

- The Picture Placeholders option, when checked, displays a box instead of a picture. Using this option speeds scrolling through a document and gives you a complete sense of the text format; however, you will not see the pictures on screen.

- Animated Text, when checked, causes animated text to display. Clearing this checkbox causes such text to display as it will look printed.

- ScreenTips turns on the pop-up help files that appear when you place your mouse pointer over one of Word's buttons.

- The Highlight option, when checked, causes highlighted text to be displayed on the screen. This highlight option refers to the new feature that lets you place color highlights on text in order to draw attention to it. It does not refer to the highlight that occurs when you select text for manipulation.

- The Bookmarks option, when checked, causes bookmarks and links to be displayed in grayed brackets. This option is useful when you want to see where bookmarks and linked information appear.

- The Field Codes option, when checked, causes fields to display as the text codes that create the field rather than as the result of those codes. In a date field, for example, you see the instructions for creating the date rather than the date itself. This option is useful if you know how to work with field codes and need to see the codes to make adjustments.

- The Field Shading drop-down list box allows you to select whether—and if so, when—Word displays nonprinting shading around fields. You can select from Never, When Selected, and Always. When Selected is the default.

- The Wrap to Window option, when checked, causes the text to be wrapped at the current document window border. You can use this option to avoid the annoying horizontal scroll when you are typing on a line wider than the current window can display; however, using this option does not give you an accurate view of your document's layout.

The remaining two groups in this tab are fairly self-explanatory. The Window group offers check boxes that control whether the Status Bar, Horizontal Scroll Bar, and Vertical Scroll Bar are displayed. It also provides a spin box that lets you set the Style Area Width, which displays the style of each paragraph at the left of the workspace. The Nonprinting Characters group provides check boxes that control whether the named nonprinting characters are displayed on the screen. Use these controls to set up your display so that your workspace is comfortable and familiar.

Edit

The Edit tab (see Figure 8.13) controls how Word behaves when you use editing features, including when you edit pictures. These controls determine which keys perform certain editing functions and how drag-and-drop features work.

The Edit tab provides the following controls:

- The Typing replaces selection check box, when checked, causes a selection to be deleted when you start typing, before the characters you type appear on the screen. The net effect is that the selection appears to be

Figure 8.13

The Edit tab of the
Options dialog box

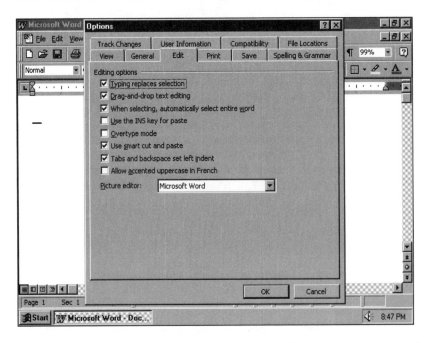

replaced by what you type. When unchecked, this control causes what
you type to appear, scrolling the selection to the left.

- When checked, the Drag-and-drop text editing option allows you to
  copy and move a selection by dragging with the mouse. When this box is
  unchecked, you must perform these operations using the Edit menu.

- When you check the When selecting, automatically select entire word
  check box, you can select an entire word by selecting just a part of it.
  When this box is unchecked, you select only the characters you have
  dragged over with the mouse.

- The Use the INS Key for paste option enables you to paste data from
  the Clipboard by pressing Ins rather than Shift+Ins.

- Overtype mode, when checked, has the same effect as pressing Ins. Each
  character you type replaces the character at the insertion point. Unchecking the box returns you to inserting new characters to the right of
  the character at the insertion point.

- Use smart cut and paste deletes unnecessary spaces when you cut information from a document or paste information into a document. If you included extra spaces at the end of a sentence in the cut operation, Word

removes the extra spaces (or adds more spaces, if necessary) to fit the context into which you paste.

- The Tabs and backspace set left indent option lets you use those keys to create a Left Indent. To see how this feature works (after you have selected it in the Edit Tab selections), place your Insertion Point at the beginning of a paragraph and press the Tab key twice. This creates a first line tab for that paragraph. Then, with the cursor at the same place, press the Backspace key. The entire paragraph indents to the first tab, but this is only useful if, for some reason, you've opted to remove the Indent icon from the Formatting toolbar.

- Allow accented uppercase in French enables Change Case and the proofing tools to suggest and insert accented uppercase letters when you are working in text formatted for the French language.

- The Picture editor drop-down list box lets you select the graphics editor you want to use to create pictures for your Word documents. The list offers the options of Microsoft Draw, Microsoft Word, PowerPoint Presentation, and PowerPoint Slide.

Save

The Save tab (see Figure 8.14) provides controls that govern Word's behavior in saving documents. These options enable you to set up automatic saving, to embed fonts in a document, and to set passwords for documents.

The Save tab gives you the following controls:

- Always create backup copy, when checked, causes Word to copy the current version of the document to a file with a BAK extension before saving any changes. You then have two versions of the document at all times: the version you opened before making changes and the version you saved with the changes.

- Allow fast saves causes Word to save only the changes to a document, not the entire file. As a result, the saving process is faster. However, your document file will become much larger if you make frequent saves into it when fast saves are enabled. As a general rule, only enable this option if your files are so large that saving them (or automatically saving them) takes longer than you like.

  NOTE. *You cannot keep a backup copy if you enable fast saves. These two options are mutually exclusive. Word enables you to check only one or the other.*

- Checking Prompt for document properties causes Word to display the Properties dialog box as you save each new document. If you have used Word 6.0, this is similar to the Summary Info feature.

Figure 8.14

The Save tab of the
Options dialog box

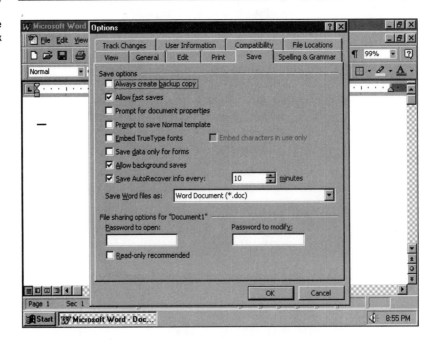

- Prompt to save Normal template, when checked, causes Word to display a dialog box that asks if you want to save changes to the NOR-MAL.DOT template each time you close Word.

- Embed TrueType fonts, when checked, causes the TrueType fonts used in your document to be stored in its file. When others open and read the document, they can see the fonts you used, even if those fonts are not installed on their computer. When this checkbox is enabled, you can also select Embed characters in use only, which causes Word to only store the characters you actually used instead of the entire TrueType font set. For instance, if you only used a single letter of a given TrueType font and you select Embed characters in use only, only that letter will be saved in the document. This can reduce the size of your document file somewhat in certain circumstances.

- The Save data only for forms check box helps you create special templates called forms, and use them to create database records. When this box is checked, the data on your form is stored in a single record, letting you import the record into a database.

    NOTE. *A form is a template that you have protected using the Protect Document command on the Tools menu. It contains tables and some special fields that you can insert using the Form Field command on the*

Insert menu. When you use a form as the template for a document, you can enter information only in the table grid and controls provided. Because the form is protected, you cannot change the rest of the document. You can save the entire form document, or only the data entered into the fields. The purchase-order template included with Word is a sample of a form.

- Allow background saves lets Word save documents in the background while you continue working. If you have disabled Allow fast saves it's a good idea to enable this feature so that you experience as little interruption as possible during save operations.

- The Save AutoRecover info every check box causes Word to save a copy of your document on the schedule of minutes that you set using the spin box. You should select this option to guard against losing parts of your document if your computer loses power or is accidentally reset. These events happen more often than you think. If you work rapidly, three minutes might be a good choice. Remember that enabling this feature is not a substitute for saving your file normally.

- Use the Save Word files as drop-down list box to select the default file format with which your files are saved. For instance, if you are using Word 97 and frequently work with people who are using Word 95, you can set this option to automatically save your files using the Word 95 format.

The File-Sharing Options group enables you to set passwords on a document. You have the following options:

- Enter a "Password to open" in the text box to keep other users from opening a document. Unless other users enter the correct password, they cannot open the document.

- Enter a "Password to modify" to prevent users from saving changes to a document. Other users can open the document, but they cannot save it without entering the correct password.

- For a moderate level of protection, check the Read-only recommended check box. When other users attempt to open the document, they see a message that recommends opening the document for reading only. However, they can open the document for both reading and writing if they want.

Track Changes

The Track Changes tab (see Figure 8.15) gives you control over the way revisions are marked in your document. You can select the color and style for each type of revision mark. You can make these choices for text inserted into a document, text deleted from a document, and text marked as revised in the margin.

Figure 8.15

The Track Changes tab of
the Options dialog box

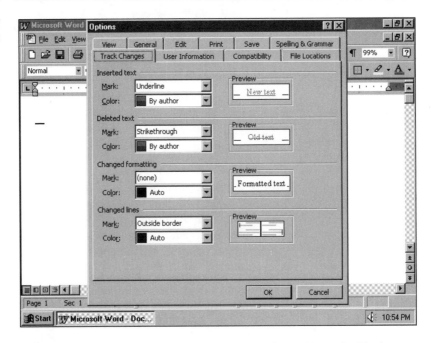

NOTE. *You can mark revisions to a document by opening the Tools menu, selecting the Track Changes sub-menu, clicking on the Highlight Changes command, and then checking Track changes while editing in the Highlight Changes dialog box. All further changes you make to the document will be formatted as specified by you in this tab. You can use the other controls in the Highlight Changes dialog box to accept revisions made to a document, to compare two documents, and to merge revisions from the revised version of a document into the original document.*

In each of the Inserted Text, Deleted Text, Changed formatting, and Changed lines groups, you can select the Mark used to identify the item and the Color used to code the item using the drop-down list boxes. In the Color drop-down list boxes, you can select to code each different author as a different color, or to select a single color for all revisions. In the Mark drop-down list boxes, you can select from the various character styles and formats offered. The preview boxes show you the effects of the changes you have made.

User Information

The User Information tab lets you set the information for the user of the system, as shown in Figure 8.16. The controls are straightforward. Enter your Name, Initials, and Mailing Address in the text boxes provided, then click on the OK button.

Figure 8.16

The User Information tab
of the Options dialog box

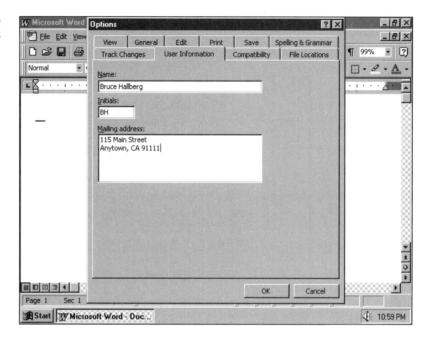

Compatibility

The Compatibility tab (see Figure 8.17) gives you the chance to change the
way Word imports files from other word processors. As a rule, you should modify the options presented here only when file conversion has not been successful. However, experimentation is relatively risk-free. You can always exit the
document without saving and reconvert it by opening the original file again.

If your converted document is not formatted as you want, perform the
following action:

1. Open the Tools menu, select the Options item, and click on the Compatibility tab.

2. Review the available conversion options and make the adjustments you
think necessary. When you click on OK, your document's formatting
will adjust to reflect the changes you have made.

After you have the look you want, click on the Default button to make
the conversion options you have selected the default options applied when
converting from that word processor (see Figure 8.18). Answer Yes to make
your changes part of the new default setting for all documents converted
from the word processor in question.

Figure 8.17

The Compatibility tab of
the Options dialog box

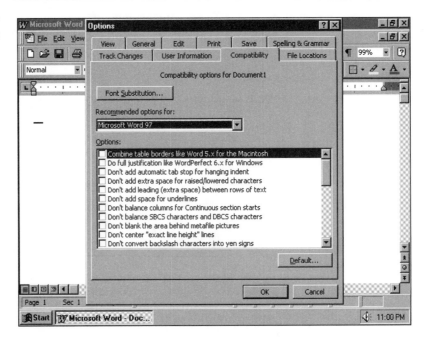

The specific controls offered by the Compatibility tab are as follows:

- The Recommended options for drop-down list box shows the word processor Word recognizes as having created the converted document. You
  can make a new selection if Word did not recognize the correct word
  processor.

- The Options list box offers 25 conversion options that Word applies in
  converting files. The options applied to your document are checked. To
  indicate that additional options should apply, check the box next to the
  description of the option. To prevent an option from applying, uncheck
  its box.

  TIP. *If you have a question about whether an option will help, try it and
  click on OK. If you do not like the changes, remove it. You can easily
  experiment using the Compatibility tab.*

- The Font Substitution button opens a dialog box for selecting fonts that
  substitute for fonts used in the document but not installed on your machine. If any substitution has taken place, clicking on this button brings
  up the Font Substitution dialog box.

  NOTE. *To use the Font Substitution dialog box, click on one of the fonts
  listed in the Missing document font list box. Open the Substituted font*

Figure 8.18

You can make the new
options the default
setting for all converted
documents

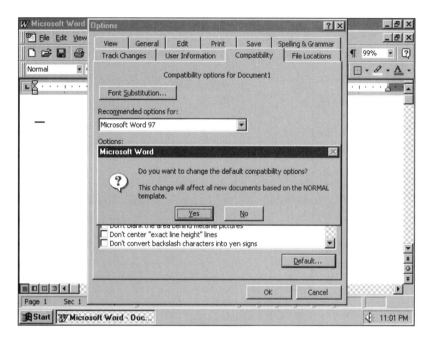

*drop-down list box and select the font you want to substitute for the
missing font. Click on the OK button to apply your changes. Click on the
Convert Permanently button to make the changes permanent for the
document. (In other words, Word no longer sees the font as having been
substituted.)*

File Locations

The File Locations tab displays a list of the directories where Word stores
eight types of files (see Figure 8.19). Using this tab, you can review these locations and make changes in the directories specified. You should make such
changes if you have moved the files from a previous directory to a new directory, as when consolidating all the clip-art images installed by various programs on your system into a single directory that all programs can access.

TIP. *If you have not installed a network, you will not see a directory for
workgroup templates.*

To change the directory specifications, follow this procedure:

1. Select the directory to change in the File types list box.

2. Click on the Modify button or double-click on the directory in the list
   box.

Figure 8.19

The File Locations tab of
the Options dialog box

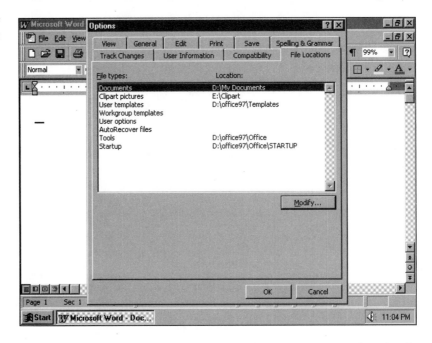

3. In the Modify Locations dialog box, either type the new location into the
   Folder name list box or use the Look in controls, which work like those
   in the Open dialog box, to specify the new directory. If you need to create a directory, click on the Create New Folder button, type the name in
   the resulting Create Folder dialog box, and click on OK. Then click on
   OK in the Modify Locations dialog box.

4. Repeat steps 1 through 3 for each change you need to make.

5. Click on the Close button in the File Locations tab.

CAUTION! *Be careful with the changes you make. Word will look for the exact
directory you specify. If you make a mistake, you might experience error
reports saying that Word could not locate certain files, or dialog boxes that
should show a list of files might be blank. If such problems occur, double-
check the file locations for accuracy.*

- *Explaining Macros*
- *Recording Macros*
- *Modifying Macros*

9

Word's Recorded VBA Macros

This chapter explains how to create word macros. You will learn how to record macros and assign them to the keyboard, menu, and toolbars. You will also learn the basics of Word Visual Basic macro programming.

More specifically, you will learn the following:

- What a macro is

- How to record a macro

- How to use the Customize dialog box to assign macros

- How to prevent common macro problems

- How to program macros

By the time you complete this chapter, you will be able to build simple macros—just by recording your actions with the menu, keyboard, toolbars, and mouse—as well as more complex and useful macros.

As explained in Chapter 5, "Understanding Word Concepts," Word is a word processor that is based on the concept of macros, or programs that emulate commands that you otherwise use. Each command that you can execute from the menu constitutes a named block of code created by the Word programmers. When you execute a command from the menu, your menu action selects the block of code by name and has it executed. As a result, the action you wanted Word to take occurs exactly as you asked it to when you selected the menu option.

This chapter extends the concept of Word macros by showing you how to create your own commands, which you can attach to the menu or to toolbar buttons. You need not think that this business of creating custom commands is beyond you. Word makes the process easy—as easy as clicking a few buttons and taking the action you wanted to make with a single command. You don't need know anything about programming to build your own macros.

■ Explaining Macros

A Word macro is a special type of document, for two reasons. First, a macro is a document that is stored as a part of a template. In that sense, a macro bears the same relationship to a template that a subdocument bears to a master document. Second, a macro consists of only certain kinds of "sentences": the names of Word commands.

The names of the Word commands make up Word's macro programming language, called Visual Basic for Applications. Visual Basic for Applications (VBA) contains quite a few additional commands that do not appear on the Word menus. These commands allow you to open special-purpose files and to create dialog boxes, and to control program flow and other programming needs. As a result, by using VBA you can make Word do anything you want it to do. You have complete control over all of Word's commands, its file-handling capabilities, even its capability to create and display dialog boxes.

TIP. *Use macros to automate the actions you repeat most frequently. If you perform a multistep action repeatedly as you work, you can use a macro to do it for you.*

There are two ways to create macros. You can sit down and figure out exactly what you want Word to do. You can read through the list of Word commands and decide which ones would accomplish the task, then you can type each of the commands into a macro file in the proper order, hoping you did not make any typing mistakes. And you would have a macro that has taken you a lot of time and effort to build, even assuming that you had gotten all the commands right and the macro works correctly.

On the other hand, you can have Word record the macro for you. First, you choose the Macro command from the Tools menu, and then select Record New Macro from the sub-menu that appears. The Record Macro dialog box appears, in which you then type the name you want to use for your new macro and choose whether the macro will be assigned to a toolbar or to a keyboard key combination. Finally, you click the OK button in the Record Macro dialog box to begin recording your actions. You then take the action you want to have automated as a macro, performing all the menu and mouse steps exactly as if you were simply using them normally. When you are finished, you click on the Stop button. You now should have a correctly built macro that does exactly what you did as you were recording your actions. Word builds a macro file for you containing all the commands necessary, and it works just as you did with the mouse and keyboard. Unless you made a mistake, your macro will not take the wrong action.

■ Recording Macros

To show you why and how to record a macro, let's examine the case of a computer-book author. When a chapter is finished and ready to send to the publisher, several tasks have to be performed. The line width of the text needs to be set to 6.5 inches throughout the document. The fields used to number figures and tables need to be updated. Since the publisher needs a text-only document, the links in the fields need to be broken. The document needs to be checked for spelling. The spacing between a period and the next sentence needs to be cut from two spaces to one. Finally, for some publishers, the document needs to be saved in Word for Windows 2.0 document format, the version that the publisher uses.

TIP. *While this example relates to only one type of document, every document has finishing steps that need to be taken once the text and layout are complete. Record these steps as a macro saved in the template for the document, and you will never forget to do any of them again.*

Odds are that on any given day the author of a chapter is going to forget to do one or more of those things (especially as deadlines approach!). The writer could use a checklist, but checklists have a way of getting lost or forgotten. The best solution for the author is to record a macro that performs all these steps and save it in the template used to create the chapter. Word then is responsible for maintaining the checklist of things to be done. The writer only needs to remember to run the end-of-chapter macro, and Word will take care of all the details.

To record such a macro, follow these steps:

1. Open the Tools menu and select the Macro option and then choose Record New Macro.

2. You see the Record Macro dialog box shown in Figure 9.1.

Figure 9.1

The Record Macro
dialog box

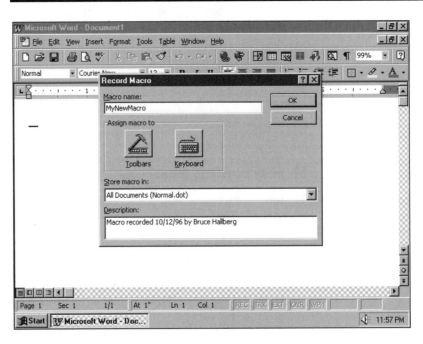

3. Enter a name for the macro in the Macro name field in the Record Macro dialog box. You cannot use punctuation or spaces for the macro name. Keep it short but descriptive. You may wish to use capital letters at word beginnings to make it more readable. For this example, type MyNewMacro.

4. Open the Store macro in drop-down list box and select the template in which the macro will be stored. If you want the macro available to all documents, store it in NORMAL.DOT. If not, store it in the template for the documents that will use it.

5. Enter a description of what the macro does, up to 255 characters, in the Description field. (A description helps protect you from forgetting what the macro does.) While the description is optional, it appears in the Description text box in the Macro dialog box, and also appears on the status bar when the macro is selected as a menu command or as a toolbar button.

6. If you want to assign the macro to a toolbar or the keyboard, click on the appropriate button in the Assign macro to group. Each button opens the Customize dialog box (discussed in detail in Chapter 8, "Customizing Word") to the appropriate tab. In this example you will assign the macro to the keyboard, so click on the Keyboard button.

7. In the Customize dialog box (see Figure 9.2), press the key combination that you want to use to run the macro. In this example, press Ctrl+Shift+E. Word displays the keys you pressed in the Press new shortcut key text box. Word also warns you if the key combination is already assigned to another command or macro. (If it is and you do not want to disturb the assignment, press Backspace to clear the text box and try again.)

8. Click on the Assign button, then click on the Close button. At this point, the Macro Recording toolbar will float above your Word screen, and the pointer will display a cassette tape below the arrow (see Figure 9.3). You are now recording your macro.

9. To record your macro, you now perform steps like the following (you can perform your own steps at this point; the following list just shows the steps that would be performed for the example being discussed):

   a. Open the **Edit** menu and choose the **Select All** option. (You select the entire text because your next actions must affect the entire text.)

   b. Drag the right margin pointer to the 6.5-inch indicator. If it is already there, click on it to set that right margin for all paragraphs.

Figure 9.2

The Customize dialog box

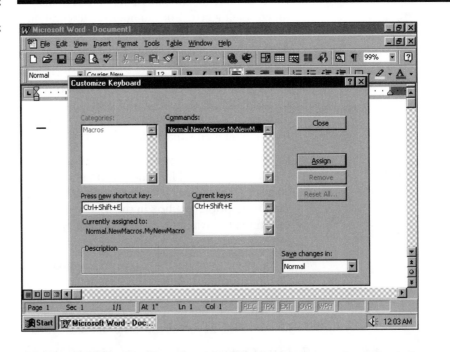

Figure 9.3

The Word screen as you record a new macro

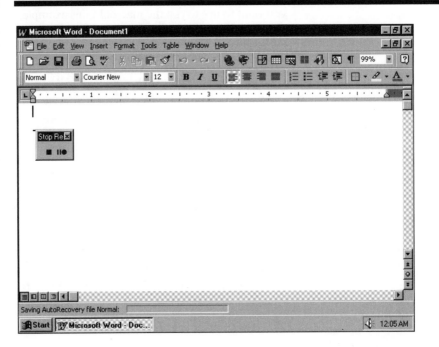

    c. Press F9 to update the figure-number fields.

    d. Press Ctrl+Shift+F9 to unlink the fields. This action converts all number fields to plain text that represents the last update of the field.

    e. Press Ctrl+Home to clear the selection and move to the beginning of the document.

    f. Click on the Spelling button on the Standard toolbar and check the spelling in the document.

    g. Open the **Edit** menu and select the **Replace** option. Enter two spaces in the **Find what** box and one space in the **Replace with** box. Click on the **Replace all** button.

    h. Open the **File** menu and select the **Save As** option. In the Save As dialog box, open the **Save As File Type** drop-down list box and select the Word for Windows 2 option. Click on the OK button.

10. Click on the Stop button on the Macro Recording toolbar. Your macro has been recorded and saved.

TIP. *If you are unsure as to the next action to perform during macro-recording, you can use the Pause button on the Macro Recording toolbar to pause the recording. You then can try out the next step until you are sure how it should go (use the Undo button if your attempts need to be reversed first). Click on the Pause button again to continue recording your well-practiced action.*

You can run your new macro in any document you create with the template that contains the macro. However, there are two cautions to consider when using this macro. First, do not use it in a document that does not have active fields. The unlink-fields action that you recorded has nothing to do under such circumstances and causes an error. Word presents a dialog box informing you that a command failed, and then exits the macro procedure, doing none of the rest of the work. Second, if you run your new macro on a document, it will name the document using the same name as the file with which you recorded the macro. You could accidentally overwrite a file.

Obviously, your macro needs to be modified slightly before it is ready for use. The next section tells you how.

■ Modifying Macros

You have seen how you can record some rather complex actions as a macro very easily. However, you also have seen how some recorded macros can have unfortunate side effects. Typically, unfortunate side effects include the following:

- Commands that cause errors when they cannot perform the intended action. Virtually every Word command and every macro you create can have this unfortunate consequence.

- Commands that record specific file names or other document-specific information.

You can easily modify your macros to resolve these side effects. To make the modifications, you need to know how to edit a macro, how to test a macro, and how to debug a macro. Fortunately, these are not complex tasks. Word makes it easy to solve both of the problems associated with recording macros.

VBA is designed to report an error every time a command cannot carry out its action, for whatever reason. The reason Word reports the error and stops the action is that it has no other instructions. However, you can add a command to each macro you record that tells Word what to do when it encounters an error.

Word also identifies document-specific information in easy-to-spot ways. Typically, if you delete the document-specific information from the command, Word carries out the command using the defaults for the document at hand. In the case of the Save As command, if the command has no file name to use, it uses the file name for the document on which the macro is operating. You can easily scan your macro commands and remove such information.

TIP. *Before you read through the next few sections, you might want to make sure that the VBA Help file is available on your computer. When you select the typical installation using Setup, this file is not installed. Double-click on either the Word or Office Setup icon and add the VBA Help file to your installation.*

Editing

The procedure for editing a macro is much like the procedure for editing a document, because a macro is just a special type of document. To open a macro for editing, follow these steps:

1. Open the Tools menu and select the Macro command, and then choose Macros from the sub-menu.

2. In the Macro dialog box, select the name of the macro to edit from the Macro name combination box (see Figure 9.4). You might need to open the Macros in drop-down list box to select the appropriate template so that your macro shows in the list box.

3. Click on the Edit button.

Figure 9.4

Preparing to edit a macro using the Macros dialog box

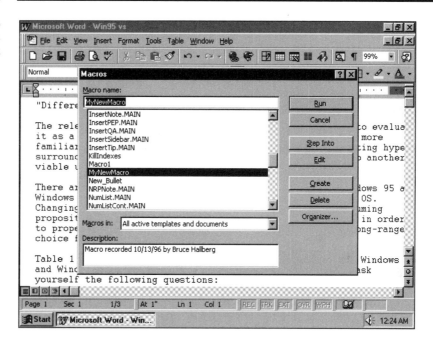

At this point, Word opens the macro and displays it as a document. Word also displays the Macro toolbar, which assists you in working with the macro. Figure 9.5 shows the MyNewMacro macro you just recorded opened for editing.

You edit a macro exactly as you edit a document: all the same editing actions apply.

It's important to avoid adding extraneous characters to a macro command, placing extra characters before the command, or misspelling a command keyword. VBA does not know how to deal with such issues, and will instead display an error message that explains that it could not understand the command. When you make changes, you want to make them with the precision of a surgeon. Go into the file, add or delete or change what you need to, and exit the file leaving the rest intact.

Figure 9.5

The MyNewMacro macro open for editing

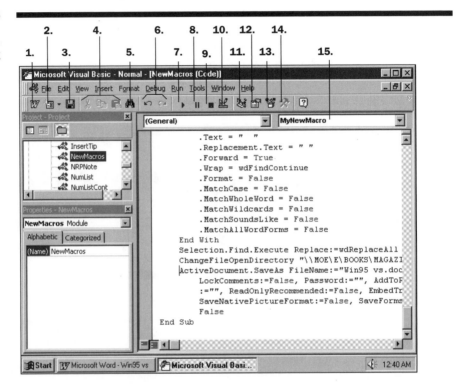

1. **View Microsoft Word**
2. **Insert UserForm**
3. **Save Template**
4. **Cut, Copy, and Paste**
5. **Find**
6. **Undo and Redo**
7. **Run Sub/UserForm**
8. **Break**
9. **Reset**
10. **Design Mode**
11. **Project Explorer**
12. **Properties Window**
13. **Object Browser**
14. **Toolbox**
15. **Active Macro**

TIP. *The active macro is the one that runs when you click on the Run Sub/ UserForm button on the Macro toolbar. The Active Macro drop-down list box (refer to Figure 9.5) always indicates which macro is active. If you have more than one macro open for editing and testing, you can change which one is active by selecting its name from this list.*

To make the specific changes necessary in the MyNewMacro macro, you need to add one statement and delete a portion of another. To solve the problem of an error being generated, you need to add a statement telling Word what to do if a statement cannot carry out its action. VBA provides a family of three such commands, each of which gives Word different directions. In the case of this macro, you want the command that cannot complete its action to give control to the next command, so that the rest of the macro can run. In other words, if a command cannot be carried out, you want to ignore that command and get on with the rest of the macro.

To add this function to your macro, perform the following procedure:

1. Position the insertion point at the end of the Sub MAIN line.

2. Press Enter to create a new line.

3. Type **On Error Resume Next**.

The line you have just added tells Word that when it encounters an error, it should continue running the macro with the next command. No dialog box will appear, and the macro will keep running until it ends. You have to type this command, as it is one of the few that you cannot record.

To solve the problem of Word using the default document name inappropriately, you need to remove document-specific information. In this macro, only one element needs to be removed. If you look at the line that begins FileSaveAs, you'll see that it contains a specification of the file name to use. If you remove that specification, Word will use the name of the file on which the macro is running instead. To solve this problem, follow these steps:

1. Find the ActiveDocument.SaveAs command near the end of the macro.

2. Select the portion of the command that says FileName:="*filename*" (where "filename" is the name found in quotes after the equal sign).

3. Press the Del key to remove that portion of the command.

Save the changes you have made in your macro by pressing the Save button on the Standard toolbar—just as you would in any other file. You can close a macro-editing window by opening the File menu and choosing the Close and Return to Microsoft Word option.

Testing

Testing your revised macro is largely a process of running the macro and verifying that it works. If it does not work, then you need to proceed to the stage of debugging. When you test your macro, you should have its editing window open to take advantage of the Macro toolbar's testing aids; however, you cannot test a macro while its editing window is the active document window. You must make a document window active and run the test from the Macro toolbar, which remains available as long as you have a macro-editing window open.

The Debug menu in the VBA editor contains a number of commands that help with testing (see Figure 9.6):

- **Step Into** causes commands to be run individually. You can step into each command, watching what it does and looking for errors in the Word document that is the target for the macro.

- **Step Over** causes a command that uses a subroutine of commands to be executed, but you do not execute the subroutine commands one-by-one.

Figure 9.6

The Debug menu of the
VBA editor

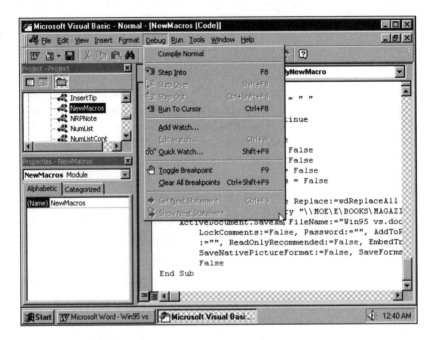

Instead, they execute at once, and you move to the next command in
your main procedure.

- **Step Out** is used when you are within a subroutine and wish to execute
  the remaining lines of the subroutine's code and return to the next command in the main program.

- **Run to Cursor** causes all commands up to the position of the insertion
  point in the VBA editor to be executed.

The remaining commands in the debugger (Add, Edit, and Quick Watch;
Toggle Breakpoint and Clear All Breakpoints; Set Next Statement and Show
Next Statement) are typically used by more advanced VBA programmers.
You should not need these commands for debugging recorded VBA macros.

Testing is a straightforward process. You run the macro, looking for an
error message or a failure of the macro to perform the action you intended.
If the macro runs correctly, you are finished with it. If it fails to run correctly,
you need to start debugging.

Debugging

Debugging can be a very difficult process. It can be tedious and time-consuming. That is why your first step in debugging should be to re-record the macro.

If this course of action solves the problem, you do not have to proceed further. If recording again does not solve the problem, use the Step Into command in the Debug menu to move through your macro line by line. You need to have both your active document and your misbehaving macro visible on your screen, and you need to follow some fairly straightforward rules.

The first rule to follow is that Word is doing exactly what you told it to do, which is not necessarily what you want it to do. You need to look first at what you told Word to do to see if you can find the problem. If a paragraph format is not set correctly, did you set it correctly in the dialog box when you recorded the macro? If fields are not updating, did you press F9 (or was it F8?) when you recorded the macro? If the file name is not correct on the save, what file name did you tell it to use? Chances are the source of the problem is something you told the macro to do that was not what you intended to say.

The second rule to follow is that Visual Basic commands consist of a name and some parameters that the command might require. The name of the command invokes the action named. Some commands take no parameters, others do. Parameters can appear as an item or list of items separated by commas in parentheses after the command name. You should check all of the parameters your commands contain to see if any contain problematic settings.

The third rule to follow is that there are just a few things, really, that can go wrong in writing a macro. The following list describes these possibilities, along with common symptoms:

- *Infinite Loops.* The macro just keeps on running and will not stop unless you click on the Stop button on the Macro toolbar. The most likely cause is a command that causes the macro to execute a second command, which in turn causes the first command to be re-executed, causing the second to re-execute, and so on. The most likely cause in a recorded macro is an incorrect On Error statement. Examine the macro carefully using the Step button on the Macro toolbar. When you have found the two statements that are calling each other, break the chain of calls in the most convenient way.

- *Misspelled Statements.* You receive a Syntax Error or a Label Not Found Error. Word cannot compensate for mistakes in typing. The best prevention for spelling errors is to record commands whenever possible. To correct syntax errors, compare what you typed, character by character, to the examples given in the Visual Basic Help file.

- *Extra Characters.* You receive any of a variety of errors, but they will all have "incorrect" or "missing" or a similar word in their description of the problem. Word is interpreting the extra characters as a part of a command and cannot make sense of the command. The solution is to compare what is in the macro-editing window, character by character, to the example in the Word Basic Help file.

- *Incorrect Information.* Your macro does not do what you want it to do, but everything else seems correct. Check the values you have assigned to the parameters of your commands: one of these is probably wrong.

Debugging a macro can be frustrating. It can be so frustrating that continuous, long efforts at it usually are unproductive. You may get trapped in a rut and not see the problem from a fresh perspective. Debugging is best done in short bursts with breaks in between. Stay with the procedures suggested above for the best results. Change only one thing at a time in your macro between each test run. If you change more than one command, you might fix the problem you had but introduce another one.

TIP. *You can prevent a command from executing by placing the characters REM, for REMark, in front of them. You can also use a single quote mark (') to accomplish the same thing.*

If all else fails, both the Word Help file and the Word manual explain how to get technical assistance from Microsoft. The good news about VBA, however, is that if you record when you can and type only when you have to, and if you follow these suggested procedures, you should rarely run into a problem with a macro that you cannot solve quickly.

- *Creating a Web Page in Word*

- *Formatting a Web Page in Word*

- *Viewing a Web Page with Online Layout View*

- *Creating a Hyperlink to a Web Page*

- *Sending a Web Page to an FTP Site*

10

Creating a Web Page with Word

THE MOST POPULAR PART OF THE INTERNET IS THE WORLD WIDE Web, a huge collection of interlinked documents called Web pages. Computers that store Web documents are usually called *Web servers,* and specific collections of Web pages that relate to a common theme or sponsor are usually called *Web sites*, but because the Web uses a protocol called *HTTP* to transfer documents, Word refers to Web servers and Web sites as *HTTP locations*. You can publish a Microsoft Office document as a Web page so that other people who surf the World Wide Web can see your document.

In order to put information on the Web, you need to have an Internet Service Provider that provides space for Web pages or access to a Web server established at your company. Your company may also have an *intranet*, a private network that supports HTTP. The documents stored on an intranet Web site are only visible to company employees, unless you set up a system for access to the network from outside the company. If your company doesn't have an intranet, you can ignore all the references to intranets in this chapter. Your Webmaster, or the person who manages the Web servers at your company, can tell you where to place your Web pages on corporate servers.

This chapter shows you how to use Word 97's new Internet-related features. You will learn how to convert a Word Document into a Web page, create a Web page from scratch in Word, and format a Web page in Word. You will be shown how to view a Web page with Word's Online Layout view, create a hyperlink to a Web page, and send a Web page to an FTP site.

Converting a Word Document into a Web Page

The hot thing on the Internet is having a personal World Wide Web page. Why would you want a Web page of your own? Suppose you want to advertise a business or hobby with a product brochure, publish your ideas for the world, tell friends what's happening in your life, or simply have a presence on the Web for the fun of it.

Companies may also want to set up Web sites to publish a newsletter or technical support data, or to simply promote their products and services.

Every Web page is basically a plain text file with formatting instructions for the text, graphics, and links that have been added to it. This file is called the *HTML source*, because the instructions are written using the Hypertext Markup Language (HTML.) The Web recognizes the HTML format.

When you convert a Word document to a Web page, Word creates the HTML source code for the new page. Word tries to include codes in the HTML source document that closely match the formatting of your Word document. Unfortunately, Word's formatting features are far more sophisticated than HTML formatting, so your Web page may not always meet your expectations. If you want more control over the appearance of your Web pages, you might want to create them from scratch, as discussed in the next section on "Creating a Web Page in Word."

NOTE. *If you want to create Web pages, your installation of Office 97 should include the Web-page authoring tools. If it doesn't, you'll need to run the Microsoft Office 97 setup program again to add them. (If you have questions, ask your company's computer guru or system administrator to assist you.)*

Here's how the Word-to-Web conversion process works:

1. Open the document you want to convert (see Figure 10.1).

Figure 10.1

A Word document

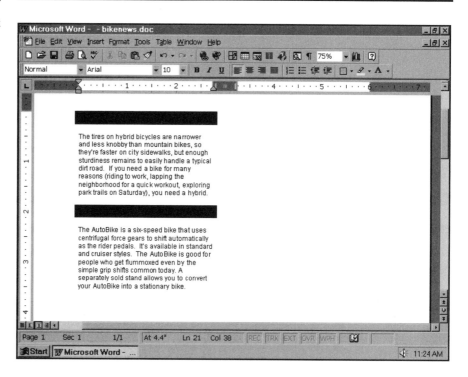

2. Choose Save As HTML from the File menu. The Save As HTML dialog box opens (see Figure 10.2). Notice the HTML Document choice in the Save As Type list.

3. Choose a location for your document from the Save In list, and type a name in the File Name text box.

4. Choose Save.

Word creates the HTML source code behind the scenes, and displays the resulting Web page in the Word window. Figure 10.3 shows an example in which Word was able to convert all the formatting from the original document, except for the borders and shading on the headings.

HTML automatically adds blank lines under paragraphs and headings. If you have too much white space in your Web page, it was caused by pressing Enter to create blank lines in your Word document. To prevent ending up with too many blank lines in your Web page, create blank lines in your Word

Figure 10.2

The Save As HTML dialog box

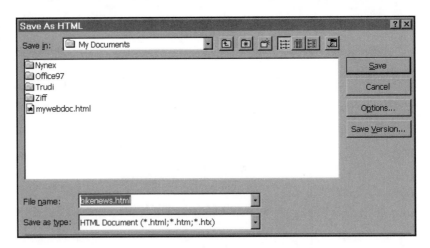

Figure 10.3

The same Word document converted to a Web page

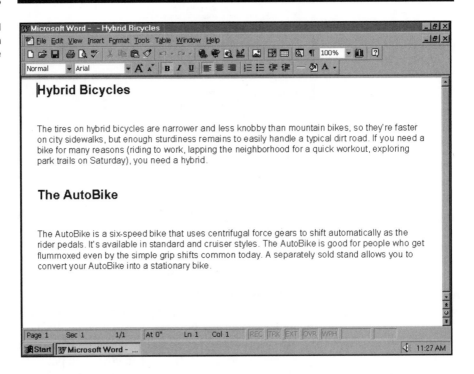

document by choosing Paragraph from the Format menu. Then increase the Spacing After setting in your Paragraph settings and choose OK. This will add spacing after each paragraph without requiring you to press Enter.

When Word displays a Web page, it automatically switches to the new Online Layout view, and modifies the menus and toolbars to include commands for working with Web pages. You can also view the Web page in a Web browser, such as Netscape Navigator or Microsoft Internet Explorer. Depending on how your browser interprets HTML codes, your Web page may look different than it does in Word.

NOTE. *When a Web page is displayed on your screen, the File, Save As HTML command changes to the Save As Word Document command to let you convert the Web page to a Word document.*

Note that the name displayed in the title bar of a Web page is not the file name, but the *title* of the document: HYBRID BICYCLES, in this example. You can change the title of a Web page in Word. To do so, display the Web page on your screen and choose File, Properties. The Document Properties dialog box will appear. Edit the title in the Title text box and choose OK.

After you convert the Word document to a Web page, you can make your Web page accessible to other people by placing it on a Web site. The easiest way to do this is by using FTP, as explained in the section on Sending a Web Page to an FTP Site later in this chapter. Once the Web page is on a Web site, you'll need to provide links to the page. If you want more information on creating and maintaining Web sites, refer to *How to Use the Internet* from Ziff-Davis Press or another book about Web design.

■ Creating a Web Page in Word

As you learned earlier in this chapter, you can convert a Word document into a Web page. However, if you want to create a good-looking Web page, the best method is designing one from scratch. Word provides two templates for Web pages:

- The Blank Web Page

- The Web Page Wizard

If you already have experience designing Web pages, then the Blank Web Page is a good choice. If, on the other hand, you need a little coaching, you can use the Web Page Wizard. As with other Wizards, this one asks you some questions, and then handles the formatting and design work for you. All you need to do is fill in the text.

To start the Web Page Wizard, choose New from the File menu. You'll see the New dialog box. Click the Web Pages tab, and double-click on the Web Page Wizard. Word will display the Web Page Wizard, as seen in Figure 10.4.

Figure 10.4

Selecting the Web page type

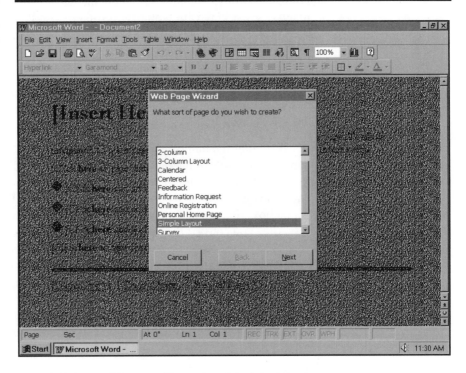

The Web Page Wizard will ask what type of Web page you want to create. Try clicking on a few different types. Word will show you a sample of the currently selected type behind the dialog box. When you've made your selection, click on the Next button.

Next, the Web Page Wizard will ask what style you want (see Figure 10.5). Again, when you click on various options in the list, Word will show you a sample of each style behind the dialog box. Once you've chosen a style, click on the Finish button.

Word creates a Web page based on your selections. If you choose to create a home page, you'll see items under Contents—Work Information, Hot List, Contact Information, and so on (see Figure 10.6). These are hyperlinks to other sections of the same Web page.

Figure 10.5

Selecting a Web page
style

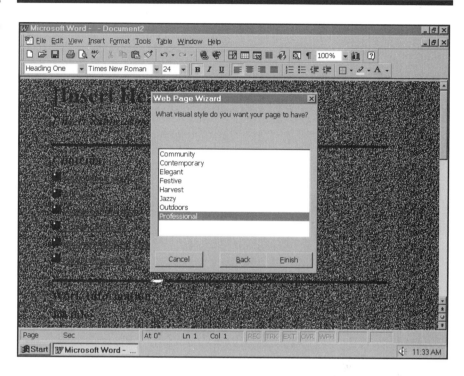

The status bar indicates the number of pages in the Web page. The text in brackets, [Insert Heading] and [Subheading], shows you where you should type. Click on these instructions to select them, and type over them with your actual text.

To finish creating the Web page, click on each hyperlink to jump to the various sections, and fill in your text. For example, when you click on Work Information, it will lead to the Work Information part of the Web page. You can also navigate through the page with the scroll bar or other standard keyboard techniques.

NOTE. *When you point to a hyperlink on a Web page, a ScreenTip contains a letter (A, B, C, etc.) that represents the name Word has used in the HTML source to refer to the hyperlink.*

After Word has jumped to the destination of the link, replace any instructions you find with actual text. For example, replace all the *[type some text]* instructions with the text you want. You can also make any changes you'd like to existing text such as the *Job title* and *Key responsibilities* headings. To jump quickly back to the top of the Web page, click on the *Back to top* hyperlink.

Figure 10.6

A sample home page with hyperlinks

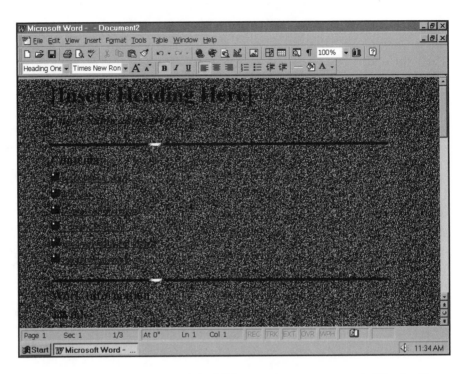

When you have completed the Web page, be sure to save it. Word will automatically choose HTML Document from the Save As Type list, and append the extension .html to the file name.

NOTE. *When you save a Web page you created using the Web Page Wizard, Word will copy any graphic images it used in the page into the folder in which you saved the page itself. If you plan to place your Web page on a Web site, you might want to save it into an empty folder, so that it will be obvious what graphics files go with the page. When you transfer the page to a Web site, transfer all the graphics files with it. The graphics files will be in GIF or JPEG format, because these are the formats in widespread use on the Web.*

■ Formatting a Web Page in Word

After you have created a Web page, you can enhance its appearance by using Word's toolbar buttons and menu commands. When you format a Web page, Word automatically inserts the appropriate codes in the HTML source. However, each browser application recognizes a slightly different set of

HTML codes, so there is no guarantee that your page will look the same in a browser as it does in Word. As of this writing, Netscape Navigator and Microsoft Internet Explorer are the two most popular browsers. If you're going to publish your page on a Web site, open it in both of these browsers to make sure it looks OK before you post it to a site. See the section on "Sending a Web Page to an FTP Site" later in this chapter.

To apply basic character and paragraph formatting to the text on your page, select the text you want to change, and use the buttons in the Formatting toolbar. For example, you can apply changes to the font, font size, font style, and text alignment. When a Web page is displayed in the Word window, Word replaces the Font Size list with the Increase Font Size and Decrease Font Size buttons. Other than that, the buttons for character and paragraph formatting are the same ones that usually appear in the toolbar (see Figure 10.7).

Figure 10.7

The Formatting toolbar can be used when a Web page is displayed in the Word window.

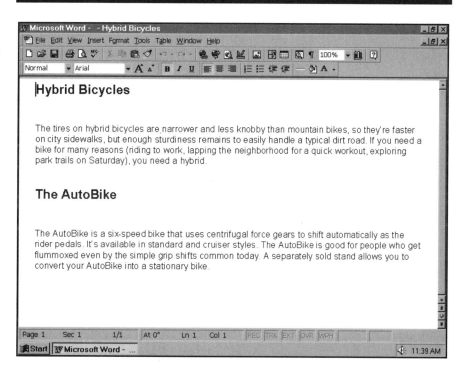

To add a horizontal line (referred to as a *horizontal rule* in HTML terminology) to the page, first place the insertion point where you want to add the line. Then click the Horizontal Line button in the Formatting toolbar. Word will add a line across the width of the page (see Figure 10.8).

Figure 10.8

A horizontal line across a
Web page

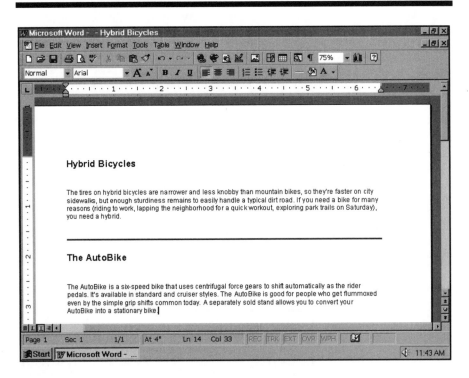

If you want to change the appearance of the line, right-click on the line
and choose Edit AutoShapes from the Shortcut menu. Make the desired
changes, and choose OK.

To add a background color or texture to the Web page, click the Fill button in the Formatting toolbar. When you see the color you want in the palette, click on it. Otherwise, choose More Colors to display the Colors dialog
box, and then select from the wide range of colors displayed. If you want to
add texture, choose Fill Effects to display a palette of textures, select a texture, and choose OK.

If you are familiar with HTML, you might want to edit the HTML
source code for your page directly to fine-tune the formatting. To do so,
choose HTML Source from the View menu. If you have any unsaved
changes, Word will prompt you to save them first before displaying the
source code.

Word will now display the HTML source code underlying your page.
Make the desired changes to the code, save them, and then choose Exit
HTML Source to return to Online Layout view. If you aren't sure how to
work with HTML code, you should use the toolbar buttons and menu commands instead.

■ Viewing a Web Page with Online Layout View

Note. To switch to Online Layout view quickly, click the Online Layout View button at the left end of the status bar.

Word's new Online Layout view shows a version of the Web page that's similar to the way it will look in a Web browser. The text is large and wraps to the View window, not the way it wraps for printing. To switch to Online Layout view, choose Online Layout from the View menu.

As you can see, the document contains large text and wraps to the window (see Figure 10.9). Use the scroll bars to see the rest of the document.

Figure 10.9

A Web page in Online Layout view

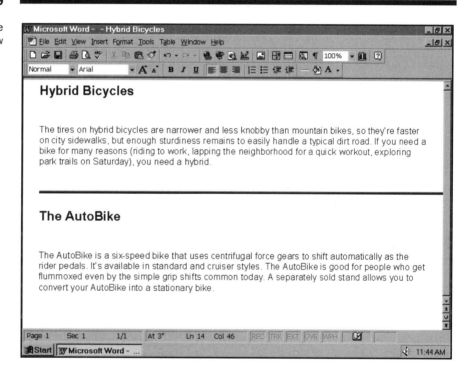

If you want to return to Normal view, click the Normal View button at the left end of the status bar.

■ Creating a Hyperlink to a Web Page

Instead of having a Web wizard put hyperlinks in your Web page, you can create your own *hyperlinks* to move to a Web page and Office documents. A hyperlink is a piece of text or graphic in a document that links to other documents or Web pages (see Figure 10.10). You can even link to a specific location in a document. When you click a hyperlink, you move to the location that the link points to. A hyperlink appears as text in a color in the document.

Figure 10.10

A hyperlink to a Web page

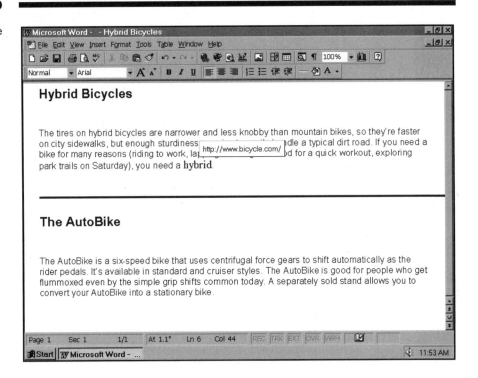

Remember that hyperlinks are useful when you're distributing your document electronically and expect people to read it on-screen. Also, make sure that your readers will be able to access the documents you link to. For example, if you link to a document on your local hard drive (C:) instead of a network drive, other people on your network won't be able to jump to the document, unless you have made the entire contents of your machine available to other users on the network.

To create a hyperlink to a Web page, first select the words or graphic image that you want to form the hyperlink. Choose Hyperlink from the Insert menu. The Insert Hyperlink dialog box will open (see Figure 10.11).

Next, enter the destination for your link in the Link to File or URL text box. If the destination is a URL, type it directly into the text box, and choose OK. If the destination is a document on your network, click on the Browse button. You will see the Link to File dialog box.

Note. You can also click the Insert Hyperlink button in the Standard toolbar to select the Insert Hyperlink command.

Figure 10.11

The Insert Hyperlink
dialog box

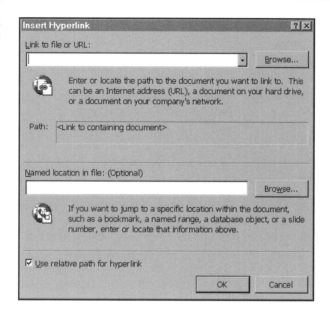

Locate and select the document you want to link to, and choose OK. The path and file name will now be displayed in the Link to File or URL text box. Choose OK to return to your document.

NOTE. *When you want to specify what part of the document you want to link to, you can use the Named Location in File text box. Some examples of named locations include a bookmark in a Word document or a named range in an Excel spreadsheet. For more information on named locations, take a look at the online help in Word or Excel.*

The text or graphic you selected in the Web page is now a hyperlink. When you point to it, the mouse pointer becomes a hand, and a ScreenTip appears listing the name of the destination file or URL.

Click on the link to jump to the destination. Word will display the destination document. If the destination is a Web page, Word will display the page in your browser. To go back to the document containing the hyperlink, click on the Back button in the Web toolbar.

Note. If the Web toolbar isn't displayed, click on the Web Toolbar button in the Standard toolbar.

When you click on a hyperlink that points to a document created in a program other than Word, Word will first load the program, then open the document within it. If the program is part of Office 97 (Excel, Access, Outlook, or PowerPoint) you'll see the Web toolbar at the top of the program window.

By default, Word automatically formats URLs you type in your documents as hyperlinks.

If you no longer want a hyperlink, right-click on the link you want to delete, and choose Hyperlink in the Shortcut menu. Choose Select Hyperlink, and then press the Delete key.

You can change the destination of a hyperlink at any time. To do so, right-click on the link, choose Hyperlink in the Shortcut menu, and choose Edit Hyperlink. Edit the destination in the Edit Hyperlink dialog box, which looks exactly like the Insert Hyperlink dialog box, and choose OK.

If Word is not automatically formatting URLs as hyperlinks, you can turn on the feature called AutoFormat As You Type Internet and Network Paths. Choose AutoCorrect from the Tools menu. The AutoCorrect dialog box will open. Click the AutoFormat As You Type tab. Then, check the Internet and Network Paths with Hyperlinks check box in the Replace As You Type area.

■ Sending a Web Page to an FTP Site

FTP (File Transfer Protocol) is a protocol for sending files between your computer and other computers on the Internet. Computers on the Net that offer files for downloading are called *FTP sites*. Using FTP is a fast and reliable way to download files from other Internet computers, and upload files of your own. It is the most convenient way of uploading (or *publishing*) Web pages you've created to a Web site.

To use FTP from Word, begin by telling Word about the FTP sites you want to access. First display either the Open or the Save As dialog box. Click the Open button on the Standard toolbar, or choose Save As from the File menu.

NOTE. *If you use FTP frequently, you should obtain a more robust and flexible FTP program—a good one you can try is CuteFTP, available at http://www.cuteftp.com.*

Click the Look In drop-down arrow (in the Open dialog box) or the Save In drop-down arrow (in the Save As dialog box) to display the list, then make your choice. The Add/Modify FTP Locations dialog box will appear (see Figure 10.12).

In the Name of FTP Site text box, type the name of the computer at the FTP site, prefaced by *ftp*. Most Web addresses begin with *www* and most FTP addresses begin with *ftp*. If you aren't sure of the correct FTP site name, ask the site's system administrator.

If you have a personal account at the FTP site, choose the User option button, and enter your user name and password. Then choose Add.

Figure 10.12

The Add/Modify FTP
Locations dialog box

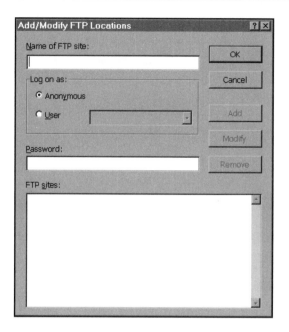

NOTE. *Many companies let people who don't have personal accounts log into their FTP site as anonymous users. Anonymous users are only given access to certain public areas of a site. Most typically, you connect as an anonymous user if you just want to download files—software, bug fixes, and so on. Anonymous users may not be able to upload files.*

You can add a site to your list of FTP locations and set it up to connect you as an anonymous user. Enter the name of the site, click the Anonymous option button, and choose Add.

Note that the FTP sites you've added appear in the list of FTP locations at the bottom of the dialog box. When you've finished adding sites, choose OK.

The new FTP locations will appear in the Look In list in the Open dialog box or the Save In list in the Save As dialog box. Notice that Word automatically appends *ftp://* to the addresses (see Figure 10.13).

Once Word knows about a site, you can use the Open dialog box to download files from the site, and you can use the Save As dialog box to upload files.

To log into an FTP site, make sure you are connected to the Internet. Next, display the Open dialog box to download a file, or the Save As dialog box to upload a file. In the Look In or Save In list, choose the FTP location.

Figure 10.13

FTP addresses in the
Save As dialog box

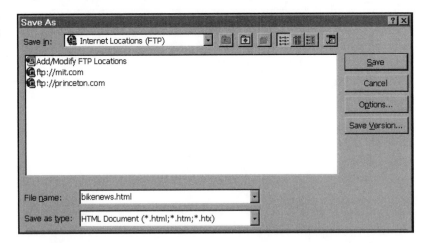

After a moment, Word will display all the folders at the FTP site. Double-click on folders until the one you want to upload to or download from appears in the Look In or Save In list.

If you're downloading a file, click on the file you want to download and choose Open. Word will then display a message box showing you its progress as it downloads the file. After the document appears on your screen, you can use File, Save As to save it onto a local drive.

If you're uploading a file, type a name for the file, and choose Save.

NOTE. *Another way to upload or download a file is to add the FTP site, and type the URL for the file in the File Name text box of the Open or Save As dialog box. For example, you could display the Open dialog box and type ftp:// ftp.mit.com/update.doc in the File Name text box to download a document called update.doc from the FTP site at mit.com.*

Word displays your password for a personal account at an FTP site on your screen in two situations. When you download a file from a personal FTP account, your password appears in the message box showing the status of the file transfer. Your password can also appear in list of recently accessed files at the bottom of the File menu, because Word includes the entire URL for files you've recently transferred via FTP. To work around this security problem, choose Options from the Tools menu, click the General tab, and decrease the number in the Recently Used File List box from four to none.

3

Excel

- *Examining Worksheets*
- *Understanding Excel's Three Types of Data*
- *Formatting Your Worksheet*
- *Mastering Borders, Patterns, and Colors*

11

Understanding Excel Worksheet Concepts

Worksheets are the primary elements that you work with when you use Microsoft Excel. Worksheets can be simple or complex, depending on your needs. To fully develop your worksheets, you need to understand all their rules, nuances, and features.

This chapter will help you do so by presenting the following topics:

- Using workbooks, worksheets, and data

- Entering text, numbers, and figures

- Formatting your worksheets

- Mastering borders, patterns, and colors

When you finish this chapter, you will be well on your way to building more spectacular and dynamic worksheets.

Look around your desk. How many piles of papers or notebooks do you have? Do you have key data placed in these piles, such as budgets, sales reports, or invoice statements? Are some of the piles vital to the success of your business, job, or home budget planning? Would you like a better way to manage some of this mess? If you answer "Yes" to these questions, you are a prime candidate for a spreadsheet program like Excel 97.

■ Examining Worksheets

Excel workbooks contain worksheets, which are like the ledger sheets you might have used in high school accounting class. Along the left side of the sheets are rows numbered 1, 2, 3, and so on, and along the top of the sheets are columns lettered A, B, C, and so on. The intersection of these rows and columns are *cells*. Worksheets contain 256 columns and 16,384 rows.

The data that you place in worksheets can be text, formulas, or numbers. Usually, *text* entries are labels, such as American Conference or December Sales Results. You also might use text entries when you have numbers and text combined, such as account codes. *Number* entries might be points scored, dollars earned, taxes paid, interest rates, or any other number that you need to store. *Formula* entries are calculations based on values that you specify, such as cells or ranges.

Selecting and Viewing Sheets

Not surprisingly, each type of data that you can enter in Excel has its own rules and features. The basic means of getting the data into the worksheets, however, is the same: You select the sheet and cell into which you want the data placed, and you type the information.

Before you enter the data, make sure that you are working in the correct workbook and worksheet. When Excel starts, a blank workbook with three blank sheets opens. Along the bottom of the workbook are tabs that let you select the sheet you want to work with. These tabs are numbered Sheet1, Sheet2, and so on. If you do not want to start a new worksheet, you can also enter data in a workbook that you have saved previously by selecting File, Open and opening the desired file. You then click on the tab to change to the sheet in which you want to enter the data, and select the cell to contain the data.

If you have more than one workbook open, you can move between workbooks by selecting Window and choosing the workbook that you want to make active. This is handy if you are cutting and pasting data from one workbook to another. You can also arrange the workbooks on your screen to make them easier to switch between by using the Window, Arrange command. When you select this option, the Arrange Windows dialog box appears (see Figure 11.1).

Figure 11.1

Use the Arrange Windows dialog box to keep your workbooks organized on-screen.

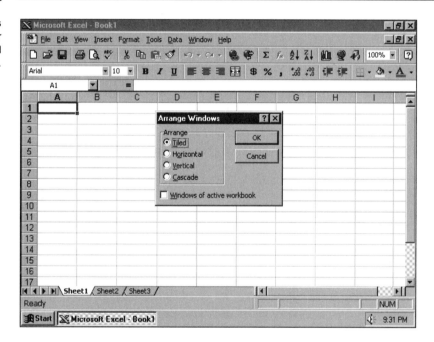

This dialog box enables you to arrange your workbooks so that they are placed vertically or horizontally (by using the Vertical and Horizontal options), tiled (by using the Tiled option), or cascaded (by using the Cascade option). You can also arrange only the windows of the active workbook by clicking in the Windows of active workbook check box. This puts the active workbook in the foreground and the inactive ones in the background.

TIP. *As with any other Windows application, you can move individual Excel workbook windows around by using the mouse and grabbing the title bar. The Arrange Windows dialog box is useful in some cases when you just cannot* *seem to set up the interface to suit your needs and you want a more automatic way of doing so.*

Hiding Workbooks

As your worksheets get more complex, or if you have several workbooks open at once, you may find that your screen feels overly cluttered. You can keep it clean by hiding workbooks or worksheets.

To hide a workbook, select the workbook that you want to hide and choose Window, Hide. The workbook disappears immediately from your screen. To reveal ("unhide") any windows that are hidden, perform the following steps:

1. Select Window, Unhide. This displays the Unhide dialog box with a list of the hidden windows (see Figure 11.2).

Figure 11.2

The Unhide dialog box keeps a list of hidden windows.

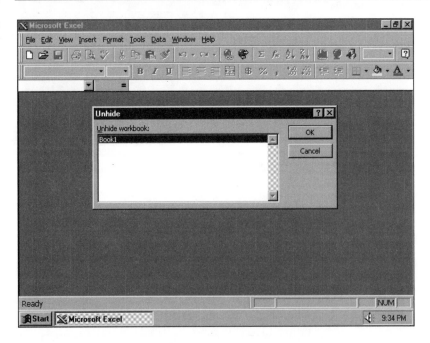

2. In the Unhide Workbook list box, click on the window you want to unhide.

3. Choose OK or press Enter. The window you want to unhide reappears on-screen in its previous size and position.

Hiding Worksheets

What if you want to hide all those other worksheets in a workbook that you are not using? To do this, you cannot use the Windows, Hide command because that hides the entire workbook, and not just a particular sheet. You have to use the Format, Sheet command instead, as follows:

1. Switch to the sheet you want to hide.

2. Select Format, Sheet. A submenu pops out to the side of the pull-down menu.

3. Choose Hide. The sheet instantly disappears.

   To unhide the worksheet, select Format, Sheet, Unhide to display the Unhide dialog box. Click on the sheet you want to unhide and choose OK or press Enter. The sheet reappears on-screen.

Locking Workbooks

You might want to keep all the windows in place, or you might want to keep other people from moving windows around if they are using your workbooks. To lock a window after you have it in place, select the Tools, Protection, Protect Workbook command to display the Protect Workbook dialog box (see Figure 11.3). In this dialog box, you can enter a password in the Password (optional) text box so that users will need a password to move the windows or modify the structure of the workbook (such as hide, unhide, delete, or move it). Click in the Windows check box so that the position of the windows cannot be changed. Click in the Structure check box to protect the structure of the workbook.

CAUTION! *Remember your password. If you forget it, you cannot unprotect your workbook.*

Moving Around in Workbooks and Worksheets

To switch between sheets in the active workbook, you simply click on the tab of the sheet you want to view. Excel offers a few other navigational tools to help you move around in your workbooks. You can, for instance, use scroll bars to move around. You can also type a cell reference to switch to that cell.

   Tab-scrolling arrows appear at the bottom of workbooks to help you move through the worksheet names in a workbook. You cannot switch to a different sheet by using the tab-scrolling arrows, but you can view the names of the sheets and then click on the sheet tab that you want to activate. Each workbook has four tab-scrolling arrows. The far-left and far-right arrows move to the first and last sheets in the workbook, respectively. The middle two arrows move one sheet to the left or right in the workbook. See Figure 11.4 for the placement of these scrolling arrows.

Figure 11.3

The Protect Workbook
dialog box

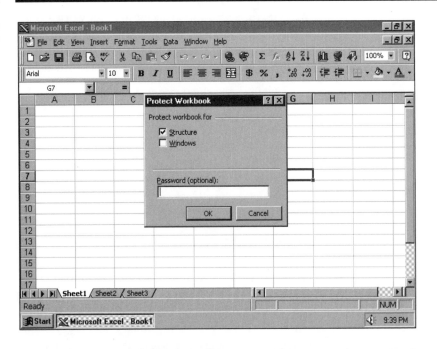

Figure 11.4

Tab-scrolling arrows help
you identify sheets in
your workbook.

1. **Scroll to last sheet**
2. **Scroll one sheet to
   the right**
3. **Scroll one sheet to
   the left**
4. **Scroll to first sheet**

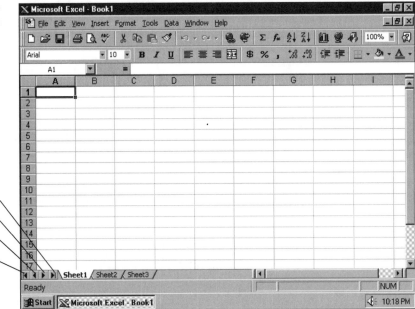

Selecting More than One Worksheet

You sometimes have to select several non-contiguous worksheets in a workbook that are not side by side—Sheet2, Sheet4, Sheet 11, and Sheet13, for example. To do this, perform the following steps:

1. Click on the tab-scrolling arrows to show the first sheet that you want to select, such as Sheet2.

2. Click on that tab (in this example, Sheet2).

3. Click on the tab-scrolling arrows to show the next sheet in the group that you want to select, such as Sheet4.

4. Click on that tab while pressing Ctrl (in this example, Sheet4).

5. Continue scrolling to the next sheet tab, using Ctrl+click to select a new sheet, until all the sheets you want are selected.

As you select the sheets, the tabs will change color to signify that you have selected them.

In other situations, you might need to select several sheets that are in order, such as Sheet3 through Sheet8. Follow these steps to select multiple contiguous sheets quickly:

1. Click on the tab-scrolling arrows to show the first sheet you want to select, such as Sheet3.

2. Click on that tab (in this example, Sheet3).

3. Click on the tab-scrolling arrows to show the last sheet in the group that you want to select, such as Sheet8.

4. Click on the last sheet name while pressing Shift. This selects all the sheets between the first and last sheets on which you clicked. Again, the tabs change color to show that they have been selected.

Using the Go To Command

If you want to move to a specific sheet in an open workbook, but you don't want to scroll through all the sheets and you know exactly the sheet and cell reference, perform the following steps:

1. Select Edit, Go To (or press F5 or Ctrl+G). The Go To dialog box appears.

2. In the Reference text box, enter the name and cell of the sheet to which you want to switch. You have to separate the name and cell with an exclamation point, like this: SCORES!H6. In this example, you are telling Excel to jump to cell H6 in the SCORES worksheet.

3. Choose OK or press Enter.

■ Understanding Excel's Three Types of Data

You might have stacks of papers on your desk and loose invoices jammed in your filing cabinet. These numbers, dates, products, inventory lists, dollars spent and received, phone numbers, addresses, and other miscellaneous words and numbers are forms of data. You need to find a way to administer all this data so that you can use it quickly and efficiently. Now that you know how to move among workbooks and worksheets, you can start entering it all, even if you have been putting it off for months (or years!).

When you finally break down all the data and see what you have, you can begin to formulate how you want it to look in your worksheets. Phone numbers and addresses, for instance, can comprise a Black Book worksheet. Sales data for the entire midwestern sales force can be put into a Midwest Sales worksheet. You even can start thinking about creating sophisticated workbooks that rely on macro or Visual Basic for Applications front ends.

TIP. *One way to get ideas on the types of workbooks and worksheets that you can build in Excel is to view the sample file that comes with Excel 97. This file is called SAMPLES.XLS, and is stored in the \Office97\Office\Examples directory.*

Using Text as Data

You can include text entries that are alphabetical characters, numbers, symbols, and spaces. Usually text entries, which can be up to 32,767 characters long in a cell, are used to label worksheets and to help readers understand the contents of the workbooks. You also can enter numbers and have them treated as text, such as addresses, numbers used as labels, and numbers that begin with 0. When you enter a number that has a leading zero, Excel deletes the 0. You can, however, retain the 0 by leading the entry with an apostrophe ('), which tells Excel that the entry is to be accepted as text. (The apostrophe does not appear in the cell.)

TIP. *Another way to enter a number as text is to select Format, Cells. This displays the Format Cell dialog box. Click on the Number tab and select the Text option in the Category list. Click on OK or press Enter. This returns you to the active worksheet, where you can enter the number and have it be accepted as text.*

Excel places text in a cell by aligning it with the left side of the cell. Numbers, on the other hand, are right-aligned. If your text entry is too large to be viewed in the default cell size, the text will be displayed over the next cell unless there is data there, in which case the text will be cut off at the border of the cell. You can correct this by resizing the cell using the formatting features explained later in this chapter.

To enter text in a worksheet, select a cell and type the text. In the following example, you enter some text and some numbers as text. Notice how text aligns on the left side of the cell.

The following exercise uses a new worksheet that you can open by choosing File, New:

1. Select File, New or click the New button on the toolbar, to create a new workbook. A new workbook with blank worksheets appears.

2. Click in the cell in which you will enter the text—for example, cell B4.

3. Type the text you want—for example, Sales. Notice how the text aligns on the left side of the cell.

4. Enter some numbers that you want to appear as text, such as the current year. To do this, add an apostrophe (') before the number: '1997. Excel interprets this data as text and does not think it is a number entry. (You'll learn about number entries in the next section.)

TIP. *By default, numbers are right-aligned in cells, and text is left-aligned. Use this visual cue to quickly see if Excel is accepting an entry as text or as a number.*

Another way to enter text (or any other data) is to use the formula bar on the formatting toolbar. To make this your default choice, turn off the in-cell editing feature. This method is nice if you don't want to see your entries made directly in the cell until you are finished entering them.

To turn off in-cell editing, use these steps:

1. Select Tools, Options. The Options dialog box will appear.

2. Click on the Edit tab to display the Edit dialog box (see Figure 11.5).

3. Click on the Edit directly in cell check box to turn it off.

4. Click on OK or press Enter.

Now, when you click or double-click on a cell to edit the contents, your insertion point will appear on the formula bar instead of within the cell. The characters are still displayed in the cell as you type. Some people find it easier to work this way.

Regardless of the location of your insertion point, when you begin entering characters, the formula bar will display four buttons (see Figure 11.6).

• The Name box on the formula bar shows you the cell reference for the selected cell. You can press the arrow to the right of the box and enter a cell reference in order to move to that cell quickly.

• The Cancel button lets you undo what you have typed before entering the data. You also can press Esc to do the same thing.

Figure 11.5

The Edit tab of the
Options dialog box

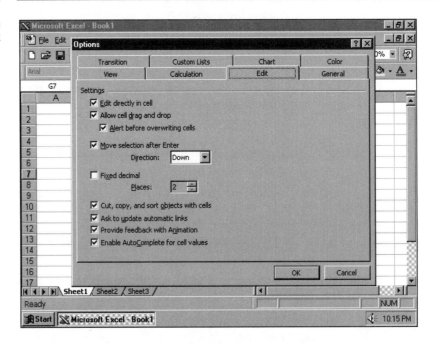

Figure 11.6

The buttons on the
formula bar (visible when
editing a cell's contents)
give you mouse-click
access to data-entry
functions.

1. **Name box**
2. **Cancel**
3. **Enter**
4. **Edit Formula**

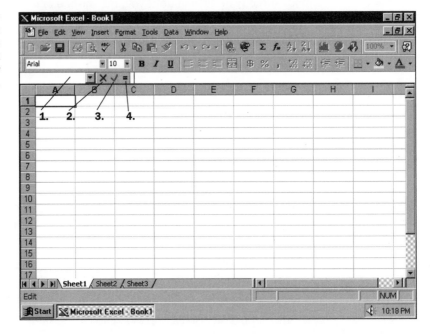

- The Enter button is used to place the entry into the selected cell, or you can press the Enter key.

- The Edit Formula button changes the formula bar to add tools that make entering formulas with functions easier. Using this feature is discussed later in this chapter.

Text entries may become lengthy and run too long for the cell in which they are contained. To avoid having text flow into other cells, you can use text wrapping to display the entry in multiple lines in one cell.

To see how the feature works, enter a lengthy string of some data in a cell. Next, select Format, Cells and click on the Alignment tab. Choose the Wrap text check box and press Enter or click on OK. The cell (along with the row) grows higher to accommodate all the data.

TIP. *You can press Alt+Enter while entering text into a cell to force a carriage return in the cell's contents. The height of the cell automatically adjusts to accommodate the lines you enter this way.*

Using Numbers as Data

For the most part, your worksheets will contain numbers. The primary function of a spreadsheet is to help you calculate, store, manipulate, and present numbers. These numbers might be dollar amounts, percentages, dates, or other values. Excel lets you enter these characters as number data: 1 2 3 4 5 6 7 8 9 0 E e . % - + / . (Later in this chapter, you are shown how to change the formatting of numbers.)

Numbers are entered the same way text is: select the cell, type the number, and then press Enter or click on the Enter box on the formula bar. Excel right-aligns the numbers in the cells. If you want to enter fractions, type an integer (such as 1 or 0), a space, the numerator, a slash (/), and the denominator: 3 1/2 or 0 5/16. The first fraction in these examples reads as *three and one-half,* and the second fraction reads as *five-sixteenths.* If you do not use an integer before the fraction, Excel thinks you are entering a date. The second example without the zero (5/16) would be read as *May 16.*

Some other forms of numbers that you might need to enter are negative numbers, dollar amounts, decimals, and very large or small numbers. Dollar amounts are entered with the dollar sign, then the number: $34.90. Decimal values are entered with the decimal point: 432.89. If you deal with large numbers, such as scientific notations, you use the form 84.3992 E+3. (*E* is the symbol that represents scientific notation.)

TIP. *To enter a number that has thousands and uses one or more commas in it, you have to put the commas in the correct place or Excel will think it is a text* *entry. The number 34,45 is not the same as 3,445 to Excel. The first is interpreted as text and the second is interpreted as a number.*

When you enter a number that does not fit in a cell, Excel automatically adjusts the width of the column so that the number can be displayed. If you narrow the column or do something else to cause the number to need more space to display than there is, Excel displays a series of ####s to indicate that the column is not wide enough (see Figure 11.7). To change the ####s to the actual numbers, you can widen the columns or change the numeric format (such as changing the font or point size of the number). To change the numeric format, you might need to change a long number to scientific notation. (Later in this chapter, you are shown how to widen columns.)

Figure 11.7

When numeric entries are too long to fit in a cell, you see a series of ####s.

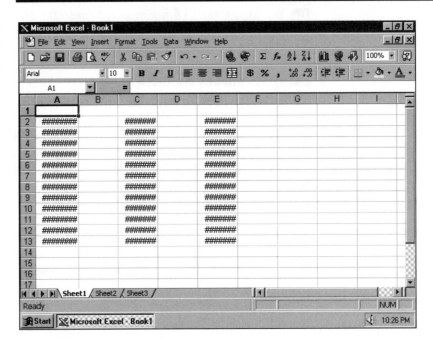

Entering Dates and Times

You might need to place actual dates and times into your worksheets, such as February 1, 1997, or 5:13 p.m. When you enter dates and times, Excel stores this data as a serial number. *Serial numbers* represent starting points that are programmed into Excel. A date serial number is computed from the starting point of December 31, 1899. A time serial number is computed using fractions of the 24-hour clock.

If you enter the date December 31, 1997, for example, the serial number is 35,795. This means that 35,795 days have passed between December 31, 1899, and December 31, 1997. If you enter a time of 12:00 noon, Excel saves it as the serial number 0.50; 5:00 p.m. is 0.70833. This means that when it is noon, half the day has passed; when it is 5:00 p.m., you have only about three-tenths of the day left.

NOTE. *Why are serial numbers used by Excel? Serial numbers make it easy to calculate dates and times you might need in your results, such as delivery times and dates or accounts payable data. All you need to think about, however, is entering dates and times the way Excel accepts them, which is in a number of different formats. You do not need to enter serial numbers, although you can if you want. Excel handles the conversion of date entries into "behind-the-scenes" serial numbers automatically.*

The secret to entering and displaying dates and times correctly is to use Excel's date and time formats. These formats are found by selecting Format, Cell and clicking on the Number tab (see Figure 11.8). In the Category list box, you can choose the type of number, including Date or Time, that you want to format. You then choose a particular style in the Type scroll box. A sample based on the data in the cell you are formatting appears in the Sample box. Using these formats, you can display dates and times in many different styles.

The way a time or date is displayed in your worksheet depends on the number format applied to the cell. When you type a date or time in a format that Excel recognizes, the cell's format changes from the General number format to a built-in date or time format. The specified format is applied to your entry (unless you change the format for that cell). Figure 11.9 shows a worksheet in which the formula bar displays the way the date was entered, but the cell displays the data according to the formatting assigned.

One of the most useful shortcuts when you are entering data is to enter the current date and time automatically in a cell. Press Ctrl+; to enter the current date, and press Ctrl+: to enter the current time.

Using Formulas as Data

The third type of data that you can enter in Excel is formulas. Formulas are simple to understand. They calculate results based on values. You can use numbers, cell references, text, or functions in formulas.

To enter formulas in your worksheets, perform the following general steps:

1. Click on the cell in which you want to include the formula.

2. Enter an equal sign (=) or other operator. Remember that Excel changes these other operators to equal signs when you enter the formula.

Figure 11.8

Use the Number tab to format dates and times.

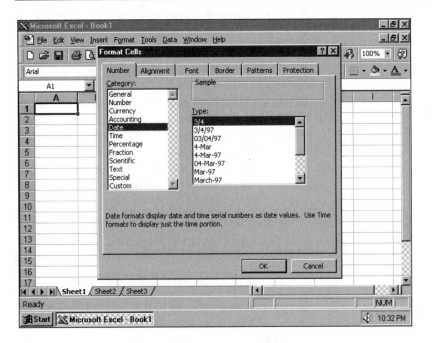

Figure 11.9

Excel reformats date displays to match your settings.

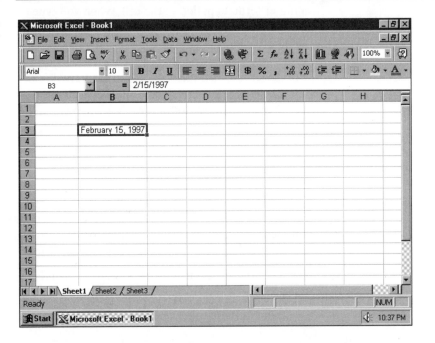

3. Enter a value, cell reference, range, or function name by typing it or selecting it with your mouse. The cell reference or range appears in the formula.

4. If the formula is complete, press Enter.

5. If the formula is not complete, enter an operator, such as +, -, or @.

6. Go back to Step 3 and continue building the formula until it is complete.

Most of the time, you use Excel formulas to calculate results of numbers. These types of formulas are called *arithmetic formulas*. Generally, arithmetic formulas calculate results by using numbers, function results, and cell addresses with one or more of the following mathematical operators:

$$= - * / \% \wedge$$

The caret ($\wedge$) operator denotes an *exponentiation operator*. An example of exponentiation is raising a number to a certain power. The formula $=5\wedge 2$ means *5 raised to the second power*, or 25.

Calculating by Order of Precedence

When you enter a formula that contains operators, you need to keep in mind the order by which Excel calculates the formula. This is called *order of precedence*, and is used by Excel to determine which part of the formula to calculate first, second, and so on.

If you have the formula $=5*3\wedge 2$, for example, it is not clear which part of the formula should be calculated first. Excel's order of precedence first calculates the exponentiation part ($3\wedge 2=9$) and then the multiplication part ($5*9$). The result of this total formula is 45.

If you calculate the parts in the opposite order, the results are quite different ($5*3=15$; $15\wedge 2=225$), so it is important to understand Excel's order of precedence when you create your formulas. Table 11.1 shows the order in which Excel calculates formulas and the operators associated with certain operations.

You might want to create formulas that do not follow the natural order of precedence. You might, for instance, want to add two numbers together and *then* multiply the sum by another number. In the order of precedence, however, Excel multiplies first, then adds. To overcome this in your formula, use parentheses to surround the numbers that you want Excel to calculate first.

If, in the preceding example, you want to add 5 and 3 and then multiply the sum by 10, set up the formula as the following:

$$=(5+3)*10$$

Table 11.1

Order of Precedence in
Formulas

ORDER	OPERATION	OPERATOR
1	Range	:
2	Intersection	Space
3	Union	,
4	Negation (such as -9)	–
5	Percent	%
6	Exponentiation	^
7	Division and multiplication	/ and *
8	Addition and subtraction	+ and -
9	Concatenation	&
10	Comparison	= < > <= >= <>

When you have more complicated formulas, you might have parentheses inside of parentheses. This is called *nesting*. Keep in mind that Excel calculates what is inside of parentheses first, and the formulas within the inner parentheses are calculated before those within the outer ones.

The following example provides some sample formulas that you can enter in a new worksheet to help you get acquainted with entering formulas.

1. In cell B4, enter **=2+2** and press Enter.

2. In cell B6, enter **=2*2** and press Enter.

3. In cell B8, enter **=2/2** and press Enter.

4. In cell B10, enter **=2-2** and press Enter.

5. In cell B12, enter **=2^2** and press Enter.

6. In cell B14, enter **=2*(2^5)** and press Enter.

Figure 11.10 shows the results of these formulas and how your worksheet should look.

TIP. *Remember to type the equal sign to start the formula. If you forget to do this and press Enter, Excel interprets your entries as text and does not calculate the formula. To edit the cell after you have entered the formula, double-click on the cell (to edit directly in the cell), or click on the cell and move your*

Figure 11.10

Entering formulas

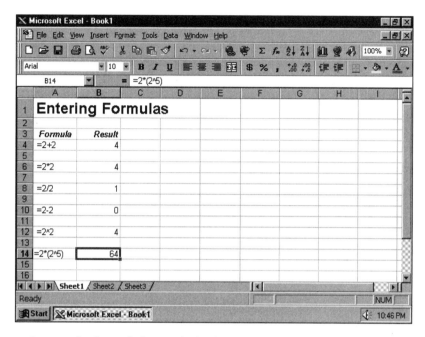

pointer to the formula bar and edit the entry there. Press Enter to have Excel evaluate the formula.

Copying and Moving Formulas

You can click on any cell that contains a formula and select Edit, Copy from the menu bar, then move the insertion point to the new cell and select Edit, Paste. The results of the calculation appear in the cell.

TIP. *A quicker way to copy a formula to an adjacent cell (one that is above, below, to the right, or to the left) is to use the mouse. Click on the cell that contains the formula and move the mouse pointer to the lower right corner of the cell border. Grab the cell handle that appears and move the selection into the cells where you want to copy the formula. Then release the mouse button.*

When you copy a formula, you usually have a number of calculations to perform in a worksheet that use the same formula but have different cell references. The worksheet shown in Figure 11.11, for example, figures out the total projected sales for January through June for a fictitious company. Cell I5 shows the total sales for Wile E. Coyote through June. The formula to calculate this result is the following, as displayed in the formula bar:

=SUM(C5:H5)

Figure 11.11

Creating a formula that can be copied

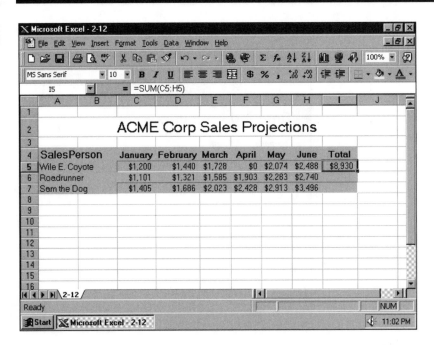

Now that you have this formula written, you can use it to add the totals for the other salespeople. When you copy the formula into another cell, Excel assumes that you want to use the same general formula, but the cell references are to be changed. That is, to calculate Roadrunner's total, you want to use cell references C6:H6, not C5:H5 as in the original formula. The other salesperson also has his or her own data that needs to be calculated.

How does Excel know which cell references to use? This is known as *relative reference format* in Excel. When you create a formula that asks Excel to "add the contents of cells C5:H5," Excel interprets this as "adding the contents of the cell six rows to the left (cell C5), to the contents of the cell five rows to the left (cell D5), to the contents of the cell four rows to the left (cell E5), to the contents . . ." until all are added and displayed in I5.

When you copy this formula from I5 to I6 to add Roadrunner's sales numbers, Excel automatically adjusts the cell references but interprets the formula in the same way. In this case, Excel interprets the formula as "add the contents of the cell six rows to the left (cell C6), to the contents of the cell five rows to the left (cell D6), to the contents of the cell four rows to the left (cell E6), to the contents . . ." until all are added and displayed in H5.

Sometimes, however, you cannot just copy a formula from one cell to another and get the correct results. This occurs when you have some references that change in a formula *(relative references)* and some that do not. Those that do not are called *absolute references.* When you use absolute references in a formula, Excel uses the specific cell reference that you enter, regardless of where you copy the formula.

You might, for example, want to add another formula to the worksheet shown in Figure 11.11 that determines the total sales quota for the next six months for each salesperson, and the quota is two-and-one-half times the total amount they produced in the first six months. This quota index is placed on the worksheet in cell C9 as 2.5. The formula is =I5*C9 and is created in J5 for Wile E. Coyote.

When you copy the formula to another cell (such as to J6 for Roadrunner) using the techniques you have learned, Excel assumes it is working with a relative reference format and you get $0 in the cells, which obviously is the wrong sales quota (see Figure 11.12). You get this result because Excel interpreted your copied formula to mean "multiply the number that is 1 column to the left by the number that is 4 rows down and 7 columns to the left." When you copy the formula to Roadrunner's row (J6), Excel cannot find a value that is "14 rows down and 7 columns to the left," so it multiplies the number 1 column to the left (in this case, $10,993) by 0.

Figure 11.12

Using relative references does not always work when copying cells.

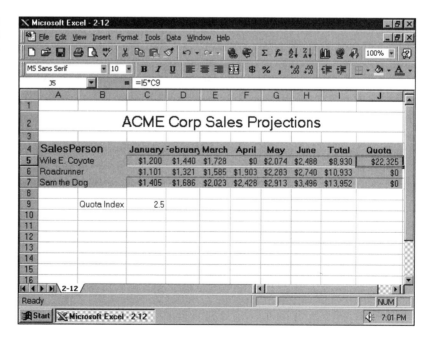

To get the correct results, use Excel's absolute reference format to anchor the number that you want to use in all the formulas. The anchored value is the cell reference that does not change, regardless of where you copy or move a formula. In the example shown in Figure 11.12, you need to anchor the quota index number (2.5) so that each salesperson's total value can be multiplied by this value. To distinguish between absolute and relative references in a formula, use a dollar sign ($) before the row and column of the cell address that you want to anchor: $C$9, for this example.

The following steps show the way to set up the example worksheet by using absolute references and then copying the formula to other cells. For this example, the figures and formulas entered in Figure 11.11 are already in the worksheet:

1. Use the numbers shown in Figure 11.11 (you could enter your own, but it is easier to follow along if you simulate the example used here).

2. In cell J5, type the formula **=I5*$C$9** and press Enter. The result of the calculation is $22,325.

   TIP. *When entering a cell reference in a formula, use the F4 key to switch between absolute and relative references.*

3. Copy the formula in cell J5 into cells J6:J7 to calculate the new quotas for the rest of the sales force. To do this, click on cell J5 and grab the handle at the bottom right side of the cell border.

4. Drag the selection down to cell J7 and release the mouse button. The new values appear in the selected cells, showing the sales quota for the rest of the staff (see Figure 11.13).

TIP. *You can use absolute references to anchor part of a cell reference. You can, for example, anchor just the column part or row part of the reference. To do this, place the dollar sign in front of the column address or the row address, depending on which part you want to anchor. You might want to do this if the column you refer to in a formula stays the same but the row changes with each calculation.*

Referencing Another Worksheet in a Formula

If you have a lot of data and you create many worksheets to store this data, you might have occasions when a formula in one worksheet needs to use data from another sheet. These *sheet references* are handy, because they mean you don't have to create redundant data in numerous sheets.

To refer to another cell in another sheet, place an exclamation mark between the sheet name and cell name. You might, for instance, write a formula in cell A9 in Sheet1 that needs to reference cell B5 in Sheet2. This reference

Figure 11.13

Copying the quota
formula using an
absolute reference
produces correct results
in this example.

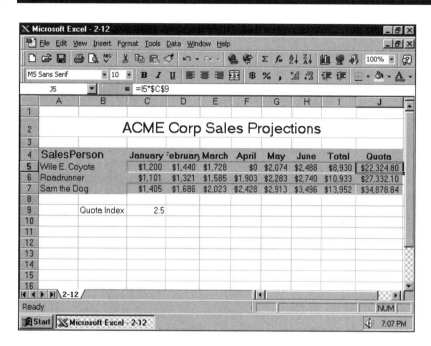

looks like SHEET2!B5. (Use the correct sheet name in place of SHEET2 if
you have named the sheet.)

TIP. *When the sheet name contains spaces, such as Sales 94, you need to place
single quotation marks around it when you are making sheet references.*

If you are not sure of the cell reference in another sheet, you can start
writing your formula and switch to the sheet that you want to reference
when you get to that part of the formula. Then use your mouse and click on
the cell or range of cells that you want in your formula. The cell or range reference appears automatically in your formula. You then can finish your formula and press Enter to calculate it.

Using 3D References

What if you have a formula that needs to reference a cell range that has two
or more sheets in a workbook? This might happen if you have identical worksheets for different sales teams, regions, or states. You also might have several different worksheets that have totals calculated and entered in identical
cell addresses. You then can add all these totals to get a grand total by refer-
encing all the sheets and cell addresses in one formula.

When you have cell ranges such as this, Excel refers to them as *3D references*. A 3D reference is set up by including a *sheet range*, which names the beginning and ending sheets, and a *cell range*, which names the cells to which you are referring. A formula that uses a 3D reference that includes Sheet1 through Sheet10 and the cells A5:A10 might look something like the following:

=SUM(SHEET1:SHEET10!A5:A10)

Another way to include 3D references in your formulas is to use the mouse and click on the worksheets that you want to include in your formula. To do this, start your formula in the cell where you want the results. When you come to the point where you need to use the 3D reference, click on the first worksheet tab that you want to include in your reference, hold down Shift, click on the last worksheet that you want to include, and select the cells you want to reference. When you finish writing your formula, press Enter.

Calculating a Formula

As soon as you enter a formula (that is, type it and press Enter), Excel automatically calculates it. You might not want Excel to do this all the time, particularly if you have created a complex, time-consuming calculation that you don't want to do right away. Or, you might want to write a formula before you get all the data in the worksheet.

To tell Excel not to calculate a formula automatically, perform the following steps:

1. Select Tools, Options. This displays the Options dialog box.

2. Click on the Calculation tab to display the calculations options (see Figure 11.14).

3. Click on the Manual option button. You also can set up Excel to calculate the worksheet automatically, except items in a table, which you can calculate manually by clicking on the Automatic except tables option.

   The Calc Now (F9) button can be used to calculate all your open worksheets. Or, you can use the Calc Sheet button to calculate only the active worksheet. You can press F9 while you are working in the worksheet to calculate all open worksheets; you do not have to open this dialog box every time you want to calculate your worksheet. Press Shift+F9 to calculate only the active worksheet.

4. When you choose the Manual option, you then can decide whether to have Excel calculate before you save the worksheet by selecting the Recalculate before save checkbox.

5. Press Enter or click on OK.

Figure 11.14

The Calculations tab in
the Options dialog box

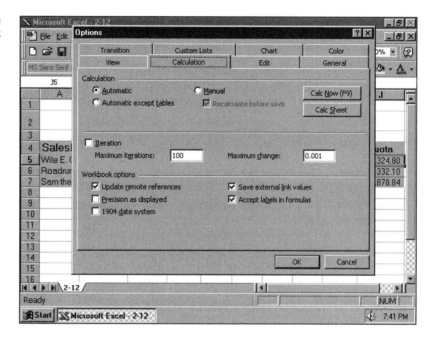

Viewing Worksheet Formulas

Excel displays the formula for a selected cell in the formula bar, and the results of the calculation in the cell. You might find this inconvenient if you
want to view all your formulas at once. To see the formula in a single cell, select the cell and press Ctrl+'. To see all the cells displayed as formulas, perform the following steps:

1. Select Tools, Options.

2. Click on the View tab to display the View options (see Figure 11.15).

3. Click on the Formulas check box in the Window Options group. This
   tells Excel to display formulas instead of values.

4. Press Enter or click on OK.

Using Arrays in Formulas

In the worksheet in the preceding examples, notice that there are several
areas that use the same formulas but have different cell references. The Total
column, for example, uses the same SUM formula to calculate each of the
employees' sales numbers.

Figure 11.15

The View tab of the
Options dialog box

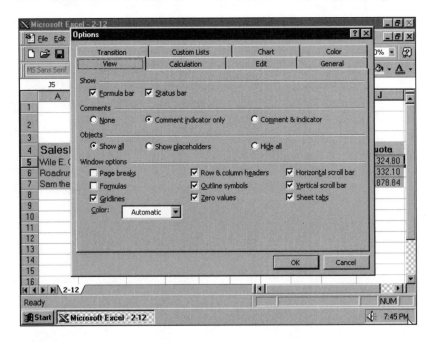

When you have situations like this, you can save system memory and time by using an *array formula,* a rectangular range of formulas that is treated as one group. Excel denotes array formulas by placing braces ({}) around them. Excel automatically places these braces; you do not have to place them yourself.

To enter an array formula, perform the following steps:

1. Select the range that you want to contain the array formula.

2. Enter the formula and use the range coordinates for the area you want to include in the array formula. You also can use the mouse to select this area.

3. Finish the formula.

4. Press Shift+Ctrl+Enter to tell Excel to make this formula an array formula. Excel places braces around the formula.

TIP. *You cannot insert cells or rows within an array, edit a single cell in an array, or delete part of an array. You can edit an array by double-clicking on the array range. Edit the array formula and press Shift+Ctrl+Enter.*

■ Formatting Your Worksheet

Once you enter your data and set up some formulas, your worksheet is functional, but it might not look very appealing. You might, for instance, want to highlight certain columns in your sheet, use color-coded cells, change fonts, or format dates, numbers, and times to improve the appearance of your worksheet.

Alignment

When you enter data into a cell, it aligns automatically to Excel's default. For text, this alignment is left-justified. For numbers, this alignment is right-justified. However, you might want to center the text or align the numbers along the left side of the cell. Excel allows you to align data in a number of different ways by using the Alignment tab in the Format Cells dialog box (see Figure 11.16). To use this option, select Format, Cells and click on the Alignment tab.

Figure 11.16

Use the Alignment tab to customize how data is displayed in selected cells.

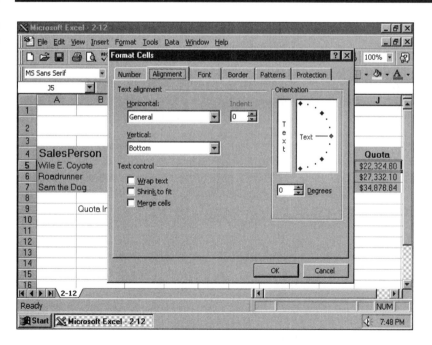

Use the Horizontal list box to select how text is aligned horizontally. You can choose from General, Left, Center, Right, Fill, Justify, and Center Across Selection. General aligns text using the default method. Left, Center, and

Right align the text accordingly. Fill causes the text in the cell to be repeated so that it completely fills the cell. Justify spreads the text out so that it meets both the left and right sides of the cell. Center Across Selection causes the text to be centered across the selected range of cells.

TIP. *The Formatting toolbar contains buttons for aligning text, including the Left, Center, and Right Align buttons. You also can center text across cells by using the Center Text in Selection button.*

Later in this chapter you are shown how to modify the height and width of rows and columns. When you do, you can change the way the cell contents are aligned vertically by using the options in the Vertical list box. You can, for instance, align the data at the top of the cell with the Top option. Use the Center option to align the data in the center of the cell. The Bottom option is used to place the data at the bottom of the cell. Justify is used to justify the data in the cell vertically.

Another problem that you can overcome easily with the alignment options is a long text entry. In Figure 11.17, for instance, the text in cell B4 overlaps several neighboring cells. To correct this problem, click in the Wrap text check box on the Alignment tab to have Excel automatically adjust the height of the cell to accommodate several lines of text. Notice in Figure 11.17 how cell B6 is large enough to contain all its text, making it easier to read.

Figure 11.17

The Wrap text option allows you to place several lines of text within a single cell easily.

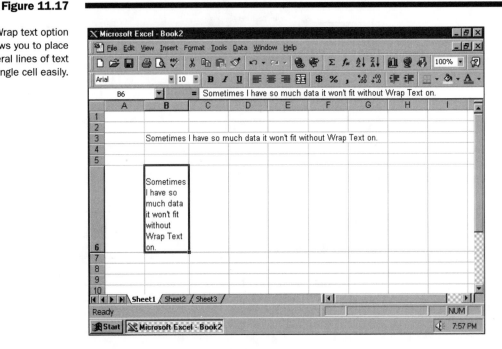

You might want to have text displayed in several different angles. This is handled by the Orientation section of the Alignment tab. The default selection is horizontal. You can choose the vertical option so that the text reads from top to bottom. Or, you might want to read the text at an angle, which you can choose with the half-clock setting in the Orientation section. (You can also manually enter in the number of degrees to rotate the text with the Degrees spin box.) These latter options are handy when you need vertical titles for reports or charts.

Tabs and Carriage Returns

Most computer users are comfortable using a word processor to type text and do elementary tasks such as tabbing and starting new paragraphs. In most word processing applications, you press Tab to tab over or press Enter to start a new paragraph. In Excel, however, these tasks are not as intuitive.

If you press Enter while you are typing text, Excel interprets this as the end of your entry and enters the contents into the cell. Similarly, when you type text and then press Tab, Excel enters what you have typed and moves over to the next cell. To place a carriage return inside a cell entry, press Alt+Enter. To place a tab inside a cell entry, press Alt+Ctrl+Tab. By using tabs and carriage returns in your cell entries, you have more control over how your final worksheet looks.

TIP. *You can delete Tab and carriage returns as you do any other character in a cell. First select the cell, press F2 for editing, and press Del to delete the Tab or return.*

Fonts

The numbers, letters, and other characters that appear on your screen all belong to a certain font. A *font* is the typeface, type size, and type style of a certain character. With Windows 95, you can use TrueType fonts, a specially designed type of font that you can resize and print with good precision. With TrueType fonts, what you see on-screen in your worksheet will be what you see when it is printed (or very close to it).

The size, type, and variety of fonts you use help make your worksheet stand out among other reports. Keep in mind that when you format your worksheets you ultimately intend to have someone (maybe just you) look over it. For this reason, make your worksheets easy to use, to the point, and functional. A functional worksheet does not have to be drab in appearance or intimidating.

You might, for instance, change the point size from the default 12 points to a larger 14- or 16-point size. You can make the text bold, italic, or underlined. Along with centering titles or justifying text, you can add these subtle formatting changes to make your text pop off the page. Compare the worksheets in Figures 11.18 and 11.19. Both contain the same data and text. Which one are you more likely to read?

Some of the most common character-enhancing options are available on the default formatting toolbar. You probably will use this toolbar throughout the time you create your worksheets and enter data. The options available to help you change your font characteristics include the following (see Figure 11.20):

- *Font drop-down list.* Use this list to choose the font for the selection.

- *Font Size list.* Use this list to change the point size of the selected entry.

- *Bold, Italic, Underline buttons.* These buttons enable you to add bold, italic, and underline font styles to your selection.

- *Alignment buttons.* These buttons let you quickly align text within cells.

- *Center across selection.* This button lets you quickly center text in the left-most cell across the entire range of cells you select.

- *Font Color.* Add a little color to your entries by changing the color of the selection from black to a number of different colors. You might, for instance, use red to denote late payments.

Figure 11.18

A worksheet without formatting enhancements

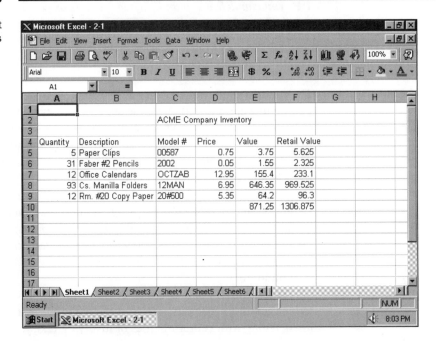

Figure 11.19

The same worksheet with
various formatting
enhancements

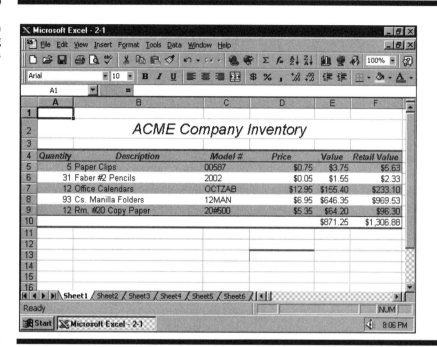

Figure 11.20

Character formatting
options on the default
toolbar

1. **Font**
2. **Font size**
3. **Bold**
4. **Italic**
5. **Underline**
6. **Left, Center, and
   Right alignment**
7. **Center across
   selection**
8. **Font color**

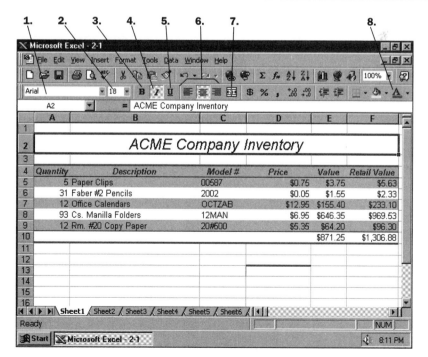

If you want to use a dialog box interface to change the selected character(s), select Format, Cells and click on the Font tab. This displays the Font tab options (see Figure 11.21):

- *Font.* This option enables you to choose the font for the selection. True-Type fonts appear with a double-T logo next to them. Printer fonts appear with a printer icon next to them.

- *Font Style.* Use this list to add character enhancements, such as regular (also known as *roman*), italic, bold, and bold italic.

- *Size.* This option enables you to select a different point size for your selection.

- *Underline.* This drop-down list helps you select the type of underlining you want for your selection, such as None, Single, Double, and Single or Double Accounting. Accounting underlines only the numbers in a cell, not the entire cell.

- *Color.* Use this list to select a color. You might want to experiment with the way different colors print. Use Automatic for black-and-white printers if you do not want to take any chances.

Figure 11.21

The Font tab options

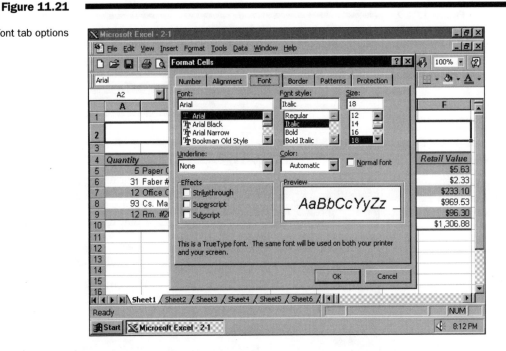

- *Normal Font.* This check box allows you to select Excel's default font.

- *Effects.* This area enables you to add Strikethrough, Superscript, and Subscript characteristics to your selection.

The Preview window in the lower right corner of the tab screen lets you view what the changes will do to your selection.

TIP. *A printer font is used to print your worksheets and charts from preinstalled fonts in your printer or in cartridges you can plug into the printer. PostScript fonts, for example, are printer fonts. You can also download fonts from your computer to the printer's memory.*

When you use a printer font, another font is used to display the characters on your screen. These screen fonts usually are installed when you install your printer in Windows 95. You might see some differences between what is on-screen and what actually prints, because the screen fonts might not always have the same font size and styles that the printer font has. You usually will use TrueType fonts when working with worksheets, but you can invest in some professional-quality printer fonts that will add much more to your final presentation.

Numeric Formats

Because spreadsheet applications are designed around conveying numeric data, the format your numbers are in is probably the most crucial part of your worksheet. The way you format your numeric data is up to you, but you should be consistent in the way you handle numbers from worksheet to worksheet in each workbook.

Ways that you might want to handle numeric data include making all negative numbers a different color, such as red or blue; and using commas to separate thousands.

Excel provides quite a few built-in number formats, and also lets you create your own number formats.

To apply a format to an individual cell or range, select that cell or range and perform the following steps:

1. Select Format, Cells to display the Format Cells dialog box.

2. Click on the Number tab to activate it (see Figure 11.22).

3. In the Category list box, click on the type of number that you want to format, such as General, Number, or Percentage. When you select a category, the choices available for that category are shown. For example, for Numbers you can choose the number of decimal places, the Thousands separator, and a format for negative numbers. If the selected cell has data, the Sample section will display that data in the highlighted format.

Figure 11.22

Use the Number tab to
select different numerical
formats for your data.

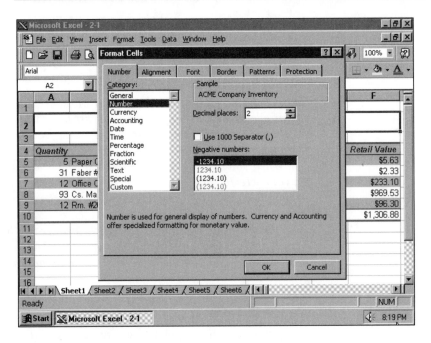

4. For more choices, choose Custom in the Category list, and the list in the
Type box changes to show a variety of custom number formats.

5. Press Enter or click on OK.

If you want a quicker way to apply common number formats, you can
use keyboard shortcuts. The following list shows the key combination and
the format code that is applied:

Key Combination	Format Code
Ctrl+Shift+~	General
Ctrl+Shift+!	0.00
Ctrl+Shift+$	$#,##0.00;($#,##0.00)
Ctrl+Shift+%	0%
Ctrl+Shift+^	0.00E+00

When you enter your numeric data, you can specify the type of format
you want applied to the number by adding certain characters, such as the dollar sign ($) and percentage sign (%). To enter a dollar amount, begin your
entry with a dollar sign, enter the numeric data, and press Enter. Excel interprets your entry as a Currency format. To enter a percent, type the number,

then add a percent sign (%) after it. Excel interprets this as the Percentage format and enters it as such.

TIP. *A quick way to display the Number dialog box is to select the cell that you want to format, click the right mouse button, and select Format Cells from the pop-up menu. This immediately displays the Format Cells dialog box, allowing you to add or change number formats.*

Modifying Columns

One of the common problems you run into with any spreadsheet application, including Excel, is the default size of the cells. They usually are too small to hold all the data you want to place in them. Excel 97 makes it easier to resize the rows and columns of your worksheets.

Recall that when you enter a number, or after a calculation is evaluated, you might have cells that contain #### characters. These characters tell you that the cell is not large enough to display the number. You need to widen the column to display the number.

You can change one or several columns by performing the following steps:

1. Select the cells in the column that you want to widen. Select a cell in each column that you want to adjust if you are resizing multiple columns.

2. Select Format, Column to display the pop-out menu shown in Figure 11.23.

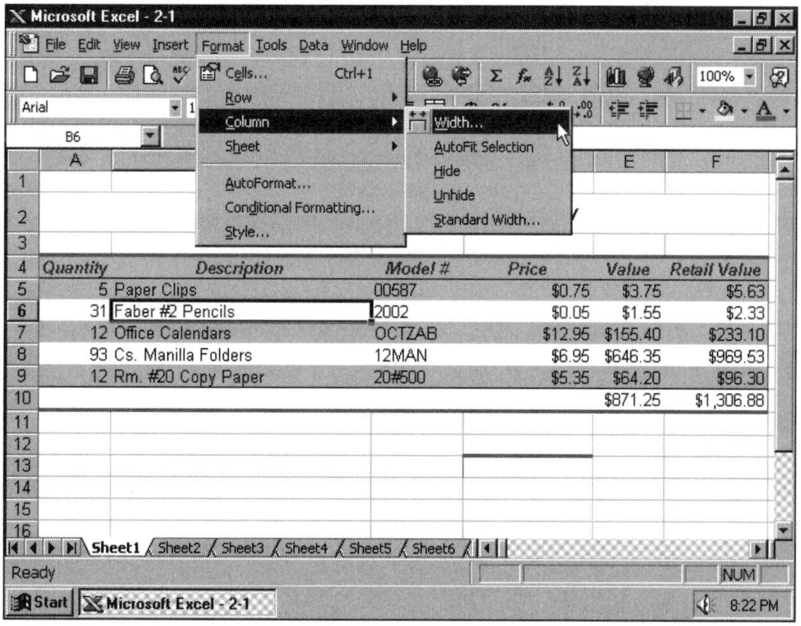

Figure 11.23

Formatting columns

The Column options provide you with the following choices:

- *Width.* This option lets you modify the selected columns to a width based on the Normal font. When you select this option, the Column Width dialog box appears (see Figure 11.24.) You can enter a specific width in the Column Width field box.

Figure 11.24

Use the Column Width dialog box to enter a specific column width.

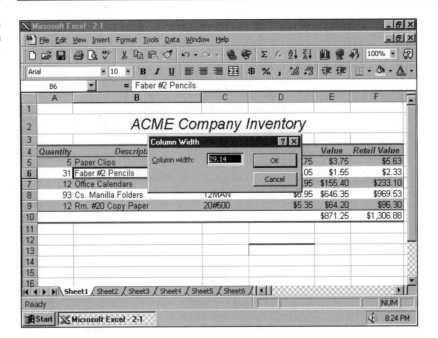

- *AutoFit Selection.* This is probably the most convenient option to use because it modifies the column widths to accommodate the widest cell contents in your selection. When you choose this option, Excel automatically increases or decreases the size of the selected columns to best fit your entries.

- *Hide.* You can hide specific columns to keep sensitive data secure. You'll learn more about this option later in this chapter.

- *Unhide.* Use this option to unhide hidden columns. This option is discussed in more detail later.

- *Standard Width.* This option lets you select the default standard column width for the selected columns. When you select this option, the Standard Width dialog box appears (see Figure 11.25). You can press Enter or click on OK to accept the default width. Or, you can change the default column width by changing the

Figure 11.25

You can change the standard column width in the Standard Width box.

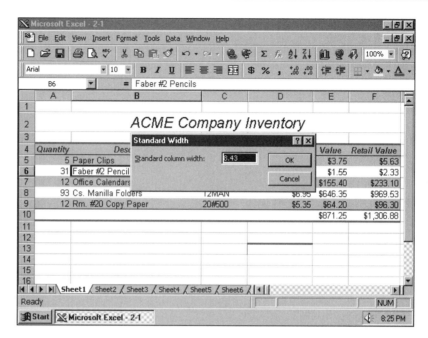

value in the Standard Column Width field box. The standard column width is 8.43 characters, the number of characters that can be displayed in the cell in the normal font.

3. Press Enter or click on OK to accept your choice.

TIP. *To change columns quickly, use your mouse. Select the columns you want to modify and move the pointer onto the column separator directly to the right of the column heading (see Figure 11.26). Drag the column left or right until the column is the width that you want. Release the mouse button.*

TIP. *If you want to fit the column to the widest cell entry, move your mouse pointer to the column heading and double-click on the right column separator. This automatically modifies the selected column to fit the widest entry.*

Hiding Columns

Sometimes you may have a worksheet that others will need to review, but you don't necessarily need to display all of the detail which factored into the result columns. You can handle this by hiding the columns containing the data that others won't find useful. To hide selected columns of data, choose Format, Column, Hide. Excel automatically hides the selected columns. To reveal a hidden column, select the cells that span the hidden column and choose Format, Column, Unhide. The hidden column appears.

Figure 11.26

Move the mouse pointer to the column separator in the column heading to modify column widths.

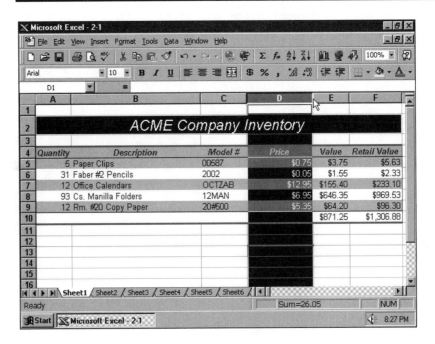

TIP. *To hide a column using the mouse, move the mouse pointer over the column separator that is to the right of the column heading you want to hide. When the pointer changes to a two-headed pointer, drag the column separator left until it is past the separator on its left.*

Reverse the process to unhide the column. Move the pointer until it touches the column separator on the right of a hidden column. The pointer then changes to a two-headed pointer with space between the two heads. Move the pointer so that its left tip touches the column separator, and drag the separator to the right. Release the mouse button, and the column is revealed.

Modifying Rows

Row size also might be a problem for the type of data you use. The standard row height, for example, usually is not large enough to display readable text or make large enough worksheet titles. You also might want to add more space between different types of numbers, such as monthly and annual totals.

You can adjust the height of rows much the same way you can columns. The standard row height is 12.75 points, enabling it to fit the default Excel font, Arial 10 point.

TIP. *If you change the point size of a font, to 20 points, for example, Excel automatically resizes the row height to fit the new font size. You do not need to adjust the row height manually.*

To change the row height of selected rows, perform the following steps:

1. Select the rows you want to resize.

2. Select Format, Row to display the pop-out menu shown in Figure 11.27.

Figure 11.27

Use the Row sub-menu to change the appearance of selected rows.

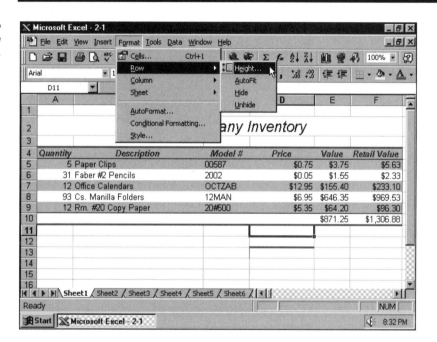

The Row options provide you with the following choices:

- *Height.* Use this option to enter a specific height for the selected rows. When you select this option, the Row Height dialog box appears (see Figure 11.28). Fill in the desired height in the Row height field box.

- *AutoFit.* Use this option to change the row height quickly to accommodate the best fit for the row. This option is nice if you don't want to mess around with changing row heights manually.

- *Hide.* This option enables you to hide selected rows. You will learn more about this later in this chapter.

- *Unhide.* This option enables you to unhide selected rows. You will learn more about this later.

Figure 11.28

Use the Row Height
dialog box to manually
adjust row height.

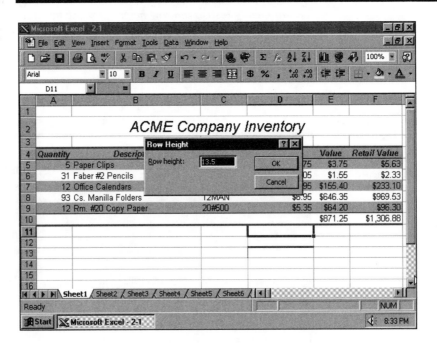

3. Press Enter or choose OK when you specify the row height in the Row
height field box.

TIP. *To change row heights quickly, use your mouse. Select the line under the
row header you want to modify and drag the pointer up or down until the row
height is what you want. Release the mouse button.*

*If you want to change the row to fit the tallest entries in a cell, move your
mouse pointer to the row heading and double-click on the row separator. This
automatically modifies the selected row to fit the tallest entry.*

Hiding Rows

If you have data entered in certain rows in your worksheets that you want to
hide, select those rows and choose Format, Row, Hide. You can reveal the
rows later by selecting the cells that span the hidden rows, as you learned earlier in this chapter.

TIP. *To hide a row using the mouse, move the mouse pointer over the row
separator that is below the row heading you want to hide. When the pointer
changes to a two-headed pointer, drag the row separator up until it is past the
separator above it.*

*Reverse the process to unhide the row. Move the pointer over the row
number that is under the hidden row until it changes to a two-headed pointer
with space between the two heads. Drag the line down to reveal the row.*

■ Mastering Borders, Patterns, and Colors

Pick up your favorite magazine and notice how the layout adds to the readability of the information. Most of the design features that professional designers employ are subtle, yet effective: colors, borders, shading, and patterns. Excel 97 helps you improve the presentation of your worksheets with these same tools.

Borders

One of the easiest ways to enhance the appearance of your worksheets is to add borders to cells or ranges of data. You can, for instance, add a border around a table of data, use borders to highlight totals, or place a border to call attention to data-entry areas on your worksheets. Excel gives you a number of different borders, as shown in Figure 11.29.

Figure 11.29

Use borders to enhance
your worksheets.

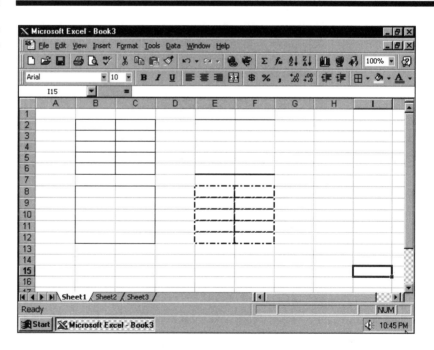

The quickest way to add a border to a selected cell or range of cells is to use the Border button on the Formatting toolbar:

1. Select the cell or range of cells that you want to enclose in a border.

2. Click on the down arrow on the Border button to display the borders list box (see Figure 11.30).

Figure 11.30

Click on the down arrow on the Borders button to display the border choices

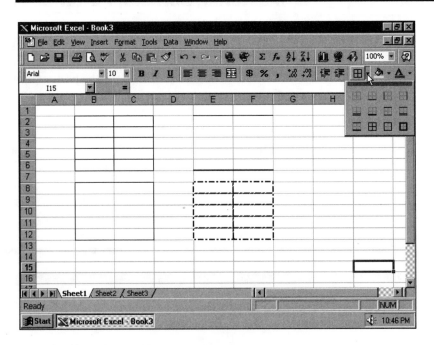

3. Pick the border style you want to use and click on it. This places the selected border around your selection.

TIP. *One of the features of Excel is the use of tear-off menus and tools. If you plan to use the Border button several times in succession, you can "tear" it off the toolbar and let it float on your desktop. To do this, click on the down arrow on the Border button, grab the dark bar at the top of the border list with your mouse, and drag it to some place convenient on your desktop. When you release the mouse button, the border list floats on your worksheet, waiting for you to use it.*

Another way to select borders for your worksheets is to use the Border tab in the Format Cells dialog box. To access this dialog box, select Format, Cell, and click on the Border tab (see Figure 11.31).

The Border tab contains the following options:

- Use the Presets section (None, Outline, and Inside) to select pre-set selections of border lines to modify.

- The Border section contains a number of buttons that let you select which lines in the border you want displayed. You can even select a diagonal line that crosses through the cell as part of a border.

Figure 11.31

Use the Border tab to fine-
tune borders.

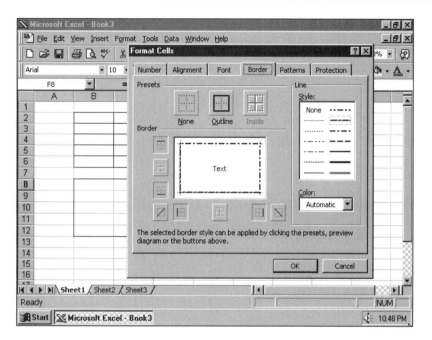

Figure 11.31

Use the Border tab to fine-tune borders.

- The Style box lets you choose from a variety of line styles.

- Use the Color drop-down list box to choose a color for your border lines.

Patterns

Another effective tool for formatting your worksheets is the use of patterns. Excel allows you to use patterns that add background effects to your lists, tables, and other entries. The patterns can be used for your print-outs and for your on-screen or visual presentations. You can, for example, output your worksheet to Microsoft PowerPoint and use it in an overhead presentation. To make your worksheets more visually stimulating, experiment with patterns until you find ones that do not overpower the information in your sheets, but instead add to their effectiveness.

To apply patterns to your worksheets, use the Patterns tab in the Format Cells dialog box. Excel gives you many different types of patterns to choose from. To add a pattern to your selection, select Format, Cells, and click on the Patterns tab (see Figure 11.32).

Click on the Pattern pull-down list box and examine the various types of patterns available to you. You can see an example of each one by clicking on it and looking at the Sample area of the dialog box. When you decide on a

Figure 11.32

Apply patterns and
shading to selected cells
with the Patterns tab.

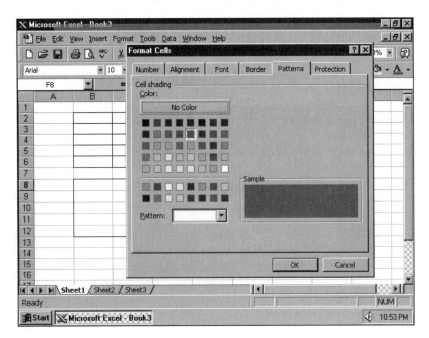

pattern, press Enter or click on OK. The pattern is applied to the worksheet
selections.

TIP. *You might want to set off a row, column, or specific cells that should not
contain any data. To help you and others keep from entering data into these
cells, use a pattern, such as a diagonal pattern, that makes it impossible to read
the data.*

Colors

As you have seen, you can apply several different formatting enhancements
to your worksheets in Excel. Probably the most effective and underused feature is color. You can brighten your on-screen presentations by effectively
using color to point out areas of interest, key data points, or data-entry areas.

CAUTION! *Although you should use as much color and shading as you can to
enhance your worksheets, you should keep in mind your printing limitations. If
you have a black-and-white printer, you cannot, of course, print color images.*

*Many times, these colors are converted to grayscale images when you try
to print them. If you have key data separated by color, such as a light blue and
a yellow, these colors usually print as similar gray tones, making it nearly
impossible to distinguish them from each other. The best way to determine*

what works best for your individual situation is to experiment with different shading and colors.

To apply colors to your cells or range of cells, perform the following steps:

1. Select the cell or range to which you want to add color.

2. Select Format, Cells.

3. If you want to add color to your border, click on the Border tab and, using the Color drop-down list box, choose the color you want. If you want to add color to your pattern, click on the Patterns tab and choose the color you want from the Color area. If you want a foreground color, click on the Pattern drop-down list box and select a color.

4. Press Enter or click on OK to apply the color to your selection.

TIP. *You also can click on the Color button on the Formatting toolbar to add color to a cell. Click on the down arrow on the button and choose the color of your choice.*

If you plan to use the Color button several times, remember to tear it off the toolbar and let it float on your workspace. To do this, click on the down arrow on the Color button to display the color list. Then, grab the color list with the mouse and drag it off the toolbar. When you release the mouse button, the color list floats on your desktop, so you can use it over and over.

- *Using Functions*
- *Using the Formula Palette*
- *Using Add-Ins*
- *Financial Functions*
- *Examining Statistical Functions*
- *Math and Trigonometry Functions*
- *Working with Text Functions*

- *Using Lookup and Reference Functions*
- *Working with Information Functions*
- *Logical Functions*
- *Troubleshooting Excel Functions*
- *Linking Functions*

12

Mastering Excel Functions

This chapter introduces you to excel 97 for windows 95 functions. *Functions* are tools you can use to analyze data and get information, which will be expressed in the form of values. These values result from a calculation or group of calculations performed on information from your worksheets. Put another way, functions help answer your questions, so that you can evaluate and examine your business, and make projections.

In this chapter, you will learn about the following:

- Using functions

- Using the Formula Palette

- Using add-ins

- Various mathematical and text functions

- Troubleshooting Excel functions

- Linking functions

If you are new to functions, you will find the first part of this chapter most helpful. If you are experienced with functions, you might want to go directly to the section containing the functions that you want to apply to your workbooks.

This chapter begins with a discussion of what functions are, and of the concepts behind them. Throughout this section you will use sample worksheets and workbooks and have an opportunity to practice using several popular functions. The use, purpose, and syntax of each function is explained step by step.

For many of the function categories available in Excel, you will learn about several functions and see examples of how to use them. The following functions are covered in this chapter:

- **Financial.** FV is the future value. CUMIPMT is the cumulative interest payment. CUMPRINC is the cumulative principal payment. EFFECT is the effective annual interest rate. AMORDEGRC is the depreciation that prorates assets for accounting periods. AMORLINC is the depreciation that calculates on the life of assets for accounting periods.

- **Statistical.** AVERAGE averages a group of values. SUM adds a group of values. MAX returns the largest number in a group. MIN returns the smallest number in a group. RANK ranks values from largest to smallest, or vice versa.

- **Math and Trigonometry.** MEDIAN returns the median in a group of values. ABS returns an absolute value for a number or range of numbers. COUNTIF counts the number of cells in a range, if they are not blank and if certain conditions are satisfied. EVEN and ODD round numbers to the nearest integer as even or odd. MOD returns the remainder of a division calculation. PI returns the value of pi. ROMAN converts Arabic numerals to Roman numerals. ROUND rounds numbers to specific levels. ROUNDDOWN rounds numbers down. ROUNDUP rounds numbers up. SUMIF adds cells based on given criteria. POWER raises a number to a specific power. PRODUCT sums a group of numbers.

- **Text.** CONCATENATE merges text from multiple locations into one item. DOLLAR formats numbers as text, with the currency format. FIXED formats numbers with a fixed number of decimal places. LEFT and RIGHT extract a certain number of characters from the left or right of a string of characters. UPPER, LOWER, and PROPER change the case for the display of text. UPPER displays in all uppercase, LOWER displays in all lowercase, and PROPER displays the first character of each word capitalized. TRIM removes spaces from strings of text.

- **Lookup and Reference.** ADDRESS returns information about the cell address of a reference. AREAS returns a value about an area in a reference. CHOOSE returns a value based on an index number and a list of values. MATCH returns the location of a string in an array. HLOOKUP returns a value for an indicated cell from the top row of an array. VLOOKUP returns a value from the left-most column of an array.

- **Information.** CELL returns information about a cell and its contents. COUNTBLANK counts blank cells in a range or array. INFO returns information about your system, environment, and setup. ISEVEN and ISODD return values of TRUE or FALSE based on whether a value is even or odd. N converts numbers to other formats for use in other spreadsheet programs. TYPE returns a numeric value based on the type of information contained in a cell.

- **Logical.** AND and IF return TRUE or FALSE values about a statement or calculation. AND needs all arguments to be true to return a TRUE value. NOT reverses the logic of an argument: true arguments become false, and vice versa. OR returns a TRUE value if any statement in a set of statements separated by OR is true (otherwise FALSE is returned). TRUE and FALSE return TRUE and FALSE as values.

- **Database and List.** SQLREQUEST allows connection with an outside data source and runs a query from Excel, returning the result as an array done without macros. SUBTOTAL returns subtotals from lists or databases.

- **Date and Time.** DAYS360 returns the number of days between two dates in a 360-day year (if your accounting year is based on 12 30-day months). WEEKDAY converts a serial number to a day of the week. YEARFRAC returns a fraction figured on the number of days between two dates.

■ Using Functions

Simple calculations, such as adding or subtracting, are performed on a number or series of numbers by using simple formulas. The simple formula SUM(A1..A5), for instance, inserts the sum of the numbers contained in the range A1..A5 into the cell containing the formula. These formulas are the foundation of many functions. Other functions use a combination of several formulas or procedures to achieve a desired result.

Functions, like formulas, all follow the same basic format:

- They must begin with an equal sign (=).

- The function name must be entered.

- Information about a cell or range of cells to be analyzed must be included.

- Arguments about what to do with the selected range of cells are entered last.

Some functions need additional information, and those examples will be discussed as they arise. For example, the following is the syntax for the AD-DRESS function, which returns a value about a cell address in a worksheet:

```
ADDRESS(row_number,column_number,absolute_number,al,sheet_text)
```

The arguments row_number and column_number are required arguments, and the remainder of the arguments are optional.

Some functions permit a variable number of arguments; for instance, you can use as many arguments in the SUM function as necessary. You can incorporate up to 1,024 arguments in a function, as long as no single string of characters in the function statement exceeds 255 characters.

Functions can be entered into worksheets manually, with a macro, or by using the Formula Palette.

■ Using the Formula Palette

One of the most exciting tools Excel 97 has is the Formula Palette, which replaces the Formula Palette found in Excel 95. It makes functions easier to use and understand by organizing them into logical categories, and by prompting you to complete the arguments required to make the function return a correct value.

The Formula Palette can opened two ways. Clicking on the Paste Function button on the Standard toolbar (see Figure 12.1) opens the Formula Palette. You can also click on the Edit Function button on the formula bar (the equal sign icon). This button works the same way as the Standard toolbar button.

You also can open the Formula Palette by choosing Function from the Insert menu. This displays the Paste Function dialog box, from which you choose a function to use; clicking on the OK button in the Paste Function dialog box opens the Formula Palette, which then helps you complete the function. A keyboard shortcut for opening the Paste Function dialog box is Shift+F3. Yet another way to open the palette is to enter the name of the function in a cell and press Ctrl+A.

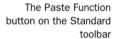

Figure 12.1

The Paste Function button on the Standard toolbar

Paste Function

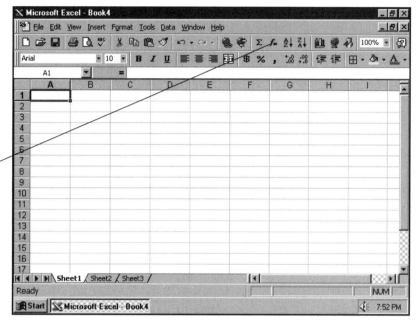

Clicking on either the Paste Function button or the Edit Function button, using the pull-down menu, and using the keyboard method all produce the same result—the Paste Function dialog box opens and allows you to choose a function, or the Formula Palette opens directly. You can see the Paste Function dialog box in Figure 12.2 and the Formula Palette in Figure 12.3.

The most recently used category of functions also appears in the Category window of the Paste Function dialog box. This is especially useful if you use a particular group of functions regularly (the list changes and maintains the last 10 functions used). When a function is highlighted, its name, a brief description, and its arguments are displayed below the category list.

After you choose a function in the Paste Function dialog box, clicking on the OK button advances you to the second step: entering arguments or instructions for calculation with the Function Palette.

If you invoke the Function Palette by typing an equal sign and the name of the function, and then pressing Shift+F3, typing the name in lowercase validates the function name. If the name is entered correctly, Excel will convert it to uppercase automatically. If the entered name is incorrect or invalid, Excel will insert a plus sign and leave the invalid name in lowercase.

Figure 12.2

The Paste Function dialog box

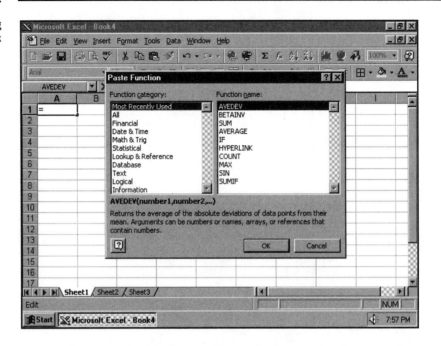

Figure 12.3

The Formula Palette

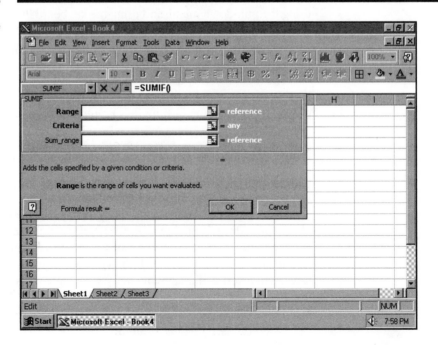

Arguments that require cell addresses or range information can be entered by keyboard or mouse. Other arguments that are not associated with specific cells on the worksheet must be entered manually. Some arguments are required for a value to be returned, and some are optional. Arguments that are required appear in bold. Optional arguments appear in regular typeface. In Figure 12.3, Range and Criteria are required arguments, while Sum_range is optional.

The buttons at the bottom of the first screen in the Formula Palette are Help, OK, and Cancel. If you get stuck on a particular function, click on the Help button. The Office Assistant will appear to walk you through either the Formula Palette or the particular function with which you are working. Cancel closes the Formula Palette completely, unless you are nesting a function. If you are nesting a function, it cancels only that function.

Tip. When you want to edit a function using the Function Palette, click on the cell containing the function to edit and press Shift+F3. This invokes the Formula Palette and takes you directly to the Step 2 of 2 dialog box, with all the arguments in the edit boxes.

■ Using Add-Ins

Some functions require add-ins to work. An *add-in* is a file that can be installed from the Tools menu, enabling additional commands and functions. The following are add-ins that come with Excel:

- AccessLinks Add-in lets you use Excel data tables as data sources for Access forms and reports.

- Analysis ToolPak is used for financial and engineering functions, and provides additional tools for statistical and engineering applications.

- AutoSave performs timed saves to disk while you work.

- Bookshelf Integration lets you use Microsoft Bookshelf with Excel workbooks.

- Conditional Sum Wizard helps you to sum certain data in Excel data lists.

- File Conversion Wizard helps you convert files into Excel 97 format.

- Internet Assistant Wizard lets you create Internet HTML pages with Excel.

- Lookup Wizard helps you find data within lists of data in Excel.

- MS Query is used to query external programs for data; it is provided for compatibility with Excel 5 but is not otherwise needed with Excel 97.

- ODBC (Open Data Base Connectivity) Add-In is a collection of worksheet and macro functions for retrieving data from external database files.

- Report Manager prints reports based on views and scenarios.

- Solver is installed at setup, allowing you to analyze what-if scenarios based on changing information.

- Template Utilities let you manipulate and work with Excel templates.

- Template Wizard with Data Tracking provides a Template Palette that accesses and tracks data.

- Update Add-In Links modifies workbooks that use links to add-ins, so that they can use built-in functions in Excel that provide the same functionality.

- Web Form Wizard assists with creating forms based on Excel worksheets that can be used to survey Internet users.

See Chapter 13 for a more detailed explanation of add-ins.

Note. Add-ins are located in the Excel LIBRARY directory or one of its subdirectories. If an add-in does not appear in the Tools, Add-Ins menu selection, Microsoft Excel Setup will help you install it.

■ Financial Functions

Excel has over 50 "canned" financial functions available for use in worksheets. Many of them require the use of add-ins. If a function does not appear, you may need to find out which add-ins are installed in the Tools, Add-Ins menu selection. A good example of financial functions is the Future Value function.

The Future Value Function (FV)

FV, the Future Value function, calculates the future value of an investment. The syntax used for this function is the following:

```
=FV(rate, nper, pmt, pv, type)
```

The required arguments are **rate** (the current percentage rate fixed for the term of the investment), **nper** (the number of periods of payment), and **pmt** (the payment amount per period). In the optional arguments, **pv** is the present value of a lump sum of future payments, and **type** is 0 or 1, depending on whether payments are due at the beginning or end of a period.

Figure 12.4 shows the process of finding the future value of a monthly $100.00 payment into an annuity that yields 10 percent over a five-year period, with payments at the end of each period.

Using the function with worksheet cell addresses rather than values typed into the Formula Palette lets you to change numbers to see the effect of different interest rates, payment amounts, or terms, without having to re-enter the entire function or go through all the Palette's steps.

To perform this calculation yourself, enter the rate of the annuity in cell I2 (expressed as an annual percentage), the number of months in cell I3, the payment into cell I4 as a negative number (negative payments are those you pay out in most Excel financial functions), and the starting value of the annuity (the *present value*, or *PV*) into cell I5.

Figure 12.4

Using the Formula Palette
to complete the FV
function

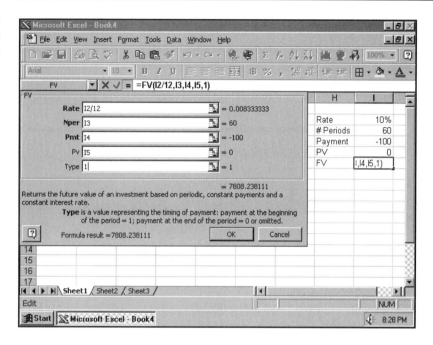

Then, enter the following in I6:

```
=FV(I2/12,I3,I4,I5,1)
```

Now you can enter all the pertinent information into your equation and see immediate results. Try performing the function using the manual typing method (use lowercase letters for function validation), and then do the same thing using the Formula Palette.

Manually typing the functions is usually more time-consuming and cumbersome than using the Formula Palette. Shorter, more frequently used functions can be faster and easier to enter using the keyboard, though. Experimenting with both methods will allow you to find the most effective way to use your software.

Notice in the formula entry that the payment value is negative. This is important to several financial functions because the functions return negative values, which can be confusing. Adding the negatives to the function cell references allows you to enter positive numbers, which might make more sense to the average user. If you are setting up a worksheet for a person who is not familiar with functions or financial analysis, this is a good idea. The negative references can be entered from the keyboard or prior to cell selection using the Formula Palette.

To use the Formula Palette to enter the FV function, you first select the cell that will contain the answer (in our example, this is I6.) Next, click on the Paste Function button in the Standard toolbar, which brings up the Paste Function dialog box shown in Figure 12.5. Select the Financial entry in the Function Category list box and then the FV function in the Function Name list box, then click on the OK button to continue. You will now see the Formula Palette shown in Figure 12.6.

Figure 12.5

Using the Paste Function dialog box to find the function you need

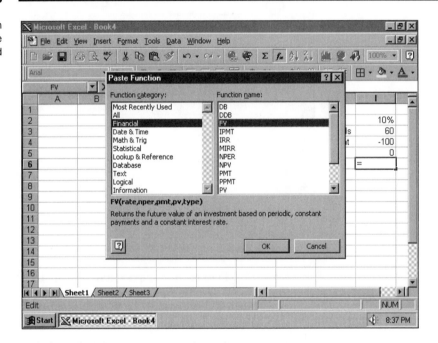

After you select the function, the Formula Palette guides you through completing it properly. For each argument of the function, you first click in the field of the argument (such as Rate) and then select the cell that contains the data for that argument with your mouse, or enter the data for the argument manually. Figure 12.4 shows you the correct entries for the FV function in the Formula Palette.

Upon completion of argument entry, the value of the FV function is displayed next to an equal sign in an area below the argument entries. In the example shown in Figure 12.4, the answer 7808.238111 appears. Use this displayed result to check your work before clicking on the Formula Palette's OK button to complete the formula.

Figure 12.6

The Formula Palette

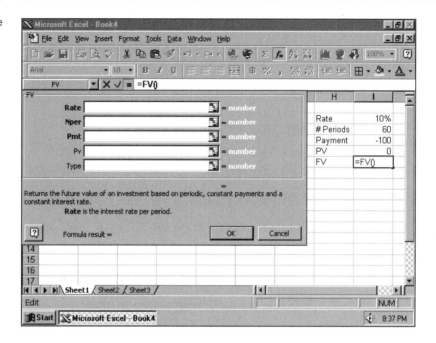

The CUMIPMT Function

The CUMIPMT function returns a value that represents the cumulative interest paid between two periods. It is one of the functions that require the Analysis ToolPak add-in.

If you borrowed $1,000.00 from the bank at a 13.5 percent interest rate for a term of two years beginning on March 1, and you want to know how much interest you have paid for a calendar year, this function does the job.

The syntax of CUMIPMT is the following:

```
=CUMIPMT(rate,nper,pv,start_period,end_period,type)
```

All the arguments are required for this function: **rate** is the interest rate, **nper** is the number of payments per period, **pv** is the present value, **start_period** is the number of the first period to calculate from, **end_period** is the number of the period to complete the calculation, and **type** is either 0 or 1 based on whether payment is made at the beginning or the end of each period.

To compose the function, enter the following:

```
=cumipmt(13.5%/12,12*2,1000,1,10,1)
```

Warning. As you enter formulas and function statements, pay close attention to spacing in the formula bar. An added space or missed comma can result in errors in the results, or in commands that do not execute.

The resulting value (shown as a negative number) is the cumulative amount of interest in the 10-month period between March and December that you paid on your $1,000.00 loan: $81.27799685.

You can use the Formula Palette to create your own interest-payment evaluation function. Then you can determine what the benefits of borrowing money over certain periods of time at various interest rates might have on your corporate or personal finances.

The CUMPRINC Function

The CUMPRINC function takes the CUMIPMT function one step further. It returns the value of the principal paid on a loan during a period of time. The two functions can be used together on one sheet because they share the same arguments and structure. Use the previous loan example and type the following:

```
=CUMPRINC(13.5%/12,2*12,1000,1,10,0)
```

This returns a value of 391.18 for the total principal paid in the 10-month period between March and December. Click on the cell, and click on the $ button in the Formatting toolbar to display the value as currency.

The EFFECT Function

The EFFECT function returns the effective annual interest rate, given the nominal interest rate and the number of compounding periods per year. For an annual interest rate of 18.25 percent that is compounded four times per year, the syntax is the following:

```
=EFFECT(18.25%,4)
```

With this function, the effective interest rate is 19.54 percent.

■ Examining Statistical Functions

Statistical functions frequently return values about arrays of data or groups of numbers. The example here provides you with a foundation of how statistical functions can help you look at data in interesting ways.

The AVERAGE Function

The AVERAGE function returns the arithmetic mean of a group of numbers. This function can have up to 30 arguments, and arguments can be names of cell ranges or of individual cells.

TIP. *Blank cells in an array to be averaged are counted and figured into the average, unless the cell has been designated as empty. Empty cells are not counted. To check or change the zero values options, select Options from the Tools menu. In the View tab, check or clear the Zero Values checkbox. The Zero values checkbox controls whether zeros display always with a zero, while blanks display as blank. Clearing this checkbox means that zero value cells are displayed as blank.*

For this example, you will create a worksheet with information about a group of salespeople. The example in Figure 12.7 shows the basic information that you will build on to learn about statistical functions.

Figure 12.7

The sales worksheet

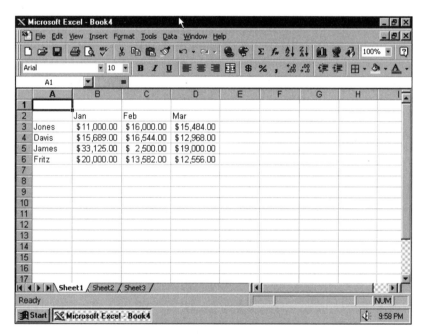

There are four salespeople listed, with three columns of information adjacent to each name. Each column represents one month's sales. To place headers on the worksheet, type Jan in cell B2. Click once with the mouse on that cell and, using the AutoFill handle, drag it across the other columns from B to D to fill in Feb and Mar. If the result is ####s across your cells, double-click on the right edge of the column header to adjust the width of the columns.

To continue formatting this sheet, highlight cells B3 to H13. This is the range of cells you will use for the statistical analysis, where currency format is important. On the Standard toolbar, click on the $ button. See Table 12.1 for the sales-worksheet data.

Table 12.1

Data for Sales Worksheet

SALESPERSON	JAN	FEB	MAR
Jones	11,000	16,000	15,484
Davis	15,689	16,544	12,968
James	33,125	2,500	19,000
Fritz	20,000	13,582	12,556

The SUM Function

In analyzing sales performance, sales totals are critical. You can add quarterly and monthly totals to your worksheet quickly by using one of Excel's most popular functions, the SUM function. It even has its own button on the Standard toolbar. In your worksheet, below the names in column A, skip one row and type **Total:** in cell A8. Then, in cell F2 of the column to the right of the Averages Column, enter **Quarterly Total** as the heading of the new column. Position the mouse on cell F3, and, holding down the left mouse button, highlight the cells to cell F6. Then move the cursor over to cell B8, hold down the Ctrl key on the keyboard, and highlight the cells from B8 to F8. You now should have two separate ranges of cells highlighted (see Figure 12.8).

Once you have your ranges highlighted, on the Standard toolbar, click on Σ, the Greek letter sigma that represents the SUM function. Excel automatically totals the number in the rows and columns you have selected, and returns the values. The SUM button on the toolbar can save a lot of time when you need to total up large worksheets and projects.

The AVERAGE Function

For this example, you will find out what the average sales amount is for each representative. Begin by clicking on the cell in the first empty column of data, on the same row as salesperson Jones. This is cell E3. On the Standard toolbar, click on the Paste Function button. Choose function category Statistical and function name AVERAGE, and click on the OK button. You now see the Formula Palette. Click inside the Number1 field in the Formula Palette, and then click on the button to the far right of the Number1 field to temporarily move the Formula Palette out of your way. You can now drag to select cells B3 through D3. Press Enter to redisplay the Formula Palette and then click on the Palette's OK button to complete the entry. The keyboard

Figure 12.8

The cells prior to clicking
the SUM button

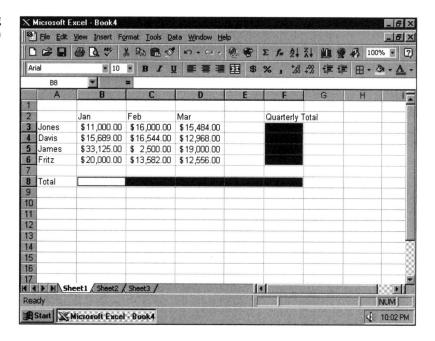

entry is **=AVERAGE(B3:D3)**. The value returned by the formula is the sum
of cells B3 through D3, divided by the number of entries in the range:
$14,161.33.

You can complete the averages for the rest of the salespeople by using
the AutoFill feature. To do this, click on E3, the cell for the average of the
first person, and position the cursor over the fill handle in the lower right corner of the cell. Then, hold down the left mouse button, and drag the pointer
down to include cells E4, E5, and E6. The averages automatically fill in for
the remainder of the sales force (see Figure 12.9).

The next step is determining what the high sales month was for each
salesperson.

The MAX Function

Of course, it is easy to look at the sheet and determine what the current high
number is for each person, but you might want to monitor these figures over a
period of months or years to determine the top month of each one. (There also
is a formula to look at the lowest month.) The MAX function is the answer.

In cell G2, type the heading **High** and press Enter. The active cell is now
G3. On the Standard toolbar, click on the Insert Function button.

Figure 12.9

The sales worksheet,
showing totals and
averages

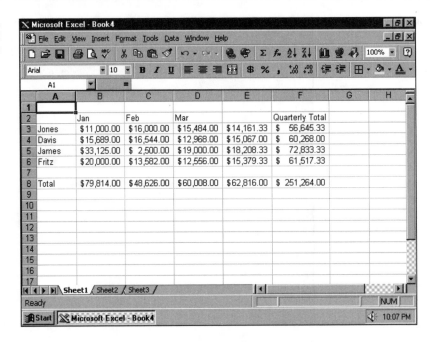

Select function category Statistical and function name MAX, and click on the OK button. The Palette prompts you for the first argument entry, which should be set to be cells B3 through D3. Click on the button at the far right of the Number1 field to shrink the Palette and then position your pointer on B3, hold down the left mouse button, and drag to cell D3. Click Enter to redisplay the Formula Palette, and then click on its OK button to complete the entry. The result, $16,000.00, is the highest value in the range for salesperson Jones.

You can use the AutoFill feature again to complete the rest of the sales staff's MAX months and provide a new entry for the MAX month for the company's total sales. Position the mouse on cell G3, click once to make G3 the active cell, and position the pointer to the lower right corner of the cell until the pointer changes to a small, black +. While holding down the left mouse button, drag the pointer down to cell G8. This action AutoFills the MAX function in all the highlighted cells, returning the maximum values for each representative and then for the entire company. (You will have a zero-value-formatted cell in G7; move to G7 and press the Del key to clean this up.) Figure 12.10 shows the result of the MAX function.

Figure 12.10

The MAX function results

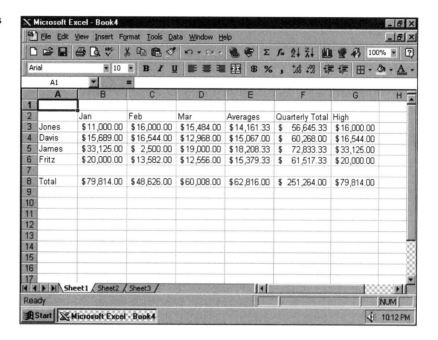

The MIN Function

The MIN function is the opposite of MAX: it returns the smallest numeric value found in a range of cells. MIN uses the same arguments and syntax.

In cell H2, type **Low** and press Enter. Your active cell is now H3. Type **=min(B3:D3)** and press Enter. The dollar amount for salesperson Jones is returned, and the active cell is now H4. Click again on cell H3 and, from the lower right corner, AutoFill the rest of the salespeople and company information with the MIN function. The MAX and MIN function columns for sales are now complete.

The RANK Function

Now that you have calculated what the highs and lows are for both the salespeople and the company, you can use the RANK function to assign a numeric rank to each person, based on his or her sales. Click on cell A2 to make it active. Type the header for that column, **Q1 Rank**, and press Enter. In cell A3, click Paste Function on the Standard toolbar. Statistical Functions should still be active, if that was the last function category used. Select RANK from the function name box, and click on the OK button.

The Formula Palette is now active, and the first argument is the number you want to rank. Because our heading was First Quarter Rank, you should choose the Quarterly Total cell for Jones, which is in cell F3. Enter F3 in the field Number and press Tab to move to the next argument. The next argument is called Ref, which indicates the numbers to compare to the first argument, or the total for the quarter.

With the Ref edit box active, enter **$F$3:$F$6**. This creates the reference for the first representative's monthly total compared to all other salespeople. Press Tab to move to the last edit box in the Formula Palette, and type **0**. Note that the result value in the Palette is now filled in.

In order to rank the remainder of the salespeople, we can use the Auto-Fill feature to drag the function to the other cells.

Tip. In the order field, Excel ranks in ascending order for non-zero characters, and in descending order for zero characters.

The MEDIAN Function

The value returned by the MEDIAN function represents the number in the middle of a set of values. In other words, half the numbers in the set have values that are higher than the median, and half have values that are lower. This is similar to averages, yet the median is not representative of a calculation on a value or values in a worksheet. It is simply the middle value from a group.

To add the MEDIAN function to our sales-analysis spreadsheet, click once on cell J2. Type the heading for this column, **Median Mo.** Press Enter, moving the active cell to I3. Enter the formula **=median(b3:d3)** and press Enter.

Figure 12.11 shows what the finished sheet should look like.

■ Math and Trigonometry Functions

Excel has almost 60 different mathematical and trigonometric functions available for use in worksheet analysis. Several of these are discussed in the following sections.

The ABS Function

The ABS function returns the absolute value of a number: that is, the number without its sign. This function can be used in calculations that require positive numbers in order to work properly. For instance, the result of =ABS(-10) is 10. The result of =ABS(10) is also 10. The ABS function always returns a positive number.

The ABS function is useful in a number of cases with Excel. Any time a function correctly returns a negative number but you want your worksheet to display a positive number, use the ABS function.

Figure 12.11

The completed Sales
worksheet showing the
MEDIAN function results

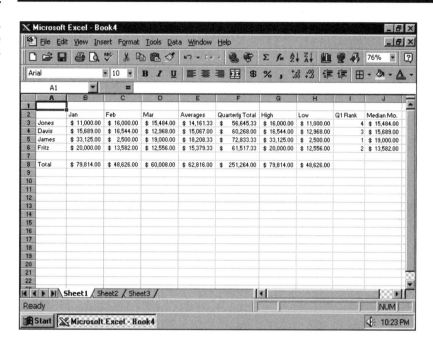

The ABS function is useful when nesting functions. Suppose you have a
SUM function that returns a negative value, such as =SUM(-10,-20) (or the
equivalent with cell references in place of the negative numbers). Using
=ABS(SUM(-10,-20)) returns 30 instead of –30.

The COUNTIF Function

The COUNTIF function examines a range of nonblank cells and counts the
number of cells that match certain criteria. In the sales worksheet example, if
each salesperson had to sell $10,000 every month to reach his or her quota,
and you wanted to have a column in your sheet that indicates how many
months they reach their goals in a certain time period, COUNTIF is the perfect function to use. The syntax of the COUNTIF function is:

```
=COUNTIF(range_to_be_counted,criteria)
```

To add this entry to your sheet, make cell K2 active by clicking on it.
Then type the heading **# Mths. > Quota** and press Enter. Next, in cell J3 use
the formula **=COUNTIF(B3:D3,">10000").**

The result is the number of months that Jones finished above quota, or
with sales over $10,000. Using AutoFill, position the mouse pointer on the
lower right corner of cell J3 until the cursor becomes a plus sign. Holding

down the left mouse button, drag the highlight box down to include cells J4, J5, and J6. The calculations will now appear.

You can use different criteria with COUNTIF. You can, for instance, use the less than (<), less than or equal to (<=), equal to (=), and greater than or equal to (>=).

You can also use COUNTIF with text entries. You can, for example, examine a range of text entries that lists sales by customer. Simply enter a customer's name for the criteria argument (surrounded by quotes as in the preceding example) to count how many sales were made to a particular customer.

The EVEN and ODD Functions

The EVEN and ODD functions are both simple and useful for certain applications. The syntax is the following:

```
=even(number)
```

   or

```
=odd(number)
```

The EVEN function takes a number, or extracts a number from a cell reference, and rounds it up to the nearest whole even number. The ODD function does the same, rounding it up to the nearest odd whole number.

This function might be useful for an inventory/ordering worksheet in which particular stock items are shipped in quantities of two only. A customer ordering one item could be notified of this upon order entry. You can accomplish this by having the quantity ordered in one column, and the shipping quantity (with the function performed on its contents) drawn from the quantity-ordered cell.

The MOD Function

MOD is a function that returns the remainder from division of a number (the remainder of a division is called the *modulo*). This calculation can be used in figuring a check digit for an account number for security purposes. For example, you might create a formula that takes a customer's telephone number, divides it by a constant number, and adds the remainder to the end of the phone number as a verification.

The syntax for MOD is the following:

```
=mod(number,divisor).
```

Using the previous example, if a customer's phone number is 555-1212 and you chose 8 as your special divisor, the formula =mod(5551212,8) will return a value of 4. The customer account number would be 55512124. The worksheet uses the MOD function and the CONCATENATE function from the Text function category. The former returns the remainder, and the latter returns the value needed for displaying the account number as one complete number. The CONCATENATE function is discussed in more detail later in this chapter.

First, set up a column for phone numbers (in this example, column A, cell 3), a column for the remainder (column B, cell 3), and a column for the new account number (column C, cell 3). When the phone number is entered in the first cell, the function automatically figures the remainder and joins the original number with the remainder in the third column.

The PI Function

PI is one of the few function selections that does not require any arguments. It can be used in formulas or calculations to return special values. The geometric equation for figuring the circumference of a circle is π (pi) multiplied by its diameter. The syntax for this calculation is the following:

```
=pi()*12
```

where the value 12 is the diameter of the circle whose circumference you wish to obtain.

The ROMAN Function

The ROMAN function takes numeric values and converts them to Roman numerals, and it can display the numerals in one of five different formats. The ROMAN function can convert numbers up to a maximum of 3,999, and it can convert only positive values. Negative values, and those exceeding 3,999, return the #value! error message.

The syntax for using the ROMAN function is the following:

```
=roman(number,style)
```

where **number** is the numeric value you wish to convert, and **style** is a number from 0 to 4. Style 0 is the Classic Roman style, and 1 through 4 are variations that yield more concise displays.

The ROUND Function

ROUND is a straightforward function that takes a number and rounds it to a specified number of decimal places. The rounding feature is important for many calculations, because the values that come from calculations might be different from the rounded number.

The syntax for the ROUND function is the following:

```
=round(number,num_digits)
```

If num_digits is less than 0, the number is rounded to the left of the decimal. If it is 0, the number is rounded to the nearest integer. If it is greater than 0, it is rounded to that number of decimal places.

The POWER Function

The POWER function returns the result of a number raised to a power. If you want to take the number 10 to the second power, for example, the keyboard entry to your selected cell is **=power(10,2)**, and the result is 100. You can accomplish the same result in Excel by typing **=10^2**.

The SUMIF Function (with PRODUCT)

The SUMIF function adds values from a list of numeric values, provided that certain criteria are met. This is an interesting function with many potential uses. Revisiting the sales worksheet used earlier in this chapter, if your company has a bonus program for salespeople that is calculated as a percentage of total sales over quota, the SUMIF function can help you calculate the bonuses automatically.

For example, if you pay a quarterly bonus of 1/2 percent of total sales for those salespeople who exceed their quota of $10,000 for a given month, the SUMIF syntax is the following:

```
=PRODUCT(SUMIF(B3:D3,">=10000"),0.5%)
```

In the example, SUMIF is nested within PRODUCT, which is a function that multiplies its arguments. The result of this function yields a number that includes only those months' sales that are greater than or equal to quota (10000), and multiplies that number by 0.5 percent, which is the bonus.

■ Working with Text Functions

Text functions, unlike many of the other function types, manipulate numbers and characters for formatting, sorting, display, and computation.

The CONCATENATE Function

The CONCATENATE function can be used in a variety of different ways to extract information from worksheets. Text can be joined to form sentences about values located in your worksheet. For example, the following text:

```
Salesperson Jones averaged 14112 for the first quarter
and exceeded quota 3 times for a bonus amount of
$211.68!
```

was extracted directly from the sales worksheet using the CONCATENATE function with this syntax:

```
=CONCATENATE("Salesperson ",$B$3," averaged ",$F$3," for the first quarter ","
and exceeded quota ",$K$3," times"," for a bonus amount of ",$M$3,"!")
```

The cell references are absolute, so the function formula can be moved anywhere in the workbook and maintain integrity.

The DOLLAR Function

The DOLLAR function converts numbers into text and formats the value as currency, with any number of decimal places. The difference between using DOLLAR and formatting numeric values as currency is that Excel converts DOLLAR-formatted cells to text. The results still can be used in formulas and calculations, because Excel also converts them to numbers when it calculates.

The FIXED Function

FIXED is a text function that formats numeric values as text with a given number of decimal places. The FIXED function also can insert commas for formatting appearance. The syntax for FIXED is the following:

```
=fixed(number,decimals,no_commas)
```

and is similar to the DOLLAR function because of its text-to-numeric conversion for calculation purposes.

The LEFT and RIGHT Functions

The LEFT and RIGHT functions extract a certain number of characters from the left or right of a string of text. If the word MICROSOFT is in cell L23, for example, and you enter the function **=left(L23,5)**, the resulting value is MICRO. If you then enter the function **=right(L23,4)**, the value is SOFT.

Tip. When joining entered text and cell references, make sure to enter the two items in separate edit boxes in the Formula Palette. This is important because the Palette places quotation marks around entered text. If you have the text "Salesperson" and the cell reference in the same edit box, the result will be Salesperson $B$3, not Salesperson Jones.

The UPPER, LOWER, and PROPER Functions

The UPPER, LOWER, and PROPER functions change the case of text strings in a worksheet. UPPER and LOWER modify the entire text string. Entering **=lower("MICROSOFT CORP")** yields microsoft corp as its value, and entering **=upper("microsoft corp")** yields MICROSOFT CORP as its value. Either all uppercase or all lowercase text using PROPER capitalizes the first letter of each word and converts, if necessary, the remaining characters in the string to lowercase.

The TRIM Function

The TRIM function removes spaces from text. This function is handy if your worksheet has received data from an external source that has added too many spaces between words in a string.

Functions related to TRIM include the following:

- CLEAN removes all unprintable characters from a text string.

- MID returns a specific number of characters from a string.

- REPLACE replaces characters within a string.

- SUBSTITUTE replaces certain characters with new ones.

■ Using Lookup and Reference Functions

Lookup and reference functions return values about locations of rows, cells, columns, and data in worksheets. They can also extract information from a table.

The ADDRESS Function

The ADDRESS function returns the location of a cell as text, given the row and column numbers. The syntax used for this function is the following:

```
=address(row_num,col_num,abs_num,a1,sheet_text)
```

where **row_num** is the number of the row, **col_num** is the number of the column, **abs_num** is a value from 1 to 4 (referring to the type of reference), **a1** is a logical value that determines if the returned value is in A1 or R1C1 format, and **sheet_text** is the name of the worksheet from which to return the value.

The abs_num argument's values are the following:

- 1=Absolute value, such as $A$1

- 2=Absolute Row, Relative Column, such as $A1

- 3=Relative Row, Absolute Column, A$1
- 4=Relative reference, A1

An example of the Address function is **=address(1,1,1,1)**, which returns the value $A$1.

■ Working with Information Functions

Information functions return values based on how a cell is formatted or what it contains.

The CELL Function

CELL returns specific information about all types of numeric formats and date formats, about whether a cell is blank or contains a label or value, and even about what or where that value is. If you need to determine what the width is for cell A3, type this formula: **=cell(width,A3)**. It can give this information by individual row and column. CELL is used for compatibility with other spreadsheet programs.

The COUNTBLANK Function

The COUNTBLANK function returns a value based on how many empty or blank cells it locates in a given array. The syntax is:

```
=COUNTBLANK(range_of_cells)
```

The function returns the number of cells within the range that are blank.

The ISEVEN and ISODD Functions

Note. ISEVEN and ISODD return a #value! message if run on a cell that contains a non-numeric value. If a number is a decimal, the ISEVEN and ISODD functions test only the integer, not the value to the right of the decimal point.

The ISEVEN and ISODD functions return the values TRUE or FALSE. ISEVEN returns TRUE if a number is even and FALSE if the number is odd. ISODD, naturally, returns FALSE if a number is even and TRUE if odd.

The TYPE Function

The TYPE function is like the INFO function, except that TYPE returns values 1, 2, 4, 8, 16, and 64 only. If a selection is a number, the value is 1. If it is text, the value is 2. If it is a formula, the value is 8; if it is an error, the value is 16; and if it is an array, the value is 64. TYPE has a simple syntax:

```
=type(value)
```

The argument value can be a cell or array reference, or a direct value entered.

■ Logical Functions

Logical functions return values based on whether certain values in a worksheet are met.

The AND and IF Functions

The AND function returns a TRUE or FALSE value based on worksheet values. This can be useful if you want to display information about a number or numbers in a worksheet. AND allows up to thirty arguments. The syntax is the following:

```
=AND(logical1,logical2)
```

Logical1 and **logical2** contain the two tests that you will perform. If both are true, the AND function returns a TRUE value. If any are false, it returns a FALSE value. You can have multiple logical tests, each one separated by commas.

An example of AND would be:

```
=AND(5<6,10>11)
```

This example would return a FALSE value, because 10 is not greater than 11.

The NOT Function

The NOT function is a simple one: it reverses the logic of an equation or argument. For example, in the formula **=not(10=11)**, the returned value is TRUE. The numbers, of course, are *not* equal. The NOT function reports FALSE for the formula **=not(10=10)**.

The OR Function

The OR function, like AND, returns a TRUE or FALSE value based on its arguments. Unlike AND, however, OR returns a TRUE value if *any* argument is true, whereas AND returns a TRUE only if *all* arguments are true.

The TRUE and FALSE Functions

The TRUE and FALSE functions are among the easiest to use of all the Excel functions, because they do not require any arguments at all. They simply return the values TRUE or FALSE when entered. You can use these functions through the Formula Palette, or they can be typed directly into a worksheet. You use these functions often when doing comparisons in formulas. For example, you could use the formula

=AND(B5=TRUE(),B6=FALSE()) to test if cell B5 is TRUE and B6 is FALSE. If both conditions are met, the AND function returns a TRUE.

■ Troubleshooting Excel Functions

Tip. As you gain more comfort with Excel functions and formulas, you might find that function entry is faster from the keyboard than through the Palette. It makes little sense to use some simple functions, such as TRUE and FALSE, with the Palette. However, the Formula Palette and some of Excel's built-in features make most function entries easier and more accurate, and error recognition faster.

The process of troubleshooting functions has improved drastically over previous releases of Excel because of the Formula Palette. The Palette provides immediate feedback and prompts you through each step of the function, which can be invaluable.

When you are troubleshooting functions, the Formula Palette can do all the formatting, typing, and arranging of function statements for you. If you invoke the Insert Function dialog box and choose the function you want to use, the entry in the formula bar is made for you before any arguments are entered. After clicking on the OK button, the arguments are displayed, and after all the required functions are completed (and prior to clicking on OK), the value is displayed below the arguments in the Formula Palette. You can see the results prior to actual entry into your worksheet.

If your function returns #value!, #name!, or another error message, you can change values by moving back through the function arguments to find the cause of the problem. For newer users of Excel, the Help button can also assist you in working through problems.

As you enter functions and determine which ones you will need to analyze your worksheets and workbooks adequately and completely, the Help button brings up specific syntax notes, tips and, in many cases, examples of ways in which functions can be used. Often mistakes in value entry can be spotted by looking at Help's examples and working back through the arguments in search of the root of the problem.

As you become more comfortable with functions, entering them from the keyboard becomes more effective. If you get in the habit of entering the formula manually, Excel converts lowercase entries to all uppercase—if they are typed correctly and are function names Excel recognizes.

■ Linking Functions

Data from one sheet in a workbook can be linked to cells located in another worksheet, another workbook, or even an external source such as a database or another spreadsheet program. Sharing information between sheets can be accomplished in a variety of ways, depending on your specific needs and application.

If you have a workbook with information related to a separate workbook, and you want to use information from the first one, the first workbook is called the *source workbook*. The sheet that receives the information from this source is called the *dependent worksheet* (or *workbook*). An *external link* refers to another Excel cell, a range of cells, or a specific named region.

To create a link between workbooks, highlight the cells that you want to link in the source workbook. From the toolbar or the Edit menu, select Copy, which places a flashing dotted line around the cells that you have selected. Click on the Window menu. Select the workbook that you want to take the selected referenced cells to, and make it the active window.

In the dependent sheet—the one you want to receive the cell references—choose Paste Special from the Edit menu. In the resulting dialog box, you can choose to copy all information about the selected cells, such as formulas, formats, values, and notes, and you can perform operations on the data. If you check All and select Paste Link in the Paste Special dialog box, the entire cell group, along with its contents, will be copied to the new worksheet. Now, any time items are changed on the original or source workbook, those changes will be passed along to the dependent reference.

When you link workbooks in this manner, Excel creates absolute references in the formulas that are transferred, so that if you move the information in the workbooks, the references to the source will remain intact. Movement in either the source or dependent workbooks is protected.

Linked formulas use this syntax:

```
{='[WORKBK.XL]Worksheet_Name'!abs_cell_ref}
```

For example, the formula {='[SALES.XLS]Sales Report'!$C$4:$D$8} in the SAMPLE1.XLS workbook is dependent on SALES.XLS workbook, Sales Report worksheet, and cells C4 to D8. When those cells are updated on the source link, the dependent links will be updated automatically.

Excel will also update dynamically any charts or related information you are using that are linked to your source reference.

■ Summary

Excel 97 contains quite a few different functions, many of which can't be covered in this book due to space limitations. You've learned about the most commonly used functions in Excel 97 in this chapter, however, and can continue your exploration on your own. You should plan on spending some time browsing through the Paste Function dialog box to learn about the other functions that are present. As you click on each function, a brief description will appear in the dialog box. By browsing the functions available in this way, you will learn what functions exist, and what sorts of things they can do for you. You can also use Excel's online Help and the Office Advisor to locate additional information about Excel's functions.

- *Installing and Removing Excel Add-Ins*
- *Using the Add-Ins*
- *Using Outlining*

13

Advanced Worksheet Capabilities

M ICROSOFT EXCEL 97 HAS SOME POWERFUL ABILITIES. THIS CHAP-
ter will introduce these abilities to you so that you can use them in
your applications. The advanced features covered in this section include several add-ins and other powerful tools that are available
to Excel users.

In this chapter, you will learn about the following:

- Excel add-ins
- Installing and removing add-ins
- Using Excel's auditing features
- Changing the appearance of your worksheet
- Using outlining

After you finish this chapter, you will know how to install add-ins, use advanced features, and apply them in applications. You'll also get a chance to use some of Excel's advanced tools, such as Auditing, Report Manager, and Pivot tables.

Add-ins in Excel are worksheet tools that bring more power to your desktop. The Excel tools covered in this chapter are AutoSave, Analysis Tool-Pak, Goal Seek, Solver, Scenario Manager, View Manager, and Report Manager. A brief description of each follows:

- AutoSave: Automatically saves your work at specified intervals.
- Analysis ToolPak: Provides a number of worksheet functions and macro functions that help with data analysis in the workbook, the Function Wizard, and the Tools menu.
- Goal Seek: Helps you find values to complete questions based on a specific outcome.
- Solver: Allows you to determine answers to complex what-if questions by analyzing cells and determining the optimum value adjustments to arrive at a desired result.
- Scenario Manager: Lets you create and analyze results from various groups of changing cells. The Scenario Manager helps you define custom assumptions and answer complex what-if questions.
- View Manager: Helps you arrange and look at your information in a variety of ways.
- Report Manager: Allows you to format information contained within workbooks, worksheets, and scenarios into organized, uniform reports.

■ Installing and Removing Excel Add-Ins

To look at the available add-ins, choose Add-Ins from the Tools menu. A list of the available add-ins appears; add-ins that are installed will have their check boxes selected. You can install a new add-in by clicking on the check box to the left of its description. Removal is just as simple. To remove an add-in that is already installed, just click on the appropriate check box to make the check mark disappear.

Many add-ins bring with them menu choices. When you install an add-in, the menu options are made available; when you remove an add-in, the options are made inactive. If you use Analysis ToolPak, you can choose from over 50 additional functions.

Selecting Add-Ins from the Tools menu brings up the Add-Ins dialog box (see Figure 13.1). Note which add-ins are currently selected. For examination, click in the check boxes currently marked with an X so that all add-ins are deselected. After you do this, close the Add-Ins dialog box by clicking on the OK button. This removes the add-ins from Excel, and changes the functions, selections, and menu selections that you can access through the various menu choices on the main toolbar, from the pull-down menus, and through several of the Wizards, such as the Function Wizard.

Figure 13.1

The Add-Ins dialog box

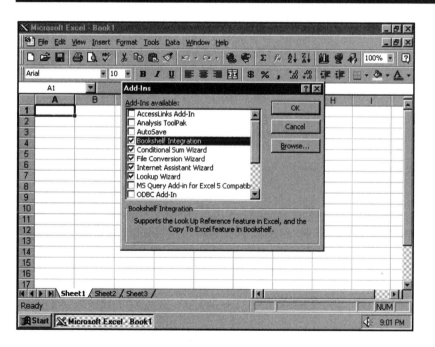

Even after you have removed all the add-ins from Excel, several of them remain available from pull-down menus, such as Solver, Goal Seek, and Scenario Manager. When they are invoked under the Tools pull-down menu, they are resubmitted to the add-ins list that Excel uses to track what is automatically loaded when starting up the software, so that the next time you use the program, the same tools are available.

Note. Using all add-ins with Excel changes the time required to load the program and may slow down other operations, such as Cut and Paste, because of the extra demands on system memory and resources.

■ Using the Add-Ins

The following sections describe the features of the Excel add-ins and get you up to speed in working with them.

AutoSave

AutoSave is one of the easiest add-ins to use, and offers one of the greatest benefits: it saves your work for you at specified intervals.

To activate AutoSave, choose Add-Ins from the Tools menu. When the Add-Ins dialog box appears, click in the AutoSave check box.

Configuring the AutoSave add-in is straightforward. Click on the Tools menu again, and if you have properly installed the add-in, AutoSave will appear in the drop-down menu with a check mark next to it. Click on AutoSave, and the AutoSave dialog box will appear with several options you can use to modify the add-in (see Figure 13.2). The default values are to automatically save your work every 10 minutes, to save the active workbook only, and to prompt the user before saving. You can also configure AutoSave to save workbooks or workspaces automatically, with or without user intervention.

Figure 13.2

The AutoSave dialog box

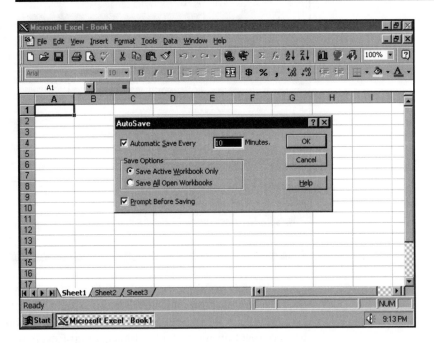

If the Prompt Before Saving check box is selected, you can save the current workbook, skip the save, cancel the operation, or get help.

If you have activated AutoSave under the default settings and you switch to another Windows application while working on an Excel workbook, the Excel title bar beneath whatever application you are running will flash when AutoSave activates, indicating that user input is required. When you switch back to Excel, the AutoSave dialog box will be in the foreground of the workbook, and the Excel title bar will stop flashing.

If you want to change the interval between saves, or save all open workbooks instead of just the active workbook, change the options from within the AutoSave dialog box. You can disable AutoSave, change the Automatic Save Every setting, choose Save Active Workbook Only or Save All Open Workbooks, and decide whether to check Prompt Before Saving. If you are working on a new workbook and have not previously saved your work, AutoSave takes you through the normal steps required to save a workbook, such as assigning a name and location for storing the workbook.

Analysis ToolPak

After you install the Analysis ToolPak, a new option appears on the Tools menu—Data Analysis, which lists the Analysis tools available in Excel.

Before you use the Analysis ToolPak, you need to organize your worksheet data as an input range, and select an output range in which to place results. The contents of the output will vary, depending on which tool you use. Excel assists you by providing labels for cells in an output range if you do not supply them.

The tools available in the ToolPak are shown in Table 13.1.

Each of the Analysis ToolPak functions has similar requirements to return values, like regular worksheet functions. All require *input values*, cells or ranges that Excel assigns as absolute values using the ROWCOLUMN reference type. In addition, you are prompted for arguments specific to the type of analysis required so that a meaningful number or report is returned as you use the functions.

The information for most Data Analysis tools can be output to a range of cells, a new worksheet ply, or its own workbook. A *worksheet ply* is simply another worksheet in your existing workbook, which you can name in the dialog box under output options, as shown in Figure 13.3.

Many of the Data Analysis tools are for exact, specific analysis, and extensive help is available in both the user's guides and Excel's online Help system. When you want more information about one of the Data Analysis tools, highlight it with the mouse and press F1 or click on the Help button.

The results generated by many of the Data Analysis tools are impressive, as typified by an Anova: Single Factor, for example. Taking a simple sample

Table 13.1

Tools Available in the
Analysis ToolPak

TOOL NAME	DESCRIPTION
Anova: Single Factor	Performs simple variance analysis based on rows or columns of data
Anova: Two Factor with Replication	An extension of the single factor Anova, which includes more than one sample for each group of data
Anova: Two Factor without Replication	Performs two sample Anova, which does not include more than one sampling per group
Correlation	Finds a correlation coefficient for a group of numbers
Covariance	Averages the deviations of two ranges of data from their respective means
Descriptive Statistics	Reports on the variability and central tendencies of data
Exponential Smoothing	Returns a value based on a prior forecast, using a constant that determines the magnitude of how strongly forecasts respond to numbers in a forecast
F-Test: Two-Sample for Variances	Compares two population groups for variance
Fourier Analysis	Solves problems in linear systems analyzing periodic data
Histogram	Calculates individual and cumulative frequencies for ranges of cell data and bins, and generates the number of occurrences of a value in a set
Moving Average	Projects values based on previous periods, such as sales or inventory
Random Number Generation	Fills cells with random numbers for a variety of different statistical uses
Rank and Percentile	Provides the percentage rank of each value in a data-set
Regression	Using the "least Squares" method, analyzes a set of observations about an event to allow forecasting of other events
Sampling	Creates a sample of data from an existing sample or population
t-Test: Paired Two-Sample Means	Compares whether two means are distinct
t-Test: Two-Sample, Assuming Equal Variances	Determines whether two sets' means are equal, assuming equal variances
t-Test: Two-Sample, Assuming Unequal Variances	Determines whether two sets' means are equal, assuming unequal variances
z-Test: Two Sample for Means	Tests the difference between two population means

Figure 13.3

Outputting in the
Covariance dialog box to
a new worksheet ply, with
new name

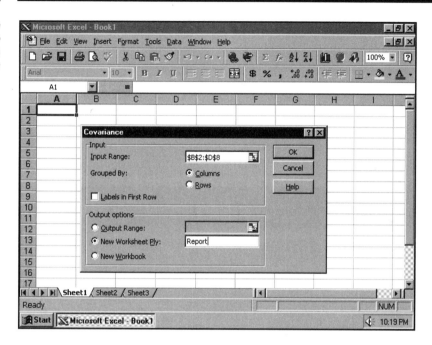

of six numbers in two worksheet cells, selecting the input range as two columns by three rows and the output range as a new worksheet ply called
Anova, the resulting report is extensive, showing the count, sum, average,
and variance, and providing an analysis of the variance in detail.

The Analysis ToolPak was developed by GreyMatter and KRISTECH
companies.

Goal Seek

Goal Seek is a handy tool that you can use to achieve a certain value in a
cell that has a formula, by adjusting the value of another cell that has a direct effect on that cell. Suppose that the sales force's total for the month
was $70,000, and that result was obtained by adding individual salespeople's
numbers for each month and displaying it in a cell below the column. You
can use Goal Seek to see how much your top representative needs to sell to
make the monthly total $80,000.

Goal Seek is invoked by choosing Tools, Goal Seek. The dialog box
prompts you to select the cell that has the formula whose result you want to
alter, then enter the value you want to reach. The final step in Goal Seek is
to select the cell whose value you want to modify to reach the goal or target
specified in the first step.

Figure 13.4 shows the Goal Seek dialog box.

Figure 13.4

The Goal Seek dialog box

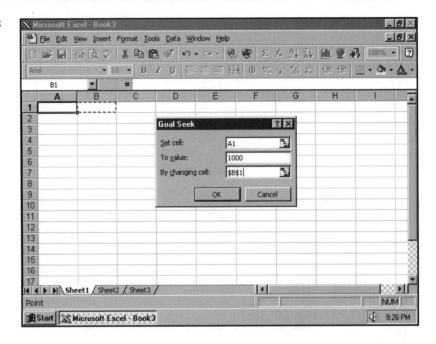

After you choose the options you want to use with Goal Seek, the Goal Seek Status dialog box appears with several options: stepping through an operation, pausing operations, and seeking additional help. This dialog box also displays the cell information, the target value, and the current value, so that as Goal Seek works, you can see the result and step through, pause, or alter it as you go. Clicking on the Pause button changes the choices to Stop and Continue.

When you click on OK in the Goal Seek Status dialog box, Goal Seek places the value found into the specified cell. If you find that this is not what you want, you can restore the values by choosing Undo Goal Seek from the Edit menu on the main menu bar. If you really can't decide what to do, choose Edit, then Redo Goal Seek, to recalculate the goal seek you just undid.

You can use Goal Seek with data tables to answer what-if questions about multiple variables against a single formula, or single variables against multiple formulas. A *data table* is an array or group of cells that shows the effects of different variables on a formula. There are two types of data tables, single-input and two-input tables. A *single-input table* takes a single variable in a formula and displays multiple values in the data table.

If you want to see the results of a varying interest rate on a loan in table format, for example, you would use a single-input data table. To make a data table, begin by entering a column of the values for which you want to see results. From the first entry in the column, go right one cell and up one cell. At this location, input the formula that contains the target cell where you want your table variables inserted—in this case, interest rates. Now, using the right mouse button, select the area that contains the variables, the formula you entered to the right and up one row, and from the Data menu, select Table.

The Table dialog box appears, and you can choose Row Input Cell or Column Input Cell. In a single-input table, you can fill in only one value (in a two-input table, you must input values for both). Your input cell, because this example uses a columnar format, is the second choice, Column Input Cell. The *input cell* is the cell whose value you want to change in the representative table of variables.

To make a two-input table, take the same column of figures and move the formula entered earlier to the cell directly above the first entry in the column. Then, directly to the right of that, enter your second variable—the length of time on a loan. Next, highlight the entire area, including the variables and formulas.

Again, choose Data, Table. For the row-input cell, choose the time frame from the main portion of the worksheet. Press Tab, or click on the next field—the Column Input Cell. Click on the percentage rate from the main area, and click on the Done button. Goal Seek fills in the values for each corresponding time frame, at each interest rate. At this point, perform the following steps:

1. Choose Data, Table.

2. For the row input, choose the time frame from the main portion of the worksheet.

3. Tab to the column-input box and click on the value for percentage rate.

4. Click on OK.

Any changes you make to the interest-rate column or the time row will be reflected automatically as you enter the numbers, which can be a valuable way to answer what-if questions.

Goal Seek can save time in doing tedious what-if analysis, offering quick solutions to questions that might take a long time to answer using trial and error.

Solver

Solver calculates answers to what-if scenarios by using adjustable cells, and even by minimizing or maximizing specific cells in order to attain the desired result.

Solver is useful for three types of problems:

- *Integer problems*. Problems that require a yes or no answer (0 or 1), or problems in which no decimal places are required. Integer problems can greatly increase the amount of time Solver needs to reach a solution.

- *Linear problems*. Problems that involve functions or operations such as addition and subtraction, or some of the built-in functions such as FORECAST.

- *Nonlinear problems*. Problems that use any algorithms, pairs of changing cells that are multiplied or divided by one another, or exponents. Growth and SQRT are two functions that might be present in a nonlinear problem.

Solver is similar to Goal Seek, but it has more options, and can answer questions of greater complexity. In addition, after Solver answers the questions you pose, you can have it generate reports based on the changes you make to your worksheets.

To start Solver, choose Tools, Solver. The Solver Parameters dialog box appears (see Figure 13.5), in which you enter the information it needs. The first item Solver needs is a *target cell:* a cell that contains a formula that you want to find a value for by altering other dependent parts of your worksheet or workbook. To select a target cell, click on the cell you want to change. If you highlight the cell you intend to change and then invoke Solver, that cell address is automatically entered in the Set Target Cell edit box.

Next, you select an Equal to parameter, Max, Min, or Value of. There is an entry box for the specific value, which is activated if you check the Value of selection. After you complete these two steps, you need to tell Solver which cells to change to arrive at the desired result, and you can use the Guess button if you need help to do this. Clicking on Guess highlights the cells on the worksheet and displays the absolute values of the cells in the box beneath the By Changing Cells text box. Guess selects all nonformula cells referred to by the formula in the By Changing Cells text box, which can save you some time.

To further customize your problem setup, you can add constraints to the equations by clicking on the Add button and choosing limits or ranges for the cells to be modified. Suppose you want to see which numbers would need to be modified for each of your salespeople to reach $80,000 sales for a month. The current sales are $55,600, but you want the values for a particular person to remain at or below a certain dollar value. You can, in the Subject to the Constraints box, add the cell reference to the person whose number you want to keep at or below the value, and indicate the Less than or equal to sign and the value.

Figure 13.5

The Solver Parameters
dialog box

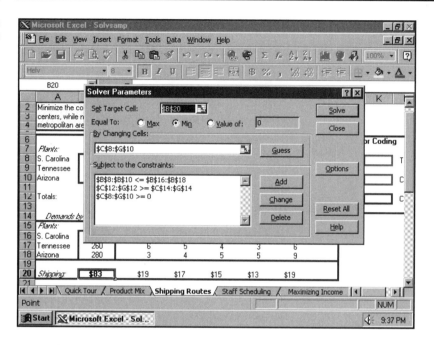

You can add multiple constraints to the equation to reach the desired goal. If you have multiple constraints and you want to change, edit, or delete them, the buttons to the right of the Constraints window turn on these functions. Clicking on the Add button brings up an empty dialog box that can be filled in with the appropriate cell, limit, and operator. Change brings up the same box, but with all the values filled in for editing. Delete prompts you to confirm the deletion of a particular constraint from the problem.

If you plan on running a similar problem against other worksheets, you can save your model problem and modify those parameters for the new problem. The Options button in the Solver dialog box presents the following options:

- *Max Time*. Limits the amount of time spent solving the problem by limiting the number of interim calculations. The default value is 100 seconds, and the maximum is 32,767. The default is adequate for most small problems. This value must be a positive integer.

- *Iterations*. Limits the amount of time Solver uses to process your problem. Again, the default is 100, which is adequate for most simple problems, and this option has the same maximum value and rules as Max Time.

- *Precision*. Determines whether the constraint cell value matches the target value or is within the upper or lower value ranges you specified. The default is 0.000001, and the number you use must be a fraction. The lower the number, the higher the precision, and the longer Solver takes to reach the solution.

- *Tolerance*. Deals with changing cells that are restricted to integers. The *tolerance* is a percentage of error allowed in a calculation in which an integer is used. A higher tolerance level increases solution speed, and this setting has no effect if there are no integer limits placed on the cells to change.

- *Assume Linear Process*. Speeds the solution if all the specified relationships are linear.

- *Show Iteration Results*. Stops Solver after each iteration and shows the results, which can be useful if you are examining a problem or troubleshooting a scenario.

- *Use Automatic Scaling*. Handy when the changing cells and the target have large-scale differences. The Estimates box specifies whether you should use Tangent or Quadratic methods to estimate target and changing cells. The Default is Tangent, but Quadratic can improve results in nonlinear problems. Derivative's choices of Forward (the default) and Central are useful if the graphical representations are not smooth and continuous. The Central method also might be useful if Solver tells you it could not improve the solution.

- *Search*. Defines whether the Newton or Conjugate gradient method of searching is used. This tells Solver which algorithm to use, and which direction to search after each iteration. The Newton method requires more memory, but results in less iteration. The Conjugate method is useful with larger problems, if memory is a problem, and can be used to step through a problem.

- The Load and Save Model buttons each bring up their own dialog boxes, and can assist you in saving additional models, or bringing them into use in other worksheets. The First Solver model is automatically saved with your work.

Solver calculations can stop for three reasons:

- The maximum time limit based on the value in the Options section for Max Time is reached.

- The maximum number of iterations or trials is reached.

- Solver solves the questions satisfactorily or runs into a problem. If Solver runs into a problem, you receive a message that Solver was unable to adequately solve your problem.

The amount of time Solver needs to operate is affected by two factors:

- The number of changing cells
- The complexity of the problem

Scenario Manager

Scenario Manager is a tool that lets you evaluate changes made to worksheets by changing information in a select set of cells. Scenario Manager tracks and maintains the input values you choose, and plugs them into the cells you request. Scenario Manager is a powerful tool for what-if analysis in a worksheet, across multiple sheets in a workbook, or across multiple workbooks.

You can activate Scenario Manager from the Workgroup toolbar or through the Tools menu. Once input, each scenario has a unique name, and its own set of changing cell information.

You can merge scenarios from sheets with other sheets to form consolidation sheets. Suppose you need to borrow money. You have a monthly payment you know you can afford, but you are not sure how much you should borrow to meet the payment. Furthermore, competing financial programs offer varying interest rates over varying terms. You can set up a model of the loan structure you want to evaluate and use Scenario Manager to evaluate for the best loan structure for your situation. If you use different scenarios to plug in different interest rates available from different banks, the Scenario Manager shows you at a glance what each program offers in terms of the final outcome. Figure 13.6 shows the model, using First in the Scenario name field.

To create the scenario, choose Scenarios from the Tools menu. The Scenario Manager dialog box appears, and any scenarios associated with the current worksheet are shown in the Scenarios list box. If there are no existing scenarios, click on the Add button to display the Add Scenario dialog box. Scenarios do not require much information, but the results can be very useful.

The scenario needs a name that can offer an indication of its purpose. The example shown previously is called First. The next box of information Scenario Manager needs is the Changing Cells box. This is the area where the variables appear on your worksheet so that Scenario Manager can provide what-if analysis.

Select the cells you want to change. If there are cells outside the contiguous range you want to include in the changing cells, use Shift+click to include them. Noncontiguous cells can be included by pressing Ctrl+click.

Figure 13.6

The Add Scenario dialog box

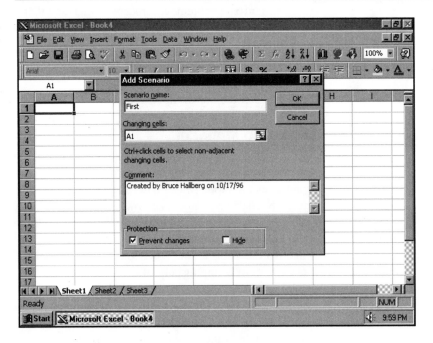

The next information box in this step is the User Comment box, which indicates the registered user's name and the date that the scenario was created or modified. Scenario Manager uses this information to track names and maintain order in the Merge function.

The last field on the Scenario Manager dialog box gives you the option of protecting the scenario by preventing any changes to it or by hiding it.

After you have filled in the fields, choose OK. The Scenario Values dialog box appears (see Figure 13.7), and you can fill in the values for the cells you want to change. When you have finished, choose OK.

You return to the main Scenario Manager dialog box, in which you should see the name of the scenario you just entered. Several buttons are available along the right side of the box:

- *Show.* Enters the results of your variables.

- *Close.* Closes the Scenario Manager.

- *Add.* Displays the Add Scenario dialog box, which you use to create a scenario.

- *Delete.* Removes scenarios.

- *Edit.* Enables you to change or modify the elements of a scenario.

Figure 13.7

The Scenario Values
dialog box

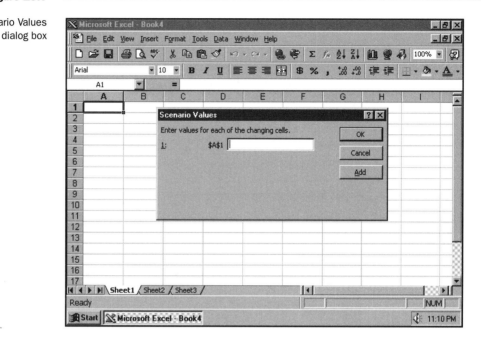

- *Merge*. Displays the Merge dialog box, which lets you select the work-book, sheet, and scenario you want to merge.

- *Summary*. Provides a new worksheet with a complete formatted summary of the variable changes.

The Summary button does some interesting things. It provides a formatted report on its own worksheet of the values that were changed and the results of the scenario. The Scenario Summary dialog box appears, and you have a choice of two different types of reports. The first is the scenario summary, which is a report on its own worksheet, showing the complete details of the scenario.

You also can put the results into a pivot table. A *pivot table* is an interactive worksheet table that you can use to organize and analyze data in a variety of ways. After you create a pivot table, you can rearrange data by dragging fields and items.

View Manager

View manager can change the way your worksheets and workbooks appear on-screen and eventually on paper without saving a separate workbook. Because Excel has a vast number of formatting options that can change the appearance of a worksheet, you might want to use View Manager to enhance your work's appearance.

The view that you save reflects current window size, in addition to many of the settings in the Options dialog box. Because each view is saved across a complete workbook, it can be helpful to use the name of the worksheet as well as a brief description.

To invoke View Manager, choose View, Custom Views.

When you choose Custom Views from the View menu, the Custom Views dialog box appears (see Figure 13.8). From this dialog box, you can select existing views of your worksheet if available. You can Add a new view, Show the effect of the view, Close the View Manager, or Delete a view.

Figure 13.8

The Custom Views dialog box

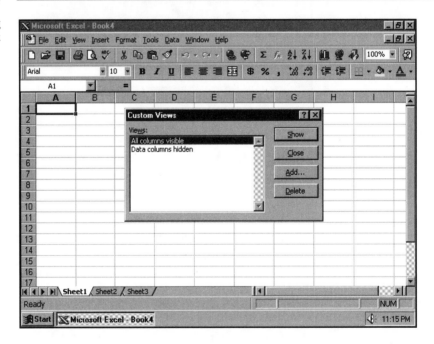

Tip. If you do not have any print settings made for a particular sheet, the entire worksheet prints.

Custom views save the print settings and displays settings for a worksheet as well as hidden column or row information. You have the option of changing these settings when you create the view in the Add View dialog box. This is done at the same time you assign a name to the view.

To set up a view, first create the look you want to use by changing the settings, zoom factors, and print settings, and hiding any columns or rows that you want to exclude from the view. After your sheet looks the way you want, choose View from the main menu and invoke Custom Views. Choose Add, and name your view. Indicate whether you want to save print settings and hidden columns or rows in the Custom Views dialog box, and click on OK to save the view of that sheet.

Report Manager

The Report Manager provides detailed reports of your workbooks in several ways. You can create customized reports from your information using the Report Manager tools.

Reports can include different views and scenarios, and a report can automatically switch between scenarios and views and print them in a specific order.

To create a report, choose Report Manager from the View menu. The main Report Manager dialog box appears, in which you can print, close, add, edit, delete, or get help.

The first step is to name the report, followed by creating a section. To do this from the Report Manager dialog box, choose Add, then name your report and tab to the section area of the Add Report dialog box. A *section* of the report is defined by simply choosing which worksheet from the workbook you want to use, and whether you want to use any predefined views or scenarios from the sheets in your reports.

After you name the report, the default values for Sheet, View, and Scenario are marked in the Section to Add group. The sheet name is the same name as the sheet that was active when you launched Report Manager. The drop-down boxes for View and Scenario are used to select available variables and representations of your workbook.

After you define a particular addition to the Report Manager, click on the Add button, and it will show up on the Print Report dialog box as well as in the Sections in this Report area.

If you want to keep an original report to show the history of a particular sheet, for example, you can choose Add in the Report Manager dialog box, and define a new report that uses your new views or scenarios.

Figure 13.9 shows Report Manager's Add Report dialog box.

When you add a new report, if you do not want to use views or scenarios in printing, you can keep the default values or uncheck the boxes to the left of the choices. Unchecking the boxes grays the selections available from the drop-down menus for each selection.

With each report you design, you can have multiple sections. In the initial stages of report design, you can update the Sections in this Report section of the dialog box after clicking the Add button next to the Section to Add group.

You might want to use different sections in a report to illustrate projected changes in business trends. If you incorporate all the selections into

Figure 13.9

Report Manager's Add
Report dialog box

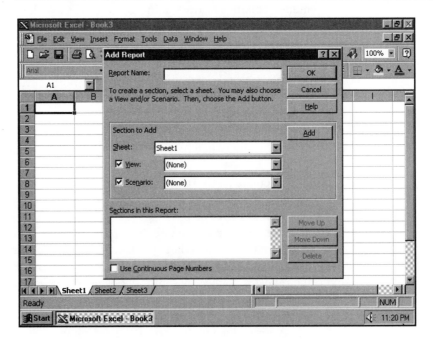

one report when you print, all will be included together. On the other hand, if you want to have the flexibility to print all the information but do not want to have all the reports print together, set up separate reports that reflect the same values.

The Add Report dialog box is also where you change the position of sections in your report, such as in what order your sections fall. If you want the report to be a single large report, you should select the Use Continuous Page Numbers check box. This option prints the page numbers across multiple sections. Unselecting this box resets the page number at each section.

NOTE. *After you define the information in the section that you want to incorporate into your report, you must click on the Add button in the Section to Add area. If you do not, an error message will appear, indicating that you cannot have a report that does not have designed sections. It becomes even more important if you add sections, however, because if you define a new section and forget to add it to the report, Report Manager will discard all your changes.*

After adding a section and clicking on OK, the Print Report dialog box is activated. To print a report, select the title of the report you want and click on the Print button. Your screen changes to each sheet, view, and scenario as it generates the report, and a standard dialog box that indicates print status appears after Excel generates the information. Upon completion, your original view, scenario, and worksheet are restored so that you can continue working.

Using Report Manager, you can set up one report to print each scenario you create, with the view options you designate for each scenario, in the order you want the reports to appear.

Using Excel's Auditing Features

Excel has auditing tools that you can use to illustrate how values are arrived at and to figure out where problems have occurred.

The Auditing toolbar provides a quick way to use some of Excel's features, using visual tools called tracers. *Tracers* are graphic displays, such as arrows, that show visually where formulas get their values. To display the Auditing toolbar, choose Auditing from the Tools menu. The last selection on the menu is Show Auditing Toolbar, and if it is already active, there is a check mark next to the selection. If you do not want the toolbar to be displayed, simply click in the Show Auditing Toolbar check box.

You can display the toolbar by choosing Toolbars from the View menu as well. The dialog box that appears shows all available Excel and add-in toolbars. If the toolbar you want is not on the list, return to the Tools menu and choose Add-Ins to make sure that the add-in you want is loaded. This displays the Add-Ins dialog box so that you can make the selection.

From the Auditing toolbar, you can select and remove tracers of different types: precedents and dependents. You can also add comments, trace errors, and show an information window.

Tracers are graphic representations that display a relationship between cells. Tracers can illustrate precedent and dependent relationships. Precedent cells are cells that are referred to directly by a formula. Dependent cells, conversely, are cells that contain formulas that refer to other cells.

Another way to describe these relationships is with the terms direct and indirect. A *direct precedent* is a cell referred to by the formula in the active cell. An *indirect precedent* is referred to by a formula in a direct precedent cell or in another indirect cell.

A *direct dependent* is a cell containing a formula that refers to the active cell, and an *indirect dependent* is a cell containing a direct dependent cell or another indirect dependent cell

In the worksheet in Figure 13.10, for example, the formula for Total in cell C6 is directly dependent on cells C2:C4. The average formula in C8 is directly dependent on the formulas in cells C6 and C7, but indirectly dependent on the values in C2:C4. The cells C2:C4 are direct precedents of the formula in cell C6. They are also indirect precedents of the formula in C8.

Figure 13.10

Samples of precedent and dependent cells

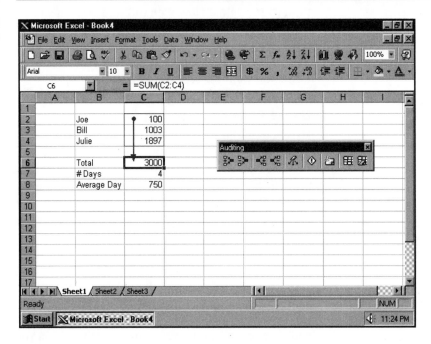

Using Auditing tools can help you understand, visualize, and trouble-shoot these concepts and the data associated with them. In the worksheet in Figure 13.10, to trace the precedents of cell C8 you begin by clicking on C8 to activate it. Then click the Trace Precedents button on the Auditing tool-bar. A box will be drawn around cells C3:C6, and a solid line will be drawn from the boxed cells to the formula in C8. Then, by clicking on the Trace Dependents button while C8 is still active, a similar line will be drawn from C6 to C8, indicating that C8 is directly dependent on C6. This action shows what the relationships are between the cells.

Another way to show this relationship is to make C8 the active cell, and click on the Trace Precedents button. The line is drawn to C6, pointing in the same direction. Click on the Trace Dependents button again to draw the box again on C2:C4, and put the arrow there as well (see Figure 13.11).

To find out which cells are dependent on which values, select cell C2. Click on the Trace Dependents button, and the arrow will point to the cell that contains the formula that is directly dependent on the value in that cell. Click on the Trace Dependents button again to draw the line to the next cell, C8, that is indirectly dependent on C2.

Figure 13.11

Tracing precedents from C8, direct and indirect

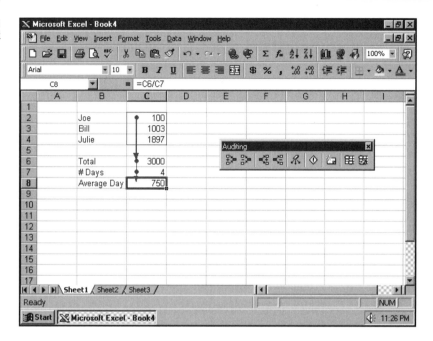

Auditing can also be useful for tracking errors in worksheets. If you have a formula that returns an error message, make the errant cell active and click on the Trace Errors button to see where the problem lies in the formula.

Excel shows tracers in three ways. The first is a solid blue line. The destination point is indicated by an arrowhead on the end of the line. On a monochrome screen, the line appears black. Errors are traced by a solid red line, or by a dotted line on a monochrome monitor. The error tracer also has an arrowhead point. The third type of tracer is a dashed black line with an icon, and is the same in both color and monochrome. This tracer refers to an external reference in another worksheet.

You can remove tracer arrows as easily as you can produce them. Press the Remove Precedent Arrows button to undo the most recent trace precedent function; the Remove Dependent Arrows button works exactly the same way.

If you press the Trace button numerous times to step through a progression of relationships as you trace, each set of arrows will be removed one at a time. You can remove all the arrows on a sheet by clicking the Remove All Arrows button.

You can add comments to your worksheets with the Auditing features. Adding comments is useful if you are going to share your work with others, as some explanation is necessary to make certain portions of the worksheet or workbook clear. It is also helpful if you are using complex formulas and references to track your work and trace your footsteps. Users—whether actual, active users, or mere receivers—of larger worksheets can also benefit from annotations and explanations.

Comments

Comments make auditing and reviewing worksheets quite a bit easier. Whether you want to remind yourself of how a portion of the worksheet operates, or need to insert questions or comments that others can read, inserted comments let you conveniently record such information.

Adding comments to worksheets is done through the Auditing toolbar. The icon of a yellow sticky-note pad denotes the New Comment button.

Choosing Comment from the Insert menu brings up the comment window for the selected cell, as shown in Figure 13.12. If you have multiple cells highlighted when you enter your comment, it will be placed in the last cell you click on.

Figure 13.12

Inserting a comment into a cell

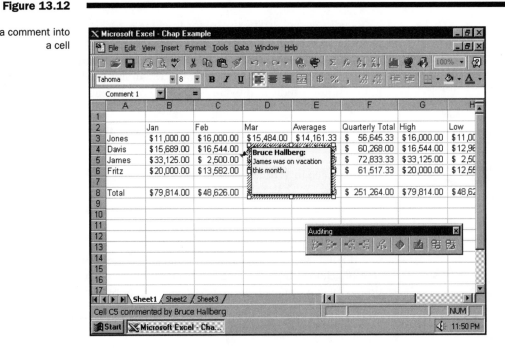

Existing comments attached to cells are indicated by a red triangle in the upper-right corner of the cell. To read a comment, simply place your mouse pointer over the cell: the comment displays automatically, just like a ScreenTip.

To copy comments from cell to cell, select the cell that has the note you want to copy. Click the right mouse button or press Shift+F10 to bring up the Cell menu. Select Copy and move the mouse to the destination cell. Click the right mouse button again and choose Paste Special. The Paste Special dialog box will appear. Click in the Comments check box to copy the comment to the new cell. You can also use the pull-down menus to copy notes.

Go To Special

The Go To Special command helps you find notes, constants, formulas that meet a particular criteria, blank cells, cells in the current region or array, cells that do not fit a pattern in a row or column, precedents or dependents (direct or all levels), the last active cell in your sheet, visible cells, or objects. The Go To Special dialog box can be accessed by pressing F5 (or by selecting Edit, Go To) and then clicking on the Special button. Figure 13.13 shows the Go To Special dialog box.

Figure 13.13

The Go To Special dialog box

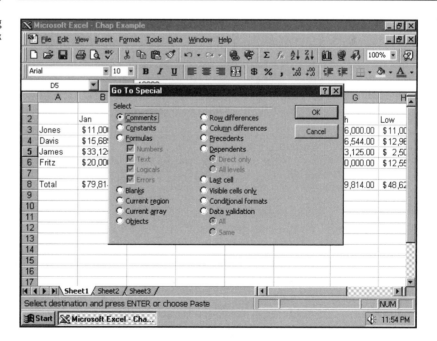

The Comments option selects all cells that contain notes (you also can press Ctrl+Shift+?). *Constants* are cells whose contents are deemed not to be a formula, so those cells whose values do not begin with an equal sign are considered to be constants, whether they are numbers or text.

The Formulas option selects cells that meet the selection criteria of values returned as numbers, text, logical, or errors. Using the Current Region option selects a range of cells as the active cell and all adjacent cells surrounded by any combination of blank rows or columns.

You can select the current array to which a cell belongs by checking the Current Array radio button, or by pressing Ctrl+/. To find cells that do not fit a pattern in a row or column based on the value in the active cell, press Ctrl+\ for rows or Ctrl+Shift+| for columns. This feature finds all the cells in a column or row that differ from the active cell at the time you select the Go To Special command.

You also can use Go To Special to find cells referred to by specific formulas (precedents) or cells with formulas that refer to selected cells (dependents). With the Go To Special dialog box options of selecting just the direct cells or all levels, you can find for precedents:

- All cells that are directly or indirectly referred to by a formula and for dependents

- All cells that contain formulas that directly or indirectly relate to cells

■ Using Outlining

Outlining is a method of creating summary reports that lets you hide or display as much information as you want. An outline can have up to eight levels of groups on both the horizontal axis and the vertical axis. One worksheet can have only one outline.

Excel can outline automatically or manually. To create an outline, first highlight or select the data you want to outline. Then choose Group and Outline from the Data menu. If your data is in a format that you can easily outline, select Auto Outline. Figure 13.14 shows the effect of automatic outlining on the sales worksheet.

The result is a grouping of related items with a row-and-column format that you can then hide, expand, or change based on the way your data is arranged. For example, if you want to show selective portions, just click on the minus signs above the lines that indicate which areas to eliminate from view in the worksheet (see Figure 13.15).

As you experiment with hiding and displaying different levels within your outline, Shift-clicking on the outline levels shows what will be hidden if you reduce the outline area.

Figure 13.14

The Auto Outline of a
worksheet

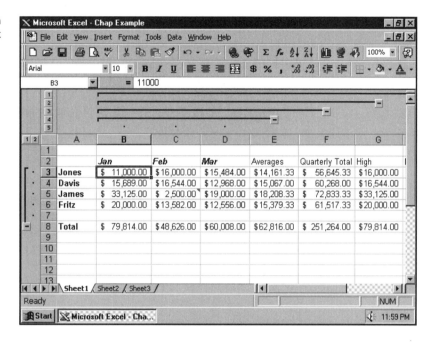

Figure 13.15

Hiding some of the detail
by eliminating an outline
level

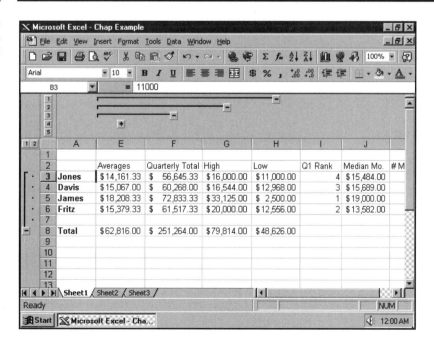

If your data is not organized in a way that you can automatically outline with ease, try the manual method. From the Data menu, choose Group and Outline, then Settings. The Settings dialog box will appear, prompting you for information about the location of summary information—whether row summaries are to be located below the detail, and if column summaries are located to the right of the detail. You can choose to have Automatic Styles, Create the outline, or Apply Styles. Apply Styles causes the built-in styles RowLevel_1 and ColLevel_1 (and so forth) to be applied automatically to the outline levels you create.

■ Summary

Excel contains extremely powerful tools that can be brought to bear on a wide variety of spreadsheet problems. In this chapter you've learned about important tools that are often overlooked by beginning users of Excel, but that can yield big dividends by saving you time in many situations.

- *Using the Excel ChartWizard*
- *Understanding Chart Types*
- *Understanding Data Organization*
- *Adding Text to Your Chart*
- *Adding a New Series to Your Chart*
- *Modifying Charts*

14

Excel Charts and Graphics

Aftter you have entered your data into a worksheet, you can use Excel's powerful charting and graphics capabilities to display this data in different ways. Excel can display data from cells in a worksheet as bar graphs, pie graphs, line charts, or in relation to other data points from other worksheets. Showing information graphically makes understanding, comparing, and evaluating data easier.

In this chapter you will learn about the following:

- Using Excel's ChartWizard
- Different types of charts
- How data organization affects your charts and graphs
- Options for setting up charts and graphs
- Building Chart Axes
- Customizing your chart by adding text
- Updating your chart by adding a new data series
- Modifying an existing chart
- Changing between chart types
- Changing the appearance of the chart you have created

Excel's charting and graphics capability goes far beyond simply showing values or data points in a graph. Using the ChartWizard, you can create presentations that can be incorporated into documents, embedded in workbooks, or even placed into a slide show. And because your data was linked to your charts at their creation, the charts are automatically updated when data in the underlying worksheet is changed.

Charts and graphs can be very simple, or they can be created to display complex relationships among data. Through the use of Excel's ChartWizard, the creation and display of a chart is made simple. Like the other Excel Wizards, the ChartWizard is a series of dialog boxes that take you step-by-step through the chart-making process, providing various options to make it quick and easy. After you have generated a chart, it can be changed to appear exactly as you want.

■ Using the Excel ChartWizard

The ChartWizard button, when clicked, leads you through four steps that result in a properly formatted chart for your data. You can select what kind of chart you want, the data area that will be charted, and a number of other chart features. When finished, you can see your completed chart and further customize it if you wish.

To create the chart in this exercise, begin by building a worksheet like the one used in previous chapters. It lists salesperson names, monthly totals for three months, and other related data.

To expedite the charting process, highlight the cells you want to represent in the graph before starting the Wizard. It's helpful to select the data to be charted before you begin, but you will also have a chance to do so during the Chart Wizard process later.

To begin creating a chart with the ChartWizard, first select the data to be charted (see Figure 14.1) and then click on the ChartWizard button. You will now see the first dialog box for the Chart Wizard, as shown in Figure 14.2.

Figure 14.1

The data that you are charting, selected in the worksheet

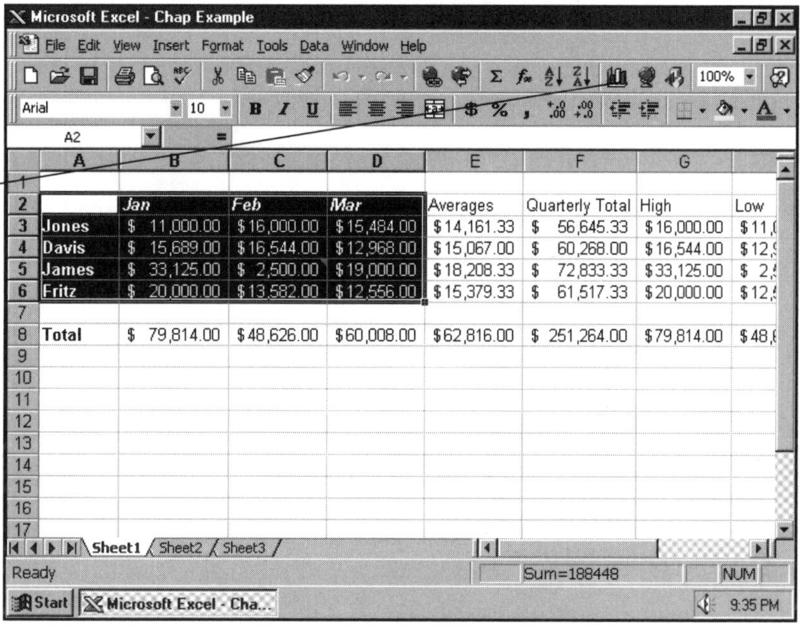

ChartWizard button

Tip. When you select a range of data points to include in your graph, be sure to include the column and row headers, as they can be used for descriptors in the chart.

Select the type of chart you want in the Chart Type window, and then select the sub-type in the Chart Sub-type window. In this example, choose the first subtype of the Column chart, as shown selected in Figure 14.2, then click on the Next button to continue.

You now see Step 2 of 4 of the Chart Wizard. The dialog box that appears contains two tabs: Data Range (which should be active) and Series. You will also see a preview of your chart, given the currently selected data range. Figure 14.3 shows you this dialog box with the Data Range tab active.

In Step 2 you can select (or reselect) the data that you will chart using the Data Range field. To do this, click in the field and then click on the hide button that appears at the far-right side of the Data range field (see Figure 14.3). The hide button gets the dialog box out of your way, letting you select the data you're interested in. When you click on the hide button, the dialog

Figure 14.2

Step 1 of the Chart Wizard lets you select your chart type and subtype.

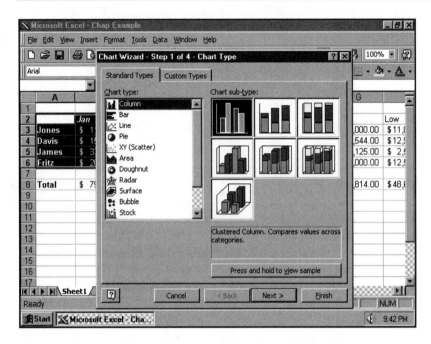

Figure 14.3

Step 2 of the Chart Wizard, where you can select the data you will chart

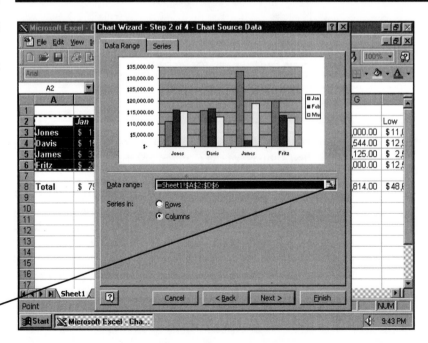

Hide button

box shrinks to a small window and reveals your worksheet, as shown in Figure 14.4. Select the data that you want to plot, and then click on the resume button again to redisplay the Chart Wizard dialog box.

Figure 14.4

Select your data and then click on the restore button to resume using the Chart Wizard.

Restore button

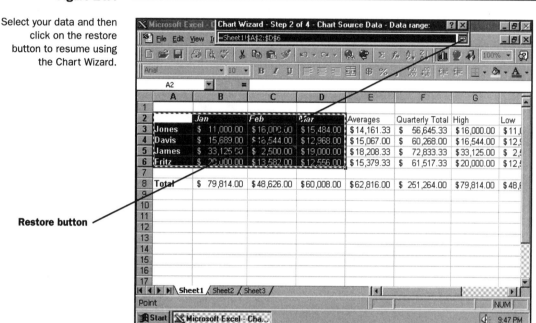

The next important choice you make in the Step 2 dialog box is whether your data series are organized in rows or columns. Your chart will look different depending on which of these options you choose. For example, if you changed the Series in option button to Rows, you would see the preview in Figure 14.5. Compare this preview to the one in Figure 14.3. Notice how choosing Columns causes the salespeople to be displayed along the bottom axis of the chart, while choosing Rows causes the months to be displayed on the bottom axis. Neither choice is inherently correct: it all depends on how you want to view the data.

Continue to Step 3 of the Chart Wizard by clicking on the Next button. You now see the Chart Options dialog box (shown in Figure 14.6) in which you can make a number of choices about how your chart displays. You will learn more about all of the chart options later in this chapter. For now, though, use the Titles tab to add a chart title ("Q1 Sales by Salesperson"), a category (X) axis label ("Salesperson"), and a value (Y) axis label ("Sales"). Click on the Next button to continue.

Figure 14.5

You may need to select either Rows or Columns, depending on how you want to display your data. Compare this preview to Figure 14.3 to see the difference.

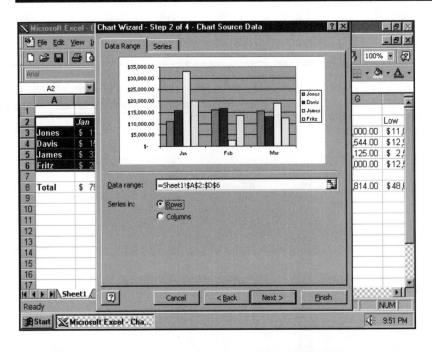

Figure 14.6

Use the Chart Options dialog box to choose formatting details of your chart.

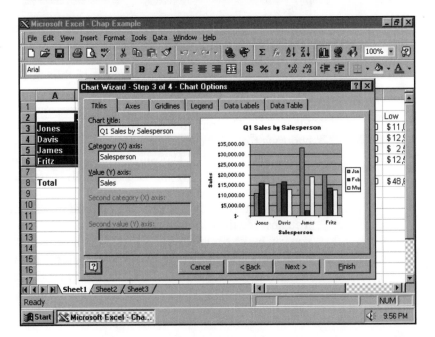

The fourth and final step of the Chart Wizard determines where the generated chart is placed. Figure 14.7 shows you the dialog box that you see for Step 4 of 4 in the Chart Wizard. You can choose to display your chart as a new sheet in your workbook, or you can embed it into an existing sheet.

Figure 14.7

Use Step 4 of 4 of the
Chart Wizard to place
your chart.

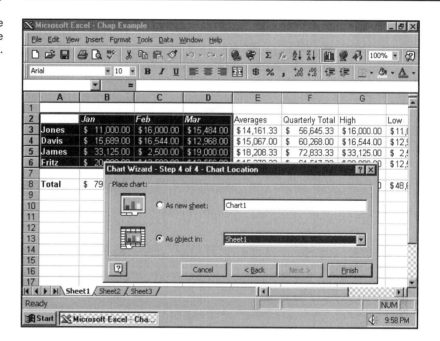

If you choose to place your completed chart as a new sheet, the sheet is created in your workbook with the name you enter in the As New Sheet field (Chart1) in Figure 14.7. If you choose to place the chart into an existing sheet as an object, it is placed into the sheet indicated by the As Object In field. Figure 14.8 shows the chart inserted as a new sheet, while Figure 14.9 shows it placed into Sheet1 as an object. Depending on your display and printing needs, both choices are useful.

Once a chart is placed into an existing sheet as an object, you can use the handles of the object to stretch the chart until it appears as you wish. You can also drag it into a new location on the sheet.

Figure 14.8

A new chart created as a separate sheet in the workbook

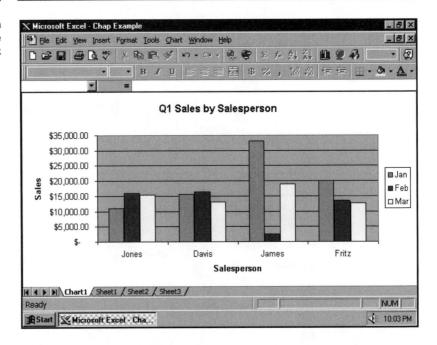

Figure 14.9

A new chart placed as an object into an existing sheet

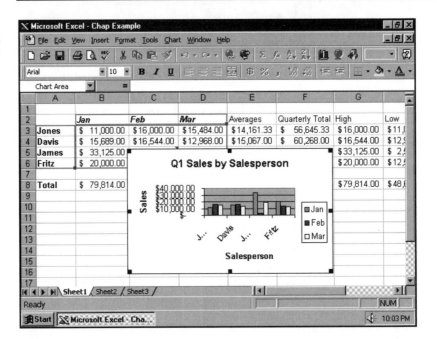

■ Understanding Chart Types

Excel has 14 basic chart types to choose from. Choosing a particular chart type is an important step in making your presentation effective and clear. The chart types are the following:

- Column chart
- Bar chart
- Line chart
- Pie chart
- XY (scatter) chart
- Area chart
- Doughnut chart
- Radar chart
- Surface chart
- Bubble chart
- Stock chart
- Cylinder chart
- Cone chart
- Pyramid chart

Choosing a chart type is crucial to communicating your information. Different types of charts tell a different story about the data, and can lead your audience to ask different questions, or to draw different conclusions. Also, different types of charts are designed for different purposes. For example, a column chart lets you easily compare different categories of data, while a line chart is designed to show changes of a value over time. X-Y (Scatter) charts show the correlation between two different measurements. And other charts are for other things. The following sections briefly discuss the different chart types available to you, and explain what each type is used to illustrate.

Column Charts

Column charts are similar to bar charts, except that their orientation is vertical instead of horizontal (see Figure 14.10). This shifts emphasis from a comparison of difference in values to an emphasis on a change over a certain period of time.

Figure 14.10

An example of a column chart

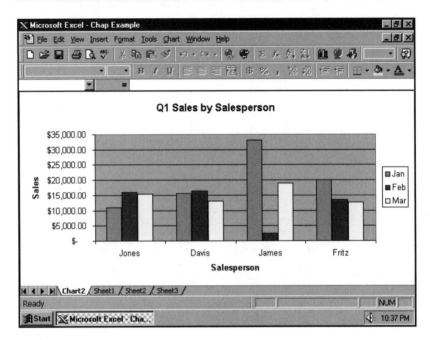

Bar Charts

Bar charts illustrate relationships among items. Use stacked bar charts to show the relationship between specific items and the rest of the dataset used to build the chart. Bar charts are organized and displayed horizontally to emphasize differences in values, as shown in Figure 14.11.

Line Charts

Line charts are great for showing trends in data over a period of time. This type of graph is similar to an area chart, but emphasizes the change of data over time in a somewhat different manner, as Figure 14.12 illustrates.

Pie Charts

Pie charts show how data points relate to a whole set of data. The pie contains only one data series, even if you have selected more than one. Figure 14.13 shows an example of the pie chart. In this pie chart, the relationship of each salesperson to the whole group is displayed in percentage figures.

Figure 14.11

An example of a bar chart

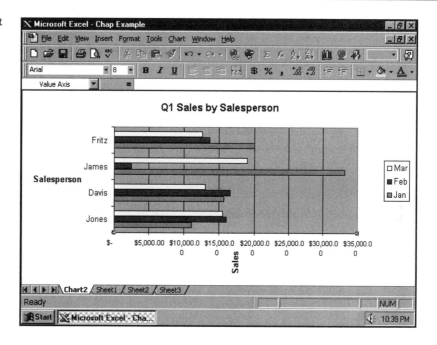

Figure 14.12

An example of a line chart

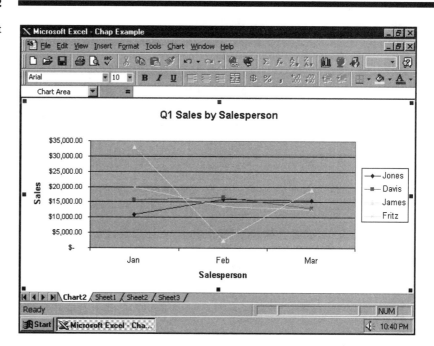

Figure 14.13

An example of a pie chart

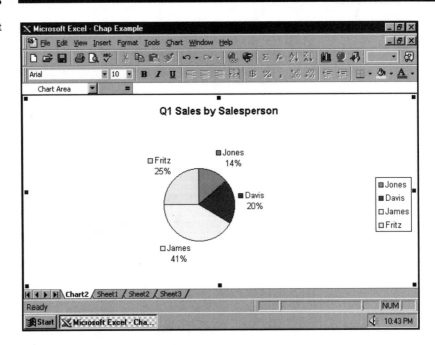

Tip. Often people who want line charts really want XY charts with lines that connect the points together (one of the sub-types of the XY, or Scatter, chart lets you do this). Line charts display changes over time, or across categories, while XY charts show a relationship between two value axes.

XY or Scatter Charts

XY or scatter charts show the relationships among data points by plotting dots on a graph relative to two or more groups of numbers as a series. The XY chart clearly shows data clusters, and is commonly used in scientific data analysis. Figure 14.14 is an example of a scatter chart.

Area Charts

Area charts show the relative change of values over a period of time. They differ from line charts in that it is easier to see the pattern of change over time, and the percentage of the total for each of the series. Figure 14.15 shows an area chart.

Doughnut Charts

A doughnut chart is similar to a pie chart, but can be used to display more than one data series at a time. Each concentric ring of a doughnut chart contains the data from a different series in the data set (see Figure 14.16).

Figure 14.14

An example of an XY
(scatter) chart

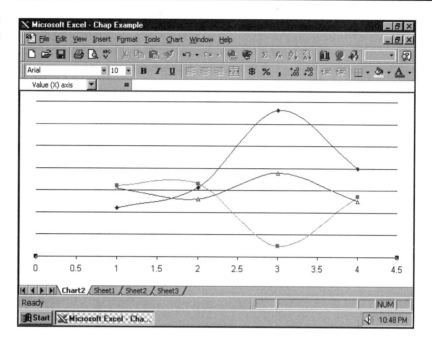

Figure 14.15

An example of an XY
(scatter) chart

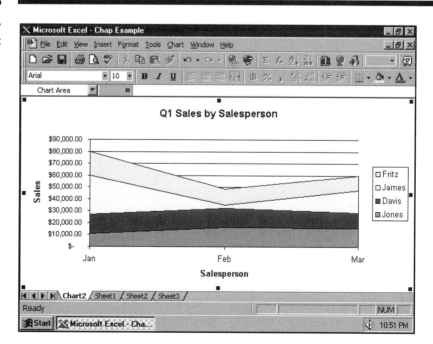

Figure 14.16

An example of a
doughnut chart

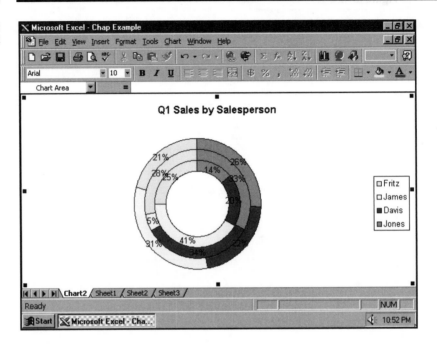

Radar Charts

The radar chart shows changes in data relative to both a central point and in-dividual data points. The value categories are scattered around the center point of the graph with lines connecting the values, as shown in Figure 14.17. Radar charts are not commonly used in the US, but are sometimes used in Europe and Asia.

Surface Charts

The surface chart shows a "flexible" continuum for displaying data (see Figure 14.18). This type of chart is useful for showing relationships among many data points.

Bubble Charts

Bubble charts (see Figure 14.19) are similar to XY (scatter) charts, but can display a third value at each intersection using the size of the bubble. The location of each bubble is determined by the two axes, while the size of the bubble can display additional data about the data point.

Figure 14.17

An example of a radar chart

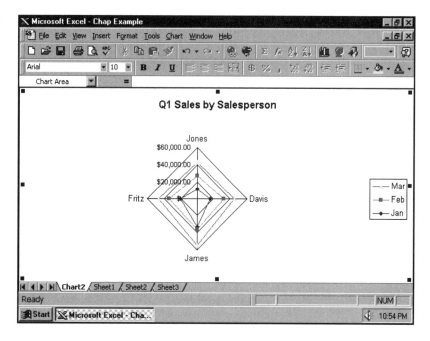

Figure 14.18

An example of a surface chart

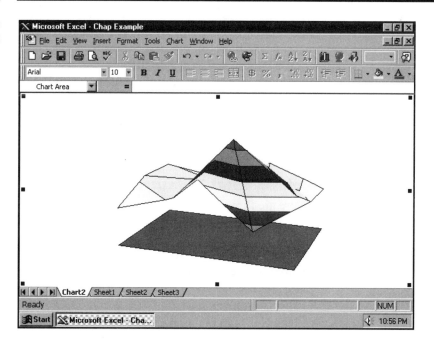

Figure 14.19

An example of a bubble chart

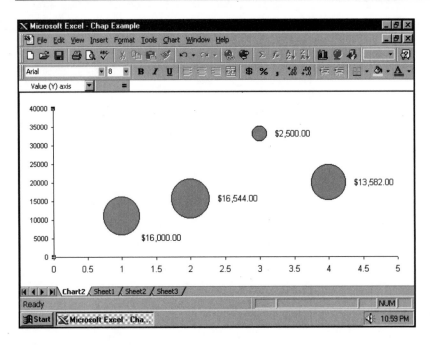

Stock Charts

Stock charts are used to plot stock market data, either for multiple companies or for one company over time. To use the stock charts, you must arrange your data in the proper order. For instance, the chart shown in Figure 14.20 is called a Volume-High-Low-Close chart, and requires four data series organized in that order. Other stock charts include High-Low-Close, Open-High-Low-Close, and Volume-Open-High-Low-Close. In the Volume-High-Low-Close chart in Figure 14.20, the columns show the trading volume, while the thin vertical line shows the high and low stock price for the day, with the small tick mark in the vertical line showing the closing price of the stock.

Column Chart Variations

There are three variations on column charts that are listed as distinct chart types: Cylinder, Cone, and Pyramid charts. These charts work just like the column chart, but look a little snazzier due to the use of the named 3-D graphic in place of the standard rectangular column. Figure 14.21 shows an example of a cone chart.

Figure 14.20

An example of a Volume-
High-Low-Close stock
chart

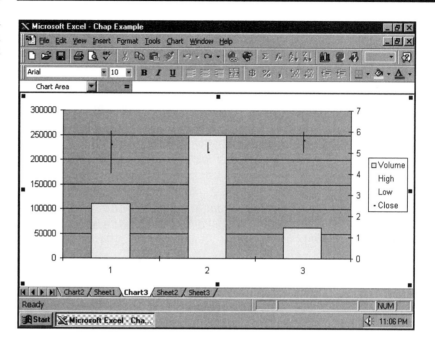

Figure 14.21

An example of a cone
chart

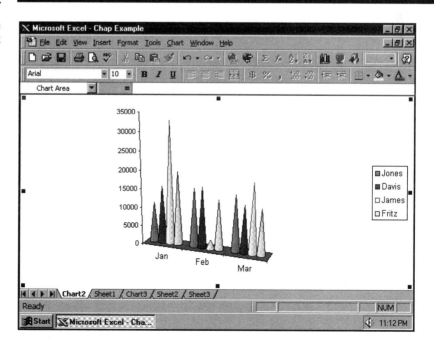

■ Understanding Data Organization

Because you have used the same worksheet data across all the different chart types, data points appear in a graph with specific relation to other data points or data series. The horizontal and vertical lines along which data are displayed are called the chart *axes*.

A two-dimensional graph shows data along two separate axes, the *X axis* and the *Y axis*. Typically the X axis is horizontal and the Y axis is vertical. The *value axis* is usually the Y axis, and the *category axis* is the X axis.

3-D charts can have two or three axes. The third axis, perpendicular to both the X and Y axes, is the *Z axis*, and it is present only in 3-D charts. While there is no such thing as a true three-dimensional screen (or printout), imagine that the Z axis is sticking out towards you.

In a two-dimensional chart, you can sometimes make a chart clearer by plotting one of the data series against a secondary axis. You usually need to do this when one or more of the series appear in radically different places on the y-axis. In cases like this, you move the data to plot against a secondary y-axis. To do this, double-click on the series you want to move. This reveals the Format Data Series dialog box for that series (see Figure 14.22). Select the Secondary axis option button on the Axis tab and click the dialog box's OK button to save the change.

Figure 14.22

Changing a data series' orientation on the Axis tab of the Format Data Series dialog box

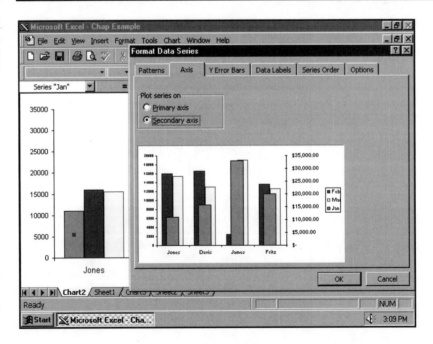

■ Adding Text to Your Chart

You can add text to your charts in a number of ways. If you decided not to include a legend in your chart, you can add one later. Legends are especially useful on large, complex graphs where they help the reader keep track of what is going on.

You can add and place a legend on your chart by right-clicking on the chart area and then choosing Chart Options from the pop-up menu. Use the Legend tab to choose whether or not to display a legend, and to determine where in the chart the legend will be placed. Once you place a legend, you can then drag it to position it where you wish more precisely.

You can also add text boxes to your graphs. A *text box* clarifies a graphic representation, emphasizes a particular point, or simply annotates some detail on your graphs.

The Excel drawing toolbar contains the Text box button. A text box can be placed next to a graph or directly within the chart. You can also simply begin typing—your text will appear in the formula bar, and when you press Enter a text box will be created in the center of your chart containing the text you typed. You can then drag the text box to anywhere on the chart.

Tip. If you add a text box on or next to a graph while the graph is not activated, the box will not move with the graph when it is moved. If, however, the graph is activated, the box and graph become one object. If you want, the box can still be moved around within the graph.

■ Adding a New Series to Your Chart

After you have defined a chart and have it displayed on a worksheet, Excel will automatically update the chart as the data within it changes. If you want to add a data point or an entirely new data series, however, you can modify the structure of your chart by following a few simple steps.

If you add a new person to your staff, for example, you will need to update the chart with that person's sales figures. To include this series of figures in this chapter's example chart, add a row with the new person's data to the worksheet. For this example, the person's name is Williams, and his sales totals for January, February, and March are 10,000, 15,000 and 20,000, respectively.

After you have entered that information into your worksheet and formatted the numbers appropriately, move back to the chart that will contain the added data and access the Add Data command in the Chart menu. You will see the Add Data dialog box shown in Figure 14.23.

Once the Add Data dialog box is visible, switch to the sheet that contains the new data and select the range. You will see the range reference appear in the Add Data's Range field. Once you have selected the range, click on the OK button to complete the operation. You will automatically return to the chart, which will contain the new information.

Figure 14.23

The example chart with
Williams's data added

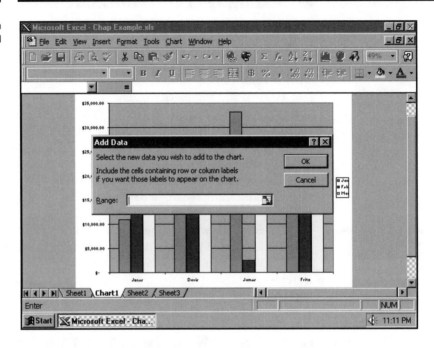

■ Modifying Charts

After your chart is in place in a given location, options are available that affect the appearance of the data.

Activating a Chart

Tip. When you activate a chart that's embedded in a worksheet by clicking in it, the choices in the Excel menu bar become chart- and graph-specific. The Format menu choices with an active graph are different from those available when a cell or range of cells is active, for example.

The first way to modify an area of a chart is to double-click on the area (legend, labels, text boxes, and so on) to be changed. Separate format options are available for each area. If you want to modify the plot or type area, bring up the formatting shortcut menu by clicking on the background of the chart and then the right mouse button (see Figure 14.24).

Double-clicking on the plot area of the graph invokes the Format Plot Area dialog box, which is one of the options available on the shortcut menu.

Making Chart Changes

You can modify most aspects of your chart with the Chart Options dialog box. Access this dialog box by choosing the Chart Options command from the Chart menu. You will see the Chart Options dialog box shown in Figure 14.25.

Figure 14.24

Using the chart's pop-up
menu

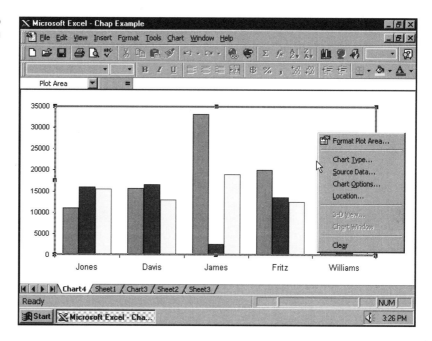

Figure 14.25

The Chart Options dialog
box

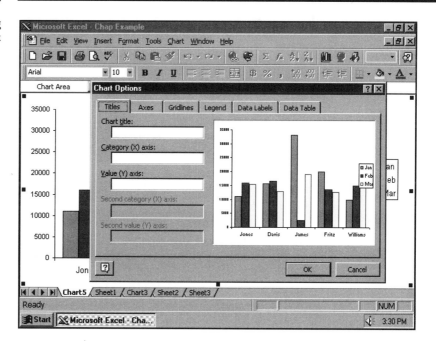

The Titles tab of the Chart Options dialog box lets you choose the titles that are present in the chart. You can type the main chart title, as well as titles for each of the available axes in the chart.

The Axes tab (shown in Figure 14.26) lets you choose which axes are visible, and also lets you control the type of the X axis. You can make the X axis automatic, category-based, or time-scale-based. The X axis changes how it spaces its tick marks depending on which of these types is chosen.

Figure 14.26

The Axes tab of the Chart Options dialog box

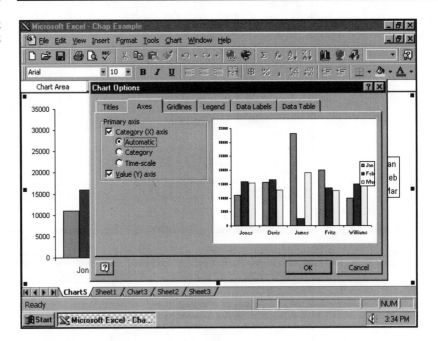

Use the Gridlines tab to choose which gridlines are shown on your chart. You can show gridlines for both the major and minor units for each of the axes in the chart. Figure 14.27 shows the Gridlines tab.

You can automatically add labels to your data points with the Data Labels tab (see Figure 14.28). In the Data Labels tab you can choose to show the actual value for each data point next to the point, its percentage of the total, its label (which is otherwise shown in the legend), a combination of its label and percent, or the size of any bubbles on the chart. Note that some of these options aren't available if they aren't appropriate for the selected chart type.

Finally, you can use the Data Table tab to insert a table containing the data charted below the chart itself. Figure 14.29 shows the Data Table tab, and the preview window lets you see how the data table will appear in the chart.

Figure 14.27

The Gridlines tab of the Chart Options dialog box

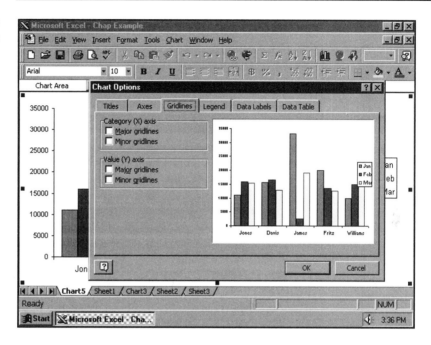

Figure 14.28

The Data Labels tab of the Chart Options dialog box

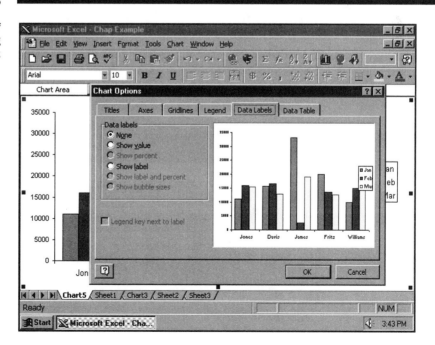

Figure 14.29

The Data Table tab of the
Chart Options dialog box

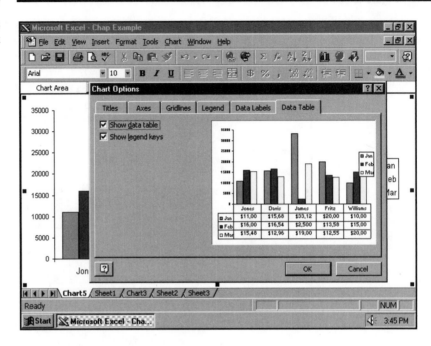

Changing the Chart Type

The Chart Type dialog box selected from the chart's shortcut menu lets you
switch the type of chart being displayed. You can choose from any of Excel's
chart types, such as doughnut, pie, area, and so on. The Chart Type dialog
box is identical to the one you see in Step 1 of the Chart Wizard.

Changing a Chart's Location

You can switch the location of a chart from being placed on a dedicated
sheet in your workbook, to being placed as an object on top of an existing
sheet, and vice versa. To do so, right-click on the chart and choose Location
from the pop-up menu. You will see the Chart Location dialog box shown in
Figure 14.30.

In this dialog box you can choose from the two types of locations available (As New Sheet and As Object In). If you choose As New Sheet, you can
name the sheet that will contain the chart, while choosing As Object In lets
you select which existing sheet will contain the chart.

Figure 14.30

The Chart Location dialog
box

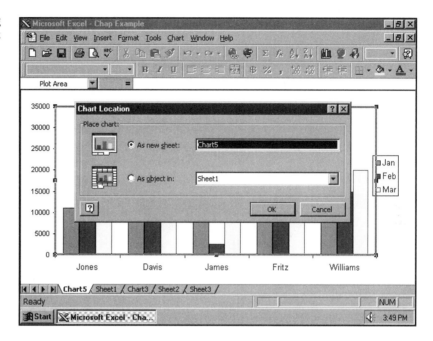

Adding Trendlines

Trendlines show trends in the data by drawing lines across data points. The line represents and displays the movement of a data point.

There are six different types of trendlines to choose from, and numerous ways to format each. Trendline types include five regression trendlines (linear, logarithmic, polynomial, power, and exponential) and a moving average trendline.

After you have inserted a trendline, you can change its pattern or type of line. Activate the line by clicking on it once, then double-click on any of the blocks on the line.

Formatting Axes

You can control a number of characteristics of the chart axes, such as how their tick marks are displayed, what font is used to display the axis labels, the scale of the axis, and how its data aligns with its tick marks. Double-click on the axis that you want to modify, or right-click on the axis and choose Format Axis from the pop-up menu. Either method will show you the Format Axis dialog box in Figure 14.31.

Figure 14.31

The Format Axis dialog
box

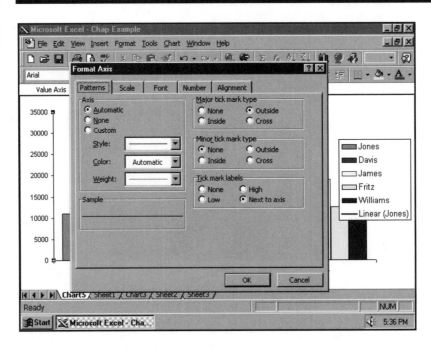

Tip. If you change the
value axis scale, be
careful that you highlight
the axis for your readers
so that they instantly
notice the changed
scale. This way you avoid
charts that might give
your readers the wrong
impression. (If you want
to see examples of such
charts, look at almost
any economic graph in
USA Today or many other
newspapers: many of
these have very small
value axis scales (for
example, the value axis
runs from, say, 793.4 to
795.3) and, at first
glance, can be
misleading.)

The Patterns tab (see Figure 14.31) lets you control how the axis is displayed. You can choose how the axis line is drawn (Style and Weight), and can choose the axis line color with the Color drop-down list box. You can also select the type of tick mark that is displayed using the option buttons on the right side of the tab. For both major and minor tick marks, you can choose from no tick marks (None), Outside ticks, Inside ticks, and Cross ticks.

The Scale tab (Figure 14.32 and Figure 14.33) of the Format Axis dialog box is frequently used. It lets you control the scale of the axis—how the values or categories are displayed.

On the Scale tab you can change the minimum and maximum scale numbers to "zoom in" on a part of the chart, leaving out other details. For instance, if you have a line chart that shows a relatively flat line, you can change the Minimum and Maximum settings so that the entire vertical area of the chart covers a very small numerical area (say from 75 percent to 76 percent instead of from 0 percent to 100 percent).

The three other tabs in the Format Axis dialog box (Font, Number, and Alignment) control how the text labels for the axis are displayed. The Font tab lets you choose the font used, the Number tab lets you choose how the numbers are formatted, and the Alignment tab lets you rotate the text.

Figure 14.32

The Scale tab of a Y axis
that lets you control
values that are charted

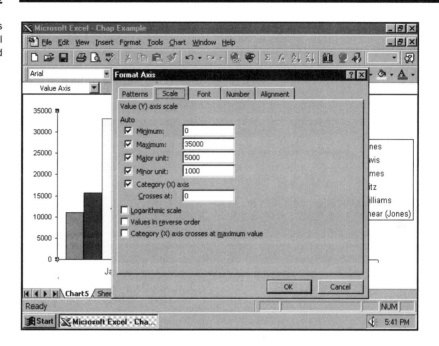

Figure 14.33

The Scale tab of an X
axis that lets you control
how categories are
displayed

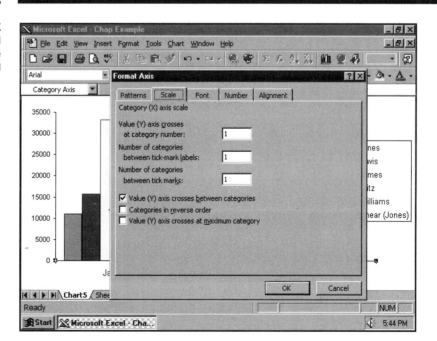

■ Summary

Excel 97 offers a number of charting improvements over previous versions of Excel. Excel 97 has done two things to the charting module: made it more powerful, and made it easier to use. It's uncommon to accomplish both goals, so Microsoft is to be commended for its work in this area.

You can use Excel's charting features to communicate your information more effectively than it would be if expressed as numbers alone. Charts are like pictures: they can be worth a thousand words (or a thousand numbers, in this case.) A properly formatted chart lets an audience instantly see the information being presented, and can often influence how they think about a particular topic. Mastering the charting features in Excel can make your work more easily understood, and help you influence your audience.

- *Using Query Wizard*
- *Importing ASCII Data*
- *Filtering Your Data*
- *Totaling and Subtotaling Lists*
- *Sorting Your Data*
- *Using Pivot Tables*
- *Automatically Formatting Your Tables*

15

Excel Data Management

Many people find that they don't need the full power (and complexity) of a database program like Access to manage most of their information. Instead, Excel's list-management features fulfill most peoples' needs. Managing data in Excel is a two-part process. First, unless you plan to type your data into Excel, you must be able to automatically bring it in from whatever source currently holds it. Second, once your data is in Excel, you will need to work with it in a variety of ways.

In this chapter, you learn about the following:

- Using Query Wizard to Query and Import Data

- Importing ASCII Data

- Sorting and subtotaling your data

- Using AutoFilter to examine parts of your data

- Improving the appearance of your data with AutoFormat

- Using pivot tables to summarize lists

Not only does Excel let you move all or selected data records from one data source into a worksheet, it gives you multiple methods for working with the data.

Being able to import and export data can lead to more effective use of office staff and increased productivity, as well as increased accuracy. It also means added power in terms of the type of information you can have in a worksheet, and in the steps for getting it there.

Excel uses Microsoft Query to perform a number of data-import and export tasks. You can use Microsoft Query directly to perform sophisticated query operations, but you can also achieve much with the Query Wizard, which uses Microsoft Query to get results but does so in a much easier-to-use fashion. In this chapter you'll learn how to use the Query Wizard.

Because Excel, Query Wizard, and Microsoft Query are very flexible, you have a chance to evaluate different ways to harness the power of importing and exporting data to and from your applications.

■ Using Query Wizard

Microsoft Query is a tool that helps you retrieve and sort data from a wide range of sources. These sources include the following:

- Microsoft Excel

- Microsoft Access

- Microsoft FoxPro

- Microsoft SQL Server

- ASCII Text

- dBASE

- Paradox

- Btrieve

Tip. If you do not have drivers for the source you need, contact Microsoft.

You need to install Query with the drivers to access these different data sources, and drivers for some of these sources come with Microsoft Query. After you use Query Wizard to access the data source you need, you can use it to sort, filter, and display information, and then send it to the application of your choice, such as Excel.

In Microsoft Query and Query Wizard, you can perform several functions that retrieve data. The most common operation is called a query. A *query* is a question about a group of data: for example, "For which customers do we have information?" or "How many customers do we have in the 12345 ZIP Code?" Microsoft Query translates your questions into a format that your computer can understand, and returns the answer as a table.

A *table* is a collection of information arranged in rows and columns. An Excel worksheet is an example of a table. Tables are usually organized by topic or by related item, such as customers, parts numbers, and the like. From a database perspective, the rows and columns equate to records and fields. A *field* is one portion of a record. Name, Address, and ZIP Code are examples of fields. A *record* is a row of related fields. A *customer record* might be a collection of 10 fields of data, all relating to one customer.

You can start Query Wizard by choosing Data, Get External Data, Create New Query. If the Get External Data option is not available on your Tools menu, select Add-ins to see whether the Query Add-in is installed. Odds are that it isn't, in which case you can use the Excel Setup program to configure it for your system.

You can also use certain external data-retrieval functions to launch Microsoft Query, such as pivot tables, which are explored in greater detail in the "Using Pivot Tables" section of this chapter.

Choosing a Data Source

For this example, start Query Wizard by choosing the Data menu, choosing the Get External Data sub-menu, and then the Create New Query command. You will see the Choose Data Source dialog box shown in Figure 15.1.

A *data source* is a definition that tells Query Wizard where to go to get its data. Each one that you want to use must be defined. The first time you use Query Wizard, you will need to define a new data source, which you do by clicking the OK button in the Choose Data Source dialog box. (Since <New Data Source> is selected in the Databases tab, you see the Create New Data Source dialog box next, in which you can define the origin of your data.)

Figure 15.2 shows the Create New Data Source dialog box. You complete this dialog box in steps, following the numbers on the left side of the dialog box. First, you enter a name that you want to use for your data source. In this example, type **dBase Example Files**. Next, you choose the driver that will be used to access the data. The drop-down list box lets you select "Microsoft

Figure 15.1

When starting Query
Wizard, you must first
select the data source
with which you will work.

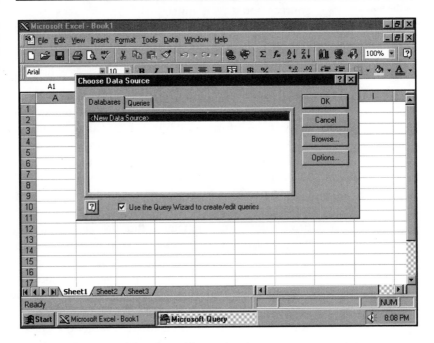

dBase Driver (*.dbf)," which you will use for this example. Next, click on the
Connect button, which brings up a dialog box from which you choose the settings appropriate for the database driver selected. Figure 15.3 shows the
ODBC dBase Setup dialog box that appears when you click on Connect with
the Microsoft dBase Driver.

In the ODBC dBase Setup dialog box, choose Version "dBase 5.0" and
use the Select Directory button to choose the \Office97\Office directory
("Office97" can be replaced in this directory name with the name of the directory where you have installed Office). Then click the OK button to return
to the Create New Data Source dialog box. Click OK again to close the Create New Data Source dialog box and return to the Choose Data Source dialog box (see Figure 15.4).

Make sure that dBase Example Files is selected, as shown in Figure 15.4, and
click on the OK button to continue. The Query Wizard will start automatically.

Using the Query Wizard

Database queries can be complex beasts, and often even experienced database
programmers have difficulty setting up queries that perform exactly as intended. Because queries can be problematic, you can use the Query Wizard to
walk you through the process, making it as quick and painless as possible.

Figure 15.2

The first step to creating a query is to select your data source. In this case you need to create a new data source before you can select one.

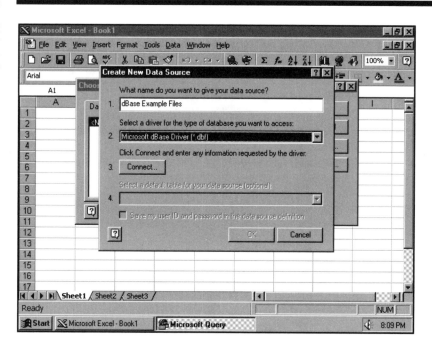

Figure 15.3

After clicking the Connect button, you will see a dialog box that lets you define the data source in more detail.

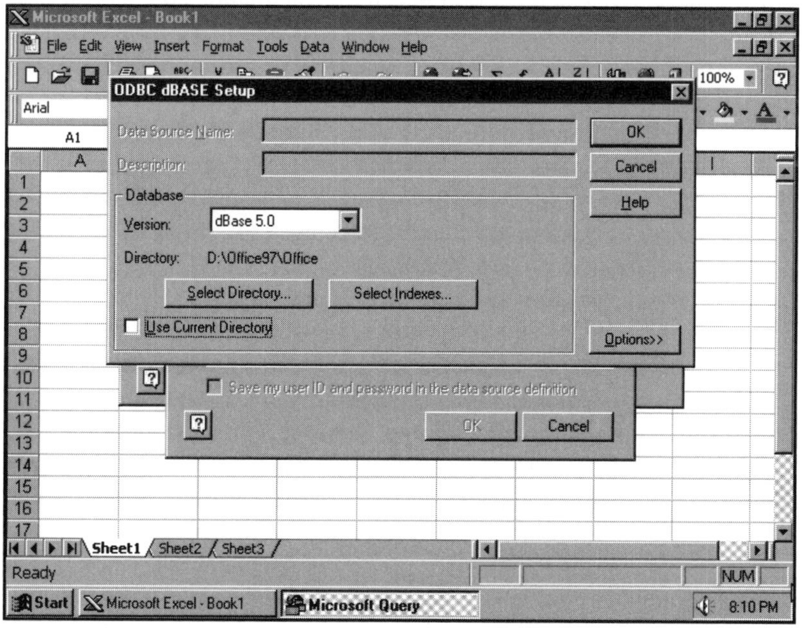

Figure 15.4

After you have successfully created a data source, it will appear in the Databases tab.

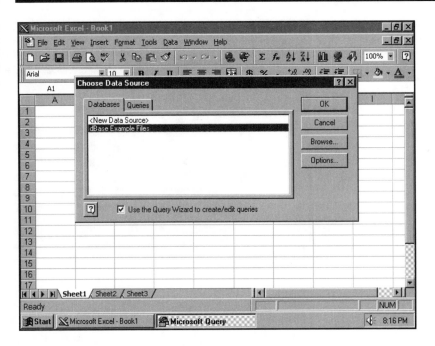

Figure 15.5 shows you the first screen of the Query Wizard, called Choose Columns. In this dialog box you choose which columns, from which database files, will be included in your query. In this example, you will retrieve a listing of all customers from the CUSTOMER database file. Click on the plus sign next to CUSTOMER to view the columns in that database and then choose each of the four CUSTOMER columns in turn by double-clicking on them. You will see the columns appear in the "Columns in your query" window as you select them. Figure 15.5 shows the CUSTMR_ID and COMPANY fields selected; CITY and REGION are not yet selected. (Be sure to select all four columns for this exercise, though.) Click on the Next button to continue to the next step.

The next step of the Query Wizard is called Filter Data. In this dialog box (see Figure 15.6) you can choose to include a subset of data, such as only customers from California, or companies whose name begins with the letter A. In this example, however, you want all of the data—so click on the Next button to continue. (You will learn how to filter data later in this chapter.)

The next step of the Query Wizard, Sort Order, lets you sort the data as it is returned to Excel. Use the Sort By drop-down list box to choose COMPANY, and make sure the Ascending option button to the right is selected. This will yield a list of companies sorted by name. Figure 15.7 shows this dialog box. After you've selected COMPANY, click on the Next button to continue.

Figure 15.5

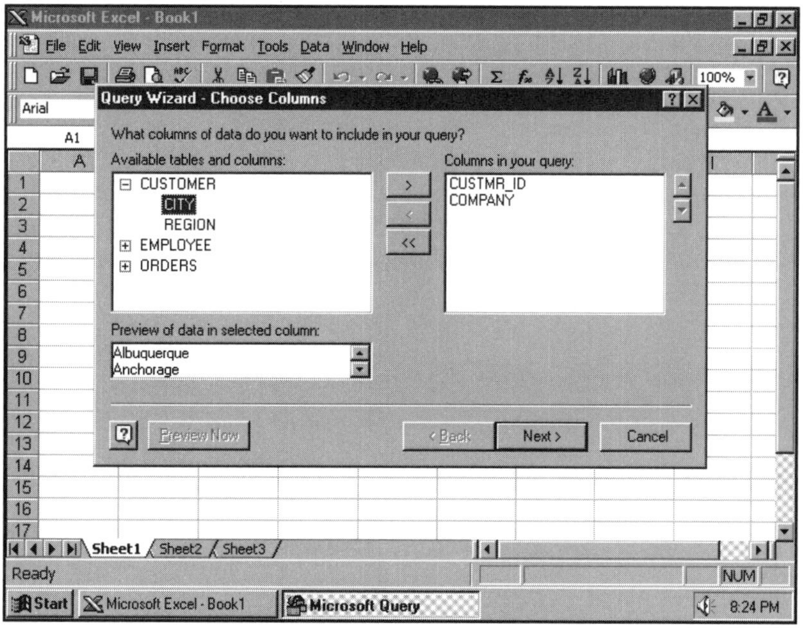

Selecting database
columns in the Choose
Columns dialog box of
the Query Wizard

Figure 15.6

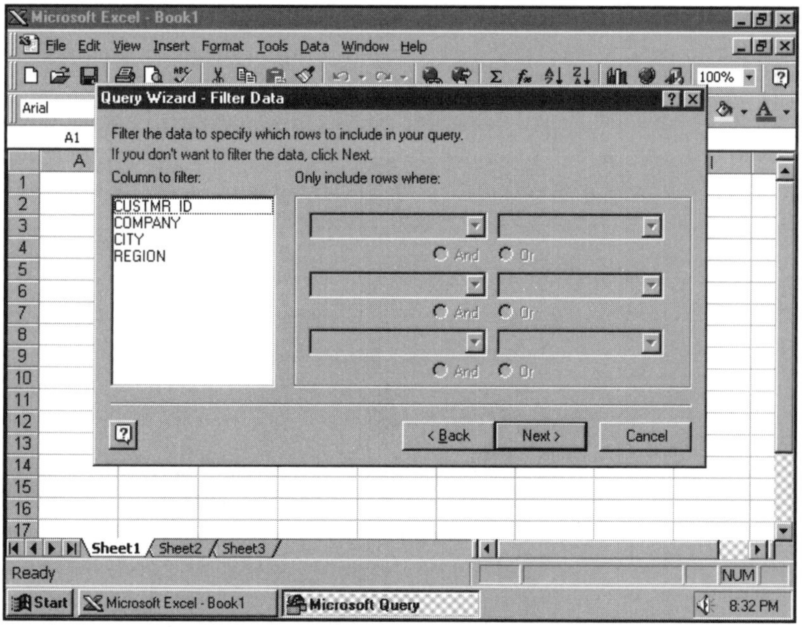

Step 2 of the Query
Wizard: Filter Data

Figure 15.7

Sorting your data using
the Sort Order dialog box

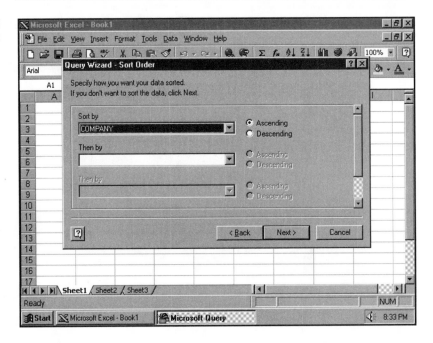

Finally, you will come to the Finish dialog box shown in Figure 15.8. At this point you have three possible actions: You can save your query for re-use in the future, you can return the data to Excel, or you can view the data or edit the query using Microsoft Query. For this simple example, first choose the Save Query button and save the query with the name **Example Query**. Then choose Return Data to Microsoft Excel and click on the Finish button.

After clicking the Finish button, you will see the Returning External Data to Microsoft Excel dialog box. Use this dialog box, shown in Figure 15.9, to determine where your retrieved data is placed. Accept the defaults of Existing Worksheet and cell A1, and click the OK button.

After a brief pause as Excel retrieves the data, you will see the requested data appear in your worksheet, as shown in Figure 15.10. The External Data toolbar will also become visible.

Selecting Data

When using the Query Wizard, you can employ the Filter Data dialog box to retrieve only selected records. Select the column name that you want to filter by, then tell Query Wizard how to select the data you want. For example, Figure 15.11 shows the Filter Data dialog box completed in such a way that only customers that are in the NY region will be retrieved.

Figure 15.8

The final dialog box of the
Query Wizard

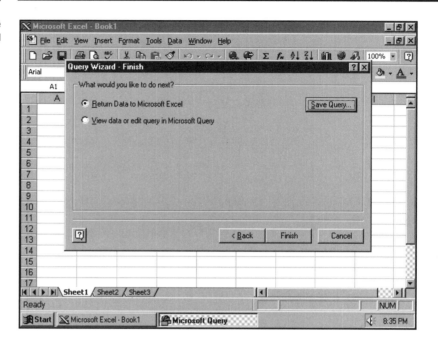

Figure 15.9

Returning External Data
to Microsoft Excel dialog
box, which lets you
choose where your data
goes

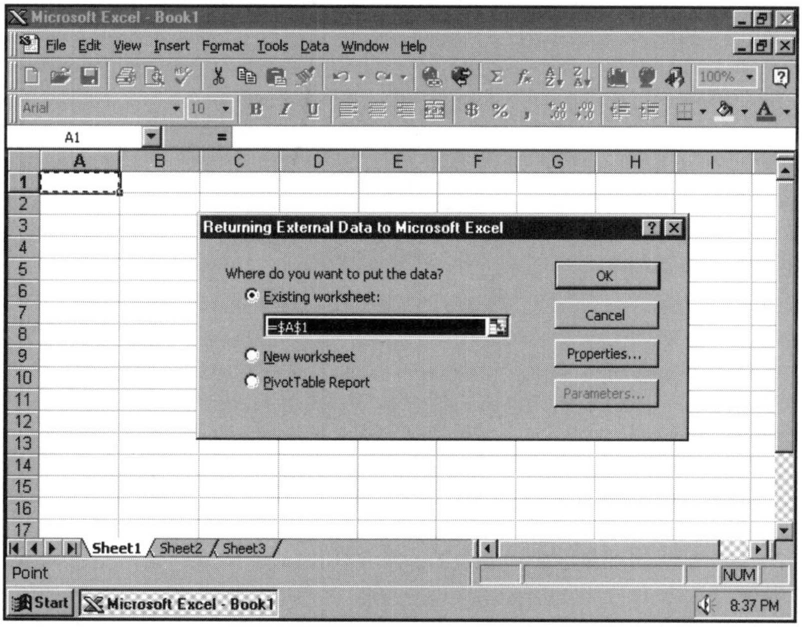

Figure 15.10

Voila! The external data has been queried successfully and returned to your Excel worksheet.

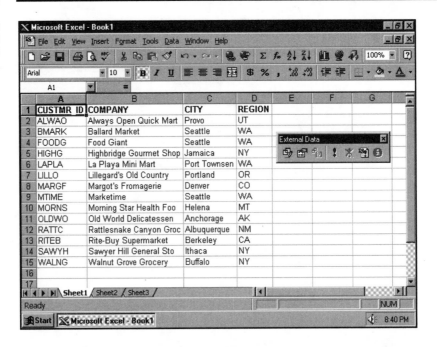

Figure 15.11

Use the Filter Data dialog box when building your query to select only certain data.

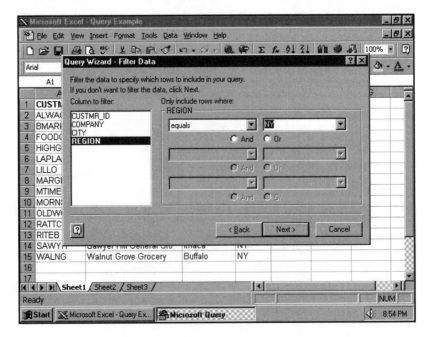

When you choose filter operations, you can select from a number of operators. You can use the equals operator to define exact matches that will be included, as shown in Figure 15.11, but you can also choose from a number of other operators. You can choose from these operators:

- Equals
- Does not equal
- Is greater than
- Is greater than or equal to
- Is less than
- Is less than or equal to
- Begins with
- Does not begin with
- Ends with
- Does not end with
- Contains
- Does not contain
- Is like
- Is not like
- Is null
- Is not null

Obviously, some operators are more useful for certain data types than others. For instance, it might make sense if you're looking for a letter or character string to look in a text field with the Begins with operator, but not in a numeric or date field.

After you choose an operator, you can click on the right-hand drop-down list box to choose from the available data, or you can type your own data into the field that you want to use with the matching operator.

You can form more complex queries in two ways. First, you can click on the And or the Or option button, and then complete the next criteria. You could enter in the query **Region equals NY or Region equals CA** to extract just records for either of those regions, for example.

The second way to form more complex queries is to add criteria for other columns: each column can have its own query criteria, if you wish. Just complete one column's criteria, then select another column in the Column to

Filter list and complete its criteria. Columns with existing criteria will display in the Column to Filter list in bold type.

■ Importing ASCII Data

Many times you will need to import data that exists in ASCII or plain text format. This usually happens when you have another program that exports its data in this format, such as an accounting system of some sort. Excel uses its Text Import Wizard to help you bring in data that isn't formatted for Excel.

To start importing data from an ASCII file, simply open it using the Open command in the File menu. Excel will recognize that the file is ASCII-based, and will start up the Text Import Wizard automatically to walk you through the process of identifying the data for Excel, as shown in Figure 15.12.

Figure 15.12

Opening an ASCII file automatically starts the Text Import Wizard.

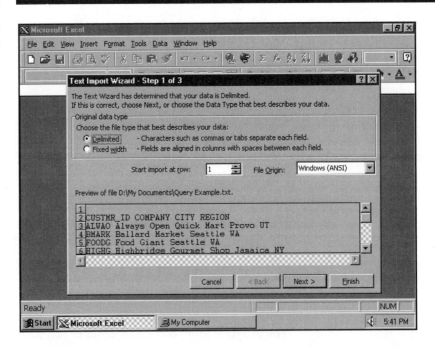

In Step 1 of 3 (see Figure 15.12), you identify these two pieces of information for Excel:

- Choose between Delimited and Fixed Width. A delimited file is one in which some character—such as a comma, space, or tab—separates each field. A fixed-width file is one in which all the fields are in exactly the same position on each line (and sometimes are all together, such that it is hard to see where each field begins and ends).

- Look in the Preview window to see what the file actually contains. If the file contains heading information, set the Start Import at Row field to the number of lines that Excel should skip. For instance, if you're importing an accounting report, the first several lines may just contain report heading information that you really don't want in your spreadsheet.

Click on the Next button to move to Step 2 of 3, shown in Figure 15.13.

Figure 15.13

In Step 2 of 3, you tell Excel how the file is laid out. This step will be different for delimited or fixed-width files.

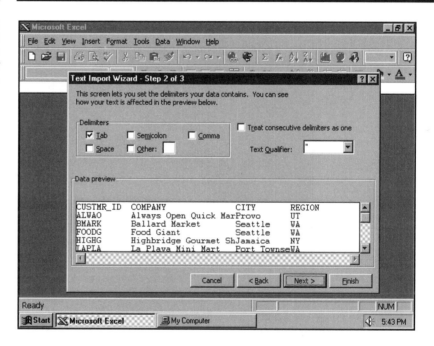

For Step 2 of 3 with delimited files, set these options:

- In the Delimiters area, choose the appropriate character that separates each field. A comma is a common delimiter character, as are tabs and spaces. You can choose multiple delimiters if your file uses them.

- The check box Treat Consecutive Delimiters as One eliminates any empty fields from your data input. Often, a null field will simply show up with, say, two commas right next to each other. Selecting this check box causes Excel to skip over those blank fields. However, choosing this check box may leave you with data that is not aligned in the same column in the final spreadsheet.

- Many ASCII files make a special point of distinguishing text fields by enclosing the text with quotation marks or some other character. This lets Excel know which fields are text, and which are simply numbers. If your file uses a special extra delimiter for text fields, choose that character in the Text Qualifier drop-down list.

Click on Next to move to Step 3 of 3, shown in Figure 15.14.

Figure 15.14

In the final step (3 of 3) of the Text Import Wizard, you identify how Excel should format each column of data.

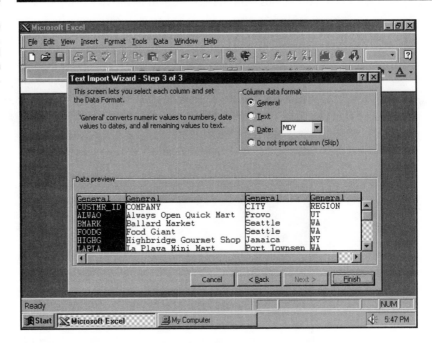

Select each column of data in Step 3 of 3, then choose the appropriate Column Data Format for each column. By default, each one will be formatted for General. However, there is a danger in letting this choice remain for some types of fields. Sometimes numeric data should be treated as text. For instance, an inventory listing might contain part numbers that lead with zeroes. If you import that column as General, the values will be entered into Excel as numbers and any leading zeroes will be lost. Prevent this problem by forcing Excel to treat such a column as text.

■ **Filtering Your Data**

Note. The AutoFilter
command is a checked
command. In other
words, when you select
it you turn AutoFilter on;
select it again and
AutoFilter is turned off.

Excel's AutoFilter tool helps you make sense of long lists of data. AutoFilter lets you quickly and easily restrict a list to show only a subset of your data.

To use AutoFilter, start with a worksheet that contains a lot of data, such as the one imported in Figure 15.15. Make sure your active cell is within the data you want to filter, then pull down the Data menu and choose Filter. This displays a submenu, in which you can find the AutoFilter command (see Figure 15.16).

Figure 15.15

Here, data captured from a telephone-call accounting system is imported with Excel's Text Import Wizard.

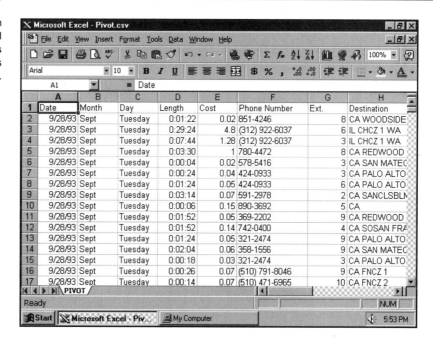

Activating AutoFilter displays arrows next to your headings. Clicking on these drop-down arrows displays lists of all the valid choices for that column (see Figure 15.17).

Tip. To return to seeing
all of your data, activate
the columns that you
filtered and choose (All)
from their lists.

When you choose to AutoFilter a column, only the lines that contain the choice you made are displayed. You can restrict what you see by combining columns in whatever way you want. In this case, for example, you could show only the calls made to a certain city, and then further restrict the listing to calls made on Tuesday.

Figure 15.16

The Data menu contains the AutoFilter command.

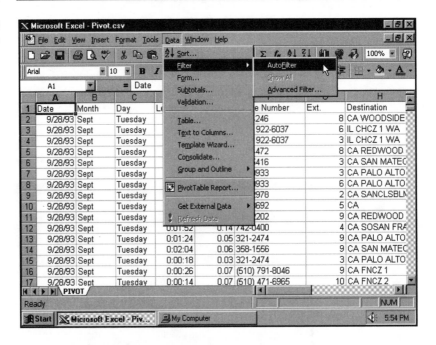

Figure 15.17

Each heading has a drop-down list arrow that lets you select from all the valid choices for that column.

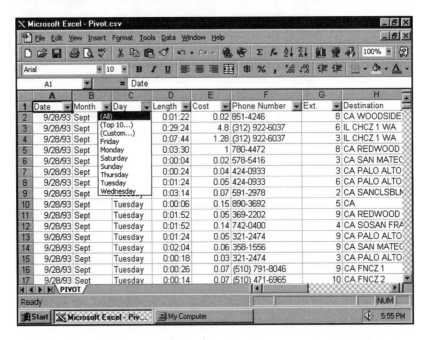

More Complex Filtering

AutoFilter also lets you ask additional questions. For one thing, each column drop-down list contains a choice called (Top 10) that displays all the rows containing the 10 most frequent choices for that column. For example, if you choose (Top 10) in the Destination field in this example, you would see a list that only showed the records for the top 10 calling destinations. Alternatively, you could find the Extension field that shows what phone in the company placed the call, and restrict the list to the 10 extensions that made the most calls. Doing this helps you focus your analysis efforts.

You can also choose custom AutoFilter choices. For any column, choose the (Custom) choice. This brings up the dialog box shown in Figure 15.18.

Figure 15.18

Use the (Custom) choice to define complex criteria.

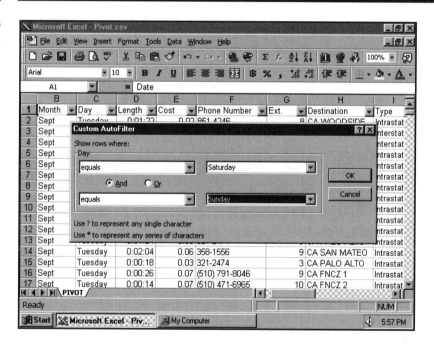

The (Custom) choice lets you define more complex criteria. In this example, you could see all calls made on weekends. Another choice would be to restrict the Cost field to amounts greater than $10.00, to see only those calls.

■ Totaling and Subtotaling Lists

Excel also lets you quickly total and subtotal your lists of data. To do this, make sure your active cell is within your data, pull down the Data menu, and choose Subtotals. This displays the Subtotal dialog box shown in Figure 15.19.

Figure 15.19

The Subtotal dialog box lets you choose how you want your data subtotaled.

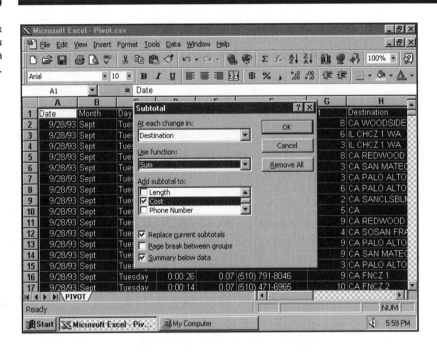

Note. Be sure to sort your data (see the next section) by the column that you want to use as your break group before performing the subtotal. The break group is the one in which you will be inserting subtotals. In this example, it is the Destination column.

In this example, when the subtotals are applied, you will see a subtotal every time the destination changes (thereby subtotaling for each different destination), and the subtotal shown will be a Sum of the values in the Cost field.

After filling in this dialog box, click the OK button to insert the subtotals. The results are shown in Figure 15.20.

Subtotals are inserted as outline levels. If you choose, you can collapse the outline levels by clicking on the minus buttons, thereby hiding the detail and leaving only the subtotals.

To remove the subtotals, reaccess the Subtotal command and click on the Remove All button.

Figure 15.20

The inserted subtotals

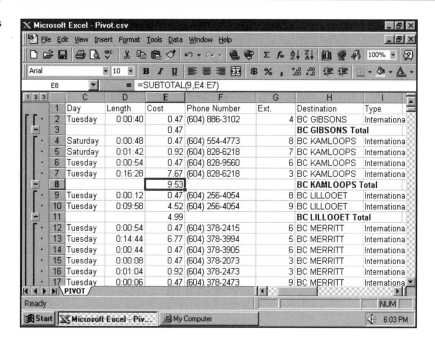

■ Sorting Your Data

Note. If your data has column-heading descriptions (and it should to make things easier), you can choose to sort by those names. On the other hand, if you do not have column headings, the Sort dialog box only displays column letters.

Excel can quickly and painlessly sort your data in a variety of ways. To access the sort feature, make sure your active cell is within your data, activate the Data menu and choose the Sort command. You will see the dialog box in Figure 15.21.

■ Using Pivot Tables

Pivot tables are tools used in Excel to summarize large lists, databases, worksheets, workbooks, or other collections of data. They are called pivot tables because you can move fields with the mouse to provide different types of summary listings: that is, the tables can change, or pivot.

Pivot tables can get their source information from a number of sources. For this discussion, you will extract data for the pivot table from external sources using the Query Wizard.

Begin with a blank worksheet. The first part of creating a pivot table is invoking the Pivot Table Wizard. This is the first button on the Query and Pivot toolbar. You can also use the PivotTable Report command in the Data

Figure 15.21

Use the Sort dialog box to sort your data in the preferred order.

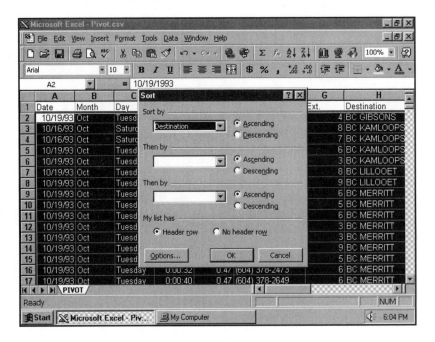

menu. The first screen of the Pivot Table Wizard is the data-source selection step. You have the following choices:

- Microsoft Excel List or Database

- External Data Source

- Multiple Consolidation Ranges

- Another Pivot Table

Choose External Data Source and click on Next. The Step 2 of 4 dialog box appears. Click on the Get Data button, which has the notation *No data fields have been retrieved*. The Query Wizard is launched.

Follow the steps involved in choosing a data source, choosing a table, and setting up a result set. Use the steps that you learned at the beginning of the chapter to create a data source for Access tables and select the OR-DERS.MDB database located in the \Office97\Office\Samples directory. Select the Invoices table and include the following fields in your query:

- Customers/CompanyName

- City

- Region

- Salesperson

- ProductName

- Quantity

- ExtendedPrice

There is no need to filter or sort the data as you use the Query Wizard to return it to an Excel sheet.

The Data is then sent to Excel through the Clipboard. The Pivot Table Wizard - Step 3 of 4 dialog box appears. Figure 15.22 shows the Pivot Table setup screen.

Figure 15.22

Setting up the PivotTable involves dragging the field buttons to positions in this dialog box.

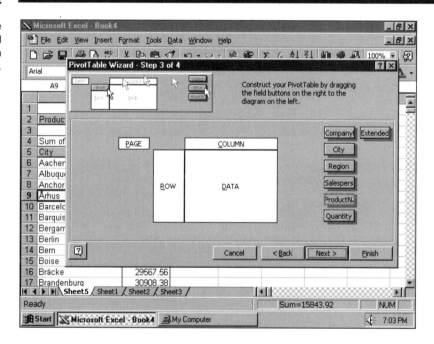

The fields that you select in your result set will appear along the right side of the dialog box. The areas of the pivot table that you will work with are Row information, Column information, Data, and Page. You can drag the selected fields into these separate areas to format tables.

In this example you'll see a basic breakdown of the data you retrieved. You will analyze product sales by region. To do this, drag the ProductName field to the Page area, the Region field to the Row area, and the Extended-Price field to the Data area. The completed PivotTable Wizard dialog box is shown in Figure 15.23.

Figure 15.23

The completed PivotTable
setup

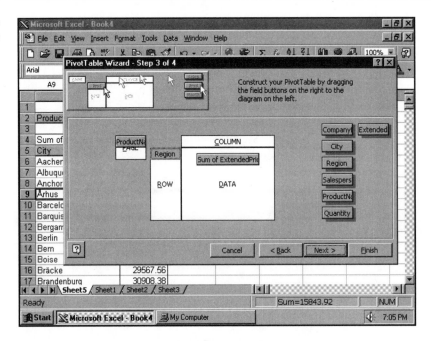

Click on Next, then click on Finish after choosing to put the PivotTable into a New Worksheet. The resulting pivot table is shown in Figure 15.24.

This relatively simple PivotTable can be used to see how much of each product the business in this example is selling in different regions. Select the product you want to examine by changing the ProductName field, using the drop-down list to the right of the field name. The instant you select it, you will see the data area of the PivotTable display the sales broken down by region, with total dollar amounts by region shown to the right of each region. A grand total for product sales to all regions is shown at the bottom of the table.

You can add and remove fields from the PivotTable by using the Wizard command from the pop-up menu that appears when you right-click on one of the PivotTable cells. This redisplays the PivotTable Wizard dialog box, in which you can arrange the data. Using this tool, you can build new or different PivotTables easily.

Using this capability, you can analyze your data differently. For example, access the Wizard command in the PivotTable's pop-up menu and arrange the fields like this: Place Region in the Page area, Salesperson in the Column area, ProductName in the Row area, and ExtendedPrice in the Data area. The completed PivotTable Wizard dialog box will be as shown in Figure 15.25.

Figure 15.24

The resulting PivotTable

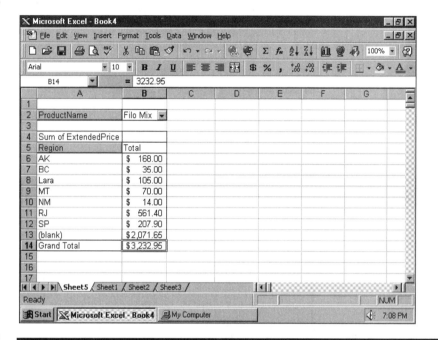

Figure 15.25

A different analysis of the data using the PivotTable Wizard dialog box

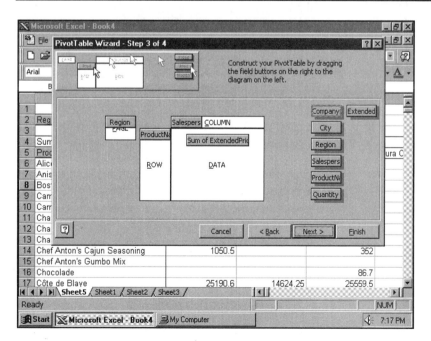

The PivotTable now shows you sales by product for each salesperson. With (All) selected in the Region field, you will see total sales across the company. You can use the Region field, however, to restrict sales shown to each individual region. Figure 15.26 shows the completed PivotTable.

Figure 15.26

The new resulting PivotTable

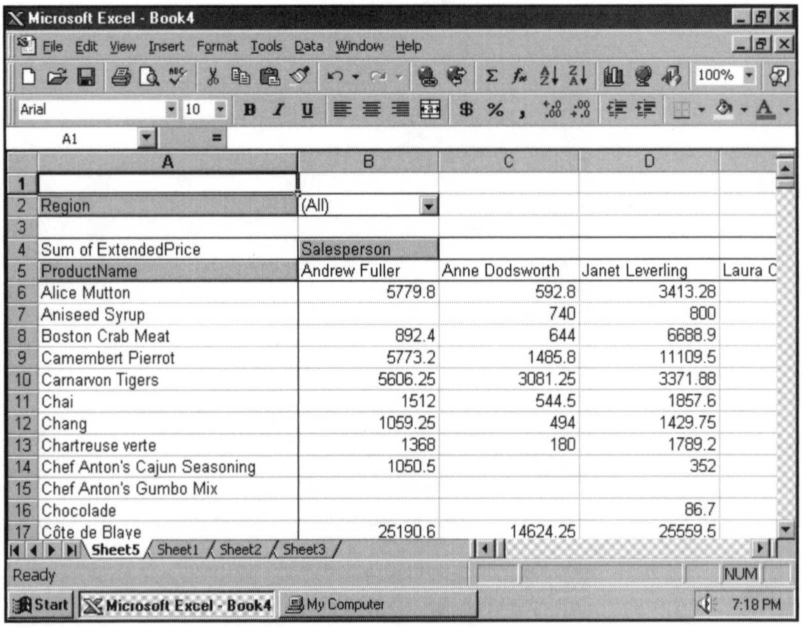

The pivot table is a very powerful analysis tool. You can summarize a vast amount of information in a friendly, informative, interactive worksheet table.

You cannot edit information in a pivot table because it maintains a link to the source data, but updating the source file does pass any new or changed information to the table. In this example, for instance, any new orders for customers will show up on the pivot table if they are entered into the source database. When the table is retrieved, the Exclamation Point button on the Query and Pivot toolbar is the Refresh Data tool. Clicking on this button performs the original query, and returns any new or changed information to your table.

If you decide you want to change the orientation of the table, you can do so dynamically by dragging the field identifiers to the desired location. As an example, if you want to see the Salesperson information in a row instead of a column, click and drag the field name for Salesperson from its present column to the Row area. The pivot table automatically reformats itself with the new information. You do not need to reaccess the PivotTable Wizard dialog box to do this: you can do it on the PivotTable directly.

You can also double-click on a field name to customize it. The customization can change where it is located; row, column or data; and how it is totaled, if at all. You also can choose to hide items.

The totals that appear on the table are figured for each subcategory in the row and for the column. When you add an additional row field, the pivot table provides a new subtotal field on the row. The same occurs with column information. The information in every row and every column is totaled. There is a grand total field for the table.

After you create your table, you can change the way it displays information in addition to dragging row, column, and page fields to new locations. By highlighting a range of cells in the detail section of the table and selecting Group from the toolbar, the pivot table combines the information into a single section. Using the Hide Detail button, you can then display just the totals.

■ Automatically Formatting Your Tables

You will generally want to format your tables to make them more pleasing to look at. Perhaps you want to print them out and make them easier to read, or perhaps you need to present the data to someone else. In any case, Excel provides an AutoFormat function that gives you several pre-designed choices.

Start with your active cell within the table you want to format, pull down the Format menu, and choose AutoFormat. This displays the AutoFormat dialog box shown in Figure 15.27.

Select each different table format to see a preview of how your table will look when formatted. When you've found a format you like, select it and click on the OK button. Your table will be formatted using the same guidelines as the preview.

NOTE. *Some printers may not handle the shading for some of the pre-defined table formats correctly. If you're working with a large amount of data, try printing just one page to make sure your printer gives you results that come out the way you want them. Then either choose a different table format and try again, or print the entire set of data.*

Figure 15.27

The AutoFormat dialog box makes formatting your data quick and easy.

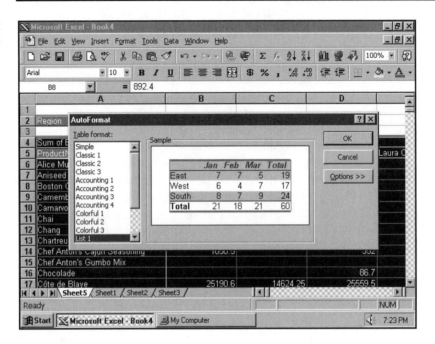

■ Summary

When you need to manage data stored in lists, you often do not need a complete database program: Excel contains features that make managing lists a snap. While you do not want to use Excel to manage lists made up of tens of thousands of records, Excel can easily handle lists of several thousand records. So long as you do not need the more sophisticated data management tools of a complete database, Excel will fit your needs. Excel is usually much more convenient to use than a full database program like Microsoft Access.

Also remember that if Excel doesn't meet your needs, you can easily move Excel lists into other formats, which can then be opened in a full database program. Access can even directly import Excel worksheets into its own databases if at some time you need its more potent data-management capabilities. Keep this in mind when you want to use Excel to manage a list of data, but aren't sure if it will handle everything you want to do. You lose little by trying, since you can always move your data if you run out of steam in Excel.

4

PowerPoint

- *Beginning a New Presentation Using the Office 97 Toolbar*
- *Bypassing the Office 97 Menu to Start PowerPoint*
- *AutoContent Wizard*
- *Using Templates*
- *Creating a Blank Presentation*
- *Open an Existing Presentation*

- *Changing the Default Page Setup*
- *Using PowerPoint Views*
- *Manipulating PowerPoint Toolbars*
- *Using Toolbar Functions*
- *Using Drawing Toolbars*
- *Working with Text within Shapes*
- *Using Alignment Tools*
- *Understanding the Masters*
- *PowerPoint 97 Is a "Living Application"*

16

PowerPoint 97 Tools and Concepts

This chapter introduces powerpoint to new users, and updates experienced users about its new features.

In a nutshell, PowerPoint creates slide shows on your computer. These can be simple presentations with text that changes on your screen after 30 seconds, or full-blown interactive multimedia tutorials, complete with write-in responses from the user and automatic connections to Web sites.

With PowerPoint, you design it as you see it. If you want text on the screen in a particular color and font, just type it in. If you want to add a picture or data table, simply open the appropriate dialog box, position it, and resize it as you wish. You may add as many slides as you like and set them to change automatically, or leave control to the viewer of your show. Slide shows can include animated text and graphics, music, and drawings that you create from over 100 shape tools. You use the same formatting tools to work with text in PowerPoint as you would in any other Office 97 application.

PowerPoint presentations can have hyperlinks: buttons to push that lead to Web sites, other slides in your presentation, or links to other documents on your network server. In fact, PowerPoint can function in an integrated way with all of your Office 97 applications. For example, Excel spreadsheets can be part of your slide show, as can Word documents. The Visual Basic tools included with PowerPoint can create programs and executables that will work in any Office 97 program. Not surprisingly, PowerPoint 97 can create entire Web Sites (see Figure 16.1). These can include sounds, videos, and "clickable" areas that will lead people to other pages in your site. Data-collection areas can be created in your site, without your having to know a stitch of CGI script. Additionally, a PowerPoint presentation can be embedded in an existing Web page. The Office 97 CD includes a free PowerPoint Animation Player. Distribute this as a browser extension to those who want to view the PowerPoint animation on your page.

If you'd rather not start a slide show from scratch, PowerPoint includes dozens of templates. These feature built-in formatting, where all you have to do is provide the text. Other templates include ideas for "brainstorming" sessions between you and your workmates, team discussion templates, and self-running information kiosks for trade shows and conferences. PowerPoint 97 does not use the term "template" as such. To open a pre-designed presentation and personalize it, you merely click on one of the four categories of presentations at the startup screen, and replace the text and pictures as you see fit.

PowerPoint can also be used to create printed material, such as certificates, calendars of events, and flyers. One special feature generates printed "speaker notes" that help guide you and your teammates during the presentation. To do so, Select File, Print and select Notes Pages or Handouts from the Print What menu.

One feature that more advanced users will appreciate is the ability to create Custom shows, with which you can make multiple versions of one major presentation, each tailored to a specific audience (see Figure 16.2). You can

Figure 16.1

The Save as HTML
dialog box

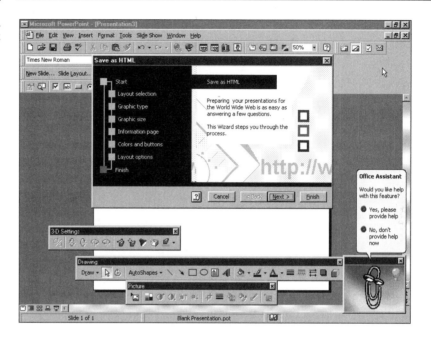

freely rearrange or add slides for various occasions without altering the "core" presentation itself. To make a Custom Show, select Slide Show, Custom Show, New.

Another advanced feature is the Meeting Minder. The presenter uses it to record notes and action points during the presentation and, at the end, to generate a final slide summing up the agreed-upon actions. The Meeting Minder's summary can be sent to Microsoft Outlook to assist with scheduling and task-assignment. PowerPoint now includes advanced 3D drawing tools, which add perspective, lighting effects, and shadows to both artwork and text. There are now over 150 Shape Tools, including algorithmic connectors, symbols, and various styles of callout boxes. Charts can be extensively labeled, and their labels can be rotated for easier viewing.

■ Beginning a New Presentation Using the Office 97 Toolbar

Open PowerPoint by selecting New Office Document from the Office 97 toolbar. From there, click Blank Presentation, and PowerPoint's New Slide screen will appear (see Figure 16.3). You'll be prompted to choose an AutoLayout from a handful of template slides that require you only to add

Figure 16.2

The Replace dialog box

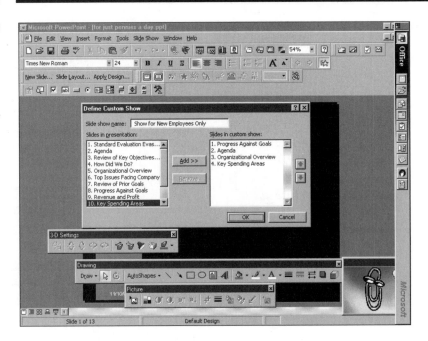

text and perhaps a graphic or two. The default AutoLayout provides simple text markers and guidance, but if you really want to go it alone without a template, use the "blank slide" provided at the lower right of the New Slide screen. (You can also start PowerPoint by selecting Microsoft PowerPoint from the Start, Programs menu).

You'll notice a brief description of the slide you are about to select at the bottom right of the New Slide screen. Some examples are "Organization Chart" and "Clipart and Text." This approach is truly geared to the person who has a meeting to catch in 20 minutes. Use one of these templates, and you won't be late. Each time you add a slide, you'll see the New Slide screen. That means you won't be locked into the same style of slide for your entire presentation. You can choose a Title Slide for Slide No. 1, and switch between many other slide types for the rest.

Moving Forward with Your Presentation

Here is a description of the tools you'll need to quickly personalize an Auto-Layout slide with your own text and artwork.

Figure 16.3

The New Slide screen featuring AutoLayout options

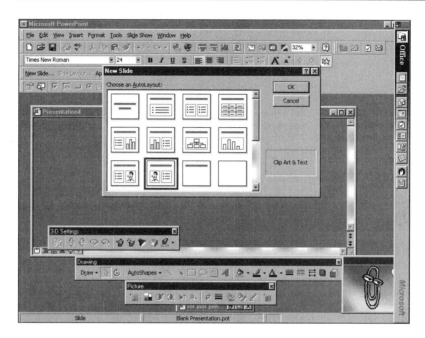

Replacing the Marker Text

If you have selected the Title slide, you'll notice the prompt, "Click to Add Title." Do so, and your text will replace the marker text, appearing in the same size and style. If you wish, replace the text style and format with others of your own choice using options from the Format menu (see Figure 16.4) or the Formatting Toolbar. Text formatting works the same way in PowerPoint as it does in other Office 97 applications. You may also format the shape the text appears in, its line width and color, and other characteristics. These features can be edited by selecting Format AutoShape from the Format menu.

The Text Box

When you clicked to replace the text, perhaps you noticed that the text box had six bounding boxes on each side and corner. These are for resizing the text box. Dragging a corner resizes the box proportionally. Dragging a bounding box on one of the sides resizes the text box along only the chosen axis.

Format AutoShape

If you double-click on the text box, you'll see that it's quite easy to change its attributes (see Figure 16.5). Double-clicking causes the Format AutoShape dialog box to appear. Here are the tools for shading the text box, and for

Figure 16.4

The Format menu

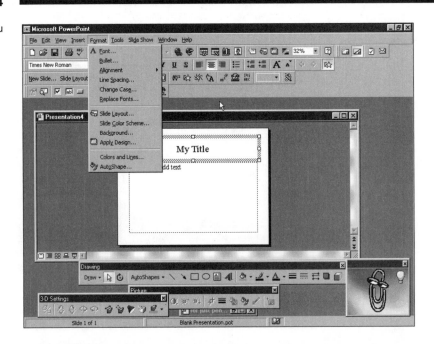

Figure 16.5

The Format AutoShape
dialog box

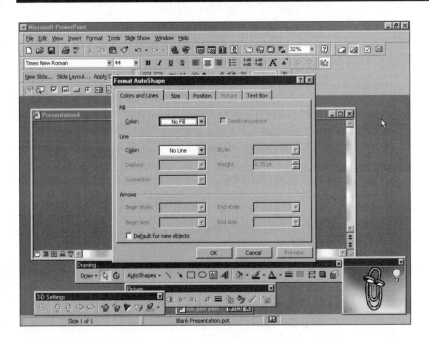

changing its border's thickness, color, and repositioning. You'll notice an option to "Word Wrap Text in AutoShape" on the Text Box tab of this dialog box. Checking this box forces your text to remain inside the box. You'll also see "Resize Text to Fit AutoShape." Enabling this feature stretches your text to fill the entire text box. Those familiar with PowerPoint 95 might wonder what happened to Text Anchor. It is now a submenu beneath the Text Box tab of the Format AutoShapes dialog box.

The Drawing Toolbar

While you have a reasonably blank slide on your screen, let's open the Drawing Toolbar. Herein lie some of the newest features of PowerPoint 97. If the Drawing toolbar is not on your screen, right-click on any blank toolbar space or select View, Toolbars. Just as with other Office 97 programs, a drop-down menu appears for selecting which toolbars should be on your desktop at the moment. If Drawing is not checked, put a check by it now. By default, the Drawing toolbar will attach itself to the bottom left of your screen. Click on AutoShapes, and see that each menu name has a submenu of shapes for just about any purpose.

Of special interest are the Action Buttons, which are like built-in hyperlinks. One provides a button that automatically starts a movie by linking to a file you specify. Another links to a sound, a slide, an Office application, or a Web site. You may place this instantly anywhere on your slide. Placing it on your screen opens a dialog box, which prompts you to supply the path for the file that you want associated with this button.

Clicking the 3D "A" opens the WordArt Gallery (see Figure 16.6). There are 36 graphic text styles you can instantly apply, or you can begin with one and edit it to build your own. Click the word "Draw" on the left side of the toolbar, and you'll see alignment and ordering commands, as well as tools to edit your shape curve by curve.

The Clipart Gallery

If you chose an AutoLayout that already had clip art in place, double-clicking on the clip art piece in your presentation will open the Clipart Gallery dialog box. If the AutoLayout you selected has no clip art, click the "picture of a man's face" icon on the Standard toolbar (the ToolTip will read "Insert Clipart"). You'll probably recognize this dialog box from working with Word 97 or other Office 97 applications. This means you'll have access to the same Clipart Gallery options and features as the other programs on the Office 97 CD.

There are, however, some PowerPoint-specific categories of clip art that will appear with the gallery. If you've performed a Typical Installation, you'll need to have the Office 97 CD in the CD-ROM drive to access all of the PowerPoint clip art.

Figure 16.6

The WordArt Gallery

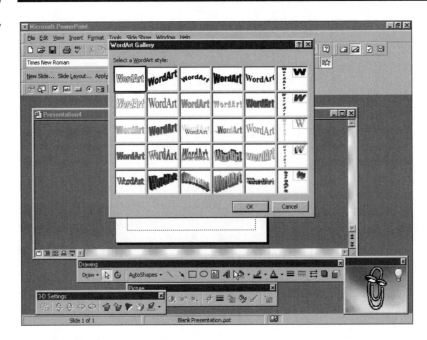

AutoClipArt

Choose Tools, AutoClipArt to access the AutoClipArt dialog box, as shown in Figure 16.7. This feature examines the text of your presentation, and provides clip art suggestions based on the presentation's content. For example, if your presentation contains the phrase "Always on Time," choosing AutoClipArt will return to you several clocks, watches, and hourglasses found in the library. Since AutoClipArt searches the vocabulary used in your presentation, it's best to wait until you've composed enough text to give AutoClipArt something to go on while it searches.

Adding a New Slide

By default, the Common Tasks toolbar is on your screen. Unless you customize it, this toolbar has three buttons: New slide, Slide Layout, and Apply design. If you click New Slide, a slide will be added after your current slide. Pick one of the more complex ones now. You'll see how to quickly set up, for example, an organizational chart, a table, or two columns of text with artwork. Figure 16.8 shows a new Organizational chart slide. Click on any line to replace the marker text with a name.

Figure 16.7

The AutoClipArt dialog box

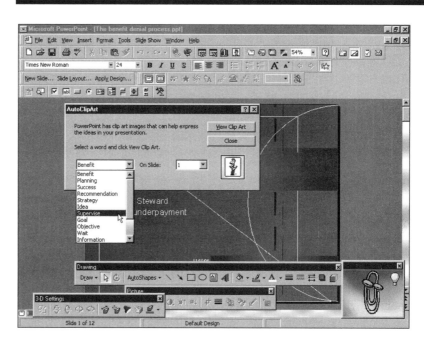

Figure 16.8

A new organizational chart slide

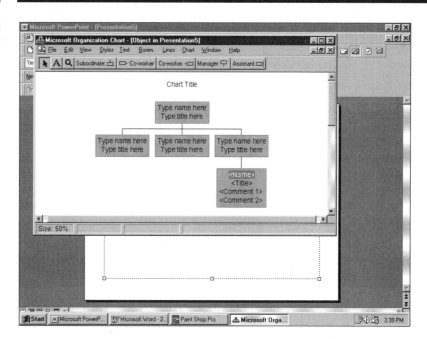

Apply Design

Select Apply design, and you'll be prompted to choose from twenty global designs (designs that apply to your entire slide show). The design you pick will be applied to your current show. The color scheme, background art, and fonts will be changed to match the new design choice (see Figure 16.9).

Figure 16.9

The Apply Design dialog box

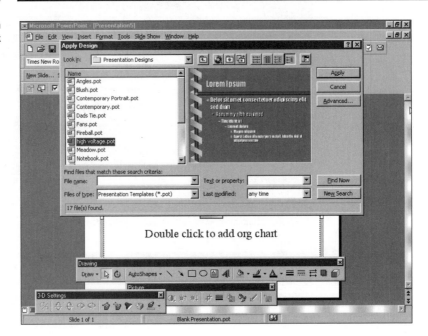

Rehearse Timing

By default, the viewer of a presentation changes slides by pressing the Space Bar. Selecting Slide Show, Rehearse Timings runs the presentation in Slide Show mode. A timer will be present at the bottom right of your screen. Rather than hit the Space Bar to change slides, click on the "forward" icon on the timer (see Figure 16.10). The amount of time each slide is present on the screen is recorded.

At the end of the show, you'll be prompted to save the timing as the new timing for the show. Answering "Yes" means that each time you run the slide show in the future, those timings will apply. You'll then be prompted to view the timings in Slide Sorter View, which displays each slide's timing. Still, even though the presentation is set up with a timer, pressing Space Bar will advance the slide during Slide Show mode viewing. To remove this option, you must select Slide Show, Set Up Show and place a check by Browse at Kiosk or Loop Continuously Until Esc is Pressed.

Figure 16.10

The Rehearsal timer in
Slide Show mode

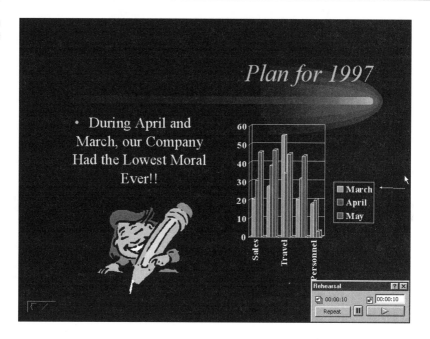

The Review Toolbox

PowerPoint 97 includes a toolbar exclusively for inserting comments onto
your slides during a presentation (see Figure 16.11). These are spontaneous
notes or points brought up during the presentation itself. The toolbar contains a link to Microsoft Outlook and Mail Recipient, so that tasks can be assigned automatically at the end of the meeting.

This toolbar can be thought of as a multimedia version of Word 97's Review toolbar. Whereas the Word 97 review toolbar contains colored markers
to highlight text entries and keep track of various editorial comments, the
PowerPoint Reviewing toolbar pastes comments on the slide screen, without
affecting any individual slide.

The Animation Effects Toolbar

The Animation Effects toolbar (see Figure 16.12) is new to PowerPoint 97.
Place it on the screen as you would any other toolbar, by double-clicking on
any blank toolbar area and placing a check by the name of the toolbar you
want available. Also, the Star icon on the far right side of the Format toolbar
turns the Animation Effects toolbar on and off. The Animation Effects toolbar will remain dim until a graphic or text frame is selected. Then each of the

Figure 16.11

The Reviewing toolbar

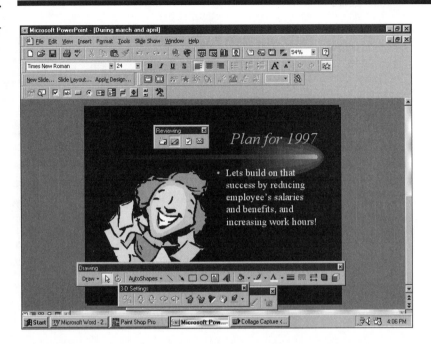

Figure 16.12

The Animation
Effects toolbar

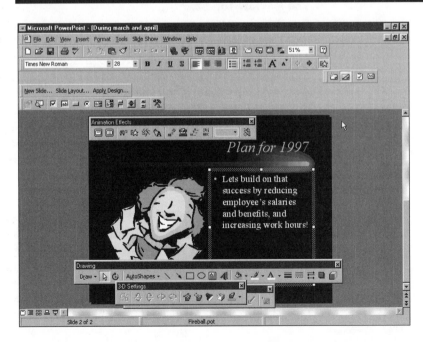

12 Animation Effect commands becomes available. Each button on the toolbar causes a particular animation to play. The animation will not run until you view the slide in Slide Show mode.

Some of the animations have a sound associated with them. For example, if you select the third icon on the toolbar, the Drive-In effect, you will see the text drive in and quickly stop. Simultaneously, you will hear screeching tires. Happily, you can use The Custom Animation button to remove the sounds, if you wish (see Figure 16.13). The Custom Animation button also allows you to combine two or more animating effects, such as Wipe Right, then Zoom Out. You can add a sound to your animation, and change the order in which you want the components of your animation to occur.

Figure 16.13

The Custom Animation
dialog box

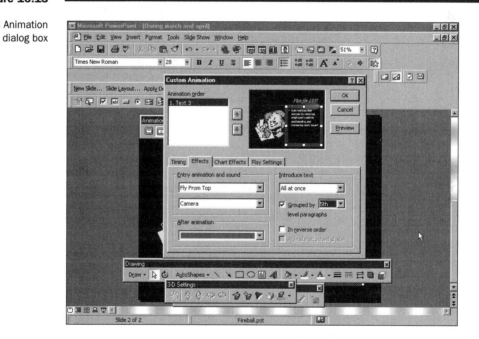

The Insert Chart Command and Editing Charts

The Standard toolbar has an Insert Chart button, and clicking it always places these two objects on the current slide (see Figure 16.14). If you already have something on the slide, this "Start up" chart and data table will be placed on top of it. The color of the bars and graphs will conform to the color scheme of your current layout.

Figure 16.14

The results of pressing the Insert Chart button

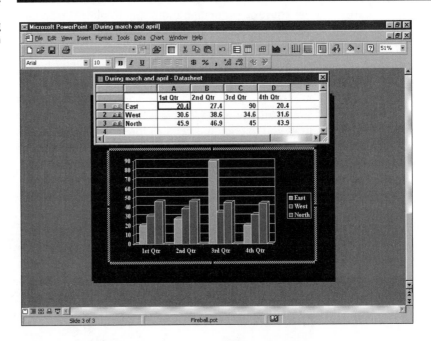

Double-clicking on each part of the chart opens a unique Formatting dialog box. For example, if you double-click on the bars of the chart themselves, you'll see options to change the bar shape, spacing pattern fill, and labeling criteria. The Legend and the chart walls each have their own Formatting dialog box, which gives you control over where the legend is placed, size and type of font used, and the types of lines used to create the chart walls.

When a chart on your slide is selected, the Standard toolbar changes. The View menu gives you access to the chart's related Data Sheet, or Data Table. You can also open the Drawing, Picture, and Word Art toolbars from there.

Of particular interest are the options found under the Chart menu of the Standard toolbar. There's Chart Type (see Figure 16.15), which allows you to present your data in one of 14 different chart types. (There are subcategories under each chart type, so there are actually more than 100 choices for chart types.) For creating your own type of chart, select the Custom Types tab found under this dialog box. The next menu item, Chart Options, allows you to change the Axis and Grids associated with how your chart is labeled.

The Data Sheet

A Data Sheet opens at the same time your chart does. You can remove this data sheet from view by Selecting View, Data Sheet. Right-clicking on the

Figure 16.15

The Chart menu is
available when a chart is
selected on your slide.

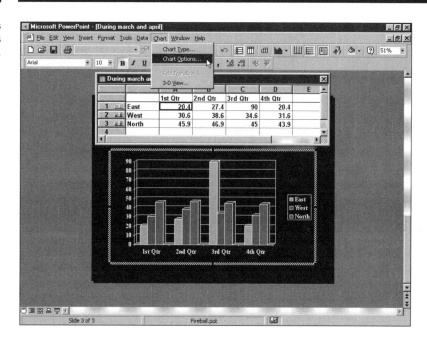

columns or rows allows merging, resizing, and cutting and pasting cells and their data.

Such menu options are also available from the Standard toolbar while the Data Sheet is selected. The Insert, Format, and Data menu items contain commands to adjust column width, change the font or numbering system, and adding up data from a series of rows or columns. Of particular interest is that double-clicking on a row or column causes the affected cells to disappear from the Chart view. This is quite helpful when you want to temporarily strip away certain fields of data in order to view others.

■ Bypassing the Office 97 Menu to Start PowerPoint

To go straight to PowerPoint itself, bypassing all the enticements to start the program through the Office 97 toolbar or Office 97 Start Menu option, you must select Start, Programs and scroll down past the Program folders and select the single-application icon, PowerPoint. The dialog box shown in Figure 16.16 will appear.

Figure 16.16

The PowerPoint
introduction dialog box

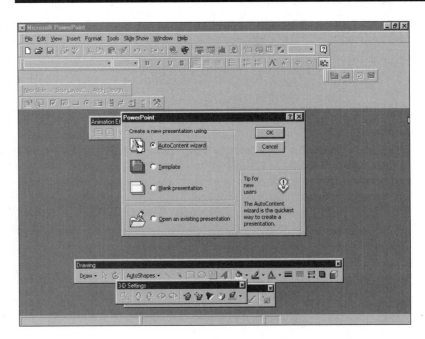

This dialog box provides four options for beginning a PowerPoint session. You can choose AutoContent Wizard, Template, or Blank Presentation, or you can choose to not have this dialog box appear when PowerPoint opens. To prevent this dialog box from appearing, open the Tools menu and select Options. The Options dialog box will appear, presenting many options to customize the way PowerPoint works. The View section includes the option Show Startup Dialog. To turn this feature off, click on the check box. For now, however, leave the setting on.

The following sections discuss the options offered in the PowerPoint dialog box and where each one takes you. By understanding these various paths when starting out, you can make the best choice for your particular task.

■ AutoContent Wizard

The PowerPoint AutoContent Wizard (see Figure 16.17) provides suggestions about the kind of information you might include in a presentation, depending on the type of presentation you are creating. To use the Auto-Content Wizard, choose File, New Presentation, and click on the Presentations tab. Select AutoContent Wizard and click on OK.

Figure 16.17

The AutoContent Wizard

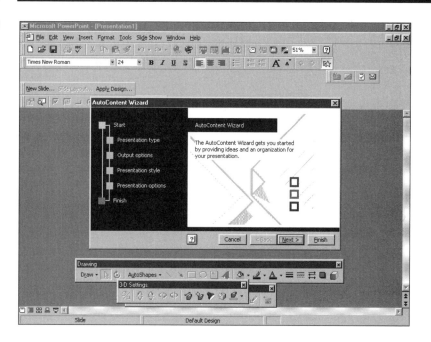

■ Using Templates

When beginning a new presentation, you might simply want to select the slide template and add slides as you work using the AutoLayouts. If this is the case, choose any of the three tabs behind the General tab in the Power-Point dialog box when it first opens. PowerPoint provides more than two dozen presentation templates, including designs for Web pages and Dale Carnegie™ Training, which gives tips on becoming a better presenter.

■ Creating a Blank Presentation

You might want to begin creating a new presentation by selecting an Auto-Layout for the first slide and working from there. You can always select a template, add objects, or choose to print outputs during or after you have finished entering slide text. When you select Blank Presentation from the initial PowerPoint dialog box, PowerPoint takes you to the AutoLayouts and asks you to make a selection. Continue to click on the New Slide button and choose an AutoLayout to build a presentation.

■ Open an Existing Presentation

To access an existing presentation, select Open an Existing Presentation from the initial PowerPoint dialog box. The Open dialog box will appear, allowing you to choose a file. You'll see a conveniently large preview screen showing the Title Slide of the selected existing presentation. Click on OK to open the file.

■ Changing the Default Page Setup

At times you might create a presentation on custom-sized paper, or need your slides to have a certain orientation. In PowerPoint, slide setup includes slide size, numbering, and orientation for slides, notes, handouts, and outlines.

If you are going to want to adjust the size of your slide or page output, it's best to do so at the beginning of your project. Changing slide sizes after text and graphics have been added can result in a distorted appearance.

Remember that whatever presentation type you ultimately choose, a PowerPoint presentation is a series of slides.

When you begin creating a new presentation, the basic PowerPoint slide will appear in the landscape position, and will be sized for letter paper (10 inches wide by 7.5 inches tall). PowerPoint allows some margin space to accommodate slide and overhead holders. To make changes to the slide setup, choose Page Setup from the File menu. The Page Setup dialog box will appear enabling you to change the slide size, numbering, and orientation.

Slide Size

PowerPoint offers five slide-size formats to accommodate various presentation types. Open the Slides Sized for list box to show the following sizes (see Figure 16.18):

- On-screen Show is used for video-screen or computer-monitor presentations.

- Letter Paper is used for presentations on 8 1/2-by-11-inch paper.

- A4 Paper is used for presentations on 210-by-297-mm or 10.83-by-7.5-inch paper. This paper is an international size.

- 35mm Slides is used for presentations on 35mm slides.

- Overhead is used for transparencies that are the size of letter paper.

- Custom is used for presentations on materials with a special, custom size.

Figure 16.18

The Slide Size drop-down menu from the Page Setup dialog box

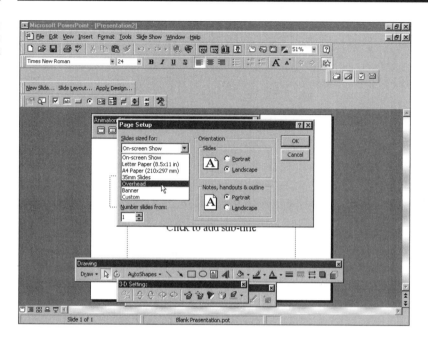

To adjust the slide height or width, click on the up or down arrow button, or select the numbers using the I-beam cursor and enter the slide size. Notice that when you click on the arrow buttons or enter numbers the slide size automatically changes to Custom.

Slide Numbering

PowerPoint numbers slides automatically, beginning with Slide 1. However, a presentation can begin with any number. You might, for example, create a presentation that is the second half of a 100-slide presentation. The slides should begin with Slide 51 to keep the order exact.

To change the beginning slide number, click on the up or down arrow button, or select the number using the I-beam cursor and enter a number.

Slide Orientation

At times you might want to create and print PowerPoint slides for use in a booklet or binder that already includes portrait-oriented pages. To keep the orientation uniform, you can change the slide setup orientation to portrait. To change the slide orientation, click on the button before Portrait or Landscape in the Page Setup dialog box.

The small sheet of paper with an *A* will adjust to show which orientation you have chosen. These same orientation changes also can be made to notes, handouts, and outline pages. Click on OK when you are finished making your selections.

■ Using PowerPoint Views

PowerPoint offers four views in which you can work on one presentation: Slide view, Outline view, Slide Sorter view, and Notes view. These views play a role in organizing an impressive presentation package. You can switch smoothly between these views while working on a presentation by using the four view buttons at the bottom of the workspace (the fifth button is for previewing a slide show), or by selecting them from the View menu (see Figure 16.19). The Status bar indicates which view you are in.

Figure 16.19

The View menu shows the four slide views

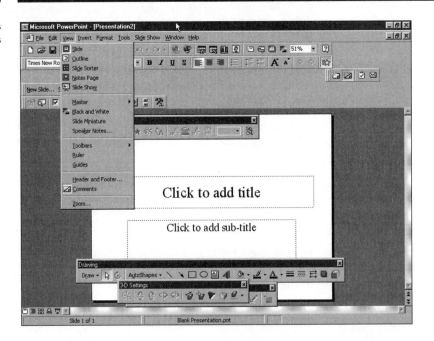

Many views share toolbars. However, the Outline and Slide Sorter views each have a toolbar that offers functions particularly useful in that view. For example, the slide transition tools appear on the Slide Sorter view toolbar, because you can apply transitions only in this view. In PowerPoint 97, notes are available to all views.

Slide View

To select the Slide view, click on the view button with the slide icon on it or choose Slide from the View menu. The Slide view is the basic PowerPoint view (see Figure 16.20). Most slide formatting and design work is done in the Slide view. PowerPoint includes many default settings in the Slide view that you can change, and that appear automatically when you begin PowerPoint.

Figure 16.20

Slide view

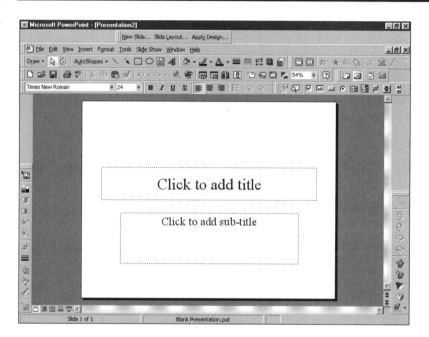

To see which toolbars are available in the Slide view, open the View menu and choose Toolbars. The Toolbars dialog box lists the toolbars available in the Slide view.

The Standard, Formatting, and Drawing toolbars are checked, indicating that they are currently in use. For a discussion of manipulating and customizing toolbars, see the section "Manipulating PowerPoint Toolbars" later in this chapter. To exit the Toolbars dialog box and return to the Slide view, click on OK.

Outline View

To select the Outline view, click on the Outline view button or choose Outline from the View menu. The Outline view shows the slide titles and text (see Figure 16.21). As shown in Chapter 15, the Outline view enables you to organize your thoughts when creating a presentation. You can insert additional text in the Outline view, create a new slide, and rearrange text or slide order.

Figure 16.21

Outline view

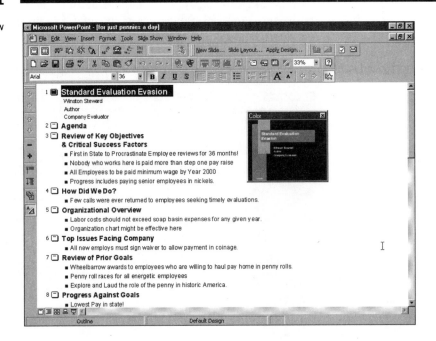

The Slide icon before each slide title indicates whether the slide contains clip art or objects not shown on the Outline. In Figure 16.21, Slide 3 has shapes inside its Slide icon, but the other slide icons do not. The clip art accounts for the shapes inside Slide 3's icon. A miniature version of the selected slide appears at the right of the screen.

The Outlining toolbar appears on the left of the screen when you select the Outline view. From the View menu, choose Toolbars to view the toolbars available in the Outline view. Notice that some of the toolbars available in Slide view do not appear as choices in the Outline view, but there is a toolbar named Outlining. Click on OK to continue.

Slide Sorter View

To select the Slide Sorter view, click on the Slide Sorter view button or choose Slide Sorter from the View menu. The Slide Sorter view shows each slide, numbered (see Figure 16.22). The Slide Sorter view lets you rearrange a presentation's slide order; delete, copy, or add new slides; and assign slide transitions to each slide. Slide transitions are discussed in Chapter 21. After

rehearsing a narration, the Slide Sorter view shows you the number of seconds that each side is programmed to appear on the screen.

Figure 16.22

Slide Sorter view

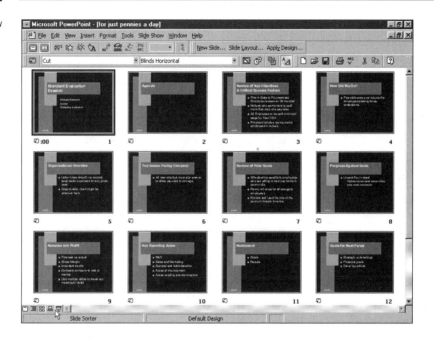

A dark box surrounds the first slide, meaning that it is selected and can
be moved, deleted, copied, or assigned a slide transition. To move a slide,
place the mouse pointer on the selected slide. Click and hold the left mouse
button, then drag the mouse pointer between Slide 2 and Slide 3 and release
the left mouse button. The mouse pointer changes to a slide icon with an
arrow pointing down when you move it. Notice that the first slide is moved,
and the slide numbering is automatically adjusted.

To select more than one slide in the Slide Sorter view, hold down the
Shift key and click on the slides you want to select. To move multiple slides,
follow the same steps outlined for moving one slide.

Deleting one or more slides is as easy as selecting the slide or slides and
pressing Del. Alternatively, you can select the slide, open the Edit menu and
choose Delete Slide. To copy a slide, select the slide and click on the Copy
button. Click the mouse where you want the copied slide to appear, and click
on the Paste button.

To add a new slide, click on the spot at which you want the new slide to
appear. If you want a new slide between the second and third slide, for example, click in the space between these slides. A large flashing cursor will appear

where you clicked the mouse pointer. Click on the New Slide button in the bottom right corner of the workspace. When the cursor is flashing, you also can open the Insert menu and choose New Slide or press Ctrl+M. Power-Point will ask you to choose an AutoLayout for the new slide, then inserts the new slide with the same color scheme and format as the other slides in the presentation.

Open the View menu and choose Toolbars to see which toolbars are available in the Slide Sorter view. Notice that there is a Slide Sorter toolbar. Click on OK.

Notes View

To select the Notes view, click on the Notes view button, or open the View menu and choose Notes. The Notes view shows a small picture of a slide with a text box below it (see Figure 16.23).

Figure 16.23

Notes view

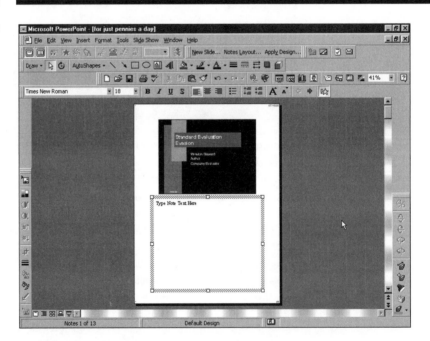

The Notes format is ideal for speaker's notes or for creating audience handouts with speaker's comments about each slide. The box beneath the slide works like a word-processing box in which you can type comments or additional information. Words wrap, just as in word-processing software. To add text in that box, click inside the box and begin typing.

PowerPoint 97 now allows you to create speaker notes and notes to yourself in other views besides the Notes view. In Slide or Outline view, select Insert, Comment, and a yellow text box will appear. You may shrink or recolor this box as you would any text box. The name of the main Presenter appears in the box. You may type any message you wish. It will remain as you move from slide to slide.

The toolbars available in the Slide view are also available in the Notes view.

■ Manipulating PowerPoint Toolbars

Located initially across the top and down the left side of the workspace, PowerPoint toolbars provide easy access to frequently used PowerPoint functions. The toolbar buttons work just like the toolbar buttons in Microsoft Word and Microsoft Excel, requiring one press to execute the function.

PowerPoint includes Tool Tips to let you know the button name and the button function. When you activate a Tool Tip, a button name appears next to the button, and a button function description appears in the status bar in the lower left corner of the workspace. To activate the Tool Tips, move the mouse pointer over a button and wait a moment. These tips help you learn and recall the functions of toolbar buttons.

As you work more frequently in PowerPoint, you will begin to recognize functions you are performing regularly. You can customize PowerPoint toolbars, just like toolbars you use in Microsoft Word and Microsoft Excel. Customization can help you work more quickly and efficiently. Methods for customizing toolbars are discussed later in this section in "Customizing Toolbars."

Like Word and Excel, PowerPoint requires you to select the text or numbers you want to change before performing a function. However, depending on the PowerPoint formatting function, you can select text or numbers in many time-saving ways. If you want to boldface a single word in a sentence, for example, you simply can place the flashing cursor within the word and click on the Bold button on the Formatting toolbar.

Floating Toolbars

When you first open PowerPoint, some toolbars are docked at the top of the workspace and down the left side. By double-clicking in the gray area in between toolbar buttons, you can float the toolbars in the workspace and move them where you like.

Move the mouse pointer between the Spell Check and Cut buttons on the top toolbar. Double-click, and watch the toolbar pop out into the slide area. Following these steps, you can float any toolbar in the workspace.

Notice the toolbar name at the top of the window and the control menu icon in the upper left corner of the window. You can float as many toolbars at one time as you would like.

Move the mouse pointer in the gray area around the buttons. Click and drag the window anywhere in the slide area. An outline of the window moves to show you where the toolbar will land when you release the left mouse button.

To remove a floating toolbar from view, click once on the X in the upper right corner of the toolbar window. To make the toolbar reappear, open the View menu and choose Toolbars. Click on the check box in front of the appropriate toolbar, and then click on OK. The toolbar will reappear floating in the workspace, because you have removed it while it was floating. To dock a toolbar, double-click on the gray space around the buttons and watch the toolbar snap into position.

Using the thickened double lines at the left side of any toolbar, you may drag toolbars to the right or left, just as you can in Word or Excel. These thickened double lines are also handles for moving toolbars to a new row or new side of the screen.

Moving Toolbars

PowerPoint lets you manipulate toolbars by dragging them out into the workspace. Move your mouse pointer into the gray space between the Spell Check and Cut buttons. Click and drag the toolbar down into the workspace. The toolbar outline will show you where the toolbar is moving. After the toolbar is well into the workspace, it will change into a square shape. When you move the toolbar down to the bottom of the workspace, it will change back to a long rectangle.

Viewing Additional Toolbars

To view additional PowerPoint toolbars, open the Toolbars dialog box by choosing Toolbars from the View menu. The Toolbars dialog box will show you which toolbars are currently visible, as well as which toolbars are available to open while in the current view. To remove a toolbar, take away the check in front of the toolbar's name by clicking inside its check box. To make a toolbar appear, click in the check box.

You can also choose to have color in the toolbar buttons, use large buttons, or hide the Tool Tips from the Toolbars dialog box. Click to add or remove the checks in the appropriate boxes. To implement your changes, click on OK. Toolbars might appear to float at first. You can move them or dock them at the top by double-clicking in the gray area around the toolbar buttons.

PowerPoint offers a shortcut to hiding or showing toolbars. To access this shortcut, move the mouse pointer over any visible toolbar and click the right mouse button. A pop-up menu will appear showing the toolbars that are available in the current view; current toolbars will have a check mark next to the toolbar name. To make a toolbar appear, click on its name to make the check appear. You also can access the Toolbars dialog box through this shortcut menu by choosing Toolbars.

Tip. You can access the Customize Toolbars dialog box through the shortcut menu by placing the mouse pointer over any current toolbar and clicking the right mouse button. Select Customize.

Customizing Toolbars

PowerPoint allows you to customize toolbars to expedite regularly used functions. Notice that PowerPoint provides extra space to the right of horizontal toolbars and at the bottom of the vertical toolbars. This extra space lets you add toolbar buttons. To customize a toolbar, select Customize from the Tools menu to display the Customize dialog box (see Figure 16.24).

Figure 16.24

The Customize dialog box's Toolbars tab

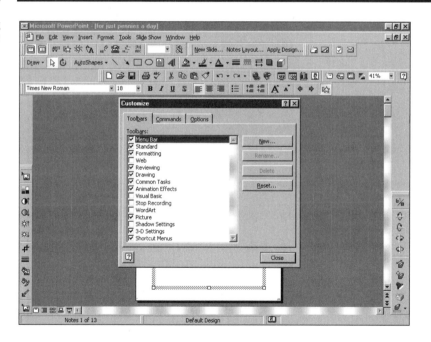

The Toolbars tab of the Customize dialog box displays categories of tools to choose from. The toolbar buttons available in those categories appear in the Buttons box. To see the buttons available in the Edit category, for example, click on Edit in the Categories list box.

Tool Tips are available on the buttons in the Customize Toolbars dialog box. Move the mouse pointer over a button in the Buttons box and wait a moment. A Tool Tip eventually appears, showing you the name of the button. To see a full description of the button's function, click on the button and view its description in the Description box (see Figure 16.25). To confirm the description you are viewing, a dotted outline will form around the appropriate button to indicate that it is selected. All of these steps are outlined in the Customize dialog box.

Figure 16.25

The Description box, for viewing a more complete description of a button's function

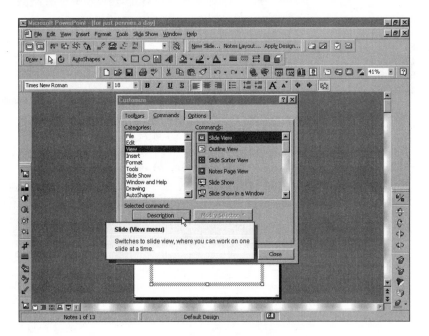

To place buttons on toolbars that are already showing in the workspace, click and hold down the left mouse button with the mouse pointer over a button. Notice that when you click and hold the left mouse button, a small plus sign (+) appears on the button. Drag the button off of the Customize Toolbars dialog box and onto the toolbar where you would like it positioned, placing the plus sign on the exact spot. Release the left mouse button and watch the button take its place where you positioned it. The button will retain its dotted outline to let you know that you still can move it to another location. To move the button again, click on it, drag it to where you want to position it, and release the left mouse button.

You can rearrange other buttons on current toolbars while the Customize dialog box is open. Click on any button, then drag the button to another location. The other buttons on the toolbar will reposition themselves to accommodate the button.

In addition to adding buttons, you can remove buttons from a toolbar with the Customize dialog box open. To remove a button, click on the button, then drag it off the toolbar and into the workspace.

If the Customize dialog box is not open, you can hold down the Alt key and drag a button off the toolbar to remove it. If you've been following along, drag the Find button off the toolbar using these steps. To copy a button from one toolbar to another, press Ctrl+Alt and drag the button to a new position. When you are done with customizing toolbars, click on Close in the Customize dialog box.

■ Using Toolbar Functions

As you can see, PowerPoint toolbars are flexible and have been designed to help you work in an efficient, comfortable manner. Now that you know how to manipulate the toolbars, you are ready to learn the functions of the buttons on four toolbars. You will recognize many of the functions, because they are identical in Word and Excel. Tool Tips can help you to review the button names and functions if you forget.

As in Word and Excel, you must select text or objects before you perform the function. PowerPoint AutoSelect is designed to select entire words rather than individual characters, so selecting text to format is easier than ever.

Button functions that are common across Microsoft Office applications are only briefly explained in the following section. This section will focus on buttons that carry functions unique to PowerPoint.

The Standard Toolbar

The Standard toolbar (see Figure 16.26) is available in every PowerPoint view. The buttons on the Standard toolbar cover the basic functions, such as Save, Cut, Copy, and Paste.

Figure 16.26

The Standard toolbar

Common Standard Toolbar Buttons

The first eight buttons on the PowerPoint Standard toolbar are basic tools also found in Word and Excel. If you know how to use these tools in other applications, you already know how to use them in PowerPoint.

When you are in PowerPoint and want to begin a new presentation while an existing presentation currently is on-screen, press the New button on the Standard toolbar. The New Presentation dialog box will appear, giving you the same options as the dialog box that appears when you first open Power-Point plus one new option, Current Presentation Format, which opens a new presentation with the same presentation format as the presentation currently on-screen.

The Open button brings up the Open dialog box, from which you can select a presentation file to open. The Save button quickly saves a presentation that already is named. If you have not named the presentation, the Save As dialog box will appear and let you name your file. The Print button brings up the Print dialog box, allowing you to print either a presentation or specific slides from that presentation. The Spelling button begins a spelling check on the current slide or on a selected slide if you are in Slide Sorter view. The Spelling dialog box works the same way as in Word and Excel.

The Cut, Copy, and Paste buttons also work just as they do in Word and Excel. In PowerPoint you need to select text or objects by clicking on them before you perform one of these functions.

The Format Painter

The Format Painter button (the button showing a paintbrush) lets you copy the format of a selected object and apply that same format to another object. This function expedites formatting and saves you time. Suppose you want to make Slide 1's title bold and italic, then decide you want the title on Slide 3 in the same format. The Format Painter is ideal for this situation because it copies entire formatting instructions.

You also can use the Format Painter to transfer slide color schemes from one slide to another in the Slide Sorter view.

The Undo Button

The Undo button reverses the last edit made to a slide. If you delete an object by mistake, for example, simply click on the Undo button to retrieve the object and place it back where it originally was. Next to the Undo arrow is a drop-down menu marked only by a small arrow facing down. This menu contains a list of the actions you have performed since you last opened or saved the current document. You can undo any or all of the items on this list. Remember, of course, that if you decide to undo an action somewhere in the middle of the list, that all the actions performed after that action will also be reversed.

The Insert Hyperlink Tool

Clicking the Insert Hyperlink Tool turns the word at the I-Bar's location into a clickable link (see Figure 16.27). You will then be shown a dialog box that prompts you to type in a URL or file location that will automatically open when that word is clicked during a presentation. The Relative Path checkbox allows you to move the files on your computer that the hyperlink refers to, as long as the folder and file structure necessary for locating *that file* stays the same. The Insert Hyperlink tool will be unavailable unless a text, chart, or art object is selected. You can only test the hyperlink operation in Slide Show Mode.

Figure 16.27

The Insert Hyperlink
dialog box

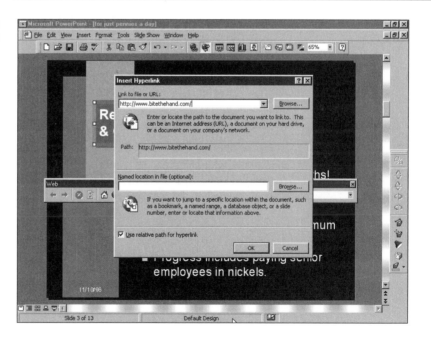

The Web Toolbar Button

Clicking the Web Toolbar Button places it on the screen. This toolbar is the same in PowerPoint as in other Office 97 applications. It contains links to your Home Web Site, a folder of Favorites, a list of the most recent sites visited, and an instant link to your default browser, labeled "Search the Web."

Adding Objects to a Slide

The following four buttons are used to insert objects on a blank slide. These buttons each work in the same way: click on the button and watch the rectangle with square resizing handles appear on the slide to show you where the new object will appear after it is created.

The objects you add to a slide using the Insert Microsoft Word Table and Insert Microsoft Excel Spreadsheet buttons are OLE/DDE objects, meaning that when the object is selected, you have access to all the editing and creating tools and menus you would have in the corresponding applications. If, for example, you insert an Excel spreadsheet on a PowerPoint slide and select it by clicking on it, you will instantly have access to Excel toolbars and menus. These tools appear where the PowerPoint toolbars are; you do not temporarily exit PowerPoint and work within Excel, then return to PowerPoint.

- The Insert Microsoft Word Table button lets you add a table to a slide conveniently. Click on the button and select the number of columns and rows you want to include in the table. When you release the left mouse button, the table will appear on the slide.

- The Insert Microsoft Excel Spreadsheet button opens a grid, just like the Insert Microsoft Word Table button. Select the columns and rows you want in the spreadsheet and release the left mouse button. The spreadsheet will appear, allowing you to add numbers and formulas.

- The Insert Chart button lets you place a graph on a slide. To insert a graph, click on the Insert Chart button on the toolbar. PowerPoint will now place an editable graph and data sheet on your slide. You can alter the size of the graph after you create it by using the square resizing handles. PowerPoint also offers an AutoLayout in which you can insert a graph by double-clicking in a designated area.

- The Insert Clip Art button lets you insert clip art on a PowerPoint slide. Just as a rectangle with black resizing handles appears when you click on the Insert Graph or Insert Organizational Chart button, this same rectangle appears when you click on the Insert Clip Art button. PowerPoint then takes you to the Microsoft Clipart Gallery.

Using Zoom Control

PowerPoint Zoom Control adjusts the distance from which you view and work on slides, notes, and outlines. Zoom Control appears on each of the four toolbars, and helps you get a closer or more distant look while you work. When altering clip art or drawing graphics in the Slide view, for example, the closer views at 66 percent and 100 percent allow you to work with more precision. To assess the overall look of the slides, you might want to step back from the slides to a 33 percent or 25 percent view.

To access the preset magnification levels, click on the down arrow to the right of the percentage.

The magnification levels available vary from view to view:

- The Slide, Slide Sorter, and Notes views have the following magnification levels: 25, 33, 50, 66, 75, 100, 150, 160, 300, and 400 percent.

- The magnification levels offered in the Outline view include 25, 33, 50, 66, 75, and 100 percent.

You also can select any of these magnification levels by choosing Zoom from the View menu. The Zoom dialog box will present some preset magnification levels, but it will also let you select a specific magnification percentage. To increase the magnification level, move the mouse pointer over the up arrow and click to increase the magnification by one-percent increments. To decrease the magnification level, click on the down arrow with the mouse pointer. You also can select the percentage with the I-beam cursor and enter the magnification you would like. Click on OK to activate the view you have chosen.

The Office Assistant Button

Click this button, and the Office Assistant will appear on the screen to the lower left of your slide.

The Formatting Toolbar

The Formatting toolbar provides functions that help you with formatting operations, such as changing fonts or italicizing text. If a data sheet, Excel spreadsheet, or clip art is selected, some features of the Formatting toolbar will be different. For example, if a data sheet is selected, the Formatting toolbar will include buttons to alter currency and percent style, and to reposition decimal points to the right or left. Since you've undoubtedly seen many similar shots of a formatting toolbar while reading this book, Figure 16.28 is a picture of the formatting toolbar while a data sheet is selected.

Choosing and Formatting Fonts

The Font list box works like the list box in Microsoft Word. Simply select the text and click on the down arrow to view the font choices. Notice the font located above the double line. PowerPoint places the fonts you used last at the top of the font list for easier accessibility as you work. Only three fonts remain at the top of the list at one time.

Figure 16.28

The Formatting toolbar
while a data sheet is
selected

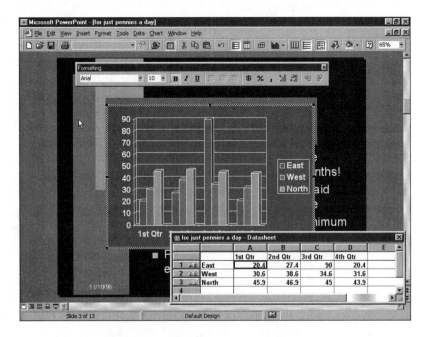

You also can change the font by opening the Format menu and choosing Font. The Font dialog box will open, allowing you to choose the desired font, font style, and size. Click on OK to exit the Font dialog box.

The Size list box drops down so that you can choose the font size you want. These font sizes are preset (for example, 12, 14, 18, or 24 points). You also can select the current font size with the I-beam cursor and then type an exact font size.

The Increase Font Size and Decrease Font Size buttons in the Formatting toolbar let you quickly change the font size of selected text by various increments.

The Bold, Italic, Underline, and Text Shadow buttons on the toolbar perform changes on selected text. PowerPoint's Bold, Italic, and Underline buttons work just as they do in Word. Simply select the text and click on the style you want to apply to the text.

The Text Shadow button allows you to add a shadow to slide text only, not to shapes or other objects. This style is especially effective in slide titles or to emphasize text. To add a shadow to text, select the text and click on the Text Shadow button.

Because you can output your presentation to color slides or overheads, color text is particularly effective. When you click on the Text Color button, a color palette will appear with the eight colors you used most recently.

Click on a color block to change the color of the selected text. If you do not see a color you like, click on Other Color for more choices. The Colors dialog box will open, showing the Standard tab.

You can even create your own color by selecting the Custom tab in the Colors dialog box to display the custom color design dialog box (see Figure 16.29). Move the black marker on the color waves to the shade of color you want. Then click on the triangular pointer along the color band and drag it up or down to select the color intensity. When you have chosen a color, click on OK, and then click on OK again to close the Other Color dialog box. This custom color will be on the color palette that appears for you to use later when you click on the Text Color button.

Figure 16.29

The Custom tab in the
Colors dialog box

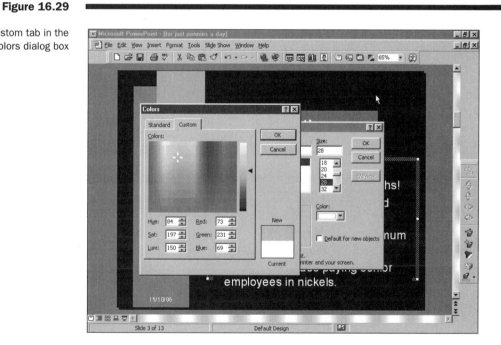

Aligning Text

The Align Left and Align Center buttons work exactly as they do in Word. Simply select the text and click on the alignment you would like. You also can access text alignment by opening the Format menu and choosing Alignment. A cascading menu will offer you four choices: left, right, center, and justify. Choose the alignment by clicking on it.

Bullets

On slides other than the title slide, PowerPoint can automatically add bullets to lists placed in the slide body text box. Notice that if you select this text, the bullet button on the Formatting toolbar is pressed. To bullet text, select the text and click on the bullet button.

Tip. As a shortcut to adding a bullet to a line of text, simply place the flashing cursor within the line, and click on the bullet button.

You are not limited to a simple dot for your bullets. To access other bullet styles, select the text, open the Format menu, and select Bullet. When the Bullet dialog box appears, click on the bullet you would like. You can select the bullet color by opening the list box under Special. Notice that if you created a custom color earlier, it also appears on this palette. Click on OK to implement any bullet formatting.

Promoting and Demoting Bullet Points

The left- and right-arrow buttons on the Formatting toolbar are the Promote and Demote buttons, respectively. These buttons allow you to create a hierarchy of text using subpoints. Suppose that on Slide 2 you wanted to move the second bullet point under the first bullet point to make it a subpoint. Click the I-beam cursor anywhere in the text, then click on the Demote button on the Formatting toolbar (see Figure 16.30).

Figure 16.30

Use the Demote button to pull Point Two under Point One in the bullet-point hierarchy.

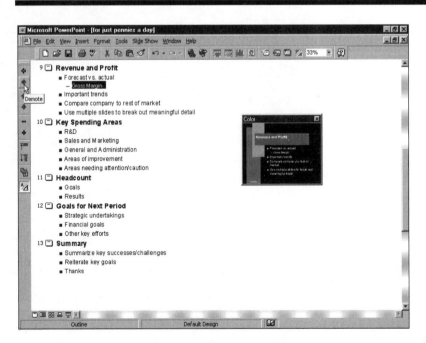

Notice how the second bullet is now indented, and has assumed a different bullet style. This bullet format is defined in the Slide Master. The Promote and Demote buttons are particularly useful in the Outline view to manipulate text and organize your thoughts.

The Outline Toolbar

The Outline toolbar (shown here with the Expand option selected) is available only in the Outline view. Change to the Outline view by pressing the Outline view button in the bottom left corner of the workspace. The Outlining toolbar will automatically appear, vertically oriented down the left side of the workspace (see Figure 16.31).

Figure 16.31

The Outlining toolbar with the Expand option ToolTip showing

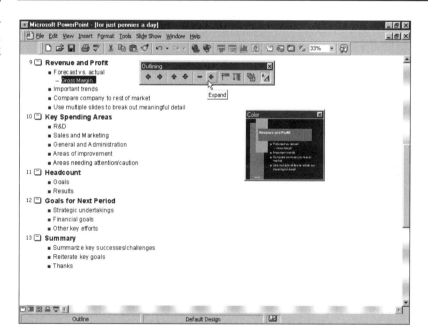

Moving Text or Slides Up and Down

The Move Down buttons rearrange text vertically by one line to eliminate cutting and pasting. To rearrange text, select the bullet point using the four-headed arrow, then click on the Move Down button.

These buttons also can be used to rearrange entire slides. To move Slide 2 into Slide 3's position, select Slide 2 by placing the mouse pointer over the slide icon until it turns into a four-headed arrow, then click.

Click on the Move Down button once and watch the slide begin its descent. Click on the Move Down button again to position all the highlighted text completely into the Slide 3 position. The slides will be automatically renumbered. You can also use these buttons to move multiple slides.

Collapsing and Expanding Selections

The Collapse Selection and Expand Selection buttons work like the Collapse and Expand buttons on Microsoft Word outlines. For example, imagine that you are currently viewing all slide titles and subpoints. To view only the title of a slide, select the entire slide and click on the Collapse Selection button. Watch the subpoints disappear. Click on the Expand Selection button to expand the slide text again.

If you are familiar with PowerPoint 95, you might be wondering what happened to the Show Titles Button. The Collapse Option has the same effect as Show Titles used to. The Show Titles and Show All buttons have been replaced by the Summary Slide option.

The Summary Slide

The Summary Slide displays the titles and main points of any slide(s) you have selected at that moment (see Figure 16.32). The Summary Slide functions as a record of the summations of all your main points. This slide can be distributed as hard copy to those attending your presentation, or it can be placed at the beginning of your show with hyperlinks to each slide referred to in the Summary. If your presentation exists as a Web site, the Summary Slide could be the basis for your home page.

Showing and Hiding Text Formatting

The Show Formatting button changes the outline text to reflect the font and font size as they appear on the slides. To revert to a default font and font size while working in the Outline view, click once on the Show Formatting button. This default text formatting option lets you see more of the outline text at one time. To change back to viewing the actual fonts and font styles, click on the Show Formatting button once again, then change to the Slide view to continue.

The Custom Toolbar

The Custom toolbar is a blank toolbar that is available for you to customize with buttons that you frequently use. To open the Custom toolbar using the right mouse button shortcut, move the mouse pointer on any current toolbar and press the right mouse button. Select Custom from the pop-up menu.

Figure 16.32

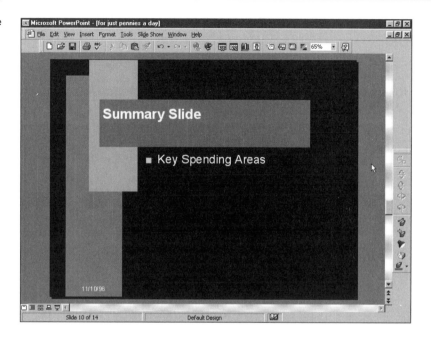

The Custom toolbar will appear as a floating toolbar. Initially it is very small, because there are no buttons on it. The toolbar will enlarge as customized buttons are placed on it via the Customize Toolbars dialog box. You can also add buttons by holding down the Alt key and moving buttons from any current toolbars to the Custom toolbar, or by using Ctrl+Alt to copy buttons from a current toolbar to the Custom toolbar.

■ Using Drawing Toolbars

Three of PowerPoint's toolbars pertain to drawing and manipulating shapes: the Drawing toolbar, the Picture toolbar, and the Word Art toolbar. You can manipulate all three drawing toolbars just as you can the others. You can dock them on either side of the workspace or at the top and bottom of the workspace. You also can customize these toolbars using the same customization techniques discussed earlier in this chapter.

The Drawing Toolbar

The PowerPoint Drawing toolbar offers many basic drawing and object-formatting tools that can help you enhance your presentations.

The Draw Drop-down Menu

The Draw drop-down menu is used to manipulate the objects on your slides. It appears on the left side of the workspace, as seen in Figure 16.33.

Figure 16.33

The Draw drop-down menu

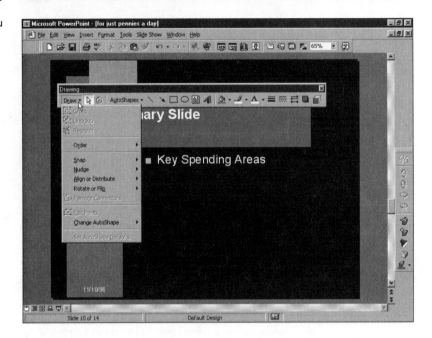

The Bring Forward and Send Backward buttons work in tandem and help you arrange multiple objects. The following steps illustrate how these buttons work. First, insert a blank slide by choosing New Slide, then another using AutoLayout. Then draw a line, a rectangle, and an ellipse on the blank slide using the techniques described earlier in this chapter. Move the objects so that they are overlapping each other.

Select the ellipse by clicking on it. You will know it is selected when the square resizing handles appear. To move the ellipse behind the rectangle, click on the Send Backward button on the Draw drop-down menu.

Grouping Objects

Right now, the three objects are separate. You can select each one individually by clicking on it. To move these objects, you would have to move them one at a time. Sometimes you will want to group objects in order to move them, or ungroup objects to edit them separately. Ungrouping objects is especially useful when altering clip art.

To group the line, rectangle, and ellipse, you must select all of them at one time. Remember, you can select one object, hold down the Shift key, and select the rest; however, PowerPoint provides a shortcut. You can drag a selection box around the objects using the cursor. To drag this selection box, place the cursor in the area to the upper left of the objects. Press and hold the left mouse button until the cursor changes to a crosshair.

Drag the crosshair so that it creates and drags a box around the three objects. A dashed outline of the box will appear to show you if you have surrounded all the objects. Release the left mouse button. All of the objects acquire square resizing handles, which lets you know that they are now selected.

Click on the Group button in the Draw drop-down menu, and notice that the square resizing handles encompass all of the objects (see Figure 16.34). At this point, you can move or resize all of the objects at one time. For example, click in the center of the rectangle and drag the mouse pointer over to the left. Notice that all the objects move together. Place the mouse pointer over a square resizing handle, grab the handle by clicking the left mouse button, and hold. Now, drag the handle in the directions that it will let you move. Notice that all of the objects either increase or decrease in size, depending on which way you move the mouse.

Figure 16.34

Using the Group command found in the Draw drop-down menu

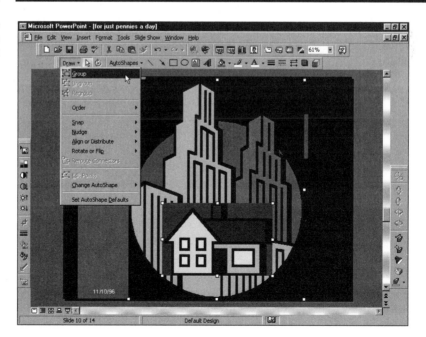

Flipping Objects

The next four buttons rotate and flip objects both horizontally and vertically. To flip or rotate a shape, select the shape using the Select tool, and select the rotation or flip direction. Experiment with the objects you have just drawn. You can rotate or flip any object, including clip art. When you are finished experimenting with objects, select them and click on the Cut button on the Standard toolbar, or press Del to remove them from the slide.

The Selection Tool

The Selection tool is used to select objects using the mouse pointer. All objects need to be selected to apply formatting. You also use the Selection tool when you want to move objects. PowerPoint reverts to the Selection tool when you finish performing a function, so sometimes it is unnecessary to click on the Selection tool button to activate it. After you draw a rectangle, for example, the mouse pointer automatically changes from a crosshair back to the Selection tool. To select multiple objects, select the first object, hold down the Shift key, and click once on the other objects you want to select.

The Free Rotate Tool

The Free Rotate tool lets you rotate any object: even text will rotate within an object. Suppose you want to rotate the rectangle you drew. Select it by clicking on it, then click on the Free Rotate tool button and move the cursor onto the slide. The cursor will change to a circular shape with a plus sign (+) in the middle. The status bar will tell you to position the cursor over any square resizing handle. When you have done this, hold down the left mouse button, and drag the object to rotate it.

To rotate an object on restricted angles, such as 45 or 90 degrees, hold down the Shift key while you rotate the object. The status bar will remind you of how to do this if you forget. Release the mouse button when you are finished rotating the object, then press Esc to exit the object-rotating mode.

The AutoShapes Button

Tip. As noted in the status bar, you can hold down the Shift key to constrain the angle when drawing a line, to draw a square when using the Rectangle tool, to draw a circle when using the Ellipse tool, or to draw a circular arc when using the Arc tool.

Click on the AutoShapes button to display a choice of shapes you can add to a slide (see Figure 16.35). Click on the shape you want to use, then drag the mouse onto the part of the slide that will receive this shape. The AutoShapes menu contains Action Buttons, which create "clickable" objects of any size. These will link the user to a file on your computer, or to a URL on the World Wide Web. AutoShapes also contains a menu of automatic Callout boxes, including speech bubbles. The special Connector shapes allow you to quickly create algorithmic charts with "IF/AND/OR" choices and branching.

Figure 16.35

The AutoShapes button, shown with the Connectors subgroup exposed

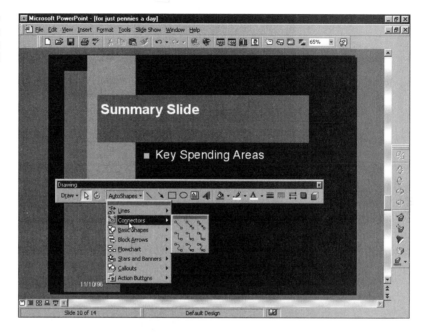

The Line, Rectangle, Ellipse, and Oval Tools

The Line, Rectangle, Ellipse, and Oval tools all work the same way. For an example, click once on the rectangle button, and move the mouse pointer onto the slide. Notice that the cursor turns into a crosshair. Click and drag the crosshair cursor down and to the right or left, depending on where you want the object on the slide. Release the left mouse button when the rectangle is the size you want.

The crosshair will immediately return to the mouse pointer. Also, Power-Point instantly attaches an object frame to the shape and provides square resizing handles for you to alter the shape.

The following procedure resizes any PowerPoint object. Move the mouse pointer over the bottom-right square resizing handle. Notice that the mouse pointer turns to arrows, showing you which way you can resize the rectangle. Grab the square resizing handle, and click and drag the mouse in the direction that you want to alter the rectangle. PowerPoint shows you an outline of the object as it is being resized to let you judge how big or small you want the object. Release the left mouse button when the object is the size you would like.

Tip. If you double-click on a drawing-tool button, you can draw shapes one after another. After drawing the first object, the crosshair remains in its crosshair shape instead of reverting to the mouse pointer, allowing you to draw another object. Press Esc to remove the crosshair.

Tip. If you accidentally alter the object's size too drastically and want to restore the object to its original proportions, press Ctrl and double-click on any square resizing handle.

Sometimes when you resize an object, it becomes difficult to keep the object proportional: a circle can become elliptical, for example, or a square rectangular. To resize an object around the center so that it maintains its proportions, hold down the Ctrl key as you drag the resizing handle. The status box also gives you this information.

The Text Box Tool

The text box tool creates a frame of any size (see Figure 16.36). To create a text box, select the Text Box tool with your pointer and "drag-and-create" a frame of any size. You may then insert text of any type or format, and may similarly format the box itself with any of PowerPoint's line width and color tools. Double-click on the box itself to access those formatting options. Type a small amount of text and double-click on it to access text-formatting tools.

Figure 16.36

The Text Box tool

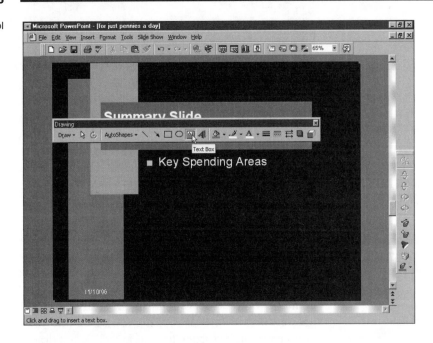

The Insert Word Art Tool

This tool converts your mouse into a tool that can drag-and-create a Word Art Object of any size. At this point, if the Word Art toolbar was not previously present, it will be now. We'll cover Word Art as a separate toolbar.

The Freeform Tool

The Freeform tool lets you draw objects with free-form lines and straight lines. To use the Freeform tool, click on the Freeform tool button and move the mouse pointer onto the slide. Just as with the other tools, the mouse pointer will turn into a crosshair when you move it into the workspace. Now, hold down the left mouse button and watch the crosshair turn into a pencil. Still holding down the left mouse button, move the mouse to draw in free-form style. Release the left mouse button, and the pencil becomes a crosshair again. Move the mouse down to draw a line. Press and hold the left mouse button to return to free-form drawing using the pencil. When you are done drawing, double-click the left mouse button. The object will immediately acquire square resizing handles, and can be altered using the same steps discussed earlier in this section.

You can use the Freeform tool to draw polygons, too. Click on the Freeform tool and move the cursor into the workspace. Using the crosshair, click the left mouse button once, but do not hold it down. Now, move the mouse to draw a line. Click the left mouse button once again to end that line, and drag the mouse to draw another line. The status bar will tell you to continue clicking for each point of the polygon, and to double-click to end your drawing.

The Fill Color Button

The Fill Color button shows a paint can that fills up a square. To access the button, you must select an object on the slide, and then click on the Fill Color button to change the object's color.

To select another fill color, click on one of the eight color blocks. To remove the fill, select No Fill. To make the fill the same color as the slide background, choose Background. PowerPoint also allows you to create a shaded fill that adds interest to any shape. To add a shaded fill, select Shaded. The Shaded Fill dialog box will open, displaying the various shading patterns.

The shading styles direct the shading within the shape. PowerPoint provides a number of patterns for spicing up a shape's fill. Click through the various Shade Styles, and watch the examples appear in miniature in the dialog box. Select the shading style you like, and click on OK.

You can also add a colored pattern inside an object. Choose Pattern to display the Pattern Fill dialog box, which presents many patterns. Click on the pattern you would like, and click on OK.

The Fill Color button will also let you select a textured fill.

You can change an object's fill color by choosing Colors and Lines from the Format menu. The Format Text Box dialog box will appear, as shown in Figure 16.37. In the Colors and Lines tab, you can change an object's fill color, line color, and line style, including dashed lines and arrowheads.

Figure 16.37

The Colors and Lines tab is found in the Format Text Box dialog box.

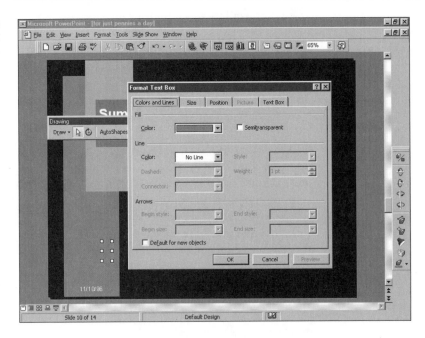

The Line Color Button

The Line Color button lets you change a line's color. With an object selected, click on the button to see the color choices, which are the same as the colors available for fill. Choose Other to custom-design your own color for the object's lines.

You can format lines by opening the Color and Lines dialog box through the Format menu and following the same steps as changing an object's fill color. The Color and Lines dialog box also lets you change the line's thickness in the Line Styles box.

The Line Style Button

Use the Line Style button to change the width or style of a line. You can choose from several thicknesses of single lines, as well as double and triple combinations of lines.

The Dash Style Button

The Dash Style button allows you to create a line made up of dotted dashes, long dashes, dash-dots, and various other dash styles.

The Arrow Style Button

The Arrow Style button applies only when you draw a line or an arc and want to place an arrowhead at one end or another, or both. To explore this feature, click on the Line button and draw a line on the slide. With the line still selected, click on the Arrow Style button, then click on the arrowhead style you want to apply to the line.

The Shadow On/Off Button

The Shadow On/Off button, which displays a rectangle with a black shadow, switches on or off to apply a shadow to an object. To shadow an object, select the object and click on the button.

To change the shadow's color, open the Format menu, choose Shadow, and select the color you would like from the Shadow dialog box. In the Shadow dialog box, you can adjust the shadow's offset direction and thickness. To increase the thickness of the shadow going up or down, click on the up or down arrow.

The 3-D Tool

This little gem hidden at the right end of the toolbar creates a world of 3-D shapes. Clicking the 3-D button shows a drop-down menu of many instant 3-D shapes. Clicking the phrase "3-D settings" beneath the ready-made 3-D shapes opens yet another toolbar (see Figure 16.38). This toolbar allows you to adjust your created object's orientation in 3-D space, as well as its surface qualities, color, thickness, and lighting settings.

The WordArt Tool

PowerPoint 97 accesses the same WordArt tools that are common to other Office 97 applications (see Figure 16.39). The same dialog box will appear, offering 30 preset WordArt creations and prompting you only to supply the text. There are no PowerPoint-specific WordArt features, however, although some improvements to WordArt in this new version will be particularly useful to PowerPoint users.

For starters, whenever you create a WordArt object with 3-D lettering, the 3-D toolbar's effects can be used to edit your object. When you create a WordArt object with depth, the 3-D toolbar will provide new surfaces, vanishing point settings, lights and shape qualities that you can add to your letters. You cannot access the 3-D toolbar from the Word Art toolbar. The only way to turn on the 3-D toolbar is to click the 3D icon at the far right of the Drawing toolbar, scroll down, and select 3-D settings. You may then use the features of the 3-D toolbar to edit your WordArt object.

Figure 16.38

You can select 3-D settings on the Drawing toolbar's 3-D tool.

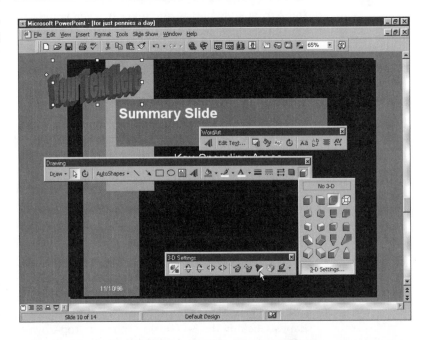

Figure 16.39

The WordArt tool

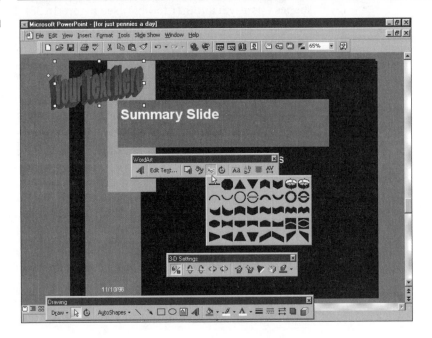

Other new WordArt features include the ability to position the text on your slide by exact numeric coordinates (from the WordArt toolbar, select Format WordArt, Position). There are many more shapes and formatting options to choose from. Character Spacing, Vertical Text, and Same Letter Height features are all accessible at the click of a button.

The Picture Toolbar

The Picture toolbar (see Figure 16.40) comes into play when editing bit-mapped pictures that you import with the Insert Picture command, or from the Pictures tab of the Clipart Gallery. The picture toolbar allows you to adjust contrast, brightness, line style, width, and color.

Figure 16.40

The Picture toolbar

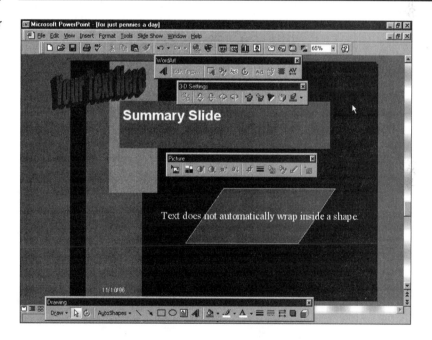

One very nice feature included on the Picture toolbar is the Set Transparency tool. Click the Set Transparency tool on any portion of your bitmap, and that color becomes transparent. This tool is helpful for allowing the main subject of a bitmap to show while the bitmap's background remains transparent, allowing the background of the slide itself to show through. The ability to make a particular color transparent is most useful for designing Web pages with PowerPoint. When designing a Web site, the time it takes to load a bitmap is of utmost consideration. If a portion of a bitmap can be made transparent, then the time required for a visitor of your Web site to load that bitmap is decreased.

■ Working with Text within Shapes

Adding text to shapes highlights words in an interesting way. Text inside of shapes can be edited just like other slide text; however, PowerPoint allows you to anchor and align text within shapes in creative ways.

Adding Text inside Shapes

To add text inside a shape, first draw the shape, right click on it, and select Add Text. You may begin typing in the default font, font size, and color. You may alter these as you would alter text features under other circumstances.

You'll quickly notice, however, that the text does not automatically stay inside the boundaries of the shape, as shown in Figure 16.41.

Figure 16.41

Text does not automatically wrap inside a shape.

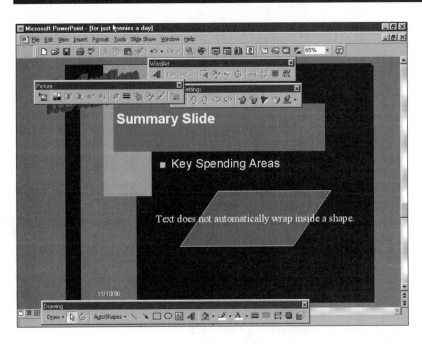

To change the behavior of text inside shapes, right-click on the shape, and select Format AutoShape. Click on the Text Box tab (see Figure 16.42). Here you can make text autowrap inside the shape, rotate the text 90 degrees at a time within a shape, and instantly shrink the shape so that it wraps closely around the text.

Figure 16.42

The Text Box tab of the
Format AutoShape
dialog box

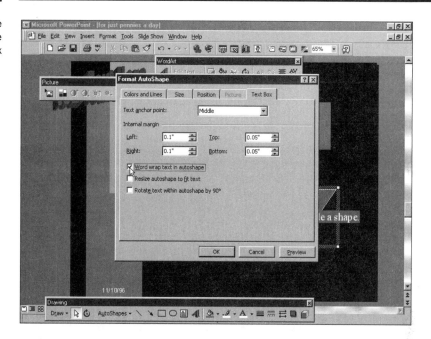

PowerPoint 95 users might wonder what happened to the Text Anchor feature. It was used to align text within shapes, and was found under the Format menu. Now Text Anchor features are relegated to a drop-down menu here in the Text tab of the Format AutoShape dialog box.

■ Using Alignment Tools

PowerPoint makes precisely aligning and positioning shapes or objects simple with its helpful tools. When you have many objects on a slide, adjusting each object individually to line up with other objects can be time-consuming. This section discusses the ways in which you can make these adjustments more easily.

Ruler

The PowerPoint Ruler is similar to the Microsoft Word ruler. You can add tabs and define text margins within text labels, or within word-processing boxes or shapes. To turn on the PowerPoint Ruler, open the View menu and choose Ruler. The Ruler is available only in the Slide and Notes views, and extends only as wide and tall as the slide size in the Slide view and the page size in the Notes view.

The PowerPoint Ruler shows you where the cursor is positioned on the slide or notes page with dotted lines that move as you move the mouse. The ruler measures in inches. On each axis, the ruler places the 0-inch mark in the center of the slide or notes page. So, if the dotted marks on each axis are on 0, the mouse pointer is positioned in the middle of the slide or notes page.

The ruler is ideal for helping you draw sizes with specific dimensions. If you want to draw a 2-by-2-inch rectangle, for example, click on the rectangle tool and position the crosshair so that you begin to draw at 0, as shown in Figure 16.43.

Figure 16.43

Positioning the rectangle tool at the zero point on the ruler

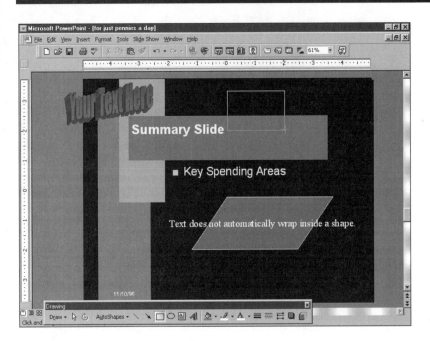

To remove the Ruler from view, open the View menu and click on Ruler to remove the check mark.

Guides

PowerPoint guides help you to align one object or multiple objects to a straight edge. To turn the guides on, open the View menu and select Guides.

Horizontal and vertical dotted lines will appear on the slide. Any shapes that you draw and move near these guides will snap to the guides.

At first, the guides appear to intersect at the center point of the slide. You can move the guides separately and reposition them to help you align objects. To move the guides, move the cursor on the dotted line and hold down the left mouse button. Notice the box that appears when you hold down the mouse button, showing the current location of the guide in inches. Move the horizontal guide up or down and the vertical guide left or right; the guide location adjusts as you move the guide. To remove the guides from view, open the View menu and select Guides to remove the check mark.

Snap to Grid

PowerPoint's Snap to Grid option helps you align objects precisely by providing an invisible grid of lines on the slide. To turn this grid on, open the Draw menu and select Snap to Grid.

To get a feel for working with the grid, draw a rectangle on the slide. Place the cursor inside the rectangle and hold down the left mouse button. Move the rectangle slowly down the slide. Notice how the rectangle seems to jump as it moves: this is the rectangle adhering to the invisible gridlines. You can temporarily override the grid by holding down the Alt key as you move the object. To turn off the Snap to Grid, open the Draw menu and select Snap to Grid to remove the check mark.

■ Understanding the Masters

PowerPoint Masters are powerful because they allow you to make formatting changes that apply to all the slides, outline pages, audience handout pages, and notes pages included in your presentation package. By making changes or additions in one place, you do not have to take the time to make changes on each individual slide or page.

PowerPoint provides Masters for slides, outlines, handouts, and notes. Handouts are paper printouts that show two or six slides on a page. Sometimes you want to give a printout of the presentation slides to audience members for their information. The Handout Master provides an easy, automatic way to prepare these pages.

Often you will want the date or a page number to appear on audience handouts or slides. The Masters are a perfect place to add these objects and to automate them for even more time savings. This section discusses each of the four PowerPoint Masters, and explains which objects can be inserted on a Master. A basic understanding of the PowerPoint Masters can help you save time when you are formatting a presentation.

The Slide Master

The PowerPoint Slide Master contains formatting information that is applied to every slide in a presentation. The Slide Master lets you conveniently change slide characteristics, such as the slide title position, the body text position, slide background colors, text formatting, and bullet formatting. By making changes in one place, you do not have to take the time to make changes on each individual slide.

To view the Slide Master, open the View menu and select Master, then choose Slide Master. Or hold down the Shift key as you click on the Slide View button. The status bar will now say Slide Master. Notice that the toolbars do not change when you switch from the PowerPoint Slide view to the Slide Master view. At this point, you can make any text-formatting changes, or add objects that you want to appear on every slide. You work in the Slide Master view just as you would in the Slide view; the difference is that additions or changes made in the Slide Master view affect every slide in the presentation.

To change text formats, select the text and make changes using the toolbar buttons or the menus. If you want every slide title to be underlined, for example, select Click to edit Master title style, and click on the Underline button on the Formatting toolbar.

Suppose you wanted to change the bullet color from yellow to pink on every slide. Click on the words Click to edit Master text styles. Open the Format menu and choose Bullet to display the Bullet dialog box. Open the Special Color list box and click on the pink color block. Click on OK, and you will see the bullet turn pink. You can change the bullet colors and styles on any level of text by following these same steps. To view these changes in the presentation, click on the Slide View button.

The Handout Master

To view the Handout Master, open the View menu and choose Master, then select Handout Master from the cascaded list. The Handout Master outlines where slides will appear if you print handouts with two or six slides (see Figure 16.44).

The Notes Master

To view the Notes Master, open the View menu and choose Master. Then, from the cascaded list, select Notes Master. The Notes Master shows a small Slide Master and a box labeled Notes Area for AutoLayouts. You can type any notes in this box that you want to appear on every note printout. However, you generally will not want to type any text here, because the notes will differ from slide to slide. You might want to add a logo or page numbers.

Figure 16.44

The Handout Master

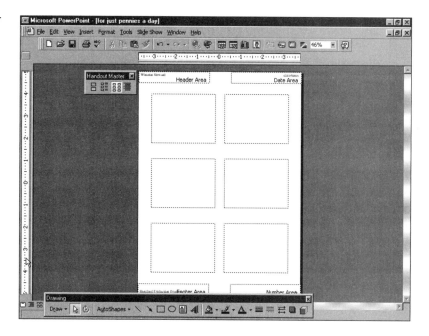

Inserting Items on the Masters

Many times you will want the date, time, or page numbers to appear on every slide, notes page, handout page, or outline page. PowerPoint Masters are the perfect place to add these items. PowerPoint even takes this process a step further by using items similar to field codes in Microsoft Word. These items automatically keep track of dates, times, and page numbers so you don't have to.

To place the date on every handout page, for example, open the View menu and choose Master. Then choose Handout Master. Select the Date area in the upper right corner. Open the Insert menu and choose Date and Time. From the dialog box (see Figure 16.45), choose the date format you want and select the Update Automatically (Insert as Field) box. The actual date will not appear until you print the handout pages.

To move the date to the lower left corner of the Handout Master, place the cursor on the gray border of the box. Click and drag the box down into the left corner. Release the left mouse button when the box is positioned where you want it.

You can format text by making selections from toolbars. Follow these same steps to insert the time or page numbers on other PowerPoint Masters. Notice the other items you can add on the Masters. All these other items come into the Masters in the same way as the date did. In many cases, however, you have to decrease or increase the size of the objects.

Figure 16.45

Inserting date and time
into a Handout Master

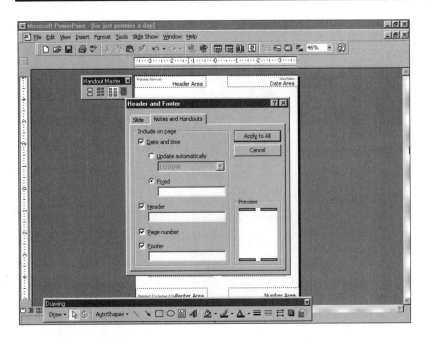

■ PowerPoint 97 Is a "Living Application"

Microsoft has striven to make information on the World Wide Web as accessible to you as anything on your personal computer. Nowhere is this blurring between online and off-line data as apparent as it is with PowerPoint 97. PowerPoint Central contains instant links to permanent Web sites that allow your existing version of PowerPoint to grow into the future, without waiting for a new update to hit the software stores. Through PowerPoint Central, you can instantly download patches and fixes; new clip art, sounds, and movies; and the newest Web tools. Just as every office environment has "living documents," such as manuals of conduct that are updated regularly, PowerPoint 97 is a "living application."

Access PowerPoint Central by selecting Tools, PowerPoint Central. You'll see the screen shown in Figure 16.46. Your first option is to search the ValuPack CD that comes with Office 97. This contains online tools for viewing PowerPoint presentations as animations on the Web; many extra templates, fonts, clip art; and patches to fix incompatibility problems between PowerPoint and older software. The next option is to browse the Web sites that Microsoft has made available for you.

Figure 16.46

The PowerPoint
Central screen

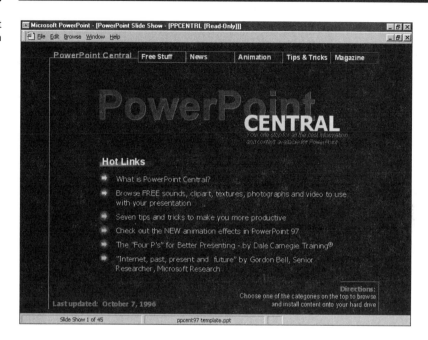

- *eUsing Color Schemes*
- *Placing a Chart on a New Slide*
- *The Standard Toolbar While a Chart Is Selected*
- *Using Microsoft Organizational Chart*
- *Adding Clip Art*
- *Exploring Further Text Editing*
- *Using the Slide Sorter Toolbar*

- *Using PowerPoint Presentation Help*
- *Meeting Minder*
- *Pack and Go*

17

Enhancing PowerPoint Presentations

POWERPOINT PROVIDES A NUMBER OF TOOLS THAT CAN HELP YOU enhance your presentations, such as mechanisms for adding color schemes and slide transitions. PowerPoint also provides tools to help you become a more effective and polished presenter, including "The Four 'P's for Better Presenting," from Dale Carnegie™ Training.

PowerPoint automates the creation of graphs and organizational charts, while keeping them professional-looking. Customizing existing clip art helps to further enhance your presentations, and makes it look as though you have hired a professional designer. Information you want to share can be quickly disseminated as the meeting closes. Responsible parties can all receive a personalized Task List, complete with an organized summary of comments that were generated during the presentation. And finally, your colleagues need not have PowerPoint 97 to enjoy your presentation. With PowerPoint Viewer, Pack and Go, and the PowerPoint Animation Player, your presentation is as portable as it is powerful.

This chapter discusses the following topics:

- Using color schemes
- Using Microsoft Graph
- Using the Organizational Chart software
- Adding and editing clip art
- Working with the Slide Sorter toolbar
- Meeting Minder
- Showing presentations on the road

Most importantly, as you perform the most common tasks required to create a presentation, PowerPoint provides continuous help.

To begin this chapter, assume that you are beginning a new presentation about learning PowerPoint. Open PowerPoint and select a blank presentation from the PowerPoint dialog box. If you currently are in PowerPoint, click on New on the Standard toolbar and select Blank Presentation. From the selection of AutoLayouts, choose Title Slide. This first slide in the Blank Presentation assumes you'll use PowerPoint's default template, which includes a white slide background and black text.

Type **Learning PowerPoint 97** for the title and **Making presentations easy!** for the subtitle (see Figure 17.1).

Tip. Shading a slide background can be particularly effective if you want to add a professional touch to a presentation. Making the top half of a slide dark can highlight a slide title. Leaving the bottom half light can make slide text pop off the screen.

■ Using Color Schemes

PowerPoint guides you through choosing a presentation color scheme by offering colors based on the slide background color. PowerPoint uses color combinations that work well together, so that you don't have to worry about creating a color nightmare. You can change the color scheme for an individual slide or for an entire presentation using the same techniques.

Adding text to a slide

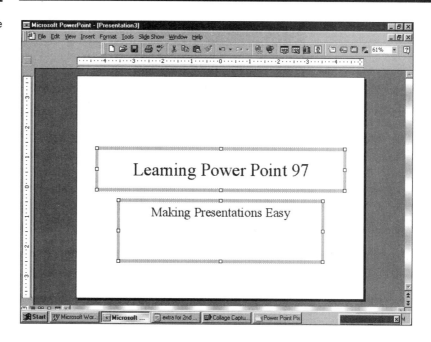

Selecting a Color Scheme

Before you select a slide background, you need to think about the conditions under which you will deliver the information. If you will be in a dark room that seats many people, for example, slides with a dark background and lightly colored text will be easy to read for audience members in the back of the room.

PowerPoint lets you select different color schemes for slides and notes. Normally, however, you will want to keep the background for notes white so that you do not detract from the slide image or text, and so you'll save a lot of printer toner.

To begin constructing a color scheme, open the Format menu and choose Slide Color Scheme.

The Slide Color Scheme dialog box will appear, displaying seven color-scheme choices. The current presentation color scheme is displayed with a box around it (see Figure 17.2). Click on any of the schemes to make it the active scheme. The color scheme includes the slide background color, text and lines color, object shadow color, title text color, object fill color, three accent colors, and hyperlink colors. A slide preview shows you where each color is used. As seen in the slide preview, the accent colors appear in objects, such as graphs.

Tip. Because you currently are in the Slide view, the Format menu offers only options that affect slides. If you were in the Notes view, the Format menu option would read Notes Color Scheme.

Figure 17.2

The Color Scheme
dialog box

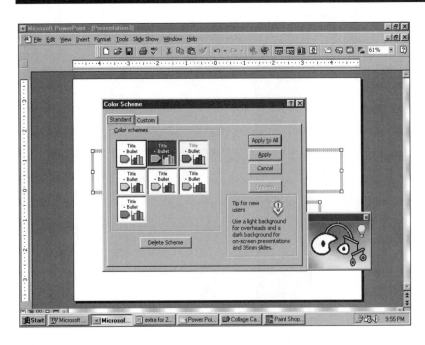

If you want to change a single color after you have picked a scheme, click on the Custom tab and choose the color of the feature you want to change (see Figure 17.3). Click on Change Color. A color palette will appear for the feature you've selected (see Figure 17.4); make a color selection and click on OK.

To create a new color, click on the Custom tab of the Color dialog box. Drag the crosshair to select a color, drag the scroll bar up or down to adjust the brightness, then click OK.

Shading

Shading can add interest to an ordinary slide background. PowerPoint lets you choose from various shading directions to highlight certain areas of the slides, depending on the slide background color you chose. To access the shading options, choose Background from the Format menu to display the Background dialog box seen in Figure 17.5.

Currently there is no shade style for the slide background. Click on the arrow below the empty text box to see the available choices for backgrounds. Choose a color for your slide's background. If none appeals to you, select More colors or Fill Effects from the menu below the color blocks. A checkbox is available to prevent any changes you make from affecting the Master Slide.

Figure 17.3

Changing the color
scheme

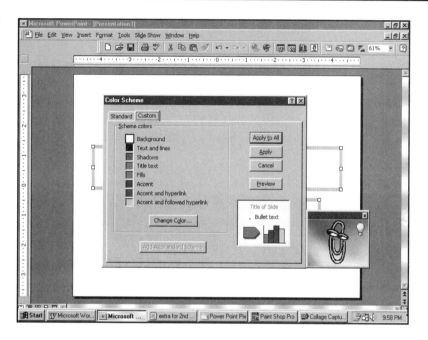

Figure 17.4

Introducing a new color
into the current palette

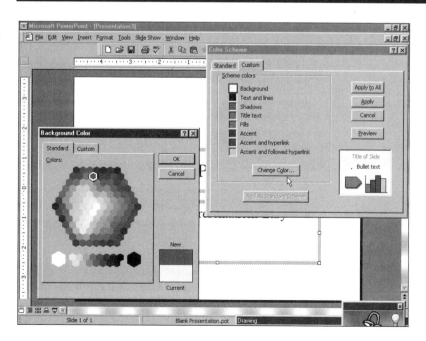

Figure 17.5

The Background dialog
box for changing slide
shading

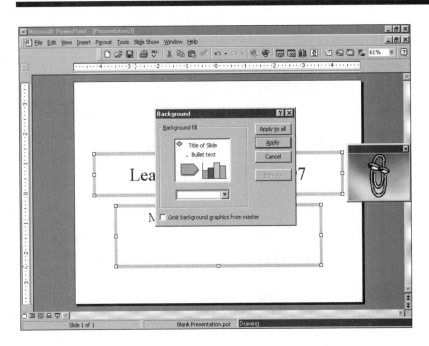

Click on Apply to change the shading style on an individual slide. To implement the shading on every slide in a presentation, choose Apply to All. To see how the shading looks on your slide, choose a shading style and variant, and click on Apply, because you currently have a single title slide.

If you want to add shading to the background of Notes pages, change to the Notes view by clicking on the Notes View button. Then, open the Format menu and select Notes Background. Experiment with a few shading styles and variants to change the background on the Notes page. You probably will want to keep the Notes Background white to keep the focus on the slide and notes.

■ Placing a Chart on a New Slide

On the second slide in this presentation, you want to present a chart showing how many new PowerPoint users there will be in the next three months. PowerPoint makes creating a chart easy. Insert Slide 2 by clicking on the New Slide button. From the AutoLayouts, select one of the Chart layouts. The new slide is inserted in your presentation, as shown in Figure 17.6.

Click on the title area and type New PowerPoint Users for the title. Double-click on the appropriate icon to add a chart.

Figure 17.6

A new slide, ready to add
a chart

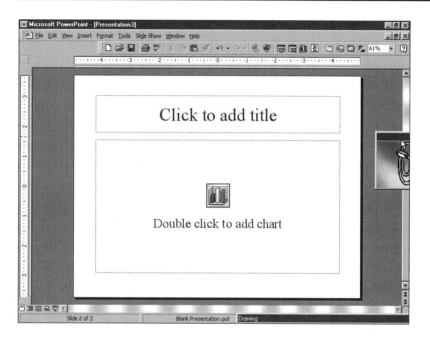

The Chart's Datasheet

The Chart opens over the PowerPoint presentation, and uses a datasheet to capture data to drive the chart. The datasheet appears on top of the chart with data already in some of the datasheet cells (see Figure 17.7). The menu bar now includes drop-down menus with commands pertaining to the chart. PowerPoint charts use their own Standard toolbar, which will be docked at the top of the workspace. Clicking on the slide underneath the chart or datasheet causes the datasheet to disappear. It will reappear when you click on the slide.

The chart's datasheet looks like a Microsoft Excel spreadsheet with rows, columns, and cells; however, the datasheet does not use formulas. You can import Microsoft Excel spreadsheet information into a datasheet, or cut and paste it into the datasheet to save time. Also, you can export datasheet information.

To change data in the cells, click once on a cell. You may then type to re-place the existing number with a new number. Just as you can select multiple cells in Excel spreadsheets, you also can select multiple cells in the datasheet. You can edit information using the Cut, Copy, and Paste buttons on the Standard toolbar, just as you edit data in Excel spreadsheets. Click on the Cut button on the standard toolbar to remove the data. Double-clicking

Figure 17.7

The chart and datasheet together: Changes in the datasheet are instantly reflected in the chart.

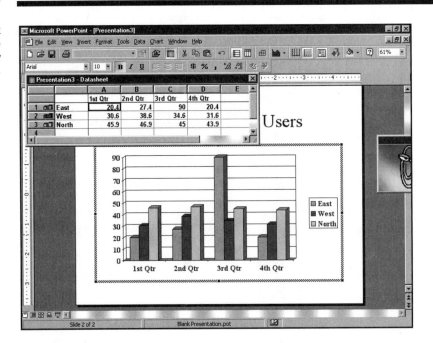

on a cell row or label temporarily hides the data. The datasheet's new totals are reflected in the chart. Until you double-click again on the temporarily hidden cell on your datasheet, you'll see less data on the chart. This allows for easier viewing of a particular target area on your chart.

To clear the current information in the datasheet, select all the cells by clicking on the button where the column and row labels intersect (see Figure 17.8), and press Del. Now the datasheet is clear for you to input new Power-Point information. Click on the cell under column A and type **January**.

Press the right-arrow key once and enter **February** under column B. Under column C, enter **March**. Click in row 1 and type **# of Users**. If the text does not fit in the column, move the mouse to the column label area, and place it right where two columns join. Pressing the left mouse button and dragging to the right will increase the size of column one, without shrinking the adjacent column (see Figure 17.9).

Let's look at a few of the unique features of the Standard toolbar as it appears when a chart is selected.

Figure 17.8

Getting ready to clear all data off the datasheet

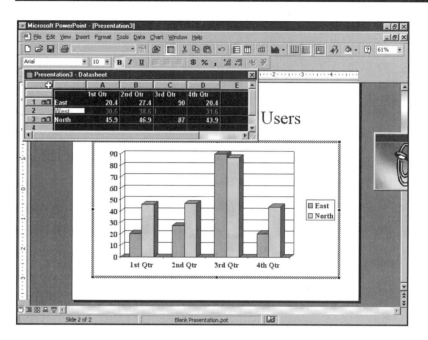

Figure 17.9

Changing the length of a column to accommodate additional text

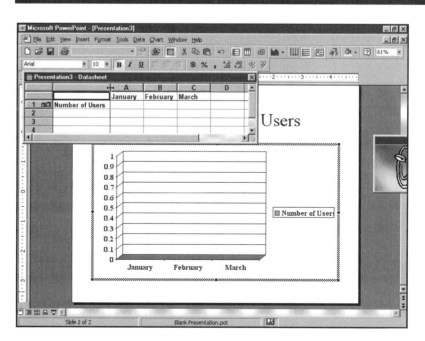

■ The Standard Toolbar While a Chart Is Selected

The Standard toolbar can quickly change your chart's formatting and appearance. Line width and color, font formatting, and the angle at which the data is read are just a few of the features editable from the Standard toolbar.

The Import File Button

The Import Data button lets you bring in data from an entire spreadsheet or from a range of cells. When you click on the Import File button, the Import File dialog box opens and allows you to select the file from which you want to obtain the data. To change the type of file you want to find, open the List Files of Type list box. To select only a range of data, enter the range in the space provided. When you have typed the file name or range, click on OK. Another dialog box might open and ask if you want to overwrite the current data in the datasheet. Click on OK or Cancel depending on your situation.

The Import File feature is quite versatile. Figure 17.10 shows Import Data formatting a text file that was composed on the fly as a table. It will become a fully functional datasheet, feeding data to the graph for your slide show.

Figure 17.10

Converting delimited text to a true chart that PowerPoint can use

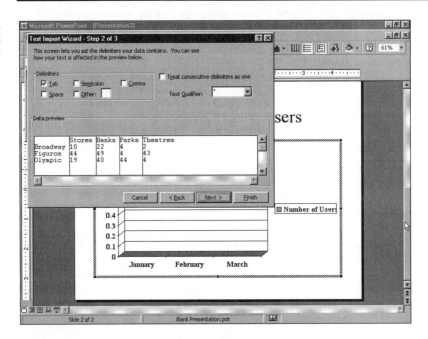

The Datasheet Button

The Datasheet button currently is pressed because the datasheet is showing. To remove the datasheet from view, click on the Datasheet button or choose Datasheet from the View menu. Removing the check mark removes the Datasheet from view. For now, however, click on the Datasheet button again to show the Datasheet.

The Editing Buttons

The Cut, Copy, Paste, and Undo buttons work just as they do on the Standard toolbar in PowerPoint. Select the text or object, then perform the function. The Undo feature that is specific to the Chart Standard toolbar does not support multiple levels of undo, whereas the general PowerPoint Undo command does.

Viewing Data by Row or Column

Currently, the new data is shown in rows. This is why the By Row button on the Standard toolbar is pressed. Click on the By Column button and see what happens. PowerPoint assumes that you want the data to be read by columns and that you want to have the different months represent individual series of data. Click on the By Row button to change "# of Users" back to the data series. You also can make this change through the Data menu by selecting either Series in Rows or Series in Columns. To remove the datasheet from view so that you can see the chart, click on the Datasheet button on the Standard toolbar.

The Data Table Toggle Button

This button lets you switch between viewing your chart as a standard chart type or viewing it as a Data Table.

Choosing a Chart Type

Currently the information is shown in a column chart. The Chart Type button on the Standard toolbar allows you to revert quickly to a default column chart, or to change the type of chart through which the data is shown. Click on the down arrow next to the Chart Type button to access the types of charts offered. Figure 17.11 shows this drop-down menu with the Radar Chart type selected.

PowerPoint 97 includes 18 unique chart types. Clicking on a Chart Type icon instantly switches the chart on the slide to the type of chart you clicked on.

If you select Chart Type from the menu instead (Chart—Chart Type), you'll have access to even more eye-catching chart styles. See Figure 17.12 for an example.

Figure 17.11

Choosing a chart type
from the Chart menu

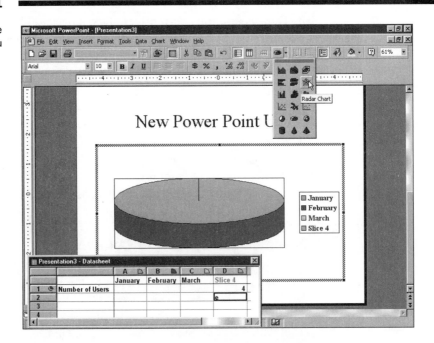

Figure 17.12

An example of a
chart type

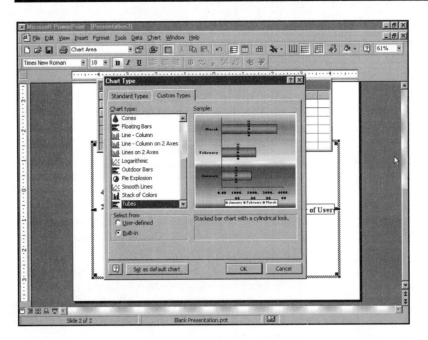

Formatting a Chart

The Horizontal Gridline button is pressed in the Standard toolbar, because these gridlines appear on the chart (although they appear vertically on the bar chart). The Legend button is pressed because a legend is currently shown on-screen. You can move the legend anywhere within the chart. The chart size might adjust to accommodate the legend. Move the cursor over the legend. Click and hold the mouse button and move the legend off the bar on the chart. Right-click on the Legend to open the Format Legend dialog box (see Figure 17.13). From here, you may edit the Legend's font, pattern, and placement properties.

Figure 17.13

The Format Legend
dialog box

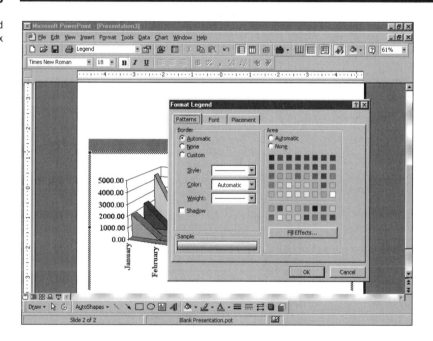

The legend has black, square resizing handles. Move the cursor over the bottom middle handle; notice the black arrows show you in which direction you can adjust the legend's size. Grab the handle and make the legend larger by dragging the mouse down. To remove the legend, click on the Legend button.

To insert a text box in the graph, click on the Text Box button and move the cursor over the chart. You cannot draw a text box anywhere outside the parameters of the chart. The mouse pointer changes to a crosshair. Drag a rectangle just as you would in PowerPoint, by holding down the left mouse button and dragging the mouse.

The Chart Drawing Toolbar

While a chart is selected, you have access to the standard PowerPoint Drawing toolbar. That means that the power to create PowerPoint's full array of Action buttons, 3-D shapes, lighting effects, and color effects is at your fingertips.

The Group Objects, Ungroup Objects, Send to Back, Bring to Front, and Shadow buttons are all available from the Draw menu on the bottom left of the toolbar. They operate just as they would on the PowerPoint main screen.

The Fill tool at the far right on the Standard toolbar functions just as it would on the main PowerPoint screen. The color boxes found in the toolbar menu become available whenever any applicable object is selected, such as the legend or the chart itself. To recolor lines, use the Line editing options found on the Drawing toolbar. Pictured in Figure 17.14 is the Fill Effects dialog box, available from the Fill menu. With it, you can select and create bitmaps and textures to fill your chart. Pictured in Figure 17.15 is a chart filled with a bitmap.

Figure 17.14

The Fill Effects dialog box

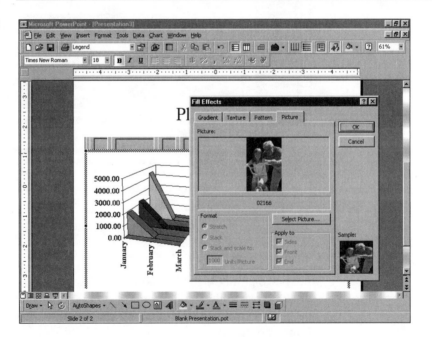

Editing the Chart

Many chart-editing options are available from the Chart menu item. While the chart is selected, click Chart—Chart Options. You'll find tools for altering the data axis (see Figure 17.16 for an example of chart data displayed at

Figure 17.15

A chart filled with a
bitmap

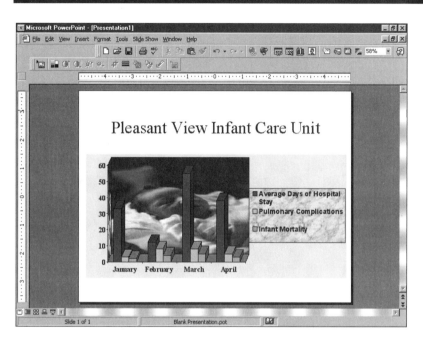

an angle), setting grid regularity, and placing title options. This menu item is where you'd come if you want to change where PowerPoint places the X and Y axis titles for your chart.

Figure 17.17 shows the 3-D View dialog box. Here you may adjust the "depth" and 3-D angle of your chart's bars or pie segments.

When the 3-D View dialog box opens, it shows a wireframe of the current chart. To change the elevation at which you view the chart, click on the up- or down-arrow button; the wireframe of the chart will reflect these changes. To change the chart's rotation, click on the rotate right or left button; the outlined chart will also reflect these changes. When the view is where you want it, click on OK. If you want to return to the original view, click on Default.

You can quickly change the way data looks on your chart by right-clicking on the axis in question (the letters going along the bottom of the chart, or the numbers moving up and down the left side of the chart). Choose Format Axis from the pop-up menu (see Figure 17.18).

The Format Axis dialog box opens. Notice the tabs running along the top of the dialog box, which are labeled Patterns, Scale, Font, Number, and Alignment. Think of these as tabbed cards that you can pull forward depending on the formatting changes you want to make. You can make changes to all of these chart aspects in one dialog box.

Tip. The Format Object dialog box in PowerPoint uses these same tabs, enabling you to make multiple formatting changes to a selected object in one dialog box.

Figure 17.16

Chart data on the lower axis displayed at an angle

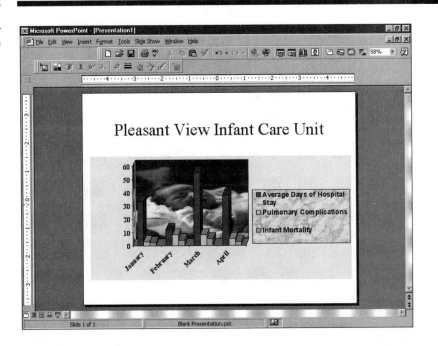

Figure 17.17

The 3-D View dialog box

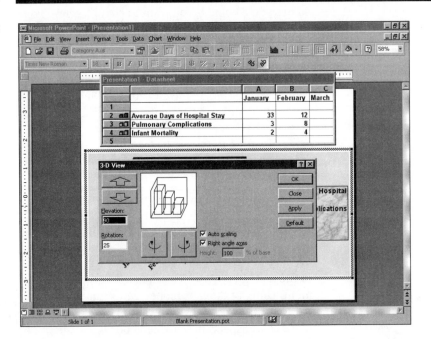

Figure 17.18

Selecting Format Axis
from the pop-up menu

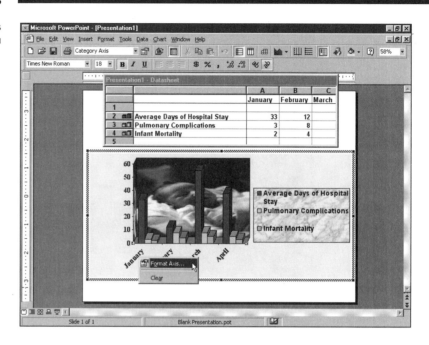

Tip. Microsoft Graph
provides many shortcut
menus that present
options related to the
selected chart objects.
Experiment by selecting
chart objects and
pressing the right mouse
button to see which
options from the
shortcut menu will
appear.

Make the text bold, then click on the tab labeled Alignment to move the Alignment tab to the front. Select the vertical text that is facing down. Click on OK to see how the text changes its orientation.

Changing Graph Colors

On the datasheet, PowerPoint shows which color represents which row or column of information; for example, any information in Row 1 is represented by a blue bar in the column chart. To better illustrate this, change the chart type to a Line Chart by clicking on the Chart Type icon on the Standard toolbar. Select Line Chart from the drop-down menu, and notice that the data lines that represent the datasheet, legend, and line chart have corresponding colors (see Figure 17.19).

Remove the datasheet so that you can view the chart. To change the color of an individual line, click directly on any line to select it. Right-click on the line and select Format Data Series. From the resulting dialog box, you can edit line color, width, shadows, and many other aspects of each information line. Were this chart a pie chart, clicking on one slice of the pie would open a similar dialog box for editing the appearance of each pie slice. PowerPoint lets you isolate a portion of your data series for closer editing. Whether dealing with a pie slice or data line, you can hold down the left

Figure 17.19

The Line color, datasheet button color, and Legend data color all correspond.

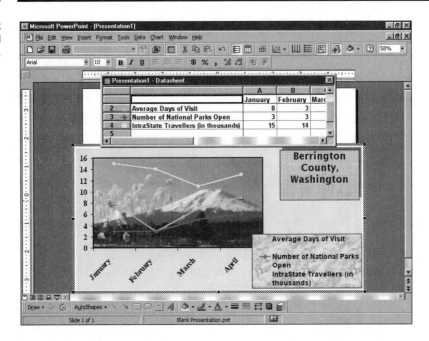

mouse button, drag the data-series piece to a new location for closer examination, and then place it back where it was.

When you are done making any formatting or data changes to the chart, click on the slide outside the chart to return to the PowerPoint presentation. The chart will position itself on the slide. If you want to access the chart again to make changes, double-click on it. To enlarge the chart once it is on the slide, grab a black resizing handle and adjust its size, just as you would for an object.

■ Using Microsoft Organizational Chart

Making an organizational chart is easy with Microsoft Organizational Chart. Instead of tediously drawing rectangles and lines, and then adding text, the chart appears before you, waiting for you to fill in names, titles, or comments.

Click on New Slide. From the AutoLayouts offered, select Org Chart. Click to add a title, and type **Potential PowerPoint Users**. Double-click where it says "Double click to add org chart," and wait for the application to open over your PowerPoint presentation. It might take some time, so don't be alarmed. When Microsoft Organization Chart opens, the beginnings of a chart will appear in the workspace (see Figure 17.20). This chart helps to get you started. To work through making a chart, you will select text and retype the information for your presentation.

Figure 17.20

The Microsoft
Organizational Chart
helps you build your own.

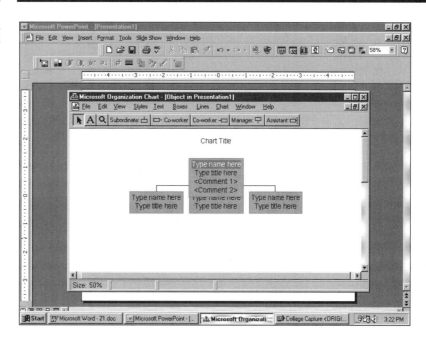

Changing Information

To change the organizational chart title, select the words "Chart Title" with
the I-beam cursor and type your text entry. You can replace the text in the organizational chart boxes in the same way. Select the top box by clicking on it,
then select "Type name here" with the mouse I-beam. Replace it with any
name you choose: Figure 17.21 shows the results of replacing both the "Type
Name Here" and "Type Company Here" text markers with new text. Select
Font from the Organizational Chart menu to change font formatting, as
shown in the example.

Notice that when you select the text, two lines of text labeled Comment
1 and Comment 2 appear. You can replace these comments with job functions or any other comments pertaining to the position. Press the down-
arrow key to select the next line of text.

When you are done filling in information in the top box, click anywhere
outside the box. The box will resize itself and any Comment line not filled in
will disappear. You may fill in the text in the other boxes using the same techniques. Edit text in a box, select the box and click the mouse I-beam inside
the box. Make any edits and click outside the box to implement the changes.

There will be times that you'll need to supplement the boxes provided
by this Organizational Chart template. We'll now discuss adding a box.

Figure 17.21

Typing a name and company into the organizational chart text marker box.

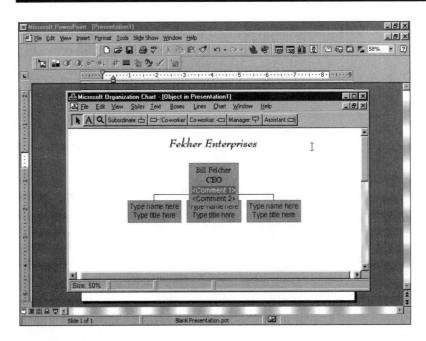

Adding a Box

As the example in Figure 17.22 shows, Mike Felcher has joined Bill Fletcher in his managerial duties at Felcher enterprises. Bill has his Assistants already in tow. Mike now wants his own team of eager subordinates to bring him coffee in the morning. Notice the toolbar at the top of the Organizational Chart window. The Add Subordinate option is selected. After clicking Add Subordinate, the mouse becomes a tiny icon representing the type of box to be added (in this case, a subordinate). After placing the icon just inside the bottom border of Mike Felcher's box, a new subordinate box is added. It can be filled in with a name, position, and comments.

Editing the Chart Style

Fonts or text colors often are used to identify levels of employees on an organizational chart. To change the characteristics of multiple boxes, you must first select them. To select more than one box, click on one box, then hold down the Shift key and click on the other boxes you want to select.

Often, however, there are many boxes with many levels of employees on an organizational chart. Selecting each box individually would be time-consuming. Microsoft Organizational Chart provides a speedy way to select multiple boxes at different levels. Suppose you wanted to select all the boxes

Figure 17.22

Making changes in your
organizational chart

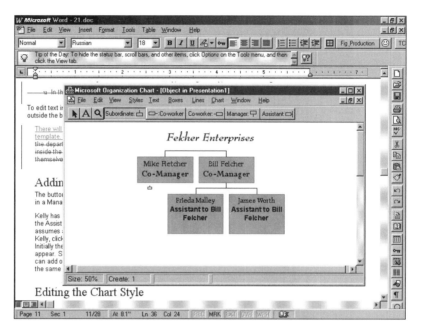

except for the Department Managers'. Open the Edit menu and choose Select: A number of choices will appear (see Figure 17.23). Because you want to select everyone except for the department managers (who are represented by the top row of boxes), choose All Non-Managers. At this point, you can make any formatting changes you would like to the selected boxes. Then, click outside the boxes to deselect them.

Microsoft Organizational Chart lets you change the format of the boxes at each level. In our example in Figure 17.24, the bottom two boxes are side-by-side with lines coming out of the tops of the boxes. You'll notice that they are selected (black in the center) and, therefore, ready for editing together as a group.

To change the format of all these boxes, open the Styles menu to display a palette of chart styles. As you can see from Figure 17.25, the Style option was used to subordinate one Assistant position to another. Now Ms. Malley has someone to bring her coffee!

Now, suppose you want to change the text color and font size for these boxes. With the four boxes selected, open the Text menu and select Color. Choose a color, then click outside the boxes to deselect them. You will see the text assume the chosen color. To change the font size, select the boxes and select Font from the Text menu. The Font dialog box will appear, allowing you to make changes to the text. To change the alignment of the text inside boxes, select the box. Open the Text menu and select the alignment: Left, Right, or Center.

Figure 17.23

Choosing what kind of organizational level box to add

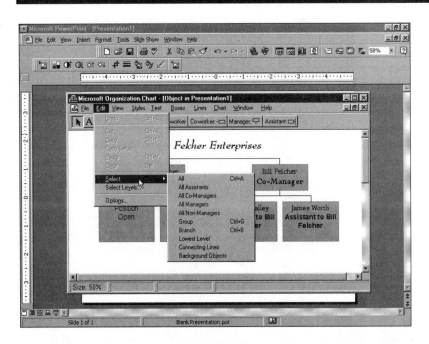

Figure 17.24

Selecting an entire level of boxes for reorganization

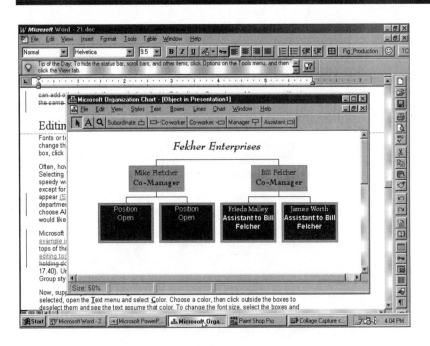

Figure 17.25

Changes in the Style option have created a new level of organization.

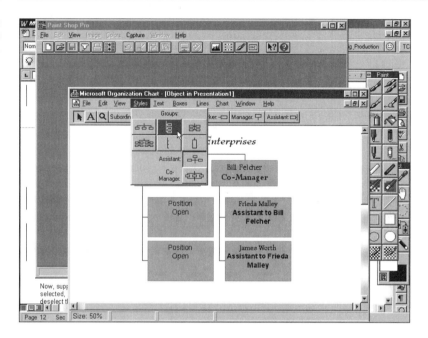

You can stylize any box even further with various borders, colors, or shadows. To make these changes, select a box or boxes and open the Boxes menu; a number of choices will appear. The first three options pertain to boxes. To change a box border, select Box Border and make a selection from the palette of borders. The remaining options work the same way.

To change the chart's background color, open the Chart menu and select Background Color. A palette of colors appears from which you can choose. Remember that this color appears on the slide, and might clash with your color scheme.

Changing the Zoom Level

Microsoft Organizational Chart enables you to view the chart at four magnification levels and provides shortcuts to access these levels:

Magnification Level	Shortcut Key
Size to Window	F9
50% of Actual	F10
Actual Size	F11
200% of Actual	F12

You also can access these views through the Chart menu. Use the button picturing a magnifying glass on the toolbar to quickly zoom into the 200% of Actual view. Click on the Zoom button, and place the magnifying glass anywhere on the chart. Click the left mouse button to zoom in. When you zoom in, the Zoom button on the toolbar will change to a button picturing an organizational chart. Click on this button, and then click anywhere on the chart to see the entire chart in the window.

Drawing Tools

Microsoft Organizational Chart provides drawing tools to help you highlight certain areas of the chart. To show the drawing tools on the toolbar, open the View menu and select Show Draw Tools (see Figure 17.26). The four tools appear as the last buttons on the toolbar. Figure 17.27 shows the Draw Tools with the mouse pointer highlighting Auxiliary Line.

Figure 17.26

Selecting Show Draw
Tools from the View menu

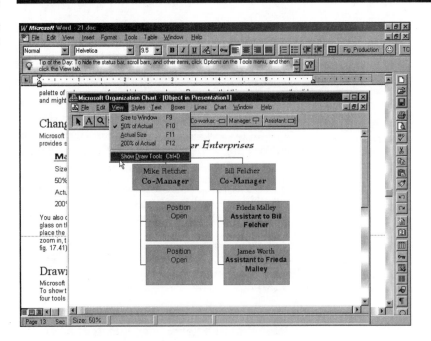

The first drawing tool shows a crosshair, and allows you to draw only vertical or horizontal lines. To draw a vertical or horizontal line, click on the button and move the cursor into the workspace; the cursor will change into a crosshair. Hold down the left mouse button and drag the mouse vertically to draw a vertical line, or drag it horizontally to draw a horizontal line.

Figure 17.27

The Auxiliary Line draw
tool selected

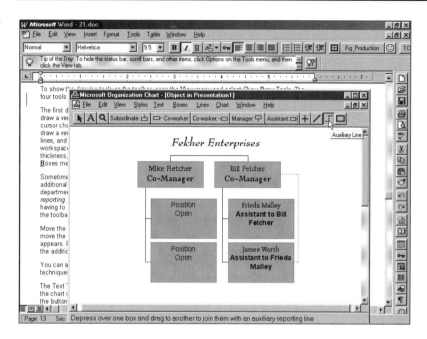

The second drawing tool is used to draw lines, and works just as it does in PowerPoint. Simply click on the button, move the cursor into the workspace to change the cursor to a crosshair, and click and drag the mouse. To change the thickness, style, or color of any line drawn on the organizational chart, select it and then open the Boxes menu. The line-formatting choices will appear at the bottom of the drop-down menu.

On an organizational chart, some boxes may need to be connected to other boxes to show additional relationships. Suppose one of the section managers occasionally reports directly to the department manager: you would want to draw a dotted line to show this unconventional channel of reporting. Figure 17.27 shows such a line, called an *auxiliary line,* connecting the lofty Bill Felcher with his Junior Assistant James Worth. In this example, the auxiliary line was fattened up a bit by selecting Line from the Organizational Chart menu, and then adjusting the Width.

You can add a rectangle to the chart by clicking on the Rectangle button and using the drawing techniques outlined in Chapter 16.

The Text Tool button just to the right of the Selection Tool button allows you to add a text label to the chart outside of a chart box. This tool works just like the Text tool in PowerPoint. Simply click on the button and move the mouse I-beam near the chart. Click the left mouse button to anchor a flashing cursor, and begin typing.

After you have created and formatted the organizational chart, open the File menu, and choose Exit and Return to Presentation. This action will close Microsoft Organizational Chart and return you to PowerPoint. The organizational chart will appear on the slide, and you can resize it using the square resizing handles.

■ Adding Clip Art

The images from the Microsoft Clipart Gallery enable you to enhance a presentation or emphasize a key point. You can rotate or flip clip art like any other object, and you can cut, copy, and paste it. Most of the time, clip art comes into the presentation either too large or in colors that do not complement your color scheme. PowerPoint lets you modify clip art extensively to make it work for your presentation. This section discusses resizing clip art and manipulating it to fit your needs.

Recategorizing Clip Art

To begin, add a new slide to your presentation by clicking on New Slide. From the AutoLayouts, select Text & Clip Art. For the title, type **PowerPoint Presentations**. Double-click on the box to access the Microsoft Clipart Gallery.

The Microsoft Clipart Gallery opens and presents images: you can see what's available by clicking the All Categories option. Scroll through the categories looking for images you might want to use. Suppose you wanted to use the School image from the Academic category in your PowerPoint presentation. You also think this image would work well in future presentations about sales techniques. In fact, moving through all the clip art, you notice that there are a number of images in different categories that would work well in those presentations. Microsoft Clipart Gallery lets you recategorize clip art into categories that you specify.

Select the image of the professor by clicking on it: a blue box will appear to show that the image is selected.

Click on Clip Properties to display the Clip Properties dialog box (see Figure 17.28). Place a check by the new category you'd like the selected clip-art piece to be available to.

Click on Edit Category list. This button takes you to the Edit Category List dialog box. In this dialog box you can create a new category and reassign the selected clip art into this category. Click on New Category. You may type in the name of a new category, as shown in Figure 17.29.

The new category will appear in the category list. Now that it exists, images from any other category can be added to this new category. Close the dialog box and return to the Microsoft Clipart Gallery dialog box.

Figure 17.28

The Clip Properties
dialog box

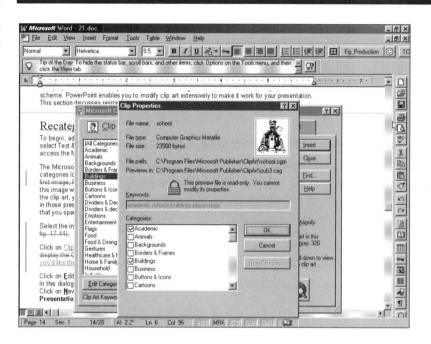

Figure 17.29

Adding a new clip
art category

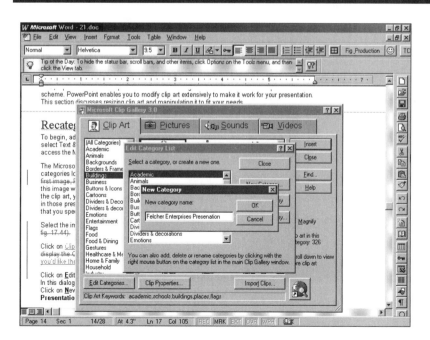

Resizing and Moving Clip Art

When the clip art is selected, a dotted line with sizing handles will surround the image. You can use the sizing handles to change the size and proportion of the image. Move the pointer over a sizing handle until the pointer turns into a double arrow. Drag the handle to change the size. To move the image, place the pointer anywhere in the selected image, and drag the entire image to a new location.

Recoloring Clip Art

PowerPoint enables you to change the colors incorporated in clip art. Suppose you wanted to change the members of the audience who are green to another color. Select the image by clicking on it, then right-click on it and choose Format Picture. You'll see the Format Picture dialog box. From there you can alter your picture's size, position on the slide, background fill and outline qualities, as well as color control. Click on the Picture tab and choose Recolor. The Recolor Picture dialog box will open, presenting all the colors found in your picture followed by options for replacing them (see Figure 17.30).

Figure 17.30

Recoloring clip art

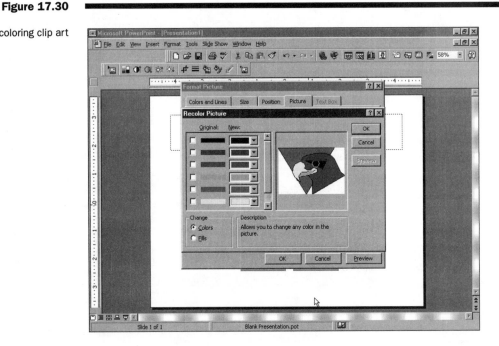

Place a check by the original color that you wish to change. Then, scroll down using the drop-down menu on the right, finally choosing a color you wish to replace the color you placed a check next to.

If you don't see a color you like, choose Other Color, which brings up a Color dialog box where you can choose from the entire spectrum of available colors.

Cropping Clip Art

At times you will want to crop an image for a presentation. To crop a picture, right click on the picture, and choose Format Picture. Click the Picture tab and choose your cropping options from the four data boxes presented (see Figure 17.31). Rather than cropping by hand, You must supply specific cropping measurements. Cropping this way provides much more precise control over your picture's appearance.

Figure 17.31

Cropping clip art

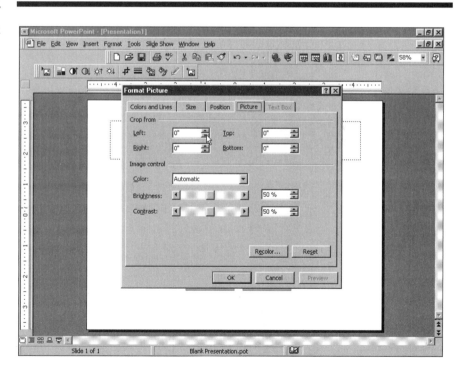

Editing Clip Art

PowerPoint clip art is composed of multiple shapes with different fill colors and shading grouped together. If you wish to separate or remove clip-art components—for example, removing the baseball bat from a baseball player's hand—you must ungroup the clip-art piece before you can move or delete its components. To do this, right-click on the clip-art piece, select Grouping, and click Ungroup, as shown in Figure 17.32. In this example, the goal was to remove the football from the football player's grasp (trying this in real life is like taking MTV from a teenager: Bodily harm can result!), and placing a cup of coffee where the football used to be. Once the football player is ungrouped, you may select individual portions of the football with the mouse pointer and delete them, one by one.

Figure 17.32

Ungrouping clip art

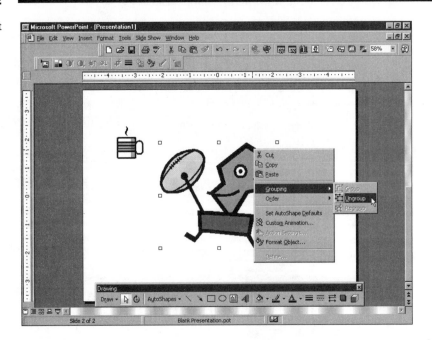

Tip. After you ungroup an image, you cannot use the Recolor or Crop Picture command through the Tools menu. Do any recoloring or cropping before you begin ungrouping the image.

If you accidentally delete part of an image, you can select Undo from the Edit menu, or click the Undo button that's on the Standard toolbar. First the pigskin has to go, followed by the outline, then the stitches, etc. You may then use your mouse pointer to draw an imaginary boundary around the football player alone, right-click on the collection, and select Group. Now drag the cup of coffee over to the player's hand and position it appropriately (see Figure 17.33).

Figure 17.33

The football player has
sacrificed his pigskin for
a good cup of coffee.

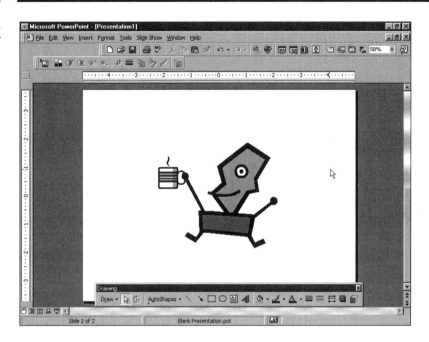

■ Exploring Further Text Editing

Now that you've mastered some text-editing basics, it's time to explore other
PowerPoint tools that make presentations quick and easy to create.

Moving Text

PowerPoint supports drag and drop. It's most helpful in the Outline or Notes
view. You can use drag and drop to reposition text just as you do in Microsoft Word. In PowerPoint, text can be moved using drag and drop on slides.
Select the text, then hold down the left mouse button until the drag-and-
drop cursor appears. Drag the text to the new location, and release the left
mouse button.

You can use the four-headed arrows to move entire lines of text directly
on a slide. Suppose you want to promote or demote bullet points on your
slide in the Outline view. You can do this using the toolbar, or you can move
the cursor over the bullet in front of the bullet you wish to promote until it
changes to a four-headed arrow. Hold down the left mouse button and slowly
move the four-headed arrow up. Do not release the left mouse button.

Notice that the four-headed arrow turns into a two-headed arrow, and a
horizontal line moves in between the bullet points. This horizontal line

shows where the selected text will be repositioned when you release the left mouse button. Release the left mouse button when the vertical line is at the top of the bulleted list, and watch this bullet point assume the top position. You can demote text using the same techniques, except that you move the four-headed arrow to the right. Select the second bullet point, and move the four-headed arrow to the right.

The subpoint now assumes the formatting defined in the Slide Master. You also can use the Promote and Demote buttons on the Formatting toolbar to indent text. With the subpoint still selected, promote the subpoint by clicking on the Promote button on the Formatting toolbar.

Spacing Lines

PowerPoint automatically uses single line spacing for text. You can override this spacing specification with the Line Spacing command from the Format menu. Figure 17.34 shows three lines of text selected on a slide. The Line Spacing command could be used to space these lines closer together or farther apart. While the text is selected, click Format—Line Spacing. The Line Spacing dialog box will appear, providing options to adjust the Line Spacing amount, and to determine whether the line spacing should affect every line of text, or only the space between paragraphs.

By default, the measurements you use to make your adjustment are tenths of a line. This is rather a blunt tool. To micro-adjust, change the drop-down menu option that reads "Lines" to "Points." This means that you will be adjusting the space between lines in picas, rather than in fractions of a line.

You can choose to change either the line spacing, or the spacing before or after paragraphs. To change the line spacing to 1.5 lines between paragraphs, click the up arrow in the line spacing box until 1.5 shows, or simply type 1.5. To see a preview of the spacing, click on Preview. You might need to move the Line Spacing dialog box off of the text box to see the preview. Click on OK to implement the new line spacing. Adjusting inter-paragraph spacing is particularly effective when you want very little text to fill a lot of slide space.

Changing Case

PowerPoint lets you switch through different cases to save formatting time. This function works the same way as it does in Microsoft Word. With the three bullet points still selected, open the Format menu and choose Change Case. The Change Case dialog box will appear, providing five options.

These options are shown in the dialog box just as they will appear on the slide. Select lowercase, for example, and click on OK: The slide text will adjust to reflect this choice. PowerPoint allows you to toggle through Sentence

Figure 17.34

The Line Spacing
command

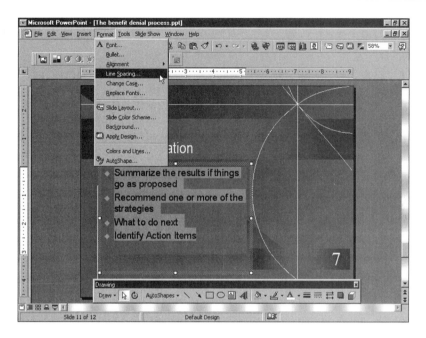

case, lowercase, and UPPERCASE using Shift+F3, just as you can in Microsoft Word. With the text currently selected, press Shift+F3 until the text turns to UPPERCASE. Using the Change Case function is especially helpful when you have a lot of text that needs to be changed.

Replacing Fonts

If a particular text box is selected, choosing Replace Fonts (see Figure 17.35) causes the entire box of text to adopt to the newly selected font. You cannot use this feature to select "a word or two" within a text box, or even to select a line or two of text. It will apply the new font to the entire box. To select a limited amount of text for formatting, try Format Painter, from PowerPoint's conventional Standard toolbar.

■ Using the Slide Sorter Toolbar

After you have created slides for a presentation, PowerPoint supplies tools to help you add even more features to the delivery. Also, PowerPoint lets you hide slides that supply information that you may need to answer audience questions, or that provide backup information to clarify a key point.

Figure 17.35

The Replace Font
dialog box

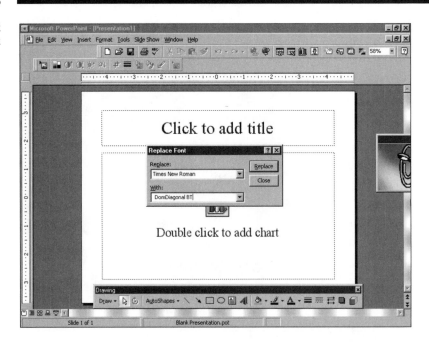

The Slide Sorter view conveniently helps you view all the slides in a presentation with slide numbers, and to insert, delete, or rearrange slides. You also can copy and paste slides. The Slide Sorter toolbar supplies the additional tools you need to apply slide transitions, create build slides, and hide slides. You can customize and move this toolbar like the other PowerPoint toolbars.

Change to Slide Sorter view by clicking on the Slide Sorter View button in the bottom left corner of the workspace to continue.

Slide Transitions

PowerPoint slide transitions add excitement during a slide show and add interest to a presentation. Instead of simply clicking through the slides, you can make a slide enter the screen from the left side or fade out when moving to the next slide. To add a slide transition to a slide, select the slide by clicking on it. A black box indicates that the slide is selected. Click on the Transition button on the Slide Sorter toolbar. The Slide Transition dialog box will appear (see Figure 17.36).

To view the effects available for the selected slide, open the Effect list box by clicking the cursor on the down arrow. Use the vertical scroll bar to view additional effects. When you get ready to make a selection, watch the

Figure 17.36

The Slide Transition
dialog box

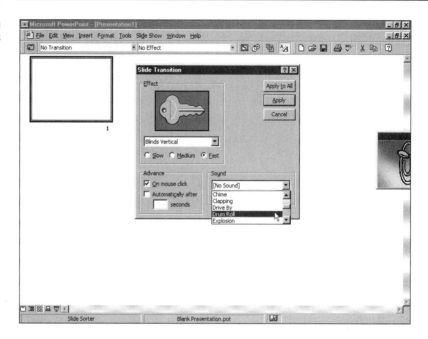

picture of the dog in the bottom right corner of the dialog box. This picture illustrates the transition so that you can get a preview. Select Checkerboard Across and watch the picture. You can regulate the speed of the transition in the Transition box: choose Slow, Medium, or Fast. The picture will preview the speed combined with the selected transition. PowerPoint 97 includes over 45 Transition effects.

PowerPoint 97 now includes sound effects that you can attach to the Transition effects. Figure 17.36, above, shows the Transition dialog box with the Sounds drop-down menu visible.

The Transition dialog box also lets you decide if you want to move through a slide show using the mouse buttons, or if you want the slides to change automatically after a certain number of seconds. You can type directly into the box. When you have made your selections, click on OK.

Back in the Slide Sorter View, a transition icon will appear under the slide to show you that there is a transition assigned to the slide. The Transition Effects box on the Slide Sorter toolbar will show you that Checkerboard Across is the current transition. If you want to change the transition, you can access the Transition Effects list box on the toolbar and make another selection. The selected slide will show you what the transition looks like when you make a selection.

Hide Slide

At times you might want to hide a slide during a slide show. For example, you might decide you don't want to share the information, but want to hold on to the slide for now. Instead of quickly clicking through the slide, which looks unprofessional and might allow the audience to read the information, PowerPoint allows you to hide slides.

To hide a slide, select the slide and click on the Hide Slide button on the Slide Sorter toolbar. Notice that a slash mark appears over the slide number to indicate that this slide is hidden. To remove the Hide Slide instructions, select the hidden slide and click on the Hide Slide button again.

Show Formatting

Sometimes you simply want to add transitions or create build slides in the Slide Sorter view. You cannot edit the information on the slides in this view. If a presentation includes many slides with a lot of clip art, working in the Slide Sorter view can become tedious and slow. PowerPoint allows you to remove the slide formatting so that you do not slow down. Click on the Show Formatting button on the Slide Sorter toolbar to remove the formatting.

Notice that the slide titles remain in the default font, so that you can identify the slides. You now can perform any Slide Sorter toolbar function more rapidly. To return to a formatted view, click on the Show Formatting button again; this feature switches on and off.

Record Narration

While in Slide Sorter View, select Slide Show—Record Narration to record speech that will play along with each slide of your presentation. The Record Narration dialog box (see Figure 17.37) allows you to trade off between high sound quality and high memory and disk space usage, or poorer sound quality and low memory and hard drive usage. You can also set up a Maximum Record Time to force yourself to keep clearly to the topic at hand while you narrate. Since recording a narration for a 25-slide presentation can require 15 to 20 megabytes of hard-drive space for storage, you are also given an opportunity to choose a hard drive and directory to store your narration in. After you are finished recording the narration for your show, you'll see the dialog box shown in Figure 17.38. This prompt lets you know that there are now defined slide lengths associated with your show, giving you an opportunity to use the Rehearse Timings feature. That helps you see if your slide-show, now timed and accompanied with narration, is appropriate for your message and audience.

Figure 17.37

The Record Narration
dialog box

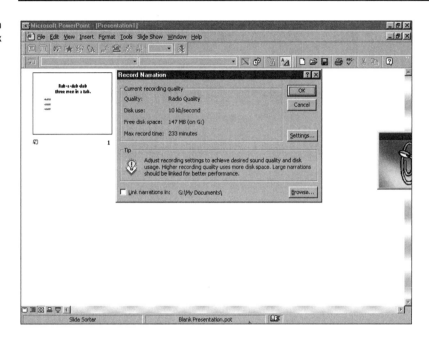

Figure 17.38

After recording a
narration, you'll be
prompted to save the
slide timings as well.

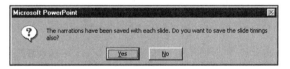

Some presenters have found that including recorded narration in a slide show greatly increases the time it takes for each slide to load. (The narration for each slide is linked with the slide itself. This is preferable to having the presentation's entire narration saved as one *very large* file.) If you have precisely timed animations that fit exactly with your voice timing, you can almost be sure that the sheer amount of memory and the hard-drive space required to load up the narration prior to each slide will throw the timing off. High amounts of RAM do not appear to prevent this timing problem. Only a disk cache large enough to keep the narration "loaded in RAM" rather forcing the computer to load from the hard drive slide after slide will really address this problem.

Action Buttons

Action buttons are available from the AutoShapes menu on the Drawing toolbar. Action Buttons are clickable buttons you can instantly apply to your slide that allow you to determine that a particular file will open when that button is clicked. That file might be a slide in the current slide show, a Web URL, or a file on your computer. These buttons are created to represent the types of links presenters typically set up on their shows, such as links to movies, to a particular document, or to a button that allows the viewer to switch to another presentation entirely. (See Figure 17.39 for the drop-down menu revealing Action Buttons.) Although a particular action button might look like a movie camera or a "fast forward" button, you will still have to provide the path itself in the Action Settings dialog box (see Figure 17.40).

Figure 17.39

The drop-down menu revealing Action Buttons

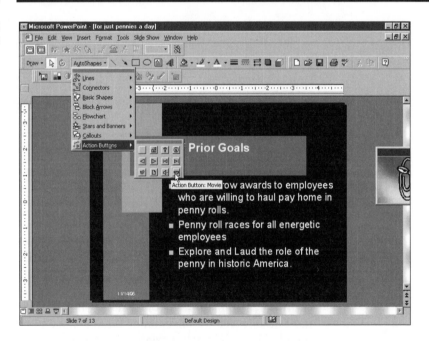

The Action Settings dialog box provides several interesting features. You can program one action to occur when the viewer hovers the mouse over the button, and yet another action to occur when the viewer actually clicks the action button. For example, you could indicate that a sound will be heard when the mouse is placed over the button, but no hyperlink action will occur until the button is actually clicked. Note also the checkbox labeled Highlight Click. This checkbox causes the button to appear to have been pressed, (pushed in) when the user clicks on it.

Figure 17.40

Selecting which file
to associate with the
Action Button

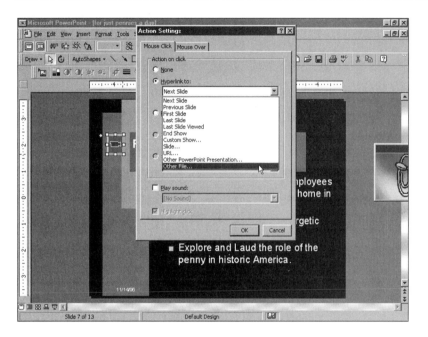

■ Using PowerPoint Presentation Help

PowerPoint provides many tools to help you perfect your delivery and to supply backup information if you get stuck. PowerPoint can track the length of a slide discussion, for example, or access files containing supportive data during a presentation.

Rehearse New Timings

Often you do not know how long it will take to show an individual slide until you are actually making the presentation. This inaccuracy can lead to rushing through the last few slides in a presentation or completely skipping over information. As you rehearse a presentation, PowerPoint can keep track of how much time you take to cover the information on a slide.

To use Rehearse New Timings, select Slide Show from the View menu to display the Slide Show dialog box. In this dialog box, you can choose to show all the slides or to show only specific slides. You also can select how to advance through slides: Choose Manual Advance if you want to use the mouse buttons or keyboard. After you have rehearsed the timing on each slide, you can choose to use those times to control the slide advancement if you do not want to use the mouse or keyboard.

To rehearse new timings, select Rehearse New Timings and click on Show; the Slide Show will begin immediately. A timer will appear in the bottom right corner of the first slide and begin timing as soon as the slide appears.

Talk through the slide just as you would during a presentation. When you are done covering a slide, advance to the next one.

When you have worked through all the slides, a dialog box will tell you the total time for the presentation. The dialog box will also ask if you want to go to the Slide Sorter view and see the timing for each slide. Click on Yes. In the Slide Sorter view, the times appear below the slides for your reference.

■ Meeting Minder

If several people view your show at different times, each can leave comments on the slides themselves. Later, you as the main presenter can compile these individual comments into minutes from your "meeting" (see Figure 17.41). These can then be assigned as Action Items (see Figure 17.42). These notes and items can be exported and scheduled as tasks via Microsoft Outlook, and the minutes themselves can be exported to Word and routed via Microsoft Mail to the responsible parties.

Figure 17.41

The Meeting Minder
in action

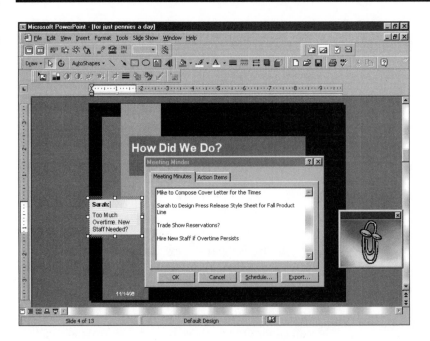

Figure 17.42

Assigning minute notes
as Action Items

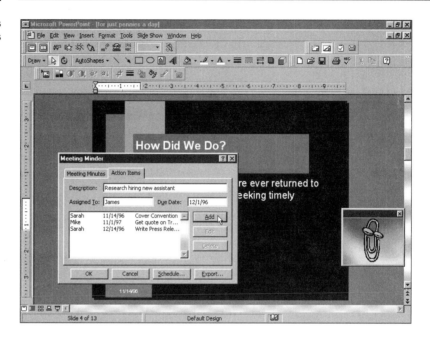

■ Pack and Go

Pack and Go lets you show a PowerPoint presentation without loading all the PowerPoint application files on a computer. Suppose you want to take a presentation on a sales call, where you will show it on a computer monitor. You don't have room to take a computer, but you know there is a computer and color monitor where the sales call is taking place. You also know that the location does not have the PowerPoint application.

PowerPoint Viewer software files fit on a single disk. You can take the software and your presentation file and load both on the on-site computer. Don't worry if the fonts you use in a presentation are not on the computer you intend to use. PowerPoint temporarily installs the fonts used in a presentation on the computer, then removes them after you are finished presenting.

To pack up your presentation and take it on the road, choose Pack and Go from the File menu. The program is a Wizard, and walks you through all the steps you'll need. Press Next to move to the next step, which is to pick the presentation you want to take. If there is a presentation loaded in PowerPoint, the dialog box defaults to it. You can also follow the instructions to pack up multiple presentations. (If you have branched slides and you don't pack up the presentation to which they're attached, you will not be able to branch when you present your show on the road.) Press Next when you have finished.

Now you have to decide where to put the files that you will need to port the presentation to another computer. Eventually the files will have to be on a disk to be moved, but you might want to put them on your hard drive in a directory you've prepared. This will let you copy the directory to a disk whenever you're traveling with your presentation. For now, choose drive A and press Next.

The next Wizard dialog box asks if you want to include linked files and fonts with the presentation or embed the fonts. If you include the fonts, you don't have to worry whether the computer you'll use has those fonts. If you embed the fonts, those fonts have to be available (but the files are smaller). It's safer to include the linked files and fonts. Press Next when you have made your choice.

The next Wizard page asks whether you want to include the PowerPoint Viewer with your portable presentation. If you do, your presentation must be run on a computer that operates with Windows NT or Windows 95. If you are going to run your presentation on a computer that is running Windows 3.1, you will have to provide the Viewer program from that system. Press Next to move on.

The last screen explains that your presentation files will be compressed and moved to drive A. Press Finish to begin the transfer.

If you make changes to your presentation, remember to run Pack and Go again.

The PowerPoint Viewer

Available on the ValuPack CD included with Office 97 (see PowerPoint Central), the PowerPoint Viewer is a program you are free to distribute to anyone. With it, anybody with a Windows 95 computer can view your presentation, even if they don't have PowerPoint. The PowerPoint Viewer has one setup file that quickly installs on the viewer's computer. After installing it, the viewer may click on the PowerPoint file itself, and the show can be viewed.

5

Access

- *Understanding Database Objects*
- *Defining Tables*
- *Relationships*
- *Sorting and Using Filters*
- *Mastering Forms Contents*
- *Using Macros*

18

Learning Access Concepts

ACCESS IS A RELATIONAL DATABASE MANAGEMENT SYSTEM
(RDBMS) A database stores information in an organized way.
Each unit of information, or record, is organized into defined
areas called *fields*. By using reports and specially posed questions
called queries, you can print mailing labels, form letters, and reports with different sets of data from the same database. You can
also examine the data in several different ways.

A phone book is an example of a database that everyone is familiar with. It organizes information. The white pages are sorted first by locality, then by last name, then by first name, then by middle initial. They are either printed as a book or delivered to you in electronic form on CD-ROM. Because we don't have control over the data in the phone book, we are limited to the structure determined by the phone company. The yellow pages provide a more user-friendly way to find information, as the records are grouped first by locality, then by a description of services, and finally are sorted alphabetically by company name.

If you had the same information in your hands as an electronic database, as the phone company does, you could search for items, reorganize its construction, and organize the data into sets of people, businesses, and addresses that would be useful for turning data into information. That is the power of a database system, and the reason that people go to so much trouble to build databases and enter data into them.

When you build your own database, first consider what information should be recorded in it. How would you like to be able to use the information? If you enter all of the address information in a field called "Address," you will not be able to sort your data by the elements of City and State. Creating and entering your data in individual fields may seem time-consuming, but it does offer you more powerful ways to use your data in the future. A good rule of thumb is to design your current database with your future needs in mind, rather than your present ones.

As we explore different features in Access, we'll use the sample database, Northwind, that is included with Microsoft Access in the Samples folder to illustrate the principles involved in working with the program.

■ Understanding Database Objects

A database contains objects that have a specific meaning and use. *Objects* are designated as tabs when you first open a database, as shown in the Database window in Figure 18.1. The objects are:

- Tables
- Queries
- Forms
- Reports
- Macros
- Modules

Figure 18.1

Database objects

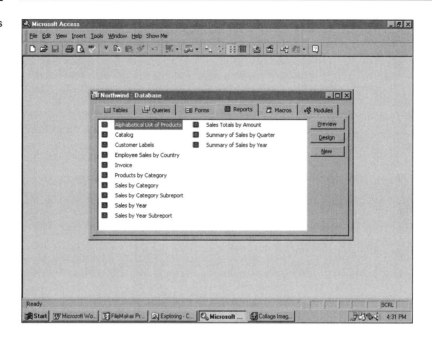

To find out more about the properties of an object, select it by clicking on its tab, pulling down the File menu and choosing Properties. Here you will find the following information, as outlined in Table 18.1.

Table 18.1

Database Properties

LABEL	WHAT IT MEANS
Name	The object's name and location.
Type	This identifies the object as a Form, Macro, Module, Query, Report, or Table.
Created	The date and time the database object was created. Note that for tables and queries this date has the same value as the DateCreated property.
Modified	The date and time when the database object was last modified. Note that for tables and queries this date has the same value as the LastUpdated property.
Attributes	This property indicates whether a database object is hidden or visible, and whether or not it can be replicated. This feature is useful if you are designing an Access database that will be used by different people in an organization, and you want to limit access to certain objects. When you click on the Hidden check box, that object will be hidden in the database window. To view hidden objects, pull down the Tools menu, choose View and click in the Hidden Objects check box. Hidden objects are grayed out in the Database window.

To examine the contents of the different database objects, click on each tab. A more concise way of getting the same information is to pull down the File menu and choose Properties. Then click on the Summary tab to display a list of the contents, as shown in Figure 18.2.

Database objects
properties summary
screen

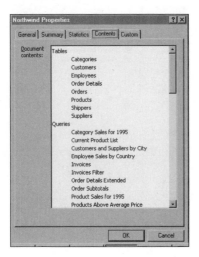

Now that you know how to find the contents of database objects, how do you know what to do with them? Each database table contains information regarding a particular subject. The Northwind database contains the following tables, shown in Figure 18.3:

- Categories

- Customers

- Employees

- Order Details

- Orders

- Products

- Shippers

- Suppliers

Each table keeps relevant information together, which makes it easier for various people to contribute to and use a database for a specific purpose. Someone from Customer Service would not need information from the Employees table, for example.

Figure 18.3

The Northwind tables

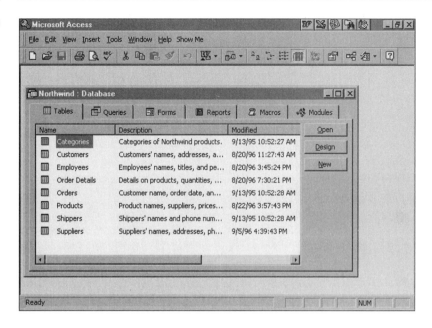

Another type of database object is called a *query*. As the name suggests, a query asks a database if it contains certain information specified by the user (see Figure 18.4). For example, you might query the Northwind database to identify the ten most expensive products. Once you have specified the information, you can save it, and use it over and over. As your database contents change, so will the results of the query.

A *report* object memorizes the way information will appear on your screen or as a print-out. Figure 18.5 shows the format used to rank the sales amounts for the past year, from highest to lowest. A report object is incredibly powerful, because once it is set up anyone who can click a mouse can extract the information and format it instantly.

A macro is a shortcut that saves you several steps. You can write macros in any of the Office programs. For example, you could write a simple macro to open a document and print a specified number of copies in one step—something that could be useful if you need to bring copies of memos or reports to weekly meetings. A list of sample macros is shown in Figure 18.6.

To run a macro, select the macro and click on the Run button.

Information may be displayed on-screen in datasheet view, which is a simple grid, or determined by a form. A *form* is an object that contains fields and graphics. For example, the employee form shown below in Figure 18.7 provides both a photo and other relevant information in a simple but effective layout.

Figure 18.4

Ten most expensive
products query

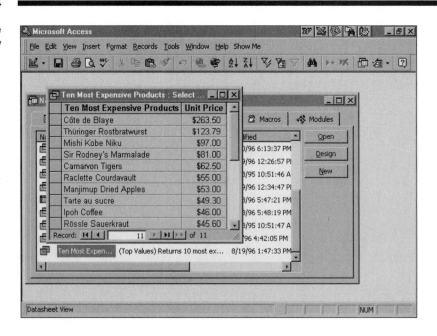

Figure 18.5

A sample sales report

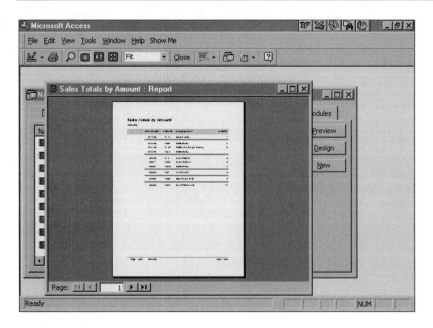

Figure 18.6

Sample macros

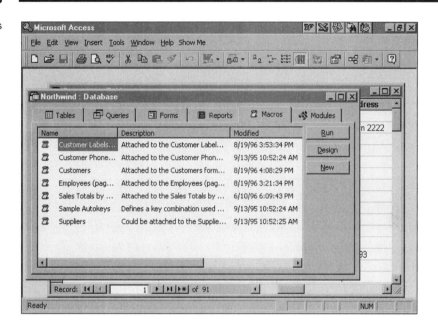

Figure 18.7

A sample employee form

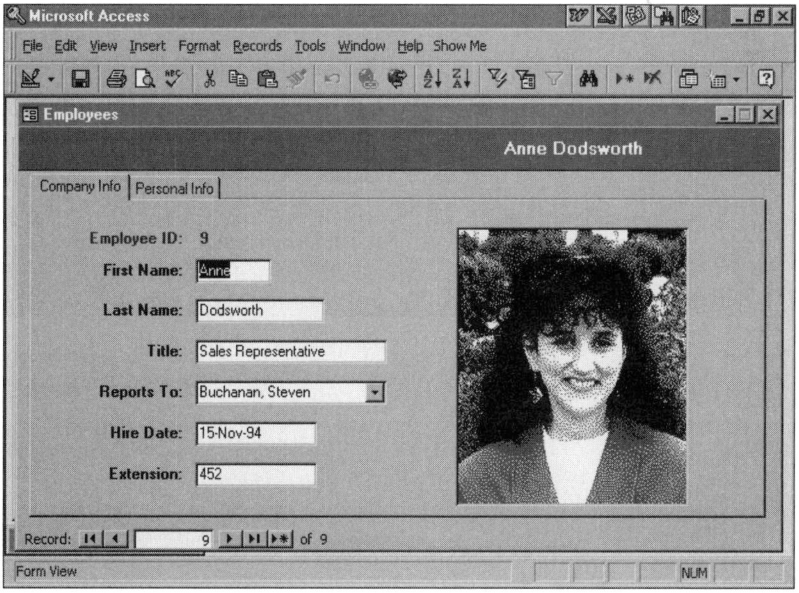

The final type of database object is the module. *Modules* are programs written in the Access Basic programming language. Figure 18.8 shows the language used to write a module that compares two databases. The Access Basic programming language is not covered in this book. If you want to use this powerful programming tool, refer to the documentation that came with your software.

Figure 18.8

A module written in
Access Basic

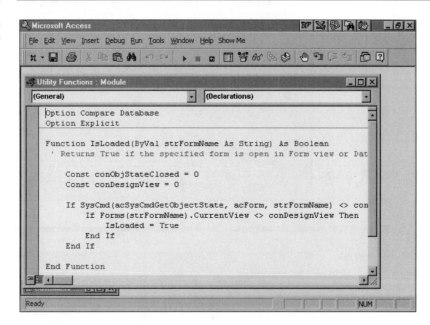

To duplicate a database object, such as a table, hold down the Control key and drag onto the database. You will now see a plus sign on your mouse pointer. Access will create a duplicate and name it Copy of (original name), as shown in Figure 18.9.

Duplicates of a database object are useful in two ways. First, you can use a duplicate as a backup copy. Second, you can experiment on a duplicate file without compromising your existing database.

Here are a few tips to help you improve your database's overall performance. While that might not seem like much of an issue now, once you have entered a sizable number of records and have established relationships, designed forms, queries, and reports, you will notice a definite slowing trend. Try some of the following steps to keep your database running rapidly:

- Place your database on your hard drive rather than on your network server.

Figure 18.9

Duplicating a
database object

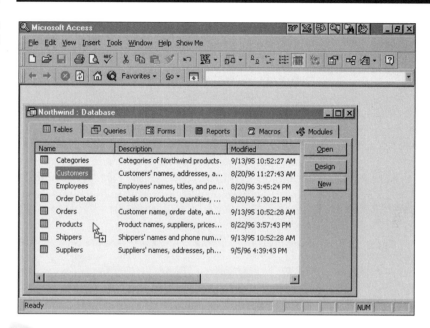

- Check the Exclusive checkbox in the Open dialog box if the database is used only by you on your PC.

- Close windows and other programs.

- Add more RAM to your computer. You can be too thin, but you can't have too much RAM. This is a relatively inexpensive way of improving the performance of your overall system.

- In the Windows Explorer, check your TMP directory for unneeded temporary files and empty your Recycle bin.

- Use a utility program such as Norton Utilities or the Windows Disk Defragmenter to optimize your hard drive at least once a month.

- Experiment with changing the virtual memory settings.

- Change your desktop to a solid color.

- Don't use software to automatically compress your hard drive.

- Move the database to a faster drive with more extra space.

■ Defining Tables

The first step in building your database is determining what information it will contain and how the database will be used in your organization. If you expect to only use Access as a contact manager or a source for labels, you may want to create one table for Customers, another for Personal, and another for Employees. If the Access database will be used by several employees or departments, it's best to organize the information into tables that reflect the way people will use it.

If you are unsure about how to begin building your database, take a look at the various ways tables are used in the sample database. To view a list of each table's contents, click on the Design tab in the Access window showing all the database objects. Access then displays a list of the fields and their characteristics, as shown in Figure 18.10.

Figure 18.10

A table in design view

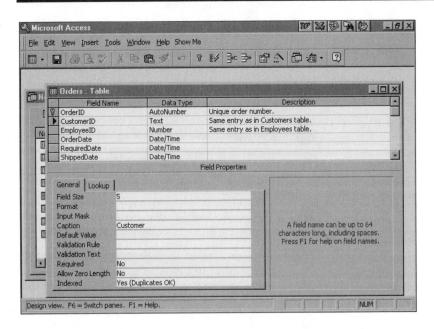

To browse the contents of an Access table, you'll need to use a combination of your mouse, resizing capabilities, and scrolling bars. When you wish to view the contents of a table, click on the Open button in the tables window. It may be that all of the data that appears in list view may not fit on your screen. The first thing you may want to do is enlarge the size of your screen. You can do this in several ways. First, you can click on the Maximize button in the top right of your screen, as shown in Figure 18.11. You can also use your mouse to drag the bottom right corner or the left or right sides of the window.

You may also find it necessary to use the scrolling bars on the right and bottom of your screen.

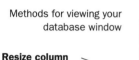

Figure 18.11

Methods for viewing your database window

Resize column

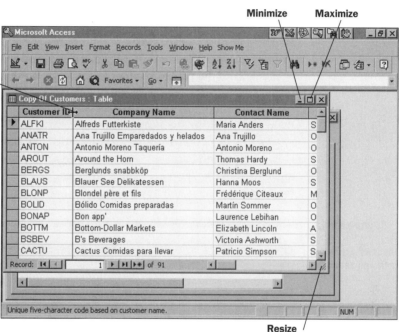

You can also expand or contract the column size. To change a column's size, click on the border of the column in the very top row. When the mouse pointer changes, drag the column to the size you desire, as shown in Figure 18.11.

■ Relationships

If Microsoft Access were a flat-file database, each table would be a separate database and information from one database could not be used to relate to information in another database. Because Access is a relational database, you are able to combine information from one table with another, and use this information in reports and queries. You do this by establishing relationships between tables based on matching values in fields or indexes. Then one record in the controlling, parent, or master table is associated with zero, one, or more records in the associated child table.

Access can be used to create different levels of relationships between tables. These relationships can be:

- One-to-one (1:1)

- One-to-many (1:M)

- Many-to-many (M:M)

To create a relationship between at least two tables, you must designate an association between common fields or indexes. To define a relationship, first designate the tables in the Relationships window, then drag a key field or index from the parent table onto the key field in the related child table. Based on the nature of the relationship, Access will assign a relationship type. However, relationships are objects, and can be altered by selecting them and adjusting their properties.

Figure 18.12 illustrates the relationships drawn between different tables in the Northwind database. Access displays relationships as lines drawn from one data table to another. Drag a table, and the relationship is preserved but the line will appear at a new angle.

Figure 18.12

Data relationships in the Northwind database

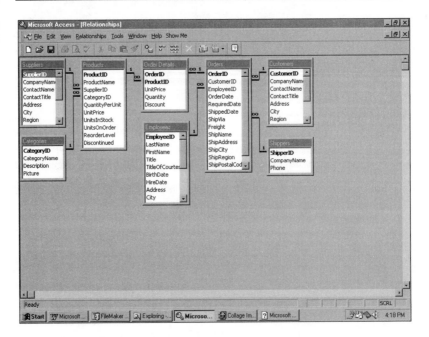

We'll look at the different types of relationships beginning with one-to-one. Before we do, let's handle some jargon. Databases are full of sterile but descriptive terms.

Primary key describes a field (or fields) whose contents are not replicated elsewhere in that particular data table. A table may have more than one key that contains unique values for each record, but only one primary key. A key that could serve as an alternate for a primary key is called a candidate key. An example of a primary key could be a unique serial number or ID number, such as a credit card or Social Security number. Primary keys are also often composed using AutoNumber fields, where the number has no meaning other than to match tables to other tables. Primary keys of that type are often referred to as surrogate keys, and they offer you the benefit of having a matching key that people don't need to see in their data, and won't be tempted to change if they do.

Foreign key describes the primary key of another database table. In many-to-many relationships, a junction table contains the primary keys of other tables. The *junction table* does not contain these fields itself: they are foreign to it. Instead, the foreign key brokers information from more than one source to create the ability to track information more completely.

Unique index describes what happens when you set the property of a primary key to No Duplicates. A unique index is used in queries for more than one table to prevent a record from being listed twice. This means that you won't have to worry about duplicate labels or form letters. In Access, a unique index is an alternate primary key that hasn't been so designated.

It is important to realize that indexes can be composed of either a single field or a combination of fields. The latter case is called a *composite index*. Access lets you define both types of indexes. Some databases allow you to create indexes from any valid expression that is record-specific, but with Access the vast majority of cases are handled by single-field or composite indexes.

The best way for you to explore creating different relationships between tables is to experiment with it yourself. Before you begin to make changes to the Northwind database, make a copy of it. We'll use this copy for experimentation. To create a replica of the database, pull down the Tools menu and choose Replication. Access then displays the alert box shown in Figure 18.13.

Click Yes as long as you have enough space on your hard drive. Access will then prompt you to save any changes you may have made during the session. If you want to keep the Northwind database clean, click No each time to create a new Design Master.

A Design Master allows you to make changes to your database's structure. You will not be able to make design changes to your previous database. While this may seem frustrating, the purpose of a Design Master is to protect the integrity of your database. As you use the Replication command again,

Figure 18.13

The replication alert box

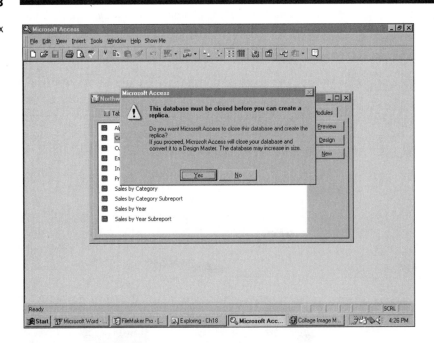

the newest file becomes the Design Master. *A database may have only one Design Master at a time.*

During the replication process, you will be prompted to make a backup copy of the database. Since a database reflects a great deal of time spent in design and the processing of a lot of information, you should make a backup on a regular basis—two times a day for a database that is heavily used, once a day for a more lightly used database. You can also drag the icon of the Access database onto of the briefcase icon on your computer's desktop. Be aware that a copy of the backup file may not be able to be synchronized or updated with the existing data in the replica set.

One-to-One Relationships

A one-to-one relationship describes a relationship between two or more tables, when the only field you have designated as related is a primary key or unique indexes. In a one-to-one relationship, only one field links to another field in another table. A one-to-one relationship is not often encountered, since this is the type of information that could often be stored in one table. An example of a one-to-one relationship would be ordering food in a Chinese restaurant. You ask for General Gau's Chicken, a unique item on the menu, and the waiter tells the kitchen to prepare another dish of "Number 19." The first time this happens will be confusing if the numbers are not printed on the menu. However, as long as you get the dinner you wanted, you will be happy. A restaurant that prints the names of the dishes and their numbers is combining the data in one table, and there is no need to designate a relationship or perform a query to get the correct information.

You might choose to set up a database with one-to-one relationships if you need to break up the information in a large database or isolate information from the person performing data entry. For example, a lab that performs testing for cancer or AIDS patients might list the results under a patient number. The unique patient number would be related to a table containing the patient's name and address information. Anonymity would be preserved, and gossip would be cut to a minimum. Figure 18.14 shows a report based on a one-to-one relationship.

Figure 18.14

The results of a one-to-one relationship

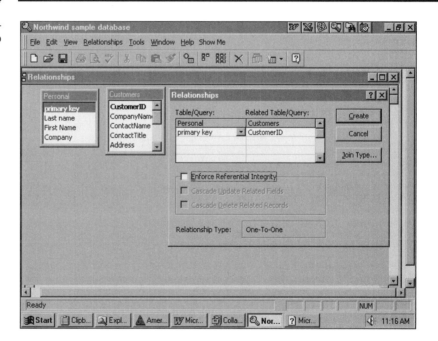

One-to-Many Relationship

Probably the most common type of relationship you'll want to build into your database is the one-to-many relationship. In a one-to-many relationship, information from one table may match many matching records in other tables. However, the information in the second table will only match one field in the first table.

In a one-to-many relationship, only one of the related fields has been designated primary key, or is used as a unique index.

To take the example of the medical lab a bit further, one table might have the lab results and a patient identifier (a primary key), and the second table might contain the patient's name and address information. The table called "Patient Info" and the table "Lab results" share the Patient identifier number. Since each patient could have a variety of medical tests on the same or different dates, if you use a one-to-many relationship, you would get an up-to-date report on all the medical tests that have been completed and logged into the central database. Figure 18.15 shows a report based on a one-to-one relationship.

Figure 18.15

The results of a one-to-many relationship

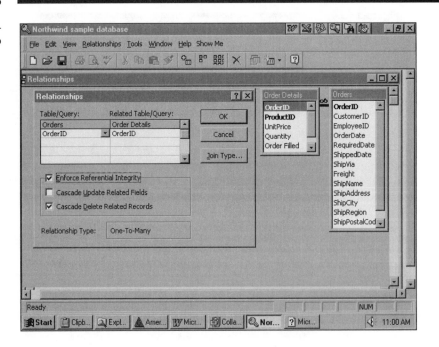

Many-to-Many Relationships

A many-to-many relationship reflects the complexity of the real world. To build a many-to-many relationship, you must use a third table that acts as a junction between another two tables. A junction table must contain a primary key from both of the other tables.

The Order Details table is an example of a junction table in the Northwind sample database. The Order Details table builds a many-to-many relationship between the Orders and Products tables, making it possible for an order to contain more than one product and for a single product to be in more than one order.

You can think of a many-to-many relationship as two one-to-many relationships coordinated by a third table. Be careful to define a primary key as a unique index. If you don't perform this step, Access may not be able to provide you with the correct information when you query the database.

Understanding Access Queries

When you bring up a table, you can get a certain amount of information from it by just scrolling through the records. Your journey through the table will be somewhat haphazard, and it won't permit you to draw complex conclusions that incorporate data from other tables.

Access has methods for filtering and sorting your data, for relating data from different tables, and for applying a combination of selection criteria and sorts to it in a query. Filters are a set of selection criteria applied to a table. Access allows for several different methods to set a filter, such as filter by form, filter by selection, and so forth; and Access allows for one filter to be set at a time. When you filter your table, you will see a selected set of records. You can filter the selected records again, and see a narrower set of records. You can think of filters as very simple queries.

With a database as powerful as Access, there are many types of queries. First, we'll look at what you can do with some simple queries, then we'll move on to more complex queries.

Simple Queries

A simple query is a set of instructions that helps you selectively find and retrieve information from your database. A simple query acts as a filter. Access comes with a Simple Query Wizard that helps you compose this type of query, as well as other query wizards. This query sorts order numbers numerically, then calculates the order subtotal amount.

To find out what goes on behind a query, select a query and open it in Design view, as shown in Figure 18.16. Here we find that the information is drawn from one table only. It's important to understand what information is going into a query. If this table reflected only East Coast sales, the president of the company might be alarmed at these figures if she were expecting a report detailing the company's national and international sales.

Microsoft Access has an elegant Query Wizard, which you should use before you decide to build more complex queries on your own. To use the Query Wizard, you must show the Query objects in your database and click the New button on the right-hand side. The New Query dialog box will appear, as shown in Figure 18.17.

Figure 18.16

A query in Design view

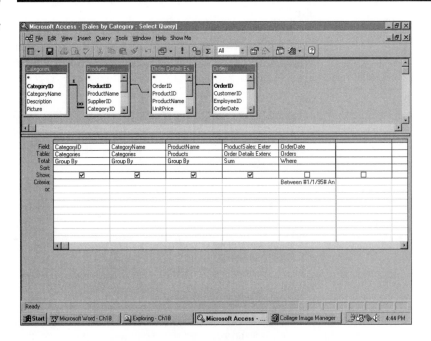

Figure 18.17

The New Query dialog box

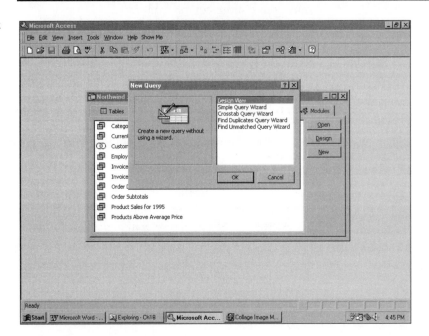

Click on the Simple Query button to display the Simple Query Wizard dialog box. Then hold down the name of the query to show a list of all queries that are incorporated in the database.

The rest is pointing and clicking. Choose the tables and fields you want incorporated into the query. Simple queries could help an organization locate suppliers near its customers, or calculate the amount of sales by individual or time period, for example.

The information is located in what is called a *dynaset* object. A dynaset object can have many properties that affect the outcome of a query. Chapter 20, "Understanding Queries," goes into much greater detail about composing and using queries.

The Access Wizard can be used to create the following types of queries:

- **Simple select query** Use the simple select query where you select the field and table information. You can also specify which calculations are to be performed.

- **Crosstab query** This query allows you to rename the labels the information is displayed under. While your job might require that you deal with products on a very specific level, your manager might want to group them under a new name. Note that you can also use a PivotTable to change the rows and columns of a report without creating a new query.

- **Find Duplicates** The Find Duplicates query helps you troubleshoot your database by locating duplicate records or field contents. It's a good idea to check your database periodically for duplicates, as you might find that data for one customer is being split into two records. This could affect the outcome of a report. The Find Duplicates Wizard locates but does not delete the duplicates.

- **Find Unmatched query** This query allows you to locate unmatched records between tables. You can use it to troubleshoot data entry, to locate all customers whose fax numbers are not listed, or to look for areas of improvement by finding all employees who have not attended a training session in Office 97, for example.

More Complex Queries

You can use more complex queries to perform actions or use custom dialog boxes. A Parameter query uses a custom dialog box to prompt the database user for specific information. You could use a parameter query to allow you to perform a query and limit the found information to a set period of time, for example, the month of May or the year 1997. By setting parameters, you are able to use the information in your Access database in a very specific fashion to help you spot trends.

If you are familiar with other databases, you may be familiar with SQL, the Structured Query Language. Because Access has a graphical interface that lets you point and click to create a query, you do not need to know how to write an SQL instruction. However, Access uses this structure when you implement a query. To view a query in SQL format, choose Open or Design, then pull down the View menu and choose SQL view. Your query will appear in the following format, as shown in Figure 18.18.

Figure 18.18

A query in SQL view

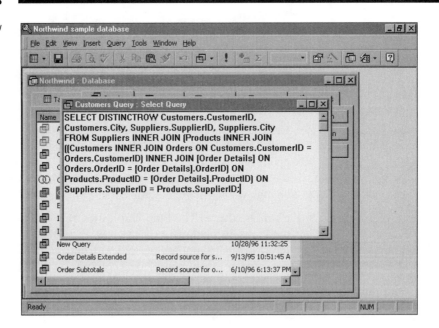

You can use the SQL information to perform several types of advanced queries, such as a Union query that combines individual fields from two or more tables or queries into one field. You can also work with a Pass through query, which allows you to work directly with another database's tables without converting them into Access.

For experiment with more advanced queries, you can try modifying an existing form or report. Another time-saver is saving an existing filter as a query. For more information on queries, refer to Chapter 20 of this book.

Users of Microsoft Access for Windows 95 should note that the Archive Query Wizard is not included in Access 97. As a workaround, users can create a make-table query to copy records into a new table.

■ Sorting and Using Filters

Sorting information means that reordering a table's contents according to a particular field. You can choose whether to sort alphabetically or numerically, and whether the order is A-Z or Z-A. When you're using information in a table that is ordered by a unique record number, the information is not presented in a readily useable fashion. For example, see the table listing the Employees of Northwind in Figure 18.19.

Figure 18.19

An unsorted database

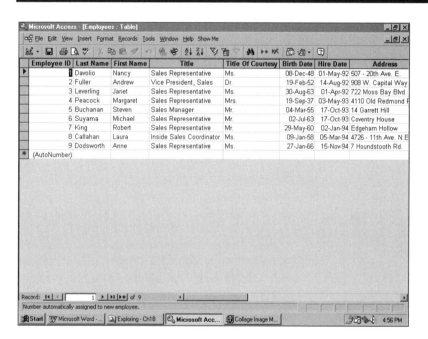

To list employees alphabetically by Last Name, click in the column you wish to sort by and pull down the Records menu. Choose Sort and A-Z. The data will now be sorted by last name, as shown in Figure 18.20.

You can also use the Sort Ascending and Sort Descending icons on the Toolbar. Note that in the sorted record all the information pertaining to each record is preserved. Sorting a database will not scramble your records.

Some things to remember about sorting are:

• A record without an entry in the field you are sorting by will be listed at the top of the search results. In other words, nothing is less than something. Finding empty fields can help you examine the completeness of your database records.

Figure 18.20

A sorted database

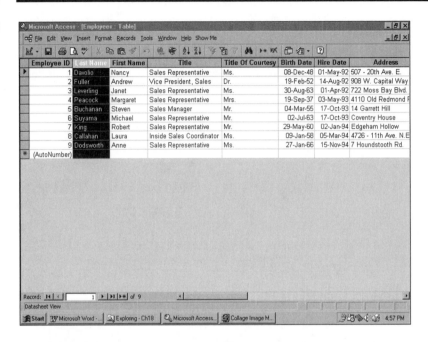

- If the field you are sorting by is a text field that contains numbers, such as a street address, the resulting sort will display the result by the first digit, then the next, as shown in Figure 18.21. When entering numbers in your data table, consider using 01, 02, 03 instead of 1, 2, 3. Otherwise, if you choose to sort by that field you will see results like those shown in Figure 18.22.

- You may want to apply a more advanced sort, where you specify several fields in order. To create a more advanced sort, pull down the Records menu and choose Filter, then Advanced Filter Sort. In the Advanced Filter Sort dialog box, shown in Figure 18.23, select the fields, their order, and whether to sort in ascending or descending order.

It may happen that when a table is set up the fields you wish to sort by are not adjacent to each other. With a bit of clicking and dragging you can change the order of the columns for your reading convenience. To move a column, select the entire column by clicking on the field name. Holding down your mouse, drag the column to its new location. You will see a small box attached to your cursor, which indicates that you are dragging and dropping. A thin, dark column will be displayed where the column will be positioned when you release the mouse.

Figure 18.21

Sorted numbers in a
text field

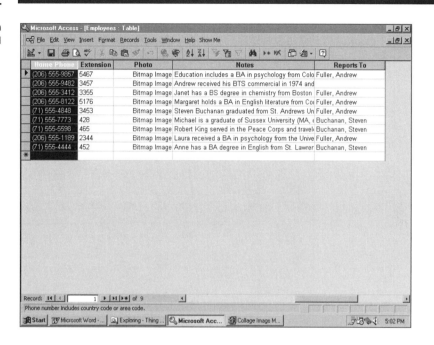

Figure 18.22

Problems sorting numbers

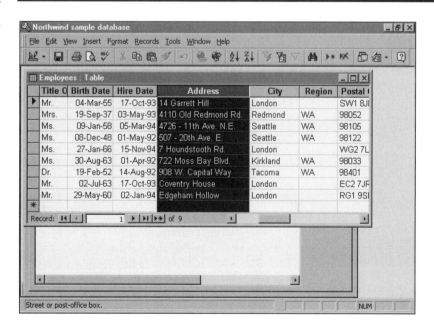

Figure 18.23

The Advanced Filter Sort
dialog box

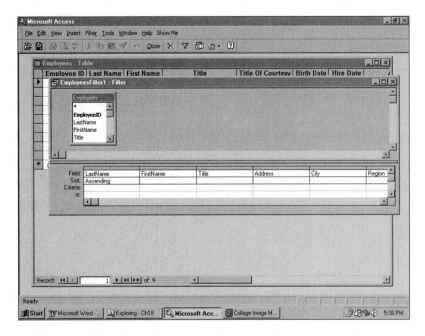

To restore your table to its previous sorted value, choose Undo Filter/
Sort from the Records menu. When you close a table to which you have
made changes, you will be prompted to save or discard any changes made to
the layout.

Filtering information differs from sorting information in that a sort reor-
ders all the records in a table, whereas a filter displays only those records
that have information in one or more specified fields. Using a filter does not
eliminate any records from your database, although the other records are
not displayed after you have used the filter. Using the Products data table
from the Northwind database, we'll use filters to provide a list of discontin-
ued items by company. A list like this could serve as a quick reference for employees handling customer orders.

After opening the Products table, pull down the Records menu and
choose Filter by Form, Filter by Selection, or Filter Excluding Selection.
When you select Filter by Form, Access will provide a form that lets you
specify your sorting criteria, as shown in Figure 18.24.

Click in the spaces to choose the fields you want to use as filters. Clicking
in a field displays a list of the field's contents. Once you enter the information in the form, pull down the Records menu and choose Apply Filter/Sort,
or click on the icon in the toolbar, as shown in Figure 18.25.

Figure 18.24

Filter by form

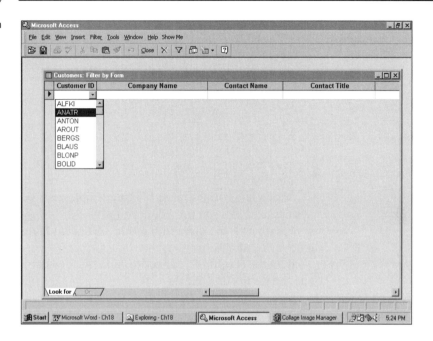

Figure 18.25

The Filter icons on the toolbar

Filter icons

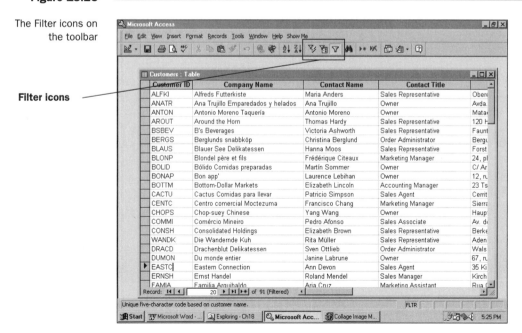

To see all of your records again, choose Remove Filter/Sort from the Records menu.

The Filter by Selection command is definitely cool. If you want to see only the information that matches the field you have currently selected, pull down the Records menu and choose Filter by Selection, or click on the command's icon on the toolbar. The results are instantaneous and gratifying.

The Filter Excluding Selection command allows you to eliminate all records containing the information in the selected field. Pull down the Records menu and choose Filter Excluding Selection, or click on the command's icon on the toolbar. Toggling between the by exception and excluding selection options allows you to see how the data looks with or without a certain element.

Using filters and sorting is more flexible than using queries. While queries are marvelous at providing you with a way to repeatedly retrieve the same data with the same formatting, sorting and filtering allows you to be more active in interpreting your data.

Use the results of your sort or filter as the basis of a new query, or to refine the results of a query.

■ Mastering Forms Contents

Typically, you should build the information in your data table first, then design the forms you need. With this strategy, you will be able to troubleshoot any problems you may have with the information in the data table before spending time designing your forms. Form design invariably takes a lot of time as you "tweak" this or that field and position. If you need to restructure your data table, you will also need to rework any forms you have created. Once you start creating forms, it's rewarding to be able to see and use your data in a graphical format instead of as a boring list.

A form contains fields from your data table. A form need not contain all the fields in a table. For example, you may want to create a form that contains limited address and phone information, like the phone list shown in Figure 18.26.

You can design different forms to suit the needs of those using your database. You can enter data from various forms (see Figure 18.27), but you should set standards within your organization. If the only data entry were to be from the Customer Phone List form, a lot of good information would not be captured.

Each form can be made up of different types of fields. Table 18.2 lists different field types and their characteristics.

Figure 18.26

The Customer Phone List form

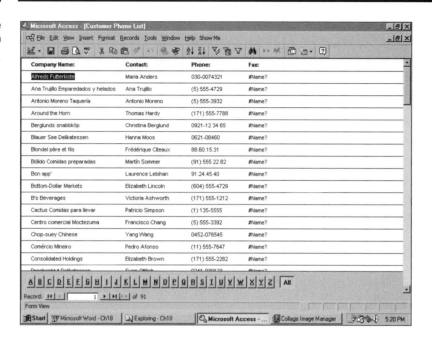

Figure 18.27

An HTML page opened in Word

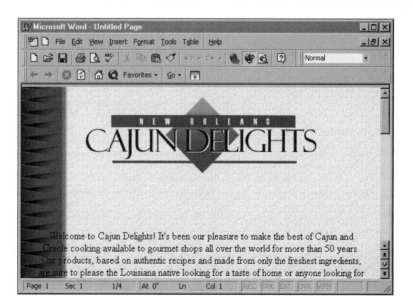

Table 18.2

Field Types and Their Uses

FIELD TYPE	PURPOSE/TIPS	LIMITS
Text	(Default) Use the text field for text, combinations of text and numbers. Even though phone numbers do not contain text, they should be formatted as text fields to prevent Access from interpreting the dash as a minus sign.	255 characters unless a smaller amount is specified
Memo	Ideal for lengthy text or combinations of text and numbers.	65,535 characters
Number	Contains numeric data which may be used in calculations. See Currency.	1, 2, 4, or 8 bytes
Currency	Data in this field involves currency values and/or numeric data with one to four decimal places, which may be used in calculations. Accuracy to 15 places before the decimal separator and to four places after the decimal.	8 bytes
Date/Time	Designates date and time values for the years 100 through 9999.	8 bytes
AutoNumber	A unique sequential number or random number assigned to a new record. You can't change the contents of an AutoNumber field.	4 bytes
Yes/No	This type of field can only have one of two values, such as Yes/No, True/False, or On/Off.	1 bit
OLE Object	An object linked to or embedded in an Access table.	Up to 1 gigabyte
Hyperlink	Text or a combination of text and numbers that is stored as text and used as a hyperlink address. There are three parts of the address: the display, the path, and the URL. Use the Insert menu to put a hyperlink address in a field.	Each part of the hyperlink may use up to 2048 characters. The hyperlink may open a document created in Word or use your modem to directly access an Internet site. Figure 18.32 shows an HTML page opened in Word.
Lookup Wizard	Use this to create a field where you can create a lookup field and choose data from another table.	Typically 4 bytes

To get a better understanding of how field types are used, select a table from the Northwind database and click on Design. Figure 18.28 displays the Orders field information in Design view. Note that the field designated as the Primary key has an icon of a key to its left.

Figure 18.28

Field information in Design view

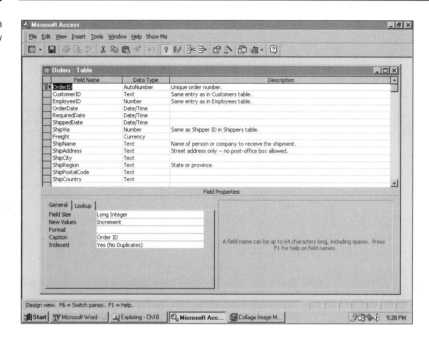

Table 18.3 comes from the Suppliers, Employees, and Products tables, which can give you a good idea of how to use the various field types.

Table 18.3

Suppliers, Employees, and Products Tables Information

FIELD	USED FOR	FIELD TYPE
SupplierID	Unique identifier for each supplier	AutoNumber
CompanyName, Address, Phone, and others	Used for text and non-mathematical numbers like phone numbers	Text
HomePage	The URL is stored as a hyperlink that will be activated by double-clicking	Hyperlink
BirthDate	Records dates and times in the correct format	Date/Time

FIELD	USED FOR	FIELD TYPE
Notes	Provides a space for additional text or documentation	Memo
TitleOfCourtesy	A predetermined list allows you to select a value without typing	Text (Lookup)
ReportsTo, CategoryID	Predetermined list allows you to choose a numerical value without typing	Number (Lookup)
Photo	An external object created with Object Linking and Embedding	OLE Object
UnitPrice	Allows value entered to be formatted as currency and used in calculations	Currency
Discontinued	Provides a simple check box for status	Yes/No
UnitsInStock	A numeric amount which will be used in calculations or summaries	Number

To change a data type, open the table or form in Design view and click on the data type to display a drop-down menu showing the available data types, as shown in Figure 18.29.

If the field has been used to create relationships, Access will display an alert, which forces you to open the Relationships window and to break the relationships with that field first.

If we only had this kind of alert in real life, we would be warned whenever we were changing the rules in the middle of a relationship! Instead we would be forced to think about whether we wanted to end a relationship in order to begin a new one under different conditions.

■ Using Macros

A macro is a memorized action or set of actions. Once you have an idea of the tasks that you perform repeatedly, you'll have a list of potential macros. Macros can be activated by a button or by selecting them from the Macro command on the Tools menu.

If you have more than one macro, you can define it as part of a macro group. If you have a lot of macros, grouping them can help you more easily locate them, or prevent you from applying the wrong one. You can also indicate what conditions are needed to run the macro. For instance, you could

Figure 18.29

A macro opened in Design view

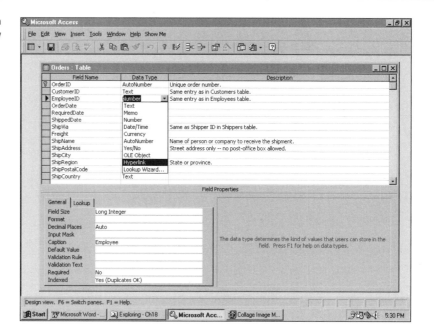

create a macro which queries a database for a Yes/No answer to the question "payment received?" If the answer is "No" and the invoice date was greater than 30 days, you could instruct Access to create statements for customers with overdue accounts. You could even add printing as the last part of the macro, as long as you supply the printer with any special paper needed.

Another useful macro might compare the contents of one database with those of another. You could use the condition that this action occurs after 8 PM at night when the computer would be unused. Of course, you'll have to leave your computer on, your network connection up (if the database is on a network), and Access open.

The Northwind database comes with several built-in macros. To get a feeling for how a macro is constructed, open a macro in Design view. The macro design window shown in Figure 18.30 is deceptively uninformative. It isn't until you click on the various fields and lines that other options present themselves.

To keep a record of what a macro does, its properties and actions, and its permission information, choose the Print command from the File menu. Having this information available in printed form can help you restore corrupt macros, try out new actions or conditions, or (gasp) rebuild a macro list that was not backed up when your computer disappeared in a theft or fire, was savaged by a virus, or was not adequately backed-up. The Print Macro Definition

Figure 18.30

Click on various fields
and lines for other options

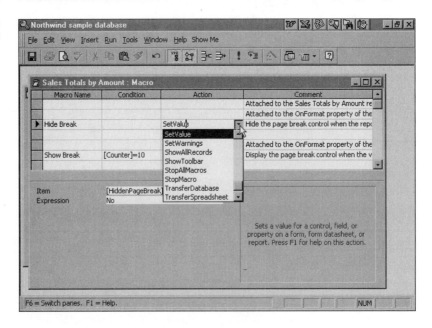

dialog box allows you to specify how much information you want included on your printout.

A macro can contain several actions. These actions are listed in the table below. For more help on macros, refer to your Microsoft Access documentation.

A word of caution about sharing your macros with others: There is such a thing as a macro virus. A macro virus is hidden in a file or template's macro. As soon as you open the file or template, the macro virus adds itself to your Normal template, infecting *every* document you save. Whenever you share a file with some one, you may be transmitting the virus to their computer. Lest you think, "this can't happen to me," be aware that even Microsoft has distributed infected files—including some given away at trade shows and through mailings. These days we have to practice "safe computing," which means that all computers should be loaded with anti-viral software, especially since we download files from the Internet. For the latest on macro viruses and free programs to battle them, check Microsoft's home page at http://www.microsoft.com or by choosing Microsoft on the Web from your Help menu.

To find out more about what each action does, choose an action. A description will be displayed in the bottom part of the window. To add the next action to your macro, move to another action row. Use comments to explain what that step is to accomplish, so that you'll be able to better adapt or trouble-shoot the macro in the future.

The only way to check the accuracy of a macro is to run it. Usually, you'll find that you need to adjust a step or two in order to get things just right. You'll need to verify each action, stop the macro when it goes wrong, fix it and try it again.

To step through a macro, open the macro in Design view. Then, click on the Step icon on the toolbar, as shown in Figure 18.31, or choose Single Step from the Run menu.

Figure 18.31

The Step icon

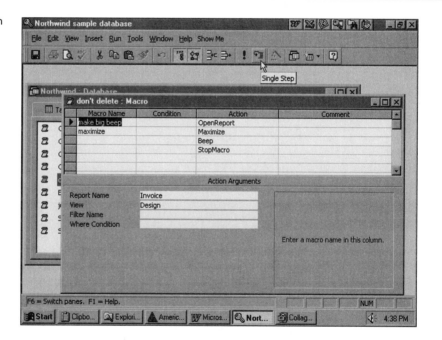

If Access can't run the macro as you have written it, you will see the alert shown in Figure 18.32. While frustrating, it actually helps you narrow down the step of the macro that needs adjusting.

The last field of the alert, Arguments, refers to information needed for an action to be complete.

Some Things You Should Know about Macros

Table 18.4 lists the limitations of certain attributes. These can hardly be thought of as limiting, but if you create a lot of macros you should be aware of them.

Figure 18.32

The macro error alert

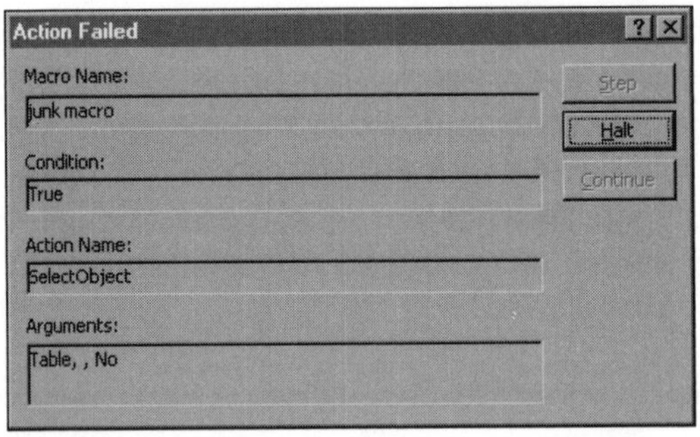

Table 18.4

Attribute Limitations

DESCRIPTION	MAXIMUM
Actions	999 actions
Condition	255 characters
Comment	255 characters
Action Argument	255 characters

Creating Useful Reports

A report is the physical representation of a database. Reports can simply list all the information in a table, or they can incorporate filters and queries. Reports answer questions and supply information in a relevant format. Double-clicking on a report opens it in Print Preview.

A useful report presents information in a way that is useful to the intended reader. The sample catalog report shown in Figure 18.33 has a lot of white space. A commercial report would need to combine more records on each page. Still, the sample catalog presents the information about each product clearly, and contains an order form at the end.

Reports typically take the form of catalogs, directories, summaries, labels, performance charts, and inventories, to name just a few popular formats.

The Access Report Wizard, which is described in more depth in Chapter 22, provides you with a good starting place for building reports. Note that no matter how elegant its layout, a report will be ineffective if the information is not accurate or has been entered consistently. A trial for those who have tried database publishing is the very quality of the information itself.

Figure 18.33

A sample catalog report in 4-page Preview view

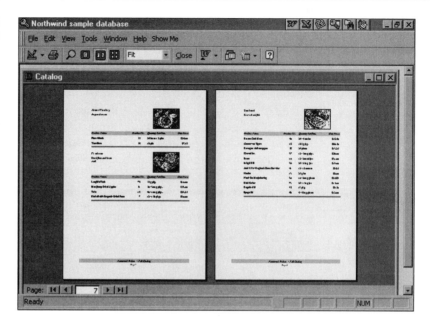

Before you are ready to create a report, check the spelling by pulling down the Tools menu and selecting the Spelling checker. Access added a nice feature to the Spelling command, which is shown in Figure 18.34.

Figure 18.34

The Access Spelling Checker dialog box

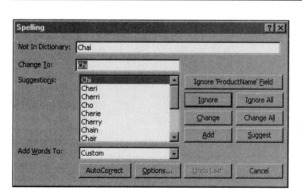

Note that you have the ability to ignore the contents of a selected field. This means that you can skip fields whose contents, such as e-mail addresses, would slow down the process. You know that you can't rely on a spelling checker alone, so you or a co-worker should proof the contents of a printed data table. In this way, you'll be able to avoid the embarrassment of errors such as "pubic" for "public" or "plague" for "plaque": both actual errors seen in real reports!

Another step in preparing your database for a report is making sure that the same information is listed under the same field for each record. If it isn't, the reader will not be able to make sense of the information you have published with great care. Often you can remedy any problem by cutting and pasting information from field to field when the table is in List view.

Another item to check is the use of abbreviations. A directory that lists Street, ST, Str, St, and St. is not as authoritative as one where all abbreviations are consistent. A quick way to clean up this sort of error is using the Replace command on the Edit menu, as shown in Figure 18.35.

Figure 18.35

The Replace dialog box

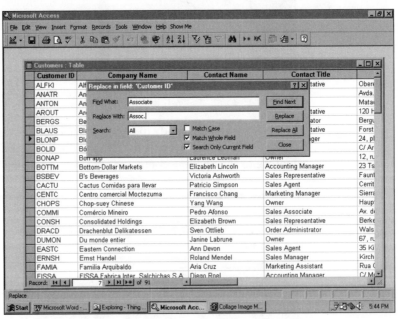

Note that you can limit the replacement to the current field and to terms that match the desired case. Although it may seem tempting to use the Replace All option, you should step through a couple of samples to make sure you are not introducing any errors into the database by replacing St. Bridget Street with Street Bridget St., for example.

Another thing that will improve the quality of your document is including information in the header or footer of the report identifying the date compiled, page number, and file name and location. With this information, one can readily discard an older report upon receiving a newer one without having to compare the information first. Your readers will love anything you can do to save them time.

A header contains information printed at the top of every page, a footer contains information printed at the bottom of every page. To create a header and footer, you need to open a report in Design view, as shown in Figure 18.36. A tool palette will also be displayed.

Figure 18.36

A report in Design view

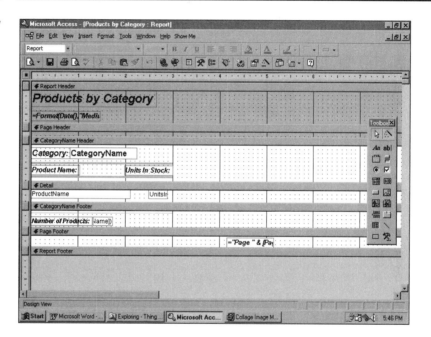

To insert header or footer information, pull down the View menu and se-lect Report Header/Footer or Page Header/Footer. Using the Insert menu, you can easily add the page number, the date, and the time. To add other in-formation, click the text tool on the palette, position your cursor. and type.

Here are some tips to help you print your reports without monopolizing the printer forever:

- Print only one copy and photocopy the rest.

- Limit the amount of information in a report; print a subset of the entire database or restrict the fields included in the report.

- Choose the graphics that will be included with care. Including graphics just because they look nice rather than for their impact is going to slow up the entire job.

- Minimize the use of color to both enhance its effect and reduce file size.

- If the report is based on several actions, such as queries and sorting, you may want to set the field property to Indexed.

- If your report can be broken up into smaller reports that can be compiled separately, you may save time by doing so.

- Use the Performance Analyzer on the Tools menu to see if your database objects can be improved.

You can create a report on your own, or you can have Microsoft Access create a report for you using a Report Wizard. A Report Wizard speeds up the process of creating a report, because it does all the basic work for you. When you use a Report Wizard, it prompts you for information and creates a report based on your answers. Even if you've created many reports, you may want to use a Report Wizard to quickly lay out your report. Then you can switch to Design view to customize it.

- *Database Design*
- *Creating Tables*
- *Field and Table Properties*

19

Access Tables

In ACCESS, AS IN ALL DATABASES, TABLES ARE THE SKELETON UPON which your database application is built. Your base tables determine how easily you can create data-entry forms, how easy it is to ask questions and get answers, and how easy it is to compose the reports that provide to others the information your data contains.

■ Database Design

In a flat-file database product, a database is a single table. This is analogous to a spreadsheet, where the columns of a worksheet represent fields and the rows represent records. In fact, many spreadsheets like Excel let you define part or all of a worksheet as a database so that you can perform the operations of a database on the data it contains.

When you work in a relational database product like Access, you create tables that describe a single thing, which is often referred to as an entity. An *entity* can be described as being associated with attributes. In a database, an entity might be a person, and all of the items that describe a person would be its attributes; or it could be some subset of that universe. An entity can also be an event, a set of properties, an action, or something that relates other entities to one another. The important factor in determining what should be an entity is that you desire to collect information or attributes about it, and that you wish to store them in your database.

Relational database theory takes entities and turns them into tables, and you store data in these tables. Then tables are related to one another so that the records in one table can be matched up with related data stored in other tables.

The so-called "Entity-Relationship" (ER) model of database analysis and design is the best-known and most widely employed construct used in relational database design. It is not the only method, however. Another popular method describes objects and the roles that they play: FORML, or Formal Object Role Modeling. FORML is alternatively called the NIAM approach, for Natural Language Information Analysis Method. In FORML/NIAM, you compose natural sentences that describe who does what to whom. The method then breaks down your information into tables and relationships.

Both ER and NIAM have a sound mathematical basis, and both can take the information you wish to describe and break it down to tables and relationships, removing redundant data. There are computer-aided software engineering (CASE) tools that can be used to enhance both approaches.

While the methods are rigorous, you still should have some sense of what your database is expected to accomplish. Creating well-crafted, robust databases still requires equal measures of theory and art. And the truth is that your own common good sense will serve you at least as well as a fancy CASE tool for any database with less than a dozen tables. Large systems, however, lend themselves best to rigorous analysis.

Database Theory and Normalization

Relational database theory and design owes its development to a branch of relational set theory, which was developed by E.F. Codd in the 1960s. Codd, and the set of rules he devised ("Codd's Rules") describe how to construct tables of related data in such a way that redundancies are eliminated and the values are stored compactly. Codd was a researcher at IBM San Jose, and his work was aimed at creating high-performance databases that not only allowed for data reduction, but provided methods for retrieving data in a flexible way so that questions could be posed and answered without the questioner having intimate knowledge of how a particular database was constructed. Today, the vast majority of database management systems (DBMS) are relational.

The process of reducing a dataset down to a set of related tables is called "normalization." Codd's Rules describe this process. In relational databases, you strive to construct tables in which each record contains a value that uniquely identifies each record in a table. That value can be in a field that has been designated as a primary index and that contains unique values, or it can be a combination of fields specified for that purpose. Access allows you to create primary indices of either a single field or a composite field. When you have a set of tables within which each has uniquely identified records, this is commonly referred to as "First Normal Form" (1NF) in database theory.

Tip. You can run the Table Analyzer Wizard to help you decide if your tables store redundant information and need to be split.

The next step in the process of removing redundant data or normalizing tables is making a table out of any attribute that can be described by two or more values. In that case, an additional table is called for. When you have created a set of tables in which no field takes a multi-valued description, you have achieved what is referred to as Second Normal Form (2NF) in relational database theory.

Third Normal Form (3NF) describes tables in which no field exists that isn't a key or index for the table that depends on any other field that isn't a key or index in the table. While there are three or four more rules in relational theory that lead up to Fifth Normal Form (5NF), where a database is fully normalized, most people and systems strive for at least this level of data reduction. More reduced databases tend to have tables with very few fields, and performance problems can occur when they are joined to create data-entry forms.

When you create a database, first carefully examine the data you wish to collect, then examine the way you wish to output that data. Often collecting forms and reports that already exist is a good way to begin. If you can visualize a way to construct tables that will make creating forms for entering your data easier, and if your table structure supports a method for outputting the reports you need, your database will probably serve you well.

How Do Relationships Work?

In Access, there are three types of relationships that you can define:

- One-to-one (1:1): This relationship matches a single record in the parent table to a single record in the child table. Relationships of this type are rare in database design.

- One-to-many (1:M): In this type, a single record in the parent table matches up to zero, one, or several records in the child table. This relationship defines the potential for multiple matches, not necessarily their occurrence.

- Many-to-many (M:M): A M:M relationship is almost always comprised of two 1:M relationships involving three tables with a join table in the middle. A *join table* might include only the two key fields necessary to match up with the fields in the two other tables, which serve the role of the child or "many" side of the relationship.

Note. Access allows you to enforce inter-table table-based rules called Referential Integrity, so that child records are not orphaned in your database.

For example, in one very common type of relationship a table is defined that stores a form's header information. That table serves as the parent, master, or controlling table in a 1:M (one-to-many) relationship with a child, detail, or transaction table, which stores line items in the form. When you want to compose your form, create a record in the parent table that is matched with unique values from a primary index or a field, through an identical value in a field or regular index of the child table that describes the line items of your form. You can create as many line items or child records as you wish for a parent record; but only one parent record may be associated with records in the child table.

Consider the Relationships window for the Northwind sample database that comes with Access shown in Figure 19.1. You can view this window by clicking the Relationships button on the toolbar when the Tables, Queries, Forms, or Reports tabs are current in the Database window. You create relationships in this window by dragging the index or field from the parent table onto the related field in the child table. If a relationship is not possible, Access will not create the join. Also, Access recognizes the type of relationship possible and creates it.

Northwind contains eight tables and seven defined relationships, all of which are on view in Figure 19.1. There are no 1:1 relationships defined. No M:M relationships exist in this system, because there is no table joining two others that is on the 1 side of both relationships. In Figure 19.1, the Relationships type window was exposed for the 1:M relationship between Category and Products by double-clicking on the join line, or by clicking once on that line and selecting the Join Properties command from the View menu. You will note that the relationship is described, as is its enforcement of Referential Integrity.

Figure 19.1

The Relationships window
with the Relationships
dialog box shown

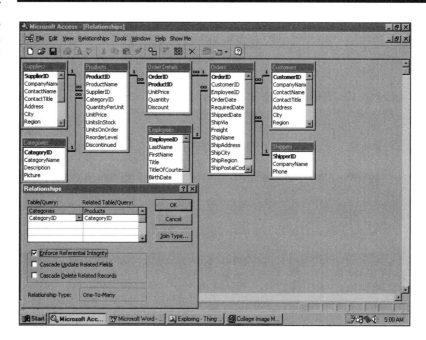

If you click the Join Type button in the Relationships dialog box, you will encounter the different types of joins that Access allows, as indicated in the Join Properties dialog box shown in Figure 19.2. A join is the method used to return matched values from a relationship, and joins have particular importance in returning a result set or dynaset for a query. Access allows the following types of joins:

- Only Equal Value: This is an equi-join where only records in which the values in the two tables match are returned.

- Include ALL Records from "<Left table name>": This is a left outer join, and all records from the left table and matching records from the right table are returned.

- Include ALL Records from "<Right table name>": This is a right outer join, and here all records from the right table and matching records from the left table are returned.

- When the two tables involved are the same table, this is called a self-join. Here records that match each other in the same table are returned.

In outer joins, Access shows an arrow pointing at the side of the join that contributes all of its records. Joins are particularly important in composing multi-table queries, and are discussed in the next chapter in more detail. By default, Access makes all joins equi-joins.

Figure 19.2

The Join Properties
dialog box

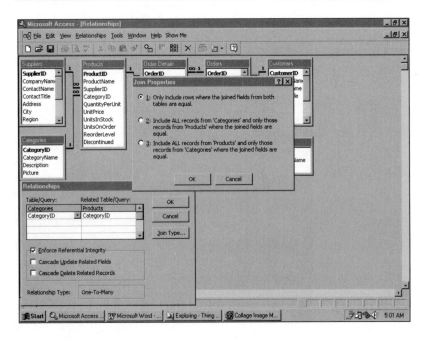

Figure 19.2

The Join Properties dialog box

■ Creating Tables

Many databases define tables as separate files, such as .DBF files in dBase or FoxPro. Access tables are objects contained inside a single Access database file. You create tables in Access in the following ways:

- By running either the Database Wizard or the Table Wizard.

- By entering data directly into a blank datasheet and specifying that the datasheet define a table.

- By designing the table in the Table Designer from scratch.

- By specifying that a query be output to a new table.

- By duplicating and renaming a pre-existing table.

- By importing a table from another source, or by linking to an outside data source.

The Database and Table Wizard

The Database Wizard has the following database templates: Address Book, Office Tracking, Book Collection, Contact Management, Donations,

Event Management, Expenses, Household Inventory, Inventory Control, Ledger, Membership, Music Collection, Order Entry, Picture Library, Recipes, Resource Scheduling, Service Call Management, Students and Classes, Time and Billing, Video Collection, Wine List, and Workout. When you run through the Database Wizard, you have the opportunity to create data-entry forms, queries, and reports.

The Table Wizard creates tables appropriate to the collection of databases that the Database Wizard offers. The Table Wizard is a very fast way of creating tables, and can be a useful starting place for modifying tables to suit your purposes. The Table Wizard lets you structure tables based on fields in existing tables, create rudimentary table relationships, and specify a primary key. Figure 19.3 shows you the first step of field selection in the Table Wizard.

Figure 19.3

The first step of the Table Wizard

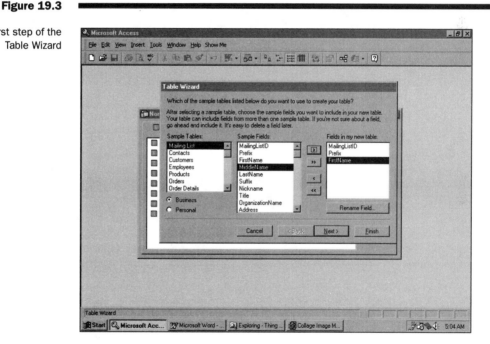

Creating Tables in Datasheet View

A datasheet is a spreadsheet-style view of your table, an example of which is shown in Figure 19.4. To open a table in Datasheet view, double-click on the table's name in the Database window, or click once and then click on the Open button. Normally you view your table's data in Datasheet view and define your table's structure in Design view, an example of which is shown in Figure 19.5. However, Access offers you a fast way of defining a table that allows you to start with a blank datasheet.

Figure 19.4

A table in Datasheet view

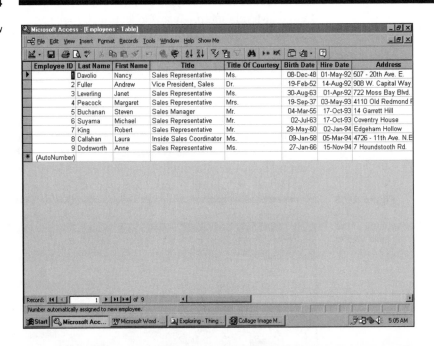

Figure 19.5

The same table in Design view

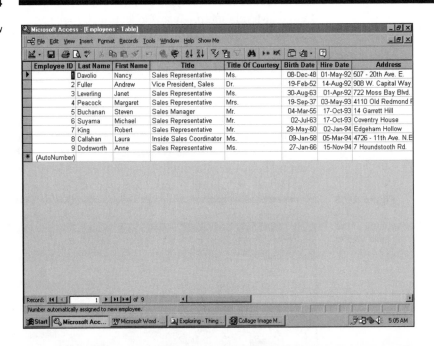

The datasheet method is a fast way to create tables, but it is limited in its capabilities. When you enter data, Access makes some assumptions based on the type of data you have entered and automatically creates fields for it. This method is best used for small tables that you will modify later. Access will not define relationships, nor will it enter any indices, data validation, or database rules using this method.

To create a table from a datasheet:

1. Click on the Tables page in the Database window, then click on the New button.

2. Select Datasheet in the New Table dialog box, as shown in Figure 19.6. A datasheet with 20 columns and 30 rows will appear with default field names. Columns become fields, rows become records.

Figure 19.6

The New Table dialog box

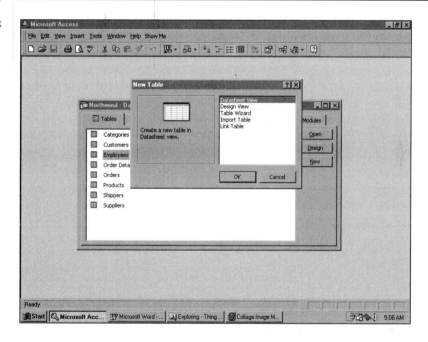

3. To rename a column heading, double-click and enter the field name(s), then press the Enter key or click elsewhere.

4. To create more columns, click on a column to the right of your new field, then select the Column command from the Insert menu.

5. Enter data into the datasheet: each column is a field, each row is a record. Since Access makes certain assumptions based on the style of

data you enter, use consistent entries for dates, times, currency, and other datatypes.

6. Click on the Save button on the Table Datasheet toolbar or select the Save command on the File menu.

7. Enter the name of the table in the Table Name text box that's in the Save As dialog box, then click the OK button.

8. An alert box will appear that asks you if Access can create a primary key. Click Yes if you haven't created a field with unique values that can identify each row of your datasheet (records in the table), or No if you have created such a field.

Access will now create the new table and save it to disk. When you have Access create the primary key, it makes an AutoNumber field with sequential numbers entered into it.

Since the Datasheet view is a special kind of data-entry form, the topic of navigating in this view and entering data is described more fully in Chapter 21.

Design View

Most of the time you open a table's structure in Design view to create it or to modify it. There are several ways of opening a table in Design view, but the following are the most common:

- Click on a table name in the Database window, then click on the Design button.

- Switch from Datasheet view to Design view by clicking on the View button on the toolbar and selecting the Design command.

- Right-click on a table name in the Database window and select the Design command.

To start a new table from scratch in the Table Design view, click the New button on the Table tab or select the Table command from the Insert menu, then select the Design view selection in the New Table dialog box, and click the OK button.

The Table Design view has two panels. The top panel lets you create new fields by entering their names into the field grid. The bottom panel displays properties that apply to the current field, as indicated in the top panel by a right-facing arrow in the field selector button. When you are done defining your fields, close the Table Design view window.

Importing and Linking Tables

Microsoft Access can import tables from other Access databases and from data created in several other databases and spreadsheets that support standard file formats. Microsoft Excel, dBase, Microsoft FoxPro, Paradox, and Lotus 1-2-3 are just some of the programs that Access can import data from. This feature allows you to create new Access tables from pre-existing data.

To create a new table by importing:

1. Open the database that will contain the linked table, and view the Database Window.

2. Select the Import command from the Get External Data submenu of the File menu.

3. In the Import dialog box, select the appropriate file format from the Files of Type drop-down list; then locate the table or spreadsheet of interest using the Look in list box.

4. Select the table or spreadsheet, then click the Import button.

Access will add the imported table to your database and display its name in the Database window as an Access file. You can repeat the process to import additional tables.

The process of linking to a table in Access is similar. When you import a table, the original table serves as the data source, and only a reference to that table is contained in your Access database. When you link to a table, you can view the table and most often you can also modify the data in that table. Access takes care of the details of opening the table and saving it in the appropriate data format.

When you import a new table, a copy of the table is created in the Microsoft Access format. The source table is left intact. When you link to a table in Access, you will see different icons for the tables in the Tables section of the Database window. A dBase table shows the dB symbol, Paradox a Px symbol, and other Access tables a datasheet icon.

By comparison, when you import a table, you create a copy of that table in your database, and Access converts the table into its own format and incorporates the data into an Access database file.

To link to a table in another format:

1. Open the database that will contain the linked table, and view the Database Window.

2. Select the Link Table command from the Get External Data submenu of the File menu.

3. In the Link dialog box, select the appropriate file format from the Files of Type drop-down list; then locate the table or spreadsheet of interest using the Look in list box.

4. Select the table or spreadsheet, then click the Link button.

5. What happens next depends on the data source you selected:

   • For Access, unencrypted Paradox tables, or spreadsheets, Access tables and spreadsheets are imported directly.

   • For encrypted Paradox tables, Access will prompt you for the password; enter the password and click OK. Access will add the linked table to your database, and display its name and an appropriate icon in the Tables page of the Database window.

   • If you have selected a FoxPro or dBase table, then a dialog box will appear asking you to associate that table with the corresponding index (.CDX or .IDX) file; for dBase you would associate the table with an .MDX or .NDX file.

6. Select the index or indexes, then click the Close button or Cancel if no index exists.

7. Enter the index that identifies each record in the Select Unique Record Identifier dialog box. Normally that index is the primary index, but it could also be candidate indexes for these two databases.

■ Field and Table Properties

In Access, fields, tables, and relationships are objects that can take properties. The properties you assign these objects add special features that may aid you in data entry, provide for data validation, give you a particular view of your dataset, and make the relationships between your data possible. The sections that follow highlight the main properties.

Field Types

You can create fields by entering the field name in the next Field Name column on the blank row of the field grid. Field names can be up to 64 letters long, and can include letters, numbers, spaces, symbols, and other special characters (with the exception of periods, exclamation points, brackets, and grave marks).

The second column, Data Types, describes the type of data contained in the field. This is a very important property, because Access can calculate, store, display, and format your data entries differently depending upon the datatype you set. Some fields impose a specific size on the field, while others allow you to define the field size in the Field Size property in the General section of the Design view. Unlike other databases, Access uses only the amount of space that your data requires for a field, and does not leave blank space that the field size requires.

For example, the currency datatype allows for up to 15 decimal places to the left of the decimal and four places to the right. When displaying currency fields, Access can make use of your currency preferences in the Regional control panel. Since this datatype defines the field size, that property is missing for this datatype. Table 19.1 summarizes the allowed datatypes in Access 97.

Table 19.1

Summary of Datatypes

DATA TYPE	STORAGE SIZE	RANGE
Byte	1 byte	0 to 255
Boolean	2 bytes	True or False
Integer	2 bytes	-32,768 to 32,767
Long (long integer)	4 bytes	-2,147,483,648 to 2,147,483,647
Single (single-precision floating-point)	4 bytes	-3.402823E38 to -1.401298E-45 for negative values; 1.401298E-45 to 3.402823E38 for positive values
Double (double-precision floating-point)	8 bytes	-1.79769313486232E308 to -4.94065645841247E-324 for negative values; 4.94065645841247E-324 to 1.79769313486232E308 for positive values
Currency (scaled integer)	8 bytes	-922,337,203,685,477.5808 to 922,337,203,685,477.5807
Decimal	14 bytes	+/- 79,228,162,514,264,337,593,543,950,335 with no decimal point; +/- 7.9228162514264337593543950335 with 28 places to the right of the decimal; smallest non-zero number is +/- 0.0000000000000000000000000001.
Date	8 bytes	January 1, 100 to December 31, 9999
Object	4 bytes	Any Object reference
String (variable-length)	10 bytes + string length	0 to approximately 2 billion
String (fixed-length)	Length of string	1 to approximately 65,400

Table 19.1

DATA TYPE	STORAGE SIZE	RANGE
Variant (with numbers)	16 bytes	Any numeric value up to the range of a Double
Variant (with characters)	22 bytes + string length	Same range as for variable-length String
User-defined (using Type)	Number required by elements	The range of each element is the same as the range of its data type

The third and last column in the field grid is the Description property. Descriptions show up in the Status bar when the field is current in a form, and they are a great help to users. The Caption property in the General section is what you use as a label for the field in the Datasheet view, as a default label when you add the field to a form, and in other instances.

Field Properties

Several of the field properties are important, and are commonly set during a table's definition. Among the most important are:

- **Field length.** This describes the number of allowable characters that may be entered into a field.

- **Format.** The Format property controls how the data you entered is displayed. Different datatypes allow for different possible formats.

- **Input Mask.** This property controls the characters that you can enter into a field. For example, you could use this property to allow 10 numbers—and only 10 numbers—to be entered into a field meant for telephone numbers.

- **Caption.** The caption is the name shown for the field in a datasheet, or as a default label on a form.

- **Default Value.** When you create a new record, this is the value that Access enters into the record. You are free to modify this value at any time. Note that this default value will not be entered into records you append to a table.

- **Validation Rule.** This is a rule that must be obeyed before the value in a field can be entered. For example, you could use an expression ">1 and <10" to force a value in this range.

- **Validation Text.** This is the text that is displayed in the alert box when a value is not valid.

- **Required.** If you set this to yes, Access requires you to enter a value in this field; that is, this field becomes mandatory.

- **Indexed.** This property indexes a field, and either allows duplicate values (a regular index) or only allows unique values (a primary or candidate index).

As you enter property cells, you may see an arrow for a drop-down list that will display allowable values; a Build button that opens the Expression Builder, which lets you create expressions that are evaluated to a value or to True or False; or both an arrow and a Build button. Depending on datatype, you may see additional properties, or some of these properties may disappear.

If the field's data come from another data source, you will want to fill in the Lookup portion of the properties sheet. Data can come from other tables, queries, and data sources, and this tab lets you define the source and how that data is handled. Lookups are particularly valuable for isolating large tables of narrowly defined data, such as zip codes or other category listings.

Tip. There are many more aspects to setting properties than can be described here. To get help on any aspect of the Table Design view, place your insertion point in that cell and press the F1 key. Access will give you context-sensitive help.

Indexes

Indexes are a very important aspect of table design. An index is a list of the values in a field or set of fields that shows where in the table the listed items may be found. The concept is identical to that of an index for a book. By defining an index, you can provide a method for quickly sorting your table when it opens, quick matching parent records to child records, optimizing query design, and other essential database functions.

There are several index types in use:

- Primary index. A primary index is used to uniquely identify the records in a table. Therefore, a primary index allows no duplicate records. A primary index shows a key symbol to the left of the field name.

  In many cases a primary index is used to match one table to another, but not always. Sometimes a primary index has a physical reality, as in Purchase Order numbers. In other instances database designers use numbers like AutoNumber (incrementing values) that have no meaning as surrogate keys. The advantage of the latter construct is that the user never needs to see the field that matches up tables in the database, and won't be tempted to change values in them if they do.

- Candidate index. A candidate or unique index is one that contains unique values only. Access lets you define an index of this kind when you enter the Yes (No Duplicates) entry into the Index property.

- Composite index. A composite index is one in which two or more fields are indexed together. The order of field selection is important, because it is the order in which they are indexed. Unlike other databases, Access does not allow indexes to be created using expressions.

- Regular index. A Regular index is one where duplicate (Yes (Allow Duplicates)) values are allowed. This index can serve as the source of the "many" values in a 1:M relationship, and will be faster at finding matches than a field used as the many match in the child table.

Creating primary indexes is easy. Simply make that field the current field, then click the Primary Key button on the toolbar. If you create a relationship based on that primary key with another table, you will first have to delete the relationship before you can delete the primary key. You delete the primary key by clicking once again on the Primary Key button.

You create other kinds of indexes by setting the Indexed property, as described above. In the case of composite indexes involving two or more fields, the easiest place to create is the Indexes dialog box shown in Figure 19.7. To view the Indexes dialog box, click the Indexes button on the toolbar.

Figure 19.7

The Indexes dialog box

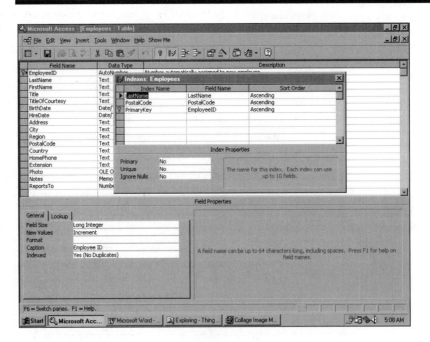

Create a composite index by entering a field name in the Field Name column on a new row, then enter the Index Name. Move to the next blank row and enter the next field name in the composite index without entering an Index Name. You can have up to 10 fields in a composite index.

The Indexes dialog box also lets you assign additional characteristics to indexes. You can assign a sort order, ascending or descending; assign primary or unique indexes; and decide whether null values are considered.

You can delete indexes in the Indexes dialog box by deleting their entries, or in the Table Design View by removing their Indexed property.

Table Properties

You have seen field properties, and how fields can be filled in with default information and have their contents validated. Tables also can have properties assigned to them, although the range of properties allowed is small. They are important nonetheless. To view a table's properties, right-click on the table name on the Table tab of the Database window to see one set of properties (Figure 19.8); and anywhere in the Table's Design View to see another (Figure 19.9).

Figure 19.8

Employee Properties

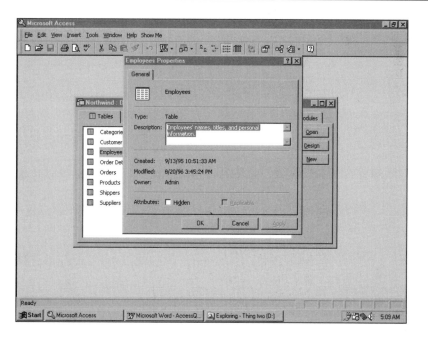

Figure 19.9

Table Properties

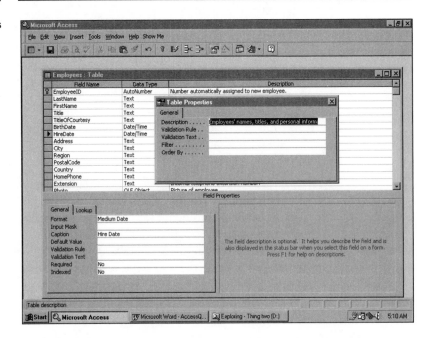

In the former case, you can use this group to decide whether the table is visible or not (you might not want it to be for a category table with static data); in the latter instance you can set a filter, a sort order, and/or table-level validation rules.

A filter lets you apply criteria to the selection of records from a table. This topic was briefly discussed in the previous chapter, and comes up again in Chapter 20. A sort order can be a field, or a group of fields separated by commas. The first field is the primary sort key in the order.

You have seen field-level validation in the table designer. Sometimes you need to provide rules that examine the contents of two or more fields at a time. These are table-level rules. Whereas field-level rules fire as soon as you try and leave the field, table-level rules are not evaluated until you try to leave the record and Access tries to autosave the data. Often table-level rules enforce business rules that are important to your database. Beyond table-level validation is the inter-table level validation provided by Referential Integrity rules.

- *What Is a Query?*

20

Understanding Access Queries

W HEN YOU DESIGN YOUR TABLES TO CONTAIN ALL OF THE DATA
you wish to collect in a relational database management system
(RDBMS), you want every conceivable piece of data to be accom-
modated. In most instances, you don't wish to see the full set of
data entered. Often you want to see a portion of the data sorted
and grouped in ways that help you calculate aggregate functions
like sums or averages, so that you can see trends and exceptions in
your dataset, and learn from them.

■ What Is a Query?

Access offers you several means of selecting data that can help you to achieve this end. The most complex and useful of these is queries, but there are other simpler constructs, like filters, that you can apply. This subject was covered in brief in Chapter 18, which overviewed Access; but it is so important to the creation of forms and reports that this chapter will expand upon the topic.

When you want to see just a subset of your records in a table, you can create a filter. A filter defines a set of records that match a criteria or set of criteria. Access lets you set a single filter for a table, which will apply to only that table. You can also set a sort for your filtered table, and you can continue to filter a filtered set of records, narrowing your selections even further. The problem is that a filter applies only to a single table, not to related tables—and you can set just one filter at a time.

When you create a query, you can specify that a result set is to be returned from a group of records in related tables, based upon the kind of join condition you specified in the relationship Join Type dialog box. Queries can provide Boolean-logic filtering records based on AND and OR conditions; queries can sort records, group records, and provide a view of your dataset that shows only the fields or tables that you select. That makes queries infinitely more valuable than filters, even though setting up a query is more complicated.

To top it off, filters can be applied to queries as well as to tables. In fact, filters are even more useful when applied to queries.

Query Recipes

A query is a recipe for selecting records from a database. Queries can work with a single table, with two unrelated tables, and with two or more related tables. They are very flexible. Queries are used as the basis for forms and reports in Access. When you run a query, you will see the records that satisfy the conditions that the query was meant to capture.

Access translates your query into a SELECT-SQL statement that runs in the background. SQL, or Structured Query Language, is a high-level database programming language that many relational databases understand and use. SQL is a codified international database standard, although there are many variants of the language. It is because Access is able to speak SQL that it can read and write to remote data sources.

Creating Queries

Access offers you a set of Query Wizards to help you quickly create queries, and especially to assist you with certain important queries. It also has a Query Design View that lets you create a Query By Example (QBE).

You can create a new query by using a Query Wizard, or by building one from scratch in the Query Design window. Both are relatively easy to use, although the Query Wizard will walk you through the process step-by-step.

Query Design View

The Query Design View offers you a method for creating query by examples. In this window you can add data sources, relate the data sources, provide criteria for selection, group sources, show or hide fields from the result set, sort, and create and enter calculated fields. Figure 20.1 shows you a labeled Query Design View window.

Figure 20.1

The Query Design View with labeled elements

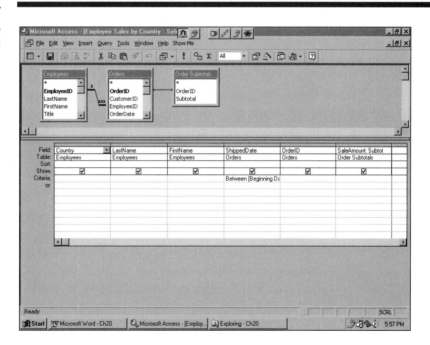

As you add tables into your query, you will see the relationships you created for your database in the Relationships window. You can either use these relationships, or delete them and create relationships appropriate to the result set you are trying to achieve.

To add tables to a query, click the Show Tables button on the toolbar or select the Show Tables command on the Query menu. The Show Table dialog box shown in Figure 20.2 will appear. This dialog box shows that you can use the base tables in your database for your query, or create queries based on other queries. When you run a query that's based on another query, you narrow the result set of the first query based on the specifications of the second query.

Figure 20.2

The Show Table dialog box

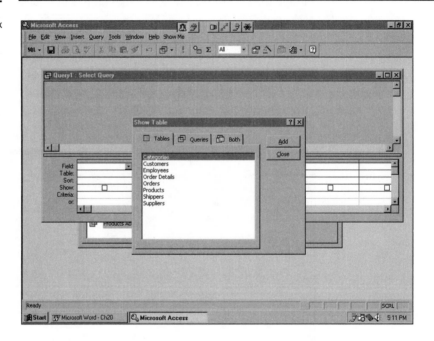

Add fields from the field list by either double-clicking on them in the field list, or by dragging them onto the field or output grid. You don't need to show a field to use it in your query. By leaving fields out of the viewed fields and creating summary fields, you can create queries that form the basis for summary reports, for example.

The lines in the output grid offer you the following information:

- **Field**. The name of the field to be used, either a field from a data source or the name of a calculated field that you create in the query.

- **Sort**. This field provides an ascending or descending sort. If you specify two or more fields, the fields on the right are sorted first, the fields on the left last. The leftmost sorted field is the primary sort key.

- **Show**. This allows you to use a field or calculation, but to also determine whether you will show the result or not.

Tip. To move between the data pane and the field grid, press the F6 key.

- **Criteria**. These are selection rules that you create. You can enter values, ranges, expressions, Boolean logic, and so forth. A Build button appears when you enter this row to let you create the expression in the Expression Builder, should you so choose. Or, by entering criteria on this row, you can expand the records you select based on these additional selection criteria.

Once you have completed your Query, you can save it to disk. What you are saving is the method for retrieving a result set, and not the result set itself.

Creating Calculated Fields in Queries

When you create a calculated column in the field grid of the Query Design View window, the result of the calculation is either used, or used and displayed to the resulting query datasheet. The calculated field is not stored to disk, but is derived data. You have the full range of Access functions at your disposal: aggregate operators such as count, average, sums, and so forth when you group your records; Boolean logic; and other calculation methods.

Any fields you name in a calculated field need to be drawn from tables or queries that have been added to your query. When you create a calculated field, Access enters Expr1, Expr2, and so on as the default field names. You can change the field name, and the field name you supply for the calculated field will then appear as the caption or column heading in the resulting datasheet of the dynaset. Do not use the name of an existing field in one of your tables for the calculated field name, or Access will get confused and return erroneous data.

Create a calculated field in a query by entering the expression for that field in the Field row beneath the field name for that calculation. If you don't enter a field name (really a column name), Access will enter the default name.

To create a calculated field in a query:

1. Open the query in the Query Design View.

2. Enter an expression in an empty field in the Field row, using brackets for field names.

3. For group or aggregate functions like SUM, AVG, COUNT, MIN, MAX, STDEV, or VAR, click the Totals (Σ) button on the toolbar to view the Totals row.

4. Change the field that must be grouped on the Group By row to Expression.

5. Enter any additional criteria or sort expressions.

6. For the calculated field, click on the Properties button in the toolbar and set the field properties.

You will see the calculated field when the query runs. If you based your calculation on a group of records using a Group By expression, then your calculation will compute the value based on those records. You do this to apply an aggregate function in a calculation.

Query Properties

Queries offer you additional properties that affect the way a query is returned, and that can change the nature of the query itself. To see a query's Property sheet, right-click anywhere on the Query Design View window and select the Properties command, or select the Properties command from the View menu. Figure 20.3 shows you this Properties dialog box with the General properties tab showing.

Figure 20.3

A Query Properties dialog box

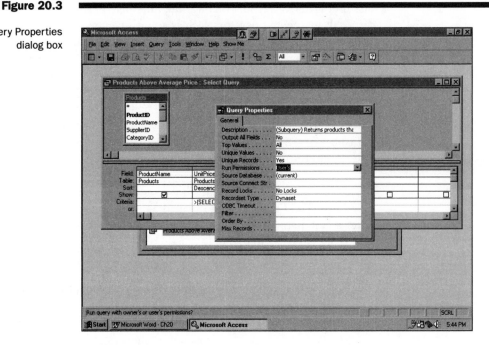

In the Properties dialog box there are some significant properties, which you may wish to set. You can specify the output fields, the number or percentages of matching records returned, unique records returned only, connect properties, a filter, and a sort order. This overlooked dialog box is a very convenient place to modify your query design. It is absolutely essential to set these parameters when accessing a large data set.

You should note that, just as with table properties, when you open the Properties sheet from the Queries tab of the Database window, you only see a description text box, and will be offered the choice to hide or reveal the results of the query.

Creating a Query in Design View

To create a new query in Query Design view:

1. Click on Query page in the Database window, then click on the New button.

2. Select Design View in the New Query dialog box, as shown in Figure 20.4.

Figure 20.4

The New Query dialog box

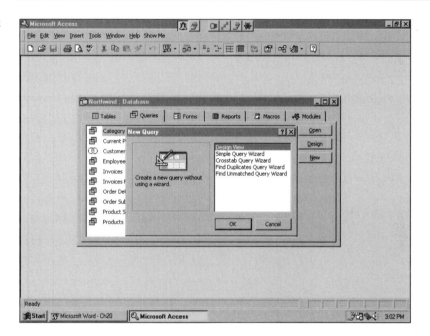

3. Select the table(s) you need in the Show Table dialog box, then click the OK button. When you add related tables, the permanent relation in the Relationships window of your database is used. But you can delete this relationship and create a new one. Relationships that you delete or create do not affect your database relationships, but help to compose the query.

4. To create a relationship between the index of the parent tables and the related field or index of the child table, click and drag a line in the top pane of the Query Design view between them.

5. Click on the field cell in the Query Design Grid, then select the field you wish to use in your query, or select the asterisk field to add all fields to your query. You can drag a field from the data-environment pane onto

the field grid if you want it to be used in the query grid, or just double-click on that field to move it onto the list.

6. Press the Down arrow key and select the Sort order for any field that you wish to sort. Fields are sorted in their order from right to left, with the left field as the primary sort key. To reorder the fields, click and drag the column header.

7. Click on the Show check box for any field you wish to see in the Query. Fields can be used in queries that do not appear in the query output.

8. Enter any filter in the Selection criteria cell for that field, and additional AND statements in the same cell; enter OR statements (expanding the range of selection) into an OR clause, or on the next line beginning with the row label OR. Figure 20.5 shows you a developed query in Query Design View.

Figure 20.5

A developed query

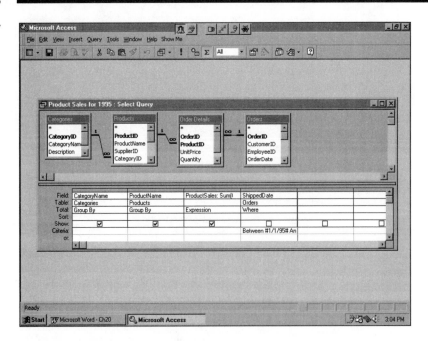

9. Click on the Save button in the Query Design toolbar, or select the Save command from the File menu.

10. Enter the name of the form in Query Name text box of the Save As dialog box (see Figure 20.6), then click the OK button.

Access will create the new query and save it to disk.

Figure 20.6

The Save As dialog box

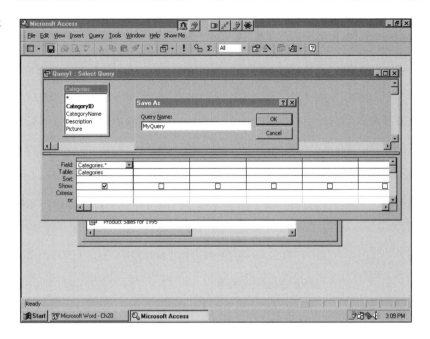

When you run a query, the data you see reflects the data that conforms to your query at runtime. You can update the data, delete, or append, or you can update the data in a result set.

The Query Wizards

You can also use one of the Query Wizards to create a new query. You can choose from the Simple Query Wizard, Crosstab Query Wizard, Find Duplicates Wizard, and Find Unmatched Query Wizard in the New Query dialog box. The purposes of these queries are as follows:

- **Simple Query Wizard**. This wizard steps you through the creation of a Select query one step at a time. You can select tables to include criteria, sorts, grouping, calculated fields with aggregate functions like sums, counts, averages, and other totals. Select queries are the most commonly defined queries.

- **Crosstab Query Wizard**. This wizard lets you summarize the values in your records by fields, arranging them in groups of records down the leftmost column of a datasheet, and organizing them by factors along the top-most column headers. A classic example of a crosstab query is one that sums up sales by month, when you have actually stored sales records by day.

If you want to create a crosstab without storing a query, you can use the PivotTable Wizard. This wizard changes column and row headings on demand.

- **Find Duplicates Query Wizard**. This wizard searches your table to see if any records exist that share the same value. You can search by field(s), and direct the output of the query to a table that removes the duplicate records.

  This query is useful in validating a field for use as a primary key, and for creating the table that contains that field as the primary key. The topic "Automatically delete duplicate records from a table" in Access's online Help system will tell you how to do this.

- **Find Unmatched Records Query Wizard**. This wizard creates a query from a table with related records in another table. You specify the tables and the matching indexes or fields. Then the query finds any orphaned child records, or childless parent records. You use this query to establish Referential Integrity conditions before imposing the rules.

The Queries Tab

You may want to take a look at the Northwind sample database's Queries tab in the Database window. This sample database contains the different types of queries you might wish to define as examples. Figure 20.7 shows you this window.

Notice that there are different types of queries stored in this window, as evidenced by the appearance of different types of icons. The icon containing two tables is a Select Query. Queries of this type include: Category Sales for 1995, Current Product List, Employee Sales by Country, and so on.

The icon with two intersecting circles indicates a Union Query, and is stored as a SELECT-SQL Statement with a Union clause. Figure 20.8 shows you the Design window for the Customers and Suppliers by City query, with its Select statement featuring a Union clause. Union queries are one example of an SQL-Specific Query, which you can create using this command on the Query menu. You can also create Pass Through queries, or create SQL queries by entering code into a text window using the Data Definition command on the SQL-Specific submenu of the Query menu.

Finally, the Quarterly Orders by Products query is a crosstab query, as indicated by the appearance of a spreadsheet-like icon on the Queries tab.

All of these queries can be created from the Design View window using commands from the Query menu.

When you click the Open button with a query selected or double-click on the query name, the query will run and be displayed in a datasheet. The Design button opens the query in the Query Design View. Finally, the New

Figure 20.7

The Queries tab of the
Database window for the
Northwind database

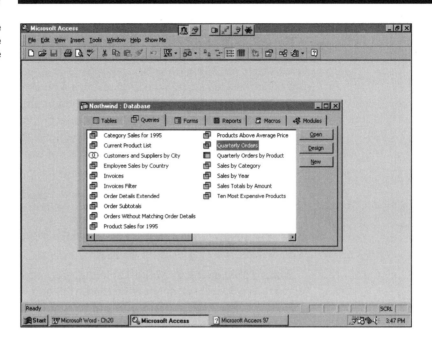

Figure 20.8

A Union query

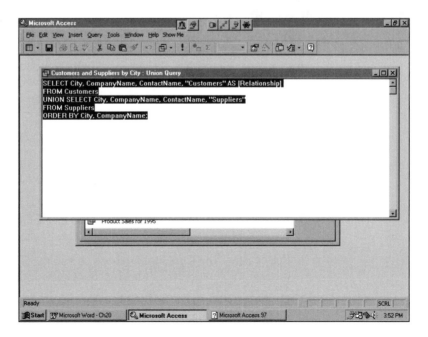

button opens the New Query dialog box, which lets you start a new query in one of several different ways.

Action Queries

Queries have an additional advantage. You can direct their output in the form of actions: the so-called action queries. You can use the result sets from queries as the basis for creating a table, appending records to a table, deleting records from a table, and updating records in a table.

Action queries collect a result set, and can use that result set to modify the records in your database in several different ways. There are four action queries:

- **Append query**. An Append query adds the records in your result set to your tables.

- **Delete query**. A Delete query removes the groups of records returned from your query from your database.

- **Make Table query**. A Make Table query creates a new table from your result set. The result set may be read from and written back to a single table, or it can write to two or more related tables.

- **Update query**. An Update query alters the information in your result set, and writes the changes back to your tables.

Append Query

Append queries let you add records to one or more tables. This is useful when you wish to transfer records from one table or set of related tables to another. You can also use the Append query to write data to the same fields in matching records between two tables.

To append the results of a query to your table:

1. Create a new query, or open an existing query in the Query Design View.

2. Click the Query Type button on the Standard toolbar, then select the Append Query command from that button menu, or select the Append Query command from the Query menu.

3. Enter the name of the source table and any related tables in the Table Name text box of the Append dialog box, as shown in Figure 20.9.

4. Select either the Current Database or Another Database radio button, pick the target table(s), then click the OK button.

5. Drag the fields from the field list that you want to append to the query-design grid, along with any fields that you will use for selection criteria.

Figure 20.9

The Append dialog box

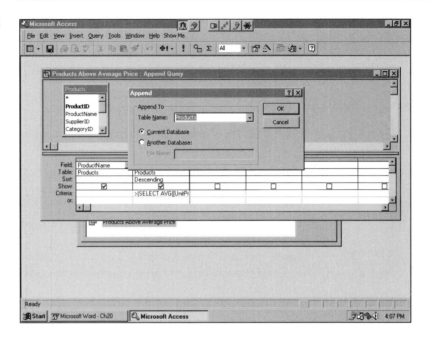

6. To retain AutoNumber values in the source table, drag the AutoNumber field onto the query-design grid. For primary keys of this type, don't drag them onto the query design grid.

7. For fields with the same name, drag the asterisk for each table to the query-design grid.

8. Enter the criteria for creating the result set in the query-design grid.

9. Click on the View button in the toolbar to preview the records to be deleted.

10. Click on the Run button (!) to append the records the table(s) you specified.

The query will now run, and the records will be appended to the table(s) you specified.

Note. When deleting tables in a 1:M relationship, if Referential Integrity requires cascading deletes, the query must be run twice: once to delete the parent table records, and again to delete the child table records.

Delete Query

You use Delete queries to remove the set of records in a result set from the table(s) you specify. This can be a single table, or related tables involved in 1:1 or 1:M relationships.

To delete records from your table(s) as the result of a query:

1. Create the query required, or open an existing query in the Query Design View.

2. Click on the Query Type button on the Standard toolbar and select the Delete Query command.

3. Double-click on the asterisk symbol in the table(s) you wish to delete records from so that they appear in the Delete row. You can also drag the asterisk onto the field list grid.

4. Specify criteria for deleting records in the Where column on the Delete row.

5. Click on the View button in the toolbar to preview the records to be deleted.

6. Click on the Run button (!) to delete the records form the table(s).

Make Table Query

Make Table queries create a table with many purposes. You can use this query to run a report, back up selected data in your database, archive records, export records, extract a dataset to improve performance in your forms and reports, and so forth. In other words, Make Table queries are quite useful.

To create a new table from a query:

1. Click the Query Type button on the toolbar, then select the Make Table Query command, or select the Make Table Query command from the Query menu.

2. Enter a name in the Table Name text box of the Make Table dialog box (see Figure 20.10), select either the Current Database or Another Database radio button, then click the OK button.

3. Drag the fields from the field list to the query-design grid that will be in the new table.

4. Enter the criteria for your result set, and any sort or show (filters) you desire.

5. Click the View button to see your result set, then click the Run (!) button on the toolbar.

6. Dismiss the dialog box, and Access will write your result set to disk as a table in the database you specified.

Update Queries

The final action query is the Update query. This query can modify records in a result set, either in a single table or in a set of related tables. This is one of the primary methods for making global changes quickly in Access, and can also be used to replace data in several records at once.

Figure 20.10

The Make Table dialog box

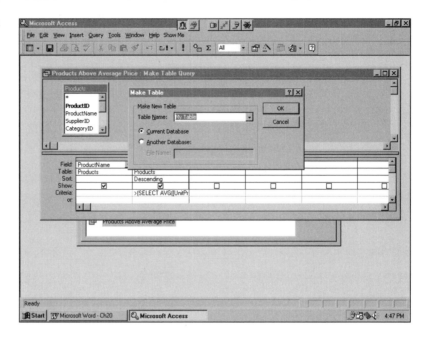

To update, modify, or change the values in a set of records as the result of a query:

1. Create a new query or open an existing query in the Query Design view.

2. Click the Query Type button on the toolbar, then select the Update Query command, or select this command from the Query menu.

3. Drag the fields from the field list to the query-design grid that will be in the new table.

4. Enter the criteria for your result set, and any sort or show (filters) you desire.

5. In the Update To row, enter the expression or value to be used as a replacement for the field(s) selected.

6. Click the View button to see a list of records that will be updated with their *old* values.

7. Then click the Run button (!) on the toolbar.

8. Dismiss the dialog box, and Access will replace the old data in your selected records with their new values in the result set you specified.

See How the Query Runs...

When you run a query, you will see the results in a datasheet window. The result of a query is called a query dynaset or, since it is often displayed in a datasheet window, a query datasheet. This is a most crucial piece of information for you to understand:

- When you display a query result in a datasheet, the information is derived from the underlying tables, and is in most cases editable.

That is, when you make changes to a dynaset, Access will write those changes back to your tables and save them to disk. You can specify that a dynaset be "read-only," but in most cases what you are trying to achieve is the ability to not only select those records, but act on them as well.

- *Form Types*
- *Creating Forms*
- *Data Entry*

21

Creating and Using Forms

D ATABASE APPLICATIONS PROVIDE FORMS FOR DATA ENTRY AND data modification. When you create forms, you can present your user with a sensible method for accessing and creating data. A form on your computer screen might appear as a purchase order, a ticket that you print, a reservation form, a questionnaire that you fill out, or any number of other things. Forms can contain buttons that perform actions, they can be dialog boxes, or they can be help screens.

Forms play a role not only in controlling what data is entered, but also in how that data is entered. A form can draw data from tables and queries, and can be structured to provide an order of data entry through its tab order. Each of the various types of controls that you place on a form can limit data entry, or aid in providing values to be entered.

■ Form Types

Figure 21.1 shows you a Order Entry form from the Northwind database. This form isn't much different in appearance from the order-entry form that you might tear off of a printed pad of order-entry forms printed for your business. But with this form, you can control what gets entered and when, auto-enter default values, perform data validation and sophisticated searches, and so forth. You can have as many line items on the form as you wish, and you can have the form calculate your great sales while contemplating your next trip to the south of France. And you can print a copy of the form, if you have a mind to.

Figure 21.1

The Order Entry form in
Form View from the
Northwinds database

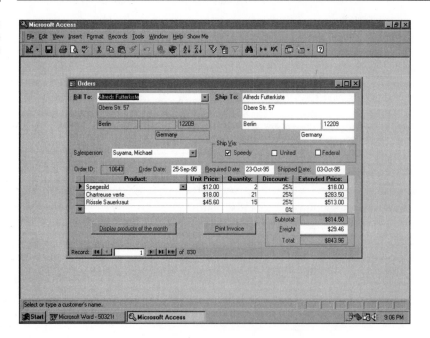

■ Creating Forms

Access provides you several methods for creating forms. You can create forms from scratch using the Form Design View, or you can create forms using the various Form Wizards that Access provides.

The Forms Tab

The Forms tab of the Database window offers you a single location from which you can access pre-existing forms, create new ones, or delete old ones. When you open the Forms tab of the Database window, you can do the following things:

- Click on the New button to open the New Form dialog box shown in Figure 21.2; then select Design View to open the Form in Design View (Access's form modification mode) or one of the Form Wizards.

- Click on the Design button to open a selected form in Design View.

- Double-click on an existing form name to open the form in Form View (Access's data entry mode); or click once to highlight the form name and click the Open button or press Ctrl+O to see your form in Form View.

- Click on a form name and press the Del key to delete a form.

Figure 21.2

The New Form dialog box

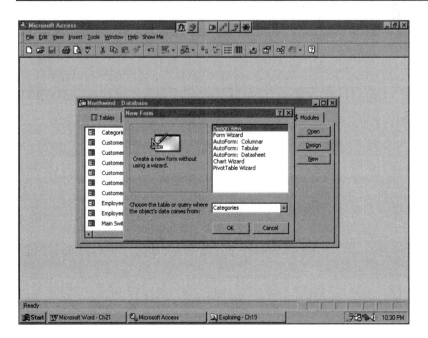

•   Select one of the commands on the View menu to alter your view of the Database window.

Design View

A form's Design View is where you go to change details of your form's construction. Figure 21.3 shows you the Order Entry form from Northwind in Design View.

Figure 21.3

The Order Entry form in Design View

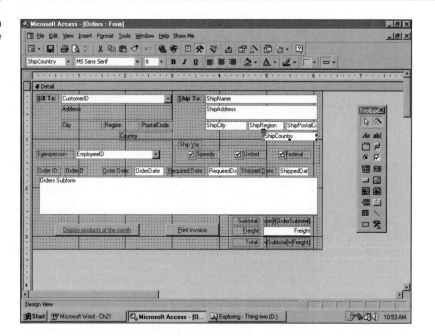

In Design View you can change the attributes or properties of a control, change a control's data source, move a control onto or off of a form, or add additional sections to a report. You can enter data into a form's Form View, but you can modify the form only in Design View. You can use the View button at the left of the toolbar or the commands on the View menu to move between these two views.

To open a blank form in Design View, do the following:

1.   Click on the Form tab in the Database window, then click on the New button.

2.   Select Design View from the list in the New Form dialog box.

3. Select the table or query that will be the data source in the Choose the table or the query... drop-down list, then click the OK button. Access will now open the blank form in Design View.

4. Click on the Save button on the Form Design toolbar, or select the Save command on the File menu.

5. Enter the name of the form in the Save As dialog box, then click the OK button.

Access will create the form and save it to disk.

Just as you can control the properties of a query to suit your purposes, forms also take properties. You can see the Property sheet of a form by clicking on the box in the selector box that has a black rectangle on it where the two rulers meet in the upper-left corner of the design surface; or you can right-click on the form and select the Properties command. Figure 21.4 shows you a form Property sheet.

Figure 21.4

A form's Property sheet

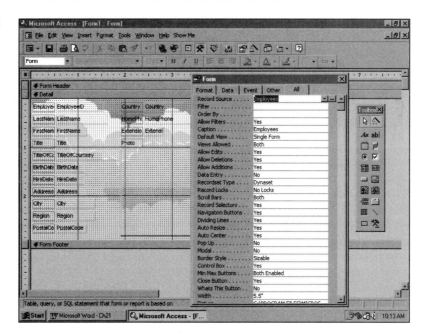

Controls

In Figure 21.3, several controls have been added to the form. Some controls are bound to fields in tables and queries; other controls, like text labels and graphics, are unbound. You can create controls by clicking on a tool in the toolbox and drawing them on the form.

You will see the toolbox when you are in the Form Design View. If the toolbox is not in view, click on the Toolbox button on the toolbar to bring it into view (see Figure 21.5).

Figure 21.5

The Toolbox button on the Design View toolbar

Toolbox button

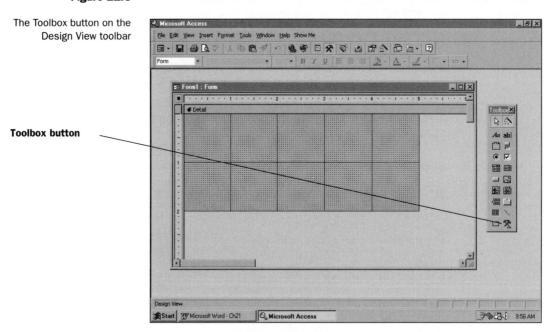

To use a tool in the toolbox, click on that tool and perform the action associated with that tool. To use a tool repeatedly, double-click on the tool to lock it. A tool stays locked until you click on another tool or press the Esc key.

You can click and drag a field from a form-field list onto your form's design surface. A default control type for that field will be created, based upon what you specified in the Table Design View. If you didn't assign a default control type for that field, then you can create the default control for that particular datatype.

Controls are edited in the Design View. You can change a shape's size by clicking and dragging a reshape handle, move the control with a click and a drag, and perform other formatting tasks. With some controls, such as text labels, you can enter new text directly. Most aspects of controls can be altered via the Property sheet.

To open a control's property sheet, select the control and click on the Properties button on the toolbar, select the Properties command on the View menu, or right-click on the control and select the Properties command from the shortcut menu.

Figure 21.6 shows you the Properties sheet for a text-box (field) control.

Figure 21.6

A text field control's Properties sheet

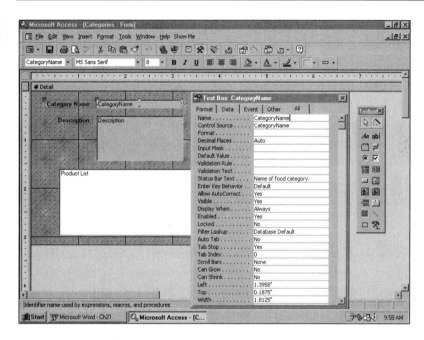

Tip. To get help on any property, make that property current and press the F1 key. Access will provide context-sensitive help. To open up a large text-editing box into which you can enter an expression, press the Shift+F2 keys. A Zoom box will appear.

To move about the Property sheet, press the Up or Down arrow key, or the Page Up and Page Down keys. Some properties contain a drop-down list of values from which you can select, while others display the Build button that opens the Expression Builder or offer both options.

Sections of a Form

A form can have up to five sections. Most forms have a detail section in which the data of an individual record is displayed. By controlling the size of the detail section versus the size of the form, you can control how many records are in view when you open the form on your monitor or print the form. In the tabular form you saw earlier, several records' data is in view. A columnar form shows only one record at a time.

Access lets you add a page header and page footer and/or a form header and a form footer to your form. Form headers and footers appear once on a display or form. The header appears at the top of the form, and the footer at the bottom. Figure 21.7 shows you a form with both page and form headers and footers added to it.

Figure 21.7

A page with both page
and form headers
and footers

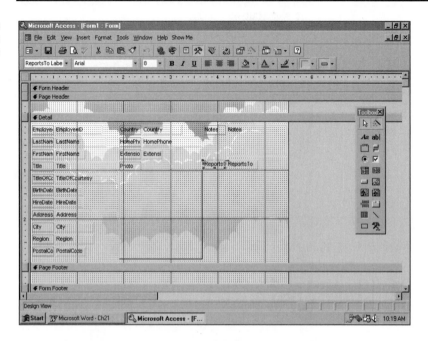

In a form that spans two or more pages, each page will print or display a page header or a page footer on each page. You will also find a page-break control in the toolbox that will help you construct multipage forms.

To insert a header or footer on your form, select the Page Header/Footer or Form Header/Footer command from the View menu. You can remove these sections by selecting the command once again to remove the check mark.

The Form Wizards

The easiest way to create a form is to use the Form Wizards. The forms these wizards build can serve as starting points in your application for the customized forms that you actually need.

To create a form using the Form Wizard:

1. In the Form tab of the Database window, click on the New button, and select the Form Wizard in the New Form dialog box.

2. Choose the data source from the table or query... drop-down list; then click the OK button.

3. Select the fields found on your form from the Available Fields list box.

4. For any related tables, select that table from the Tables/Queries list box and add its fields to the Selected Fields list box, then click the Next button.

5. For a form with two or more tables connected by a relationship, specify the parent table.

6. For the child table, select either a Form with subform(s) (grid) or a Linked form linked through a button, then click the Next button.

7. Select the form type—Tabular or Datasheet—then click the Next button.

8. Select the form style, then click Next.

9. Enter the form name in the Form text box and the subform name (or another name for the related or linked tables) into the fields provided.

10. Either save the form and Open the main form to view and enter data, or Modify the design of the forms, then click Finish.

Access will now create the new form and save it to disk.
The Form Wizards create the following types of forms:

- Columnar. In a columnar form, the fields line up on the right, and are vertically stacked with a text label just to the left of each one.

- Tabular. Tabular forms have fields in columns, with the field names as the column titles. This layout is similar to a datasheet, but not as dense.

- Datasheet. Datasheets present a spreadsheet-like layout, and are the default view for tables and queries. Datasheets aren't really forms, because you can't add controls to them or change the tab order. However, they are accessible in the Forms tab.

- Chart. The Chart Wizard creates a form with a chart on it that displays data in a field or fields. This type of form is useful for displaying trends.

- PivotTable. The PivotTable wizard creates a form with a Microsoft Excel PivotTable on it. This type of form is useful for summarizing data by categories.

An AutoForm wizard is one that runs without asking you for additional options. AutoForms exist for Columnar, Tabular, and Datasheet forms. Figures 21.8, 21.9, and 21.10 show you these three form types, respectively.

■ Data Entry

You move through a form by pressing the Tab key to move forward and using the Shift+Tab keystroke to move backward. This is called the *tab order* of a form. The natural tab order of a form is from left to right, and from top to bottom, based on the top left corner of a control. You can set the tab order of a form in Design View for any type of view except the datasheet.

Figure 21.8

The Columnar form

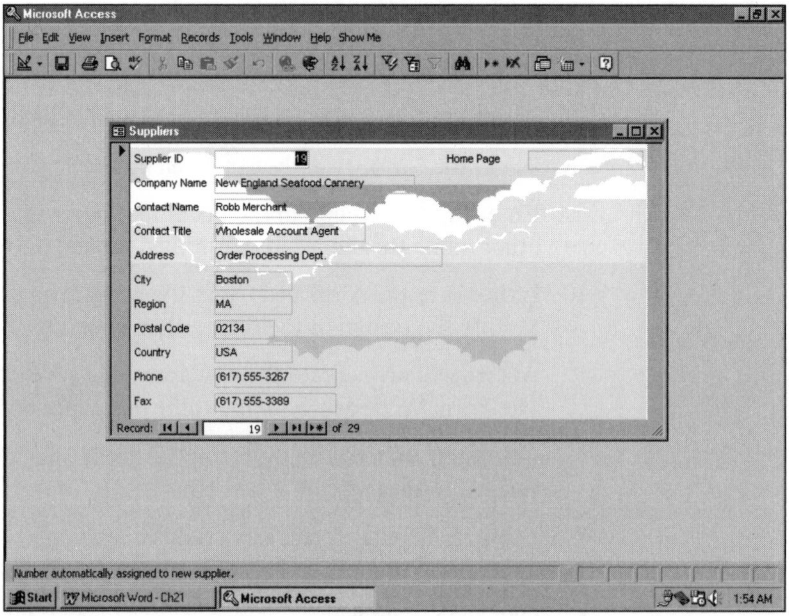

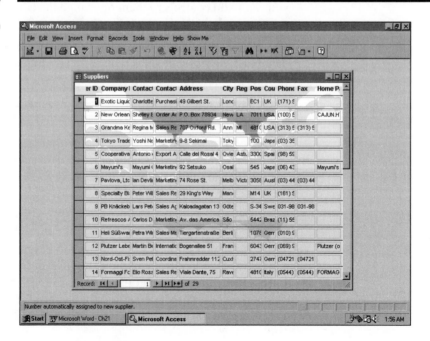

Figure 21.9

The Tabular form

Figure 21.10

The Datasheet

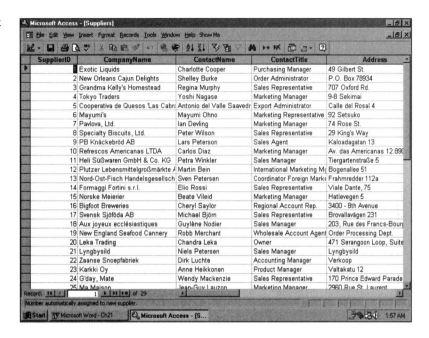

To set a form's tab order, do the following:

1. Select the Tab Order command from the View menu.

2. In the Tab Order dialog box (see Figure 21.11), click and drag the selector boxes into the order that you wish to place the fields in the tab order. Alternatively, you could click the AutoOrder button to have the default tab order restored.

To remove a field from the Tab Order, set the field's Tab Stop property to No. The number in the tab order will be indicated by the Tab Index property value.

Navigating a Datasheet

You can move through a datasheet using the Tab key and the Arrow cursor keys. Additionally, you can click anywhere on the datasheet and make that location current. When you click in the bottom blank record, you will create a new record as soon as you enter data into one of the fields and try to move the focus away from that field in the datasheet.

Datasheets offer additional methods for navigation and data entry. Table 21.1 summarizes the methods used to navigate a datasheet.

Figure 21.11

The Tab Order dialog box

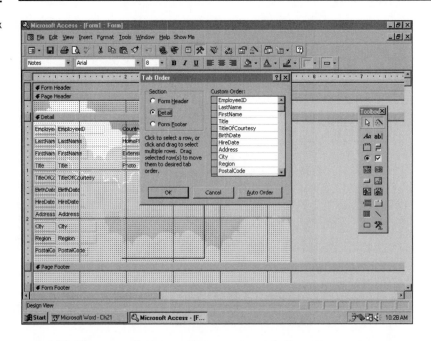

Table 21.1

Methods for Navigating
a Datasheet

TO NAVIGATE IN DATASHEET VIEW	DO THE FOLLOWING
To advance a field to the right	Press the Tab keystroke
To move a field to the left	Press the Shift+Tab keystroke
To advance to the next record	Press the Tab key on the last field in a record
To go back when you are moved to the rightmost field in the previous record	Press the Shift+Tab keystroke in the leftmost field of the current record
To move to the first record	Click on the First record button in the Navigation button section
To move to the previous record	Click on the Previous record button
To move to the next record	Click on the Next record button
To move to the Last record	Click on the Last record button
To move to the first blank record	Click on the First Blank or new record button
To move to a particular record	Double click on the record number text box, enter a record number, then press the Enter key

If you are in a multiuser application, you should know that Access will lock the record of the first user who reads the record. You can read a record that has a record lock, but you cannot modify the data contained in that form until the first person has moved on from that record.

In a datasheet, a triangle in the record-selector box indicates which record is current. You will see a pencil icon when you are editing a record and you have the lock, or a circle with a slash (the lock symbol) when someone else has the record lock.

Navigating Forms

When you bring a form into view in the Form View, you will see navigation buttons on it. Those navigation buttons also appear on a datasheet in the Datasheet View. You can use those buttons to move backwards or forwards in a record, to go to the first or last record, to go to the first blank record at the end of your table, or to go to any record number you choose. Figure 21.12 shows you a labeled Navigation bar.

Figure 21.12

The labeled Navigation bar

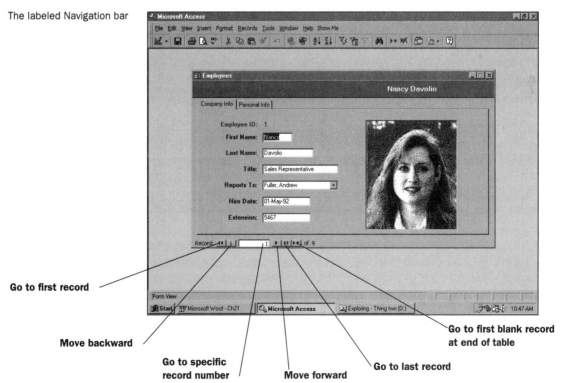

Go to first record

Move backward

Go to specific record number

Move forward

Go to last record

Go to first blank record at end of table

To navigate between fields and records in a form's Form View, you can use the methods summarized in Table 21.2.

Table 21.2

Methods for Navigating a Form

TO NAVIGATE IN FORM VIEW	DO THE FOLLOWING
To advance a field in the Tab order	Press the Tab key
To move back a field in the Tab order	Press the Shift+Tab keystroke
To advance to the first field in the Tab order on the next record from the last field in the Tab order	Press the Tab key
To move to the last field in the Tab order in the previous record from the first field in the Tab order	Press the Shift+Tab keystroke
To move to the first record	Click on the First record button in the Navigation button section
To move to the previous record	Click on the Previous record button
To move to the next record	Click on the Next record button
To move to the last record	Click on the Last record button
To move to the first blank record	Click on the First Blank or new record button
To move to a particular record	Double-click on the record number text box, enter a record number, then press the Enter key
To move to other records in a form or subform	Move the scroll bar to view other records and click in any record or field of interest.
To move between a form and subform	Press the Tab key on the last field in the Tab order of the form
To move from the first field on a subform back to the last field on the main form	Press the Ctrl+Shift+Tab keystroke.
To move from the last field on a subform to the next field in the main form, or to the first field in the next record of the main form	Press the Ctrl+Tab keystroke

- *Understanding Report Types*
- *Creating Reports from Scratch*
- *Using the Report Wizard*
- *Previewing and Printing Your Report*

22

Building Reports

W HEN YOU NEED TO PROVIDE ATTRACTIVE PRINTED OUTPUT OR
information about groups of records in Access, a report is your
best approach. You can print datasheets and forms, and to some
extent you have control over the nature of such output, but with
the Report Design tool you can do a lot more.

■ Understanding Report Types

Report view contains many of the same features that you learned about in the previous chapter on forms. You can create a report that summarizes your company's balance sheet, prints a letter for any number of records, prints mailing labels, and more. As with forms, you can open a report in Design View and create a report from scratch, or you can use one of the Report Wizards to create a report based on your answers to a number of questions.

Reports can be based on either tables or queries, use some or all of your records, and can be filtered and sorted as you wish. Reports are different from forms in that they provide you with a means to group records and to calculate results based on these groups. You can also use calculated fields in reports. It is these differences that this chapter focuses on.

Another key difference between reports and forms is that forms are meant for data output, and not for data entry. When you run a form, the data you see is from your base tables, and it is updateable (modifiable). In a report, the data you see is static and can only be viewed or printed.

There are fewer differences between reports and forms than there once were in database applications. In Access, you can now save a form as a report, and in many cases you can structure a form so that it looks like a report.

■ Creating Reports from Scratch

The report writer or report-formatting tool in Access is called the Report Design View. This tool allows you to create a report format suitable for your purpose. Reports are created in a Design View, and the results can be previewed in either the Layout Preview or Print Preview mode.

To create a report from scratch:

1. Click on the Report tab of the Database window.

2. Click on the New button to view the New Report dialog box.

3. Select Design View and in the Choose… list box the table or query that the report will be based on; then click OK. The Report Design view appears, as shown with labeled elements in Figure 22.1.

4. Add any desired controls to your report, additional sections or bands (see the next section for an explanation of these terms).

5. Save your report.

You can switch between the different views of a report by using the Design View, Layout View, or Print Preview View command on the View menu, or by selecting these commands from the View button's drop-down menu on left side of the toolbar.

Figure 22.1

The Report Design View
with labeled elements

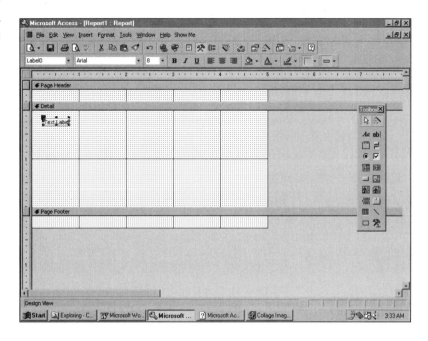

Report Sections

An Access report can have up to seven different types of sections in it. Five of
these sections are familiar to you from the last chapter on forms. Two additional
sections—Group header and Group footer—require additional explanation.

In brief, here are the sections you can add to a report:

- **Report header**. This section prints once at the beginning of a report.
  Often it contains a cover page, table of contents, executive summary, or
  other "print once, print first" material.

- **Page header**. A page header section prints at the top of each and every
  page. Report titles, page numbers, column headers, and other information that must be repeated on each page is placed here.

- **Group header**. This section appears at the beginning of a group of
  records, and is based upon a sort of the field's values or an expression
  that groups the records as specified by the group header. Typically, you
  see group titles and other text labels, column headers, totals, and other
  items that the group of records that follow requires in the group header
  section.

- **Detail section**. The detail section prints once for each record that is viewed in the report. A detail section often includes text labels and fields, but it can also include calculated fields.

- **Group footer**. This footer comes after a group of records, sorted by a field or expression. Text labels, column footers, calculated fields, running totals, subtotals or other totals are often placed in group footers.

- **Page footer**. A page footer section prints at the bottom of each and every page. Report titles, page numbers, column footers, and other information that must repeat on each page is placed here.

- **Report footer**. This section prints once at the end of a report. Often it contains a glossary, an index, or other "print once, print last" material.

You can add these bands in pairs by selecting the corresponding commands from the View menu:

- Page Header/Footer

- Report Header/Footer

If a header or a footer appears in Design View, you can choose to remove it from view. To remove any section from view, remove all controls from the section, and click and drag on the band bar until there is no space defined by the part.

Figure 22.2 shows you a report in Design View; Figure 22.3 shows you that same report in Print Preview View.

Adding Calculations to Reports

If you have a calculated field in a query upon which your report is based, that calculated field can be added directly to your report. The same expression that you entered into the Query Design grid will be calculated and displayed.

You are not limited to calculations from your data source, as you can add additional calculations to your report. Calculated fields that you define on your report are calculated at the report's run time. Most often these calculations are created to provide the calculation of an aggregate function such as a COUNT, AVERAGE, SUM, DSUM, and so on.

When you base a report's calculations on a field from a query, you can use the name of the field from the query as the name you use for the control. Any expression that isn't based on a particular field, such as SUM or DSUM, must repeat the expression on the control in the report.

To create a calculated control in a report:

1. Create a report or open an existing report in Design View.

Figure 22.2

A report in Design View

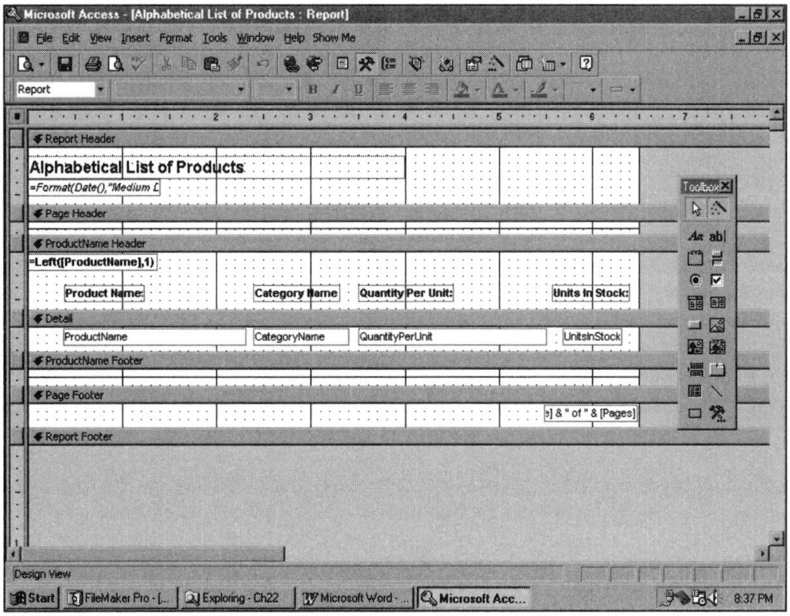

Figure 22.3

The same report in Print Preview View with the sections labeled

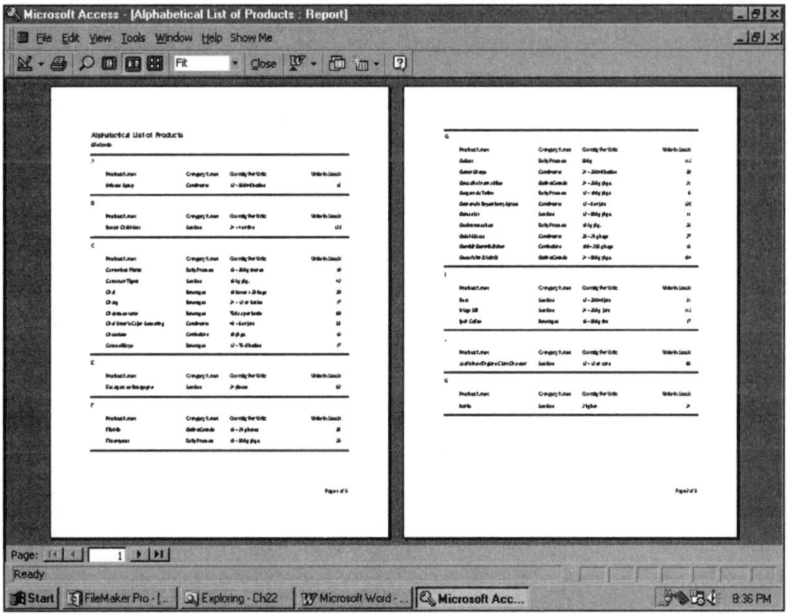

2. Click on the tool in the toolbox for the type of control that will contain the calculation. Most often this will be a text field, but calculations can be placed in toggle buttons, option groups, option buttons, check boxes, command buttons, subforms, and so on.

3. For a text-box control, enter the expression for the calculation directly into the control on your design surface.

4. For controls that don't permit direct entry of calculations, click on the Properties button on the toolbar or select the Properties command from the View menu to open the Properties sheet.

5. Enter the expression into the ControlSource property.

In order for a control to take a calculation, it must have a ControlSource property associated with it. For example, labels do not have this property and cannot display a calculated result.

When you click in the ControlSource property, you will see the Build button. This button opens up the Expression builder, into which you can place any valid Access function or operator, values, fields, or identifiers, preceded by an equal (=) sign. If you need additional room in which to construct your expression, use the Shift+F2 keystroke. Figure 22.4 shows you a ControlSource property and the corresponding Zoom box.

Figure 22.4

A ControlSource property for a calculated field, with the Zoom box open

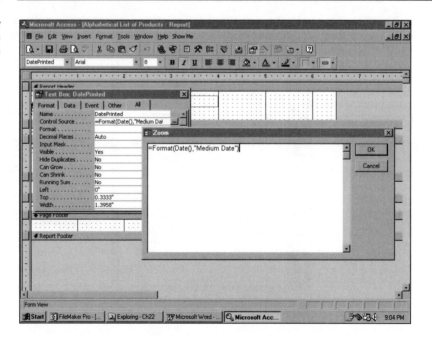

Group Calculations

Adding a calculation that displays an expression based on a group of records isn't much different from adding that calculation for every record on a header or footer, or for an individual record on the detail section. The main difference is the placement of the calculated control on a group header or group footer, and the proper sorting of the underlying dynaset by the appropriate group or expression upon which the calculation depends.

To add a group calculation to a report:

1. Open the report in Design View.

2. Click on the control in the toolbox that you desire, and create the control on the design surface.

3. To sum or average a group of records, add a text box or bounded text box to the group header or footer.

4. To sum or average all records, add a text box to the report header or report footer.

5. Click on the Properties button on the toolbar or select the Properties command from the View menu to open the Properties sheet.

6. Enter the expression, starting with an equal sign, in the ControlSource property box.

   For a count of the number of records in group, do the following:

- Place the control in the group header or footer section.

- In the Property sheet, set the Name property to RecordCount; the ControlSource to =1; and the Visible property to No.

   For a running sum of records, do the following:

- Add the control to the group footer.

- In the Property sheet, set the RunningSum property to Over Groups (resets at 0 after a group), or to Over All (runs throughout the report); and set the ControlSource property to the name of the control in the detail section that tracks the total (e.g. =[RecordCount]).

Since reports are based on your tables or queries, when you change a query's group or sort you can affect whether your report will continue to function correctly. You may also wish to group and sort a report based upon tables. Therefore, you need to know how to add groups to your report, and how to adjust the ones that are already part of your report structure.

To manually change the sort and grouping order in a report:

1. Open the report in Design view.

2. Click on the Sorting and Grouping button on the toolbar, or select the Sorting and Grouping command from the View menu. The Sorting and Grouping dialog box will appear, as shown in Figure 22.5.

Figure 22.5

The Sorting and Grouping
dialog box

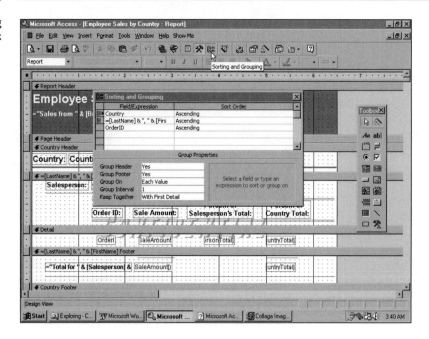

3. To move a sort or group, click and drag the row selector for the field or expression that you wish to move in the report. Access will rearrange the Group Header and Footer sections appropriately. You must adjust the controls on your report manually.

4. To add a group header or footer, enter "Yes" for the property of that sort in the Group Properties section at the bottom of the dialog box. Unlike page or report headers/footers, you can add and remove group headers and group footers individually.

5. Set the Group, Group Intervals, and Keep Together properties; then click the Close box.

◼ Using the Report Wizard

The Report Wizard offers you an easy method for creating nicely formatted reports, which will be based on your answers to questions posed in each step of the wizard. This wizard will create a report based on a single table or query, or on a set of related tables.

Even if you don't get exactly the report you wanted, the Report Wizard's output will provide a good starting place for your ultimate report.

To create a report using the Report Wizard:

1. Click on the New button on the Report tab of the Database window.

2. Select the Report Wizard in the New Report dialog box.

3. Select the table or query that will be the data source from the Choose the table or query drop down list (see Figure 22.6) then click the OK button.

Figure 22.6

Selecting the Report
Wizard from the New
Report dialog box

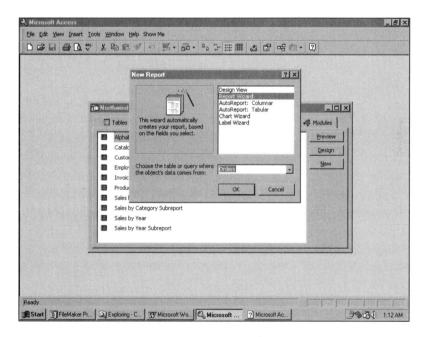

4. Select the fields from the table or query that will appear on your form by selecting them in the Available Fields list box and clicking the Move button to place them in the Selected Fields list box, as shown in Figure 22.7.

5. Select related table(s) from the Tables/Queries list box, and add the fields of interest to the Selected Fields list box.

6. Click the Next button to proceed to Step 2.

Figure 22.7

Selecting fields for your
report from the first table
or query

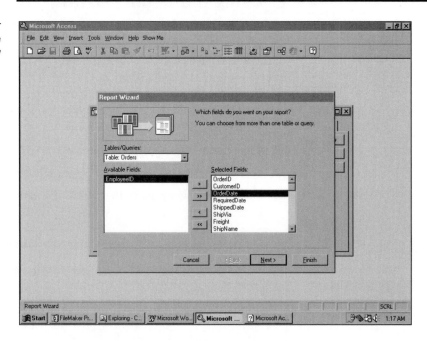

7. For any report involving a relationship, indicate which is the parent or controlling table for the dataset, as shown in Figure 22.8, then click the Next button.

8. Select the group field(s) in the proper order from top to bottom, then click the Next button. The Report Wizard will show you a graphic representation of your grouping levels, as shown in Figure 22.9.

9. If you wish to sort your data, select the sort field(s) with the top field as the primary sort key, as shown in Figure 22.10. Note that grouped fields are already sorted, and will not appear on the list of fields.

10. Click the Sort button for ascending or descending sorts.

11. Click on the Summary Options button to open the Summary Options dialog box shown in Figure 22.11.

12. Click the Summary Options button to open the Summary Options dialog box and select the types of summaries you desire in either the Detail and Summary or in the Summary section alone.

13. Click on the OK button followed by the Next button to view the layout and orientation selection step.

14. Select a layout for your report, as shown in Figure 22.12, then click the Next button.

Figure 22.8

Setting the controlling
table in a relationship

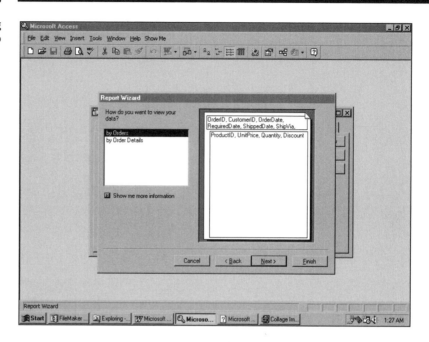

Figure 22.9

The grouping options

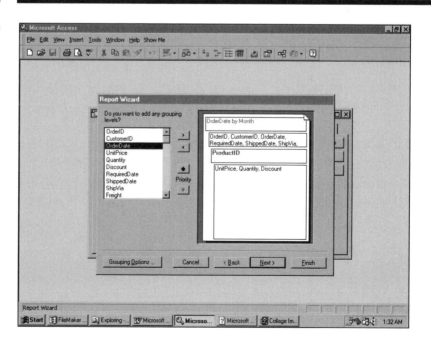

Figure 22.10

The sorting options

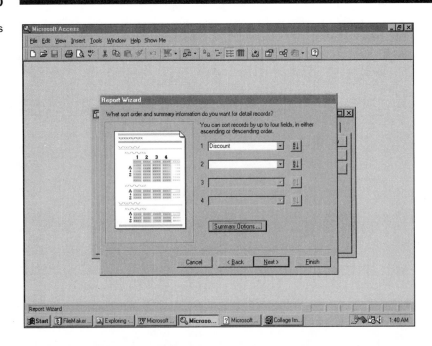

Figure 22.11

The Summary Options
dialog box

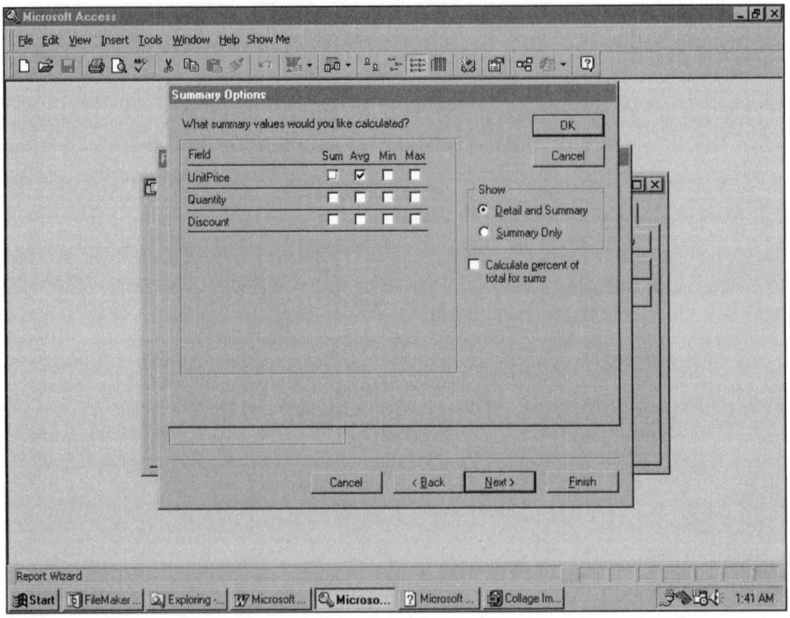

Figure 22.12

The report layout
selection step

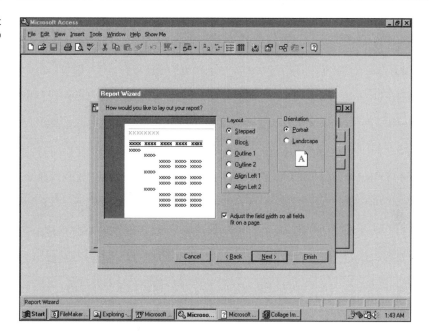

15. Select a presentation style, as shown in Figure 22.13, then click the Next button.

16. In the final step of the Report Wizard, enter a title and click on Preview the Report or Modify the Report's Design, as shown in Figure 22.14. Then click the Finish button.

The new report will now be created, and the file will be saved to disk. In this instance, Preview refers to the Layout Preview mode; Modify opens the report in the Report Design View. Figure 22.15 shows you a two-page Layout Preview of the report constructed in this exercise.

There are four additional Report Wizards, each of which generates a specific report type. The AutoReport (Columnar) and AutoReport (Tabular) wizards generate a report with almost no input. You specify the table or query upon which the report is based, and the wizard does the rest. Figure 22.16 and Figure 22.17 show you a two-page view of the Columnar and Tabular reports, respectively.

Access offers two additional Report Wizards that you can try: the Chart Wizard and the Label Wizard. In the Chart Wizard, you select a data source, the field you wish to chart, and the chart type. Figure 22.18 shows you the possible chart types you can select from. In the example, the Sales by Category query was selected as the data source in the Northwind database.

Figure 22.13

The presentation style
selection step

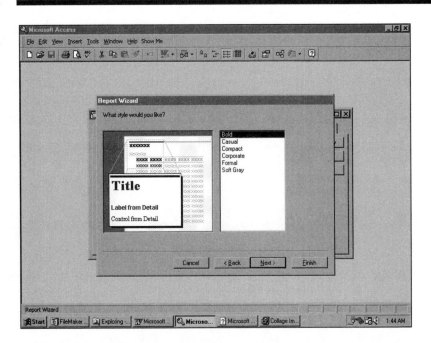

Figure 22.14

Naming and saving
the report

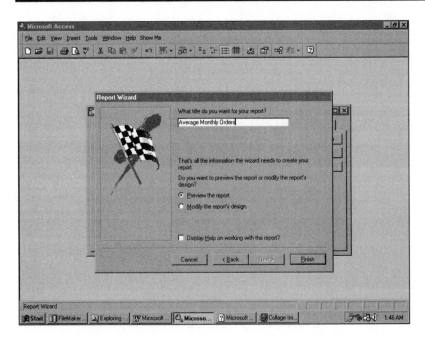

Figure 22.15

Naming and saving
the report

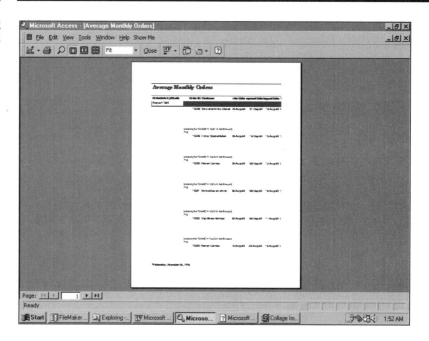

Figure 22.16

The AutoReport
(Columnar) wizard output

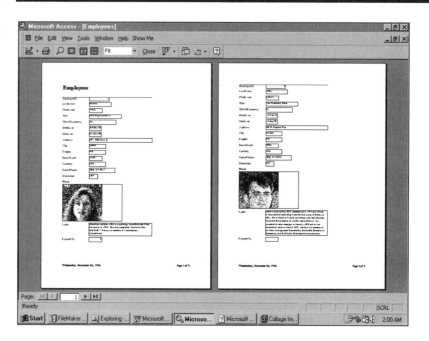

Figure 22.17

The AutoReport (Tabular)
wizard output

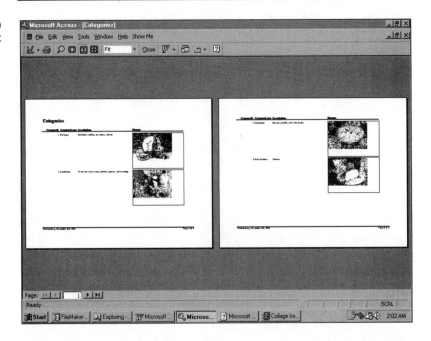

Figure 22.18

The different chart
types afforded by
the Chart Wizard

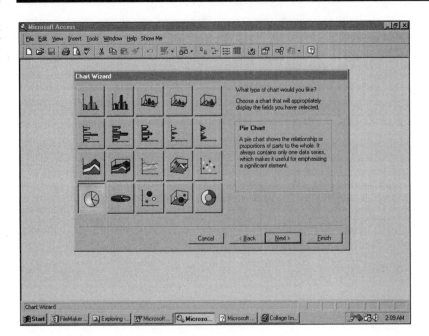

Mailing Labels

Labels are nothing more than specialized reports that repeat across or down a page. If you are using a standard-size Avery label, or a label that is an Avery equivalent, you can easily use this wizard to create your labels with no modification at all. Furthermore, if the data source contains just those records you wish to print out as labels, then you can run the report and print your labels in a matter of moments.

The Label Wizard gives you control over what appears on your mailing labels. You run the Label Wizard in almost the same manner that you run the Report Wizard itself.

To create a mailing label:

1. Select the Label Wizard in the New Report dialog box, then select the table or query that will supply the data for the labels in the Select table or query drop-down list box, and click the OK button.

2. Select the Avery label you desire, the unit of measurement, and whether the label is continuous or sheet-fed, as shown in Figure 22.19. Then click the Next button. Or, click the Customize button and then the Edit button to reveal the Edit Label dialog box shown in Figure 22.20.

Figure 22.19

Selecting an Avery label in the Label Wizard

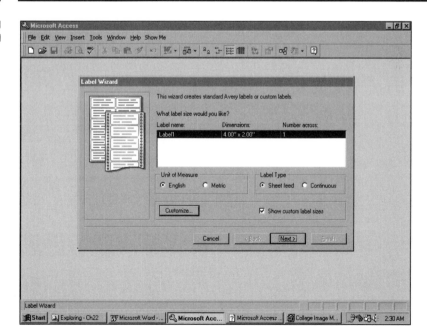

Figure 22.20

The Edit Label dialog box

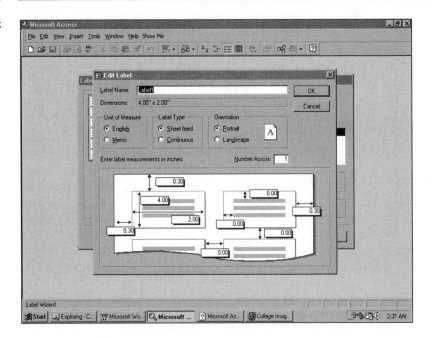

3. Select the font, size, and color of your text, then click the Next button.

4. Create a sample label by adding fields from the Available fields list box, and typing any spaces and carriage returns (press the Enter key), as shown in Figure 22.21; then click Next.

5. Select the sort field(s), with the top field as the primary sort key (see Figure 22.22). Then click the Next button.

   For example, to sort by name, use last name on top and first name below it. Or use the zip code or postal-code field as your sort field.

6. Enter a name for your label, then preview it in Layout Preview View or modify it in the Report Design View.

   Access saves your label to disk.

   If you will be using a dot-matrix printer, you will need to adjust the page setup. If you are printing labels on tractor-feed stock, the procedure for adjusting the page setup is as follows:

1. Select the Printers command from the Settings menu of the Start menu.

2. Select the printer you will use, then select the Properties command from the File menu.

Note. In Layout Preview you will only see some of your records, and your sort might not be properly displayed.

Figure 22.21

The sample mailing label,
with fields, spaces, and
carriage returns

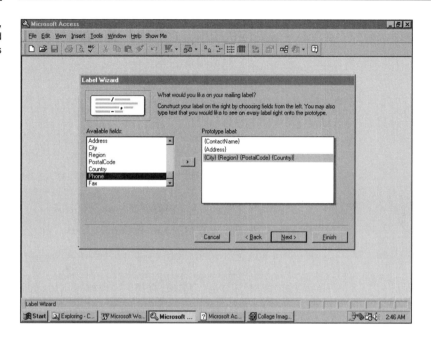

Figure 22.22

The Sort step of the
Label Wizard

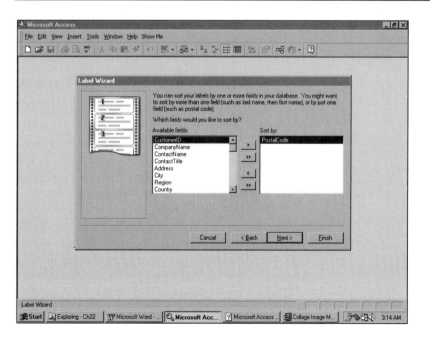

3. Click on the Paper tab, and click on the Custom icon in the Paper Size section.

4. Enter the size of your label in the User-Defined Size dialog box. Use a width from the left edge of the leftmost label to the right edge of the rightmost label. Use a length from the top of the first label to the top of the second.

5. Exit the Printer Properties dialog box.

A label layout has no header or footer, only a detail section. To create a label from scratch, use the following settings in the Page Setup dialog box:

- the Page tab to the Use Specific Printer you will use; the printer Source to User-Defined Size; and the source for label stock to Tractor, Cassette, AutoSelect tray, or whatever is appropriate.

- the Columns tab to Same as Detail in the Column Size section.

- For a layout with more than one label across on the Columns tab, enter the number of labels across in the Number of Columns text box; the amount of space between the bottom of one label and the top of another in the Row Spacing text box; and the space between the right edge of one label and the left edge of the next in the Column Spacing text box. Also specify whether the Column Layout is Down, then Across; or Across, then Down.

- If you're using a dot-matrix printer, specify the paper size as a User-Defined Size, as described in the numbered list above.

■ Previewing and Printing Your Report

When you print a report, it is almost always a good idea to preview your printed report. This is especially true when you are formatting the report, and equally true when you need to see if the groups you have established and the calculations contained in your report are functioning properly. Access makes it easy to preview your report, and offers you two separate modes for doing so.

In Layout Preview, you can preview a few of your first records. Layout Preview is especially useful when you want to see if your formatting is correct, but you don't want to spend a lot of time waiting for your report to run. When a report is based on complicated calculations or on large data sources, a Print Preview can take a long time to process.

Layout Preview suffers from one important defect: Since the selected first group of records may not establish your groups and sorts, it is possible and even probable that what you see in the preview window will not be representative of your final report's data. For this reason, when you are deal-ing with small datasets you are best advised to use Print Preview instead.

You are probably familiar with the Print Preview mode from other Win-dows programs. In this view, all of your records have been processed, and what you see is what you would print to the printer that is currently selected. If you change your printer or output device, then what you see in the Print Preview window changes as well.

You can use the toolbar buttons to switch your preview view, the page icons to switch your page view, zoom to change the magnification level, links to other Microsoft Office products, and so on.

To preview a report in Print Preview mode:

- Select the report in the Database window and click on the Preview button.

- With a report open in view or selected, select the Print Preview com-mand from the View button at the left of the standard toolbar, or select the Print Preview command from the View menu.

There are numerous shortcuts to working in Print Preview View, such as clicking on a zoomed page and going to a 100-percent view, and vice versa. Table 22.1 details some of the shortcuts most commonly used in Print Pre-view View.

Table 22.1

Print Preview Shortcuts

TO DO THIS	PRESS THIS
To open the Print dialog box	P or Ctrl+P
To open the Page Setup dialog box	S
To zoom in or out on a part of the page	Z
To cancel Print Preview or Layout Preview	C or Esc
To move to the page number box; then type the page number and press Enter	F5
To view the next page (when Fit To Window is selected)	Page Down or Down arrow
To view the previous page (when Fit To Window is selected)	Page Up or Up arrow
To scroll down in small increments	Down arrow
To scroll down one full screen	Page Down
To move to the bottom of the page	Ctrl+Down arrow
To scroll up in small increments	Up arrow

Table 22.1 (Continued)
Print Preview Shortcuts

TO DO THIS	PRESS THIS
To scroll up one full screen	Page Up
To move to the top of the page	Ctrl+Up arrow
To scroll to the right in small increments	Right arrow
To move to the right edge of the page	End or Ctrl+Right arrow
To move to the lower-right corner of the page	Ctrl+End
To scroll to the left in small increments	Left arrow
To move to the left edge of the page	Home or Ctrl+Left arrow
To move to the upper-left corner of the page	Ctrl+Home

Outlook

- *Adding Appointments*
- *Adding Meetings*
- *Adding Tasks*
- *Managing Contacts*
- *Creating Events*
- *Tracking Projects*
- *Messaging with Outlook*

- *Using Outlook Notes*
- *Journaling with Outlook*
- *Printing Items*

23

Outlook Basics

W ITH MICROSOFT OUTLOOK, YOU CAN MANAGE TASKS AND INFOR-
mation on your desktop. Not only can you improve the way you
control your own time, but you can share this management information with others through e-mail, over a company network or in
print. You can also use Microsoft Outlook to archive past entries—a useful tool for project management.

Open Microsoft Outlook by double-clicking on its desktop icon, as shown in Figure 23.1.

Figure 23.1

Microsoft Outlook icon on the desktop

When you open Microsoft Outlook, you get a glimpse of the many powerful features loaded into this compact little program, as shown in Figure 23.2. The main components of Microsoft Outlook are:

- Inbox
- Calendar
- Contacts
- Tasks
- Journal
- Notes
- Deleted items

Information from other Microsoft Office programs can be used within Outlook.

Figure 23.2

The Microsoft Outlook
main screen

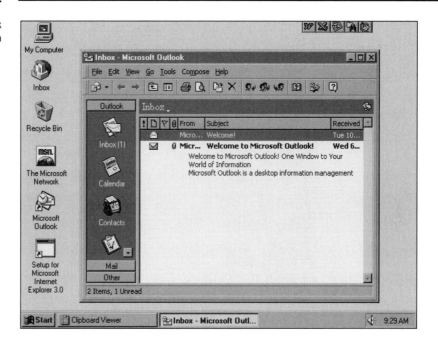

Tip. You can use Office to preview the contents of other Office documents without opening them in Word, Excel, or Access.

To use Outlook, enter the information you need to keep track of, such as appointments, things to do, and events. This section helps you to start using Outlook as a basic personal information manager. The following chapter provides more in-depth information.

■ Adding Appointments

Keeping track of appointments and deadlines is quite a task. With Outlook, the deadlines don't shift, but we're less likely to overlook appointments and more likely to schedule our time successfully, as it's easy to see when items from the task list collide with other time restraints. In Outlook, an appointment is something for which you schedule time that does not require the presence of other people.

To add appointments, click on Microsoft Outlook, then click on the Calendar icon in the left scrolling bar or pull down the Go menu and choose Calendar. The Calendar module will be displayed, as shown in Figure 23.3.

To enter an appointment directly on the calendar, click on the appropriate date in the calendar, then scroll to the correct time and type your appointment. If you need to reserve a block of time for the appointment rather

Figure 23.3

The Outlook Calendar module

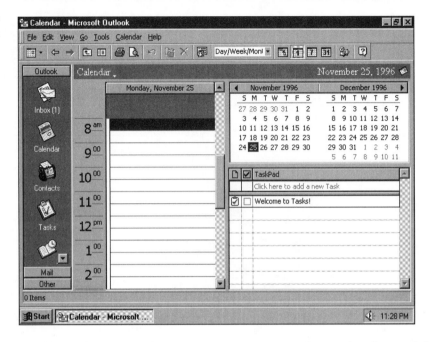

than just make a note of it, position your mouse at the starting time and drag down to the completion time.

You can also enter an appointment in the calendar by pulling down the Calendar menu, as shown in Figure 23.4.

Choose New Appointment, and your screen will display the New Appointment dialog box, as shown in Figure 23.5.

Type the name of the appointment, its location, and its starting and ending times. If you need to, you can have Outlook provide on-screen reminders. For tasks that happen on a regular basis, choose Recurrence from the Appointment menu.

To edit an appointment, click on the day and time, and then make any needed corrections. To delete a selected appointment, pull down the Edit menu and choose Delete.

Tip. Instead of typing in the exact date and time for the starting and ending times, type "next Friday" or "noon." The Autodate feature allows Outlook to interpret your typed text.

■ Adding Meetings

In Outlook, a meeting is a type of appointment that involves other people and resources. Setting up a meeting is quite simple. From the Calendar module, pull down the Calendar menu and choose New Meeting Request. The New Meeting Request dialog box will now be seen, as shown in Figure 23.6.

Figure 23.4

The Calendar menu

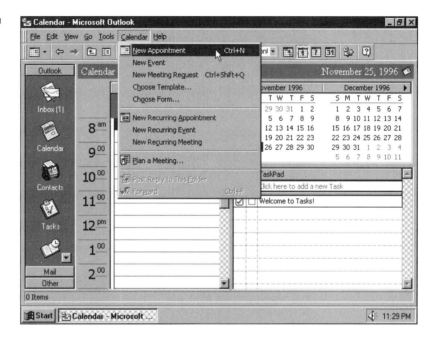

Figure 23.5

The New Appointment
dialog box

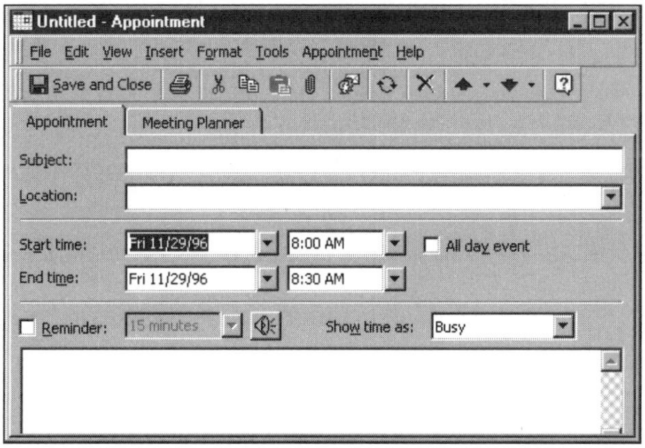

In the Appointment tab, enter the names of anyone who should be invited to the meeting. You can use this information to e-mail the other attendees.

For more meeting-scheduling options, click on the Meeting Planner tab, as shown in Figure 23.7.

Figure 23.6

The New Meeting
Request dialog box

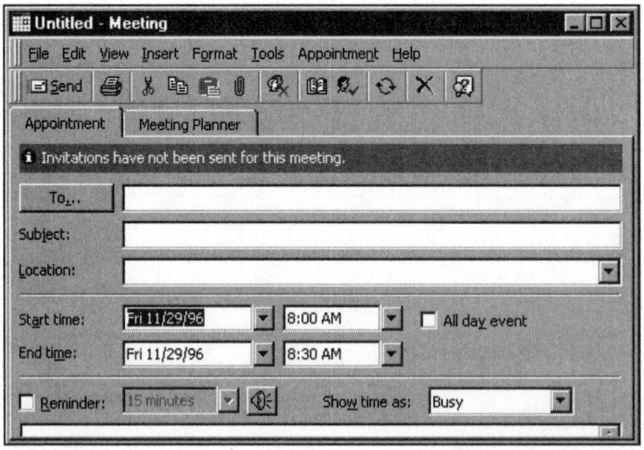

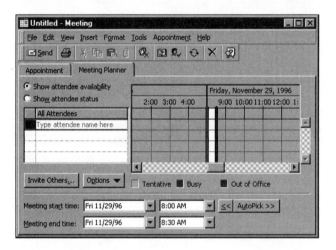

Figure 23.7

The Meeting Planner
dialog box

Use the Meeting Planner to set a meeting time and date, reserve a room
or other resources, and list the people to be invited. If you have e-mailed
meeting invitations, you will find the responses in your Inbox. If the response
is poor, use the Meeting Planner to select another time.

To edit a meeting, open the Meeting Planner and add or change any
needed persons or resources. To delete a selected meeting, pull down the
Edit menu and choose Delete.

■ Adding Tasks

Long before Outlook, computer users composed To Do lists in word processors or on scribbled pieces of paper. With Outlook, we now have an integrated way to combine our meeting obligations and task lists.

In the main Outlook window, click on the Tasks icon in the left-hand column. The Tasks window will pop up, as shown in Figure 23.8.

Figure 23.8

The Tasks window

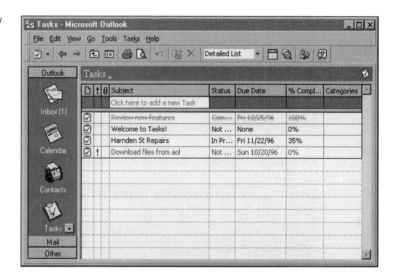

The Tasks window lists all tasks. To show that a task has been completed, click on the checkmark icon and a line will be drawn through the text. To add a new task, pull down the Tasks menu and choose New Task. The New Task dialog box will appear, as shown in Figure 23.9.

Complete the task and status information. When you exit the Task view and return to the Calendar view, you are reminded of the tasks appropriate to each day by the list in the lower right corner.

To edit a task, double-click on the task itself and make any needed changes. To delete a selected task, pull down the Edit menu and choose Delete.

■ Managing Contacts

If you're working at your computer while you're on the phone, there's no longer any excuse for not organizing your list of contacts and their phone, e-mail, and address information. To move to the Contacts module, click on the Rolodex icon in the left-hand column of the Outlook main window. The main Contacts window will appear, as shown in Figure 23.10.

Figure 23.9

The New Tasks dialog box

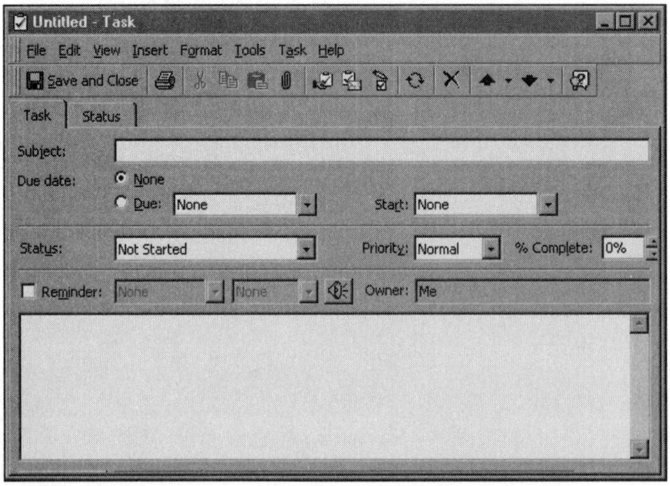

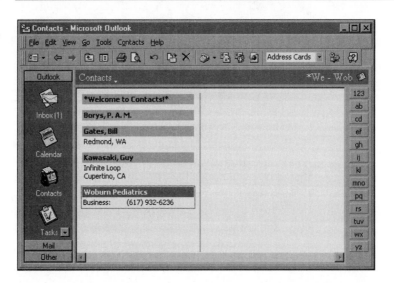

Figure 23.10

The Contacts main
window

To add a contact, pull down the Contacts menu and choose New Contact.
The alphabetical listings on the right-hand side allow you to scroll through
your address book swiftly. The Contacts main window automatically displays
the name of the person to which the software is registered. Double-click on
the name to bring up the Contacts dialog box, as shown in Figure 23.11.

Figure 23.11

The Contacts dialog box

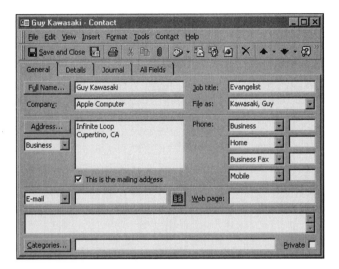

Click on the General tab and enter the basic information: name, company, address, title, phone numbers, e-mail addresses, etc. Under the Details tab you can add more specific information, including the name of a person's spouse and his or her birthday! The All Fields tab allows you to customize the fields you enter, and even to create custom fields that can make Outlook much more relevant to your needs. To enter additional records, pull down the File menu and choose New.

To edit any information in the Contacts area, select the record you want to modify, bring up the appropriate field, and retype over the existing information. To delete information, select the information you wish to delete and press the Delete key. To delete an entire record, select the record in the contact list, pull down the Edit menu, and choose Delete.

■ Creating Events

Events in Outlook are classified as activities that last a day or more. Annual events, such as birthdays or anniversaries, are the first that come to mind. Business events may include training sessions or vacations. Unlike appointments, which occupy blocks of time on one's calendar, events are displayed as banners under the date, as shown in Figure 23.12.

To create an Event, choose the Calendar mode, then pull down the Calendar Menu and choose New Event. The New Event dialog box will appear, as shown in Figure 23.13 below.

Figure 23.12

An event displayed as a banner

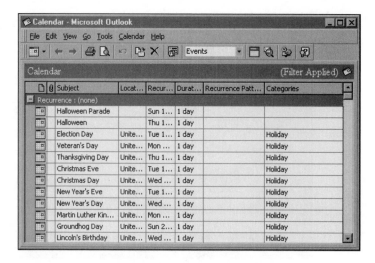

Figure 23.13

The New Event dialog box

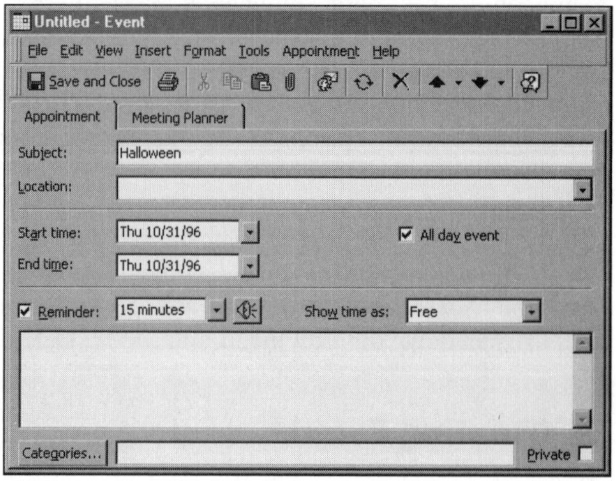

As you type in the information regarding the event, note that you can also set up a reminder for up to three days into the future. This gives you ample time to get the suit from the cleaners or send out that all-important birthday or anniversary card.

■ Tracking Projects

The task feature helps you stay informed about the things you need to do. In the real world you can delegate tasks, and you can also do so in Outlook. Using Outlook in this way works best over a network, although you can use it to document when work gets done. If you are not on a network, print out the form and have it filled out by those responsible for the task's completion.

When you receive a task in your Inbox, you have the option of accepting the task and becoming its owner, refusing it, or passing it on to someone else. That also sounds a bit like the real world, doesn't it?

When a task is refused, it is returned to its sender. After a task is accepted, the sender can receive a status report, but may not change any of the project details—changes can only be made by the person in charge of completing the task.

Outlook does not permit you to assign a project to a group. To receive status reports in your Inbox, you'll need to break out the task into discrete units. For example, the task "Preparing training materials" could be split between a writer, a subject-matter expert, a proofreader, and a clerk.

■ Messaging with Outlook

Like the rest of Windows 95, Outlook is optimized to work over a network. That's why e-mail capability is at the very heart of this organizational tool. All received messages all appear in your Inbox, with the top item in the left scrolling window as shown in Figure 23.14.

Figure 23.14

The Inbox

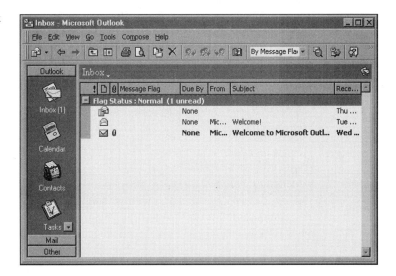

Previewing Messages

If you're a busy person, you may not want to read all of your messages. To find out what the gist of a message is and whether it's destined for your hard drive or your recycling bin, use the preview function. To preview the first lines of an e-mail message in your Inbox, pull down the View menu and choose Format View. The Format Table View dialog box will appear, as shown in Figure 23.15.

Figure 23.15

The Format Table View
dialog box

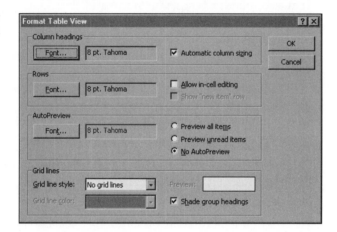

Now click on the Preview Unread radio button. When you click OK, your Inbox will display the first few lines of each message, as shown in Figure 23.16.

Reading and Replying to Messages

To read a message in your Inbox, double-click on the message. The message window will pop up, as shown in Figure 23.17.

As you read the message, note that you have some additional options in the message window. You can reply to the message or forward it to another person by clicking on the appropriate button. If the message is important but you don't have time to deal with it now, pull down the Edit menu and choose Mark as Unread. Your message will reappear in your Inbox.

Deleting Messages

Receiving messages and memos is wonderful—until they start cluttering up your hard drive. To delete a message, select it in your Inbox, pull down the Edit menu and choose Delete. To select more than one message, hold down the Shift key as you click on the messages you wish to delete.

Figure 23.16

The Inbox with message previews

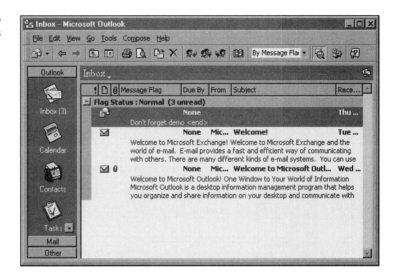

Figure 23.17

An opened message

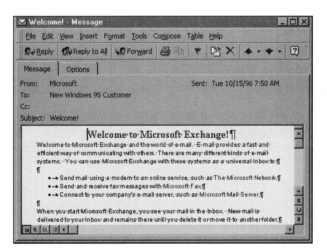

■ Using Outlook Notes

Of the products that have revolutionized this century, disposable diapers, white-out, and those sticky little pieces of yellow paper are among my personal favorites. Suddenly it became fun and convenient to post little reminders. Outlook has a feature called Notes that emulates these sticky notes.

To use Notes, click on the Notes icon in the bottom of the left-hand scrolling window. The Notes window will appear, as shown in Figure 23.18.

Figure 23.18

The Notes window

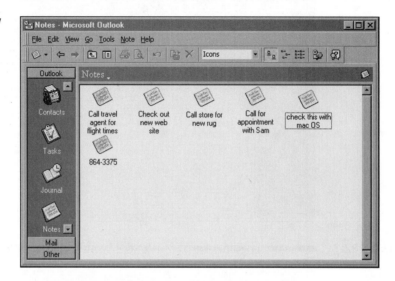

To create a new note, pull down the Notes window and choose New Note. A form in the shape of a yellow sticky note will appear. You may type directly onto the note. You can send these notes to others on your network. When you return to the Notes window, you will see all the notes there.

■ Journaling with Outlook

Because you document so many of your tasks and information using Outlook, it's only natural to expect that you would be able to keep a journal of your activities. To move to the Journal view, click on the Journal icon in the left scrolling window. The journal takes the form of a timeline, as shown in Figure 23.19.

The journal scrolls back only as far as August 24, 1996 (the release date for Windows 95). Each day, your activities are automatically logged in. Each file that you work on and its complete path is noted, as is the amount of time you worked on each task or file.

With this amount of information, you can easily track your time and productivity. Even better, Outlook provides a shortcut to the documents you were working on, as shown in Figure 23.20. You no longer have to guess the names and locations of files you worked on previously.

Figure 23.19

The Journal view

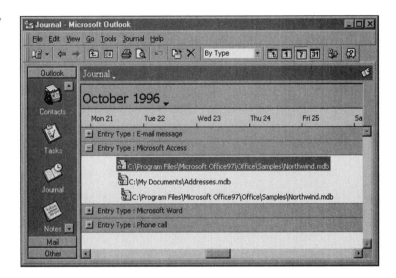

Figure 23.20

A journal page with document shortcut

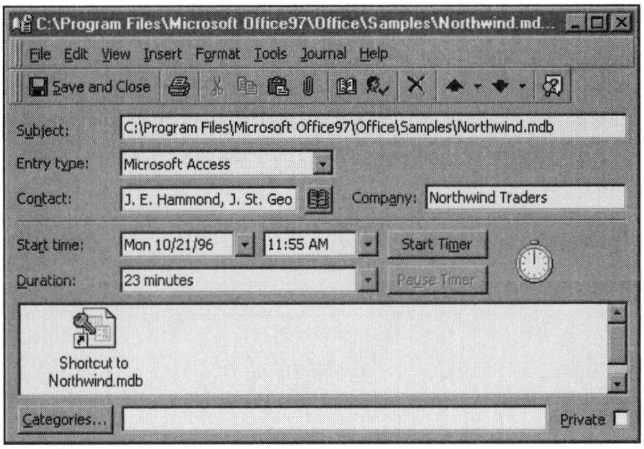

To document other tasks, such as phone calls, pull down the Journal menu and choose New Journal Entry. The Journal Entry dialog box will appear, as shown in Figure 23.21.

Complete the dialog box with as much detail as you need. Use the large rectangular space at the bottom of the dialog box for notes. At the bottom right-hand side of the dialog box you can indicate whether or not you want to share this information with others or keep it private.

Figure 23.21

New Journal Entry
dialog box

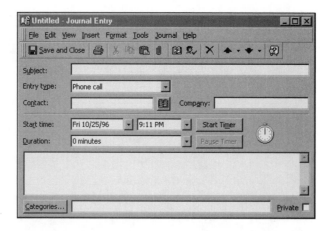

■ Printing Items

The power of Outlook comes mainly from its ease-of-use and its tight integration with e-mail capabilities. Without powerful printing capabilities, Outlook would leave all the valuable information on the desktop.

As a rule, you should always use the Print Preview command on the File menu before you are ready to print. Previewing your printed items often saves time, trees, and frustration.

Printing messages from your Inbox is fairly straightforward. Once you view the document in Print Preview, click on the printer icon in the Print Preview window, or pull down the File menu and choose Print. You will be able to select the number of copies, and you can limit printing to odd or even pages. Some documents may be printed out in more than one format—a nice feature.

To print a Task list, switch to the Task module. Pull down the File menu and choose Print. The tasks print out in a grid fashion—not a fancy layout, but a useful list to bring to meetings.

To print information from the Contacts module, decide on the Page Layout that best meets your needs. To select a layout, pull down the File menu and choose Page Setup. A hierarchical menu will appear on the right showing the following selections: card style, small booklet style, medium booklet style, memo style, and phone directory style. Choose the layout that best meets your needs. You will be able to make some modifications, including the font, in the Page Setup dialog shown in Figure 23.22.

Figure 23.22

The Page Setup dialog box

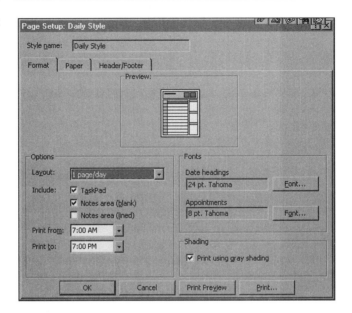

Because the Outlook Calendar function is integral to many tasks, there are several layouts to choose from in the Page Setup command. These are the Daily style, Weekly style, Monthly style, Trifold style, and Memo style. If none of these styles answer your needs exactly, you can edit them. Be aware that a Monthly printout style will not be able to contain as much detail as a Weekly printout style.

Journal entries must be selected before printing: otherwise you would end up with piles of useless printed pages. Check the Print Preview window to be sure that you have selected the appropriate journal entry. Journal entries print out in the form of a memo, as shown in Figure 23.23, and do not resemble their visual-timeline on-screen display.

Printing out the Outlook Notes can be very helpful. In the Print dialog box you can indicate whether you want each note to print out on its own page, or if you want to combine them on a page.

To document a project you may want to print out copies of documents in your Inbox, your task list, and status reports. Selected contact information would also round out the printed documentation.

You can place header and footer information to indicate the date and time of the printout. This strategy allows you to manage your printouts with more efficiency and confidence. Always be sure to save your file before you print it out. If you are willing to spend much time in Outlook, be sure that

Figure 23.23

Previewing the printed
journal entry

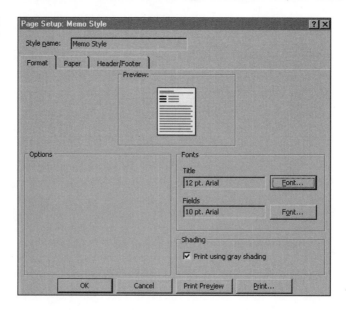

you back up the file on a regular basis. Also make a habit of keeping a printout. If disaster ever strikes you and your computer, you will be able to use it
to reconstruct your records.

- *Controlling the Folders*

24

Learning Outlook

Mⁱᶜʳᵒˢᵒᶠᵗ MICROSOFT OUTLOOK MAY BE INSTALLED VIA EITHER A NETWORK or the Office 97 CD. Before you begin, be sure to have your CD containing the program ready, and quit any open programs.

To install programs in Windows 95 or later, click on the Start menu on the bottom of your screen, choose Settings, and then choose Control panels. In the Control Panels window, click on Add/Remove Programs. The Add/Remove Programs Properties window will appear, as shown in Figure 24.1.

Figure 24.1

The Add/Remove Programs Properties window

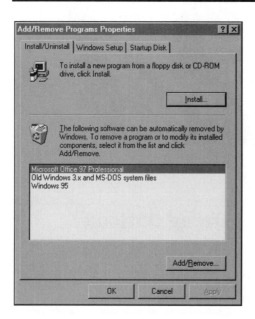

Click on the Install/Uninstall tab, then click on Add/Remove. The installer will give you further information and directions.

During the Setup program, Outlook will scan your computer to see if a user profile already exists. If you are working on a network, the administrator will have already created one. If you are working on a standalone PC and do not use a password to get into your computer, the Setup program will create a user profile for you. Information in your user profile documents whether you have an e-mail account or Internet connection, and if you have a personal folder. Outlook also needs to know what your information service is—this involves whether or not you are connected to the Microsoft Network, use Microsoft Exchange Server, or use personal folders.

If you know you are going to use Outlook in a networked setting that will incorporate e-mail, you may want to set up the network first so that you can test it. You can add or change your e-mail capabilities at any time, but you will have to add them to your user profile if you have already installed Outlook.

■ Controlling the Folders

One of the best ways to get organized is to make sure that you understand where the information is located, where it will be stored, and how you can access it. Boring, but true.

Reordering and Naming the Folders

A Personal folder is a file located on your computer's hard drive, not on a network server. Your Personal folder is identifiable by its .pst extension. Like other folders, your Personal folder can contain other folders, messages, forms, and files. If you wish, you can have incoming e-mail messages sent directly to your Personal folder. Because it serves so many valuable uses, you should make regular back-ups of your Personal folder file.

When customizing Microsoft Outlook, be sure to fully explore your options. To see these options, pull down the Tools menu and choose Options. A many-tabbed dialog box will appear, on your screen, as shown in Figure 24.2.

Figure 24.2

The Options dialog box

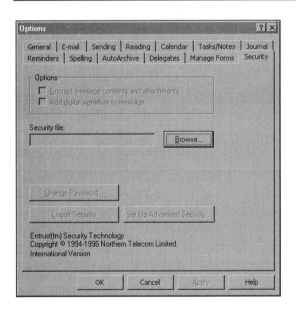

The tabs cover the following options:

- **General:** Use this screen to customize which folder Outlook should open in. The Inbox is a good choice if you use e-mail. On a standalone PC, the calendar might be a more useful choice. Here you can make decisions on how to handle deleting information and how to set up your modem. The General window is shown in Figure 24.3.

Figure 24.3

The General tab of the Options dialog box

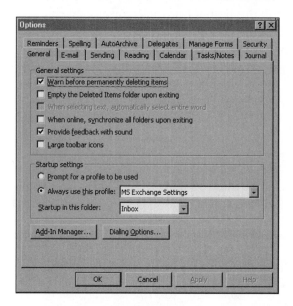

•   **E-mail:** Use this screen only if you use e-mail. Here you can customize how new items are handled and whether you want to use Word to read your new messages. The E-mail options window is shown in Figure 24.4.

•   **Sending:** These options are only of use to those with e-mail. Here you can set options for handling new messages, tracking messages, and implementing decisions about how and where to save messages. The Sending options screen is shown in Figure 24.5.

•   **Reading:** More options for those using e-mail. Here you can customize how to reference messages you are replying to, and set options for when to forward messages. The Reading options screen is shown in Figure 24.6.

•   **Calendar:** Everyone should take a look at the options in this window. Here you can indicate how many days appear in the work week, and what day the week starts on. You can also customize the hours displayed in the calendar—a nice option if your workday isn't 9 to 5. If you've ever forgotten anything, you may want to explore setting some of the reminder settings so that Outlook will provide on-screen prompts. Don't forget the buttons on the bottom of this screen either: you can add holidays in your calendar, set the time zone and, if you are on a network, set up some nifty advanced scheduling features. The Calendar options screen is shown in Figure 24.7.

Figure 24.4

The E-mail tab of the
Options dialog box

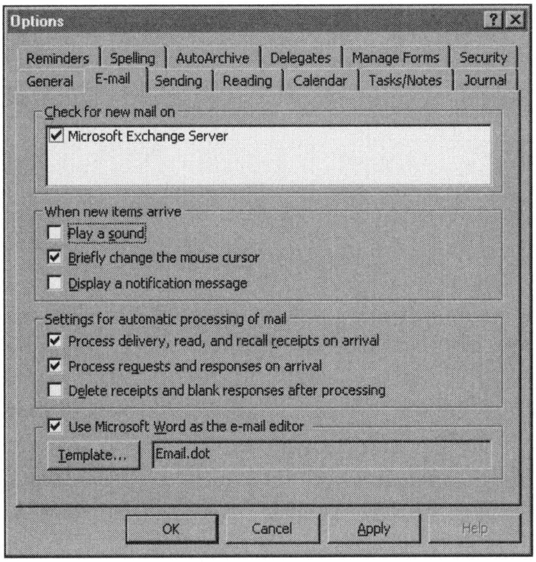

Figure 24.5

The Sending tab of the
Options dialog box

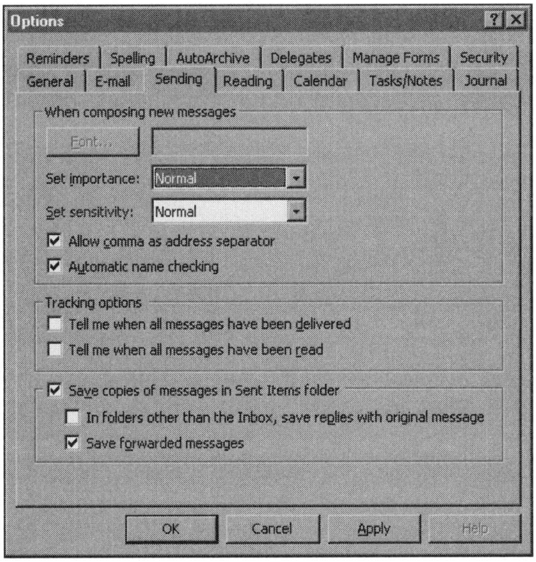

Figure 24.6

The Reading tab of the
Options dialog box

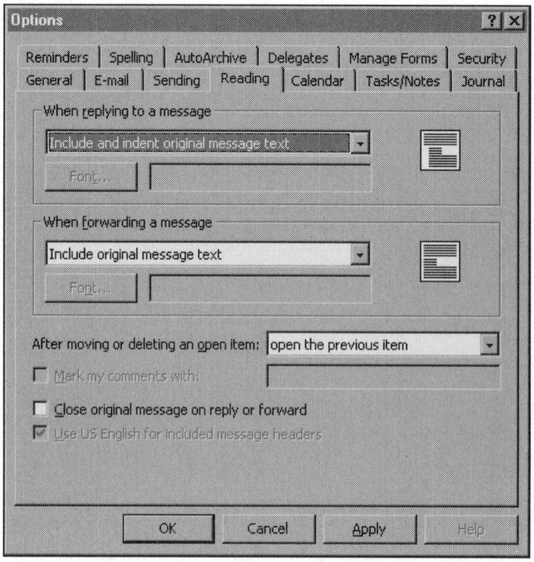

Figure 24.7

The Calendar tab of the
Options dialog box

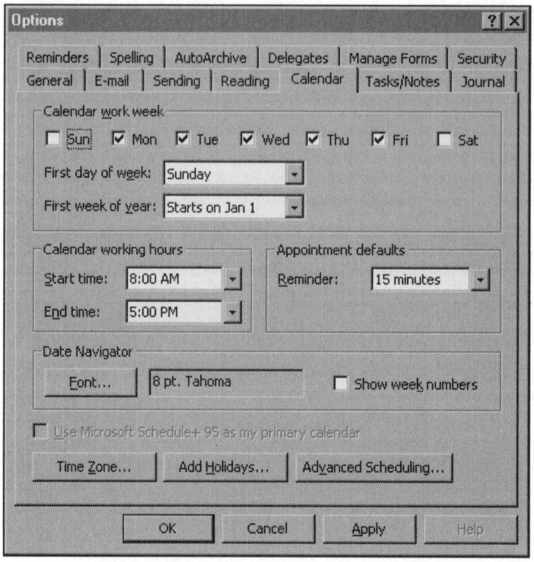

- **Tasks/Notes:** Here you have some powerful options for customizing the appearance of unfinished and completed tasks, and for the compilation of a status report. You can also change the color of the sticky notes, specify whether they include the time and date, and choose the font used. The Tasks/Notes options screen is shown in Figure 24.8.

Figure 24.8

The Tasks/Notes tab of the Options dialog box

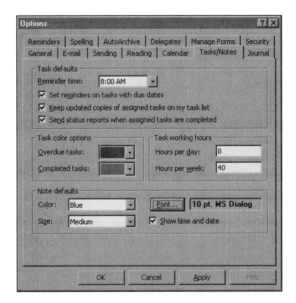

- **Journal:** The Outlook Journal keeps track of files you have worked with, e-mail, messages, and tasks, and may be limited to certain contacts. You could have the Journal record all client information, but disregard personal information. The Journal options screen is shown in Figure 24.9.

- **Reminders:** The two settings in Reminders allow you to display a reminder and choose whether or not to play a sound with the reminder. The Reminders options screen is shown in Figure 24.10.

- **Spelling:** The options in this window can save you a bit of embarrassment. You can specify whether to always check your spelling, whether to check before a message is sent, and whether to ignore uppercase letters and numbers. Another nice feature is the ability to specify ignoring text that you are quoting in a reply. The Spelling options window is shown in Figure 24.11.

- **Auto Archive:** Use this area to configure the frequency and location of archived backups. Outlook is preconfigured to perform an archive at startup every two weeks, so you might as well make your own settings here. The AutoArchive window is shown in Figure 24.12.

Figure 24.9

The Journal tab of the
Options dialog box

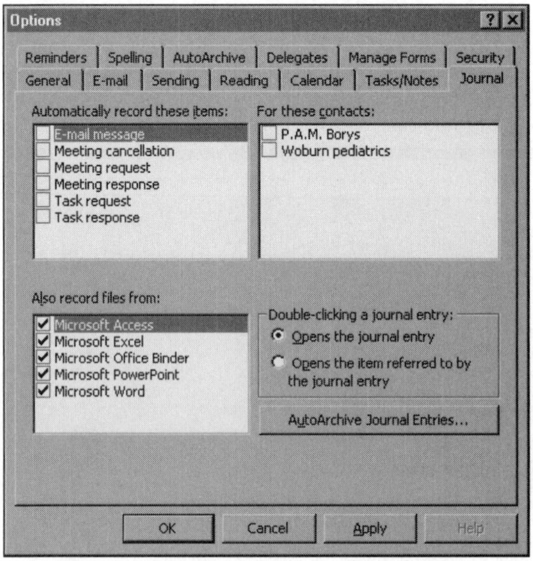

Figure 24.10

The Reminders tab of the
Options dialog box

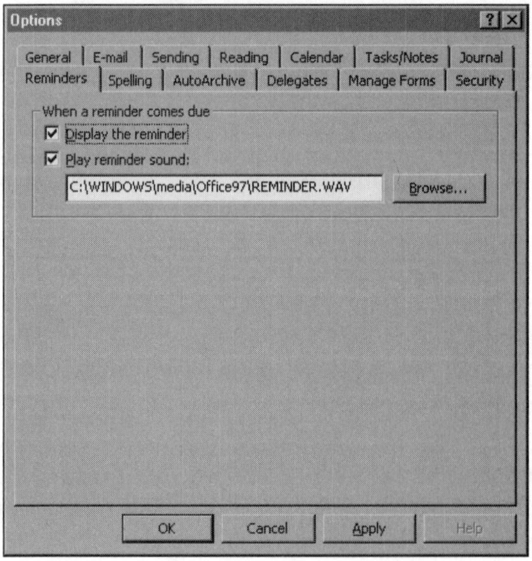

Figure 24.11

The Spelling tab of the
Options dialog box

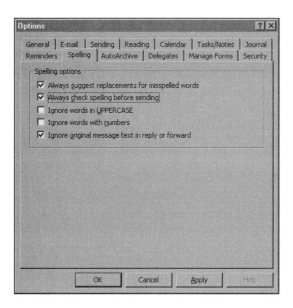

Figure 24.12

The Auto Archive tab of
the Options dialog box

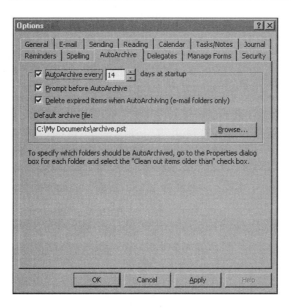

- **Manage Forms:** Click on the Manage Forms tab, then click on the Forms Manager button to display the screen, which allows you to import other forms into Outlook. To import forms, you'll need to locate the folder on the right that contains them. Then click on the Install button to move them to the left scrolling window. Uncheck the hidden checkbox to see which forms you have added. Choose Show Categories to view a description of the form's purpose. The Forms Manager window is shown in Figure 24.13.

Figure 24.13

The Forms Manager screen

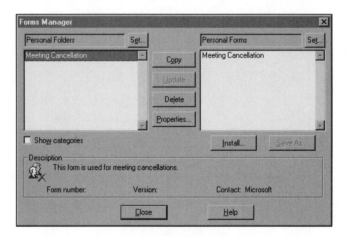

Now that you have customized Outlook, please make a backup copy!

Mastering Outlook Views

Outlook's different modules are presented visually, so it's hard to think of each module as a folder. To view the folder list in Outlook, click on the Inbox, then pull down the View menu and choose Folder list. A list of the folders used in Outlook will appear, as shown in Figure 24.14.

Click on a folder, and you will see a reduced size version of that module's contents. If you want to work this way, be sure to maximize the screen size by either clicking the maximize icon in the top right corner of your screen or grabbing the edge of the screen with your mouse and dragging it wider.

To create a new folder, click on the parent folder in the list, pull down the File menu, and choose Folder, create subfolder. Type in the folder name and description, then click Outlook.

In the sample below, I created two new folders: Miscellaneous, which is a subfolder of the personal folder; and Subrosa Journal, which is a subfolder of the Journal folder (see Figure 24.15).

Figure 24.14

The list of folders

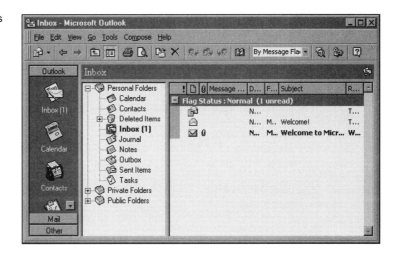

Figure 24.15

The folder list with
new folders

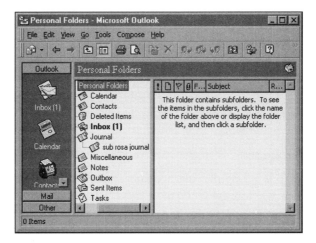

To add a folder to the left scrolling area of the Outlook window, click on a folder. Pull down the File menu and choose Add to Outlook Bar. Then click Outlook: the item will be automatically added. The folders displayed will reflect the latest activity.

One major advantage Microsoft Outlook has over other organizational tools is that it gives users the ability to view the information in a given folder in several views. Each folder contains different types of information, so some views are specialized. Read this list over carefully, because it will suggest ways of working more effectively—in your own style.

Inbox

Your Inbox stores incoming messages. Outlook's views allow you to view your messages according to different criteria. To view the Inbox options, pull down the View menu and choose Current View. The hierarchical menu will display the following options:

- **Messages:** Messages are displayed in a list in the Inbox.

- **Messages with AutoPreview:** The first three lines of the message text are displayed.

- **By Message Flag:** Messages are grouped by message flag. The due date for follow-up action for the message flag is also displayed, if appropriate.

- **Last Seven Days:** Only the messages received in the last seven days are displayed.

- **Flagged for Next Seven Days:** Only the messages that display a message flag requiring follow-up within the next seven days are displayed.

- **By Conversation Topic:** Messages are grouped by subject.

- **By Sender:** Messages are grouped by sender.

- **Unread Messages:** Only messages that are unread, or marked as unread, are listed.

- **Sent To:** Messages that you have sent are listed by the names of the recipients.

- **Message Timeline:** Chronologically ordered icons show the messages you have sent on a timeline.

Calendar

Outlook's Calendar incorporates much useful information. Outlook's views allow you to view your calendar information according to different criteria. To view the Calendar options, pull down the View menu and choose Current View. The hierarchical menu will display the following options:

- **Day/Week/Month:** Choose this view to display your appointments, events, and meetings by the day, week, or month. This view is familiar, as it resembles a pocket calendar or personal planner. A list of tasks is also included.

- **Active Appointments:** Choose this view to display all commitments (and their details) that begin today and extend into the future.

- **Events:** Use this view to display a listing of all events and pertinent details.

- **Annual Events:** Use this view to display yearly events and pertinent information in a list.

- **Recurring Appointments:** Use this view to list recurring appointments and their details.

- **By Category:** If you record category information, you can display calendar items by category.

Calendar TaskPad

The Calendar's TaskPad can be viewed in several ways: see Figure 24.16 for an example. To view the TaskPad options, pull down the View menu and choose TaskPad view. The hierarchical menu will display the following options:

- **All Tasks:** Choose this view to see a list of all tasks.

- **Today's Tasks:** Choose this view for a list of tasks due on or after today.

- **Active Tasks for Selected Days:** Choose this view to help plan your time and to view tasks that are on the days you have selected. If you select several nonadjacent days, Outlook will display only the active tasks for the first day you have selected.

- **Tasks for Next Seven Days:** Choose this view to display any tasks for the next seven days that have not been completed.

- **Overdue Tasks:** Use this view to see if anything has escaped your attention. Outlook will display any incomplete tasks with expired completion dates.

Figure 24.16

The TaskPad

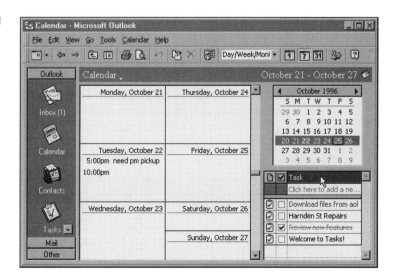

- **Tasks Completed on Selected Days:** Use this view to show your boss how productive you are. In this view, Outlook lists all completed tasks for the days you have selected.

Contacts

The contact information you enter in Outlook is organized into named fields, and Microsoft has designed some very useful views for the Contact module. To use these views from the Contact module, pull down the View menu and choose Current View. The following list displays to the right of the menu:

- **Address Cards:** Use this view to emulate a Rolodex with one mailing address plus business and home phone numbers.

- **Detailed Address Cards:** Use this view to capture more complete information, such as business and home addresses, additional phone numbers, and other details.

- **Phone List:** Use this view for a company phone list with company name, business phone number, business fax number, and home phone number.

- **By Category:** If you use categories, you can create a contact list ordered by categories. The contacts under each category will be alphabetically sorted.

- **By Company:** Use this view to create a company directory list organized by company and containing job title, company name, department, business phone number, and business fax number.

- **By Location:** Create a geographical contact list sorted by country containing company name, state, country, business phone number, and home phone number.

To improve the way Outlook sorts a view, pull down the View menu and choose Group by. The Group By dialog box will appear, as shown in Figure 24.17.

To select a field to sort by, click on the top scrolling box. If you want to perform additional sorting criteria, select other fields from the additional scrolling lists. I found this helpful when I modified the Contact view by location, which sorted entries by nation. Instead, I selected State as the primary sorting key and Company name as the secondary sorting key.

Tasks

The Tasks window provides more room for detail than the TaskPad, which is part of the calendar module. To use any of the views below, click Tasks. Pull down the View menu and select Current View, then select the desired view from the hierarchical menu to the right. All views will display the task icon, subject, and due date at minimum. Other views provide more details. The Tasks window is shown in Figure 24.18.

Figure 24.17

The Group By dialog box

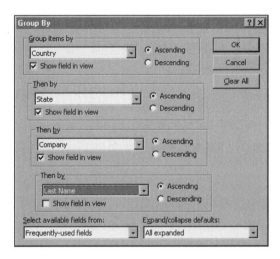

Figure 24.18

The Task window
Detail view

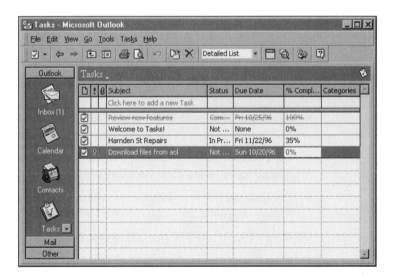

- **Simple List:** Use the simple list to view tasks that remain to be completed.

- **Detailed List:** Use this detailed view to document task priority, percentage complete, and other details.

- **Active Tasks:** Use this view to list all incomplete tasks.

- **Tasks for Next Seven Days:** Choose this view to display any tasks for the next seven days that have not been completed.

- **Overdue Tasks:** Use this view to see if anything has escaped your attention. Outlook will display any incomplete tasks with expired completion dates.

- **By Category:** If you use categories, this is a great way to group the types of tasks you need to accomplish.

- **Assignment:** Use this view only if you delegate tasks to others. Information includes only those tasks which have been assigned to others, and is sorted by task owner and due date.

- **By Person Responsible:** Use this view to list tasks which have been delegated. The list is sorted by task owner and by due date.

- **Completed Tasks:** Use this view to list tasks that have been marked complete.

- **Task Timeline:** Use this view to create a timeline on which tasks are represented by icons, and displayed in chronological order by start date. Tasks without explicit start dates will be positioned on the timeline according to their due date.

Journal

Outlook stores a record of your actions in the Journal module. You can view this information as a timeline organized by date. To use the other views from the Journal module, pull down the View menu, choose Current View, and make a selection from the hierarchical list that pops up:

- **By Type:** Choose this view to see all journal entries arranged by type on a timeline.

- **By Contact:** Employ this view when you want to view all journal entries organized by contact name on a timeline.

- **By Category:** If you assign categories as you work in Outlook, use this view to organize all journal entries by category on a timeline.

- **Entry List:** This view puts journal entries in a list.

- **Last Seven Days:** Use this view to see all journal entries from the last seven days in a list.

- **Phone Calls:** Use this view to provide a record of all phone-call journal entries you have entered in Outlook. An example of this view is shown in Figure 24.19.

Figure 24.19

The Journal
phone-call view

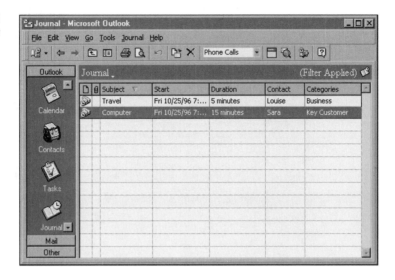

Notes

One problem with those sticky notes is that you end up with quite a bit of clutter when you use more than two. Outlook provides you with several options for viewing notes, which makes using them much more effective. From the Notes module, pull down the View menu, choose Current View, and make a selection from the pop-up menu on the right.

- **Icons:** Use this view to have Outlook display Notes by icons according to creation date.

- **Notes List:** Use this view to obtain a list of notes sorted by creation date.

- **Last Seven Days:** Use this view to create a list of notes made in the last seven days.

- **By Category:** If you use categories, use this view to order notes by category. Each category list is then sorted by creation date. An example of this view is shown in Figure 24.20.

- **By Color:** If you choose different colors of notes for different tasks, you can use this view to sort notes in a list by color. Each color list is then sorted by creation date.

Figure 24.20

Viewing Notes by category

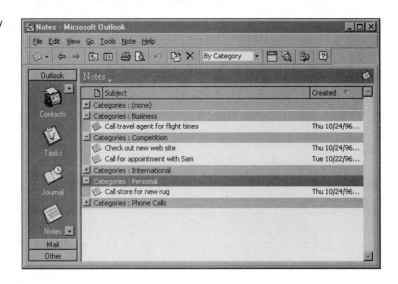

Other

As we've seen, the views offered in Outlook extend the usefulness of this program. Since the standard complaint regarding personal information managers is that they don't adequately reflect the needs of the individual using them, Microsoft has also enabled users to customize views to meet their own needs.

Before you begin customizing, consider whether or not you are sharing information across a network. If so, you may want to speak to your network administrator first. In this way, the administrator can decide whether to implement these changes on a wider scale, and will be better able to answer the "Why is my screen different?" question.

When you create custom views, you determine how the information is grouped and sorted. You can also customize the column settings.

To customize a view, first select the module you want to work from. Pull down the View menu and choose Define Views. The Define Views dialog box will appear, as shown in Figure 24.21.

To create a new view, click New, and the Create a New View dialog box will appear to show you your options (see Figure 24.22).

We recommend that in your first attempts at customization you copy an existing view and experiment by modifying its information and presentation. This way you'll be able to gain an appreciation of what happens when you change the fonts used. If you are on a network, be sure that the fonts used are shared by all other computers you are sharing Outlook information with.

Figure 24.21

The Define Views
dialog box

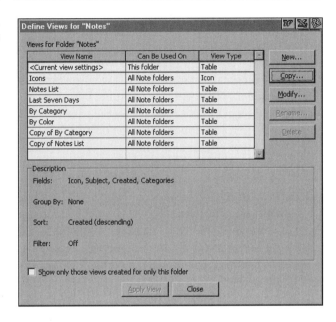

Figure 24.22

The Create a New View
dialog box

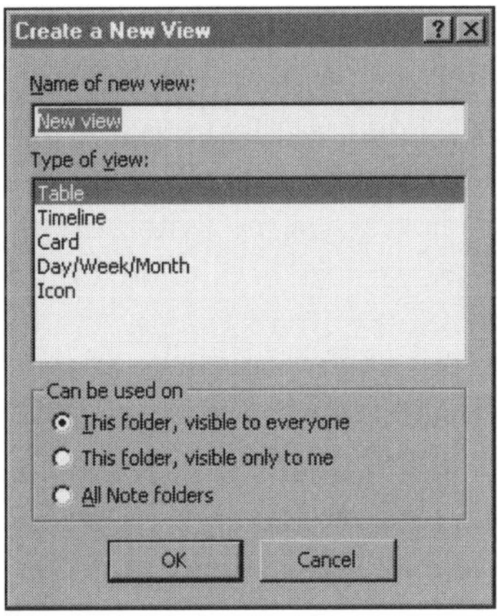

Exchanging Data

One way to exchange information is copying it from one document or program and pasting it into another document or program.

Microsoft Office programs are smart about sharing information with each other. You can paste information from Excel into Word, and your formatting will survive. When you cut or copy to another program the information is pasted, if possible, in a format that the receiving program can edit. If you set up a document with Word and separate the columns with tabs, you can paste this information into Excel and the information will be poured into Excel's rows and columns. Even a report generated in Access can be pasted into Excel, with each column representing a field value and each row representing a complete record. In many cases you will be able to edit the information you have pasted in. When you can't edit the information, it will be treated as an embedded object that is editable by the parent program, which will be launched when you double-click the object.

Sometimes programs are not capable of sharing information. In this case, information pasted into a destination document cannot be updated or changed.

You can use the source program to edit embed-.5 ded objects. If the information can't be inserted, it will be pasted as a static picture that cannot be edited.

If you're in doubt as to how much information will be pasted into a document, pull down the Edit menu of the destination program and choose Paste Special. There you will be able to make several choices about the information to be pasted.

Updating Other Folders with Outlook

Keeping information updated is a must. You can synchronize (update) another folder with Outlook very easily. But be sure that you have a backup first, lest you overwrite the wrong data. First, choose an Outlook folder, such as your Inbox. Then pull down the Tools menu and choose Synchronize. Click on This Folder to update the information. To update all information before you log off, specify this option by pulling down the Tools menu, selecting the General tab and clicking on the Synchronize all folders checkbox. Each time you use the Synchronize command, Outlook creates a log file detailing the action in the Deleted Items folder.

Text Files and other file types

It's easy to share text files with the following file types listed in Table 24.1.

There are several file types that can be used to import data to or export data from Outlook. Table 24.2 lists the programs, the file types, and the import/export compatibility for each. Other file filters may become available: Check with Microsoft's web site **Error! Bookmark not defined.** if you need a specific filter.

Please note that the filters ACT! 2.0; ECCO Pro 3.0, 3.01, or 3.02; Side-Kick 1.0/95; Journal, and Notes are on the Office 97 CD-ROM and are not automatically installed with Outlook. If you have access to the World Wide Web from your Office computer, pull down the Help menu, select Microsoft on the Web, and click Free Stuff.

Table 24.1

Text File and Format Types for Importing to and Exporting from Outlook

FORMAT	FILE EXTENSION	IMPORT TO OUTLOOK	EXPORT FROM OUTLOOK
Comma Separated (DOS)	.txt	Yes	Yes
Tab Separated (DOS)	.txt	Yes	Yes
Tab Separated (Windows)	.txt	Yes	Yes
Rich text (Windows)	.rtf	Yes	Yes
Comma Separated (Windows)	.csv	Yes	Yes

Table 24.2

File and Format Types for Importing to and Exporting from Outlook

PROGRAM	FILE EXTENSION	IMPORT TO OUTLOOK	EXPORT FROM OUTLOOK
Microsoft Schedule+ 1.0	.cal	Yes	No
Microsoft Schedule+ 95	.scd	Yes	No
Microsoft Exchange Personal Address Book	.pab	Yes	No
ACT! 2.0 for Windows	.dbf	Yes	No
ECCO 3.0, 3.01, or 3.02	.eco	Yes	No
SideKick 1.0/95	.skcard	Yes	No
Lotus Organizer 1.0, 1.1, 2.1	.org, .or2	Yes	No
Microsoft Access	.mdb	Yes	Yes
Microsoft Excel	.xls	Yes	Yes
Microsoft FoxPro	.dbf	Yes	Yes
dBASE	.dbf	Yes	Yes

Sharing information with Public Folders

You can share documents and other information by putting it in a place where everyone on your network can see it—in a public folder. To set up public folders, you must use Microsoft Exchange Server, and you must have permission to read items on the network. If you are in doubt about either of these, speak to your network manager. Public folders can include custom views, forms, custom fields, and rules.

Public folders can store any type of file or Outlook item. All information in a public folder will be shared with all those on your network who have read permission, so there are some things that should not be placed in a public folder—your resume, for instance! Besides being an ideal place to store files that will be needed by others in your workgroup, public folders can be a location for your group to share ideas. Of course, the most obvious use—housing Outlook information—means that others in your workgroup will be apprised of meetings and tasks, and will have access to a central contact list.

Other Systems

The beauty of Outlook is that it is optimized to work across a network. But what if your company still thinks that "sneakernet," the transporting of files by hand-carried floppy disk, is high-tech? Also, if your computer is hooked up to a modem and your recipient has an e-mail address, you will be able to send files and messages to their Internet account or America Online.

You can transport files by floppy or modem, but be sure that the recipient has a program to open the files with. I composed a Note file and saved it as an RTF file. I opened the same file on a Macintosh. When I double-clicked on it, it was opened by a program called SimpleText and was quite garbled. When I launched Microsoft Word for the Mac and then opened the file, I was able to view the note, because Word has a translator for RTF files. The note appeared as a Word document, the formatting as a note on colored paper was lost in the conversion.

Mail Merge with Outlook and Word

When you perform a mail merge, you take a file that contains layout information and marry it to another file of information to produce a third unique file, which contains the sense of one and the substance of another.

Microsoft Word can use another Word file or a file from Access, Outlook, or Excel as the data document. If you plan on frequently creating merged documents like form letters and labels, you need to consider how complicated the merging will be. If you will be drawing information that needs to be calculated or sorted, it may be better to use a data document from Access or Excel.

The Mail Merge Helper is available to you when you pull down Word's Tool menu and choose Merge. It will step you through each part of the mail-merge process. Word also has a wizard for merging letters and labels, which you may find helpful.

If you only need to merge some of the names and addresses from the Outlook Contact module, create a new contacts folder with the information to be merged.

Archiving Your Data

If you are foolish enough to get on several mailing lists and go away on vacation, you can be sure that junk mail will have piled up in your absence. After your vacation, you'll have the task of trying to decide what to keep, what to throw out, and what needs your immediate attention.

In the same way that your physical mailbox gets cluttered, the contents of your Outlook mailbox can get out of hand. Outlook provides you with the ability to discard the messages you don't want, and to store others for future reference or back-up.

Archiving vs. AutoArchiving

When you make a conscious decision to archive some items, pull down the File menu, then choose Archive. This will transfer aged items to a special storage file. AutoArchiving is an Outlook feature that automatically archives items at pre-set intervals. Microsoft Outlook AutoArchives several folders as a default. The folders and their time periods are:

- Calendar (6 months)

- Tasks (6 months)

- Journal (6 months)

- Sent Items (2 months)

- Deleted Items (2 months)

Inbox, Notes, and Contacts modules that you may use often are not set to AutoArchive when you first install Outlook.

To specify the settings for archiving and AutoArchiving, pull down the File menu and choose Properties. The Properties dialog box will appear, as shown in Figure 24.23.

Near the bottom of the dialog box, clear the check box if you do not want Outlook to perform an AutoArchive.

Select a folder, then pull down the File menu to choose archive. You will see the dialog box shown in Figure 24.24. In this dialog box, you need to choose the specific folders and/or subfolders you wish to archive. Click on the calendar for a pop-up screen, and choose the date that will act as the starting date for the archive.

To adjust your AutoArchive settings, pull down the Tools menu and click on the AutoArchive tab.

Be aware that if you want any files other than the Outlook information to be included in an archive, these files must be stored in a mail folder.

Archiving removes items from their original location and places them in an archive document. An archive reflects the current status of your folder

Figure 24.23

The Properties dialog box

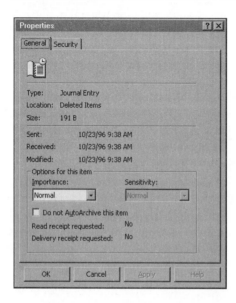

Figure 24.24

The Archive dialog box

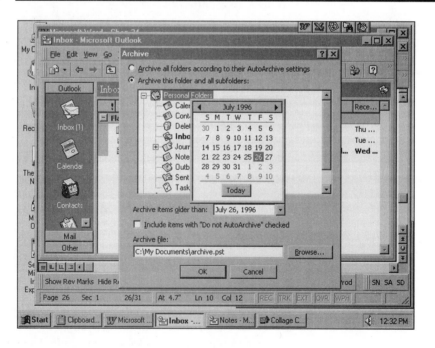

structure. Even empty folders are included in an archive. Exporting Outlook information copies the information, possibly to a different format in another program or location. When you export information, you still have a copy of the original file.

Retrieve Archived items

To retrieve information from an archive file, you'll need to either import the archive file by using the import command on the File menu, or add the archive file to your user profile. Adjusting your user profile will involve adding another information service to your profile. When this is done, the archive file is attached to your mailbox.

Some Effective Habits of Highly Organized People

No, this isn't a section on management. The traits below were adapted from *The Organized Executive*, a book by Stephanie Winston. These work habits can be made even more efficient with Outlook, so Table 24.3 reviews the ways you might be able to save time and effort on the following tasks.

Table 24.3

Using Outlook to Become More Efficient

Standardize repetitive tasks to save time	Use the Event feature on your calendar to note recurring events. Handle the same type of task the same way: for instance, consider using Outlook to dial phone numbers so you can effectively keep notes on the conversation within Outlook and post reminders on your calendar.
Consolidate actions by grouping tasks	If Outlook just doesn't feel right to you, consider using some of the other templates provided, or customizing the appearance and content of the forms.
Delegate effectively	From the tasks module, pull down the Task menu and choose New Task Request. Here you can name the task, specify how much time it should take, indicate its urgency, send it via e-mail, and receive a status report on its progress.
Make the most efficient use of their surroundings	
Devote an appropriate amount of time for each task	Use the Calendar, Task, and Notes modules to keep you from forgetting other commitments or spending too much (or too little) time on a project or task.
Save time by planning ahead	Use the Calendar feature to record events, recurring appointments, and scheduled meetings. If you need to block out times where you won't be interrupted, designate a block of time as "busy."

With all these features at your fingertips, what else can they teach you at the Harvard Business School?

- *Understanding Outlook Networking*
- *Setting Outlook Options*
- *Controlling Access to Your Information*
- *Using Meeting Features*

25

Networking Outlook

In the beginning, a personal information manager (PIM) revolutionized only a single person's ability to manage time. Office 97 builds on the improved networking capabilities introduced in Windows 95. If your computer is on a network—that is to say, it is physically connected to other computers—you may be able to use Outlook to improve how an entire group of people manages its time and resources.

■ Understanding Outlook Networking

Networks may take several forms. In a *peer-to-peer* network, computers are physically connected to each other, and one user can share information located on another user's hard drive. Each machine on the network is the equal to another: they are all peers.

In a *client-server* network, however, a *server* (typically a more powerful machine with a large hard drive) serves information and programs to *clients*, individual computers connected to the network. Only information that is either stored on the server or transmitted through it can be shared with others. Typically, when information or programs on the server are being accessed by many people at the same time, the speed of the network slows dramatically. If all the information is located on the server and the network "goes down" or "crashes," you will all have an extended coffee break, because you won't be able to get at that information. If a peer-to-peer network goes down, only the users sharing information with each other are affected. Other individual computer users are able to keep working with the information on their hard drives.

It's important to understand that for computers to be able to share information, there has to be some type of connection: either a physical connection, like a cable; or an electronic connection, like an e-mail service. E-mail, short for electronic mail, uses a computer, modem, telephone line, and special software. With e-mail, you can type a message and send it to the recipient's e-mail address. When you send the message, the recipient has to open his or her Inbox and double-click on the message to read it.

People tend to regard e-mail as an electronic version of the traditional postal service. Paper mail is private, to be opened by the addressee only, and its contents are protected by an envelope. E-mail, on the other hand, can easily be read by others, and you should consider that your boss or network administrator may have a password that enables him or her to read all of your e-mail. While our legislators decide how to treat the contents of e-mail, follow this basic rule: Never put anything in an e-mail message that must remain private, or that might embarrass you.

It is easy to copy a message and forward it to someone else, which can cause untold embarrassment—as the following true story indicates. At one company, someone made an alluring video that she attached to an e-mail message sent to her lover. When sending the message and file, she inadvertently copied the message to others in her workgroup. The little movie was soon widely viewed, which caused a lot of embarrassment, and affected the credibility of both employees.

Another source of embarrassment comes from sending off messages too quickly. All too often, e-mails that are otherwise thoughtful are larded with misspellings and unclear thoughts. If you feel angry, go ahead and type that angry message—but don't send it. "Flames" (angry messages) have a way of being copied and commented on, and even printed out and thumb-tacked on office walls. They generally do more to harm to the sender than the recipient.

Being connected is fun, and it's a great way to share information. It's best to use e-mail and networking judiciously. If you are sending constant e-mails, you are filling up someone's Inbox, taking up their time, and interrupting their chain of thought.

■ Setting Outlook Options

Outlook is new to the Office suite of software products, and serves as the unifying piece that connects program to program or co-worker to co-worker. Outlook has a number of options, each of which can be used very effectively in certain settings. Read Table 25.1 to determine which features could be useful in your organization.

Table 25.1

Networked Features of
Outlook 97

FEATURE	USE IT TO...
Customizable Views	Customize the group, sort, and column settings for your workgroup.
Attendee list	View a list of others attending a meeting to which you have been invited.
AutoDial	Have Outlook dial phone numbers you have added to your contact list.
Phone call tracking	Keep notes on a call and track the call's duration.
Delegate Access and folder permissions	Provide another person with the authority to control who gets access to your Outlook folders and to send mail on your behalf. You can also use this feature to assign read, modify, or create permissions in your public and private folders via the Microsoft Exchange Server.
E-mail	Notify others of meetings and tasks, send attached files, and do general messaging.
Group scheduling	View available meeting times, schedule meetings, and send invitations.
Public folders	Store and share information with others on your network.
Assign a task	Create a record of the tasks you have delegated via Outlook e-mail. Outlook compiles a status report on every task accepted by its recipient. Otherwise, the task is returned to the sender, or can be given to another person.
Voting	Create, send, and tally votes to a multiple-choice question sent via e-mail, such as, "which toppings do you want on your pizza? Plain, Mushroom, Eggplant."
Outlook Forms	Create forms used for data entry or display.

If you don't have Outlook installed on a company network, you can still use Outlook with Internet e-mail. The Table 25.2 shows some of the creative ways you can use Outlook's Internet capabilities.

Table 25.2

Networked Features of
Outlook 97

FEATURE	USE IT TO...
AutoNameCheck	Automatically look up any names or addresses that you type in messages.
Contact World Wide Web page access	Maintain the URL for a contact's Web page.
Hyperlinks in mail messages	Create a hyperlink within a message that will enable the message's recipient to click the link and move to that address.
Internet mail and meeting requests	Send and receive Internet mail requests for meetings by using an Internet Service Provider (ISP) or Microsoft Exchange Server's Internet Mail Connector.
Organize Web pages in a public folder	Collect Web pages for a group to share, and keep track of how often these pages are used, when they are updated, who owns the pages, and more.
World Wide Web favorites	Quickly open your Web browser and go to your favorite Web pages from the Favorites Shortcut on the Outlook Bar. Store Web page addresses in public folders to share with a workgroup or organization.

■ Controlling Access to Your Information

As long as you are connected by network or modem, you can set up Outlook to take advantage of these features. Because company policies on network communications and user settings vary, have your network guru set up Outlook on each networked computer. Discuss who should have access or "permissions" to view various types of files. This is done by changing the user profile in the Policy Editor—something not to be tried by the inexperienced. The Table 25.3 lists the levels of permission, and what each allows a user to do. The Microsoft Exchange Server is needed to use public folders or share private folders.

If you find that you are frustrated in your ability to use Outlook over a network, you should check your permission level and speak to your boss about getting the privileges you need. You may have different levels of permission for different folders.

Table 25.3

Outlook Permissions

WITH THIS LEVEL OF PERMISSION	YOU CAN...
Owner	Own a folder, which means you can create new items; read, modify, and delete any folder contents; and assign permissions to others on the network. You can also change the file structure by adding subfolders.
Publishing Editor	Do everything an owner can do, except change permissions.
Editor	Do everything the Publishing Editor can do, except create subfolders.
Publishing Author	Read items and files; create subfolders; and create, edit, and delete new items and folders.
Author	Work only on items that you create. You edit and delete your documents.
Reviewer	Read anything in the folder.
Contributor	Create new items and files, but you may not view the folder's content list.
Custom	Do anything specified by the owner of the folder.
None	Do nothing in this folder.

To grant other people access to your folders, use the Delegate Access feature, which is only available with Microsoft Exchange Server. You *must* be connected to the server to proceed any further. To check on the status of the Microsoft Exchange Server, pull down the Tools menu, choose Options, then click on the General tab. Finally, click on the Add-Ins Manager button to open the Add-Ins Manager, as shown in Figure 25.1.

Figure 25.1

The Add-Ins Manager

NOTE. *If the Microsoft Exchange Server is not on your list, you must install it. Speak to your network administrator about how to do this.*

To set permissions for a folder, pull down the View menu and choose Folder List to open the folder list, as shown in Figure 25.2.

Figure 25.2

The folder list

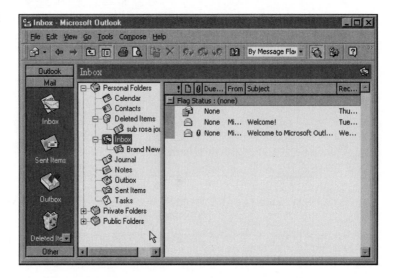

Select the folder you wish to share, pull down the File menu, and either choose Properties or right-click on the folder icon to bring up the Properties screen. Click on the Permissions tab, click the Add button and type the name of the person you are granting privileges to, and click on the Add button, as shown in Figure 25.3.

Now, click the name you just added, and select the desired permissions in the Roles box.

If the Properties dialog is grayed out, Microsoft Exchange has not been set up properly. To set multiple permissions, pull down the Tools menu, select Options, and then click on the Delegate Access tab.

When you delegate access to your folders, you make it possible for someone else to work on your behalf. You determine the level of authority they have, and can change this level at any time. Delegating access is handy if you're just too busy to handle things yourself, if you're on vacation, or if you want to see how someone else would handle additional responsibilities.

If you want to send an e-mail message notifying someone that he or she has just been given delegate status, make sure there is a check by the Automatically send a message to delegate summarizing these permissions checkbox.

Figure 25.3

Adding privileges in the
Properties dialog box

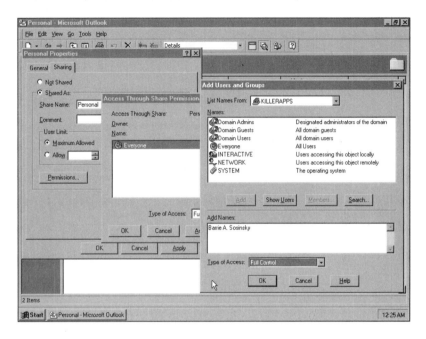

You can add more than one delegate by choosing more names in the Add
Users dialog box.

To send your delegate copies of meeting requests and responses, grant
the delegate Editor status and place a checkmark in the Delegate receives
copies of meeting-related messages sent to me check box.

To accept meetings or tasks for the manager, delegates must have Editor
status in a manager's Calendar or Tasks folder as well as Reviewer status in
the manager's Inbox.

The only time a delegate does not need the two permissions above is
when a manager puts a checkmark by the Send meeting requests and responses only to my delegates, not to me check box on the Delegates tab.

■ Using Meeting Features

Outlook's calendar module boasts an effective set of meeting tools, which
can help just about anyone who's trying to avoid having to be in two meetings at the same time. To use the features, you must be in the calendar. Pull
down the calendar menu and choose New Meeting Request. Outlook will display the untitled screen shown in Figure 25.4.

Figure 25.4

The New Meeting
Request dialog box

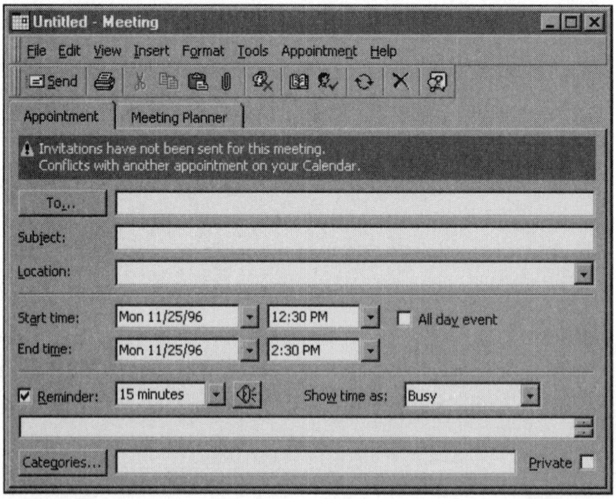

Click on the To: field, and Outlook will display the Select Attendees and Resources dialog box, as shown in Figure 25.5. Any entries you have made in your Contact list or any other address book will be available. If you can't locate a name quickly, click on the Find button at the bottom of the screen to display any names containing the letters you type.

Figure 25.5

The Select Attendees and
Resources dialog box

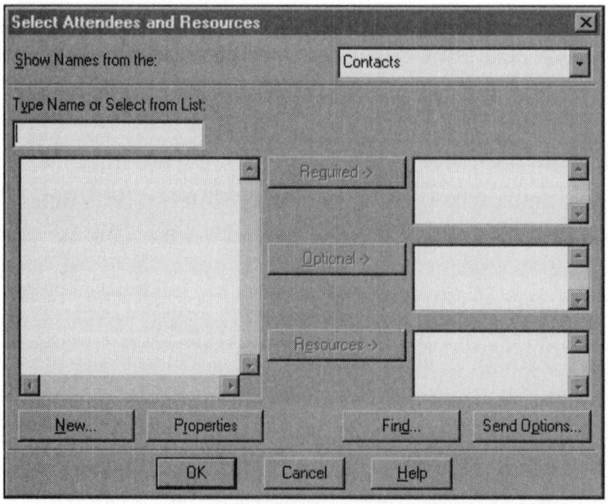

Use the Required field to indicate who must be at the meeting. If someone's attendance is not mandatory, click Optional. By listing the room and any other required items, such as projection equipment, in the Resources box, you can help make meetings more successful. Now click OK to return to the new meeting request form, and complete the time and date information, as shown in Figure 25.6.

Figure 25.6

The New Meeting dialog box with meeting information

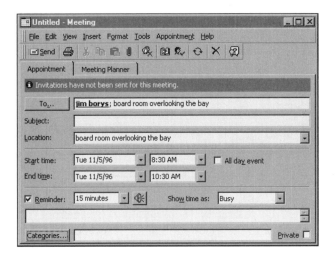

At this point, all that's left is to send the information—unless, of course, you want to track how much meeting time is spent on a given project or subject. To track this kind of information, you need to use categories. The Categories field is on the bottom of the New Meeting Request window. If you know the category, you can simply type it. Otherwise, click on the Categories bottom of the screen. Drag the screen a bit larger if the Category button is obscured. The Categories screen is displayed in Figure 25.7.

Click on a category, or type a new one and click the Add button to create more useful categories. Using categories is like using any filing system: it's only worthwhile if it's done in a systematic way. Be sure to notify others of the categories to use for various projects.

If you want to keep a meeting, its topics, and its attendees private from others who have access to your calendar, click on the Private button on the bottom right of the screen.

Using the Meeting Planner

To use the meeting planner, either click on the Meeting Planner tab of the Request New Meeting dialog box, or pull down the Calendar menu and choose Meeting Planner. You must be in the Calendar mode to access this command.

The Meeting Planner relies on everyone in your workgroup using their calendars to indicate time that is free, busy, or tentatively scheduled; and to

Figure 25.7

The Categories screen

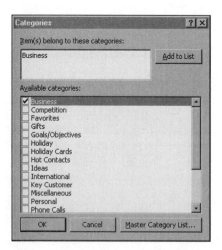

indicate events or other appointments. If people who need to come to meetings are not keeping their calendars up-to-date, you will have very mixed results with the Meeting Planner. If someone in your group does not keep e-mail in the Inbox, that person will not be aware of meetings, appointments, or schedule changes. It's always a good idea to follow up e-mail with a personal confirmation—especially if someone has been out of the office.

The Meeting Planner displays the time commitments of others as you type each name in the All Attendees field with the Show Attendee Availability option checked. To use the AutoPick feature, enter the date of the meeting and the desired attendees' names, then click on AutoPick. A vertical set of lines will be positioned to delineate a possible meeting time, as shown in Figure 25.8. You can drag the bars to new locations, widen them to extend the meeting's duration, or click the AutoPick button again.

The start and end times for the meeting will be displayed; you can also type new information here to change a meeting time. If the time isn't working out right, click the Show Attendee Status button to show the importance of invited attendees, as shown in Figure 25.9. If attending the meeting is optional for some people, you may be able to reschedule the meeting better to meet the needs of those who really must be there. When you are finished, send the meeting invitation by clicking the Send button on your Toolbar or by pressing Ctrl+Enter.

If you want potential attendees to issue the equivalent of an RSVP to you, pull down the Appointment menu and choose Request Responses. When you check on the status of each attendee later, you will be able to see if they have accepted, declined, or ignored your message.

Figure 25.8

The Meeting Planner with
drag bars

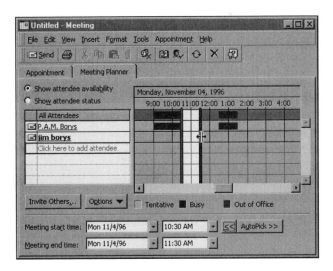

Figure 25.9

The Show Attendee
Status screen

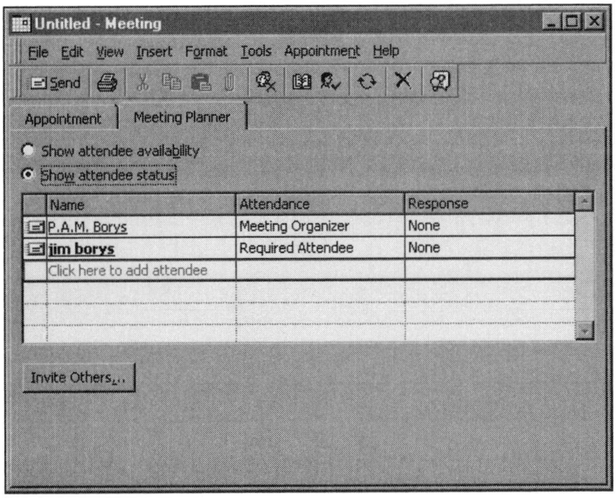

Rescheduling and Canceling Meetings

While the Meeting Planner may seem like so much magic, it's really not.
Gathering people together takes a lot of work, not to mention the ability to
compromise. You need to be able to cancel or reschedule meetings. To "unin-
vite" someone, click on the Cancel Invitation icon shown in Figure 25.10, or
pull down the meeting menu and choose Cancel Invitation.

Figure 25.10

The Cancel Invitation icon

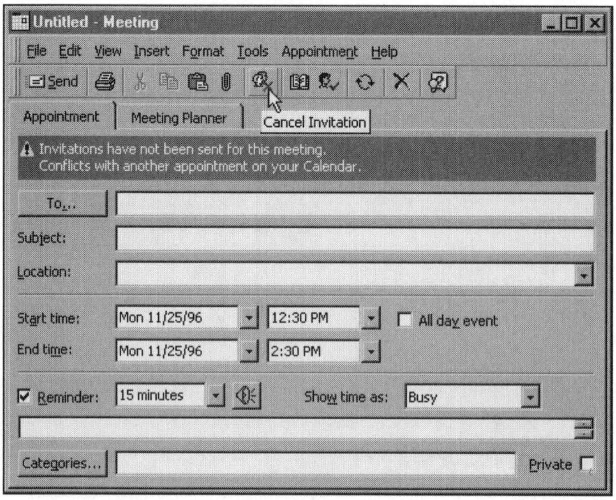

To reschedule a meeting after you have already invited people, you first need to open the Meeting file. Make any needed changes to the Appointment tab, and select the information you need to change. Click the OK button, and click Save and Close.

Remember, when working with appointments, events, and meetings, you must first click the Calendar in the Outlook Bar. Table 25.4 summarizes some of the common tasks associated with using meetings and events in Outlook.

Table 25.4

Summary of Meeting
Functions

FUNCTION	TYPE	DO THIS...
Create	Meeting	Choose New Meeting Request from the Calendar menu
Create	Recurring appointment	Choose New Recurring Appointment from the Calendar menu
Create	Recurring meeting	Choose New Recurring Meeting from the Calendar menu.
Create	Event	Choose New Event from the Calendar menu.
Create	Annual/recurring event	Choose New Recurring Event from the Calendar menu.
Create	Task from appointment	Drag the appointment to the Tasks icon on the Outlook Bar.

FUNCTION	TYPE	DO THIS...
Delete	Appointment, event, or meeting	Click on the appointment, event, or meeting; pull down Edit menu; and choose Delete.
View	Date/week	Pull down the Go menu, and choose Go to Date.
View	By day/week/ month	Pull down View menu, choose Day, Week, or Month.
Change	Appointment/ event to recur	Click on the appointment or event. Pull down the Appointment menu, choose Recurrence, and specify details.
Change	List of events	In the Current View box, click Events. Make your changes directly in the table, or double-click on an event to make changes.
Change	List of annual events	Pull down View menu, select Current View, and choose Annual Events. Type changes in the table, or double-click on the event itself.
Change	Recurring appointment	Pull down View menu, select Current View, and choose Recurring Appointments. Type changes in the table, or double-click on the event itself.
Forward	Meeting request	Open the meeting in question, add the name of the new person, and save changes.
Reschedule	Appointment/ meeting	Drag and drop the appointment or meeting from its original date and time to the new date or time.
Resend	Meeting request	Open the meeting and make changes. Pull down the File menu and choose Send.

7

Office Data Sharing and Integration

- *Examining DDE Links and Their Uses*
- *Using Macros to Control DDE*

26

Examining Dynamic Data Exchange

D YNAMIC DATA EXCHANGE (DDE) IS AN INTERNAL COMMUNICA-
tions protocol Windows uses to allow one application to exchange
data with another application. Normally used to transfer information
between applications, DDE can also be used within an application.

This chapter covers the following topics:

- Examining DDE links
- Using DDE links
- Creating links with menu commands
- Hot links and internal links
- Using macros to control DDE

DDE lets you not only share information between applications, but also send commands from one application to another to control the behavior of the receiving application. Thus, DDE is a tool that implements the Windows standards for both integration and interoperability.

DDE creates a *link*—a communication channel, rather like an open telephone line, through which data is sent. When DDE links are live, both the sending (server) and receiving (client) applications are open. While the server data is being edited, you can see the data being transferred in real time: as data in the server document changes, an hourglass icon flashes briefly as the other application is updated automatically through the link. You can size the application windows so that, with the two documents side by side, you can watch the entire process.

■ Examining DDE Links and Their Uses

Windows offers two ways to implement Dynamic Data Exchange. The first is through the application's regular interface: you execute directly, from the application's menus, any commands to create and edit links between one application and another. In the second method, you write code in an application's macro language: Only through the macro programming construct can you send instructions that control another application's behavior. This chapter teaches you how to create links with each method.

Typically, you use DDE to perform the following kinds of automated data transfers:

- Query the data in one application from inside another, and return a result. The query can produce a one-time (static) return of data, or can be set to update the data in the destination document when the query is run again.

- Convey a stream of data into an application in real time, such as sending stock market quotes into a spreadsheet.

- Link information contained in a compound document to the information's source so that the destination document is updated automatically whenever the source data is changed. Examples of this type of link, sometimes called a *persistent link,* are discussed throughout the chapter.

A Practical Example of Using an Automatic Link

Suppose, for example, that you regularly prepare a summary sales report, and send it at specific intervals to company managers: once a week to sales managers, twice a month to department heads, and once a month to the chief financial officer. These reports are based on sales figures that you track and total every day in Microsoft Excel. You can create a boilerplate report for each manager using Microsoft Word, including in each report a link to the range in your Excel worksheet that shows the running sales total.

Note. A DDE link creates a pointer to the source data. The link is document-to-document (another way of saying file-to-file) rather than document-to-application, as is the case with OLE-embedded data. Chapter 27 discusses OLE in more detail.

As you update the figures in Excel every day, the updated total will be sent automatically through the DDE link to the report documents. Whenever you open the Word documents to print and send them to the appropriate managers, the documents will reflect the latest data from the Excel worksheet.

After you have established a DDE link, you normally do not need to take any further action to maintain it. But when the source file is moved elsewhere on the system or its name is changed, you must edit the link manually to tell the destination document the source's new location or name. You will learn more about editing links later in this chapter (see the "Managing Links" section).

Different Flavors of DDE

Not all Windows applications support DDE. Some, such as screen savers and font managers, do not need DDE capability. DDE support generally is found in high-end word processors, spreadsheet programs, database applications, fax-generating applications, desktop-publishing programs, and electronic-mail packages.

Windows applications that support DDE can do so as a client, as a server, or as both. A *client application* requests or receives information from another application. A *server application* supplies information to another application.

Most applications that support DDE do so in a way that is readily accessible to the user, using commands on the application's menus and the familiar Clipboard copy-and-paste metaphor. You can think of this as *end-user DDE.* Other applications require that you access their information through macros written in a programming language. To do this, you must understand the inner workings of their DDE implementation. You can think of this method of creating DDE links as *programmed DDE.* Microsoft Word, Excel, Lotus WordPro, and WordPerfect are examples of applications that have their own macro languages and can access other applications through programmed DDE.

How to Discover Whether an Application Supports DDE

To find out whether the Windows application you use (such as Microsoft Word, Lotus WordPro, WordPerfect, Excel, or PowerPoint) supports end-user DDE, pull down the menus and look for commands such as Paste Link, Paste Special, or Links. These commands usually are on the File or Edit menus. The presence of these commands indicates that the application supports DDE, using the Clipboard to create the links.

NOTE. *One advantage to using a software suite, such as Microsoft Office, is that all of the programs in it will tend to function very similarly with regard to features such as DDE links. Other applications will generally interface just fine with Office applications, but their implementations might work somewhat differently, depending on how the applications have been programmed and designed.*

Selecting the Paste Special command from Microsoft Word's Edit menu (see Figure 26.1) brings up the Paste Special dialog box (see Figure 26.2). In this dialog box, you can select a data type and click on the Paste Link button. If the data type you choose cannot be linked, the Paste Link button will be grayed out.

Figure 26.1

The Paste Special command in Word

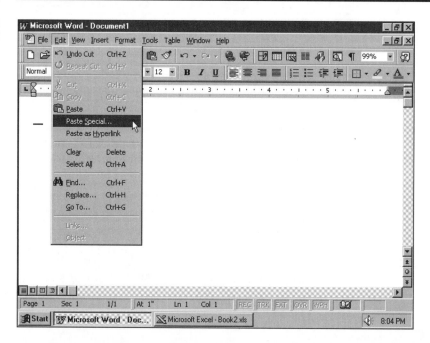

Figure 26.2

Word's Paste Special
dialog box

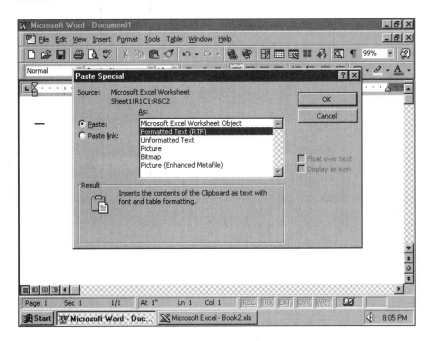

The Paste Special command in Microsoft Excel works in two different ways, depending on the source of data on the Clipboard. When you copy cells from the Excel worksheet to the Clipboard, the Paste Special command invokes a dialog box (see Figure 26.3) that allows you to paste the data back into the worksheet in several Excel-specific ways.

When the data on the Clipboard is from an external source, however, Excel's Paste Special command works the way it does in Word, offering you various linking options (see Figure 26.4).

NOTE. *If your application has a macro language, the DDE commands should be documented in either the language command reference or in the online Help. If you do not see menu commands that refer to linking, and your program does not have a macro language, consult the documentation or the vendor to find out whether and in what form DDE is supported.*

These minor inconsistencies between applications can make DDE seem too complicated or too obscure to use. The obstacle to creating DDE links disappears, however, when you remember that because end-user DDE is a Clipboard function, a reference to links appears on one or more menus—usually File and Edit—in applications in which end-user DDE is available.

Figure 26.3

Excel's internal Paste
Special dialog box

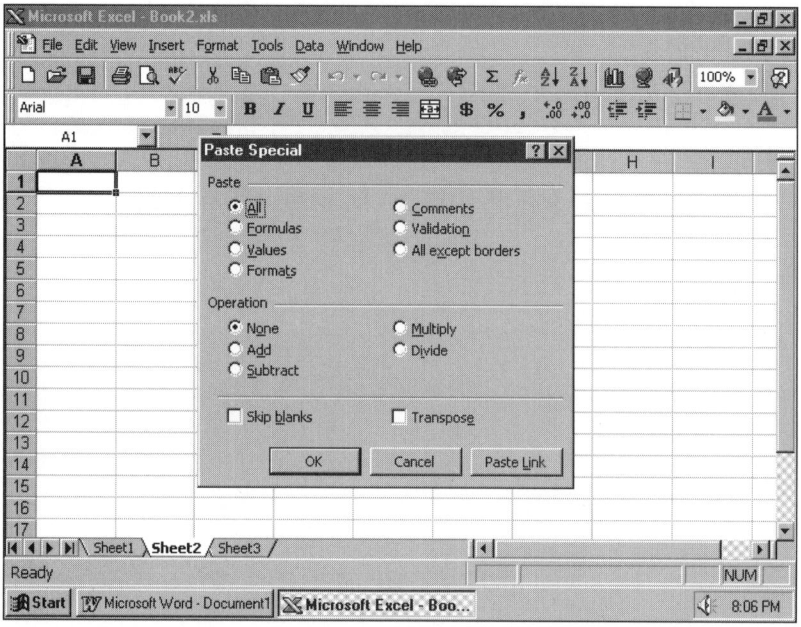

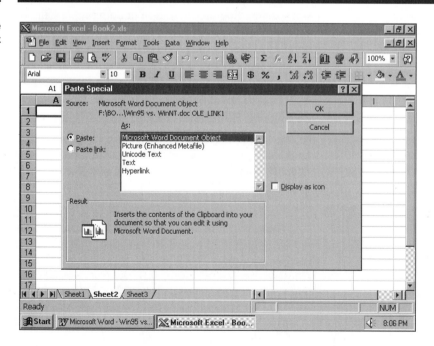

Figure 26.4

Excel's external Paste
Special dialog box

Parsing a DDE Link

Whether you create a DDE link through the menu commands or in a macro, the link always has three parts. To keep track of where the linked information is located and what it refers to, the system needs to know the following three elements:

- Application

- Topic (sometimes called *file name*)

- Item

Application is Windows's alias for the program (WinWord, for example, when Word for Windows is the server). *Topic* typically is the file name of the source document, and *item* is the information in that document to which the link points. In the case of a spreadsheet, the item is the range, expressed by either a row-and-column address or, if you have named the range, by a name. In the case of a word processor such as Word or WordPro, the item is a bookmark name that the application assigns automatically or that you create. In addition to telling the client document where to look for updated source data, these placeholders allow you to jump from the destination document to the linked information in the source document, if your application permits.

Using Menu Commands to Create Links

The following example displays the linking process in action. This example shows you how yet another program implements its DDE-related menu commands.

To copy a block of text from a Word document to the Clipboard, highlight the text and select Copy from the Edit menu (see Figure 26.5).

Open Microsoft Outlook, start a new e-mail message, then pull down its Edit menu, choosing the Paste Special command.

Note. When nothing is on the Clipboard, the Paste commands are grayed out to indicate that they are not available or applicable.

When you choose the Paste Special command and then choose the Paste Link option in the dialog box, the text will be pasted into the Exchange message, and a link that points to the original text in Word is established. You can verify the link by selecting the box that contains the linked text, then using the Links command in Outlook's Edit menu. This displays the Links dialog box that contains the current link information, as shown in Figure 26.6.

NOTE. *Because each open DDE channel requires system memory, the number of links that can be maintained in any document is limited. Factors governing the limit include how much memory is installed on the system and the claims made upon that memory by other resources currently active in the Windows session. Name and save a server document before you create a link. Otherwise, you will have to edit the link later with the source document's name.*

Figure 26.5

Copying data from Word

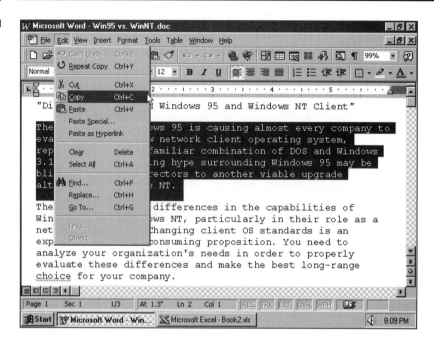

Figure 26.6

Outlook's Links dialog box displays the current link.

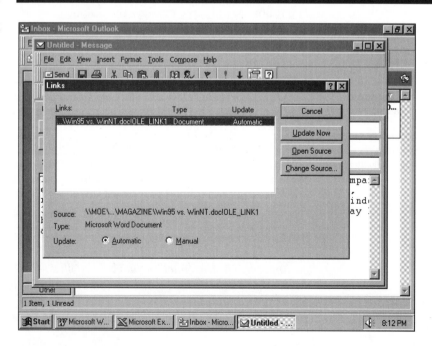

Managing Links

Can you tell, just from looking at a document, whether it contains links? If it does, can you tell where they are? Sometimes the answer is yes, sometimes it's no—and sometimes you must do a bit of sleuthing.

Word allows you to explore the links for which it is acting as server. As other applications do, Word creates a bookmark for each server link—these are DDE items. But because Word lists these items as bookmarks in the document, you can use the Go To command in the Edit menu (choosing the Bookmark option) to go to them (see Figure 26.7). Word names the bookmarks OLE_LINK*n*, where *n* is an automatically incremented number. When you go to a bookmark, Word will highlight the block of text to which the bookmark refers. Note that if you delete links, Word will not renumber the remaining bookmarks.

Figure 26.7

Finding links in Word
using the Go To dialog
box with Bookmark
selected

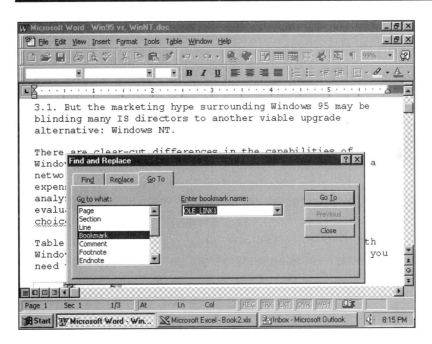

TIP. *To ensure that Excel's DDE links behave as you want them to, choose Options in the Tools menu and make sure that the Ignore Other Applications check box on the General tab is cleared (in other words, you generally don't want Excel to ignore other applications). To choose whether all links in an individual worksheet should be updated automatically, select the Calculation tab in the Options dialog box, and then check or clear the Update Remote References check box.*

In Excel, the formula that describes the link appears in the Formula bar when you select the linked object or cell that contains the object (see Figure 26.8).

Figure 26.8

Excel displays link information in its Formula bar.

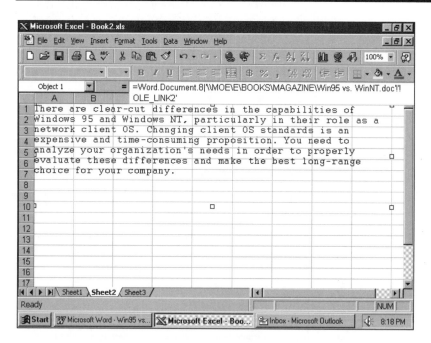

No matter how programs display links, you can always access the links in the document through a menu command. In Office applications, look for the Links command on the Edit menu. Other programs will use slightly different methods.

Each of these commands opens a dialog box that lists the document's links and their attributes. In this dialog box you can update individual links, change their status from automatic (active) to manual (inactive) and back again, cancel or unlink them (leaving the latest result in the document as static text), and edit them. Figure 26.9 displays Word's Links dialog box. The figure clearly shows the three parts of a DDE link: the application, the file name (often called the topic), and the item.

In this example, you use the Links dialog box to edit the file name (topic) after you name and save the worksheet.

NOTE. *Word not only provides the usual options, but also allows you to jump directly to the source of the link. You can do this by choosing Open Source from the Links dialog box or by selecting the command (named, for example,*

Figure 26.9

Word's Links dialog box

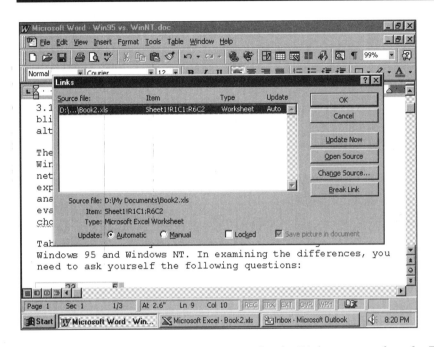

Linked Worksheet Object) that appears under the Links command on the Edit menu when a linked object is selected. The best way to edit a link, in general, is to use the Change Source button in the Links dialog box. With Excel, you can edit the link directly in the formula bar. Just be sure to press Ctrl+Shift+Enter to save the revised link as an array formula.

Understanding Hot Links

Not only does the terminology and placement of DDE-related menu commands vary from program to program, but discrepancies also exist in the way programs respond to DDE messages. Although DDE links ordinarily are well-behaved, you need to be aware of some problems you might encounter.

A *hot* (or automatic) link is one that automatically updates the destination document after the linked information in the source document is changed. A *warm* (or manual) link is one that the user must manually update when the source information is changed. A warm link is sometimes referred to as a *manual link* or an *inactive link*; a hot link is also called an *automatic link* or an *active link.*

Normally, links are hot when you first create them. But because their status can change under certain circumstances—sometimes without the user being aware that what was once a hot link is now a warm one that must be updated manually—you might need to experiment to determine just how your applications operate in this regard.

Even the most reliable end-user DDE link, such as the one you create when you paste-link ranges from Excel into Word, has one small problem. Start with both applications closed. Open Word first. It correctly reads the changed Excel source data from the disk and automatically updates the link. Then launch Excel and open the linked worksheet. Make changes in the source data.

Word does not update the link automatically. You have to update the link manually, either through the menu and dialog box commands, or by placing the cursor anywhere in the linked data and pressing F9, which is Word's Update Fields key. The link becomes a manual link—even though it is still flagged as automatic in the Links dialog box that appears when you select Links from Word's Edit menu.

To make sure that the link remains truly automatic, open the linked Excel worksheet and modify it *before* you open the Word document.

Despite the peculiarities mentioned in this section, DDE links are a powerful way to share data between Windows applications, and are indispensable for certain kinds of real-time data transfers.

Working with Internal Links

Word and Excel permit you to create internal links. In Word, an internal link is actually a reference to a bookmark.

If you copy Word text to the Clipboard and then use Paste Special to place it somewhere else in the same document as a linked object, Word will automatically assign a bookmark name to the text block, as it does when Word is the server for a regular DDE link. In the case of an internal link, the bookmark name is OLE_LINKn; the number n increases incrementally each time you create an internal link.

Internal links in Word are hot—they are updated automatically, although it may take a while, as the links update in the background. You can force an immediate update to the links in either of two ways. You can select the field(s) by putting the cursor anywhere in the text or anywhere in the field and pressing F9, the Update Fields key. Or you can choose Links from the Edit menu and then, in the Links dialog box, select the link(s) to be updated and press the Update Now button.

In Excel, you can Copy and Paste Link a cell or range of cells to different parts of the worksheet or to another worksheet. (Note that if you copy a range, the range will be pasted as an array.) In this way, you create a reference to the row-and-column or named-range address of the original cell(s). This internal link updates automatically when the source data is changed.

■ Using Macros to Control DDE

Now that you have explored the nature of DDE links and how to create and manage them by using menu commands, the next step is understanding how macros can perform many of these tasks for you, truly automating the integration and interoperability of Windows applications.

Looking At DDE Commands: Examples from Excel and Word

Although the exact form of a DDE command can vary from one macro language to another, similarities exist. Table 26.1 lists the most commonly used DDE commands. To find the exact commands for your application, including the Microsoft Office suite, check the online programming reference.

Table 26.1

Common DDE Commands

COMMON COMMAND NAME	ACTION
DDEInitiate	Starts DDE conversation with another application
DDEExecute	Sends a command to another application with which you have initiated conversation
DDEPoke	Sends data to another application with which you have initiated conversation
DDERequest	Requests data from application with which you have initiated conversation
DDETerminate	Terminates conversation with other applications
DDETerminateAll	Terminates all conversations with other applications

Using Macros

Frequently you do not have to create a persistent link, because you do not need an ongoing flow of data from one application to another.

The following Word VBA macro queries an Excel worksheet for a particular piece of data. The macro also illustrates how you can control the behavior of one application from inside another. A highly sophisticated macro might exercise even more precise control by sending extensive formatting instructions, instructions for the sizing and placement of open windows, and so on.

Using RequestFromExcel

The Word VBA macro RequestFromExcel can easily be created in Word. To see how the macro operates, create a new Word document, pull down the

Tools menu, and select Macro. On the Macro dialog box, type Request-FromExcel into the Macro Name field, and then click on the Create button. In the window that appears, type the following program code. Normally, the Word VBA macro's lines are not numbered. Line numbers are included here to help you follow the explanation of the code that follows.

```
1.   Sub RequestFromExcel()
2.   On Error GoTo Bye
3.   ChanNum = DDEInitiate(App:="Excel", Topic:="System")
4.   DDEExecute Channel:=ChanNum, Command:="[OPEN(" & Chr(34) & "E:\My
       Documents\GetStuff.xls" & Chr(34) & ")]"
5.   DDETerminate Channel:=ChanNum
6.   ChanNum = DDEInitiate(App:="Excel", Topic:="GetStuff.xls")
7.   DDEPoke Channel:=ChanNum, Item:="R2C3", Data:="Office 97 SuperGuide"
8.   DDEExecute Channel:=ChanNum, Command:="[Save]"
9.   Bye:
10.  DDETerminateAll
11.  End Sub
```

The macro does the following:

- Launches Excel. A more refined version would check first to see whether Excel were running and, if it were not, would run it automatically.

- Asks which files are open. Open files include the global macro sheet and any other macro sheets and add-ons in the XLSTART subdirectory.

- Sees whether the worksheet you want is open; if it is not, instructs Excel to open it.

- Requests information from the worksheet.

- Inserts the requested information into the Excel sheet.

- Ends by closing the DDE channels, which are no longer necessary.

In the following explanation of RequestFromExcel's code, each number refers to the corresponding line of code in the macro:

1. VBA's standard opening line for a subroutine.

2. If executing any part of the macro is a problem, the macro branches to the label Bye: (see line 9) so that the command on line 10 (DDETerminateAll) is executed before the macro exits.

3. Launches Excel at its system level, and returns the number of the DDE channel thus opened to the numeric variable ChanNum.

4. Opens the GetStuff.XLS file in Excel. The syntax, which is complex, must be followed exactly. The command enclosed in square brackets (in this case, the OPEN command) is transmitted to Excel in the style of

and with the punctuation required by its own macro commands. Chr$(34) tells Excel that the quotation marks that enclose the text are literal quotes.

5. The DDE channel that communicated with Excel in order to open the file is now closed. We no longer want to communicate to Excel, but want to communicate with the now-open file instead.

6. Now that Excel has opened the required file, a new DDE channel must be opened to communicate with it. In this line, the macro is communicating with the file, not the application.

7. The DDEPoke command inserts the data "Office 97 SuperGuide" into the item "R2C3" in Excel. R2C3 corresponds to cell C2.

8. DDEExecute is used to save the modified file.

9. The Bye: label is used if an error is encountered in the preceding lines of the macro. An error causes the macro execution to jump to this line.

10. All DDE channels are closed with DDETerminateAll.

11. VBA's standard subroutine closing line.

This is a very simple macro that illustrates how DDE communications between applications can be programmed. If you were really designing this macro, there are a number of improvements you would want to make to it:

- You would check first to see if Excel is running before invoking it. If it was running, you would branch the macro around the DDEInitiate command.

- You would check to see if the file you wanted was already open before invoking the Open command in Excel with the second DDEInitiate command.

- You might first check to see what data was in the destination cell, if that was an important step in your application.

The possibilities for improving on this macro are virtually endless. However, the core of DDE communications is demonstrated, and can serve as a basis for your own further explorations of this powerful automation tool.

- *Understanding the Terminology*
- *Creating and Editing OLE Objects*
- *Understanding Object Packager*
- *Using Object Packager*
- *Examining Multimedia and OLE*

27

Exploring Object Linking and Embedding

IN THIS CHAPTER, YOU WILL LEARN WHAT OBJECT LINKING AND Embedding (OLE) is, and how it is different from Dynamic Data Exchange (DDE.) You will learn a step-by-step process for creating and editing OLE objects. You will learn about the following topics:

- Understanding the terminology

- Creating and editing OLE objects

- Understanding Object Packager

- Using Object Packager

- Examining multimedia and OLE

You do not need programming skills to take full advantage of OLE's capabilities. OLE is easy to use, yet enormously powerful. In fact, you do not need to know anything at all about its complex underpinnings to enjoy its benefits.

With the advent of OLE, pronounced "oh-LAY," the ideal of giving users an effortless way to integrate Windows applications is a reality. OLE goes beyond mere data-sharing: it enables one application to share another application's tools as well.

Office 97 applications support a version of OLE called OLE 2. This version of OLE was introduced in Office 95, and improves the way in which different applications interact to create and work with compound documents. (The definition of a "compound document" will be discussed shortly.)

■ Understanding the Terminology

The following three terms are important to your understanding of how OLE works:

- **Compound Document**: A single document made up of parts created in more than one application.

- **Container Document**: A document containing either embedded or linked data, such as objects.

- **Object**: Any piece of data that can be manipulated as a single entity, such as a picture, chart, or section of text.

A compound document is made up of parts created in more than one application. This document is a container for those different parts, which are called objects. Note that the container document is always the client in OLE transactions.

Understanding the Compound Document

As you learned in Chapter 26 to create a DDE link you first must open the server application and the source document, copy information to the Clipboard, and use the Paste Link command to paste it to the destination document. You also can program the DDE communication with a macro. Although you don't usually have to worry about the link after it has been established, you might face difficulties if you want to access, edit, and update the source data. If you move or rename the source document (or, in some cases, move or rename *items*, such as spreadsheet cells or ranges) you must edit the information that Windows needs to maintain the link.

You can perform most of the tasks required to integrate information from one Windows application into another application from within the container document. You might need to leave the container document, however, to edit the linked information at its source. The source information is external to the container document.

Not so with OLE! OLE permits your work to be truly document-centered. You do not need to leave the container document to edit an embedded object. In fact, under most circumstances, you never have to leave it at all. You can initiate an OLE operation directly from within the container document. You just need to know the type of object you want to embed.

If your application can act as an OLE client, you can access a list of available object types from the menu bar. You might need to use a different procedure for each application, though. Look for an Insert menu, and a command on that menu called Object. If they cannot be found, you might need to choose the Insert Object command from an application's File or Edit menu, for example. A list of available objects will be displayed, such as in the Word Object dialog box shown in Figure 27.1.

Figure 27.1

Word's Object dialog box, and the list of object types you can embed

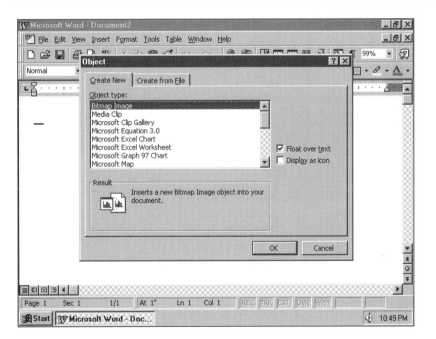

Understanding OLE Servers and Clients

Note. Modifying a drawing, changing numbers in a spreadsheet, and reformatting text all are forms of editing for which OLE can be used.

To describe the utility of OLE, Microsoft adopted the phrase, "The right tool for the right job." You create text in a word-processing program, develop numeric data in a spreadsheet, chart that data in a charting program, and create bitmaps in a paint program or illustrations in a drawing program. Each application is optimized for the kind of tasks you ask it to perform. After you create an object in any of these applications, you can embed the object in a container document created in another application.

Note. DDE links point to a source outside the current document. OLE objects reside within the current document.

In the [embedding] section of WIN.INI, you can see a list of the object types available on your system, along with the application Windows uses to edit those objects (see Figure 27.2). Keep in mind, however, that Windows 95 relies on its new registry files instead of the settings in WIN.INI, and newer applications will only store their settings in the registry. WIN.INI still exists for compatibility purposes with applications not yet fully upgraded to use Windows 95's newer features.

Figure 27.2

The [embedding] section of WIN.INI

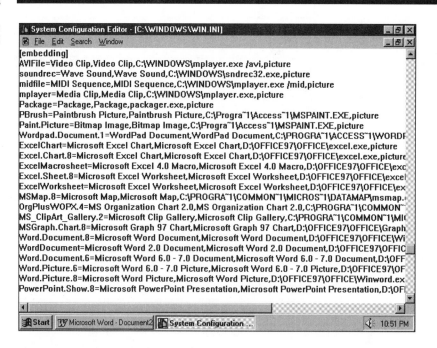

To use OLE, you do not need to know what Windows is doing behind the scenes. You do not need to know which application will create the object (the server application), nor which application will be used to edit it. To edit an embedded object, just double-click on the object, or choose an edit command from the menu. Windows will then open the server application, in which it places a copy of the embedded object and brings it to the foreground on top of the container document. You now can edit this copy of the object. After you finish, Windows will ask whether you want to update the original in the container document. After you click on OK, the object is updated and the server application closes.

Many new Windows applications and some revisions of older applications incorporate OLE technology. Because user demand is high, *OLE-compliant* is a phrase that sells software. CorelDRAW!, WordPerfect, PowerPoint, Word, and Excel are examples of high-end applications that can act as both OLE server and client.

In addition to standalone applications that have OLE server capabilities, a number of mini-applications (sometimes called *applets*) are designed to be used exclusively as OLE servers under Windows. Note that you can use the applets only from within an OLE client, not as independent programs. Examples of such applets are Microsoft's Equation 3.0, WordArt, Graph 97, and Microsoft Map. If you try to run an OLE server applet as if it were a standalone program (by clicking on the name of the EXE file in Windows Explorer, for example), you will receive an error message, such as "Sorry, Microsoft Draw can only run from within a destination application."

You might want to take data you developed independently in a standalone application and embed it in another application. To do so, follow the same copy, paste, and link procedure you use to create DDE links, with one exception: choose Embedded Object from the Paste Link (or Paste Special) dialog box. The data remains an entity in the original file, but has no link to the embedded object in your container document. Editing the original data does not update the embedded object. You can, however, edit the embedded object directly from within the container document.

You will find that working with embedded objects is simpler than working with links. Note that you can initiate the embedding procedure in one of two ways. You can create the object in the server application and paste it into the container document. Or, you can choose a command from the container document's menu that gives you direct access to the server application.

Because an embedded object does not have an independent life—it is not stored in any external file—you must consider when to embed an object and when to link one. In general, you link an object if the server data needs to be shared with more than one client, and you embed an object when the object is to be used in only one container (client) document.

■ Creating and Editing OLE Objects

This section teaches you how to create and edit OLE objects, step by step. The first example uses two of the accessory applications that come with Windows—Paint and WordPad. The second and third examples use Word and Excel, and the fourth uses only Word.

Embedding a Paint Object in WordPad

The first OLE example uses two of the accessory applications that come with Windows—Paint and WordPad.

To create the embedded Paintbrush object in a WordPad document, perform the following steps:

1. Choose Object from the Insert menu in WordPad.

2. You will see the Insert Object dialog box shown in Figure 27.3. Choose Paintbrush Picture from the Object Type list. Windows will launch Paint automatically. Looking at the title bar of the Paint window shown in Figure 27.4, you can see that this is an embedded object in WordPad rather than a normal blank Paint file.

Figure 27.3

Choosing Paintbrush Picture from the Object Type list box

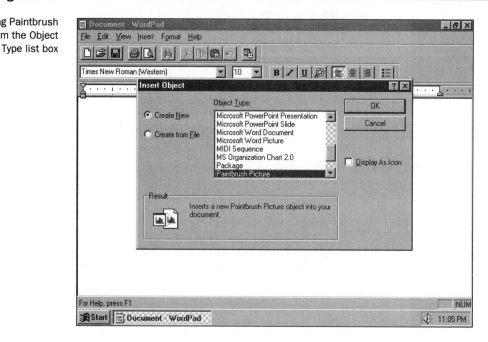

Figure 27.4

Paint is now an
OLE server.

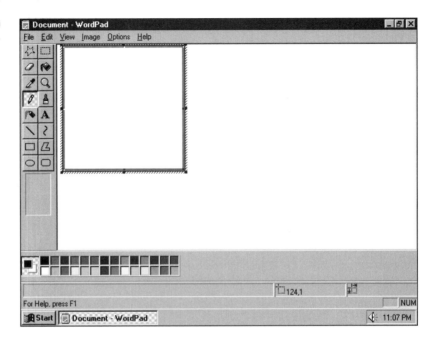

3. Create your drawing and then simply click outside of the drawing area to return to your WordPad document. Notice when you do that the Paint toolbar and menus change back to the WordPad menus. Figure 27.5 shows the completed, embedded drawing.

4. To modify the drawing, double-click on it. When you do, you'll see the Paint toolbars and menus reappear.

The procedure is that simple. All applications that support OLE perform these operations in a similar manner. In all cases, the system does the work of choosing the editing tools and loading the object for you. You do not have to leave the container document. Document-centered computing is a reality, thanks to OLE.

Embedding New Excel Data as an Object in Word

To create an Excel worksheet object directly from within a Word document (the container document), perform the steps in the following example. First, make sure that you have Word running, and then begin a new document by selecting File and choosing the New command.

1. From the new document in Word, select Object from the Insert menu (see Figure 27.6) to display the Object dialog box.

Figure 27.5

The Paint object completed in WordPad

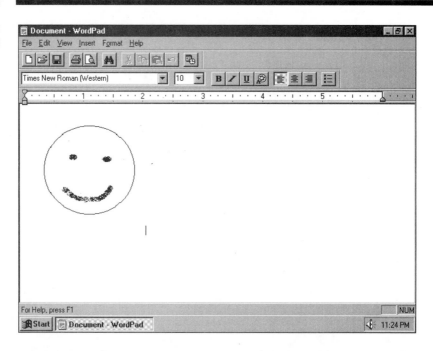

Figure 27.6

Word's Insert menu

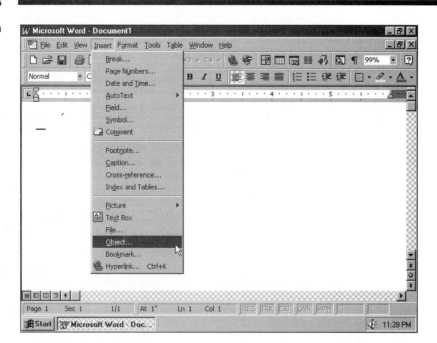

2. Make sure the Create New tab is open. From the Object Type list, choose Microsoft Excel Worksheet (see Figure 27.7) and click on the OK button.

Figure 27.7

Choosing an Excel
Worksheet object
to embed

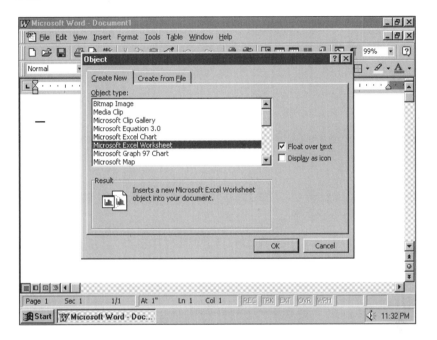

NOTE. *The list of Object Types in the various Insert Object dialog boxes illustrated in this section might not look like the list you see when you follow these examples on your own system. Remember that when you install an application that can act as an OLE server, Windows places the appropriate information about that application in the Registry Database and includes the application in the [embedding] section of your WIN.INI file. When you are working on your computer, the Object Types list will reflect the OLE servers you have installed.*

The worksheet is then created within the Word document. You can use the worksheet and Excel's tools as you usually do (see Figure 27.8). This capability is evident if you look at the formula bar. The highlighted cell shows the result of summing the two values above it.

3. To return to working in "native" Word, click outside the embedded Excel sheet. You will see Word's menus and toolbar return, as shown in Figure 27.9.

Figure 27.8

The embedded worksheet gives you access to "native" Excel.

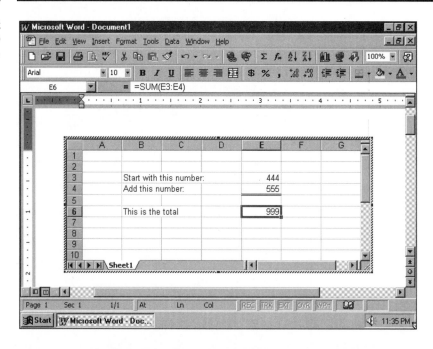

Figure 27.9

Clicking outside the embedded object returns you to the container document.

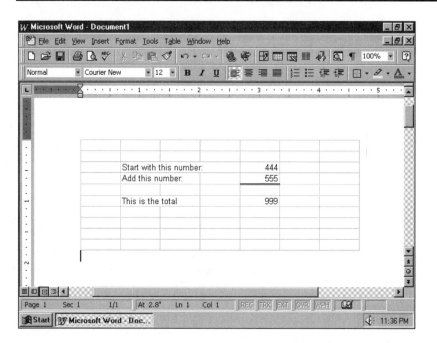

Embedding Word Text in Another Word Document

This example shows you what happens if you embed Word text in a Word document. Why would you want to do this? Perhaps you want to annotate a document, but find Word's comments too small and difficult to read, and marking the revisions is too cumbersome.

Annotating with embedded text has the advantage of making the place at which the annotations occur highly visible to the reader, as you can see in Figure 27.10. You can view or edit the linked document by double-clicking on it. To return to the main document from a linked document, choose Close and Return to Document from the File menu.

Figure 27.10

Icons can represent embedded documents.

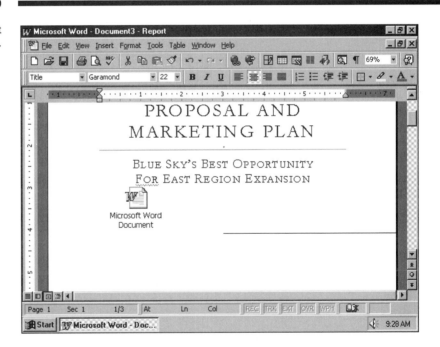

You can create these embedded text objects by using one of two procedures from within the container document. You can copy text from another document and choose Microsoft Word Object from the Paste Special dialog box (you'll also have to select the Display as Icon check box). You also can choose Object from the Insert menu, and from the Object Type list box choose Word Document. Remember to set the Display As Icon checkbox if you want the embedded document displayed that way.

■ Understanding Object Packager

As is apparent from the preceding discussion, the number of OLE-compliant Windows applications is growing. However, what do you do if you want to embed in a container document information from an application that does not talk OLE's language? What if you need to access a DOS application while you are working in a Windows document, for example? Object Packager provides a means to accomplish this task.

Object Packager, which is OLE-compliant, wraps itself around another application that is not OLE-compliant. Object Packager then contains information about the source that the source itself cannot provide. You then embed this "package" into your container document. Object Packager can wrap itself around Windows applications that are not otherwise OLE servers and can even act as a mechanism for embedding DOS applications, DOS commands, and batch files.

To see how Object Packager works, suppose that you manage a small office in which everybody has a computer that runs Windows, but in which the computers are not networked. You need to find out what each PC has in its CONFIG.SYS file.

You decide to put a memo on a floppy disk that is distributed to each user. The memo on the disk asks the users to access their CONFIG.SYS file by double-clicking on the icon in the memo (which represents an object packaged in the memo). When they double-click on the embedded icon, their CONFIG.SYS file will automatically be opened for them. They can then copy the contents of the file into the Word document by simply using the familiar copy and paste commands. After each user adds the information to the document and returns the disks to you, you will have a complete record of all CONFIG.SYS files on your office's computers. The users had to do little more than load the Word document to provide you the information you requested.

■ Using Object Packager

The following example shows you how to create a Word document into which access to Notepad, which is not an OLE-compliant application, can be embedded. You use Object Packager and have it load your CONFIG.SYS file. Object Packager lets you represent a Windows or non-Windows object as an icon in your compound document.

Creating a Packaged Object

The first thing you must do to use the Object Packager is open or create a container document. Then, to create a packaged object from within the container document, perform the following steps:

1. Begin by creating a new document in Word. From the Insert menu, choose Object to display the Object dialog box. From the Object Type list box in the Create New tab, choose Package and also set the Display As Icon checkbox before clicking the OK button. Figure 27.11 shows the Object Packager in the Word document.

Figure 27.11

The Object Packager window

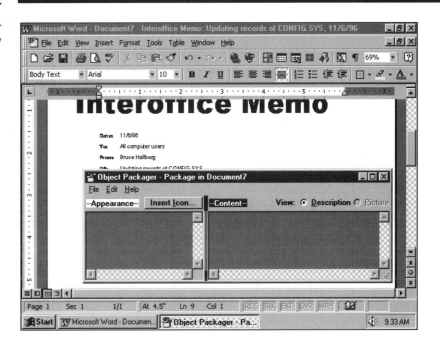

The Object Packager is divided into two windows, placed side by side. You specify the content of the package in the right window and the appearance of the package in the left window. The content window of the package usually displays a brief description of the package contents. The appearance window displays the icon to be used to represent the package after it is embedded in a document.

2. You can choose the object to be packaged via several methods. This example uses the command-line method, where you specify an actual command to be executed when the object is opened. Choose Command Line from the Edit menu to display the dialog box in Figure 27.12.

Figure 27.12

Packaging a command
line in Object Packager

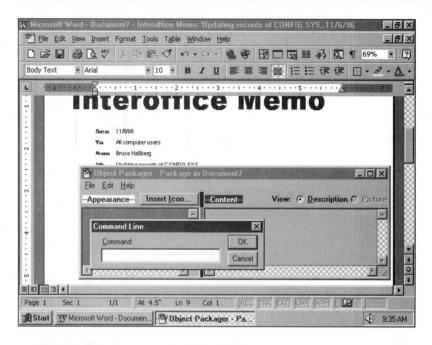

The following command will load NOTEPAD with the CONFIG.SYS file:

```
C:\WINDOWS\NOTEPAD.EXE C:\CONFIG.SYS
```

NOTE. *If you choose a simple file name to use with the Object Packager, that file name must be associated with an application in order for the object to function correctly. So, if you were to embed, say, CONFIG.SYS, and *.SYS isn't associated with an application on your system, you will get an error message when trying to open the final embedded package.*

Object Packager does not know which icon to associate with CON-FIG.SYS. You can choose any icon on your system, whether it resides in an EXE file, a DLL library, or independently as an icon, which is a file with an ICO extension.

Note. The appearance of an OLE package is the icon that you want inserted in the document. The content is the command or the file name of the application that is to be packaged.

3. To choose an icon, click on the Insert Icon button in the Appearance window of Object Packager. The child window shows you the default for the object you have chosen (or Windows makes its best guess.) Use the scroll bar to choose an icon from Windows's standard collection or click on the Browse button to load another file that contains an icon. The Insert Icon dialog is shown in Figure 27.13.

Figure 27.13

Windows includes a
standard collection of
icons that you can use
for Object Packager.

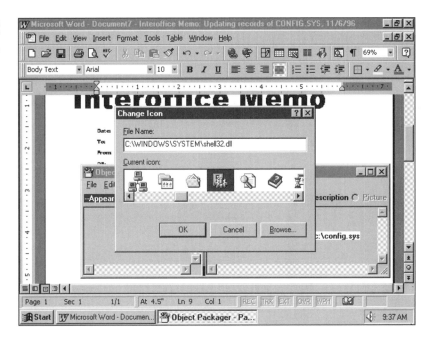

4. After you have chosen an icon, you can choose Exit from the Object
   Packager's File menu. Then, click on OK when asked if you want to
   update the object. Figure 27.14 shows the packaged object embedded in
   the completed document.

Double-clicking on the icon activates the package. (In this example, it
opens the CONFIG.SYS file with Notepad.) If you want to edit the package's content or appearance, you must select the icon with a single mouse
click and choose Package Object from Word's Edit menu.

Choosing the Content of a Package

In the previous example, you told Object Packager which object to package
by typing a command line. Alternatively, you can choose Import from Object
Packager's File menu. This opens a drive and directory window, and from
here you can choose a file to embed. This can be an executable file or a document file. If it is a document file, when you choose the icon embedded in
your container document, Windows launches the application and loads the
file. You also can drag a file from File Manager and drop it into the Contents
pane of the Object Packager dialog box.

DOS programs, of course, are not OLE-compliant, but thanks to Object
Packager you can access a DOS program directly from within your Windows

Figure 27.14

The completed document with the labeled object embedded

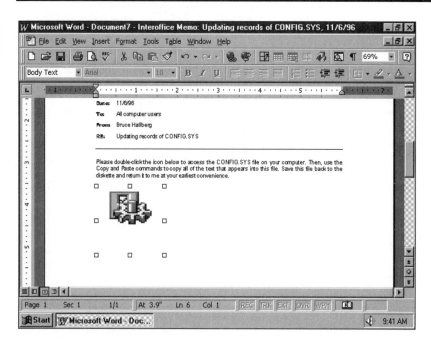

application container document. If you run that DOS program in a window, you can even copy information from it and paste the data directly into the container document.

■ Examining Multimedia and OLE

A new category of applications that rely heavily on OLE has exciting potential for Windows users—*multimedia*. By using the Windows operating system's multimedia extensions, developers of hardware and software that display sound, video, and animation images on-screen now have the software connections to bring these capabilities to Windows.

You must, however, have additional hardware to use parts of multimedia technology, such as sound and video boards, CD-ROM players, and so on. Windows comes with an OLE server for sound bites, for example, but you must have a sound board installed in your system (and external speakers that connect to it) to play back the files that Sound Recorder knows how to embed.

You also can plug a microphone into an installed sound board to record voice or other sounds, and you can create and play back MIDI synthesizer music. With the appropriate hardware, you can embed video clips from a tape or feed real-time, live video directly from a television set.

Even with relatively simple and inexpensive sound hardware you can reap some benefits from linking sound to your documents via OLE. For instance, Figure 27.15 shows a letter that has both an embedded graph as well as an embedded recording of a message from the chairman. The reader of this document has only to double-click on the graph icon in order to view the graph using its native application, or to double-click on the microphone icon to hear the recorded comments from the chairman. Using these technologies can enliven documents and make them more powerful. But, of course, these benefits will not be widely available until more PCs have such hardware built in.

Figure 27.15

Enlivening Windows applications with embedded sound and graphics

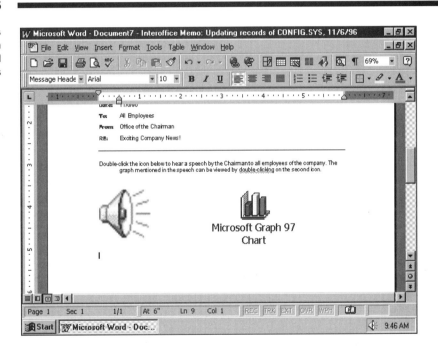

- *Sharing Files on a Network*
- *Maintaining Security*
- *Setting Up Workgroup Templates*

28

Workgroup Computing with Office

Many PEOPLE USE MICROSOFT OFFICE AT WORK AND, CONSE-quently, interact with others in the company who also use Office. Wouldn't it be nice if Office helped you work more collaboratively within your company? What if it let you manage shared files more effectively, for example? Fortunately, it does all this and more.

In this chapter, you'll learn about the following:

- Sharing Office files on a network

- Tracking control information for shared files

- Preserving the security of your files

- Sharing Workbooks in Excel

- Creating customized templates for your workgroup

One of the biggest benefits that networks bring companies is the ability to rapidly share and process information within workgroups. Most tightly knit groups within a company that use a network use shared areas on a common server to store and access files. This greatly expands the ability of the workers in the department to get their jobs done, particularly in organizations that ask every worker to get more done with less. Taking advantage of the power of your network to help peers work more smoothly together can pay large, if subtle, dividends.

The Office suite of applications supports this model of information-sharing. Individual applications let you take advantage of features that make working together easier and more manageable.

■ Sharing Files on a Network

If you often work on files that are stored in areas to which many others have access, you will often try to open a file that someone else is already working on, or they will try to open a file that you are using and changing. This simple and common occurrence can result in confusion.

Note. The figures in this section use Microsoft Word for their examples. All the Office applications, however, behave the same way when they deal with already opened files.

All Office applications warn you when you try to open a file that someone else is already using. When someone first opens a file for editing, that file is locked on the server so that another user cannot modify it while it's locked. Office helps you to deal with this gracefully by warning you with the dialog box shown in Figure 28.1.

You have three ways to deal with the dialog box shown in Figure 28.1. You can select Cancel and try again later, hoping that the file is free then; you can call the other person on the phone (if you know who it is) and ask them to close the document so you can use it; or you can click on the OK button and make a copy of the document.

Making a copy of the document means that whatever is saved to the disk at that moment will be loaded into your computer, with the indicator "(Copy)" appearing after the file name in the title bar of the application. You can then freely edit the file.

Figure 28.1

When you try to open a file that someone else is using, you will see this dialog box.

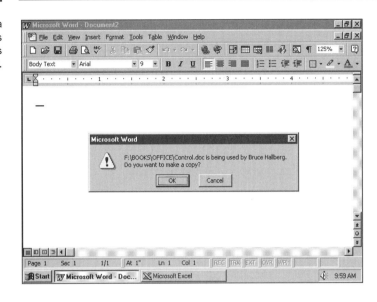

When you try to save the file, two possible things will happen:

- If the file is still open by another user, you'll see the dialog box shown in Figure 28.2. This dialog box means that you'll have to save the file under a different file name, or save it to a different directory than the original. Selecting OK will bring up the Save As dialog box automatically so you can choose a new file name or location.

- If the other person editing the file has finished their work and closed their copy, you'll see the dialog box shown in Figure 28.3. This dialog box tells you that someone else has edited the file, and that it probably contains changes that are not reflected in your copy of the file. If you proceed with saving your copy of the file using the Yes button, your changes will overwrite their changes, and their changes will be lost.

Note. The person's name that appears in the dialog box shown in Figure 28.2 is generated by the name stored in the Options dialog box of the user's Office application. For this reason, you should not use a generic name there, such as your company name.

Using Word's Workgroup Features

Word contains two features that make collaborating on word-processing documents easier: comments and tracked changes.

Comments are notes attached to specific parts of a document's text. These notes are marked with the writer's name or initials. To insert a comment, access the Insert menu and choose Comment. Type your comment in the window provided, then click the Close button to save your comment note.

To view existing comments, simply use your mouse to position your on-screen pointer over the text. Comments will appear with a yellow

Note. The name used for the comments is controlled via the Options dialog box's User Info page.

Figure 28.2

Office applications prevent you from overwriting another user's work in progress.

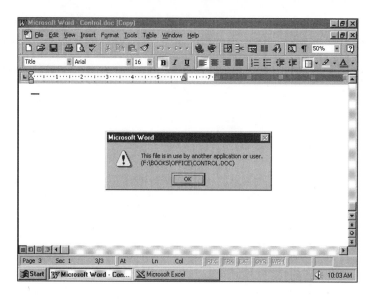

Figure 28.3

If the other user has finished with their changes, you must decide whether your changes should overwrite theirs or not.

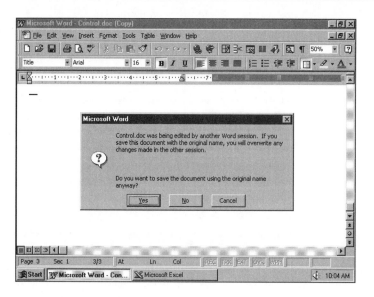

background behind text to which a comment is attached, as shown in Figure 28.4.

Figure 28.4

Reviewing a comment is as simple as moving your pointer onto the text that has been commented upon.

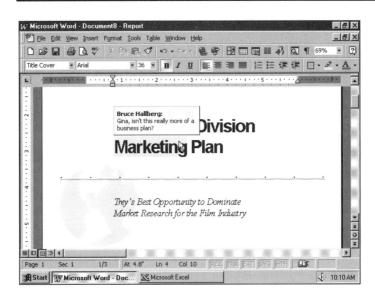

Word also contains a feature that automatically keeps track of revisions to a document. You enable this feature by selecting the Track Changes submenu in the Tools menu. Then, choose Highlight Changes to control the Track Changes feature. The Highlight Changes dialog box is shown in Figure 28.5, and a document with some revisions is shown in Figure 28.6.

The Highlight Changes dialog box has three checkboxes. "Track changes while editing" allows any changes made to the document to be tracked. "Highlight changes on screen," when selected, displays the revisions as colored strikeouts and insertions (shown with underline and in color). When "Highlight changes on screen" is cleared, you'll see the document as if all the revisions have been accepted. "Highlight changes in printed document" controls whether any tracked changes are printed, or if the printout simply prints the finished document as if the changes had been accepted.

The Options button in the Highlight Changes dialog box lets you control how tracked changes are displayed on screen. Figure 28.7 shows the Track Changes options dialog box. For each type of revision, you can choose how the revision is formatted and what colors are used.

When you receive a document that includes revisions you want to review carefully, use the Accept or Reject Changes command found in the Track Changes submenu of the Tools menu. This displays the Accept or Reject

Figure 28.5

The Highlight Changes dialog box controls how changes to a document are tracked and displayed.

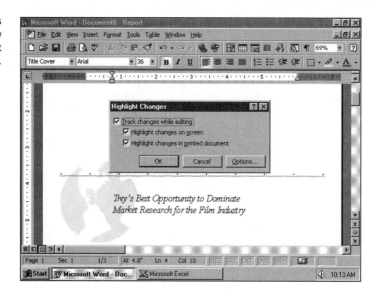

Figure 28.6

A simple deletion and addition shown as a highlighted change to the document

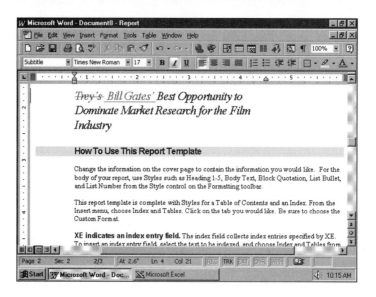

Figure 28.7

The Track Changes dialog box controls how tracked changes are formatted.

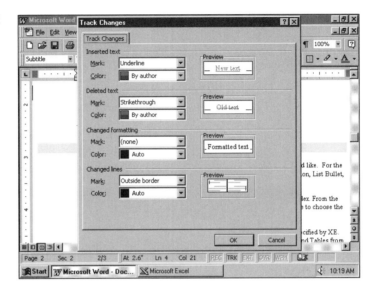

Changes dialog box shown in Figure 28.8. Use the two Find buttons to locate the changes to the document, and the Accept and Reject buttons to either make individual changes permanent, or reject them and return a changed segment to its original form. You can speed the process with the Accept All or Reject All button.

Sharing Excel Workbooks

Excel 97 has improved Excel's ability to allow multiple people to modify a workbook simultaneously. This feature is called Shared Workbooks. New to Excel 97 are the following features of Shared Workbooks, previously called Shared Lists in Excel 95:

- Changes from multiple users can now be consolidated automatically at intervals that you specify

- You can track changes made by different users for many days

- Each user can format the document and make other choices (such as printing choices) that are used for their own version of the open workbook

You set up the Shared Workbooks feature by opening the file you want to share and then choosing the Share Workbook command on the Tools menu, which brings up the Share Workbook dialog box shown in Figure 28.9.

Figure 28.8

Use the Accept or Reject Changes dialog box to see who has made what changes, and when they made them.

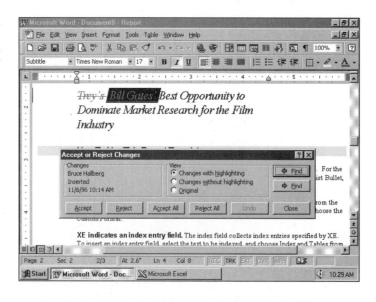

Figure 28.9

The Share Workbook dialog box lets you control how workbooks are shared.

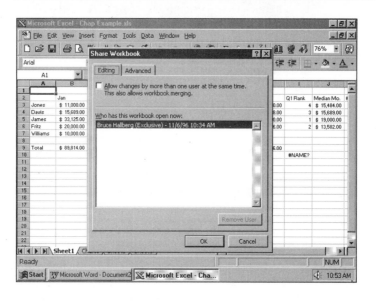

To allow simultaneous access to a workbook, set the "Allow changes by more than one user at the same time" checkbox. After doing so, you can set further options on the Advanced tab shown in Figure 28.10.

Figure 28.10

The Advanced tab of the Share Workbook dialog box

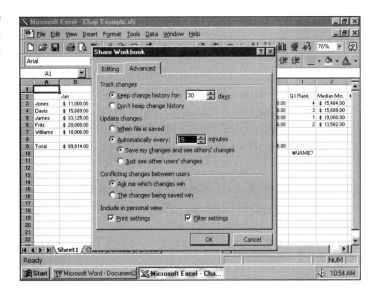

The Advanced tab contains the following options:

- Use the Track Changes section to control how long changes to the workbook are tracked. You need to enable "Keep change history for" to see merged changes from other users.

- The Update Changes section controls how changes made by multiple users are consolidated back to the main document. You can choose to see changes whenever the file is saved, or in minute-based intervals.

- The "Conflicting changes between users" section controls how changes that conflict, such as would happen when two users change the same cell to different values. Generally, this should always be set to "Ask me which changes win."

When two people work on a shared workbook, if Person 1 makes a change to a cell and saves the workbook, and then Person 2 also saves their copy of the workbook, Person 2 will see any changes that Person 1 has made. The changes will be highlighted with a comment indicator in the workbook that shows Person 2 the change that Person 1 made (and accepts these changes as a matter of course).

However, if Person 1 and Person 2 both change a cell to different values, a conflict arises. The second person to save the workbook when an entry conflicts will see the Resolve Conflicts dialog box shown in Figure 28.11. They will need to resolve the conflict using this dialog box before their version of the workbook can be saved.

Figure 28.11

Conflicts in Shared Workbooks bring up the Resolve Conflicts dialog box.

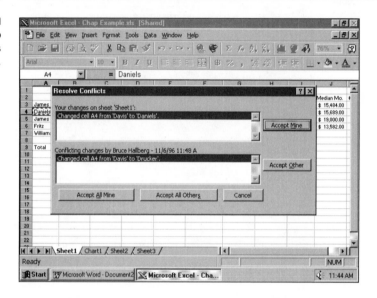

In the Resolve Conflicts dialog box, you can review conflicts individually by selecting them in the two windows, and then clicking either the Accept Mine or Accept Other button. If there are many changes that you want to accept from the same editor, you can use the Accept All Mine and Accept All Others buttons. Clicking on the cancel button cancels your save of the document; you cannot save your version until you resolve the conflicts.

When you reject another person's changes in favor of your own, that person will see your changes when they save the workbook. At that point, no conflict will arise for them: your changes will simply be updated into their copy of the workbook, along with the change comment discussed earlier.

Excel offers two tools that let you manage Shared Workbooks more easily: the ability to view who is using the file at any given time, and the History sheet.

When you're working on a shared workbook, you can see who else is working on it by accessing the Shared Workbook command in the Tools menu. The Editing tab (see Figure 28.12) shows you who has the file open for editing, and when they opened it.

Figure 28.12

The Editing tab shows
you who has the file open
at any given time.

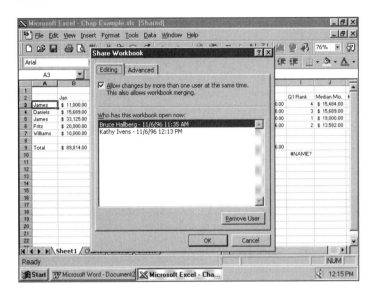

Excel also lets you keep track of any changes in the file, providing a sort of audit trail that can help you sort out problems, or simply maintain a record of changes. To see this record, follow these steps:

1. Pull down the Tools menu and choose the Track Changes submenu. Select the Highlight Changes command. You will see the dialog box shown in Figure 28.13.

2. Use the When drop-down list to choose what changes you see. You can choose "Since I last saved," "All," "Not yet reviewed," and "Since date...."

3. Use the Who drop-down list to choose whose changes will be shown. You can select "Everyone," "Everyone but me," and each user's name individually (they are listed in the drop-down list).

4. Use the Where drop-down list to select cells that will be shown. Leaving this blank causes all cells to be included.

5. Use the two checkboxes at the bottom of the Highlight Changes dialog box to control where changes are displayed.

6. Click the OK button to close the dialog box and display the changes you selected.

Figure 28.13

Excel's Highlight Changes
dialog box

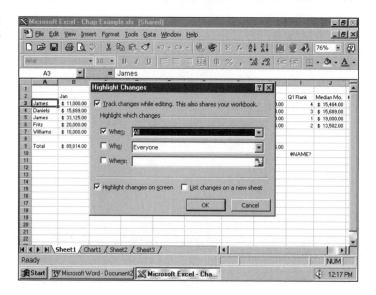

If you choose "List changes on a new sheet," a new sheet called History is inserted into your workbook that details all changes selected by the options in the Highlight Changes dialog box. Figure 28.14 shows an example of a History worksheet.

Setting Document Properties

One of the tricks to making effective use of Office applications in a shared environment involves using the file properties to track information about a particular file. With these properties, you can track such items as:

- Author

- Subject

- Keywords

- Comments

- Custom properties, such as editor, client name, and a host of other choices

To access the file's properties, pull down the File menu and choose Properties. The Summary tab contains the main tracking information, as shown in Figure 28.15.

Figure 28.14

The History sheet shows
you detailed records of
changes made to a sheet.

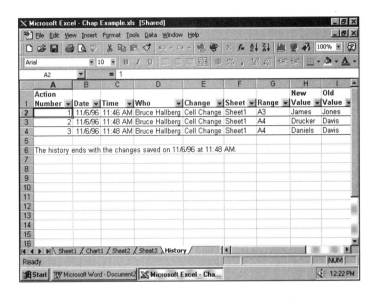

Figure 28.15

You can save summary
information about the
files you work on in the
Summary tab.

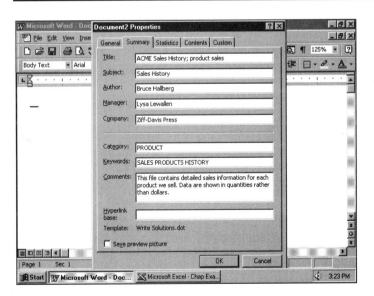

Office applications also include a host of custom file properties that you can make good use of. These are found in the Custom tab of the Properties dialog box, and are shown in Figure 28.16.

Figure 28.16

The Custom tab lets you track more detailed information about your files.

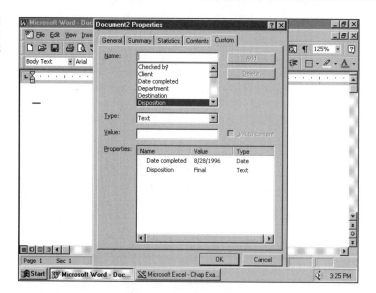

Access the custom file properties choices using the Name drop-down list, or type in your own property in the Name field. There are over 25 different default properties available to you. After choosing a custom property, choose its data type in the Type drop-down list (you may choose from Text, Number, Date, or Yes/No). Then, type the information into the Value field. Finally, click on the Add button to store the property. Existing properties will appear in the Properties window.

You can develop some more complicated mechanisms using the Link to Content check box. When selected, you can link a property to data contained in the file itself. For instance, you can reference named cells in Excel, or bookmarks in Word. You must have defined the named cells or bookmarks first, however. After they have been defined, you can click the Link to Content checkbox, and then choose the bookmark or named cells in the Source drop-down list. (Source will appear in place of the Value field when Link to Content is selected.)

When you use the Link to Content feature, the property is linked to the content so that you can search based on the property, and the property value may have a changing value. Consider, for example, a series of Excel workbooks that all have a total linked to a file property. With this feature enabled, you could search for files in which that total meets certain criteria. These search parameters can be set by clicking the Advanced button in the File Open dialog box.

Routing Files

If you use Microsoft Outlook or a compatible e-mail system, you can route your Office files to others in the company from within the individual Office applications. Access this feature by choosing Send To in the File menu, and then choosing Routing Recipient in the submenu that appears. You will see the Routing Slip dialog box shown in Figure 28.17.

Figure 28.17

Use the Routing Slip dialog box to control distribution of a document to other people.

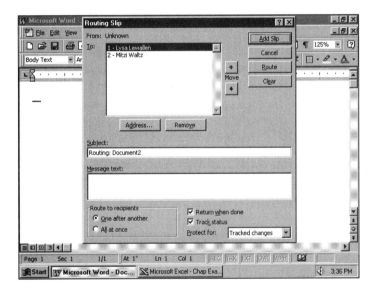

Add recipients using the Address button. Type a subject and message text in the named fields so that the recipients will know why they are getting the file. Then, choose your routing method. You can choose to send the file to "All at once" or "One after another." Selecting the Track Status check box causes an e-mail message to be automatically sent to you each time a recipient forwards the file on to the next person. You can choose to have the file automatically sent back to you once the last person is finished with it by checking the Return When Done checkbox. Also, consider using the Protect For list box to ensure that the copies the recipients receive are automatically protected, so that their changes will be visibly tracked in the document.

After filling in the Routing Slip, choose the Add Slip button to store it, or the Send button to put it in your e-mail Outbox.

■ Maintaining Security

When you work in a shared environment, protecting the security of your documents is important. You can protect many of your Office files with file-specific passwords.

Word and Excel let you use passwords to control access to your files. Outlook and Access have much more complicated security. PowerPoint does not use password protection.

To add a password to a Word or Excel file, simply choose the Save As command in the File menu. Then, click on the Options button to reveal the dialog box shown in Figure 28.18.

Figure 28.18

Use the Save options to add password protection to your files.

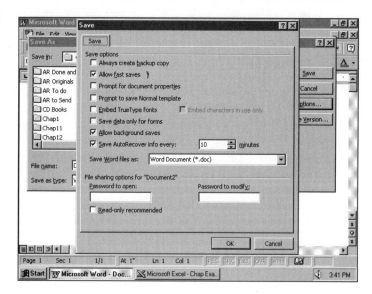

There are two different passwords you can set: Password to Open and Password to Modify. Password to Open denies access to the file entirely unless the individual knows the password. Password to Modify lets anyone open the file in read-only mode, but they can only make changes to the file if they know the password.

You also can specify that a file be Read-Only Recommended. If this check box is selected, Excel or Word warns the person opening the file that they should open it in read-only mode. Although they have the choice of opening it with write access, this check box reminds them that they should be careful in doing so.

■ Setting Up Workgroup Templates

In any of the Office applications, when you create a new file using the New command in the File menu, you see a tabbed dialog box that lists possible files and templates on which you can base your new file. Office creates the standard tabs and files when you first install it.

A workgroup may have many additional files for use within the group. You can create special Workgroup Templates that contain these group-specific files. When you do so, they also appear in the New File dialog box as if they were part of Office.

To set up a Workgroup Templates collection, first create a folder on a shared disk for your template folders. In that main folder, create a subfolder for each tab you want to appear in the New File dialog box. In this example, a Workgroup Templates folder was created in the root directory, and in that a My Workgroup folder was created. Whatever names you assign to the sub-folders will be used as the names for the tabs in the New File dialog. Place all of the template files that your group uses in each subfolder.

After this is done, each user in the group can set up their system so that it automatically uses that shared location for group-specific templates. To do so, follow these steps:

1. Make sure the Office Toolbar has been started.

2. Click in the control menu of the Office Toolbar (the upper left corner) and access the Customize command.

3. Move to the Setting tab.

4. Select the Item Workgroup Templates Location, then click on the Modify button to set it. You will see a modified File Open dialog box in which you can locate the folder that contains the templates. In this example, you choose the folder directly from the root directory called Workgroup Templates. Click on the Add button when done.

5. Close the Customize dialog box.

After setting this property, any time you use the File, New command in any Office application or from the Office Toolbar, you will automatically see tabs that contain your workgroup templates.

8

Microsoft Office and the Internet

- *What Is the Internet?*
- *What Is the Web?*
- *What Is an Intranet?*
- *Creating and Using Hyperlinks*
- *Browsing within Office Applications*

29

Introducing the Internet, Intranets, and the Web

O FFICE 97 IS THE FIRST VERSION OF OFFICE TO SUPPORT THE WORLD Wide Web as an integral part of the product. Before you use Office to interact with the Web, however, you'll need a solid understanding of how the Internet, Intranets, and the Web work.

In this chapter, you'll learn:

- What is the Internet?
- What is the Web?
- What is an Intranet?
- How to browse the Web with Office 97 applications
- Using Word to summarize Web pages

The key to effectively using the Web is to first understand exactly how it works. As you'll see in this chapter, it's really not very complicated. In fact, it's surprisingly simple: anyone can use the Web, and more importantly, anyone can create his or her own Web pages for publication on either the World Wide Web or a company-wide Intranet. In the three chapters that make up this section, you'll learn how to do all of this.

■ What Is the Internet?

The Internet is, simply put, a collection of tens of thousands (perhaps hundreds of thousands) of computers scattered all around the world that are connected together. Originally, the Internet was created by the Department of Defense as a way to link together universities doing defense-related research. Then the Internet grew to encompass universities and other higher-education centers around the country, and even private companies doing related research. The Internet continued to grow, until many people started accessing it from their office and home computers, and started doing things on the Internet besides research. Now the Internet is becoming the preferred medium for delivering a whole host of services: news, weather, marketing information, investment tools, computer software and hardware support, and many others.

The computers that make up the Internet are connected using various types of long-distance and local communications lines. Some are connected over a simple modem using a dial-up telephone line. Others are connected with T-1 lines (also called DS-1 lines), which are roughly the equivalent of 55 28,800-bps modems. Others are linked using even faster digital communications lines. Each computer is connected to the Internet at whatever speed the site's owners can afford and justify, given their needs. All the computers on the Internet are linked together in a virtual spider's web of network connections.

Originally the Internet was used to simply access other computers using two core tools: Telnet and FTP. Telnet is a program that allows users to communicate with a remote system over the Internet as if they were using a terminal connected directly to that remote computer. FTP lets you transfer files between a local computer and a remote system. Other tools have been developed over the years, of course. However, the "tool" that really brought the Internet into its own was the World Wide Web.

■ What Is the Web?

The concept behind the Web is pretty simple: What if you could have a collection of documents, each one containing text and graphics, that is designed in such a way that you can link information from one page to another? For example, you might be looking at a page on your screen about Europe, and a link on the page might take you to travel agents who can help you plan a trip to France. All you would need to do is click on the link with your mouse to go to the related pages. Or perhaps you might be reading an article about elections, and the president's name is highlighted: click on the name, and you're taken to a biography of the president. If you think about this simple but powerful concept, the possibilities are virtually endless.

This is exactly what the Web is: a collection of documents, just like word processing documents, in which the authors have embedded links to other pages that contain related information. Web documents, usually just called pages, can be stored on any computer on the Internet. Often, you might be accessing a computer near your home, but when you click on a link on a page stored there, you're suddenly (and unknowingly) transported to reading a page stored on a computer located on the other side of the world. No fuss involved: it just happens automatically.

The concept behind the Web—the linking of information on different pages—is called *hypertext*. The idea is to make plain text come alive by linking information in a document. Web pages are designed using a format called HyperText Markup Language, abbreviated as HTML. HTML documents use simple commands written in HTML to describe fonts, graphics, and links to other pages. It's up to the designer of a particular page to decide what the page contains. It's just like designing a document with word processing software: you can include text, graphics, or references to other pages. You can have small pages that fit easily on a single screen, or very large pages that are many screens long.

NOTE. *HTML files can be browsed (read) by any computer that supports a Web Browser (browsers are available for just about all types of computers). Because the HTML format wasn't designed for any single computer platform, it provides a standard way for different types of computers to share information. For example, a page designed on a computer running Windows 95 can be viewed just as easily on a Macintosh, or a Sun workstation, or an*

OS/2-based computer. If you use Office 97 to create HTML pages, other people don't need Office 97 to view your pages: they just need a Web browser and a way to access the pages you create.

Links from one Web page to another look different than the regular text on the page. Usually, links appear in a different color from normal text, and change color after you've used them. Links on Web pages, called hyperlinks, are typically underlined to help you distinguish them from surrounding text. Sometimes a hyperlink will be part of a graphic image. For instance, a small image might be shown on a page, but when you click on it, a larger version appears.

■ What Is an Intranet?

Just about all companies need to publish information for their employees, and facilitate communication between their employees. This information can include policies and procedures, employee handbooks, telephone listings, press releases, and so on. The idea behind an Intranet is to use exactly the same tools that you use for the Internet, except you store the HTML pages on a server or servers within the company, and they are accessible only to employees within the company. That's really all there is to Intranets—they're just like the Internet, but much smaller, and built to cater to a specific company's needs.

■ Creating and Using Hyperlinks

Office 97 now supports hyperlinks. In Office 97, you can use hyperlinks when designing Web pages, but they can also be used in standard Office 97 documents to link Office 97 documents together.

To create a hyperlink in an Office 97 document, pull down its Insert menu and choose Hyperlink from the menu. You will see the dialog box shown in Figure 29.1.

Use the Link to file or URL to insert the name of the file to which you want to link. You can use a filename or a Uniform Resource Locator (URL), such as

```
http://www.microsoft.com
```

Click the Browse button to locate the file you want to link to, or simply type the file's name into the field. When you click on the Browse button, you will see a standard File Open dialog box called Link to File. It will let you locate a file. The Link to File dialog box also has a Search the Web button that can help you locate a URL on the Web.

Figure 29.1

The Insert Hyperlink
dialog box

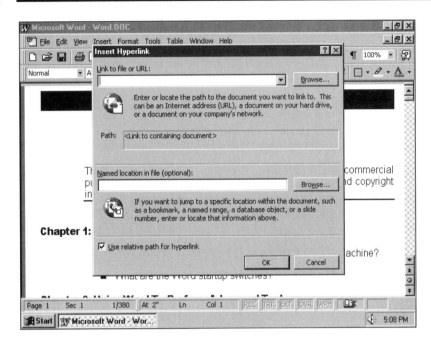

You can also insert a hyperlink into a particular position within a file using the field called Named location in file. In this field, you can choose a Word bookmark, a named range in Excel, or a slide number from a Power-Point file to create and place the hyperlink.

The Use relative path for hyperlink checkbox determines how the hyperlink refers to the destination document. When checked, the path for the file to which you are linking is stored using a relative pathname instead of an absolute pathname. You should generally leave this checkbox set, unless you're certain that you'll never need to move the set of linked documents to a different directory.

Hyperlinks, once inserted, appear in blue text and are underlined. When you move the mouse pointer over a hyperlink, the pointer changes into a hand with a pointing finger. A single click of the mouse will instantly load the document referred to by the hyperlink.

■ Browsing within Office Applications

You usually use a dedicated Web browser to read Web documents, such as Microsoft Internet Explorer or Netscape Navigator. However, you can also use Word, PowerPoint, or even Excel and Access to browse Web pages. You might use one of these applications instead of a browser if you want to use a page's content within a document in that application. For instance, if you use Excel to open a Web page that contains a table, it will be easier to copy and paste that information into an Excel workbook.

Office 97 applications let you access special Web toolbars that make browsing within those applications easier. Figure 29.2 shows a Web page as seen from Word with its Web toolbar visible. The other Office applications use the same Web toolbar.

Figure 29.2

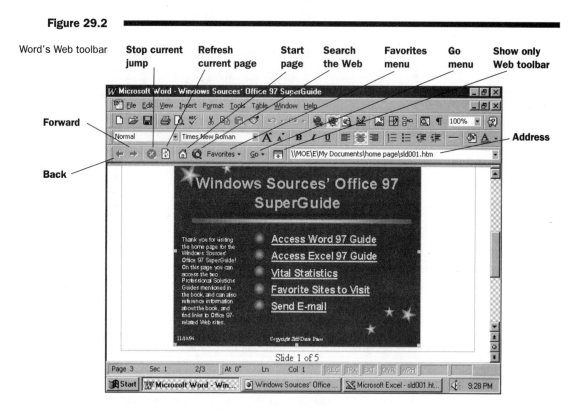

Word's Web toolbar

Stop current jump

Refresh current page

Start page

Search the Web

Favorites menu

Go menu

Show only Web toolbar

Forward

Back

Address

Tip. When you encounter a long Web page that is filled primarily with text, you can use Word's AutoSummarize feature to prepare a shortened version of the page.

The Web Toolbar works much like the one found in Microsoft Internet Explorer. You can use the Back and Forward buttons to back up through the pages you've viewed, or to move forward again. The Stop Current Jump button cancels the loading of a page you've selected (you might want to do this if the page is taking too long to load). Clicking Refresh causes a page to be updated with new data: often your computer will remember what was on a page when you viewed it before, and will display this old page instead of the current copy. Use the Home button to jump to your home page, and the Search the Web button to bring up a standard search form for the World

Wide Web. Clicking the Show Only Web Toolbar button is useful when you want to devote the maximum available screen space to viewing a Web page. Finally, use the Address field to type in the Web address for a page you want to view.

- *Word*
- *PowerPoint*

30

Creating Web Pages with Office

Each office 97 application has a different level of ability to create Web pages. Word can be used to create many different types of Web pages, while PowerPoint is good for creating personal home pages and for publishing presentations to Web pages.

In this chapter, you'll learn about creating Web pages with Office 97, including:

- Using Word's Web Page Wizard

- Publishing PowerPoint presentations to the Web

Creating Web pages with Office 97 is fast and easy, as you'll see in this chapter.

■ Word

For creating general-purpose Web pages, Word is the best choice. There are two ways to create Web pages with Word:

- Design the page using Word's formatting commands, tables, backgrounds, and Hyperlinks, and then save the results out to HTML files.

- Use Word's Web Page Wizard to take a lot of the drudgery out of creating Web pages, and then modify the results of the Web Page Wizard to suit your specific needs.

In this section you'll learn about using both of these methods, starting with the easier method—using the Web Page Wizard—and then moving on to creating Web pages manually with Word's Web Page Authoring tools.

Creating Web Pages Automatically with Word

The easiest and fastest way to create Web pages with Word is to use the Web Page Wizard, a tool designed to provide a Web-page design shortcut. Once the Web Page Wizard generates a page that you've specified, it's up to you to make adjustments so that the page contains the information and graphics that you want.

To begin using the Web Page Wizard, choose the New command from Word's File menu. Then, select the Web Pages tab shown in Figure 30.1.

There are three choices available to you on the Web Pages tab:

- Blank Web Page opens a blank Web page that's already formatted for HTML and has Word's Web Page Authoring tools activated on Word's menus.

- More Cool Stuff is a Web page with links to Microsoft's Word Web Site. The page can be used to access the site and download additional Web templates and tools for Word.

- Web Page Wizard starts the wizard, which leads you through a series of choices in order to build your Web page template.

Figure 30.1

The Web Pages tab in
Word's New dialog box

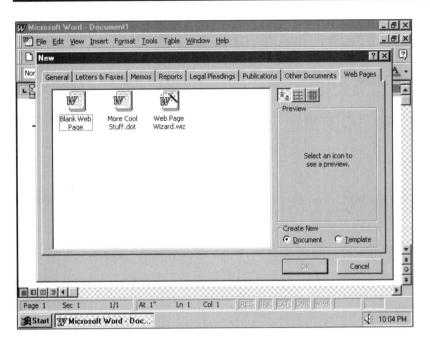

Choose Web Page Wizard and click on the OK button. A sample Web
page will appear, along with the Web Page Wizard dialog box shown in Figure 30.2.

Selecting one of the possible Web page types shown in the Web Page
Wizard dialog box causes a sample of that type of page to appear. By choosing each one in turn, you can more easily select the type of page you want to
start with. In this example, 3-Column Layout has been selected before clicking on the Next button to move forward in the Wizard. You would then see
the next dialog box of the Web Page Wizard, in which you can select the style
of Web page you want to create. The list of styles is shown in Figure 30.3.

As before, you can choose each style in turn to preview the style. After
you've found a style that appeals to you, click on the Finish button to create
the Web page. In this example, the style Community was chosen before clicking Finish.

Once you have a completed page, you can begin customizing it to suit
your needs. Each of the items listed can be replaced with text of your own,
and the existing blue underlined text can be replaced with hyperlinks to sites
or documents of your choice.

Figure 30.2

The Web Page Wizard dialog box

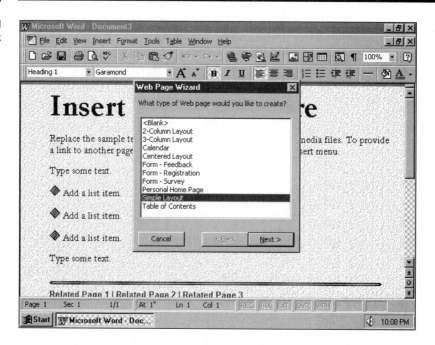

Figure 30.3

The Web page built by the Web Page Wizard

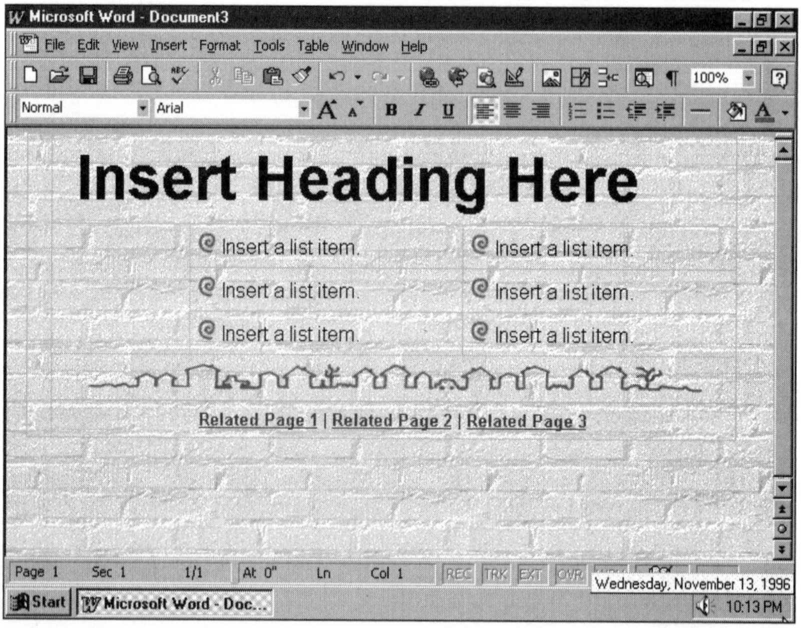

Finishing Up Web Pages Built by the Web Page Wizard

To complete a Web page built by the wizard, you will need to do several things:

- Replace any text on the page with text you choose

- Readjust the table, if necessary, to reflect the new information

- Insert any necessary hyperlinks

Replacing the text on the page is quite easy: simply select the text with the mouse and type in the replacement text.

Tip. To make the borders of a table inserted into an HTML document visible when the page is viewed, right-click on one of the borders of the table and choose the **Borders** command from the pop-up menu. You can then choose a line weight for displaying the table on the Web.

If you follow this example along on your own computer, you'll see that the list items are in a table. The table guidelines are visible as very dim hairlines surrounding each element of the page. The table, unless you have specified otherwise, will be invisible to Web browsers looking at the page: the table exists only as an alignment tool. When you change the text of the items on the page, you may need to readjust the table accordingly. Do this by carefully moving your mouse over the table borders until the mouse pointer changes to a pointer with arrows. Then drag the table border under the mouse to its new position.

The blue, underlined text you see on the Web Page Wizard-generated pages does not yet represent hyperlinks. The text has been formatted to look like hyperlinks, but these links are not yet active. To make them active, follow these steps:

1. Select the text for one of the pseudo-hyperlinks.

2. Type in replacement text that tells the reader where the hyperlink will take them.

3. While the text is selected, access the Hyperlink command from the Insert menu. You will see the Insert Hyperlink dialog box shown in Figure 30.4.

4. In the Link to File or URL field, type the name of the file where the hyperlink should take the reader, or the URL of the Web page where they should be taken. (URLs are usually in the form *http://www.sitename.com/ filename.html.*) After entering this information, click the OK button to create the hyperlink.

Figure 30.5 shows a Web page that was completed using these steps.

Creating Web Pages Manually with Word

Word 97 can be used to create Web pages using standard Word document tools. When you're happy with the results, you can save the document in HTML format and post it to a location that others can access with Web browsers.

Figure 30.4

Use the Insert Hyperlink
dialog box to indicate to
where a hyperlink points.

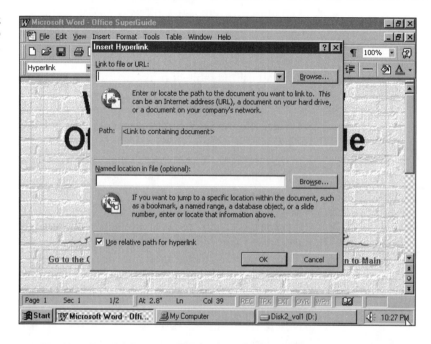

Figure 30.5

A sample Web page
created using the Web
Page Wizard and then
customized

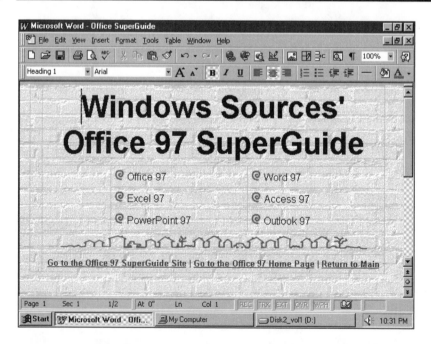

The key tools you use in Word to create Web pages manually include:

- Online Layout View (selected automatically when working with HTML documents)

- Hyperlinks to other pages

- Word's Web Authoring Tools, discussed in this section

The best way to start creating a Web page manually is to use the New command in the File menu of Word, and then choose the Web Pages tab. Choose Blank Web Page from the dialog box and click OK to create a blank Web page, as illustrated in Figure 30.6.

Figure 30.6

A blank Web page created with the File, New command

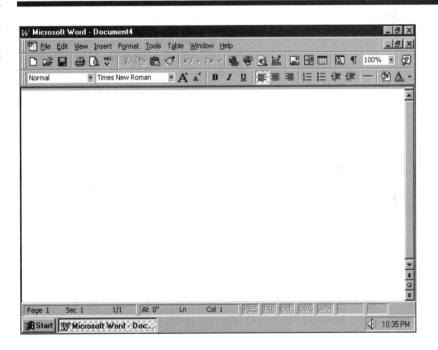

Tip. When working on a Web page, you can use the Web Page Preview command in the File menu to automatically load the current page into your Web browser, allowing you to preview exactly how it will appear to someone looking at the page on the Internet.

If you want to create a Web page from an existing Word document, open the document in Word and then choose Save as HTML from Word's File menu. This saves a copy of your document in HTML format and, more importantly, it activates Word's Web Page Authoring commands (Word's menus change when you are working with an HTML document). Also, you will be automatically placed into Online Layout view, which simulates how the page will appear when viewed with a Web browser.

Using Web Page Authoring Tools

Word has a number of tools that help you build Web pages. Many of these can be found on Word's Insert menu when you're working on an HTML document. These tools are:

- **Horizontal Line**. This places a horizontal line on your Web page, and displays a dialog box from which you can choose from many different graphical formats for the line. Figure 30.7 shows the Horizontal Line dialog box.

Figure 30.7

The Horizontal Line dialog box in Word

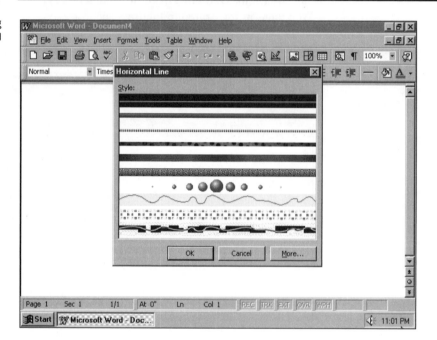

- **Picture**. This command lets you create pictures on your Web page. When chosen, a sub-menu appears that lets you choose to create the picture from clip art, from a file, from browsing a Web art page on the Internet (you will be connected automatically to the chosen page), from a scanned image, or from a chart. Pictures you create in this fashion will be saved in GIF format by default, unless you choose to create the picture from a file formatted in JPEG (JPG) format, in which case the file will be saved in that format.

- **Video**. This choice lets you insert a video movie file that has been formatted with an .AVI, .MOV, .MOVIE, .MPG, .MPEG, or .QT extension. Examples of such movies are located on the Office 97 CD-ROM in the \CLIPART\MMEDIA directory. Note that Web browsers accessing a page with a movie on it must support playing that movie format, and you should be very conscious of the size of the movie file. The movie file will have to be transmitted to the viewer's machine in order to play, and some movie files are quite large.

- **Background Sound**. You can insert background sounds in HTML documents that play when the page is loaded by a browser with sound capabilities. Most current browsers, including Internet Explorer and Navigator, support such sounds if the client computer has a sound card installed.

- **Scrolling Text**. You can use the Scrolling Text command to insert text boxes with text that scrolls on the screen. These can liven up a Web page, and do not consume too much bandwidth to transmit.

Another key element of most Web pages is a background graphic image. You can set these images for HTML documents by accessing the Background command in the Format menu. Doing so displays the submenu shown in Figure 30.8.

Figure 30.8

The Background submenu for HTML pages

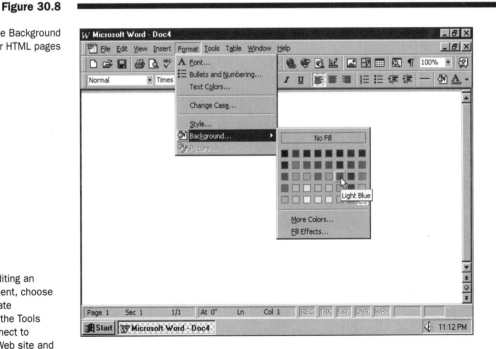

Tip. When editing an HTML document, choose the AutoUpdate command in the Tools menu to connect to Microsoft's Web site and automatically update your Web Page Authoring tools with updated versions, if any are available.

In the Background submenu you can choose a background color for your Web page. You can also choose the Fill Effects command, which allows you to choose from a number of attractive background textures. The Fill

Effects dialog box is shown in Figure 30.9. Fill Effects are only visible when you are viewing a page in Online Layout view.

Figure 30.9

The Fill Effects dialog box

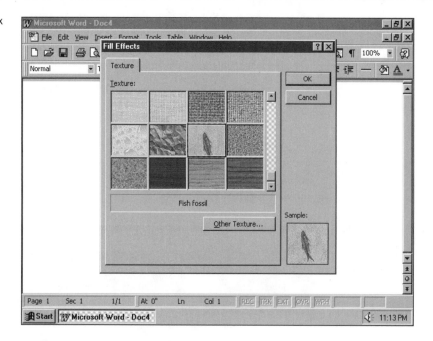

Saving Word Web Pages

When you finish creating a Web page with Word, you need to save it before placing it on a Web server. When you save a Web page, you will be saving not only the HTML document, but all of the embedded graphic images as well. It's important that you keep the graphics (which appear as .GIF and .JPG files) together with the .HTML file. Otherwise, the graphic elements of the page will not load when the page is viewed.

■ PowerPoint

PowerPoint 97 lets you take PowerPoint presentations and save them in HTML format for viewing on the Web. You can begin with any finished presentation, choosing the Save as HTML command from PowerPoint's File menu. You will see the Save as HTML Wizard shown in Figure 30.10.

The Save as HTML Wizard will walk you through a series of choices you must make as PowerPoint saves the presentation into a format readable by

Figure 30.10

PowerPoint's Save as
HTML Wizard

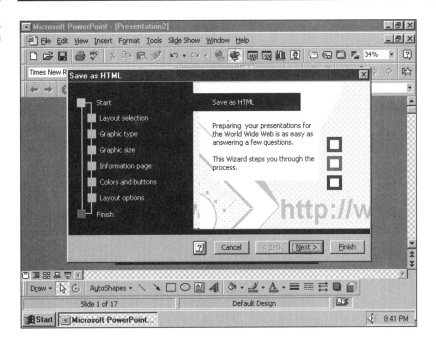

Web browsers. Clicking the Next button in the Wizard moves you through
each step.

The first step of the Save as HTML Wizard is Layout selection, as shown
in Figure 30.11. PowerPoint can save the choices you make as you use the
Save as HTML Wizard, and can apply those choices on successive uses. The
first dialog box of the Save as HTML Wizard lets you bypass certain dialog
boxes by selecting a previous format. Since this is the first time you have
used the Wizard, no formats have been saved. You will need to choose New
Layout before clicking on the Next button.

After choosing New Layout and choosing the Next button, your next
step is choosing whether or not your Web presentation will use frames (see
Figure 30.12). Frames are regions on Web pages that let the reader access
multiple "pages" of information on a single page. In the case of PowerPoint's
Save as HTML Wizard, choosing Browser Frames in the dialog box shown in
Figure 30.12 would cause the outline of the presentation to appear in a separate frame of the Web page. This outline could be used to jump between
pages of the presentation. However, you should be careful about using
frames, as older Web browsers may not support them. On the other hand,
most current browser versions *do* support frames, and since browsers are essentially free, most people use the latest versions as a matter of course. In
this example, choose Browser Frames and click the Next button to continue.

Figure 30.11

Layout selection in the
Save as HTML Wizard

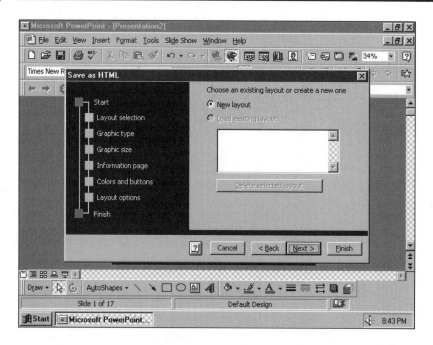

Figure 30.12

Choosing frames in the
Save as HTML Wizard

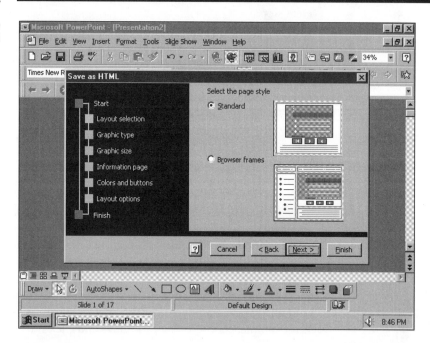

You will now see the Graphic type dialog box shown in Figure 30.13. You can choose between GIF and JPEG formats for static graphic images on your Web page. There are trade-offs involved in this choice. Generally, GIF images look clearer online than JPEG images, but they're also larger. Therefore, GIFs will cause the Web page to load more slowly. JPEG images have the added benefit of letting you choose between high compression levels and high quality: the lower the number in the Compression Value field, the smaller the JPEG files will be, and the poorer the resulting quality.

The Graphic type dialog box will also let you save any animations in the presentation as PowerPoint animations. If you choose this, the readers of your page will be prompted to download the PowerPoint Animation Player if they have not already done so. For this example, choose JPEG and make sure that the Compression Value field is set to 100 percent, which yields the highest quality.

Figure 30.13

Choosing the graphic type in the Save as HTML Wizard

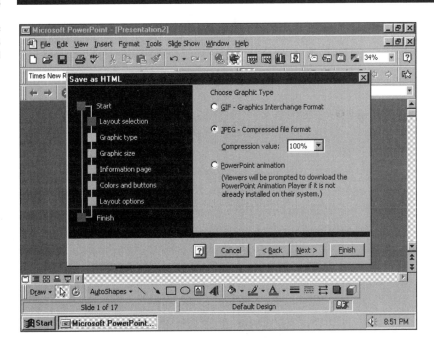

Tip. You might want to experiment with the different settings. Save your presentation three times, choosing a different graphic format each time—save each version into a different directory. Then use your Web browser to see how each version behaves. You can also examine the size of the resulting .JPEG and .GIF files to strike the perfect balance between quality and size (remember that size affects the speed of your page).

The next step lets you choose the graphic size used for your Web page (see Figure 30.14). You can choose to optimize your page for typical resolutions that might be used by people who view the presentation online. Common screen resolutions are shown: 640 by 480, 800 by 600, 1024 by 768, and 1280 by 1024. The trade-off here is that if you choose a larger screen size, the graphic images will also have to be larger to accommodate it. The larger the images, the larger the image files. Generally, 800 by 600 is a good choice: most newer computers can support that resolution.

Figure 30.14

Choosing the target screen size in the Save as HTML Wizard

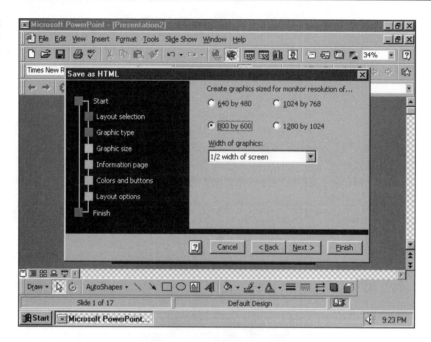

The next dialog box, shown in Figure 30.15, lets you enter data for an Information page. You can enter your e-mail address; your home page address, if you have one; and other information about yourself. If you fill out these fields, the information you specify will automatically be placed on a page of your presentation. You can select Download Original Presentation to provide a hyperlink that allows the reader to download the actual PowerPoint file on which the Web pages are based, and you can select the Internet Explorer download button to include a button on the presentation that lets the reader easily download the latest version of Microsoft Internet Explorer.

Next, you will see the Colors and Buttons page shown in Figure 30.16. Here you choose the default colors for your Web-page presentation. Generally, you should accept the Use Browser Colors option to conform with the color choices made by page readers. Otherwise, select Custom Colors and then use each of the buttons to change different color aspects of the page. Set the Transparent Buttons checkbox to cause the background colors for your page to show through the player buttons that will be automatically placed on your pages.

Figure 30.15

The Information page of
the Save as HTML Wizard

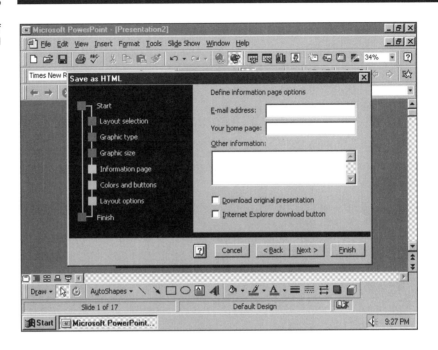

Figure 30.16

The Colors and Buttons
page of the Save as
HTML Wizard

In the next step, shown in Figure 30.17, you choose the style of control buttons that are used for the page. You can choose from three graphic button styles, or you can choose a text button (the Next Slide option).

Figure 30.17

Selecting a button style in the Save as HTML Wizard

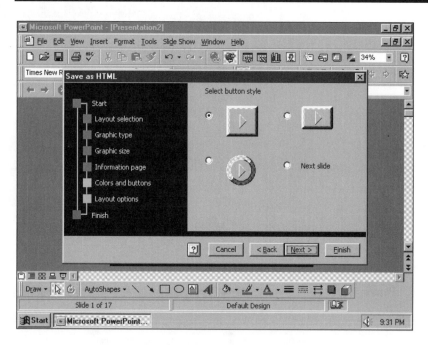

If you've developed slide notes for your presentation, you can choose to include them on your Web pages automatically with the Define framed layout options page shown in Figure 30.18.

Near the end of the Save as HTML Wizard process, you're prompted to name a folder where the presentation should be saved (see Figure 30.19). Type a folder name into the field provided, or use the Browse button to locate a folder.

After entering the name of the folder that will contain your HTML pages, the wizard's final screen lets you click the Finish button to complete your choices and save the presentation. However, you will see one final dialog box, as shown in Figure 30.20. This is where you can assign a name for the choices you made using the Save as HTML Wizard. In the future, you can select this name instead of walking through all of these steps again. Enter a name, and click on the **Save** button to save your choices.

Your presentation is now saved as a series of HTML pages, along with associated graphic files, in the directory you specified. You can browse the result by opening your Web browser and opening the Index.HTM file (see Figure 30.21).

Figure 30.18

Choosing to include slide notes with the presentation

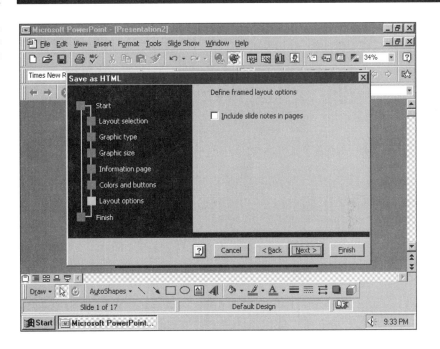

Figure 30.19

Choosing a destination folder for your HTML pages

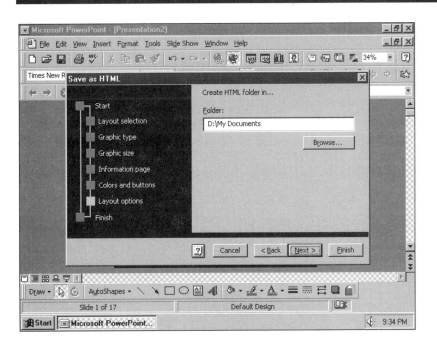

Figure 30.20

Saving the choices you
made in the Save as
HTML Wizard dialog boxes

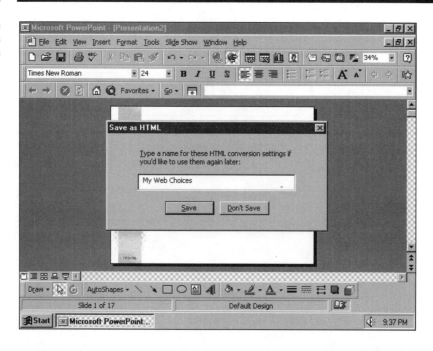

Figure 30.21

The saved presentation's
opening page

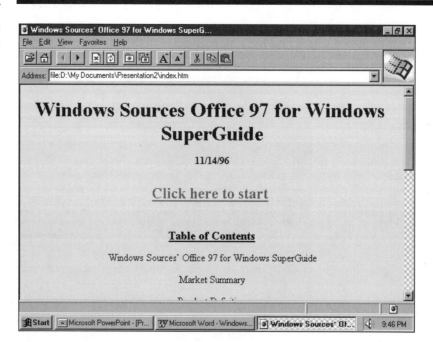

Creating Home Pages with PowerPoint

PowerPoint 97 includes an AutoContent Wizard you can use to create your own home page. When PowerPoint starts, you will see the dialog box shown in Figure 30.22. Choose AutoContent Wizard and click the OK button.

Figure 30.22

Choosing the
AutoContent Wizard when
PowerPoint starts

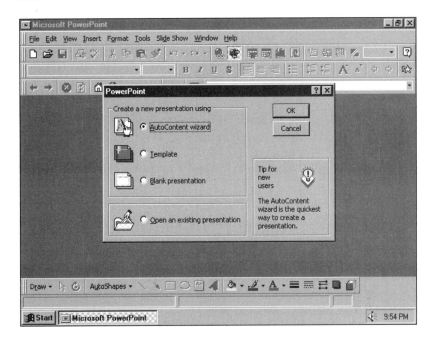

You will now see the AutoContent Wizard. Click the Next button to choose a presentation type for the Wizard, and then click on the Personal button. Choose Personal Home Page from the right-hand window, and then click on the Next button.

From the Output options dialog box that appears next, choose Internet, Kiosk before moving on to the next step. You will then be prompted for Presentation options, in which you can place additional information for your page, such as any copyright notices, the date you last updated the page, and your e-mail address.

After you have made these choices in the AutoContent Wizard, a series of pages will be created for you in PowerPoint. These will provide a starting point for creating your personal home page. For each slide, replace the text with information of your own. When you're done, click on the Save as HTML button in PowerPoint's File menu and follow through the Save as HTML Wizard discussed in the previous section. Voilà!

■ Index